"He has a great gift. He has the gift to inspire." —Bill Clinton,
former president of the United States

"Tony Robbins is a human locksmith—he knows how to open your mind to larger possibilities. Using his unique insights into human nature, he's found a way to simplify the strategies of the world's greatest investors and create a simple 7-step system that anyone can use on the path to the financial freedom they deserve." —Paul Tudor Jones II,
founder, Tudor Investment Corporation, and legendary trader
with 28 consecutive years of positive returns for his investors

"Tony Robbins has influenced millions of people's lives, including my own. In this book he offers you insights and strategies from the world's greatest investors. Don't miss the opportunity to experience the life-changing value of this book." —Kyle Bass,
founder of Hayman Capital Management and investor who turned
$30 million into $2 billion in the middle of the subprime crisis

"In this book, Tony Robbins brings his unique talent for making the complex simple as he distills the concepts of the best investors in the world into practical lessons that will benefit both naïve investors and skilled professionals." —Ray Dalio,
founder and co–chief investment officer, Bridgewater Associates,
#1 largest hedge fund in the world

"*Money: Master the Game* will be a huge help to investors . . . Tony Robbins dropped by my office for a 40-minute appointment that lasted for four hours. It was the most provocative, probing interview of my long career, a reaction shared, I'm sure, by the other souls with strong investment values and sharp financial minds who populate this fine book. This book will enlighten you and reinforce your understanding of how to master the money game and, in the long run, earn your financial freedom." —John C. Bogle,
founder, the Vanguard Group and the Vanguard index funds,
#1 largest mutual funds in the world

WHAT THE WORLD'S GREATEST FINANCIAL LEADERS ARE SAYING ABOUT TONY ROBBINS . . .

"This book is not the typical financial book in any way. It is packed with wisdom and vital philosophies to enrich your life. A lot of books out there have more sizzle than steak to offer. Tony's is different. This book will change your life." —Dr. David Babbel, *professor of finance, Wharton School of the University of Pennsylvania*

"In this book, Tony masterfully weaves anecdote and expertise to simplify the process of investing for readers—priming their financial education and helping them effectively plan for their future." —Mary Callahan Erdoes, *CEO, J.P. Morgan Asset Management, $2.5 trillion in assets under management*

"Tony Robbins needs no introduction. He is committed to helping make life better for every investor. Every investor will find this book extremely interesting and illuminating." —Carl Icahn, *Billionaire Activist and Investor*

"A gold mine of moneymaking information!" —Steve Forbes, *publisher of* Forbes *magazine and CEO of Forbes, Inc.*

"I have spoken at Tony's financial events several times in the last few years, for which he pays me a fee. But upon closer reflection, I should be the one who pays him a fee. He has the incredible talent of taking complex knowledge from leading financial experts and converting it into simple steps that the average man can apply to achieve financial security and freedom." —Marc Faber, *winner of Barron's Roundtable and publisher of the* Gloom, Boom & Doom *report*

"You can't meet Tony Robbins, and listen to his words, without being inspired to act. This book will give you the strategies to create financial freedom for yourself and your family." —T. Boone Pickens, *founder, chairman, and CEO at BP Capital and TBP; predicted oil prices accurately 18 out of 21 times on CNBC*

"Robbins's unrelenting commitment to finding the real answers to financial security and independence, and his passion for bringing the insights of the ultrawealthy to the average man, is truly inspiring. This book could truly change your life."

—David Pottruck,
*former CEO of Charles Schwab
and bestselling author of* Stacking the Deck

"If you're looking for answers and you're committed to creating financial freedom for yourself and your family, then Tony Robbins is your man. Get this book, change your life."

—Farnoosh Torabi,
award-winning author of When She Makes More:
10 Rules for Breadwinning Women

"Sitting in the back of Financial Destiny nearly twenty years ago, I was a student of Tony Robbins's who had a dream to help teach and empower one million women to be smarter with money. Thanks to Tony, a year later I would be speaking on stage at his events, writing *Smart Women Finish Rich*, and ultimately creating a program that would reach millions of women worldwide. Today there are more than seven million copies of my Finish Rich books in print, translated into 19 languages. Tony changes lives, and he will change yours. I, like you, will be reading *MONEY* cover to cover, and sharing it with my friends."

—David Bach,
nine-time New York Times–*bestselling author;
titles include* The Automatic Millionaire,
Start Late, Finish Rich, Smart Women Finish Rich,
and Smart Couples Finish Rich; *founder of FinishRich.com*

"We've been selected by *Forbes* as the most innovative company in the world for four consecutive years. Our revenues are now over $5 billion annually. Without access to Tony and his teachings, Salesforce.com wouldn't exist today."

—Marc Benioff,
founder, chairman, and CEO of Salesforce.com

"Tony's power is superhuman . . . He is a catalyst for getting people to change. I came away with: It's not about motivation as much as it is allowing people to tap into what's already there."   —Oprah Winfrey,
Emmy Award–winning media magnate

"Tony Robbins's coaching has made a remarkable difference in my life both on and off the court. He's helped me discover what I'm really made of, and I've taken my tennis game—and my life—to a whole new level!"
—Serena Williams,
18-time Grand Slam tennis champion and Olympic gold medalist

"I was afraid that my success would take something away from my family. Tony was able to turn it around and show me that I've helped millions of people. Probably the most intense feelings I've ever had."
—Melissa Etheridge,
two-time Grammy Award–winning singer and songwriter

"No matter who you are, no matter how successful, no matter how happy, Tony has something to offer you."   —Hugh Jackman,
Emmy– and Tony Award–winning actor, producer

"If you want to change your state, if you want to change your results, this is where you do it; Tony is the man."   —Usher,
Grammy Award–winning singer, songwriter, entrepreneur

"Working with Tony Robbins, I felt unstoppable. From that moment on, there was zero doubt in my mind about what I wanted and how I was going to achieve it. I was so clear about what I wanted that I made it happen: I became world champion."   —Derek Hough,
dancer, choreographer, and five-time winner of ABC's Dancing with the Stars

"Tony Robbins is a genius . . . His ability to strategically guide people through any challenge is unparalleled." —Steve Wynn, *CEO and founder of Wynn Resorts*

"Before Tony, I had allowed myself to be put in a position of fear. After meeting Tony, I made a decision not to be afraid anymore. It was an absolutely game-changing, life-altering experience. I'm so excited and thankful for Tony Robbins and the incredible gift that he gave me." —Maria Menounos, *actress, journalist, and TV personality*

"What Tony really gave me, a kid sitting on Venice Beach selling T-shirts, was to take risks, take action, and really become something. I'm telling you as someone who has lived with these strategies for 25 years: I'll come back for more again, and again, and again." —Mark Burnett, *five-time Emmy Award–winning television producer*

"What does this man have that everyone wants? He is a 6'7" phenomenon!" —Diane Sawyer, *former* ABC World News *and* Good Morning America *anchor*

"Tony Robbins helps you take that first step to making real change in your life. I have a pretty good life, but all of us have aspects of our lives that we want to make greater. It's life changing. It really is." —Justin Tuck, *defensive end, Oakland Raiders, and two-time Super Bowl champion*

"Tony Robbins knows the rhythm of success. He is an incredible source of inspiration, and his methods have improved the quality of my life. I only work with the best, and Tony is the best." —Quincy Jones, *Grammy Award–winning musician, producer*

"Tony Robbins provides an amazing vehicle for looking at your life, mapping out a mission, and determining what's holding you back and what you need to move forward." —Donna Karan, *legendary fashion designer, founder DKNY*

90

MONEY

MASTER THE GAME

7 SIMPLE STEPS TO
FINANCIAL FREEDOM

TONY ROBBINS

SIMON & SCHUSTER

NEW YORK LONDON TORONTO SYDNEY NEW DELHI

This book is designed to provide information that the author believes to be accurate on the subject matter it covers, but it is sold with the understanding that neither the author nor the publisher is offering individualized advice tailored to any specific portfolio or to any individual's particular needs, or rendering investment advice or other professional services such as legal or accounting advice. A competent professional's services should be sought if one needs expert assistance in areas that include investment, legal, and accounting advice.

This publication references performance data collected over many time periods. Past results do not guarantee future performance. Additionally, performance data, in addition to laws and regulations, change over time, which could change the status of the information in this book. This book solely provides historical data to discuss and illustrate the underlying principles. Additionally, this book is not intended to serve as the basis for any financial decision; as a recommendation of a specific investment advisor; or as an offer to sell or purchase any security. Only a prospectus may be used to offer to sell or purchase securities, and a prospectus must be read and considered carefully before investing or spending money.

No warranty is made with respect to the accuracy or completeness of the information contained herein, and both the author and the publisher specifically disclaim any responsibility for any liability, loss, or risk, personal or otherwise, which is incurred as a consequence, directly or indirectly, of the use and application of any of the contents of this book.

At the time of this publication, the author is in discussions with Stronghold Wealth Management to enter into some type of business partnership. However, at this time, the author is not an owner of Stronghold, nor does he have any type of referral for compensation relationship.

In the text that follows, many people's names and identifying characteristics have been changed.

Simon & Schuster
1230 Avenue of the Americas
New York, NY 10020

Copyright © 2014 by Anthony Robbins

All rights reserved, including the right to reproduce this book or portions thereof in any form whatsoever. For information address Simon & Schuster Subsidiary Rights Department, 1230 Avenue of the Americas, New York, NY 10020

First Simon & Schuster hardcover edition November 2014

SIMON & SCHUSTER and colophon are registered trademarks of Simon & Schuster, Inc.

For information about special discounts for bulk purchases, please contact Simon & Schuster Special Sales at 1-866-506-1949 or business@simonandschuster.com

The Simon & Schuster Speakers Bureau can bring authors to your live event. For more information or to book an event contact the Simon & Schuster Speakers Bureau at 1-866-248-3049 or visit our website at www.simonspeakers.com.

Interior design by Ruth Lee-Mui

Manufactured in the United States of America

10 9 8 7 6 5 4 3 2 1

Library of Congress Cataloging-in-Publication Data has been applied for.

ISBN 978-1-4767-5780-3
ISBN 978-1-4767-5787-2 (ebook)

To those souls who will never settle for less than they can be, do, share, and give

CONTENTS

SECTION 3

WHAT'S THE PRICE OF YOUR DREAMS?
MAKE THE GAME WINNABLE

SECTION 4

MAKE THE MOST IMPORTANT *INVESTMENT*
DECISION OF YOUR LIFE

SECTION 5

UPSIDE WITHOUT THE DOWNSIDE:
CREATE A LIFETIME INCOME PLAN

The future has many names. For the weak, it's unattainable.
For the fearful, it's unknown. For the bold, it's ideal.
—VICTOR HUGO

To avoid criticism, say nothing, do nothing, be nothing.
—ARISTOTLE

MONEY

MASTER THE GAME

FOREWORD

_____

As a former litigator with years of experience working around Wall Street firms, it's fair to say that a few liars, crooks, and con artists have crossed my path. Since both the legal and financial fields cultivate their share of professional hustlers, I've learned to quickly separate the good actors from the bad.

I am also a skeptic by nature. So when Tony Robbins sought me out for this project because of the company I founded in 2007, HighTower, I was curious but wary. _Is there really anything new to say about personal finance and investing? And is Tony Robbins the man to say it?_

I was, of course, aware of Tony's tremendous reputation as America's number one life and business strategist. And like many, I knew that he has worked with everyone from US presidents to billionaire entrepreneurs, transforming their personal and professional lives along the way.

But what I didn't know until we met was that Tony Robbins _is_ the real thing. The _man_ lives up to the hype of the _brand._ His authenticity was evident, and his passion was contagious. Rather than rehash the sins of the financial industry, Tony came to this project with the goal of democratizing financial services and offering tactics and solutions that had previously been appreciated and used by only the wealthiest investors.

Tony and I hit it off right away because we share a mission of helping empower people to make better, more informed financial decisions. That's the heart of my company, and it's what drives me personally. While the financial crisis of 2008 brought to light the conflicts and injustices inherent in the financial system, few people could come up with real-world, practical solutions that would actually make a difference for individuals and families.

Why? Because there's an inherent conflict in the system. **The largest financial institutions are set up to make a profit for themselves, not their clients.** Investors may think they are paying fees for high-quality, unbiased advice. Instead, they are all too often paying for the privilege of being offered a small sample of "suitable" investment products and services that are in constant conflict with improving the firm's bottom line.

HighTower is a solution to these problems, and that's why Tony originally came to interview me for this book. We offer only investment advice, and we have a platform of leading technology, products, and solutions that meet advisors' and investors' needs. We do not engage in the many toxic activities that create conflicts of interest within the major banks. We brought together some of the nation's best financial advisors. Simply put, we built a better model for transparent financial advice.

Tony's mission is to organize and bring to the masses the most honest and practical financial solutions—some of them are even "secrets." He understands that people need more than knowledge—they need a clear road map to a financially secure future.

The guidance provided within these pages is the result of unprecedented access to the leading minds in the financial world. I don't know of anyone other than Tony who could pull off such a feat. Only Tony, with his wide range of client relationships, his contagious enthusiasm, and his unrelenting passion could have convinced these individuals—among the best in the industry—to share their knowledge and experience.

Like me, these people trust Tony to capture their thinking and simplify it for a broad audience. And because Tony's passion lies in empowering people, he is able to take these conversations from theory to reality, offering tools that nearly anyone can use to improve his or her financial situation.

Tony challenged me to look at the solutions we had created for wealthy investors and figure out a way to make them available and applicable to the general public. I'm proud to say that we are deeply engaged in a variety of projects, and we are excited about the positive impact that together we will have on so many people.

True to his calling, Tony is using this book to empower individual investors while simultaneously helping those who have slipped through the cracks or been left behind by society. While two-thirds of Americans are concerned they won't have enough to retire, two million people have lost access to food stamps in the past year. Many of these individuals don't know where their next meal will come from.

Tony has stepped in to help fill the gap. He's spoken openly about his own experience with homelessness and hunger, and is committed to improving the lives of these often-forgotten populations. Tony is personally committed to feeding 50 million people this year, and is working to double that effort—feeding 100 million people—through matching contributions for next year and in the years ahead.

Tony has also partnered with Simon & Schuster to donate copies of his bestselling guide *Notes from a Friend: A Quick and Simple Guide to Taking Charge of Your Life* to those who are in need and just starting to embark on a new path of empowerment. His goal is to feed minds *and* bodies.

I am honored, humbled, and grateful to be a part of this project and eager to see the change we can enact together. I'm excited for you, the reader. You're about to meet the force of nature that is Tony Robbins and go on a journey that will truly be life changing.

—ELLIOT WEISSBLUTH,
founder and CEO, HighTower

INTRODUCTION

I first met Tony Robbins 25 years ago inside a cassette tape. After watching an infomercial on late-night TV, I took the plunge and bought his 30-day self-improvement program *Personal Power*. I listened to his tapes every day during my one-hour commute to and from Oracle Corporation, back and forth between my home in San Francisco and our office in Redwood Shores. I was so moved by Tony's words that one weekend I stayed home and did nothing else but listen again to all 30 days in just two days, and I quickly understood that Tony was truly an amazing person, and his ideas were unlike anything I had ever experienced before. *Tony transformed me.*

At the age of 25, as the youngest vice president at Oracle, I was massively successful—or so I thought. I was making more than $1 million a year and driving a brand-new Ferrari. Yes, I had what I thought was success: a great home and an incredible car and social life. Yet I still knew I was missing something; I just didn't know what. Tony helped me to bring awareness to where I was, and helped me start defining where I really wanted to go and the deeper meaning of what I wanted my life to be about. It wasn't long before I went to Tony's special intensive weekend program called Unleash the Power Within. That's where I really refined my vision and committed to a new level of massive action. With that, I dove deeper into Tony Robbins's work and launched full-force on my journey to create and build Salesforce.com.

I applied Tony's insights and strategies and built an amazing tool called V2MOM, which stands for vision, values, methods, obstacles, and measurement. I used it to focus my work, and ultimately my life, on what I really wanted. The V2MOM program took five of Tony's questions:

1. What do I really want? (Vision.)
2. What is important about it? (Values.)

3. How will I get it? (Methods.)
4. What is preventing me from having it? (Obstacles.)
5. How will I know I am successful? (Measurements.)

Tony said to me that the quality of my life was the quality of my questions. I soon began to model everything in my life, my work, and my future simply by asking these basic questions and recording my answers. What happened was amazing.

On March 8, 1999, the first day that we started Salesforce.com, we wrote a V2MOM, and today all of our 15,000 employees are required to do the same thing. It creates alignment, awareness, and communication, and it's all based on what Tony has taught me over the last two decades. Tony says repetition is the mother of skill—that's where mastery comes from—and so we keep writing and improving our V2MOMs. It's one of the reasons *Forbes* magazine just named Salesforce.com the "World's Most Innovative Company" for the fourth year in a row, and *Fortune* magazine says we are the "World's Most Admired" software company, as well as the seventh "Best Place to Work" in 2014. Today we produce $5 billion a year in revenue, and we continue to grow.

I can truly say that there would be no Salesforce.com without Tony Robbins and his teachings.

This book you are about to read, with its 7 Simple Steps to Financial Freedom, has the potential to do the same thing for you that Tony Robbins's *Personal Power* audio program did for me. It is going to bring Tony's wisdom into your life (along with the wisdom of 50 of the most brilliant financial minds in the world!) and give you the tools you need to make your life even better. As you read *Master the Game*, I am sure you will translate what Tony is saying into your own life, and create your own methods to achieve success and realize freedom.

When Tony told me the title of this book, the first thing I said was, "Tony, you're not about money! You're about helping people create an extraordinary quality of life!"

I soon discovered this book really isn't about money, it is about creating the life you want, and part of that is deciding what role you want money to play in it. We all have money in our lives; what matters is that you master money and it doesn't master you. Then you are free to live life on your own terms.

One of my closest mentors, General Colin Powell, former secretary of state and chairman of the Joint Chiefs of Staff, said this about money: "Look for something you love to do and you do well. Go for it. It will give you satisfaction in life. It could mean money, but it may not. It could mean a lot of titles, but it may not. But it will give you satisfaction." General Powell and Tony Robbins are saying the same thing. The real joy in life comes from finding your true purpose and aligning it with what you do every single day.

General Powell also urged me to consider the role of money as I pursued my vision of creating a software company that would change the world. He told me that the business of business was not just to make a profit but also to do good—to do good while doing well. Tony Robbins's focus on contribution, even 25 years ago, also made a strong impression on me and influenced my thinking. When I started Salesforce.com, I aimed to do three things: (1) create a new computing model for enterprises now called "cloud computing"; (2) create a new business model for enterprise software based on subscriptions; and (3) create a new philanthropic model that tightly integrates the success of a company with its ability to give back.

What has resulted over the last 15 years is a company that today has completely transformed the software industry and achieved a market capitalization of more than $35 billion. However, the best decision I ever made was putting 1% of our equity, 1% of our profit, and 1% of our employees' time into a philanthropic pursuit called Salesforce Foundation. It has resulted in more than $60 million in grants to nonprofits all over the world, more than 20,000 nonprofits using our product for free, and our employees contributing more than 500,000 volunteer hours to their communities. All of this happened once Tony helped me build the tools to gain clarity about what I really wanted to build, give, and become. And nothing has made me happier or brought me more satisfaction and joy in my life.

That's also why I have joined Tony in his quest with the nonprofit Swipeout program to provide meals to more than 100 million people a year; provide clean, disease-free water to more than 3 million families a day; and to work to free both children and adults from slavery.

I've sent my parents, my closest friends, and my most important executives to Tony's seminars to study his work, and they have all said the same thing: "Tony Robbins is one of a kind, and we are lucky to have him in our lives." Now, with *Money: Master the Game*, Tony will open the same door for you that he opened for me. I am confident that with him as your coach, you too will transform your life and find a path to gain everything you really want!

—MARC BENIOFF,
founder and CEO of Salesforce.com

WELCOME TO THE JUNGLE: THE JOURNEY BEGINS WITH THIS FIRST STEP

IT'S YOUR MONEY!
IT'S YOUR LIFE!
TAKE CONTROL

Money is a good servant but a bad master.
—SIR FRANCIS BACON

Money.

Few words have the power to provoke such extreme human emotions.

A lot of us refuse to even talk about money! Like religion, sex, or politics, the topic is taboo at the dinner table and often off-limits in the workplace. We might discuss *wealth* in polite company, but *money* is explicit. It's raw. It's garish. It's intensely personal and highly charged. It can make people feel guilty when they have it—or ashamed when they don't.

But what does it really mean?

For some of us, money is vital and crucial but not paramount. It's simply a tool, a source of power used in service of others and a life well lived. Others are consumed with such a hunger for money that it destroys them and everyone around them. Some are even willing to give up things that are far more valuable to get it: their health, their time, their family, their self-worth, and, in some cases, even their integrity.

At its core, money is about power.

We've all seen how money can have the power to create or the power to destroy. It can fund a dream or start a war. You can provide money as a gift or wield it as a weapon. It can be used as an expression of your spirit, your creativity, your ideas—or your frustration, your anger, your hate. It can be used to influence governments and individuals. Some marry for it—and then find out its real price.

But we all know that on some level it's an illusion. Money isn't even gold or paper today, it's zeros and ones in banking computers. What is it? It's like a shape-shifter or a canvas, assuming whatever meaning or emotion we project on it.

In the end, money isn't what we're after . . . is it? What we're really after are the feelings, the emotions, we *think* money can create:

> that feeling of empowerment,
> of freedom,
> of security,
> of helping those we love and those in need,
> of having a choice, and
> *of feeling alive.*

Money is certainly one of the ways we can turn the dreams we have into the reality we live.

But even if money is just a perception—an abstract concept—it doesn't feel that way if you don't have enough of it! And one thing is for sure: **you either use it, or it uses you. You either master money, or, on some level, money masters you!**

How you deal with money reflects how you deal with power. Is it an affliction or a blessing? A game or a burden?

When I was choosing the title of this book, a few people were actually outraged at the suggestion that money could be a *game*. How could I use such a frivolous term for such a serious topic! But, hey, let's get real. As you'll see in the pages to come, the best way to change your life is to find people who've already achieved what you want and then model their behavior. Want to master your finances? Find a financial master and imitate how he or she deals with money, and you will have found a pathway to power.

I can tell you right now, I have interviewed many of the wealthiest people in the world, and most of them *do* think of money as a game. Why else would anyone work ten or 12 hours a day after they've made billions of dollars? And remember, not all games are frivolous. Games are a reflection of life. Some people sit on the sidelines, and some play to win. How do you play? I want to remind you, this is a game that you and your family can't afford to lose.

My promise to you is this: if you will stay with me and follow the 7 Simple Steps in this book—the steps that have been distilled from the world's most successful financial players—you and your family will win this game. And you can win big!

But to win, you have to know the rules and learn the best strategies for success from those who have already mastered the game.

The good news is that you can save years of time—and in a few minutes—by simply learning the pitfalls to avoid and the shortcuts to experiencing lasting success. The financial industry often works to make this topic feel incredibly complex, but in reality, once you get past the jargon, it's relatively simple. This book is your opportunity to stop being the chess piece and become the chess player in the game of money. I think you're going to be very surprised at how, with an insider's understanding, you can easily transform your financial life and enjoy the freedom you deserve.

So let's get to it. Just imagine what life would be like if you had mastered this game already.

What if money didn't matter?

How would you feel if you didn't have to worry about going to an office every morning, or paying the bills, or funding your retirement? What would it be like to live your life on your own terms? What would it mean to know you had the opportunity to start your own business, or that you could afford to buy a home for your parents and send your kids to college, or have the freedom to travel the world?

How would you live your life if you could wake up each day knowing there was enough money coming in to cover not only your basic needs but also your goals and dreams?

The truth is, a lot of us would keep working, because that's the way we're wired. But we'd do it from a place of joy and abundance. Our work would continue, but the rat race would end. We'd work because we want to, not because we have to.

That's financial freedom.

But is it a pipe dream? Is it really possible for the average person— more importantly, for *you*—to make this dream a reality?

Whether you want to live like the 1% or just have the peace of mind from knowing that you won't outlive your savings, the truth is you can always find a way to make the money you need. How? The secret to wealth is simple: Find a way to do more for others than anyone else does. Become more valuable. Do more. Give more. Be more. Serve more. And you will have the opportunity to earn more—whether you own the best food truck in Austin, Texas, or you're the top salesperson at your company or even the founder of Instagram.

But this book isn't just about adding value—it's really about how to go from where you are today to where you truly want to be, whether that's financially secure, independent, or free. It's about increasing the quality of your life today by developing the one fundamental skill that the vast majority of Americans have never developed: the mastery of money. In fact, 77% of Americans—three of every four people—say they have financial worries, but only 40% report having any kind of spending or investment plan. **One in three baby boomers have less than $1,000 saved!** Polls show that fewer than one in four trust the financial system—with good reason! And stock ownership has been hitting record lows, particularly among young people. But the truth is, you don't *earn* your way to freedom. As you'll see later in this book, even multimillion-dollar earners such as *Godfather* director Francis Ford Coppola, boxer Mike Tyson, and actress Kim Basinger lost it all because they didn't apply the fundamentals that you'll soon be learning. You have to be able to not only hold on to a portion of what you earn for your family, but, more importantly, multiply what you earn—making money while you sleep. **You have to make the shift from being a consumer in the economy to becoming an owner—and you do it by becoming an investor.**

Actually, a lot of us are already investors. Maybe you first got into the game when Grandma bought you a few shares of her favorite stock just for being born, or perhaps your employer auto-enrolled you in the company's 401(k), or maybe you first became an investor when a friend told you to forget the Kindle and buy Amazon stock instead.

But is this enough? If you're reading this now, my guess is that you know the answer: no way! I don't have to tell you it's not your parents' and grandparents' investment world. The plan used to be so simple: go to college, get a job, work your butt off, and then maybe get a better job with a bigger corporation. After that, the key was to find a way to add value, move up the ladder, invest in company stock, and retire with a pension. Remember pensions? A promise of a never-ending income for life? They've become relics.

You and I both know that world is over. We live longer now on less money. New technologies keep coming online, stoking a system that often seems designed to separate us from our money instead of helping us grow it. As I write these words, interest rates on our savings hover near zero, while the markets rise and fall like corks on the ocean. Meanwhile, we're faced with a financial system of limitless choices and mind-boggling complexity. **Today there are more than 10,000 mutual funds, 1,400 different ETFs, and hundreds of global stock exchanges to choose from.** It seems like every day we're pitched more and more complex investment "instruments" with an alphabet soup of acronyms: CDOs, REITs, MBSs, MLPs, CDSs, CETFs . . .

WTF?

How about HFT? That's short for *high-frequency trading*, where 50% to 70% of the tens of millions of trades that churn through the market each day are now generated by high-speed machines. What does that mean for you? It takes only a half second, or about 500 milliseconds, to click your mouse to complete your E*Trade order. In that short time, the big boys with the supercomputers will have bought and sold thousands of shares of the same stock hundreds of times over, making microprofits with each transaction. Michael Lewis, bestselling author of the HFT exposé *Flash Boys: A Wall Street Revolt*, told *60 Minutes*, "The United States stock market, the most iconic market in global capitalism, is rigged . . . by a combination of the stock exchanges, the big Wall Street banks, and high-frequency traders . . . They're able to identify your desire to buy shares in Microsoft and buy them in front of you and sell them back to you at a higher price!" How fast are these guys? One HFT firm spent a quarter of a billion dollars to straighten the fiber-optic cables between Chicago and New York, reconstructing the landscape and literally terraforming the earth to shave 1.4 milliseconds off its transmission time! But even that's not fast enough. Some trades already take place in microseconds—that's a *millionth* of a second. Soon HFT technology will allow these trades to happen in nanoseconds— a *billionth* of a second. Meanwhile, they're laying cable on the ocean floor, and there's even talk of solar-powered drones acting as microwave relay stations to connect exchanges in New York and London.

If all of this leaves you reeling, I'm with you. What are your chances of competing with flying robots trading at the speed of light? **Where do you turn to find a path through this high-tech, high-risk maze of choices?**

> An expert is an ordinary man away from home giving advice.
> —OSCAR WILDE

The problem is, when it comes to money (and investing), everybody has an opinion. Everybody's got a tip. Everybody has an answer. But I'll give you a hint: they rarely have one that will really help you. Have you noticed how beliefs around money are like religion and politics? Conversations can get intense and emotional. Especially online, where people without any real knowledge or mastery will promote their own theories and criticize others' strategies with such vehemence, even though they have no proven track record. It's like a psychologist on Prozac telling you how you can have a fulfilled life. Or an obese person telling you how to get thin and fit. I tend to separate pundits into those who *talk the talk* and those who *walk the walk*. I don't know about you, but I'm sick and tired of hearing from all these "experts" who tell us what to do, but haven't produced results in their own lives.

If you thought you were going to hear from another investment guru making crazy promises, you came to the wrong place. I'll leave that to the financial entertainers who scream at you about buying the hottest stock, or implore you to save your money and put it in some mythical mutual fund. You know the one, where they promise you'll continuously compound your money with 12% annual growth. **They dole out advice that too often has no basis in reality, and often they don't even invest in the products they push.** Some of them might sincerely think they're helping, but people can be sincere and be sincerely wrong.

I want you to know I'm not one of those "positive thinkers" who's going to pump you up with a false view of the world. I believe in intelligence. You have to see things as they really are but not worse than they are—that view of life only gives you the excuse to do nothing. You may know me as the "smiling guy with the big teeth" on TV, but I'm not here to tell you to do a bunch of affirmations—I'm the guy who's focused on helping you dig deep, solve real problems, and take your life to the next level.

For 38 years, I've been obsessed with finding strategies and tools that can immediately change the quality of people's lives. I have proven their effectiveness by producing measurable results where others have failed. So far I've reached more than 50 million people from 100 different countries through my books, videos, and audio programs, and another 4 million in live events.

What I've known from the beginning is that **success leaves clues. People who succeed at the highest level are not lucky; they're doing something differently than everyone else does.** I'm interested in those people: those who have a relentless hunger to learn and grow and achieve. Don't get me wrong. I'm not deluded. I'm aware there are very few people in the world who are fit and healthy and who sustain it. Most people don't have decades of sustained love and passion in their intimate relationships, nor do they experience ongoing gratitude and joy. There are very few people who maximize their business opportunities. And there are even fewer who start with little or nothing and become financially free.

But a few do! A few *do* have great relationships, great joy, great wealth, and endless gratitude. I have studied *the few who do versus the many who talk.* If you want to look for obstacles, what's *wrong* is always available. But so is what's *right*! I am a hunter of human excellence. I seek out those individuals who break the norms and demonstrate to all of us what's really possible. I learn what those few extraordinary individuals do that's different from everybody else, and then emulate them. I find out what works, and then I clarify it, simplify it, and systematize it in a way to help people move forward.

Ever since the dark days of 2008, when the global financial system nearly melted down, I've been obsessed with finding a way to help everyday people take control of their money and fight back against a system that's often been rigged against them. The fix has been in for years, and it hasn't gotten a whole lot better with all those so-called reforms on Capitol Hill. In some areas, it's gotten worse. To find answers, I interviewed 50 of the most brilliant, influential players in the world of money. In this book, you won't get talking heads, and you won't get my opinions, either. You'll hear it straight from the masters of the game: self-made billionaires, Nobel laureates, and financial titans. Here's just a sampling of a few of the masters of money that you will be learning from in the pages ahead:

- John C. Bogle, the 85-year-old sage with 64 years of stock market history and the founder of the Vanguard Group, the number one mutual fund company in the world;
- Ray Dalio, founder of the largest hedge fund on the planet, with $160 billion in assets;
- David Swensen, one of the greatest institutional investors of all time, who grew Yale University's endowment from $1 billion to more than $23.9 billion in less than two decades;
- Kyle Bass, a man who turned $30 million in investments into $2 billion in two years during the subprime crisis;
- Carl Icahn, who has outperformed Warren Buffett, the market, and virtually everyone else in the last one-, five-, and ten-year cycles;
- Mary Callahan Erdoes, whom many consider to be the most powerful woman in finance. She oversees more than $2.5 trillion as CEO of J.P. Morgan Asset Management; and
- Charles Schwab, who led a revolution to open up Wall Street to individual investors, and whose iconic company now has $2.38 trillion under management.

I'll put you in the room with these and many other superstars who get consistent results, decade after decade, in up markets and down, booms and busts. Together we will uncover the core secrets to their investment success and see how to apply them even to the smallest amount of money.

And here is the key: I wrote this book based on timeless wisdom of the most successful investors in the world. After all, none of us knows which way the economy will be headed by the time you're reading this book. Will there be inflation or deflation? A bull market or a bear? **The idea is to know how to survive and thrive in any market condition. These *real* experts will explain how.** Plus, they'll be opening their portfolios to show you the mix of investments that they rely on to weather every storm. And they'll answer this question: If you couldn't pass on any of your financial wealth to your children, but only a set of principles, what would they be? That could be the greatest inheritance of all, and you don't have to be one of their kids to get it!

The secret of getting ahead is getting started.
—MARK TWAIN

Get ready, because together we're about to go on a journey through 7 Simple Steps to financial security, independence and freedom! Whether you're a millennial just starting out, a baby boomer facing retirement, or a sophisticated investor looking to keep your edge, this book will offer you a practical blueprint for setting and achieving your financial goals and help you break free from whatever limiting behaviors might be holding you back from true abundance. We'll explore the psychology of wealth, something I've studied and taught for nearly four decades. We'll tackle the money mistakes people make, zeroing in on what keeps them from following through on their best-laid plans. And to make sure you get the results you desire, I've gone to the best behavioral economists on earth to find **solutions that really work— small, simple adjustments that automatically trigger you to do what others need discipline to maintain; strategies that can make the difference between retiring comfortably or dying broke.**

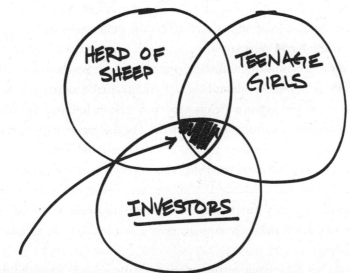

© 2013 Behavior Gap

Let's face it: so many smart and accomplished people have put aside this area of money because it seems so complicated and overwhelming. One of the first people I gave this manuscript to to review is a brilliant friend named Angela who has accomplished mastery in many areas of her life—but never in the area of money. She told me that people thought she was amazing because she'd sailed 20,000 miles of ocean in some of the roughest seas on small sailboats. But she knew she neglected her finances, and it embarrassed her. "It seemed so confusing, and I couldn't be competent. I already felt defeated, so I gave up, even though it's not in my nature." But she found that by following the 7 Simple Steps in this book, she could finally get control of her finances, and it was easy and painless! "Gosh, I could save for my future just by cutting a few things that don't give me joy," she told me. Once she started thinking about saving, she was able to set up an automatic investment account, and by chapter 2.8, she had already transformed her life.

A few days later, she came in to see me and said, "I got my first-ever brand-new car."

I asked her, "How did you do it?"

She said, "I began to realize that I was spending more money on my old car for repairs and gas than it cost me to finance a brand-new car!" You should have seen the look on her face when she pulled up in a shiny new pearlescent white Jeep Wrangler.

So I want you to know that this book is not just about how to have a comfortable retirement, but also about how to have the quality of life you desire and deserve today. You can live life on your own terms while you simultaneously lock in your future quality of life as well! The feeling of empowerment and inner strength and certainty that you experience when you master this area of your life will spill into everything else: your career, your health, your emotions, and your relationships! When you lack confidence about money, it unconsciously affects your confidence in other areas too. But when you take charge of your finances, it empowers you and excites you to take on other challenges!

What holds us back from getting started on the road to financial freedom? For a lot of us, like my friend Angela, it's the feeling that we're in over our heads. We've been taught to think, "This is too complex" or "This is not my field." Frankly, the system is *designed* to be confusing, so that you'll give up control to the "professionals" who reap enormous fees by keeping you in the dark. You're going to learn in the chapters ahead how to prevent that from happening, and, most importantly, I'm going to show you that investing your way to freedom isn't confusing at all.

One reason people succeed is that they have knowledge other people don't. You pay your lawyer or your doctor for the knowledge and skills you don't have. They also have their own special language that can at times keep them insulated from the rest of us.

For example, in the medical world, you might hear that 225,000 people have died "iatrogenic deaths" in the past year. According to the *Journal of the American Medical Association* (*JAMA*), it's the third largest cause of death in the United States. *Iatrogenic.* How's that for a hundred-dollar word? It sounds important, but what does it even mean? Is it a rare tropical disease? A genetic mutation? No, *iatrogenic* actually refers to an inadvertent death caused by a doctor, or a hospital, or an incorrect or unnecessary medical procedure.

Why don't they just come out and say so? Because it doesn't serve a medical institution's interests to put it in plain language a layperson can understand. The financial world has its own jargon too, with special words for things that are really additional fees disguised in language that would make it impossible for you to realize it is taking much more of your money than you would ever imagine.

I hope you'll let me be your translator as well as your guide on this journey. Together we'll break the code and cut through the complexity that keeps most of us feeling like outsiders in the world of finance.

Today there is so much information that even the most sophisticated investors can feel overloaded. Especially when we realize what's being pushed on us often has nothing to do with our needs. Say you're having some mild chest pains, and you Google the word *heart*. What do you see? It's not something about the heart attack you might want to deal with right now. Instead, you get Heart, the music group that hasn't had a hit in 20 years. How does that help you?

My plan is to serve you by becoming your personal financial search engine—a *smart* search engine, one that will filter through all the superflu-ous, even harmful financial information out there to deliver simple, clear solutions.

Before you know it, you'll be an insider too. You'll learn why chasing returns never works, why nobody beats the market long-term,[1] and why the vast majority of financial experts don't have a legal responsibility to serve your best interests. Crazy, right? You'll learn why the returns advertised by mutual funds are not the returns you actually earn. You'll find solutions that could add literally millions of dollars to your lifetime of investing returns—statistical studies show that you can save between $150,000 and $450,000 just by reading and applying the principles of section 2 of this book! You'll be putting money back in your own pocket, not the "fee factories." You'll also learn about a proven way of growing your money with 100% principal protection, and tax free to boot (IRS-approved). This vehicle is finally avail-able to individual investors like you.

And here's what truly sets this book apart: I don't just tell you about investment strategies that the ultrawealthy have and that you can't afford or access; I've found ways to make them affordable and accessible for you! Why should the privileged few be the only ones to tap into extraordinary opportunities? Isn't it time that we level the playing field?

Remember, *it's your money*, and it's time for you to *take control*.

A moment's insight is sometimes worth a life's experience.
—OLIVER WENDELL HOLMES, SR.

Before we go on, let me tell you what moved me to write this book. If you've watched any of the coverage of my work over the years, or if you've read any of my previous books, you probably know my track record for creating mas-sive and measurable change—helping people lose 30 to 300 pounds, turning around relationships that seem to be at their end, helping business owners grow their companies 30% to 130% in a year. I also help people overcome

---

1. Except for a few "unicorns," a tiny and exclusive group of "financial wizards" that the general population does not have access to, but I'll introduce you to in the chapters ahead.

enormous tragedies—from couples who've lost a child, to soldiers coming back from Afghanistan with post-traumatic stress disorder. **My passion is helping people create real breakthroughs in their relationships, their emotions, their health, their careers, and their finances.**

For nearly four decades, I've had the privilege of coaching people from every walk of life, including some of the most powerful men and women on the planet. I've worked with presidents of the United States as well as presidents of small businesses. I've coached and helped transform the performance of sports stars, from the early days with hockey great Wayne Gretzky to today's superstar Serena Williams. I've had the privilege to work with award-winning actors with the coolness of Leonardo DiCaprio and the warmth of Hugh Jackman. My work has touched the lives and performances of top entertainers from Aerosmith to Green Day, Usher to Pitbull to LL Cool J. And billionaire business leaders as well, such as the casino magnate Steve Wynn and the internet wizard Marc Benioff. In fact, Marc quit his job at Oracle and began building Salesforce.com after attending one of my Unleash the Power Within seminars in 1999. Today it's a $5 billion enterprise and has been named the "World's Most Innovative Company" by *Forbes* magazine for the last four consecutive years. So obviously **my clients don't come to me for motivation. They have plenty of that already.** What they get from me are strategies that help them hit the next level and keep them at the top of their game.

In the financial arena, since 1993 I've had the honor to coach Paul Tudor Jones, one of the top ten financial traders in history. Paul predicted the October 1987 Black Monday crash—still the largest single-day US stock market decline (by percentage) ever. While markets plummeted around the world and everyone else was losing his shirt, Paul as much as doubled his investors' money in 1987. He did it again in 2008, bringing his investors nearly a 30% positive return while the market plummeted 50%! My job working with Paul is to capture the principles that guide all his decisions. Then I put them into a system that he uses daily and, most importantly, at critical times. I'm not a positive-thinking coach. Quite the opposite: I'm a prepare-for-anything coach. I've been in touch with Paul, tracking his trading every day through a roller coaster of market conditions. From the tech bubble of the late 1990s to 9/11. From the growth in real estate and the collapse of the subprime market to the financial meltdown of 2008. I've been there during the subsequent European debt crisis as well as the largest one-day percentage crash in gold prices in three decades in 2013.

In spite of the diversity of these financial challenges, in 28 full consecutive years, Paul has never had a single losing year. I've been working with Paul for the last 21 of those years. He is truly unmatched in his ability to find the way to victory. I've had the privilege of being shoulder-to-shoulder with him while he made money consistently, no matter how volatile the market. Through him, I've learned more about the real world of investing and how decisions are made in tough times than I could get from a hundred MBA courses.

I'm also incredibly blessed to not only work with Paul during this time but also consider him one of my dearest friends. What I love and respect about Paul is that he not only creates financial results for himself but also is one of the most extraordinary philanthropists in the world. Over the years, I've watched him grow the Robin Hood Foundation from the simple idea of harnessing the power of free markets to alleviate poverty in New York into what *Fortune* magazine has called "one of the most innovative and influential philanthropic organizations of our time." So far Robin Hood has distributed more than $1.45 billion in grants and initiatives, changing millions of lives in the process.

I've also learned my own lessons along the way, some through the pain of my own trials and errors—which this book is designed to help you avoid as much as possible. I've earned my own scars on Wall Street. I took a company public when I was 39 years old and watched my personal net worth soar to over $400 million in a few weeks—and then plunge back to earth with the dot-com crash of 2000!

But that stock market "correction" was nothing compared with what we've all been through in recent years. The meltdown of 2008–09 was the worst economic crisis since the Great Depression. **Do you remember how it felt when it looked like our financial world was coming to an end?** The Dow Jones Industrial Average plunged 50%, dragging down your 401(k) with it. The bottom fell out in real estate, and the price of your home may have plummeted by 40% or more. Millions of people lost the gains from a lifetime of hard work, and millions more lost their jobs. During those terrible months, I received more phone calls from a greater variety of people needing help than ever before. I heard from barbers and billionaires. People would tell me they were losing their homes, their savings were gone, their children couldn't go to college. It just killed me because I know what that feels like.

I've worked hard and been blessed with financial success, but it wasn't always that way. I grew up with four different fathers in California's dusty San Gabriel Valley. I can vividly remember, as a kid, not picking up the phone or answering the door because I knew who was there—it was the bill collector, and we had no money to pay him. As a teenager, I was embarrassed to have to wear school clothes we bought for 25 cents at the thrift shop. And kids can be pretty brutal when you are not "hip." Today the thrift-store shopping would be a sign of coolness—go figure! And when I finally got my first car, a beat-up 1960 Volkswagen bug, the car had no reverse, so I parked on a hill, and there was never enough money for gas. **Thankfully, I didn't buy the theory that this is just how life is. I found a way to overcome my circumstances.** Because of my own experiences, I can't stand to see anybody suffer. It makes me crazy. And 2008 brought more needless economic suffering than I had seen in my lifetime.

In the immediate aftermath of the stock market crash, everybody agreed that something had to be done to fix the system. I kept waiting for those promised changes to happen, but years later it was still business as usual. And the more I learned about the roots of the financial crisis, the angrier I got. My personal tipping point came after I watched an Academy Award–winning documentary called *Inside Job*, narrated by Matt Damon, about the Wall Street gunslingers who took crazy risks with our money and nearly toppled the economy. And their penalty? We the taxpayers bailed them out, and somehow the same cast of characters was put in charge of the recovery. By the end of the film, I was seething with frustration, but I converted my anger into a question: "What can I do?"

This book was the answer.

There is no friend as loyal as a book.

—ERNEST HEMINGWAY

It wasn't an easy decision. I haven't written a major book in almost 20 years. Last year, on average, I was on a plane once out of every four days traveling to more than 15 countries. I run a dozen companies and a nonprofit. I have four children, an amazing wife, and a mission I love and live. To say my life is full would be an understatement. Both *Unlimited Power* and *Awaken the Giant Within* were international bestsellers, and that was enormously gratifying, but I haven't felt compelled to write again until now. Why? I love live events! I love the total-immersion experience, the immediacy and flexibility of communicating with 5,000 to 10,000 people at a time, going deep and keeping their focused attention for 50 hours in a weekend. And that in a day and age when most people won't sit for a three-hour movie that someone spent $300 million to make. I can remember vividly Oprah telling me that she couldn't stay for more than two hours—and 12 hours later she was standing on a chair and shouting to the camera, "This is one of the greatest experiences of my life!" Usher told me he loved my work, but certainly he wouldn't last through an entire weekend. Just like Oprah, he ended up having the time of his life. Fifty hours later he said to me, "This is like going to one of the greatest concerts of my life! I was writing notes like crazy, and you made me laugh my ass off!"

My live-event experience is filled with so much emotion, music, excitement, and profound insights that people are moved to take massive action. They don't just think, they don't just feel, they *change, they transform.* And my body language and my voice are essential to my style of teaching. So, I've got to confess, when I sit down to write words on a page, I feel like there's a gag over my mouth and one hand tied behind my back! Heck, I found that I could reach more than ten million people through one TED Talk alone.

So what made me change my mind?

The financial crisis caused tremendous pain, but it also made us reevaluate what's most important in our lives—things that have nothing to do with money. **It was a time to get back to basics, to the values that have sustained us through troubled times before.** For me, it made me remember the days when I was sleeping in my car homeless and searching for a way to change my life. How did I do it? Books! They helped to establish me. I've always been a voracious reader: as a young man, I decided I was going to read a book a day. I figured leaders are readers. I took a speed-reading course.

I didn't quite read a book a day, but over seven years, I did read more than 700 books to find the answers to help myself and others. Books on psychology, time management, history, philosophy, physiology. I wanted to know about anything that could immediately change the quality of my life and anyone else's.

But the books I read as a child made the deepest impression. They were my ticket out of a world of pain: a world with no compelling future. They transported me to a realm of limitless possibilities. I can remember Ralph Waldo Emerson's essay on self-reliance, and the lines "There is a time in every man's education when he arrives at the conviction that envy is ignorance; that imitation is suicide; that he must take himself for better, for worse, as his portion." Another was a book by the philosopher James Allen, *As a Man Thinketh*, echoing the biblical proverb "As a man thinketh, so his heart will be." It came to me at **a time when my mind was a battlefield filled with fear.** *He taught me that everything we create in our lives starts with thought.*

I devoured biographies of great leaders, great thinkers, great *doers*, like Abraham Lincoln, Andrew Carnegie, John F. Kennedy, and Viktor Frankl. I realized that the great men and women of the world had experienced pain and suffering much greater than my own. They weren't just lucky, or even fortunate; somehow there was something in them, an invisible force that would not let them settle for less than they could do, or be, or give. **I realized that biography is not destiny; that my past was not equal to my future.**

Another favorite was an American classic from 1937, Napoleon Hill's *Think and Grow Rich*. Hill spent two decades in the early 20th century interviewing 500 of the world's most accomplished individuals, from Andrew Carnegie, to Henry Ford, to Theodore Roosevelt, to Thomas Edison, finding out what made them tick. He discovered that they all shared a relentless focus on their goals, and a combination of burning desire, faith, and persistence to achieve them. Hill's message that ordinary people could overcome any obstacle to success gave hope to a generation of readers struggling through the Great Depression. *Think and Grow Rich* became one of the best-selling books of all time.

Napoleon Hill's quest has been an inspiration to me. Like his classic, this book is modeled on seeking out the best of the best in the world, from

Warren Buffett to Sir Richard Branson—and including the man that experts in the field have called the Edison of our day: Ray Kurzweil, who invented the first digital music synthesizers, the first software to translate text into speech; he's the man behind Siri on your iPhone. He developed a device that allows the blind to walk the streets and read road signs and order from any menu. Today Ray is head of engineering development for Google. But I wanted to write a book that went beyond the psychology and science of achievement to come up with a real plan, with real tools that you could use to build a better future for yourself and your family. It would be a handbook, a blueprint, an owner's manual for the new economy.

As I began to reassociate to the power of a book, I thought, "I need to put these answers in a form that's available to anyone." And with today's technology, this book has a few great advantages to help push you along the way. It has electronic segments where you can go online to see some of the men and women I interviewed and hear their words. We have an app that's designed to trigger you to walk through the 7 Simple Steps so you don't just learn the ideas but follow through and get the financial freedom you truly deserve.

By the way, **when I began this adventure, people told me I was crazy.** Many so-called experts—and even friends!—warned me I was nuts to try to bring the complex world of finance to a wide audience. Even my publisher begged me to write about anything else.

But I knew I could pull it off if I found the best voices to guide the way. Most of the people I've interviewed here do not give interviews, or if they do them, they're extremely rare. They might speak in Davos, Switzerland, at the World Economic Forum, or for the Council on Foreign Relations, but bringing their knowledge to the general population, in their voices, has never been done before. Sharing their critical insights in a way that anyone could act on became the mission of this book.

I've been honored to have great relationships with some of the most influential people in the world: friends in high places who were willing to make a few calls on my behalf. Before long I found doors opening to me, and I was getting access to the masters of the game.

Welcome to the jungle . . .

—"WELCOME TO THE JUNGLE," Guns N' Roses

So where do I start? I decided to start with a person who most people have never even heard of, even though he's been called the Steve Jobs of investing. But ask any of the world's financial leaders, whether they're the chairwoman of the Federal Reserve, the head of an investment bank, or the president of the United States, and they all know about Ray Dalio. They read his weekly briefing. Why? Because governments call to ask him what to do, and he invests their money. Same with pension funds and insurance companies. He's the founder of Bridgewater Associates, the world's largest hedge fund, with $160 billion in *assets under management (AUM)* at a time when a large hedge fund might manage $15 billion. It used to take a net worth of $5 billion and an initial $100 million investment just to get in the door. But don't bother trying; he won't take your money—or anybody else's—at this point.

Ray Dalio came from an unlikely background, born in Queens, New York, to a jazz musician father and a homemaker mother. He started as a caddy who picked up his first stock tips at the local golf course. Now he's worth about $14 billion and is the 31st richest man in the United States. How did he do it? I had to find out! Here's a man whose Pure Alpha fund, according to *Barron's*, has lost money only three times in 20 years, and in 2010 he produced 40% returns for his key clients. Over the life of the fund (since launching in 1991), he's produced a 21% compounded annual return (before fees). If there's anyone I wanted to ask, "Can the average investor still make money in this crazy, volatile market?" it was Ray. So when he told me, "There's no question you can still win," I was all ears! How about you?

It's not that easy to get access to Ray Dalio. But as it turns out, Ray already knew who I was, and he was a fan of my work. One afternoon I sat down with him in his surprisingly modest house on a wooded island off the Connecticut coast. He got right to the point, telling me that individual investors like you can win—but only if you don't try to beat the pros at their own game.

"What they gotta know, Tony, is you *can* win," he said. "But you can't do it by trying to beat the system. You don't want to try. I have fifteen hundred employees and forty years of experience, and it's a tough game for *me*. **This is poker with the best poker players on earth.**"

Ray is 65 years old, speaks with a soft New York accent, and uses his hands like a conductor when he talks. He reminded me that poker, like playing the markets, is a zero-sum game. For every winner, there has to be a loser. "As soon as you're in that game, you're not just playing poker against the guys across the table. It's a world game, and only a small percentage of people make real money in it. They make a lot. They may take money away from those who are not as good at the game," he said. "So I would say to your investors, the average guy: you don't want to be in that game."

I asked Ray, "If you're telling people they can't compete in this game, should they be thinking twice about letting someone else play *for* them? What about the brokers and mutual fund managers who say they can get you better returns?"

"You think you're going to a doctor, but they're not doctors," he told me. We're trained to throw our total faith into doctors and do whatever they tell us without thinking, hoping they have all the answers. But Ray Dalio says that typical money managers are not going to help you win because they don't have the skills or resources to play in the big game, either. "If they did, you wouldn't have access to them.

"The Olympics is easy compared with what we do," Ray continued. "This is more competitive. You can go to your broker-dealer, and you think you have to say, 'Is that a smart guy?' He might be smart. He might care about you. **But you've got to ask, 'How many gold medals has he won?'** You have to be very, very careful, because there are so many people who'd give you advice, but they have to be good enough to be able to take it away from the best in the game."

So what's the answer?

"Instead of trying to compete, you've gotta learn **there is a passive way to win.** There's a way to *not* put all your eggs in one basket. It's a system to **protect yourself against all downsides,** because the best investors know they're going to be wrong, no matter how smart they are."

Wait a second! Ray Dalio, who gets a compounded return of 21%, can still be wrong?

"That's right, Tony, I'm gonna be wrong," he said. "We're all gonna be wrong. So we gotta set up a system that protects us from that."

So, at the end of nearly three hours together, it was time for the big question: "Ray, what is that system?" And Ray said to me, "Tony, the last time

I took money, you had to have a five-billion-dollar net worth to get access to my knowledge and the minimum investment was one hundred million. It's really complex, and it changes a lot."

I said, "C'mon, Ray. You just told me that nobody new can get access to you anyway. I know how much you care about people. If you couldn't pass on your money to your children, and you could pass on only a set of principles or a portfolio—a system that will allow them to make money in good times and bad like you have—tell me what that would look like for the average investor?"

We went back and forth a bit, and in the end, guess what? He walked me through the sample ideal portfolio, the exact investment mix that would help you maximize returns with the least amount of downside volatility in any market.

What's a portfolio? If you're not familiar with the term, it's just a collection of diverse investments that you put together to try to maximize your financial returns. Ray revealed a simple system of what to invest in and in what percentages and amounts. And when we looked back in history, we found that by using his strategy, you would have made money 85% of the time over the last 30 years (1984 through 2013)! That's only four losing years in the last 30 years (1984 through 2013)—with a maximum loss of 3.93% in a year (and an average negative year of just 1.9%). And one of those four down years was just 0.03%, which most would chalk up to a breakeven. In 2008 you would have been down just 3.93% when the rest of the market lost 51% (from peak to trough)—all by just doing what Ray has shared with us. The plan he shared here has averaged a return of just under 10% per year (net of fees), and it's an investment plan that you can easily set up for yourself! And it's only *one* of the systems from the world's greatest investors that you'll learn when you get to section 6, "Invest Like the .001%: The Billionaire's Playbook."

Now, I know you want to jump ahead right now and look up the portfolio, but I want to remind you, there are 7 Simple Steps you have to follow to make this work. If you haven't figured out where you're going to get the money to invest, you haven't figured out what your goals are, and you don't know what the rules of the game are, then access to the best portfolio in the world will be worthless. So stay with me, and let's stay in sequence. There's a method to my madness!

How valuable is that information from Ray Dalio? If others have to have $5 billion to get access, and it cost you only the price of this book, then it's not a bad return on investment!

As exciting as it was to learn his investment system, what I found most interesting about Ray is how he looks at the world. He sees it as a jungle, and his life as a constant, exhilarating battle.

"The way I look at life, Tony, we all have something we want, something that represents a greater quality of life. But to get there, you have to go through a jungle filled with challenge. If you pass through it, you get to the life you desire. It's like I'm on one side of the jungle," he told me. "And you could have a terrific job, a terrific life if you can cross that jungle. But there are all of these dangerous things and they can all kill you. So, do you stay on one side and have a safe life, or do you go into the jungle? How do you approach that problem?"

Ray goes into the jungle with very smart and trusted friends by his side, always asking, "*What don't I know?*" "This is the key thing," he said. **"What has been very successful for me through my whole life is to not be arrogant about knowing, but to embrace the fact that I have weaknesses; that I don't know a lot about this, that, and the other thing. The more you learn, the more you realize you don't know."**

Is that ever the truth! And I was a living example. I went into this book thinking I knew what I was doing. After all, I'd had decades of experience. But during my four-year quest to meet the best investors on earth, I've been humbled over and over again by how much I didn't know. And I found that unlike the talking heads who claim to have all the answers, the best are essentially humble. Like Ray Dalio, they'll tell you what they think and then admit they could be wrong.

> Riches are not an end of life, but an instrument of life.
> —HENRY WARD BEECHER

As my journey continued, I found my mission was evolving. At each stop along the way, I was discovering tools, opportunities, and investment products available to ultrawealthy people that the average person never hears about. And ironically, some of the best ones have very little risk, or they have limited risk with what they call *asymmetric risk/reward*—which means the investors get a big upside potential for very little downside exposure. And that's what the "smart money" lives for.

It was exciting for me to find out about these opportunities and take advantage of some of them, because at this stage of my life, I'm old enough, fortunate enough, and well off enough financially to have those choices. But my sons and my daughter don't, and some of my dearest friends don't, and, most important, likely neither do you (unless you've got tens of millions stashed away and you're just reading this to see where Ray Dalio puts his money).

So I changed from being just a passive information gatherer in the world of investing to becoming a passionate advocate for my friends and readers. **I wasn't just going to tell you about something that wealthy people get to do; I wanted to open up these opportunities for everyone.** So I looked for companies that have focused exclusively on the ultrawealthy and then worked to convince them to create new opportunities for investors at any economic level or any age level. I've worked to highlight their services, and in some cases, I've gone all in and partnered with them to help create new products that will be available to you for the first time. But what I'm most proud of is that I've persuaded many of them to open up their services for people who are not wealthy—for free! In the pages that follow, you'll learn about a revolutionary strategic venture between Stronghold Wealth Management and HighTower, the fifth largest investment advisory firm in the United States, which provides transparent, conflict-free advice to the ultrawealthy. It will now provide some of the same extraordinary planning services at no charge to you, regardless of how much you have to invest. You will learn how to access a complimentary online platform that will allow you to test-drive your broker and see if you're truly overpaying for underperformance. I'm hoping this could be the beginning of a sea change in the world of personal finance, a real leveling of the playing field for the first time.

Why in the world do they do this? First, it's the right thing to do. People need to know what they are truly paying for. Second, they know that people with lots of money didn't always start out with lots of money. It's the secret to wealth, remember? Do more for others than anybody else does. And if

HighTower does this for you at this stage of your life, they're betting you won't forget them in the future. You'll become a raving fan and a loyal client forever.

You get the help you need today for no money and HighTower gets a future client. That's financial synergy. An opportunity to create the elusive win-win that rarely shows up in the world of Wall Street.

> Kindness in words creates confidence. Kindness in thinking
> creates profoundness. Kindness in giving creates love.
> —LAO-TZU

One of the great gifts of "mastering the game" is not only being able to win but to have enough to make a difference for others. No matter how difficult our situation may be, there are always people who are suffering more. When someone creates wealth, it's his or her privilege, and, I believe, his or her responsibility, to give back to those who are just beginning the journey or those who have experienced tragedies that have knocked them off the path. As I will share with you later, my family was the recipient of a simple act of kindness when we literally had no food, and that changed my entire perspective on people and life. It helped shape who I am today.

So for decades I have worked to give back by feeding more than 2 million people a year through my Anthony Robbins Foundation, and for the last few years, my wife and I have personally matched all their contributions.

Today I'm proud to say that a kid who started with no food personally helps 4 million people a year to feel cared for and fed. In total, over 38 years, I've had the honor to feed 42 million people.

I want to use this book as a vehicle to help you develop enough wealth—both physical and emotional—so that you can be a force for good through your economic contributions as well as your time. I will tell you, though, if you won't give a dime out of a dollar, you won't give $1 million out of $10 million. The time to give is now! When I had nothing, I began this process. The reward is that if you give, even at the times when you think you have very little, you'll teach your brain that there is more than enough. You can leave scarcity behind and move toward a world of abundance.

So I'd like to get you started on this path. As you read this book, know that you are not only helping yourself create a new financial future, but you are helping those 17 million American families who face hunger every day.[2]

How? I decided to do more in one year than I have in my entire lifetime. In the name of my readers, at the time of this publication, I am donating 50 million meals to the men, women, and children in this country who suffer from homelessness. You'd be surprised who these people are. Yes, some have been scarred by memories of serving in war and some are mentally or physically challenged. But millions are people just like you and me who had a normal life and then the loss of a job, a health problem, or a family loss pushed them over the edge to where they could not meet their financial obligations. Most Americans are only a few lost paychecks away from insolvency. So together let's reach out to help.

As I was writing this book, Congress slashed $8.7 billion from the food stamp budget. I witnessed firsthand the devastating impact this had on the volunteers and nonprofit organizations that work in the fight against hunger. That's why I put up 50 million meals, and I'm using my influence to get matching funds so that we can provide 100 million meals to feed the hungry. You're welcome to join in and help, but know this: because you bought the book, the one you are holding in your hand or reading on your iPad, you're personally feeding 50 people. My hope is that by the end of this book, you'll be inspired to make a small direct donation on your own as well. I have information in the last chapter on how you can use your "spare change to help change the world." There are so many simple and enjoyable ways in which you can give and create a legacy you can feel truly proud of.

Whew, this has been quite a full chapter! I know it's a lot, but hopefully it doesn't feel long! Do I have you hooked on what's really possible for your life now? Can you imagine what it will feel like to take yourself from where you are today to where you really want to be? What would it be like to have your experience of money no longer be a source of stress but rather a feeling of excitement and pride? I promise you the feelings you will have as you

2. Feedingamerica.com

conquer this area of your life will create a new momentum not only with financial success but also in other areas of life that matter even more! Are you ready?

One final note, if you've read this far, I want to compliment you because, unfortunately, you're in the top 10% of people who buy a nonfiction book. That's right: statistics show that fewer than 10% of people who buy a book ever read past the first chapter. How insane is that? I wrote this book to be simple but also to give you the opportunity to go deep—to master the game, to arm you with the skills to master your financial world once and for all. It's not meant to be a "little red book of investing." So I want to invite you now, and challenge you, to commit to take the full journey with me through these pages. I promise you the rewards you will reap will last for decades to come.

So turn the page and let me first give you a quick overview of what it will take to have an income for life—a paycheck that gives you the life you have (or the lifestyle you desire) without ever having to work again. Once you achieve this, you will work only if and because you want to. Let's grab an outline of the road ahead and discover the 7 Simple Steps to Financial Freedom.

THE 7 SIMPLE STEPS
TO FINANCIAL FREEDOM:
CREATE AN INCOME FOR LIFE

A journey of a thousand miles begins with a single step.

—LAO-TZU

Tell me something: Have you ever had that experience, you know . . . the completely humiliating experience of playing a video game against a child? Who always wins? The child, of course! But how does she do it? Is she smarter, quicker, stronger?

Here's how it works. You're visiting your niece or nephew, and she or he will say, "Come play it with me, Uncle Tony!"

You immediately protest, "No, no, I don't know this game. You go ahead and play."

And they say, "C'mon, it's easy! Just let me just show you." Then they shoot a few bad guys when they pop up on the screen. You still resist, so they start pleading. "C'mon! C'mon! Please, please, please!" You love this kid, so you give in. Then she says the simple words that tell you you're being set up: "You go first."

So you decide you're gonna make it happen! You're going to show this kid a thing or two. And then what? *Bam! Bam! Bam!* In 3.4 seconds, you're dead. Shot in the side of the head. Smoked.

Then the kid takes the gun, and suddenly it's *bam-bam-bam-bam-bam!* The bad guys are dropping from the sky and whizzing around every corner in hyperspeed. The kid is anticipating every move and picking them off— and about 45 minutes later, you get your second turn.

Now you're ticked off, and even more committed. This time you last a full five seconds. And she goes another 45 minutes. You know the drill.

So why do these kids always win? Is it because they have better reflexes? Is it because they're faster? No! **It's because they've played the game before.**

They already have one of the greatest secrets to wealth and success in life: **they can anticipate the road ahead.**

Remember this: anticipation is the ultimate power. Losers react; leaders anticipate. And in the following pages, you'll learn to anticipate from the best of the best: the Ray Dalios and the Paul Tudor Joneses and the army of 50 other extraordinary financial leaders who know the road ahead. They're here to help you anticipate the problems and challenges on the path to financial freedom so you don't get hurt along the way. Like Ray Dalio says, it's a jungle out there, full of things that can kill you financially, and you need trusted guides to help you get through it. With their help, we're going to lay out a plan that will help you anticipate the challenges, avoid unnecessary stress, and arrive at your ideal financial destination.

I want to give a quick overview of where we're going and how this book is set up, so you can make the best use of it. But before we do that, let's be clear about our true purpose. **This book is committed to one primary outcome: to set you up so you have an income for life without ever having to work again. Real financial freedom!** And the good news is, it can be achieved by anyone. Even if you're starting out in debt, deep in the hole—no exaggeration—with a little bit of time, consistent focus, and the right strategies applied, you can get to financial security or even independence in a few years.

Before we walk through the steps, let's first take a look at why being financially secure used to seem so simple. What's changed? And what do we need to do? Let's start with a little history lesson.

> You can be young without money, but you can't be old without it.
> —TENNESSEE WILLIAMS

Everything about your financial life seems so much harder these days, doesn't it? I'm sure you've wondered why it is so difficult to save money and retire comfortably. We've come to treat retirement as a given in our society;

a sacrosanct stage of life. But let's not forget that retirement is a relatively new concept. The idea has really served only a generation or two—for most of us, our parents and grandparents. Before their time, folks generally worked until they couldn't.

Until they died.

Do you remember your history? When was Social Security invented? It was created under Franklin Delano Roosevelt during the Great Depression, when there was no social safety net for old and sick people. And "old" was a different concept back then. The average life expectancy in the United States was 62 years. That's all! And Social Security retirement benefits were supposed to kick in at age 65, so not everybody was expected to collect, or at least not for very long. In fact, Roosevelt himself didn't live long enough to cash in on his benefits (not that he would have needed them). He died at the age of 63.

The Social Security Act eased the suffering of millions of Americans during a time of crisis, but it was never intended to become a replacement for retirement savings—just a supplement to cover the most basic needs. And the system wasn't designed for the world we live in today.

Here's the new reality:

There's a 50% chance that, among married couples, at least one spouse will live to the age of 92 and a 25% chance that one will live to 97.

Wow! We are closing in on a life expectancy of age 100 pretty damn quick.

And with longer lives, we expect longer—much longer—years for our retirement. Fifty years ago, the average retirement was 12 years. Someone retiring today at age 65 is expected to live to 85 or longer. That's 20-plus years of retirement. And that's the average. Many will live longer and have 30 years of retirement!

> It is not realistic to finance a 30-year retirement with 30 years of work. You can't expect to put 10% of your income aside and then finance a retirement that's just as long.
>
> —JOHN SHOVEN, Stanford University professor of economics

How long do *you* expect to live? All the breakthroughs we're seeing in medical technology might add years to your life—decades, even. From stem cell technology, to 3-D printing of organs, to cellular regeneration, technologies are exploding onto the scene. You'll hear about them in chapter 7.1, "The Future Is Brighter Than You Think." It's a blessing, but are you ready? Many of us are not.

A recent survey conducted by Mass Mutual asked baby boomers to name their number one fear.

What do you think it was? Death? Terrorism? Pestilence?

No, the number one fear of baby boomers was outliving their savings.

(Death, by the way, checked in a distant second.)

The baby boomers have a right to be scared, and so do millennials. According to an Ernst and Young study, 75% of Americans can expect to see their assets disappear before they die. And the Social Security safety net—if it survives into the next generation—won't provide a reasonable standard of living on its own. The current average benefit is $1,294 per month. How far do you think that will stretch if you live in New York, Los Angeles, Chicago, or Miami? Or how long will the equivalent system work in your country if you live in London, Sydney, Rome, Tokyo, Hong Kong, or New Delhi? **No matter where you live, if you don't have another source of income, you could end up the best-dressed greeter at Wal-Mart.**

It's obvious that we'll need to stretch our retirement income longer than ever before—smack in the middle of a flat economy at a time when many are struggling to recover lost ground.

How have we responded to this growing emergency? A lot of us find the problem so painful and overwhelming that we just block it out and hope it goes away. According to EBRI, the Employee Benefit Research Institute, 48% of all working Americans haven't even calculated how much money they'll need to retire. Yep, 48%! That's an astounding number: almost half of us have yet to take one of the first steps toward planning for our financial futures—and our time of reckoning is coming.

So what's the solution? It starts with taking Step 1: make the most important financial decision of your life. **By the time you finish this book, you'll**

not only have an automated plan for saving and investing, but also you'll know how to create income without having to work.

Wait a second! That's too good to be true, you're thinking. And anything that sounds too good to be true probably is, right?

Yet I'm sure you know there are some exceptions to the rule. What would you say if I told you that today there are financial instruments that will let you make money when the markets go up and not lose a penny when they go down? Twenty years ago, it would have been impossible for ordinary investors to imagine such a thing. But investors using these tools in 2008 didn't lose a dime or even a night's sleep. I have this kind of security and freedom for my family. It's an amazing feeling to know you'll never run out of income. And I want to make sure you have it for yourself and your family as well. In this book, I will show you how to create a guaranteed lifetime income stream.

A paycheck for life without ever having to work again.

Wouldn't it be great to open up your mail at the end of the month, and instead of finding a statement with an account balance you're hoping hasn't gone down, you find a check in its place? Imagine this happening every month. That's income for life, and there's a way to get it.

In section 2, we'll show you how to build your investments into a sizeable nest egg—what I call a *critical mass*—that will enable you to make money even while you sleep! With a few simple strategies, you'll be able to create a guaranteed income stream, allowing you to build, manage, and enjoy your own personal "pension" on your own terms.

It's probably hard for you to imagine that there's a structure available today that can deliver for you:

- 100% principal protection, meaning that you can't lose your investment.
- The returns in your account are directly linked to the upside of the stock market (for example, the S&P 500). So if the stock market goes up, you get to participate in the gains. But if the market goes down, you don't lose!
- You also have the ability to convert your account balance to a guaranteed income that you'll never outlive.

You can stop imagining—it's here! It's one of the opportunities that's now available for investors like you. (And you will find out about it in chapter 5.3.)

To be clear, I'm not suggesting here that, even with income for life, you'll want to stop working when you reach the traditional retirement age. Chances are you won't. Studies show that the more money you earn, the more likely you are to keep working. It used to be that the goal was to get rich and retire by the age of 40. Now the goal is to get rich and work until you're 90. Nearly half of all individuals who earn $750,000 per year or more say they will never retire, or if they do, the earliest they would consider it is age 70.

How about the Rolling Stones and Mick Jagger at age 71—still rockin' the world?

Or think of business moguls like Steve Wynn at 72.

Warren Buffett at 84.

Rupert Murdoch at 83.

Sumner Redstone at 91.

At those ages they were all still running their businesses and crushing it. (Probably still are.) Maybe you will be, too.

But what happens if we can't work, or don't want to work anymore? Social Security alone is not going to be much of a cushion for our retirement. With 10,000 baby boomers turning 65 every day and the ratio of old to young getting more and more lopsided, it may not even be around, at least as we know it. In 1950 there were 16.5 workers paying into the Social Security system to support one person getting benefits. Now it's 2.9 workers per recipient.

Does this ratio sound sustainable to you?

In an article titled "It's a 401(k) World," Thomas Friedman, the *New York Times* columnist and bestselling author, wrote, "If you are self-motivated, wow, this world is tailored for you. The boundaries are all gone. But if you're not self-motivated, this world will be a challenge because the walls, ceilings and floors that protected people are also disappearing. . . . There will be fewer limits, but also fewer guarantees. Your specific contribution will define your specific benefits much more. Just showing up will not cut it."

As for those sweet employee pensions our parents and grandparents counted on in retirement, they too are going the way of blacksmiths and telephone operators. **Only about half of America's private sector workforce is covered by any kind of retirement plan at all, and most of those are now do-it-yourself, take-all-the-risk models.**

If you're a municipal, state, or federal employee, you might still enjoy a government-backed pension, but with every passing day, there are more folks, like those from Detroit to San Bernardino, wondering if that money will be there when it's their time to collect.

So what's your retirement plan? Do you have a pension? A 401(k)? An IRA? Today about 60 million Americans participate in 401(k) plans, totaling over $3.5 trillion. But they can be a bad, even disastrous deal for you if you're in one of the high-fee plans that dominate the market. That's why, if you are in a 401(k) plan, you've got to read chapter 2.5, "Myth 5: 'Your Retirement Is Just a 401(k) Away.' " What you'll learn and the simple changes you can make could transform your life—giving you peace of mind and the certainty you need today—and mean the difference between retiring early and not being able to retire at all.

DEATH AND TAXES: THE ONLY CONSTANTS

Not to be outdone by volatile markets (moving faster than the speed of light, literally), exorbitant (and hidden) fees, and an outdated pension system, let's not forget about our good old friend the tax man. Oh, the tax man. He'll take up to 50% (or more!), thank you very much—on everything you earn. If you thought hidden fees were the only drag on accumulating wealth, you've missed the biggest culprit of all.

We all know the drag of taxes, to some degree, but few realize just how big a bite taxes take from our ability to achieve financial freedom. Sophisticated investors have always known this: it's not what you earn, it's what you keep that matters.

The greatest investors in the world understand the importance of tax efficiency. Just how destructive can taxes be when compounded over time?

Let's try a metaphor: say you've got one dollar, and somehow you're able to double it every year for 20 years. We all know this game. It's called compounding, right?

After year one, you've doubled your dollar to $2.
Year two: $4.
Year three: $8.
Year four: $16.
Year five: $32.

If you had to guess, what do you think your dollar has grown to by year 20?

Don't cheat and peek ahead. Take a moment and guess.

Through the magic of compounding, in just two decades your dollar turns into (drumroll, please): $1,048,576! That's the incredible power of compounding!

As investors, we want to tap into this power. But, of course, the game is not that simple. In the real world, Caesar wants to be paid first. The tax man is looking for his piece. So what's the impact of taxes on the same scenario? Once again, take a guess. If you're fortunate enough to pay only 33% in taxes per year, what do you think your dollar has now grown to after taxes in 20 years?

Again, take a moment and really guess.

Well, if the tax-free number was $1,048,576 . . . hmmm. With 33% tax, would that be about $750,000? Or even $500,000? Think again, Kemosabe.

Now let's look at the next column and see the incredible dollar-draining power when we take out money for our taxes each year before compounding—doubling our account. Assuming an annual tax rate of 33%, at the end of those same 20 years, the actual net amount you'll end up with is just over $28,000!

That's right, $28,000! A difference of over $1 million—and that doesn't even account for state taxes! In some states, such as California, New York, and New Jersey, you can expect the total to be significantly smaller still.

Sure, this dollar-doubling, dollar-draining scenario is based on returns you'll never see in the real world—but it illustrates what can happen when we neglect to consider the impact of taxes in our financial planning.

Given the way things are going in Washington, do you think taxes are going to be higher or lower in the coming years?

(You don't even have to answer that one!)

In section 5, I'm going to give you the "in" that until now was available only to sophisticated investors or ultra-high-net-worth individuals. I'm going to show you what the smartest investors already do—how to take taxes out of the equation, using what the *New York Times* calls "the insider's secret for the affluent." It's an IRS-approved method to grow your money tax free, and you don't have to be rich or famous to take advantage of it. It could literally help you achieve *your* financial independence 25% to 50% faster, depending upon your tax bracket.

> No person is free who is not master of himself.
>
> —EPICTETUS

But plan or no plan, the future is coming on fast. According to the Center for Retirement Research, 53% of American households are "at risk" for not having enough money in retirement to maintain their living standards. That's more than half! And remember, more than a third of workers have less than $1,000 saved up for retirement (not including pensions and the price of their home), while 60% have less than $25,000.

How can this be? We can't blame it all on the economy. The savings crisis started long before the recent crash. In 2005 the personal savings rate was 1.5% in the United States. In 2013 it was 2.2% (after topping 5.5% at the height of the meltdown). What's wrong with this picture? We don't live in isolation. **We know we need to save more and invest. So why don't we do it? What's holding us back?**

Let's start by admitting that human beings don't always act rationally. Some of us spend money on lottery tickets even if we know the odds of winning the Powerball jackpot are 1 in 175 million, and that we are 251 times more likely to be hit by lightning. In fact, here's a statistic that will blow your mind: the average American household spends $1,000 a year on lotteries. Now, my first reaction when I heard this from my friend Shlomo Benartzi, the celebrated professor of behavioral finance at UCLA, was, "That's not possible!" In fact, I was recently at a seminar and asked the audience how many had bought a lottery ticket. In a room of 5,000 people, fewer than 50 raised their hands. If only 50 people out of 5,000 are doing it and the average is $1,000, then there are plenty of people buying *way* more. By the way, the record is held by Singapore, where the average household spends $4,000 a year. Do you have any idea what $1,000, $2,000, $3,000, $4,000 set aside and compounded over time could be worth to you? In the next chapter, you're going to discover how little money it takes to have a

half million to one million dollars or more in retirement that requires almost no time to manage.

So let's turn to behavioral economics and see if we can't find some little
tricks that could make the difference between poverty and wealth. Behavioral economists try to figure out why we make the financial mistakes we
do and how to correct them without even our conscious awareness. Pretty
cool, huh?

Dan Ariely, renowned professor of behavioral economics at Duke University, studies how our brains fool us regularly. Human beings evolved
to depend on our sight, and a huge part of our brain is dedicated to vision. But how often do our eyes deceive us? Have a look at the two tables
below.

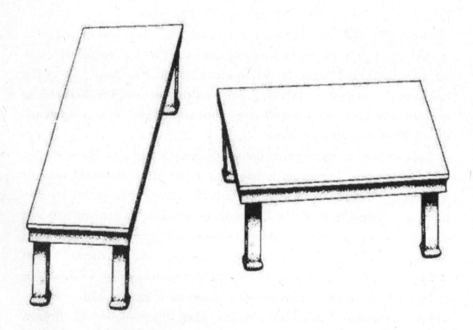

If I asked you which table is longer, the narrow one on the left or the fat
one on the right, most people would naturally pick the one on the left. And
if you were one of them, you'd be wrong. The lengths of both tables are
exactly the same (go on, measure them if you don't believe me). Okay, let's
try it again.

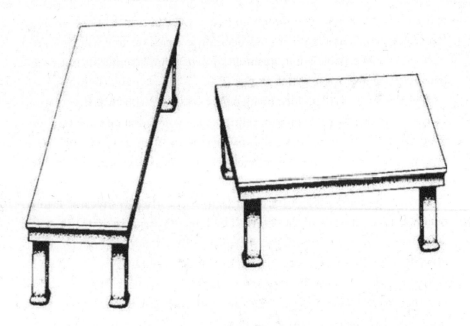

Which table is longer this time? Wouldn't you bet anything that the one on the left is still longer? You know the answer, and yet your brain continues to deceive you. The one on the left still looks longer. Your eyes haven't caught up with your brain. "Our intuition is fooling us in a repeatable, predictable, consistent way," Ariely said at a memorable TED Talk. "And there is almost nothing we can do about it."

So if we make these mistakes with vision, which in theory we're decent at, what's the chance that we don't make even more mistakes in areas we're not as good at—financial decision making, for example? Whether or not we think we make good financial decisions, or poor ones, we assume **we're in control of the decisions we do make.** Science would suggest we're not.

Just like the visual illusions we're susceptible to, Ariely told me later in an interview that he chalks up many of our decision-making mistakes to "cognitive illusions." A case in point: If you were to walk into your local Department of Motor Vehicles tomorrow and be asked the question "Do you want to donate your organs?" what do you think you would say? Some of us would immediately say yes, and think ourselves selfless and noble. Others might pause or balk or be turned off by the gruesomeness of the question and decline. Or maybe you'd punt and say you need time to think about it. Regardless, you'd assume that your decision is based on free will. You are a competent and capable adult, qualified to determine whether or not to donate your organs to save a life.

But here's the thing: a lot of it depends on where you live. If you are in Germany, there's about a one-in-eight chance you'll donate your organs—about 12% of the population does. Whereas in Austria, Germany's next-door neighbor, 99% of people donate their organs. In Sweden, 89% donate, but in Denmark, the rate is only 4%. What gives? Why such a disparity?

Could it be about religion, or a fear factor? Is it based on culture? It turns out the answer is none of the above. The huge disparity in donor rates has absolutely nothing to do with you personally or your cultural heritage. It has everything to do with the wording on the form at the DMV.

In countries with the lowest donor rates, like Denmark, there is a small box that says, "Check here if you want to participate in the organ donor program." In countries with the highest rates, like Sweden, the form says, "Check here if you *don't* want to participate in the organ donor program."

That's the secret! Nobody likes to check boxes. It's not that we don't want to donate our organs. That little bit of inertia makes all the difference in the world!

If a problem is too overwhelming, we tend to just freeze and do nothing. Or we do what's been decided for us. It's not our fault. It's the way we're wired. The problem with organ donation is not that people don't care, it's that they care so much. The decision is difficult and complicated, and many of us don't know what to do. **And because we have no idea what to do, we just stick with whatever is chosen for us," says Ariely.**

This same sense of inertia, or picking what has been chosen for us, helps explain why only a third of American workers ever take advantage of available retirement plans. It explains why so few of us have made a financial plan for our futures. It seems complicated. We're not sure what to do, so we punt, or we do nothing at all.

Ariely told me that when it comes to the physical world, we understand our limitations and build around them. We use steps, ramps, and elevators. "But for some reason, when we design things like health care and retirement and stock markets, we somehow forget the idea that we are limited," he said.

"I think that if we understood our cognitive limitations in the same way that we understand our physical limitations, even though they don't stare us in the face in the same way, we could design a better world."

Remember what Ray Dalio said about going into the jungle, that the first thing he asked himself was, *"What don't I know?"* If you know your limitations, you can adapt and succeed. If you don't know them, you're going to get hurt.

My goal in this book is to wake people up and give them the knowledge and the tools to take immediate control of their financial lives. So I've created a plan that won't trip you up because it's too complex, or too hard, or time intensive. Why? Because, as we've seen from those DMV forms, **complexity is the enemy of execution.** That's why I've divided this plan into 7 Simple Steps and created a powerful new smart phone app, completely free, to guide you through them. You can download it right now by going to www.tonyrobbins.com/masterthegame. You can check off your progress as you go, and celebrate your victories along the way. The app will support you, answer your questions, and even give you a nudge when you need it. Because you're going to get excited and have the best intentions, and then a few distractions or an attack of inertia can knock you off target. This automated system is designed to prevent that. And guess what? **Once you're done, you're done. After your plan is in place, you'll have to spend only an hour or so once or twice a year to make sure you're on course.** So there's no excuse not to stay on the path to a lifetime of financial security, independence, and freedom—and have plenty of time to enjoy the things that really matter to you!

Hopefully, by now your mind is churning. I know I've given you a lot to think about so far, but I'm committed to creating lasting breakthroughs in your financial life, and I want you to get a clear picture of the road ahead. So let's take a quick walk through the 7 Simple Steps to Financial Freedom.

If you belong to a generation raised on blogs and tweets, my guess is that you're saying: "Why don't you just put these 7 Steps—and, for that matter, the whole book!—in one paragraph for me, or even an infographic?" I could do that. But *knowing* information is not the same as *owning* it and following through. Information without execution is poverty. Remember: we're drowning in information, but we're starving for wisdom.

So I want to prepare your mind for each of the steps that are coming. In this way, you'll be ready to take the necessary actions that will guarantee that your path to financial freedom is realized.

This book is designed to give you mastery over a subject that torments most people because they've never taken the time to master the fundamentals that would set them free. And mastery means going deep. Anyone can read something, remember it, and feel like he or she has learned something. **But true mastery requires three levels.**

The first is cognitive understanding. It's your ability to understand the concept. Any of us can get it. And many of us already have a *cognitive* understanding of personal finance and investing. But that and $3 will almost buy you a cup of coffee at Starbucks! What I mean is that information by itself is not valuable. It's only the first step.

You start getting real value when you reach the second step: emotional mastery. That's where you have heard something with enough repetition, and it's stimulated enough feelings inside you—desires, hungers, fears, concerns—that now you become conscious and capable of consistently using what you've learned.

But the ultimate mastery is physical mastery. That means you don't have to think about what you do; your actions are second nature. **And the only way to get it is through consistent repetition.** My great teacher, Jim Rohn, taught me that **repetition is the mother of skill.**

I'll give you a perfect example of where I fell short in this area. In my early twenties, I decided I wanted to get a black belt in martial arts, and I had the privilege of meeting and becoming dear friends with the grand master Jhoon Rhee. He's the man who brought Tae Kwon Do to this country and who trained both Bruce Lee and Muhammad Ali in the art. I told him I wanted to gain my black belt in the shortest time in history, and I was willing to do whatever it took in terms of practice, commitment, and discipline to break the record. He agreed to travel on the road with me to complete my training. It was brutal! I'd often finish a seminar and arrive at one o'clock in the morning for my training, and then work with the master for another three or four hours. I would have to get by on four hours of sleep at most.

One night, after a particularly long period of practicing the same exact move at least 300 times, I finally turned to my teacher and asked, "Master, *when* can we go on to the next move?" He looked at me sternly and said, "Oh, grasshopper, this *is* the next move. The fact that you can't tell the difference between the move you made this time and the one you did before shows you are still a dabbler. Those fine distinctions are the difference between a master and an amateur. And mastery requires this level of repetition. With each repetition you must learn more," he said with a smile.

Do you see my point? This book was not designed for you to skim through in an afternoon.

As you read, you'll notice that this book is unlike anything you've encountered before because it reflects my unique style of teaching. You'll be asked a lot of questions, and you'll sometimes see facts and phrases that you've read before. There will be a lot of exclamation points! This isn't an editing mistake! It's a technique designed to mark out key ideas and to build knowledge into your mind, body, and spirit so that action becomes automatic. That's when you'll start seeing results and reaping the rewards that you desire and deserve. Are you up for the challenge?

And remember: this is not just a book, it's a blueprint. Each section is designed to help you understand exactly where you are in financial terms and help you close the gap between where you are now and where you truly want to be. This work is designed to arm you, not just for today but for the rest of your life. I know you'll come back at different stages to take things to the next level.

SECTION 1:
WELCOME TO THE JUNGLE:
THE JOURNEY BEGINS WITH THIS FIRST STEP

Like all great adventurers, we'll start by getting oriented for the trip. In chapter 1.4, you'll learn more about the psychology of wealth, what holds us back, and some simple cures. You'll uncover what it is you're really investing for, and unleash the power of the best financial breakthrough strategies. Then, in the next chapter, we blast off. Here **you'll take the first of the 7 Simple Steps and make the most important financial decision of your life. This chapter is a must read.** You'll learn how, with even the smallest amount of money combined with the miracle power of compounding, you can absolutely become financially independent in your life without ever having to make a fortune in annual income. You'll activate this system by deciding on a portion of your income to save and invest for compounded interest. You'll become not just a consumer in the economy but also an owner—an investor with a stake in the future. You'll learn how to build your own automated "money machine," a system that will generate income for you for a lifetime while you sleep.

SECTION 2:
BECOME THE INSIDER:
KNOW THE RULES BEFORE
YOU GET IN THE GAME

Maybe you've heard that old expression, "When a man with money meets a man with experience, the man with the experience ends up with the money, and the man with the money ends up with the experience." Now that you've decided to become an investor, this section explains the critical rules of the game so that you don't fall prey to those players with all the experience. This road map shows the way through the investment jungle that Ray Dalio was talking about, with the worst danger zones marked with big red Xs. These are the marketing myths—some people call them investment lies—that are often designed to systematically separate you from your money. You'll learn why the returns the mutual funds advertise are not the returns that you actually receive. I know it sounds crazy, but the 1% fee that you think is the total cost you're paying is really only one of more than ten potential fees, and that your average mutual fund might be eating up 60% of your potential returns over time! Remember, in this short section alone, you'll save between **$250,000 and $450,000 minimum,** back in your pocket without getting any better returns over your investment lifetime! And you'll see that this amount is all documented—based on studies, not based on my opinion or funny math. We'll also discuss the deceptions that can be a part of *target-date funds* and *no-load funds*, and arm you with a real understanding of how to protect yourself from firms that often tailor these products and strategies for *their* maximum profit—not yours! By the end of this section you'll have taken your second step, and even if you only have a small amount of money, you'll be investing it like an insider.

SECTION 3:
WHAT'S THE PRICE OF YOUR DREAMS?
MAKE THE GAME WINNABLE

Together we'll explore your financial dreams, and set some realistic goals that will make the game truly winnable. Most people have no idea how much money they'll need to achieve financial security, independence, and freedom. Or the giant numbers they have in their heads are so intimidating that they never even start a plan to get there. But in chapter 3.1, you'll figure out what you *really* want, and it's going to be exciting—especially when you realize that your dreams may be closer than you think. You'll not only dream, but you'll turn those dreams into reality—a plan—in chapter 3.2. It's going to be different for everyone, and we have the software to customize it for you. You can do it online or on your app, where you can keep it and change it as many times as you want until you find a realistic and achievable plan. And if you're not getting to your dreams fast enough, we're going to show you five ways to speed it up in section 3. By the time you've taken Step 3, you'll not only know how to build wealth for your future retirement, but how to enjoy it along the way.

SECTION 4:
MAKE THE MOST IMPORTANT
INVESTMENT DECISION OF YOUR LIFE

Now that you're thinking like an insider, you know the rules of the game, and you've learned how to make the game winnable, it's time to make the most important *investment* decision of your life: Where do you put your money and in what proportions? *Asset allocation* is what every Nobel Prize winner, every hedge fund manager, every top institutional investor, bar none, told me was the key to successful investing—yet virtually 99% of Americans know little or nothing about it. Why? Maybe it seems too complicated. But in chapter 4.1, I'm going to make it simple and also show you where to go to have an expert assist you online. Proper asset allocation means dividing up what you're investing into buckets that are secure and give you peace of mind, versus buckets that are riskier but may have greater potential for growth. It's the ultimate bucket list! And when you complete Step 4, you'll not only know how to *become* wealthy, but how to *stay* wealthy.

SECTION 5:
UPSIDE WITHOUT THE DOWNSIDE:
CREATE A LIFETIME INCOME PLAN

What good is investing if you don't have any money to spend? Most people have been so conditioned to focus on putting more money in a 401(k) plan or building their retirement account they forget that they'll need to draw it down as income some day. And since account balances fluctuate (remember, they don't just go up!), we must create and protect our income plan. Remember 2008? How do you protect yourself from the next crash? How do you set up a portfolio that avoids getting whipsawed? How do you know you won't end up outliving your money, which is so many people's number one fear? You may be blessed with a long life, but it may not feel like a blessing if you run out of money. In this section we'll offer specific insights into one of the best-kept secrets in the financial community and help you develop a guaranteed lifetime income plan—a certain revenue stream that can form the foundation for true financial peace of mind. **We'll explore creative ways you can stop or drastically limit losses and increase your gains**—using the investment vehicles favored by banks, large corporations, and some of the world's wealthiest individuals. What do they know that you don't know? It's how to have the upside without the downside, and to make sure your gains aren't eaten away by taxes.

SECTION 6:
INVEST LIKE THE .001%:
THE BILLIONAIRE'S PLAYBOOK

We'll hear what's good and what's challenging about the state of the global economy—how we got here and what may be coming next—from some of the clearest and most influential thinkers in the financial world. **Then you'll meet the masters of the game, 12 of the most colorful and brilliant minds in finance, and learn what has guided them through every economic condition.** We'll ask **Paul Tudor Jones** how he made a 60% monthly return in 1987 by predicting the Black Monday crash, when the market was burning down around him. And how, 21 years later, he was able to make nearly 30% when the market lost nearly 50% and the world seemed to be falling apart again. Plus we'll look at how he has avoided losses and managed to have 28 straight profitable years in every conceivable market, never losing a dime. Some of the people you'll be meeting in our "Billionaire's Playbook," such as **Charles Schwab, Carl Icahn, T. Boone Pickens, Ray Dalio,** and **Jack Bogle,** struggled when they were growing up—they weren't born with a silver spoon in their mouth. So how did they make it to the top? We'll ask what money means to them, and we'll peek into their actual portfolios. By the time you've finished Step 6, you'll know how the .001% invests.

SECTION 7:
JUST DO IT, ENJOY IT, AND SHARE IT

Here we'll come up with an action plan to help you live a better, fuller, richer, more joyful life. And we'll talk about what to do to stay on target. I guarantee we'll blow your mind with some of the breathtaking new technologies that will make even the *near* future better than you think. This is the opposite of what most people believe. According to an NBC–*Wall Street Journal* poll, 76% of Americans—an all-time record—think that their children's lives will be worse off than their own! But you're going to get an insider's look at what's coming from some of the most brilliant minds of our time. We'll hear from my friends Ray Kurzweil, the Edison of our age, and Peter Diamandis, creator of the X Prize, about new technologies coming online: 3-D printers that will transform your personal computer into a manufacturing plant, self-driving cars, exoskeletons that enable paraplegics to walk, artificial limbs grown from single cells—innovations that will dramatically change our lives for the better in the very near future. I'm hoping this will inspire you, and also show you that even if you somehow screw up and don't get your financial act together, you'll still have a better quality of life. And for those with the resources, you're looking at a future of limitless possibilities.

We'll wrap up with the simple fact that the secret to living is giving: sharing with others not only gives you a greater quality of life but also brings you a greater experience of joy. And you'll learn about new technologies that make giving painless and fun. As you feed your mind and build your own wealth, my hope is that you'll do well enough to help others. And remember, you're my partner in giving now. And as you're reading, someone in need is being fed.

> I don't believe people are looking for the meaning of life as
> much as they are looking for the experience of being alive.
> —JOSEPH CAMPBELL

I've made these 7 Simple Steps to Financial Freedom as clear and simple as possible for you. Now it's up to you to take action and follow through each of the seven steps, one at a time, to get the job done.

What do you need to see it through? What works best for you? Let's create a simple plan together now. Some of you might sit down and read the whole book over a long weekend—and if you do, then you're as crazy and as obsessed as I am, a brother or sister on the path! If you don't have a weekend to spare, consider taking a chapter a day or a section a week. Immerse yourself a little bit at a time for a few weeks and you'll get it done. Whatever it takes.

This is a journey of a lifetime, a journey worth mastering! If you're with me, let the journey begin!

TAP THE POWER:
MAKE THE MOST IMPORTANT
FINANCIAL DECISION OF YOUR LIFE

My wealth has come from a combination of living in
America, some lucky genes, and compound interest.
—WARREN BUFFETT

Let's kick it in gear now. It's time to begin our journey by tapping the power that can create real wealth for anyone. It's not some get-rich-quick scheme, and it's not what most people think will make them financially free or wealthy. Most people are looking to make some "big score"—a financial windfall—and then they think they'll be set.

But let's face it, we're not about to *earn* our way to wealth. That's a mistake millions of Americans make. We think that if we work harder, smarter, longer, we'll achieve our financial dreams, but our paycheck alone—no matter how big—isn't the answer.

I was reminded of this fundamental truth on a recent visit with the noted economist Burton Malkiel, author of one of the classic books on finance, *A Random Walk Down Wall Street.* I went to see Malkiel in his office at Princeton University because I admired not just his track record but also his no-nonsense style. In his books and interviews, he comes across as a straight shooter—and the day I met him was no exception. I wanted to get his insights on some of the pitfalls facing people at *all* stages of their investment lives. After all, this was the guy who helped create and develop the concept of index funds—a way for the average investor to match, or mimic, the markets; a way that anyone, even with a small amount of money, can own a piece of the entire stock market and have true portfolio diversity instead of being stuck with the ability to buy only a small number of shares of stock in one or two companies. Today this category of investments accounts for over **$7 trillion** in assets! Of all the people I'd planned to interview for this book, he was one of the best-qualified to help me cut through the clutter and doublespeak of Wall Street and assess our current investment landscape.

What's the biggest misstep most of us make right from the start? Malkiel didn't even hesitate when I asked him. He said the majority of investors fail to take full advantage of the incredible power of compounding—the multiplying power of growth times growth.

Compound interest is such a powerful tool that Albert Einstein once called it the most important invention in all of human history. But if it's so awesome, I wondered, why do so few of us take full advantage of it? To illustrate the exponential power of compounding, Malkiel shared with me the story of twin brothers William and James, with investment strategies that couldn't have been more different. He gives this example in one of his books, so I was familiar with it, but to hear him tell it *live* was an incredible experience—a little like hearing an 81-year old Bruce Springsteen play an acoustic version of "Born to Run" in his living room. The story supposes that William and James have just turned 65—the traditional retirement age. William got a jump-start on his brother, opening a retirement account at the age of 20 and investing $4,000 annually for the next 20 years. At 40, he stopped funding the account but left the money to grow in a tax-free environment at the rate of 10% each year.

James didn't start saving for retirement until the ripe old age of 40, just as his brother William stopped making his own contributions. Like his brother, James invested $4,000 annually, also with a 10% return, tax free, but he kept at it until he was 65—25 years in all.

In sum, William, the early starter, invested a total of $80,000 ($4,000 per year × 20 years at 10%), while James, the late bloomer, invested $100,000 ($4,000 per year × 25 years at 10%).

So which brother had more money in his account at the age of retirement?

I knew where Malkiel was going with this, but he told the story with such joy and passion that it's like he was sharing it for the very first time. The answer, of course, was **the brother who'd started sooner and invested the least money.** How much more did he have in his account? Get this: *600% more!*

Now, step back for a moment and put these numbers in context. If you're a millennial, a Gen Xer, or even a baby boomer, pay close attention to this message—and know that this advice applies to you, no matter where you are on your personal timeline. If you're 35 years old and you suddenly grasp the power of compounding, you'll wish you got started on it at 25. If you're 45, you'll wish you were 35. If you're in your 60s or 70s, you'll think back to the pile of money you could have built and saved if only you'd gotten started on all that building and saving when you were in your 50s and 60s. And on and on.

In Malkiel's example, it was **William, the brother who'd gotten the early start and stopped saving before his brother had even begun, who ended up with almost $2.5 million.** And it was **James, who'd saved all the way until the age of 65, who had less than $400,000. That's a gap of over $2 million!** All because William was able to tap into the awesome power of compounding for an additional 20 years, giving him an insurmountable edge—and saddling him with the family dinner checks for the rest of his life.

> The man on top of the mountain didn't fall there.
>
> —VINCE LOMBARDI

Not convinced that compound interest, over time, is the only sure way to grow your *seed of money* into the *bumper crop of financial security* you'll need to meet your future needs? Malkiel shared another favorite story to bring home his point—and this one's from our history books. When Benjamin Franklin died in 1790, he left about **$1,000** each to the cities of Boston and Philadelphia. His bequests came with some strings attached: specifically, the money was to be invested and could not be touched for 100 years. At that point, each city could withdraw up to $500,000 for designated public works projects. Any remaining money in the account could not be touched for another 100 years. Finally, 200 years after Franklin's death, **a period of**

time that had seen stocks grow at an average compounded rate of 8%, each city would receive the balance—which in **1990 amounted to approximately $6.5 million.** Imagine that $1,000 grows to $6.5 million, with no money added over all those years.

How did it grow? Through the power of compounding!

Yes, 200 years is a long, long time—but **a 3,000% rate of return** can be worth the wait.

Malkiel's examples show us what we already know in our hearts to be true: that for most of us, **our earned income will never bridge the gap between where we are and where we really want to be.** Because earned income can never compare to the power of compounding!

> Money is better than poverty, if only for financial reasons.
> —WOODY ALLEN

Still think you can earn your way to financial freedom? Let's take a quick look at how it's worked out for some of the highest-paid people in the world:

Legendary baseball pitcher Curt Schilling earned more than $100 million in an incredible career that included not one but two World Series championships for the Boston Red Sox. But then he poured his savings into a videogame startup that went bankrupt—and brought Schilling down with it. "I never believed that you could beat me," Schilling told ESPN. "I lost."

Now he's $50 million in debt.

Kim Basinger was one of the most sought-after actresses of her generation, torching the big screen with indelible roles in such films as *9½ Weeks, Batman,* and *L.A. Confidential,* which earned her an Academy Award as best supporting actress. At the height of her A-list popularity, she earned more than $10 million per picture—enough to spend $20 million to buy a whole town in Georgia.

Basinger ended up bankrupt.

Marvin Gaye, Willie Nelson, M.C. Hammer, Meat Loaf—they sold millions of albums and filled stadiums with adoring fans. Francis Ford Coppola? He packed theaters as the director of *The Godfather,* one of the greatest

American films, which—at least for a while—held the all-time box office record with gross ticket sales of $129 million.

All had near-brushes with bankruptcy—Coppola, three times!

Even Michael Jackson, the "King of Pop," who reportedly signed a recording contract worth almost $1 billion and sold more than 750 million records, was forced to the brink of bankruptcy in 2007, when he was unable to pay back a $25 million loan on his Neverland Ranch. *Jackson spent money like he would never run out—until he finally did.* At his death two years later, he reportedly owed more than $300 million.

Do you think any of these ultra-megastars imagined a day when the money would stop flowing? Do you think they even *considered* preparing for such a day?

Have you ever noticed that no matter how much you earn, you find a way to spend it? By these examples, it's clear to see that you and I are not alone. We all seem to have a way of living up to our means—and some of us, I'm afraid, find a way to live *beyond* our means. We see this most of all in the stars who take the biggest falls—like the rich-beyond-their-dreams prizefighters who hit the canvas with a thud. Just look at the up-and-down-and-out career of **former heavyweight champ Mike Tyson, who made more money in his time than any other boxer in history—nearly a half billion dollars—and went bankrupt.**

But five-division world champion Floyd "Money" Mayweather Jr. is about to beat Iron Mike's earning record. Like Tyson, Mayweather fought his way up from hardscrabble beginnings. In September 2013 he scored a guaranteed purse of $41.5 million for his bout against Saúl "Canelo" Álvarez—a record amount that grew to more than $80 million based on pay-per-view totals. And that was just for one fight! Before this giant payday, he'd already topped the *Sports Illustrated* "Fortunate 50" list ranking the richest athletes in the United States. I love Mayweather personally. He's an extraordinarily gifted athlete—with a work ethic like few alive. He's also incredibly generous with his friends. There is a lot to appreciate in this man! But Mayweather had fought his way to the top of this list before, only to lose his fortune to wild spending sprees and bad investments. He is reported to spend so recklessly, he's known to carry around a backpack filled with

$1 million in cash—just in case he needs to make an emergency donation to Louis Vuitton.

Like so many achievers, the champ is smart as a whip, and my hope is that he is following better investment practices today, but according to no less an authority on money than 50 Cent, Mayweather's former business partner, the champ has no income outside of fighting. The rapper summed up the boxer's financial strategy in plain terms: "It's fight, get the money, spend the money, fight. Fight, get the money, spend the money, fight."

Sound like a ridiculous strategy? Unfortunately, we can all relate at some level. *Work, get the money, spend the money, work*—it's the American way!

> Before you speak, listen. Before you write, think. Before you spend, earn.
> Before you invest, investigate. Before you criticize, wait. Before you pray,
> forgive. Before you quit, try. Before you retire, save. Before you die, give.
> —WILLIAM A. WARD

Here's the $41.5 million question: If these individuals couldn't build on their talents and blessings and *earn their way to financial freedom*, how can *you* expect to earn your way?

You can't.

But what you *can* do is make a simple change in strategy and embrace a whole new mind-set. You have to take control and harness the exponential power of compounding. It will change your life! **You have to move from just working for money to a world where money works for you.**

It's time to get off the sidelines and get into the game—because, ultimately, we must all become investors if we want to be financially free.

You're already a financial trader. You might not think of it in just this way, but if you work for a living, you're trading your time for money. Frankly, it's just about *the worst trade you can make*. Why? You can always get more money, but you can't get more time.

I don't want to sound like one of those tearjerker MasterCard commercials, but we all know that life is made up of priceless moments. Moments that you'll miss if you're trading your time for money.

Sure, from time to time, we all need to miss a dance recital or a date night when duty calls, but our precious memories aren't always there for the taking.

Miss too many of them, and you might start to wonder what it is you're *really* working for, after all.

THE ULTIMATE ATM

So where do you go if you need money and you're not a world champion fighter with a backpack of large bills? What kind of ATM do you need to complete *that* transaction?

Right now, I'm betting, the primary "money machine" in your life is *you*. You might have some investments, but let's say you haven't set them up with income in mind. If you stop working, the machine stops, the cash flow stops, your income stops—basically, your financial world comes to a grinding halt. It's a zero-sum game, meaning that you get back just what you put into it.

Look at it this way: you're an ATM of another kind—only in your case, the acronym might remind you of that lousy "time-for-money" trade. You've become an **Anti–Time Machine.** It might sound like the stuff of science fiction, but for many of you, it's reality. You've set things up so that you give away what you *value* most (time) in exchange for what you *need* most (income)—and if you recognize yourself in this description, trust me, you're getting the short end of the deal.

Are we clear on this? **If you stop working, you stop making money.** So let's take *you* out of the equation and look for an alternative approach. Let's **build a money machine to take your place**—and, **let's set it up in such a way that it makes money while you sleep.** Think of it like a second business, with no employees, no payroll, no overhead. Its only "inventory" is the money you put into it. Its only product? **A lifetime income stream that will never run dry**—even if you live to be 100. Its mission? To provide a life of financial freedom for you and your family—or future family, if you don't have one yet.

Sounds pretty great, doesn't it? If you set up this *metaphorical machine* and maintain it properly, it will hold the power of a thousand generators. It will run around the clock, 365 days a year, with an extra day during leap years—and on the Fourth of July, too.

Take a look at the accompanying graphic, and you'll get a better idea how it works.

As you can see, the "machine" can't start working until you make **the most important financial decision of your life. The decision? What portion of your paycheck you get to keep. How much will you pay yourself**—*off the top*, **before you spend a single dollar on your day-to-day living expenses?** How much of your paycheck can you (or, more importantly, will you) leave *untouched*, no matter what else is going on in your life? **I really want you to think about this number, because the rest of your life will be determined by your decision to keep a percentage of your income today in order to always have money for yourself in your future.** The goal here is to enable you to step off the nine-to-five conveyor belt and walk the path to financial freedom. The way to start off on that path is to make this simple decision and begin to tap into the unmatched power of compounding. And the great thing about this decision is that *you* get to make it. *You*! No one else!

> I can't afford to waste my time making money.
> —JEAN LOUIS AGASSIZ

Let's spend some time on this idea, because the money you set aside for savings will become the core of your entire financial plan. Don't even think of it as savings! I call it your **Freedom Fund,** because freedom is what it's going to buy you, now and in the future. Understand, this money represents just a portion of what you earn. It's for you and your family. Save a fixed percentage each pay period, and then invest it intelligently, and over time you'll start living a life where your money works for you instead of you working for your money. And you don't have to wait for the process to start working its magic.

You might say, "But Tony, where do I come up with the money to save? I'm already spending all the money I have." We'll talk about a simple yet extraordinary technique to make saving money painless. But in the meantime, let me remind you of my friend Angela, the one who realized she could drive a new car for half the money she was spending on her old car. Well, guess what she did with 50% of the money she was paying out? She put it toward her Freedom Fund—her investment for life. When we started, she thought she couldn't save anything; the next thing you know she was saving 10%. Then she even added an additional 8% from her savings on the cost of the car for short-term goals as well! But she never touches the 10% of her income that is locked in for her future!

MONEY MACHINE

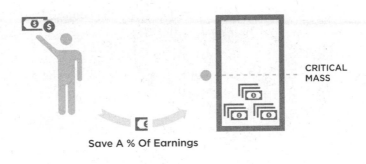

Save A % Of Earnings

Save A % Of Earnings

In the end, it doesn't matter how much money you earn. As we have seen, if you don't set aside some of it, you can lose it all. But here you won't just set it aside stuffed under your mattress. You'll accumulate it in an environment you feel certain is safe but still offers the opportunity for it to grow. You'll invest it—and, if you follow the Money Power Principles covered in these pages, you'll watch it grow to a kind of tipping point, where it can begin to generate enough in interest to provide the income you need for the rest of your life.

"I'd like to make a deposit."

You might have heard some financial advisors call this pile of money a *nest egg*. It is a nest egg, but I call it your money machine because if you continue to feed it and manage it carefully, it will grow into a critical mass: a safe, secure pile of assets invested in a risk-protected, tax-efficient environment that earns enough money to meet your day-to-day expenses, your rainy-day emergency needs, and your sunset days of retirement spending.

Sound complicated? It's actually pretty simple. Here's an easy way to picture it: imagine a box you'll fill with your investment savings. You'll put money into it every pay period—a set percentage that *you* get to determine. **Whatever that number is, you've got to stick to it. In good times and bad. No matter what. Why? Because the laws of compounding punish even one missed contribution.** Don't think of it in terms of what you can afford to set aside—that's a sure way to sell yourself short. And don't put yourself in a position where you can suspend (or even invade) your savings if your income slows to a trickle some months and money is tight.

What percentage works for you? Is it 10%? Or 15%? Maybe 20%? There's no right answer here—only *your* answer. What does your gut tell you? What about your heart?

If you're looking for guidance on this, experts say you should plan to save at least a minimum of 10% of your income, although in today's economy many agree 15% is a far better number, especially if you're over the age of 40. (You'll find out why in section 3!)

> Can anybody remember when the times
> were not hard and money not scarce?
> —RALPH WALDO EMERSON

By now you might be saying, "This all sounds great in theory, Tony, but I'm spread thin enough as it is! Every penny is accounted for." And you wouldn't be alone. Most people don't think they can afford to save. But frankly, we can't afford not to save. Believe me, all of us can find that extra money if we *really* have to have it right now for a real emergency! The problem is in coming up with money for our *future* selves, because our future selves just don't seem real. Which is why it's still so hard to save even when we know that saving can make the difference between retiring comfortably in our own homes or dying broke with a tiny bit of financial support from the government.

We've already learned how behavioral economists have studied the way we fool ourselves about money, and later in this chapter I'll share some of the ways we can trick ourselves into doing the right thing automatically! **But here's the key to success: you have to make your savings automatic.** As Burton Malkiel told me during our visit, "The best way to save is when you don't see the money in the first place." It's true. Once you don't even see that money coming in, you'll be surprised how many ways you find to adjust your spending.

In a few moments I'll show you some great, easy ways to automate your savings so that the money gets redirected before it even reaches your wallet or your checking account. But first, let's look at some real examples of people living from paycheck to paycheck who managed to save and build real wealth even when the odds were against them.

DELIVERING MILLIONS

Theodore Johnson, whose first job was with the newly formed United Parcel Service in 1924, worked hard and moved his way up in the company. **He never made more than $14,000 a year, but here's the magic formula: he set aside 20% of every paycheck he received *and* every Christmas bonus, and put it into company stock.** He had a number in his head, a percentage of income he believed he needed to save for his family—just as you will by the end of this chapter—and he committed to it.

Through stock splits and good old-fashioned patience, **Theodore Johnson eventually saw the value of his UPS stock soar to over $70 million by the time he was 90 years old.**

Pretty incredible, don't you think? And the most incredible part is that he wasn't a gifted athlete like Mike Tyson or a brilliant director like Francis Ford Coppola—or even a lofty corporate executive. He ran the personnel department. But he understood the power of compounding at such an early age that it made a profound impact in his life—and, as it turned out, in the lives of countless others. He had a family to support, and monthly expenses to meet, but to Theodore Johnson, no bill in his mailbox was more important than the promise of his future. He always paid his Freedom Fund first.

At the end of his life, Johnson was able to do some beautiful, meaningful things with all that money. He donated over $36 million to a variety of educational causes, including $3.6 million in grants to two schools for the deaf, because he'd been hard of hearing since the 1940s. He also set up a college scholarship fund at UPS for the children of employees.

Have you heard the story of Oseola McCarty from Hattiesburg, Mississippi—a hardworking woman with just a sixth-grade education who toiled for 75 years washing and ironing clothes? She lived simply and was always careful to set aside a portion of her earnings. "I put it in savings," she explained of her investment philosophy. "I never would take any of it out. I just put it in. It just accumulated."

Oh, boy, did this woman's money accumulate. **At 87 years old, McCarty made national news when she donated $150,000 to the University of Southern Mississippi to start a scholarship fund.** This woman didn't have the compelling screen presence of a Kim Basinger or the distinctive musical talent of a Willie Nelson, but she worked hard and knew enough to see that her money worked hard, too.

"I want to help somebody's child go to college," she said—and she was able to do just that, on the back of her good diligence. There was even a little left over for a small luxury item: she bought an air conditioner for her house.

All the way at the other end of the spectrum, we see the rousing example of Sir John Templeton, one of my personal role models and one of the greatest investors of all time. I had the privilege of meeting John and interviewing him several times over the years, and I'm including our last interview in our "Billionaire's Playbook." Here's a little background. He didn't start out as "Sir John." He came from humble beginnings in Tennessee. John had to drop out of college because he couldn't afford the tuition, but even as a young man, he recognized the incremental power of compounded savings. *He committed to setting aside 50% of what he earned*, and then he took his savings and put it to work in a big way. He studied history and noticed a clear pattern. **"Tony, you find the bargains at the point of maximum pessimism,"** he told me. "There's nothing—*nothing*—that will make the price of a share go down except the pressure of selling." Think about it. When things are going well in the economy, you might get multiple offers on your house and you'll hold out for the highest price. In bull markets, it's hard for investors to get a good deal. Why? When things are going well, it's human nature to think they're going to continue going well forever! But when there's a meltdown, people run for the hills. They'll give away their homes, their stocks, their businesses for next to nothing. By going against the grain, John, a man who started with practically nothing, became a multibillionaire.

How did he do it? Just when Germany was invading Poland in 1939, plunging Europe into World War II and paralyzing the world with fear and despair, he scraped together $10,000 to invest in the New York stock market. He bought 100 shares of every company trading under $1, including those considered nearly bankrupt. But he knew what so many people forget: that night is not forever. Financial winter is a season, and it's followed by spring.

After WWII ended in 1945, the US economy surged, and Templeton's shares exploded into a multibillion-dollar portfolio! **We saw the same kind** of growth happen as the stock market soared from the lows of March 2009 to more than 142% growth by the end of 2013. But most people missed it. Why? When things are going down, we think they're going to go down forever—pessimism takes over. I'll show you in chapter 4.4, "Timing Is Everything?," a system that can help you keep your head and continue to invest when everyone else is afraid. It's in these short, volatile periods that astronomical returns really become available.

I took those insights to my Platinum Partners, an exclusive mastermind group I'd started to support my foundation, and shared with them some of the potential opportunities in front of them. **Take the Las Vegas Sands Corp. listed on the New York Stock Exchange. On March 9, 2009, its stock price had dropped to $2.28 a share. And today it's $67.41— a 3,000% return on your money!**

That's the power of learning to invest when everyone else is afraid.

So what can we learn from Sir John Templeton? It's amazing what research, faith, and action can do if you don't let everybody else's fears paralyze you. This is a good lesson to remember if, as you're reading these pages, we're going through more tough financial times. History proves that those "down and scary times" are the times of greatest opportunities to invest and win.

He knew if he could set aside half of his meager earnings, he'd stake himself to where he could take full advantage of any investment opportunities. But even more important, he became one of the world's leading philanthropists, and after he became a British citizen, the Queen of England knighted him for his efforts. Even in death, his legacy of giving continues: each year, the John Templeton Foundation gives away more money in grants "to advance human progress through breakthrough discoveries"—about $70 million—than the Nobel Prize Commission awards in a decade.

And what's the great takeaway of Theodore Johnson's story? You don't have to be a financial genius to be financially free.

The lesson of Oseola McCarty's life? Even a day laborer can pinch enough pennies to make a meaningful difference.

The lesson of these three wise investors? **By committing to a simple but steady code of savings, by drawing down on your income each pay period and *paying yourself first*, there's a way to tap the power of compound savings and let it take you to unimaginable heights.**

The most difficult thing is the decision to act, the rest is merely tenacity.
–AMELIA EARHART

So how much will you commit to set aside? For Theodore Johnson, that number was 20%. For John Templeton, it was 50%. For Oseola McCarty, it was simply a case of *penny wisdom*: putting those pennies in an interest-bearing account and letting them grow.

What about you? Got a number in mind? Great! It's time to decide, it's time to commit. **It's time to take the first of the 7 Simple Steps to your Financial Freedom! The most important financial decision of your life needs to be made right now! It's time for you to decide to become an investor, not just a consumer. To do this, you simply have to decide what percentage of your income you will set aside for you and your family and no one else.**

Once again, this money is for you. For your family. For your future. It doesn't go to the Gap or to Kate Spade. It doesn't go to expensive restaurants or a new car to replace the one that's still got 50,000 miles to go on the odometer. Try not to think of it in terms of the purchases you're not making today. Focus instead on the returns you'll reap tomorrow. Instead of going out for dinner with friends—at a cost, say, of $50—why not order in a couple pizzas and beers and split the cost among your group? Trade one good time for another, save yourself about $40 each time out, and you'll be way ahead of the game.

What's that, you say? **Forty dollars doesn't sound like much?** Well, you're right about that, but do this once a week, and put those savings to work, and you could take years off your retirement time horizon. **Do the math: you're not just saving $40 a week, but this one small shift in your spending can save you approximately $2,000 each year**—and with what you now know, **that $2,000 can help to harness the power of compounding and help you to realize big, big gains over time. How big? How about $500,000 big? That's right: *a half million dollars!*** How? If you had Benjamin Franklin's advisors, they'd tell you to put your money in the market, and if you too generate an 8% compounded return over 40 years, that $40 weekly savings ($2,080 per year) will net you $581,944! More than enough to order an extra pizza—with everything on it!

Are you starting to see how the power of compounding can work for you, even with just a few small, consistent actions? **And what if you found some more aggressive savings than $40 a week? Even $100 could mean a $1 million difference at the time you would need it most!**

Remember, you can't begin to tap into the awesome power of compounding until you commit to this all-important savings piece. After all, you can't become an investor until you have something to invest! It's basic: the foundation for creating wealth, the difference between being a wage earner and an investor, and it starts with setting aside a portion of your income that you lock away automatically and keep for yourself and your family.

So what will it be? 10%? 12%? 15%? 20%?

Find your threshold and circle it.

Highlight it.

Click on it.

Commit to it.

Make it happen.

And automate it!

How do you automate it? You can start by downloading our free app from www.tonyrobbins.com/masterthegame. It's a great way to begin your journey by setting in place automatic reminders to capture your commitments and make sure you implement your new plan! If you haven't done it yet, do it now! It will help guide you through the following easy steps:

- If you get a regular paycheck, you'll most likely be able to set up an automated plan with a call to the human resources department, instructing it to send a specific percentage of your paycheck—that you and you alone choose—directly to your retirement account.
- If you already have automatic deductions going into your 401(k), you can increase the amount to the percentage you've chosen. (And in the following sections of this book, I'll show you how to make sure your retirement plan is set up in such a way that you can actually "win" this game, to make sure you're not paying hidden fees and that your money is free to grow in a compounded environment—ideally, tax-deferred or tax free for maximum growth.)

Got that taken care of? Outstanding!

- But what about if you're self-employed, or if you own your own business or work on commission? No problem. Just set up an automatic transfer from your checking account.

What if you don't have a retirement account—a place to put your dedicated savings? Simple: stop right now, jump online, and open up a savings or retirement account with a bank or financial institution. You can check out this link with lots of choices to help you locate one that's a good fit for you (www.tdameritrade.com or www.schwab.com), or you can find one on our app. Or, if you're feeling low-tech and looking to roll up your sleeves and get started in a hands-on way, simply walk down the street and visit your banker.

When's a good time to get started on this? Would *now* be a good time? Go ahead, I'll wait . . .

> If you don't want to work, you have to work to earn
> enough money so that you won't have to work.
> —OGDEN NASH

Great, you're back. You got it done. Congratulations! You've just made **the most important financial decision of your life**—the first of the 7 Simple Steps to Financial Freedom. Now you're on your way to converting your dreams into reality.

In the pages ahead, I'll share with you some of the safest, most certain strategies to grow your money—in a tax-advantaged way! But for now let's just lock down this basic savings piece, **because your financial future will flow from your ability to save systematically.** Most of you probably know this, on some level. But if you know it, and you're *still* not doing anything about it—well, then you just don't know it. **Contrary to popular wisdom, knowledge is not power—it's *potential* power. Knowledge is not mastery. *Execution* is mastery. Execution will trump knowledge every day of the week.**

> I hate losing more than I even want to win.
> —BRAD PITT as Oakland A's general manager Billy Beane in *Moneyball*

What if, after everything you've just learned, you still haven't taken that first step to set aside a percentage of your earnings to save for compounded interest? Is there something holding you back? What's really going on? Could it be that you're not systematically saving money because it feels like a sacrifice—a loss—instead of a gift to yourself today and in the future? In my search for answers, I met with Shlomo Benartzi of the UCLA Anderson School of Management. He said, "Tony, the problem is people feel like the future is not real. So it's hard to save for the future." Benartzi and his colleague, Nobel Prize winner Richard Thaler of the University of Chicago, came up with an amazing solution called Save More Tomorrow (SMarT) with a simple but powerful premise: if it hurts too much to save more money now—just wait until your next pay raise.

How did they come up with it? First, Shlomo told me, they had to address the challenge of immediate gratification, or what scientists call **"present bias."** He gave me an example: when he asked a group of students whether they wanted a banana or some chocolate for a snack when they met again in two weeks, a full 75% said they wanted a banana. But two weeks later, with the choices in front of them, 80% picked the chocolate! **"Self-control in the future is not a problem,"** said Shlomo. It's the same with saving, he told me. "We know we should be saving. We know we'll do it next year. But today we go and spend."

As a species, we're not only wired to choose today over tomorrow, but also we hate to feel like we're losing out on something. To illustrate the point, Shlomo told me about a study in which monkeys—our not-so-distant cousins—were given an apple while scientists measured their physiological responses. Enormous excitement! Then another group of monkeys was given two apples. They also displayed enormous excitement. And then one change was made: the monkeys that were given two apples had one taken away from them. They still had one apple, but what do you think happened? You guessed it. They were angry as hell! (Scientifically speaking.) Think this happens with people, too? In fact, how often does this happen with the average person? We forget what we already have, don't we? Remember this study when I tell you the story of a billionaire named Adolf Merckle in the next chapter. You'll have a flash of insight.

The bottom line is, if we feel like we're losing something, we avoid it; we won't do it. That's why so many people don't save and invest. Saving sounds like you're giving something up, you're losing something today. But you're not. It's giving yourself a gift today of peace of mind, of certainty, of the large fortune in your future.

So how did Benartzi and Thaler get around these challenges? They came up with a simple system to make saving feel painless. It aligns with our natures. As Shlomo said in a TED Talk, "Save More Tomorrow invites employees to save more maybe next year—sometime in the future when we can imagine ourselves eating bananas, volunteering more in the community, exercising more, and doing all the right things on the planet."

Here's how it works: you agree to automatically save a small amount of your salary—10%, 5%, or even as little as 3%. (This is a number so small you won't even notice the difference!) Then you commit to saving more in the future—but only when you get an increase in pay. With each pay raise, the percentage saved would automatically get a little larger, but you wouldn't feel it as a loss, because you never had it in the first place!

Benartzi and Thaler first tested the Save More Tomorrow plan almost 20 years ago at a company in the Midwest where the blue-collar workers said they couldn't afford to squeeze another dime out of their paychecks. But the researchers persuaded them to let their employer automatically divert 3% of their salaries into a retirement account, and then add 3% more every time they got a pay raise. The results were amazing! After just five years and three pay raises, those employees who thought they couldn't afford to save were setting aside just under a whopping 14% of their paychecks! And 65% of them were actually saving an average of 19% of their salaries.

When you get to 19%, you're approaching the kinds of numbers that made Theodore Johnson, the UPS man, incredibly wealthy. It's painless, and it works. It's been proven time and again.

Let me show you the chart that Shlomo uses to illustrate the impact that each increase in savings will have on an employee's lifestyle.

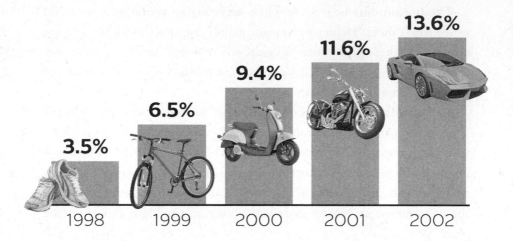

At 3%, there's an image of a pair of sneakers—because that's all you'll be able to afford if you save only 3%! At 4%, there's a bicycle. It goes all the way up to 14%, where there's a luxury car and the clear message that life is great! That's a big difference!

Now 60% of larger companies are offering plans like Save More Tomorrow. Find out if yours does, and if not, show this book to the HR department and see if you can get one put in place.

Of course, you'll still need to go out and actually "earn" your raise—your boss isn't likely to hand it to you just because you've asked nicely. But once you do, you're free to earmark the full amount of the raise, or just a portion, depending on your circumstances. In some cases, if you work for a matching company, your employer will help to effectively double your contribution— and you'll be well on your way soon enough. In fact, below is a link to an online Save More Tomorrow calculator that will allow you to see the impact on your own financial future: www.nytimes.com/interactive/2010/03/24/your-money/one-pct-more-calculator.html.

If your employer doesn't offer the plan, you can set one up with America's Best 401k, and many other 401(k) systems. You could start out with 5% (although I would encourage you to start with no less than 10%, if at all feasible) automatically going into your Freedom Fund, and then commit to 3% more every time you get a raise. Go online or make one phone call, and it will be happening for you. You could do this today and lock in your future in the most painless way possible. There's no excuse for you not to do it! You can even go to our app, where we've prewritten an email that you can send to your boss or head of HR so you can put this process to work for you right away. How's that for easy? Do it *right* now!

But what if you're self-employed? What if you own your own business, and you feel like you need to put every cent into it? Believe me, you'll find a way. What if there was a new tax that came out, and you had to pay 10% more, or even 15% more to the government? You'd hate it! You'd scream bloody murder! But you'd find a way to pay it. So think of this percentage as a tax you "get to pay"—because the money doesn't go to Uncle Sam but to your family and future self! Or think of yourself as a vendor who's got to be paid first. If it has to be done, you'll do it. But in this case, it's something you're setting aside that is yours and your family's to keep forever, right? And remember, you want to automate it. **That's the whole secret: earn more, spend less, and automate it.**

LIKE LETTERS OF FIRE ACROSS THE SKY

As a young man, I came across George Samuel Clason's classic 1926 book *The Richest Man in Babylon*, which offered commonsense financial advice told through ancient parables. I recommend it to everyone. Over the years, one passage has stayed with me: **" 'A part of all I earn is mine to keep.'** Say it in the morning when you first arise. Say it at noon. Say it at night. Say it each hour of every day. Say it to yourself until the words stand out like letters of fire across the sky. Impress yourself with the idea. Fill yourself with the thought. Then take whatever portion seems wise. Let it be not less than one-tenth and lay it by. Arrange your other expenditures to do this if necessary. But lay that portion first."

> No one would have remembered the Good Samaritan if
> he'd only had good intentions. He had money as well.
> —MARGARET THATCHER

Lay that portion first, my friend. And then *act on it*! It doesn't matter what the number is, just get started. Ideally, it shouldn't be less than 10%. But as time goes by, make the number mean something.

THE NEXT STEP

Now that you've set up an automated investment plan—your Freedom Fund, your new money machine—there may be two questions burning in your mind: First, where do I put this money? And second, how much am I going to need to achieve financial security or freedom? We're going to answer both of those questions clearly. And the answers are going to come from the best financial achievers in the world.

But first we need to understand what you're really investing for. What's behind your personal desire for financial freedom? And what does wealth really mean *to you?* What are you really after? So let's take a quick moment—just a few pages—to look at how *you* are going to master money.

MONEY MASTERY: IT'S TIME TO BREAK THROUGH

Gratitude is the sign of noble souls.
—AESOP

Money is one of the ways we can turn the dreams we have into the reality we live. Without enough money, or a true scarcity of it, life can feel miserable. But when you have money in your pocket, does everything automatically get better? I think we all know the answer.

Money can't change who we are. All it does is magnify our true natures. If you're mean and selfish, you have more to be mean and selfish with. If you're grateful and loving, you have more to appreciate and give.

Take a moment and think back to the financial meltdown of 2008. Trillions of dollars of stock and home values evaporated into thin air. Millions of jobs were lost in a matter of months. What did you experience? How did it hit you? How did it affect your family? How about your friends? Some of us reacted with fear, some with anger, some with resignation, some with resolve. All these responses were not about money but about *us*. These events shined a light on what money really means to us. What power we give it. Whether we let money control us, or whether we take control of it.

YOUR MONEY OR YOUR LIFE

One of the most powerful examples I know from that time is a gentleman named Adolf Merckle. In 2007 he was the 94th richest man in the world, and the richest man in Germany, with a net worth of $12 billion. He owned the largest pharmaceutical company in Europe, and then he expanded his empire into manufacturing and construction. He was proud of what he'd accomplished. He was also something of a speculator.

In 2008 he decided to make a bet in the stock market. He was so certain that Volkswagen was going down, he decided to short the company. Just one problem: Porsche made a move to buy Volkswagen, and the stock price shot up, not down. Almost overnight, Merckle lost nearly three-quarters of a billion dollars on that single gamble.

To make matters worse, he desperately needed some cash to pay off a huge loan. But in 2008, banks weren't loaning money to anyone: not you, not me, not billionaires—not even other banks.

So what did Merckle do? Search for new financing? Cut his expenses? Sell some companies at a loss? No. When he realized he'd lost a total of $3 billion and was no longer the richest man in Germany, that he had failed his family, he wrote a suicide note and walked in front of a speeding train.

That's right. He killed himself.

In a tragic irony, his family discovered only a few days later that the loans he sought had come through, and his companies were saved.

Did Adolf Merckle die because of money? Or did he die because of what money *meant* to him? For Merckle, money was an identity. It was a source of significance. The loss of his status as the richest man in Germany was too much to bear, and he felt like a failure—even though there was still $9 billion left in his pocket!

You might be thinking, *"What a waste."* But it may be a little too easy for us to judge this man. How often have we attached our identity—or our future prospects—to money at some level? Probably more than we'd all like to admit.

THE BILLIONAIRE WHO WANTS TO DIE BROKE

On the other hand, there are people like Chuck Feeney, an Irish-American from Elizabeth, New Jersey, and a self-made billionaire. Have you ever tried to get through an airport, anywhere in the world, and found yourself lured into a room full of shiny bottles of liquor and perfume and other tax-free luxury items? Duty Free Shopping (DFS). That's Chuck Feeney's idea. He started with nothing in 1960 and ended up with a sales empire worth $7.5 billion.

At one point, *Forbes* had listed him, like Merckle, as one of the richest men in the world. But Feeney was so humble, you would never have known it. Most of his life, he didn't own a car or a home. He flew coach and wore a plastic watch. Like Merckle, his bank account was dwindling—right now he's in his 80s, and Feeney has just over $1 million left to his name. But the big difference between him and Merckle is that instead of trying to hold on to every last penny, Chuck Feeney *gave* away all his money.

This is a guy who, for the last 30 years, has made it his mission to take this vehicle called money and use it to change lives everywhere. His philanthropy reaches all over the world, from helping to create peace in Northern Ireland, to fighting AIDS in South Africa, to educating kids in Chicago.

The most amazing thing about Feeney is that he did it all anonymously. Feeney wanted no credit. In fact, only recently has word gotten out that he's the man behind all these incredible projects. And he's still going! Chuck Feeney says his goal is to bounce the last check he writes.

Obviously money meant very different things for Adolf Merckle and Chuck Feeney. What does money *really* mean to you? Do you use money, or does money use you? Like I've said from the beginning: if you don't master money, at some level, it's going to master you.

THE ULTIMATE GOAL: GIVING BACK

For me, money was always out of reach as a child. It was always a source of stress because there was never enough of it. I remember having to knock on the neighbor's door to ask for food for my brother and sister and me.

Then, on Thanksgiving Day when I was 11 years old, something happened that changed my life forever. As usual, there was no food in the house, and my parents were fighting. Then I heard someone knocking at the front door. I opened it a crack and saw a man standing on the steps with grocery bags filled with enough food for a big Thanksgiving dinner. I could hardly believe it.

My father always said that nobody gave a damn about anybody. But all of a sudden someone I didn't know, who wasn't asking for anything in return, was looking out for us. It made me think, "Does this mean that strangers care?" And I decided that if strangers care about me and my family, I care about them! "What am I going to do?" I promised myself that day, I was going to find a way, somehow, someday, to give back and pay it forward. So, when I was 17, I saved my money from working nights as a janitor and went out on Thanksgiving and fed two families. It was one of the most moving experiences of my life. It lifted my spirit to see faces turned from despair to joy. Truly, it was as much a gift to me as it was to them. I didn't tell anybody what I was doing, but the next year, I fed four families. Then eight. I wasn't doing it for Brownie points, but after eight, I thought, "Man, I could use some help." So I enlisted some friends, and they got into it too. It grew and grew. Now my foundation feeds 2 million people every year in 36 countries, through our International Basket Brigades. Would I have known the joy of giving if it wasn't for that terrible Thanksgiving when I was 11? Who knows? Some would call it luck or fate or plain old good fortune. I see the hand of God in it; I call it grace.

Here's what I know: I learned the joy of giving, and it had nothing to do with money. Money is simply a vehicle for trying to meet our needs, and not just our financial needs. Much of our life is guided by the beliefs we develop over the course of time; the story we create about what life's about, how we're supposed to be, what we're supposed to do or give. Ultimately, what's going to make us happy or fulfilled. Everyone has a different "happy." Some people find happiness pleasing others, while others find happiness in power and domination. Others define their happy as a billion dollars. Some think the way to happiness and a meaningful life is to get closer to God and give up everything material. Still others think the ultimate idea of happiness is freedom.

Whatever emotion you're after, whatever vehicle you pursue— building a business, getting married, raising a family, traveling the world—whatever you think your nirvana is, I have found it's only an attempt by your brain to meet one or more of six human needs.

These six basic needs make us tick. They drive all human behavior and are universal. They are the force behind the crazy things (other) people do and the great things we do. We all have the same six needs, but how we value those needs, and in what order, determines the direction of our life.

Why are the six human needs so important to understand? Well, if you're going to build wealth, you've got to know what you're really after—what you're building it for. Are you looking for wealth to feel certain and secure? Are you chasing wealth to feel special and unique? Or are you looking to have a sense of contribution—you want to do things for others in a way you've never been able to do before? Or maybe all of the above?

If you value certainty as the most important need in your life, you're going to move in a very different direction, act differently in relationships, in business and finance, than if love is your number one need. If we get underneath what you're really after, it's not money at all. **What you're really after is what you think money is going to give you.** Ultimately, it's a set of feelings. And beneath those feelings are needs.

NEED 1:
CERTAINTY/COMFORT

The first human need is the need for Certainty. It's our need to feel in control and to know what's coming next so we can feel secure. It's the need for basic comfort, the need to avoid pain and stress, and also to create pleasure. Does this make sense? Our need for certainty is a survival mechanism. It affects how much risk we're willing to take in life—in our jobs, in our investments, and in our relationships. **The higher the need for certainty, the less risk you'll be willing to take or emotionally bear.** By the way, this is where your real "risk tolerance" comes from.

But what if you're totally certain all the time? **If you knew what was going to happen, when it was going to happen, how it was going to happen.** You knew what people were going to say before they said it. How would you feel? At first you'd feel extraordinary, but eventually you'd be what? Bored out of your mind!

NEED 2:
UNCERTAINTY/VARIETY

So, God, in Her infinite wisdom, gave us a second human need, which is **Uncertainty.** We need variety. We need surprise.

Let me ask you a question: Do you like surprises?

If you answered "yes," you're kidding yourself! **You like the surprises you want. The ones you don't want you call problems!** But you still need them to put some muscle in your life. You can't grow muscle—or character—unless you have something to push back against.

NEED 3:
SIGNIFICANCE

The third is **Significance,** that basic human need that drove Adolf Merckle. We all need to feel important, special, unique, or needed. So how do some of us get significance? You can get it by earning billions of dollars or collecting academic degrees—distinguishing yourself with a master's or a PhD. You can build a giant Twitter following. Or you can go on *The Bachelor* or become one of the next *Real Housewives of Orange County.* Some do it by putting tattoos and piercings all over themselves and in places we don't want to know about. You can get significance by having more or bigger problems than anybody else. "*You think* your *husband's a dirtbag? Take mine for a day!*" Of course, you can also get it by being more spiritual (or pretending to be). Unfortunately, one of the fastest ways to get significance—that costs no money and requires no education—is through violence. If someone puts a gun to your head, in that instant he becomes the most significant thing in your life, right?

Spending a lot of money can make you feel significant, and so can spending very little. We all know people who constantly brag about their bargains, or who feel special because they heat their homes with cow manure and sunlight. Some very wealthy people gain significance by hiding their wealth. Like the late Sam Walton, the founder of Wal-Mart and for a time the richest man in America, who drove around Bentonville, Arkansas, in his old pickup, demonstrating he didn't need a Bentley—but, of course, he did have his own private fleet of jets standing by.

Significance is also a moneymaker—that's where my dear friend Steve Wynn has made his fortune. The man who made Las Vegas what it is today knows people will pay for anything they believe is "the best"—anything that makes them feel special, unique, or important; anything that makes them stand out from the crowd. He provides the most exclusive, luxurious experiences imaginable in his casinos and hotels—they are truly magnificent and unmatched in the world. He's got a nightclub called XS (what else?) that is the hottest spot in Las Vegas. Even on a weeknight, it has a line out the door. Once you're in, you have the privilege of purchasing an ordinary bottle of champagne for $700, or if you want to step up and show everyone you're a player, you can spend $10,000 for a special "Ono cocktail" of rare vintage cognac and fresh orange juice that comes with a white-gold necklace. Hey, it comes to your table with a sparkler, just so everybody knows you're significant (and out of your mind).

NEED 4:
LOVE AND CONNECTION

The fourth basic need is **Love and Connection.** Love is the oxygen of life; it's what we all want and need most. When we love completely, we feel alive, but when we lose love, the pain is so great that most people settle on connection, the crumbs of love. You can get that sense of connection or love through intimacy, or friendship, or prayer, or walking in nature. If nothing else works, you can get a dog.

These first four needs are what I call the needs of the personality. We all find ways to meet these: whether by working harder, coming up with a big problem, or creating stories to rationalize them. The last two are the needs of the spirit. These are more rare—not everyone meets these. When these needs are met, we truly feel fulfilled.

NEED 5:
GROWTH

Number five is **Growth.** If you're not growing, you're what? You're dying. If a relationship is not growing, if a business is not growing, if *you're* not growing, it doesn't matter how much money you have in the bank, how many friends you have, how many people love you—you're not going to experience real fulfillment. And the reason we grow, I believe, is so we have something of value to give.

NEED 6:
CONTRIBUTION

That's because the sixth need is **Contribution.** Corny as it may sound, **the secret to living is giving.** Life's not about *me*; it's about *we*. Think about it: What's the first thing you do when you get good or exciting news? You call somebody you love and share it. Sharing enhances everything you experience.

Life is really about creating meaning. And meaning does not come from what you get, it comes from what you give. Ultimately, what you get will never make you happy long term. But who you become and what you contribute will.

Now, since this is a book about your money, think about how money can fulfill the six human needs. Can money give us certainty? You bet. Variety? Check. Obviously it can make us feel important or significant. But what about connection and love? In the immortal words of the Beatles, money can't buy you love. But it can buy you that dog! And it can, unfortunately, give you a false sense of connection because it attracts relationships, although not always the most fulfilling kind. How about growth? Money can fuel growth in business and in learning. And the more money you have, the more you can contribute financially.

But here's what I truly believe: if you value Significance above all else, money will always leave you empty unless it comes from a contribution you've made. And if you're looking for significance from money, it's a high price to pay. You're looking for big numbers, but it's unlikely you'll find big fulfillment.

The ultimate significance in life comes not from something external but from something internal. It comes from a sense of esteem for ourselves, which is not something we can ever get from someone else. People can tell you you're beautiful, smart, intelligent, the best, or they can tell you that you are the most horrible human being on earth—but what matters is what *you* think about yourself. Whether or not you believe that deep inside you are continuing to grow and push yourself, to do and give more than was comfortable or you even thought possible.

There is nothing more significant than growing and giving. So while money is an extraordinary vehicle to meet many of our six needs, it's not the only one. When you are pursuing money, don't forget why you are pursuing it. You're trying to meet some emotional and psychological desires. Underneath those emotions are the needs that must be fulfilled for your life to be extraordinary.

When the astronauts went to walk on the moon, imagine the journey they went on. From being a small child dreaming of someday flying to outer space, to the day when Buzz Aldrin and Neil Armstrong stood on the moon, looking back at that extraordinary view of planet Earth that we've all seen only in pictures. They were the first human beings to do it in the entire history of the species—how incredibly significant.

What happened next? Ticker-tape parades. Shaking the president's hand. They were heroes. And then what? What do you do after you've walked on the moon, and you're only 39 years old? If you've studied the history of the astronauts, or read their biographies, you'll know that many of them became extremely depressed. Why? Because the only way they could find adventure was by traveling into space or all the way to the moon. They forgot how to find adventure in a simple smile.

I'm not going to preach to you anymore, but I wanted to take this short time to say that while it's time to master your money, don't wait to master yourself. **The fastest way to feel connection, a sense of how significant your life is, a deep sense of certainty and variety, and put yourself in a state where you can give to others, is to find a way each day to appreciate more and expect less.** The wealthiest person on earth is one who appreciates.

I interviewed Sir John Templeton for the first time when I was 33 years old. Remember, he was the multibillionaire who started with nothing and made all of his money when everyone else was afraid, during the worst times in history: WWII, Japan after the war, and in the late 1980s and early 1990s when massive inflation hit parts of South America. When others were fearful, he went out and invested. I asked him, **"What's the secret to wealth?" And he said, "Tony, you know it, and you know it well. You teach it to everyone. It's gratitude."** When you're grateful, there is no fear; when you're grateful, there is no anger. Sir John was one of the happiest and most fulfilled human beings I have ever known. Even though he passed in 2008, all these years later his life continues to inspire others.

If you want to be rich, start rich. What can you be grateful for today? Who can you be grateful for today? Could you even be grateful for some of the problems and the pain that you've been through in your life? What if you took on the new belief that everything in life happens for a reason and a purpose, and it serves you? What if you believed in your heart of hearts that life doesn't happen to you, it happens for you? That every step along the way is helping strengthen you so that you can become more, enjoy more, and give more. If you'll start from that place, money won't be the source of your pleasure or your pain. Making money will just be a fun journey of mastery, and wealth a great vehicle to achieve what matters most in life.

But as long as money is such a part of our lives, let's get right back on the money track. As heartfelt as this chapter has been, not all the people you'll meet along the financial path will be operating from the benevolent place of Growth and Contribution! You're going to be entering a world that is filled with people and organizations that too often will be looking to take advantage of your lack of experience and understanding. So I want to prepare you for what's ahead. **Before we discuss where to put your money and what to look for, I have to show you what to look *out* for.**

There's a reason why most investors do not make money over time. I want to arm you with the knowledge that will both protect you and allow you to maximize the growth of your investments **so you can achieve true Financial Freedom faster than you can imagine.** The peace of mind you deserve will soon be yours. Turn the page . . .

SECTION 2

BECOME THE INSIDER:
KNOW THE RULES
BEFORE YOU GET IN THE GAME

BREAK FREE: SHATTERING THE 9 FINANCIAL MYTHS

Remember the golden rule: he who has the gold makes the rules.
—UNKNOWN

You have to learn the rules of the game, and then
you have to play better than anyone else.
—ALBERT EINSTEIN

I know that you want to jump right in and learn where to put your money to obtain financial freedom. And I want to dive in and show you! I absolutely light up when I see someone really "get it" and come to understand and embrace that the game is truly winnable. But it's not enough to just save your money, get a great return, and reduce your risk. You have to know that there are a lot of people looking to take a piece of your wealth. **The system is riddled with loopholes—what I would call landmines—that can blow up your financial future.** So in this section, we're going to go through 9 Myths—you might call them lies—that have been marketed to you over the years. And if you aren't aware of them—if you don't see them coming—they will systematically destroy your financial future.

This next section is where this book starts to pay off! In fact, if you have the average American salary of $50,000 per year, and currently save 10% of your income and invest that money over time, you'll save $250,000 over your investment lifetime by just part of what you will learn in this section. That's five years of your current lifestyle, at your current income, without having to work a single day! And that is statistically proven, not a number I'm pulling out of a hat. If you make only $30,000 per year and save just 5% of your income each year, you'll still save $150,000 over your investment lifetime. That's a half decade's worth of your current income without having to work for it. If you're in the $100,000-plus category, this section could put $500,000 to $1 million back in your pocket over your lifetime. Sounds like a massive promise, huh!? I will let the numbers do the talking in the pages ahead.

It's a short section, so pay attention because you're going to want to take immediate action. By shattering these myths, you will be able to immediately "stop the bleeding" in areas where you never thought you needed to. Knowing these 9 Myths will protect you and insure that you get to the level of financial freedom that you're truly committed to. Let's begin!

WELCOME TO THE JUNGLE

Whether you are a seasoned investor or just beginning to see yourself as an investor, the jungle that Ray Dalio so vividly described holds the same dangers for all of us. **But most of the danger lies in the fact that what you don't know *can* hurt you.**

THE OFFER

I want you to imagine that someone comes to you with the following investment opportunity: he wants you to put up 100% of the capital and take 100% of the risk, and if it makes money, he wants 60% or more of the upside to come to him in fees. Oh, and by the way, if it loses money, you lose, and he still gets paid!

Are you in?

I'm sure you don't need any time to think this through. It's a no-brainer. Your gut response has to be, "There's no way I'm doing this. How absurd!" The only problem is that if you're like 90% of American investors, you've invested in a typical mutual fund, and, believe it or not, these are the terms to which you've already agreed.

That's right, there is $13 trillion in actively managed mutual funds[3] with 265 million account holders around the world.

---

3. According to the website Investopedia: "Active managers rely on analytical research, forecasts, and their own judgment and experience in making investment decisions on what securities to buy, hold, and sell. The opposite of active management is called passive management, better known as 'indexing.' "

How in the world do you convince 92 million Americans to participate in a strategy where they willingly give up 60% or more of their potential lifetime investment upside with no guaranteed return? To solve this riddle, I sat down with the 85-year-old investment guru Jack Bogle, the founder of Vanguard, whose 64 years on Wall Street have made him uniquely qualified to shed light on this financial phenomenon. His answer?

"Marketing!

"Tony, it's simple. Most people don't do the math, and the fees are hidden. Try this: if you made a onetime investment of $10,000 at age twenty, and, assuming 7% annual growth over time, you would have **$574,464** by the time you're nearly my age [eighty]. *But*, if you paid 2.5% in total management fees and other expenses, your ending account balance would only be **$140,274 over the same period.**"

"Let's see if we've got this straight: you provided all the capital, you took all the risk, you got to keep $140,274, but you gave up $439,190 to an active manager!? They take 77% of your potential returns? For what?"

"Exactly."

Money Power Principle 1. Don't get in the game unless you know the rules! Millions of investors worldwide are systematically marketed a set of myths—investment lies—that guide their decision making. This "conventional wisdom" is often designed to keep you in the dark. When it comes to your money, what you don't know *can*—and likely will—hurt you. Ignorance is not bliss. Ignorance is pain, ignorance is struggle, ignorance is giving your fortune away to someone who hasn't earned it.

A FAILED EXPERIMENT

It's not just high-cost mutual funds that are the problem. The example above is just a peek under the sheets at a system designed to separate you from your money.

Without exception, every expert I have interviewed for this book (from the top hedge funds managers to Nobel Prize winners) agrees that the game has changed. Our parents didn't have a fraction of the complexity or dangers to deal with that we have today. Why? They had a pension—a guaranteed income for life! They had CDs that paid conservative but reasonable rates—not the 0.22% you would be paid at the time of this writing, which won't even keep up with inflation. And some had the privilege of putting small investments into blue-chip stocks that paid steady dividends.

That ship has sailed.

The new system, which really got rolling in the early '80s with the introduction of the 401(k), is an experiment that's now been conducted for the most part on the single largest generation in US history: the baby boomers. How is this experiment working?

"This do-it-yourself pension system has failed," said Teresa Ghilarducci, a nationally recognized expert in retirement security at the New School for Social Research and an outspoken critic of the system as we know it. "It has failed because it expects individuals without investment expertise to reap the same results as professional investors and money managers. What results would you expect if you were asked to pull your own teeth or do your own electrical wiring?"

What's changed? We exchanged our guaranteed retirement pensions with an intentionally complex and often extremely dangerous system, filled with hidden fees, which gave us "freedom of choice." And somehow, in the midst of working your tail off, providing for your family, staying in shape, and taking care of the important relationships in your life, you are supposed to become an investment professional? You're supposed to be able to navigate this labyrinth of products, services, and unending risk of your hard-earned money? It's near impossible. That's why most people give their money to a "professional," often a broker. A broker who by definition works for a company that is *not* required by law to do what's in your best interest (more on this baffling concept in Myth 4). A broker who gets paid to funnel your money to the products that may be the most profitable for him and/or his firm.

Now, let me be clear: this is *not* another bash-Wall-Street-book. Many of the large financial institutions have pioneered some extraordinary products that we will explore and advocate throughout this book. And the vast majority of people in the financial services industry care intensely for their clients, and more often than not, they are doing what they believe to be the best thing. Unfortunately, many don't also understand how the "house" reaps profits whether the client wins or not. They are doing the best they can for their clients with the knowledge (training) and the tools (products) they have been provided. **But the system isn't set up for your broker to have endless options and complete autonomy in finding what's best for you. And this could prove costly.**

Giving up a disproportionate amount of your potential returns to fees is just one of the pitfalls you must avoid if you plan on winning the game. And here is the best news yet:

THE GAME IS STILL WINNABLE!

In fact, it's more than winnable—it's exciting as hell! Yes, there are major challenges and more pitfalls you must avoid, but consider how far we have come. Today, with the click of a button and a minimal charge, you can invest in just about anything you want anywhere in the world you want. "It's easier than it's ever been to do pretty well," said James Cloonan in a recent *Wall Street Journal* article. Cloonan is founder of the nonprofit American Association of Individual Investors. "You just have to decide to do the right thing."

Heck, just 35 years ago "you had to spend hours in a public library or write away to a company just to see its financial statements. Brokerage costs and mutual-fund fees were outlandish; tax rates were larcenous," wrote Jason Zweig in his *Wall Street Journal* article "Even When Stocks Make You Nervous, Count Your Blessings."

Aside from high-frequency traders, technology has made the world of investing a much more efficient space for all of us. And this fits perfectly with the millennial generation, which wouldn't accept anything less. "For us, it's all about convenience!" exclaimed Emily, my personal assistant, who is a "straight-down-the-fairway" millennial. "There is no tolerance for slow or inefficient. We truly want everything to be at the touch of a button. We order everything on Amazon; we lift one finger, and it's done. I can stream a movie on Netflix. I can get a car registration online. I can buy stocks online. I can do my presentation online. This morning I took a picture of my check and had it in my bank account by six—I didn't even have to get out of my pajamas."

THE HOUSE HAS THE EDGE

Steve Wynn, the billionaire gambling mogul credited with transforming Las Vegas into the entertainment capital of the world, is one of my dearest friends. The casinos he's built are considered to be some of the most magnificent playgrounds in the world. Through it all, he's made his fortune from one simple truth: the house has the edge. But by no means does he have a guaranteed victory! On any given night, a high-rolling gambler can take millions out of Steve's pocket. And they can also leave if his "house" doesn't completely captivate them. On the other hand, nearly all mutual fund companies have a stacked deck. They are the ultimate casino. They've captured you, you're going nowhere, and they are guaranteed revenue whether you win or not.

TWICE BURNED

After 2008, when the US stock market lost more than 37%, the financial world was completely changed for most Americans. Even five years later, a survey from Prudential Financial showed that 44% of American investors still say they would never put their money in the stock market again, while 58% say they lost faith in the market. But the insiders are still in the game. Why? Because they know better. They know the "right" way to play the game. They know that today there are powerful tools and strategies that have never existed before. Get this:

Today you can use a tool, issued and backed by one of the largest banks in the world, that will give you 100% principal protection guaranteed by its balance sheet *and* allow you to participate in 75% to 90% of the upside of the market (the S&P 500) without being capped! That is not a misprint. You can participate in up to 90% of the upside, but if the market collapses, you still get back 100% of your money! Sounds too good to be true? And if a product like this did exist, you would have already heard of it, right? Wrong. The reason? In the past, to *even hear* about this, you had to be in the top 1% of the 1%. These are not "retail" solutions, where they sit on the shelf. These are custom designed for those with enough money to partake.

This is just one example of how, as an insider, you'll soon know the new rules of how to achieve wealth with minimal risk.

Risk comes from not knowing what you're doing.
—WARREN BUFFETT

THE ROAD LESS TRAVELED

CONQUER THE MOUNTAIN OF FREEDOM

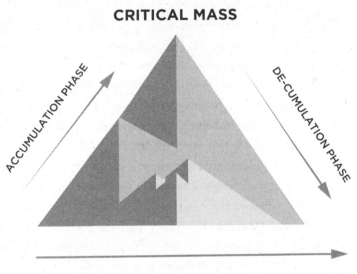

The journey ahead is one that requires your full participation. Together we are going to climb this mountain called Financial Freedom. It's your personal Mount Everest. It won't be easy, and it will require preparation. You don't head up Everest without a very clear understanding of the dangers that lie ahead. Some are known, and some could sneak up on you like a violent storm. So before we set foot on the mountain, we must fully grasp what's on the path before us. One false step could mean the difference between wondering how you will pay next month's mortgage and an abundant life, free of financial stress. We can't ask someone to climb it for us, but we also can't do it alone. We need a guide who has our best interests at heart.

THE PINNACLE

The core concept of successful investing is simple: Grow your savings to a point at which the interest from your investments will generate enough income to support your lifestyle without having to work. Eventually you reach a "tipping point" at which your savings will hit a critical mass. This simply means that you don't have to work anymore—unless you choose to—because the interest and growth being generated by your account gives you the income you need for your life. This is the pinnacle we are climbing toward. The great news is that if you become an insider, today there are new and unique solutions and strategies that will accelerate your climb and even protect you from sliding backward. But before we explore these solutions in more depth, let's map out our journey with more clarity.

There are two phases to your investing game: the *accumulation phase*, in which you are socking away money for growth, and the *decumulation*, during which you are withdrawing income. The journey up the mountain will represent our accumulation phase with the goal of reaching the pinnacle, or critical mass. The goal is to stay on top of the mountain as long as we can. To take in the views and breathe in the fresh air of freedom and accomplishment. There will be many hurdles, obstacles, and, if you're not alert, even lies, that will prevent you from reaching the peak. To ensure our best chance of success, we will flush these out in the pages to come.

And when we enter the second act of our life, when it's time to enjoy what we made, we will have the freedom to work only if we want to. At this stage we will ski down the mountain and enjoy ourselves. Spending time with the ones we love, building our legacy, and making a difference. It's during this phase that we will eliminate the number one fear of baby boomers: the fear of outliving our money. This second phase is rarely discussed by the asset management industry, which is focused on keeping money invested.

"It's not about having some arbitrary amount of money in your account on some given day," exclaimed Dr. Jeffrey Brown, professor of finance at the University of Illinois and consultant to the US Treasury and the World Bank. "I think a lot of people are going to get to retirement and suddenly wake up and realize, 'You know what? I did a fairly good job. I have all this money sitting here, but I don't know how long I am going to live, and I don't know what my investment returns are going to be, and I don't know what inflation is going to be. What do I do?' "

After I read one of his recent *Forbes* columns, I called Dr. Brown to see if he would be willing to sit down and share specific solutions for investors of all shapes and sizes. (We'll hear from Dr. Brown on how to create income for life and even how to make it tax free in his interview in section 5, "Upside Without the Downside: Create a Lifetime Income Plan.") And who better to outline the solution than the man who is not only a top academic expert but was also one of only seven people appointed by the president of the United States to the Social Security Advisory Board.

BREAK THE CHAINS

In the words of David Swensen, one of the most successful institutional investors of our time, to have unconventional success, you can't be guided by conventional wisdom. Let's shatter the top nine financial myths that misguide the masses, and, more importantly, uncover the new rules of money, the truths that will set you financially free.

Let's start with the biggest myth of all. . . .

MYTH 1:
THE $13T LIE:
"INVEST WITH US.
WE'LL BEAT THE MARKET!"

The goal of the nonprofessional should not be to pick winners—neither he nor his "helpers" can do that—but should rather be to own a cross section of businesses that in aggregate are bound to do well. A low-cost S&P 500 index fund will achieve this goal.

—WARREN BUFFETT, 2013 letter to shareholders

When you look at the results on an after-fee, after-tax
basis, over reasonably long periods of time, there's almost
no chance that you end up beating the index fund.

—DAVID SWENSEN, author of *Unconventional Success*
and manager of Yale University's more than $23.9 billion endowment

FINANCIAL ENTERTAINMENT

When you turn on the financial news today, you can see that it is less "news" and more sensationalism. Talking heads debate with zeal. Stock pickers scream their hot picks of the day while sound effects smash, crash, and "ka-*ching*!" through our living room speakers. Reporters film "live on the scene" directly from the trenches of the exchange floor. The system, paid for by advertisers, breeds the feeling that maybe we are missing out! If only we had a hot tip. If only we knew the next "must-own" mutual fund that would surely be the "5 star" comet. (Mutual funds are rated between 1 and 5 stars by rating authority Morningstar.)

Chasing returns is big business. Personal finance writer Jane Bryant Quinn once referred to this sensational hype as "financial porn." Luring us into glossy pages where the centerfolds are swapped with five-star ratings and promises of carefree walks on the beach and fishing off the dock with our grandkids. The bottom line is that advertisers are fighting to get a grasp on our money. The war for your assets rages on!

So where *do* you put your money? Who *can* you trust? Who will protect you and get you the best return on your investment?

These are the immediate questions that are sure to come to mind now that you've committed to becoming an investor—now that you've committed to socking away a percentage of your income. So where do most people put their money for the long haul? Usually the stock market.

And the stock market has indeed been the best long-term investment over the past 100 years. As Steve Forbes pointed out at one of my financial events in Sun Valley, Idaho, in 2014, "$1 million invested in stocks in 1935 is worth $2.4 billion today (if you held on)."

But the moment you open an IRA or participate in your 401(k) plan at work, there will be a jolly salesman (or sales process) telling you to park your money in a mutual fund. And by buying an actively managed mutual fund, what exactly are you buying? You are buying into the fund manager in hopes that his or her stock-picking abilities will be better than yours. A completely natural assumption, since we have insanely busy lives, and our method of picking stocks would be the equivalent of throwing darts!

So we hand over our money to a "five-star" *actively managed* mutual fund manager who by definition is "actively" trying to beat the market by being a better stock picker than the next guy. But few firms will discuss what is sometimes called the $13 trillion lie. (That's how much money is in mutual funds.) Are you ready for this?

An incredible 96% of actively managed mutual funds *fail to beat the market* over any sustained period of time!

So let's be clear. When we say "beat the market" as a whole, we are generally referring to a stock *index*. What's an index, you ask? Some of you might know, but I don't want to risk leaving anyone in the dark, so let's shed a little light. An index is simply a basket or list of stocks. The S&P 500 is an index. It's a list of the top companies (by market capitalization) in the United States, as selected by Standard & Poor's. Companies like Apple, Exxon, and Amazon make up the list. Each day, they measure how all 500 stocks performed, as an aggregate, and when you turn on the news at night, you hear if the market (all the stocks on the list collectively) was either up or down.

So instead of buying all the stocks individually, or trying to pick the next highflyer, you can diversify and own a piece of all 500 top stocks simply by investing in a low-cost index fund that tracks or mimics the index. One single investment buys you a piece of the strength of "American capitalism." In a way, you are buying into the fact that over the past 100 years, the top-tier companies have always shown incredible resiliency. Even through depressions, recessions, and world wars, they have continued to find ways to add value, grow, and drive increasing revenues. And if a company fails to keep making the grade, it falls off the list and is replaced with another top performer.

The point here is that by investing in the index, you don't have to pay a professional to try picking which stocks in the index you should own. It's effectively been done for you because Standard & Poor's has selected the top 500 already. By the way, there are number of different indexes out there. Many of us have heard of the Dow Jones index, for example, and we will explore others soon.

TEN THOUSAND OPTIONS

There are 7,707 different mutual funds in the United States (but only 4,900 individual stocks), all vying for a chance to help you beat the market. But the statistic is worth repeating: 96% will fail to match or beat the market over any extended period. Is this groundbreaking news? No, not to insiders. Not to the smart money. As Ray Dalio told me emphatically, "You're not going to beat the market. No one does! Only a few gold medalists." He just happens to be one of those medalists honest enough to issue the warning "Don't try this at home."

Even Warren Buffett, known for his incredibly unique ability to find undervalued stocks, says that the average investor should never attempt to pick stocks or time the market. In his famous 2014 letter to his shareholders, he explained that when he passes away, the money in a trust for his wife should be invested only in indexes so that she minimizes her cost and maximizes her upside.

Buffett is so sure that professional stock pickers can't win over time that he was more than happy to put his money where his mouth is. In January 2008 Buffett made a $1 million wager against New York–based Protégé Partners, with the winnings going to charity. The bet? Can Protégé pick five top hedge fund managers who will collectively beat the S&P 500 index over a ten-year period? As of February 2014, the S&P 500 is up 43.8%, while the five hedge funds are up 12.5%. There are still a few years left, but the lead looks like the world's fastest man, Usain Bolt, running against a pack of Boy Scouts. (Note: for those unfamiliar with what a hedge fund is, it is essentially a private "closed-door" fund for only high-net-worth investors. The managers can have total flexibility to bet "for" the market and make money when it goes up, or "against" the market, and make money when it goes down.)

THE FACTS ARE THE FACTS ARE THE FACTS

Industry expert Robert Arnott, founder of Research Affiliates, spent two decades studying the top 200 actively managed mutual funds that had at least $100 million under management. The results are startling:

From 1984 to 1998, a full 15 years, only eight out of 200 fund managers beat the Vanguard 500 Index. (*The Vanguard 500, put together by founder Jack Bogle, is a mirror image of the S&P 500 index.*)

That's less than 4% odds that you pick a winner. If you've ever played blackjack, you know the goal is to get as close to 21 without going over, or "busting." According to Dan and Chip Heath in their *Fast Company* article "Made to Stick: The Myth of Mutual Funds," "by way of comparison, if you get dealt two face cards in blackjack (each face card is worth 10, so now your total is 20), and your inner idiot shouts, 'Hit me!' you have about an 8% chance of winning!"

Just how badly does chasing performance hurt us? Over a 20-year period, December 31, 1993, through December 31, 2013, the S&P 500 returned an average annual return of 9.28%. But the average mutual fund investor made just over 2.54%, according to Dalbar, one of the leading industry research firms. Ouch! A nearly 80% difference.

In real life, this can mean the difference between financial freedom and financial despair. Said another way, if you were the person who simply owned the S&P 500, you would have turned your $10,000 into $55,916! Whereas the mutual fund investor, who was sold on the illusion that he or she could outperform the market, ended up with only $16,386.

Why the huge performance gap?

Because we buy high and sell low. We follow our emotions (or our broker's recommendations) and jump from fund to fund. Always looking for an edge. But when the market falls, when we can't take the emotional pain any longer, we sell. And when the market is up, we buy more. **As a famous money manager named Barton Biggs observed, "A bull market is like sex. It feels best just before it ends."**

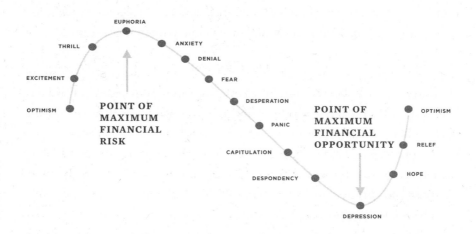

WISDOM OF AGES

At 82 years young, Burt Malkiel has lived through every conceivable market cycle and new marketing fad. When he wrote *A Random Walk Down Wall*

Street in 1973, he had no idea it would become one of the classic investment books in history. The core thesis of his book is that market timing is a loser's game. In section 4, we will sit down and you'll hear from Burt but for now what you need to know is that he was the first guy to come up with the rationale of an index fund, which, again, does not to try to beat the market but simply "mimics," or matches, the market.

Among investors, this strategy is called *indexing* or *passive investing*. This style is contrary to active investing, in which you pay a mutual fund manger to actively make choices about which stocks to buy or sell. The manager is trading stocks—"actively" working with hopes of beating the market.

Jack Bogle, founder of the behemoth Vanguard, subsequently bet the future direction of his company on this idea by creating the first index fund. When I sat down with Jack for this book, he echoed why Vanguard has become the largest index mutual fund manager in the world. His best single rant: "maximum diversification, minimal cost, and maximum tax efficiency, low turnover [trading], and low turnover cost, and no sales loads." How's that for an elevator pitch!

SHORTCUT

Now, you might be thinking that there must be some people who can beat the market. Why else would there be $13 trillion in actively managed mutual funds? Mutual fund managers certainly have streaks where they do, in fact, beat the market. The question is whether or not they can sustain that advantage over time. But as Jack Bogle said, it all comes down to "marketing!" It's our human nature to strive to be faster, better, smarter than the next guy. And thus, selling a hot fund is not difficult to do. It sells itself. And when it inevitably turns cold, there will be another hot one ready to serve up.

As for the 4% that do beat the market, they aren't the same 4% the next time around. Jack shared me with what he says is the funniest way to get this point across. "Tony, if you pack 1,024 gorillas into a gymnasium, and teach them each to flip a coin, one of them will flip heads ten times in a row. Most would call that luck, but when that happens in the fund business we call him a genius!" And what are the odds it's the same gorilla after the next ten flips?

To quote a study from Dimensional Fund Advisors, run by 2013 Nobel

Prize–winning economist Eugene Fama, "*So who still believes markets don't work? Apparently it is only the North Koreans, the Cubans, and the active managers.*"[4]

This part of the book is where anyone reading who works in the financial services industry will either nod in agreement or figure out which door they will prop open with these 600 pages! Some will even be gathering the troops to mount an attack. It's a polarizing issue, without a doubt. We all want to believe that by hiring the smartest and most talented mutual fund manager, we will achieve financial freedom more quickly. After all, who doesn't want a shortcut up the mountain? And here is the crazy thing:

As much as everyone is entitled to his own opinion, nobody is entitled to his own facts!

Sure, some mutual fund managers will say, "We may not outperform on the upside but when the market goes down, we can take active measures to protect you so you won't lose as much."

That might be comforting if it were true.

The goal in investing is to get the maximum net return for a given amount of risk (and, ideally, the lowest cost). So let's see how the fund managers did when the market was down. And 2008 is as good a place to start as any.

Between 2008 and early 2009, the market had its worst one-year slide since the Great Depression (51% from top to bottom, to be exact). The managers had plenty of time to make "defensive" moves. Maybe when the market was down 15%, or 25%, or 35%, they would have taken "appropriate measures." Once again, the facts speak for themselves.

Whether the fund manager was trying to beat the S&P Growth Index, made up of companies such as Microsoft, Qualcomm, and Google, or trying to beat the S&P Small Cap Index, made up of smaller companies such as Yelp, once again, the stock pickers fell short. According to a 2012 report titled *S&P Indices Versus Active Funds Scorecard—SPIVA*, for short—the S&P 500 Growth Index outperformed 89.9% of large-cap growth mutual funds, while the S&P 500 Small Cap 600 Growth Index outperformed 95.5% of small-cap growth managers.

---

4. Active managers rely on their own judgment and experience in making investment decisions on what stocks or bonds to buy, hold, and sell. They believe its possible to outperform the market with this approach.

THE UNICORNS

Now, having made it clear that almost nobody beats the market over time, I will give one caveat. There is a tiny group of hedge fund managers who do the seemingly impossible by beating the market consistently. But they are the "unicorns," the rarest of the rare. The "magicians." The "market wizards." Like David Einhorn of Greenlight Capital, who is up 2,287% (no, that's *not* a typo!) since launching his fund in 1996 and has only one negative year on his track record. But unfortunately, it doesn't do the average investor any good to know they are out there, because their doors are closed to new investors. Ray Dalio's fund, Bridgewater, hasn't accepted new investors in over ten years, but when it did, it required a minimum investment of $100 million and $5 billion in investable assets. Gulp.

Paul Tudor Jones, who hasn't lost money in over 28 years, called his investors recently and sent back $2 billion. When a hedge fund gets too big, it's harder to get in and get out of the market—harder to buy and sell its investments quickly and easily. And being slow means lower returns.

Before you begin to think this is a glowing report on hedge funds, let me be clear. For the fifth year in a row, ending in 2012, the vast majority of hedge fund managers have underperformed the S&P 500. According to the financial news site Zero Hedge, in 2012 the average fund returned 8% as opposed to 16% for the S&P 500. In 2013 hedge funds returned an average of 7.4%, while the S&P 500 soared 29.6%, its best year since 1997. I am sure their wealthy clients weren't too pleased. And to add insult to injury, they usually charge 2% per year for management, take 20% of the overall profits, and the gains you do receive are often taxed at the highest ordinary income tax rates. Painful.

THE BIGGEST BANK IN THE WORLD

No matter what aspect of life, I am always looking for the exception to the rule, as that's where outstanding tends to live. Mary Callahan Erdoes fits that bill. In an industry dominated by men, she has risen to the top of the financial world. Wall Street is a place where performance speaks louder than words, and Erdoes's performance has been extraordinary. Her consistent breakthrough results have led her to become the CEO of J.P. Morgan Asset Management, and she now oversees portfolios that total more than $2.5 trillion—yes, trillion with a *t*!

We had a fantastic interview for this book, and she shared some profound wisdom, which we will cover in section 6. But when I brought up the studies that no manager beats the market over time, she was quick to point out that many of J.P. Morgan's fund managers have beaten the market (in their respective classes) over the past ten years. Why? The examples she provided didn't lose as much as the market when the market went down. This difference, she says, is what provided the edge they needed to stay ahead. Erdoes and many industry experts agree that certain less-developed, or emerging, markets provide opportunities for active managers to get "an edge." They have the opportunity to gain an even greater advantage in *frontier markets*— places such as Kenya and Vietnam—where information isn't as transparent and doesn't travel as fast. Erdoes says this is where a firm such as J.P. Morgan has massive reach and resources, and can use its on-the-ground contacts in the community to give it valuable insights in real time.

According to Jack Bogle, there is no empirical basis to show that active management is more effective for all the major asset classes: large-cap growth, value, core, mid-cap growth, and so on. But it does appear that these frontier markets present opportunities for active management to sometimes outperform. Will they continue to outperform going forward? Only time will tell. We do know that every active manager, from Ray Dalio to J.P. Morgan, will be wrong at some point in their attempt to outperform. Therefore, developing a system and a proper asset allocation is crucial. We will address this in Section 4. It will be up to you to evaluate them for yourself, and don't forget to take into account the fees and the taxes (which we will discuss in the next chapter).

ALL WEATHER

You might be reading this book in a bull market, a bear market, or a sideways market. Who knows? The point is that you need to have your investments set up to stand the test of time. An "All Weather" portfolio. The people I have interviewed have done well in both good times and bad. And we can all count on ups and downs in the future. Life isn't about waiting for the storm to pass; it's about learning to dance in the rain. It's about removing the fear in this area of your life so you can focus on what matters most.

WHEN, WHERE, AND HOW?

So what does the All Weather portfolio look like? "Where do I put my money, Tony?!"

First, you don't have to waste your time trying to pick stocks yourself or pick the best mutual fund. A portfolio of low-cost index funds is the best approach for a percentage of your investments because we don't know what stocks will be "best" going forward. And how cool to know that by "passively" owning the market, you are beating 96% of the world's "expert" mutual fund managers and nearly as many hedge fund managers. It's time to free yourself from the burden of trying to pick the winner of the race. As Jack Bogle told me, in investing it feels counterintuitive. The secret: "Don't do something, just stand there!" And by becoming the market and not trying to beat it, you are on the side of progress, growth, and expansion.

So far we have referred many times to "the market" or the S&P 500. But remember that the S&P 500 is only one of many indexes or markets. Most have heard of the Dow Jones Industrial Average. There are others, such as a commodities index, a real estate index, a short-term bond index, a long-term bond index, a gold index, and so on. *How much of each to buy is critical and something we will get to in section 4.* In fact, how would you like to have Ray Dalio tell you what his ideal allocation would be? The strategy he shares in the pages ahead has produced just under 10% annually and made money more than 85% of the time in the last 30 years (between 1984 and 2013)! In fact, when the market was down 37% in 2008, his portfolio model was down only 3.93%! I sure wish I had known this back then!

Or how about David Swensen, the man who took Yale's endowment from $1 billion to more than $23.9 billion while averaging 14% annually? He too shared his ideal allocation for you in the pages ahead. Priceless information all captured in section 6, "Invest Like the .001%: The Billionaire's Playbook."

So if you look at these experts' models without fully understanding asset allocation, it's like building a house on a weak foundation. Or if you focus on asset allocation before knowing your goals, it will be a complete waste of time. And maybe most importantly, if we don't protect you from the people looking to take a good chunk of your wealth, all is lost. That's why we are uncovering the 9 Myths—Step 2 in our 7 Simple Steps to Financial Freedom—so that you become an "insider." So that you will know the truth. And the truth will set you free.

IT PAYS TO BE A STAR

Even after everything we have showed you about actively managed mutual funds, there are undoubtedly those who will say, "Tony, I have done my research, and not to worry. I only invest in five-star funds, nothing less." Oh, really?

According to Morningstar, over the decade ending December 2009, roughly 72% of all fund deposits (about $2 trillion) flowed to four- and five-star funds. For those who aren't familiar, Morningstar is the most popular and thorough service for evaluating mutual funds, and they apply a five-star ranking system to their past performance. Brokers are starry-eyed as they share with you the next hot fund.

David Swensen told me that "the stars are so important that mutual fund companies are quick to eliminate funds which fall below the four-star threshold. For the five-year period ending in 2012, 27% of domestic equity funds and 23% of international equity funds were either merged or liquidated; a common practice to eliminate a poor track record from a family of funds."

It's routine for mutual fund companies to set up multiple new funds to see which one is hot and euthanize the others. As Jack Bogle explains, "A firm will go out and start five incubation funds, and they will try and shoot the lights out with all five of them. And of course they don't with four of them, but they do with one. So they drop the other four and take the one that did very well public with a great track record and sell that track record."

Imagine we could adopt this practice in our own investing life? What if you could pick 5 stocks and if four went down and only one went up, you could pretend all your losers didn't happen? And then tell your friends that you are the hottest stock picker since Warren Buffett.

In addition, the lackluster performance of these four- and five-star supernovas (dying stars) is well researched in a *Wall Street Journal* article entitled

"Investors Caught with Stars in Their Eyes." A study was done in which the researchers went back to 1999 and studied the ten-year *subsequent* performance of those who bought five-star funds. Their findings? "Of the 248 mutual stock funds with five-star ratings at the start of the period, just four still kept that rank after 10 years."

How many times have you picked a shooting star only to watch it burn out? We all have at some point. And here we see that it's because we had less than 2% odds that the shooting star wouldn't fizzle into darkness. We all want the guy with the hot hand, but history tells us that it's the hot hand that will inevitably turn cold. Isn't that why Vegas always wins!?

An "insider" knows that chasing the highflyer is chasing the wind. But it's human nature to chase performance. It's almost irresistible. Yet the "herd" mentality quite literally results in financial destruction for millions of families, and I know that if you are reading this book, you are not willing to fall victim any longer. You're becoming an insider now! And what other cool strategies do "insiders" use? Let's find out.

UPSIDE WITH PROTECTION

In the past 100 years, the market was up approximately 70% of the time. But that leaves 30% of the time that the market was down. So while investing in the indexes is a great solution for a portion of your money, *it shouldn't be for all of your money.* Markets are volatile at times so it only makes sense that you will want to protect a portion of your portfolio if or when the markets take another big dive. Heck, there have been two 50% hits since 2000.

One exciting strategy we will introduce allows us to make money when the market (index) goes up, yet it simultaneously guarantees that we will not lose our original investment if the market goes down. The catch? You don't get to capture or participate in *all* of the gains.

Most are in disbelief when I explain that there are tools out there that can guarantee that you don't lose while still giving you the ability to participate in market "wins." Why haven't you heard of them? Because they are typically reserved for high-net-worth clients. I will show you one of the only places where the average investor can access these. Imagine your friends with their baffled and even suspicious looks when you tell them you make money when the market goes up but don't lose money when it goes down.

This strategy alone can completely change the way you feel about investing. It's your safety rope while climbing the mountain when everyone else is "white knuckling" it with hope. Imagine the feeling of certainty, of peace of mind, knowing that you aren't at risk. How would this change your life? How would you feel when you open up your monthly statements? Would you be gritting your teeth or feel calm and collected?

We've only scratched the surface of the incredible insights and tools that lay ahead, so you must stay tuned. But for now, we can remember the following:

- Stocks have by far been the best place to be for long-term growth over time.
- Stocks are volatile. In the pages ahead, you will learn from the "market masters" how to "smooth out the ride" by investing in and diversifying across multiple different indexes.
- Don't be sold that someone is going to beat the market. Instead, align yourself with the market! Once you put your indexing plan in place (which we will do step by step), you won't have to spend your time trying to pick which stock to buy because the index will have done it for you. This will save you a tremendous amount of time and angst in trying to pick a winner.
- Begin to think like an insider! Never again will you tolerate the "herd" mentality in your own life.

FEES ON FEES

By tapping into the power of indexing, by passively owning the market, you are also combatting our second myth. Nearly every person I ask doesn't know *exactly* how much he or she pays in fees. I'll admit, I also didn't know at one stage in my life. The fee factories have become masterful at either hiding the fees or making them appear negligible. "No big deal." Nothing could be further from the truth. When climbing the mountain of financial freedom you will need every bit of forward progress to succeed. You can't afford to take two steps forward and one step back by letting excessive fees drain your account. So the *real* question is: Are you funding *your* retirement or *someone else's*? Turn the page now and find out!

MYTH 2:
"OUR FEES?
THEY'RE A SMALL PRICE TO PAY!"

The mutual fund industry is now the world's largest skimming operation,
a $7 trillion trough from which fund managers, brokers, and other insiders
are steadily siphoning off an excessive slice of the nation's household,
college, and retirement savings."

—SENATOR PETER FITZGERALD, cosponsor of the Mutual
Fund Reform Act of 2004 (killed by the Senate Banking Committee)

INSULT TO INJURY

Nothing is more infuriating than to be told one price but then realize that
you are paying another. You agree on the price of a new car, but when it
comes down to signing the documents, a couple thousand in fees magically
appear. Or you check out of a hotel and discover an additional resort fee, a
tourism tax, a wireless internet fee, fees for towels—you get the point.

It's frustrating. We feel trapped. We feel snowed. Strong-armed or simply
deceived into paying more than we should. With the help of fine print, the
$13 trillion mutual fund industry is hands down the most masterful in the
craft of hiding fees.

In a *Forbes* article entitled "The Real Cost of Owning a Mutual Fund,"
Ty Bernicke peels back the layers to dissect the *actual* cost and arrives at a
heart-stopping total:

The average cost of owning a mutual fund is 3.17% per year!

If 3.17% doesn't sound like a big number to you, think of it in light of
what we just learned about becoming or owning the market. For example,
you can "own" the entire market (let's say all 500 stocks in the S&P 500) for
as little as 0.14%—or as the investment world calls it, 14 basis points (bps).

That's just 14 cents for every $100 you invest. (Just a quick FYI for you insiders: there are 100 basis points in 1%, so 50 basis points is 0.5% and so on.)

Owning the entire market is accomplished through a low-cost index fund such as those offered through Vanguard or Dimensional Fund Advisors. And we already know that owning the market beats 96% of all the mutual fund "stock pickers" over a sustained period. Sure, you might be willing to pay 3% to an extraordinary hedge fund manager like Ray Dalio, who has a 21% annualized return (before fees) since launching his fund! **But with most mutual funds, we are paying nearly 30 times, or 3,000%, more in fees, and for what? Inferior performance!!!** Can you imagine paying 30 times more for the same type of car your neighbor owns, and it goes only 25 mph to boot!

This is exactly what is happening today. Two neighbors are both invested in the market, but one is shelling out fistfuls of cash each year, while the other is paying pennies on the dollar.

SAME RETURNS, DIFFERENT RESULTS— THE COST OF IGNORANCE

Three childhood friends, Jason, Matthew, and Taylor, at age 35, all have $100,000 to invest. Each selects a different mutual fund, and all three are lucky enough to have equal performance in the market of 7% annually. At age 65, they get together to compare account balances. **On deeper inspection, they realize that the fees they have been paying are drastically different from one another. They are paying annual fees of 1%, 2%, and 3% respectively.**

Below is the impact of fees on their ending account balance:

Jason: $100,000 growing at 7% (minus 3% in annual fees) = **$324,340;**

Matthew: $100,000 growing at 7% (minus 2% in annual fees) = **$432,194;** and

Taylor: $100,000 growing at 7% (minus 1% in annual fees) = **$574,349.**

Same investment amount, same returns, and Taylor has nearly twice as much money as her friend Jason. Which horse do you bet on? The one with the 100-pound jockey or the 300-pound jockey?

"Just" 1% here, 1% there. Doesn't sound like much, but compounded over time, it could be the difference between your money lasting your entire

IMPACT OF FEES

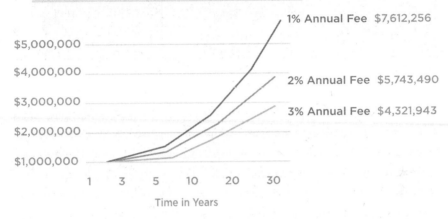

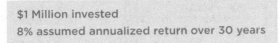

$1 Million invested
8% assumed annualized return over 30 years

1% Annual Fee $7,612,256

2% Annual Fee $5,743,490

3% Annual Fee $4,321,943

$5,000,000

$4,000,000

$3,000,000

$2,000,000

$1,000,000

1 3 5 10 20 30

Time in Years

life or surviving on government or family assistance. It's the difference between teeth-clenching anxiety about your bills or peace of mind to live as you wish and enjoy life. Practically, it can often mean working a full decade longer before you can have the freedom to quit working if you choose to. As Jack Bogle has shown us, by paying excessive fees, you are giving up 50% to 70% of your future nest egg.

Now, the example above is hypothetical, so let's get a bit more real. Between January 1, 2000, and December 31, 2012, the S&P 500 was *flat*. No returns. This period includes what is often called the "lost decade" because most people made no progress but still endured massive volatility with the run-up through 2007, the free fall in 2008, and the bull market run that began in 2009. So let's say you had your life savings of $100,000 invested. And if you simply owned, or "mimicked," the market during this 12-year period, your account was flat and your fees were minimal. But if you paid the 3.1% in average annual fees, and assuming your mutual fund manager could even match the market, you would have paid over $30,000 in fees!!! So your account was down 40% (only $60,000 left), but the market was flat. **You put up the capital, you took all the risk, and they made money no matter what happened.**

I AM SMARTER THAN THAT

Now, you might be reading along and thinking, "Tony, I am smarter than that. I looked at the 'expense ratio' of my mutual fund(s), and it's only one percent. Heck, I even have some *'no load'* mutual funds!" Well, I have some swampland in Florida to sell you! In all seriousness, this is the exact conclusion they want you to arrive at. Like the sleight-of-hand magician, the mutual fund companies use the oldest trick in the book: misdirection. They want us to focus on the wrong object while they subtly remove our watch! The expense ratio is the "sticker price" most commonly reported in the marketing materials. But it certainly doesn't tell the whole story . . .

And let me be the first to confess that at one stage in my life, I thought I was investing intelligently, and I owned my share of the "top" five-star actively managed mutual funds. I had done my homework. Looked at the expense ratios. Consulted a broker. But like you, I am busy making a living and taking care of my family. I didn't have the time to sit down and read 50 pages of disclosures. The laundry list of fees is shrouded within the fine print. It takes a PhD in economics to figure it out.

PhD IN FEES

Just after the 2008 crash, Robert Hiltonsmith graduated with a PhD in economics and decided to take a job with policy think tank Dēmos. And like all of us, nothing he learned in college would prepare him for how to create a successful investment strategy.

So, like most, he started making dutiful contributions to his 401(k). But even though the market was rising, his account would rarely rise with it. He knew something was wrong, so he decided to take it on as a research project for work. First, he started by reading the 50-plus-page prospectus of each of the 20 funds he invested in. Incredibly boring and dry legalese designed to be, in Hiltonsmith's words, "very opaque."[5] There was language he couldn't decipher, acronyms he hadn't a clue what they stood for, and, most importantly, a catalogue of 17 different fees that were being charged. There were also additional costs that weren't direct fees per se but were passed onto and paid for by the investors nonetheless.

To better shroud the fees, Wall Street and the vast majority of 401(k) plan providers have come up with some pretty diverse and confusing terminology. Asset management fees, 12b-1 fees/marketing fees, trading costs (brokerage commissions, spread costs, market impact costs), soft-dollar costs, redemption fees, account fees, purchase fees, record-keeping fees, plan administrative fees, and on and on. Call them what you want. They all cost you money! They all pull you backward down the mountain.

After a solid month of research, Hiltonsmith came to the conclusion that there wasn't a chance in hell that his 401(k) account would flourish with these excessive and hidden fees acting as a hole in his boat. In his report, titled *The Retirement Savings Drain: The Hidden & Excessive Costs of 401(k)s*, he calculated that the average worker will lose $154,794 to 401(k) fees over his lifetime (based on annual income of approximately $30,000 per year and saving 5% of his income each year). A higher-income worker, making approximately $90,000 per year, will lose upward of $277,000 in fees in his/her lifetime! Hiltonsmith and Dēmos have done a great social good in exposing the tyranny of compounding costs.

DEATH BY A THOUSAND CUTS

In ancient China, death by a thousand cuts was the cruelest form of torture because of how long the process took to kill the victim. Today the victim is the American investor, and the proverbial blade is the excessive fees that slowly but surely bleed the investor dry.

David Swensen is the chief investment officer of Yale's endowment. He has grown the fund from $1 billion to more than $23.9 billion, and he is considered to be the Warren Buffett of institutional investing. When I sat

---

5. Robert Hiltonsmith and his research were featured on a terrific *Frontline* documentary called *The Retirement Gamble*, which first aired on PBS on April 23, 2013.

down with him in his Yale office, I was enlightened yet angered when he shared the *real* truth regarding the "fee factories" that are slaughtering Americans. David shared, "Overwhelmingly, mutual funds extract enormous sums from investors in exchange for providing a shocking disservice." Later in the book, we will sit down and look over David's shoulder at his portfolio recommendations, but it doesn't matter how great your strategy is if excessive fees are eroding the path beneath your feet.

The "asset gathering" complex and the actively managed mutual funds they peddle are, for the most part, a disastrous social experiment that began with the advent of the 401(k) in the early '80s. The 401(k) was not a "bad" concept. It was a good idea for those who wanted to put extra money away. But it was just meant to be a supplement to a traditional pension plan. Today there is over $13 trillion in managed mutual funds, much of which is held in retirement accounts such as 401(k)s and IRAs. They were supposed to get us to our retirement goals. They were supposed to beat the market. But not only do they rarely beat the market, a significant majority are charging astronomical fees for their mediocrity. The aggregate of these fees will ultimately cost tens of millions of people their quality of life and could very well be the number one danger and destroyer of your financial freedom. Sound like an overstatement?

Jack Bogle, founder of Vanguard, says, "I think high costs [eroding already lower returns] are as much of a risk for investors as the [economic situation] in Europe or China."

IT GETS WORSE

So let's recap. Not only will the vast majority (96%) of actively managed mutual funds *not* beat the market, they are going to charge us an arm and leg, and extract up to two-thirds of our potential nest egg in fees. But here is the kicker: they are going to have the nerve to look you in the eye and tell you that they truly have your best interests at heart while simultaneously lobbying Congress to make sure that is never the case.

THE TRUTH/SOLUTION

First, you need to know how much you are paying! I recommend visiting the investment software website Personal Fund (www.PersonalFund.com) for its cost calculator, which analyzes each of your funds and looks beyond just the expense ratio to the additional costs as well.

Keep in mind, these calculators can only estimate the fees. They can't take into account other costs such as taxes because each person's tax bracket may differ. You may also own the mutual fund inside your 401(k), in which you won't be paying taxes on the growth but instead will be paying a "plan administrator." Some 401(k) plans are low-cost, while others are hefty with expenses. The average plan administrator charges 1.3% to 1.5% annually (according to the nonpartisan Government Accountability Office). That's $1,300 for every $100,000 just to participate in the 401(k). So when you add this 1.3% for the plan administration to the total mutual fund costs of 3.17%, it can actually be *more* expensive to own a fund in a tax-free account when compared with a taxable account (a whopping total of 4.47% to 4.67% per year)!!!

Think about it: you are saving 10%, but half of it is being paid in fees. How insane is that? But as you'll learn here, you don't have to be caught in this trap. By becoming an insider, you can put a stop to this thievery today. Fees this high are the equivalent of climbing Everest in flip-flops and a tank top. You were dead before you got started.

ADD 'EM UP

Nontaxable Account	Taxable Account
Expense ratio, 0.90%	Expense ratio, 0.90%
Transaction costs, 1.44%	Transaction costs, 1.44%
Cash drag, 0.83%	Cash drag, 0.83%
—	Tax cost, 1.00%
Total costs, **3.17%**	Total costs, **4.17%**

"The Real Cost of Owning a Mutual Fund," *Forbes*, April 4, 2011

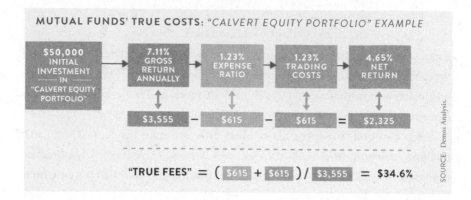

MUTUAL FUNDS' TRUE COSTS: *"CALVERT EQUITY PORTFOLIO" EXAMPLE*

$50,000 INITIAL INVESTMENT IN "CALVERT EQUITY PORTFOLIO"	7.11% GROSS RETURN ANNUALLY	1.23% EXPENSE RATIO	1.23% TRADING COSTS	4.65% NET RETURN
	$3,555 −	$615 −	$615 =	$2,325

"TRUE FEES" = ($615 + $615)/ $3,555 = $34.6%

SOURCE: Demos Analysis.

ESCAPE

To escape the fee factories, you must lower your **total annual fees** and associated investment costs to 1.25% or less, on average. This means the cost of the advice (a *registered investment advisor* to help you allocate appropriately, rebalance your portfolio periodically, and so on) *plus* the cost of the investments should ideally be 1.25% or less. For example, you might be paying 1% or less to the registered investment advisor and 0.20% for low-cost index funds like those offered through Vanguard (for a total of 1.2%). *And* the 1% paid to the advisor as a fee can be tax deductible. Which means your "net" out-of-pocket cost is close to half, depending on your tax bracket. Most Americans use a typical broker where the commissions aren't deductible, nor are those expensive fees the mutual fund charges. (We will discuss the difference between a broker and a registered investment advisor shortly. You don't want to miss this one!)

In section 3, we will show you step by step how to dramatically reduce your fees and legally reduce your taxes. And all that money you save will accelerate your path to financial freedom.

NEVER AGAIN

Now that you know how the game is played, now that you have looked behind the curtain, make the decision that you will never be taken advantage of again. **Resolve right now that you'll never again be one of the many. You're becoming an insider now.** You are the chess player, not the chess piece. Knowledge is power, but execution trumps knowledge, so it's what you do from here that will matter. Yes, I will show you exactly *how* to reduce your fees, but you must decide to take the necessary action. You must declare that you will *never again* pay insane fees for subpar performance. And if this book can save you 2% to 3% per year in unnecessary fees, we just put hundreds of thousands of dollars, maybe even millions, back in your pocket. **Said another way, this could get you to your goal that much quicker and save you 5 to 15 years of accumulation time so that you can retire sooner if you so choose.**

By simply removing expensive mutual funds from your life and replacing them with low-cost index funds you will have made a major step in recouping up to 70% of your potential future nest egg! How exciting! What will that mean for you and your family? Vanguard has an entire suite of low-cost index funds (across multiple different types of asset classes) that range between 0.05% and 0.25% per year in total "all-in" costs. Dimensional Funds is another great low-cost index fund provider. If you don't have access to these low-cost providers in your 401(k), we will show you how to make that happen. And while low-cost index funds are crucial, determining how much of each index fund to buy, and how to manage the entire portfolio over time, are the keys to success. We will cover that in the pages ahead.

Now that you have resolved to take action, to whom do you turn? Who do you trust as a guide? Going back to your broker to help you save on fees is like going to your pharmacist to help you get off meds. How do you find conflict-free advice? And how do you know that the guidance you're getting isn't in the best interest of the person on the other side of the desk? Turn the page to uncover Myth 3, and let's get answers to these pressing questions. . . .

BREAK IT DOWN

If you really want to know how badly you're being abused through hidden fees, take a moment and review a sample list below of some of the core fees and costs that impact your mutual fund investments:

BREAKOUT OF FEES

1. **Expense Ratio.** This expense is the main "price tag"—the number they want us focused on. But it certainly doesn't tell the whole story.

According to Morningstar, US stock funds pay an average of 1.31% of assets each year to the fund company for portfolio management and operating expenses such as marketing (12b-1 fees), distribution, and administration. Many of the larger funds have realized that a 1% ballpark expense ratio is where they want to come in so that investors don't flinch and brokers have a good story to sell—I mean, *tell*.

2. **Transaction Costs.** Transaction costs are a broad, sweeping category and can be broken down further into categories such as brokerage commissions, market impact costs (the cost of moving the market as mutual funds trade massive market-moving positions), and spread costs (the difference between the bid-and-ask or the buy-and-sell price of a stock). A 2006 study by business school professors Roger Edelen, Richard Evans, and Gregory Kadlec found that US stock mutual funds average 1.44% in transaction costs per year. This means that these transaction costs are perhaps the most expensive component of owning a mutual fund, but the industry has deemed it too tough to quantify, and thus it goes unreported in the brochures.

3. **Tax Costs (or 401[k] Costs).** Many people are excited about the "tax-deferred" treatment of their 401(k), but for most employees, the tax cost has been swapped out with "plan administrative" fees. These are charged *in addition* to the fees paid to the underlying mutual funds, and according to the nonpartisan GAO (Government Accountability Office), the average plan administrator charges 1.13% per year! If you own a mutual fund in a taxable account, the average tax cost is between 1.0% and 1.2% annually, according to Morningstar.

4. **Soft-Dollar Costs.** Soft-dollar trading is a quid pro quo arrangement whereby mutual fund managers choose to pay inflated trading costs so that the outside firm executing their trades will then rebate the additional cost back to the fund manager. It's a rewards program for using a particular vendor. The frequent flier miles of Wall Street. The fund manager can use these funds to pay for certain expenses such as research and reports. These are costs the fund manager would otherwise have to pay, so the net result is that you and I pay! These are simply well-disguised increases in management revenue that hit the bottom line. They're unreported and nearly impossible to quantify,

so we aren't able to include them in our equation below, but make no mistake, it's a cost.

5. **Cash Drag.** Mutual fund managers must maintain a cash position to provide daily liquidity and satisfy any redemptions (selling). Since cash is not invested, it doesn't generate a return and thus hurts performance. According to a study titled "Dealing with the Active," authored by William O'Rielly, CFA, and Michael Preisano, CFA, the average cost from cash drag on large-cap stock mutual funds over a ten-year time horizon was 0.83% per year. It may not be a direct fee, but it's a cost that takes away from your performance.

6. **Redemption Fee.** If you want to sell your fund position, you may pay a redemption fee. This fee is paid to the fund company directly and the US Securities and Exchange Commission (SEC) limits the redemption fee to 2%. Like the world's most expensive ATM, it could cost you $2,000 to get back *your* $100,000!

7. **Exchange Fee.** Some funds charge a fee to move or exchange from one fund to another within the same family of funds.

8. **Account Fee.** Some funds charge a maintenance fee just to have an account.

9. **Purchase Fee.** A purchase fee, not to be confused with a front-end sales load (commission), is a charge to purchase the fund that goes directly to the fund company.

10. **Sales Charge (Load) or Deferred Sales Charge.** This charge, typically paid to a broker, either comes out when you purchase the fund (so a smaller amount of your initial deposit is used to buy shares in the fund) *or* you pay the charge when you exit the fund and redeem your shares.

MYTH 3:
"OUR RETURNS?
WHAT YOU SEE IS WHAT YOU GET"

Surprise, the returns reported by mutual funds
aren't actually earned by investors.
—JACK BOGLE, founder of Vanguard

Most people are familiar with the boilerplate disclaimer that past
performance doesn't guarantee future results. Far fewer are aware
of how past performance numbers themselves can be misleading.
—"HOW FUNDS MASSAGE NUMBERS, LEGALLY,"
Wall Street Journal, March 31, 2013

LIPSTICK ON A PIG

In 2002 Charles Schwab ran a clever TV ad where a typical Wall Street sales
manager is giving a morning pep talk to his boiler room. "Tell your clients
it's red hot! *En fuego!* Just don't mention the fundamentals—they stink." He
wraps up his morning sermon by dangling courtside tickets to the Knicks
for the winning salesman and gives his final send-off: "Let's put some lip-
stick on this pig!"

GET MY GOOD SIDE

In 1954 Darrell Huff authored a book entitled *How to Lie with Statistics*. He
points to the "countless number of dodges which are used to fool rather than
to inform." Today the mutual fund industry has been able to use a tricky
method to calculate and publish returns that are, as Jack Bogle says, "not actually earned by the investors." But before we explain this masterful "sleight
of pencil" magic, let's first understand the illusion of average returns.

Below is a chart showing a hypothetical market that is up and down like a roller coaster. Up 50%, down 50%, up 50%, and down 50%. This produces an *average* return of 0%. And like you, I would expect that a 0% return would mean that I didn't lose any money. And we would both be wrong!

As you can see by the chart, if you start with an actual dollar amount (let's use $100,000), at the end of the four-year period, you are actually down $43,750, or 43.75%! You thought you were even, but instead you're down 43.75%! Would you ever have guessed this? Now that you're an insider, beware! Average returns have a built-in illusion, spinning a performance enhancement that doesn't exist.

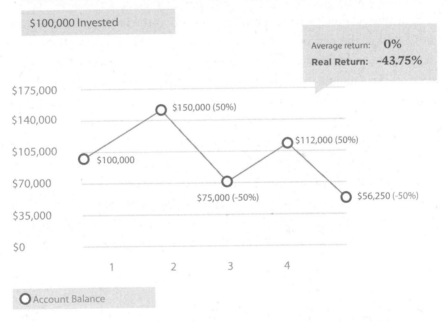

MARKET PERFORMANCE

$100,000 Invested

Average return: **0%**
Real Return: **-43.75%**

- $150,000 (50%)
- $100,000
- $112,000 (50%)
- $75,000 (-50%)
- $56,250 (-50%)

$175,000
$140,000
$105,000
$70,000
$35,000
$0

1   2   3   4

○ Account Balance

In a Fox Business article titled "Solving the Myth of Rate of Return," Erik Krom explains how this discrepancy applies to the real world: "Another way to look at it is to review the Dow Jones since 1930. **If you add up every number and divide it by 81 years, the return 'averages' 6.31%;** however, if you do the math, **you get an 'actual' return of 4.31%.** Why is this so important? If you invested $1,000 back in 1930 at 6.31%, you would have $142,000, at 4.31% **you would only have $30,000."**

THE SCALES ARE WEIGHTED

Now that we see that average returns aren't a true representation of what we earn, sit back and relax because the grand illusion isn't over yet. The math magicians on Wall Street have managed to calculate their returns to look even better. How so?

In short, when the mutual fund advertises a specific return, it's not, as Jack Bogle says, "the return you actually earn." Why? Because the returns you see in the brochure are known as *time-weighted returns*. Sounds complicated, but it's not. (However, feel free to use that to look brilliant at your next cocktail party!)

The mutual fund manager says if we have $1 at the beginning of the year and $1.20 at the end of the year, we are up 20%. "Fire up the marketing department and take out those full-page ads!" But in reality, investors rarely have all their money in the fund at the beginning of the year. We typically make contributions throughout the year—that is, out of every paycheck into our 401(k). And if we contribute more during times of the year when the fund is performing well (a common theme, we learned, as investors chase performance) and less during times when it's not performing, we are going to have a much different return from what is advertised. So if we were to sit down at the end of the year and take into account the "real world" of making ongoing contributions and withdrawals, we would find out how much we *really* made (or lost). And this real-world approach is called the *dollar-weighted return*. Dollar-weighted returns are what we actually get to keep whereas time-weighted returns are what fund managers use to fuel advertising.

Jack Bogle has been a continual proponent of changing this rule. He believes that investors should see how much they actually earned (or lost) based on their own personal situation (contributions and withdrawals included). Sounds like common sense, right? But it's no surprise why mutual funds are resistant. Bogle says: "We've compared returns earned by mutual fund investors—dollar-weighted returns—with the returns earned by the fund themselves, or time-weighted returns, and the investors seem to lag the fund themselves by three percent per year." Wow! **So if the fund adver-tises a 6% return, its investors achieved closer to 3%.**

THE TRUTH AND THE SOLUTION

Average returns are like profile photos for online dating. They paint a better portrait than the reality! If you know the amount you started with in your investment and you know how much you have now, you can go to a website such as Moneychimp (www.moneychimp.com/calculator/discount_rate_calculator .htm), and it will show you exactly what the actual return is on your money over that period of time.

You must also remember that the returns reported by mutual funds are based on a theoretical person who invested all his money on Day 1. This just isn't true for most so we can't delude ourselves into believing that the glossy brochure returns are the same as what we have actually received in our account.

THE PATH IS CLEAR

Nobody said climbing a mountain would be easy. But it's a heck of a lot easier when you have a machete called "truth" to hack away the lies and grant a clear view of the path ahead. As an insider, you are no longer flying blind.

You now know that stock-picking mutual funds don't beat the market over any sustained period (especially after you account for fees and taxes).

You also know that fees *do* matter. And that by lowering your fees, you can get back as much as 60% to 70% of your future potential nest egg. How will this awesome truth impact your future?

And finally, you know that average returns don't paint the real picture. Actual returns matter. And you now have the simple tools to calculate them.

Your journey to financial freedom has more than begun. You are hitting your stride, and the truths you have learned so far will separate you from being one of the "sheeple."

FLYING SOLO

As I have taught people these tools, I often notice that people feel as though they can no longer trust anyone. In a sense, they feel betrayed, as they become enlightened and start to understand the *real* rules of the game. They think they must now handle everything on their own and become an island unto themselves because "nobody can be trusted." This just isn't true. There are a number of incredible financial professionals who are full of integrity and committed to their clients' futures. I have an amazing advisor whom I trust implicitly to act in my best interests, and together we review and manage my investments. Like you, I am insanely busy and don't have the time or desire to spend my days managing the details of my portfolio. In reality, if done properly, a brief quarterly or twice-a-year review is all that is needed to go over your objectives and rebalance the portfolio.

So how do you know the difference between a salesman and a trusted advisor? Between a broker and a guide? Myth 4 will help us quickly determine if the person on the other side of the desk is working for you or the name on their company's letterhead. As "Deep Throat" from the Watergate scandal said:

"Follow the money. Always follow the money."

MYTH 4:
"I'M YOUR BROKER, AND I'M HERE TO HELP"

"It is difficult to get a man to understand something, when his salary depends on his not understanding it."
—UPTON SINCLAIR

LET ME GET THIS STRAIGHT

So let us recap:

The mutual funds sold to me are charging me astronomical fees that could strip me of up to 70% of my future nest egg.

Over any sustained period of time, 96% of actively managed mutual funds are underperforming the market (or their benchmarks).

I am being charged 10 to 30 times what it would cost me to own a low-cost index fund and "become," or mimic, the market.

The returns the mutual funds are selling are typically way better than the returns I actually receive since they are marketed as time-weighted returns, *not* dollar-weighted returns. Dollar-weighted returns are what we actually get to keep/spend, whereas time-weighted returns are what fund managers use to fuel advertising.

And as the grand finale, your broker will look you in the eye and tell you that he has your best interests at heart. Because more than likely, he sincerely believes he is helping you. He doesn't understand, nor has he even been educated about the impact of what we described above. Heck, he is probably following the same advice he is giving you for his own personal finances.

CHOMP! CHOMP!

How in the world can the vast majority of Americans be dying the death of a thousand cuts but not rise up, vote with their pocketbooks, and take their hard-earned money elsewhere? The answer is, they've been kept in the dark for decades. Most people I talk to are highly suspicious of the financial services industry as a whole and its desire to "help" you succeed. They've been burned before. Yet in the face of a constant barrage of conflicting information and marketing hype, they quickly become overwhelmed. Not to mention the demands of daily life. Many have put their financial lives on autopilot and have accepted being part of the herd. "Hope" has become their strategy.

There's a social comfort in knowing that you're not alone. It reminds me of watching the Discovery Channel and the wildebeest that cautiously approaches the crocodile-infested water for a drink just minutes after the jaws of a croc clamped down on his buddy! Is the animal stupid? No! The animal knows that without water it will die in the blistering African sun so it takes a calculated risk. Most of us feel the same way. We know we can't sit on the sidelines, on the edge of the riverbank, because inflation will destroy us if we just sit on our cash. So, alongside our neighbors and colleagues, we journey down to the water with trepidation, and when we least expect it: *chomp!*

A Black Monday. A dot-com bubble. Another 2008.

All the while, the brokerage firm with which we entrusted our family's quality of life is taking no risk and reaping record compensation year after year.

As I write this in early 2014, the market prices have continued to grow. From 2009 through the end of 2013, the market was up 131% (including dividend reinvestment). That's the fifth largest bull market in history. People are seeing their account balances rise and are getting comfortable again. Mutual fund managers and executives are raking it in. But the crocs are still feeding.

PROTECTION FROM WHOM?

In late 2009 Representatives Barney Frank and Chris Dodd submitted proposed regulation called the "Dodd-Frank Wall Street Reform and Consumer Protection Act. One year later, after intense lobbying by the financial services community, a version of the bill passed with far less teeth than the original. But nobody stopped to ask the obvious question: *From whom or what exactly do we need protection?*

From the people we trust to manage our financial future? From the brokers who sell us expensive mutual funds? From the managers themselves, who play legal but shady games to line their pockets? From the high-frequency traders who are "front running" the market and pinching millions one penny at a time? In the last couple years alone, we have seen rogue traders cause billions in losses for banks; large firms such as MF Global misappropriate client funds and ultimately declare bankruptcy; insider trading convictions from one of the world's largest hedge funds; and bank traders criminally prosecuted for rigging LIBOR (London Interbank Offered Rates), the world's most widely used benchmark for short-term interest rates.

"WITH MY BRAINS AND YOUR MONEY, WE HAVE NOTHING TO LOSE OTHER THAN YOUR MONEY."

THE CHEF DOESN'T EAT HIS OWN COOKING

We are continually sold and influenced by those who "do as I say, not as I do." In a sobering 2009 study released by Morningstar, in tracking over

4,300 actively managed mutual funds, **it was found that 49% of the managers owned no shares in the fund they manage.** That's right. The chef doesn't eat his own cooking.

Of the remaining 51%, most own a token amount of their funds when compared with their compensation and total net worth. Remember, these guys earn millions, sometimes tens of millions, for their skills:

- 2,126 own no shares in the fund they manage.
- 159 managers had invested between $1 and $10,000 in their own fund.
- 393 managers invested between $10,001 and $50,000.
- 285 managers invested between $50,001 and $100,000.
- 679 managers invested between $100,001 and $500,000.
- 197 managers invested between $500,001 and $999,999.
- 413 managers invested more than $1 million.

So the obvious question is, if the people who manage the fund aren't investing in the fund they run, why in the world would I? Good question!!!

The chef doesn't eat his own cooking if the ingredients are bad or if he knows what the kitchen *really* looks and smells like. These fund managers are smart—they work under the hood.

WHERE ARE THE CUSTOMERS' YACHTS?

Fred Schwed Jr. was a professional trader who quit Wall Street after losing a lot of his money in the crash of 1929. In 1940 he wrote the investment classic *Where Are the Customers' Yachts?, or A Good Hard Look at Wall Street.* The joke behind the title has been retold many different ways over the years, but in Schwed's version, a successful Wall Street broker named William Travers is admiring the many beautiful yachts while on vacation in Newport, Rhode Island. Each yacht he inquires about happens to belong to a broker, banker, or trader.

He asks, "Where are the customers' yachts?"

Nearly 75 years have passed since this story was first published, but it could have been written yesterday!

WHOM TO TRUST

We have all seen numerous variations of the same commercial. The husband and wife, looking concerned, sit across the desk from their financial advisor. And with the wisdom of a grandfather and the look of a man who has weathered many storms, the hired actor assures them that with his help, they will be just fine. "Don't worry, we've got your back. We'll get your kids through college. We'll get you that sailboat. We'll get you that vacation home." The insinuation is loud and clear: "Your goals are our goals. We're here to help." But the real question is:

Are your interests *really* aligned?

Does the person with whom you trust to plan you and your family's future have every incentive to operate in your best interest? Most would think "yes"—and most would be wrong. And the answer to this question may be the difference between failing or succeeding in your journey to Financial Freedom. When climbing the mountain, how would you feel if your guide was more concerned about his own survival than yours? As David Swensen reminded me, "Your broker is not your friend."

THE SUITABILITY STANDARD

And here is the truth: the financial services industry has many caring people of the highest integrity who truly want to do what's in the best interest of their clients. Unfortunately, many are operating in a "closed-circuit" environment in which the tools at their disposal are preengineered to be in the best interests of the "house." The system is designed to reward them for selling, not for providing conflict-free advice. And the product or fund they sell you doesn't necessarily have to be the best available, or even in your best interest. **By legal definition, all they have to do is provide you with a product that is "suitable."**

What kind of standard is "suitable"? Do you want a suitable partner for life? "Honey, how was it for you tonight?" "Eh . . . the sex was suitable." Are you going to be promoted for doing suitable work? Do you fly the airline with a "suitable" safety record? Or better yet, "Let's go to lunch here; I hear the food is suitable."

Yet, according to David Karp, a registered investment advisor, the suitability standard essentially says, "It doesn't matter who benefits more, the client or advisor. As long as an investment is suitable [meets the general direction of your goals and objectives] at the time it was placed for the client, the advisor is held free of liability."

THE GOLD STANDARD

To receive conflict-free advice, we must align ourselves with a *fiduciary*. **A fiduciary is a legal standard adopted by a relatively small but growing segment of independent financial professionals who have abandoned their big-box firms, relinquished their broker status, and made the decision to become a registered investment advisor. These professionals get paid for financial advice and, by law, must remove any potential conflicts of interest (or, at a minimum, disclose them) and put the client's needs above their own.**

By way of example, if a registered investment advisor tells a client to buy IBM and later that day he buys IBM in his own personal account for a better price, he *must* give the client his stock at the lower price trade.

Imagine having investment advice where you knew that the law protected you from your advisor steering you in a specific direction or to a specific fund to make more money off of you.

One huge additional advantage? The fee you pay a fiduciary for advice may be tax deductible, depending on your tax bracket. So a 1% advisory fee could really be closer to 0.5% when you take into account the deduction. Contrast this with the 2% or more you pay to a mutual fund manager, *none* of which is tax deductible.

FINDING A FIDUCIARY

If there is one single step you can take today to solidify your position as insider, it's to align yourself with a fiduciary; an independent registered investment advisor (RIA for short).

Most people I ask don't know whether "their investment guy/gal" is a broker or a legal fiduciary, but nearly everyone believes that his investment person should have his best interests at heart. And as I mentioned before, they typically do have his clients' interests in mind but they are operating within a framework that rewards them for selling. And, by the way, you'll never hear them referred to as "brokers." They are called registered representatives, financial advisors, wealth advisors, vice president of this, that, or the other thing. In fact, the *Wall Street Journal* reported finding in excess of two hundred different professional designations for financial advisors—more than half of which are not tracked by the Financial Industry Regulatory Authority (FINRA), which oversees how investments are pitched to investors. Many of these financial service "credentials" are pure window dressing and do not impart a fiduciary duty.

NOT ALL ADVICE IS GOOD ADVICE

Aligning yourself with a fiduciary is, by all accounts, a great place to start. But this does not necessarily mean that the professional you select is going to provide good or even fairly priced advice. And like any industry, not all professionals have equal skill or experience. In fact, 46% of financial planners have no retirement plan! That's right. The cobbler's kid has no shoes! Over 2,400 financial planners were surveyed anonymously in a 2013 study by the Financial Planning Association, and close to half don't practice what they preach. Heck, I can't believe they admitted it!!! Truth is, we are living in uncharted territory. With endless complexity, central banks printing money like crazy, and even some governments defaulting on their own debt, only the elite advisors of the planning industry know how to navigate these waters.

THE BUTCHER AND THE DIETITIAN

A good friend of mine recently forwarded me a YouTube video entitled *The Butcher vs. the Dietitian*, a two-minute cartoon that effectively and succinctly highlighted the major difference between a broker and a legal fiduciary. The video made the glaringly obvious point that when you walk into a butcher shop, you are *always* encouraged to buy meat. Ask a butcher what's for dinner, and the answer is always "*Meat!*" But a dietitian, on the other hand, will advise you to eat what's best for your health. She has no interest in selling you meat if fish is better for you. Brokers are butchers, while fiduciaries are dietitians. They have no "dog in the race" to sell you a specific product or fund. This simple distinction gives you a position of power! Insiders know the difference.

I did a little digging, and the man behind the video was Elliot Weissbluth, a former litigator who 15 years ago became incensed by the conflicts of interest in the investment industry and made it his mission to provide an alternative to the brightest and most successful advisors and independent firms. In other words, choosing independence should not mean a sacrifice in sophistication and access to the best solutions. His great idea caught fire, and HighTower is now one of the largest independent registered investment advisors in the country, with nearly $30 billion in assets and 13th on *Inc.* magazine's list of fastest-growing companies. The explosive growth of High-Tower shows that clients want a dietitian. They are sick of being sold meat and then realizing that their health is in jeopardy.

I interviewed Elliot for this book and we have since developed a great friendship. I didn't have to twist Elliot's arm to leave frigid Chicago and join me for a day of 78-degree weather at my home in Palm Beach.

AN AUDACIOUS PROPOSAL

Together we sat on my back lawn overlooking the ocean and had a long conversation about the myths being marketed and injustices being done to the average investor. Elliot has a unique passion, a fervency, to serve investors by eliminating the self-interest and inherent conflicts that have become the norm in big firms. From Day One, he made the commitment to full disclosure, full transparency, and conflict-free advice in every aspect of the business. And by not accepting payments or kickbacks for selling a product or service, his firm stands in a position of true power and integrity. Firms compete to work with HighTower, and all of the benefits are passed down to the client. What's really powerful is how Elliot grew the business. First, he built a unique platform that no one thought was possible. Then he recruited the best "corner office" advisors from the biggest firms and gave them the path to the moral high ground—the opportunity to quit working for the house and work *only* for the client. And by giving them the freedom not to have to serve two masters, they could do whatever was in the client's best interest, at all times, in all transactions.

There was only one problem:

HighTower was built to service only the wealthiest Americans.

In fact, *all* of the top advisors in the industry are focused on the wealthy.

Makes sense, right? If you manage money, you want to manage fewer clients who have more money. This arrangement maximizes your own profitability. Too many small accounts means lots of overhead and cost. It's just not an efficient way to do business.

In spite of all that, I decided to drop a challenge on Elliot . . .

LET'S BLAZE A TRAIL

"Elliot, I want you to figure out a way to deliver the same fully transparent, conflict-free advice to anyone who wants the service, not just the wealthy. There has to be a way, Elliot," I said, leaning forward on the edge of my chair. "You care so passionately about justice and fairness that your own mission calls you to do this for everyone." Elliot sat back in his chair. He expected a simple interview and was now being asked to deploy some serious resources! And perhaps more importantly, I challenged him to figure out how to deliver some of the solutions that are normally reserved for folks with ultrahigh net worth. It was quite a challenge. To democratize the best investment advice coupled with the best available solutions. "Oh, and one more thing, Elliot: I think you should make a complimentary review service that is entirely free! People need to know how they are being treated!" Elliot took a few deep breaths. "Geez, Tony! I know you think big, but to gear up and make this available to everyone, at no charge? Come on!" I just smiled and said, "Yes, crazy, isn't it! No one else is going to do this. Nobody is showing how people are overpaying for underperformance. My guess is that we could show them using technology! You have the resources and the will to make this happen if you commit yourself!" I let the conversation end by simply asking him to take some time to think about the impact of what this could mean for people's lives and to get back in touch once he had fully thought it through.

IT'S DOABLE

Elliot returned to Chicago and gathered his troops. After much deliberation, and with a deep determination to find a way, Elliot called me back. After his team reviewed some patented technology we could utilize, he was convinced this could be a game changer. But he had one request. He would want to partner with an extraordinary chief investment officer. One with decades of experience and the values to match. A captain of the ship not afraid of uncharted waters. I knew just the man . . .

Ajay Gupta is the founder and chief investment officer of Stronghold Wealth Management, a firm that provides "white-glove" service for those of ultrahigh net worth. He is also my registered investment advisor and has been managing my family's money for over seven years. He spent almost two decades within the world's largest brokerage firms as the classic corner-office success story. Ajay came to the proverbial fork in the road. His choice? Either leave the brokerage world behind and carry the fiduciary flag or continue to walk the line of trying to be a dietitian within the walls of a butcher shop. I asked Ajay what was the pivotal moment of decision. "It came as a result of total frustration," he confessed. "There were investments that I knew were best for my client, but the firm wouldn't allow me to access them because they weren't 'approved.' I didn't want to steer my client to an inferior investment just so I could earn more. I treat my clients as my family, and I realized that no longer could I make choices by the constraints imposed by someone in a far-off ivory tower." Ajay's commitment was not just in words. He gave up a seven-figure bonus to leave and start his own firm. Not surprisingly, his entire team and client base followed him. After years of extraordinary performance and service, Ajay's departure from the brokerage world earned him the notice of Charles Schwab (a major service provider to independent investment advisors). He received a surprise call from the Charles Schwab headquarters letting him know that Chuck had selected him to represent the face of the more than 10,000 independent RIAs in Schwab's national media campaign. Subsequently, Ajay arranged for Chuck and me to meet, as he agreed to be one of the 50 financial moguls interviewed for this book.

When I introduced Ajay and his team at Stronghold to Elliot, it was an incredible alignment of values. What was amazing was how the sum of the whole was drastically greater than its parts. They began a monumental collaborative effort. For nearly a year, Ajay and Elliot worked together with a common goal: to democratize the best investment advice and help Americans wake up to their right to, first, know what they have been sold and then make the switch to receive transparent advice. And Stronghold Financial (a new division of Stronghold Wealth Management) was born. So in addition to serving those of high net worth, Stronghold now serves everyone regardless of how much he or she has to invest.

LOOK UNDER THE HOOD—FOR FREE!

My biggest "ask" from Ajay and Elliot was to make it possible for anyone, not just the wealthy, to be able to tap into top-tier advice, research, and planning. But I wanted them to do it for free!!!!

Most financial planners charge $1,000 or more to analyze your current investment assets, assess how much risk you're taking, quantify your *true* fees, and put together a new asset allocation. Stronghold's patented system accomplishes this in just five minutes—and it's completely free! Here is a bit more how it works:

When you visit the website, www.StrongholdFinancial.com, the system will allow you to "link" all of your accounts (even your 401[k] and accounts you have scattered at multiple firms). It will then analyze every holding you own, every fee you are paying, every risk you are taking. It will give you a comprehensive analysis and a new asset allocation. It will also reveal some of the unique strategies we will review in section 5 and compare them to your current approach. You can take this complimentary info and implement it on your own (and the company doesn't charge a dime). Or, if you decide to move forward, with the click of a button, you can transfer your accounts and have Stronghold manage your wealth, so long as you meet the minimum account size. For those who become clients, there is a team of fiduciary advisors that are available by phone to guide you in your journey and answer any questions you may have. There are no commissions, just a fee, which is based on your total portfolio value. So whether you have $2,500 or $25 million doesn't matter. Advice that was previously reserved for those of high net worth is now at your fingertips! And if you would prefer to work with someone in your local area, Stronghold has a network of independent advisors in all 50 states who are aligned with the same principles and have access to some of the unique solutions we will review in the pages ahead.

I am extremely proud of what Elliot, Ajay, and I have worked together to create: a complimentary service that can impact the entire population! And, quite frankly, it exists only because we were so frustrated by a system that often uses deceit and manipulation as weapons against investors. It's time for a changing of the guard. So while I am not currently an owner in Strong-hold, at the time of publication we are in conversations about how I can become a partner and align further with its mission of serving investors with extraordinary advice and investment solutions.

FINDING A FIDUCIARY

I don't want you to get the impression that Stronghold is the only fiduciary. There are thousands out there, and many of them are outstanding, so I would like to give you five key criteria for finding your own fiduciary. Below you will also find a link to the National Association of Personal Financial Advisors (NAPFA). This will allow you to search the country for any fee-only advisor you choose. One caveat: just because they are on the list doesn't mean they are skilled. Like any profession, be it a doctor or a teacher, there is a wide range of competency. In addition, in the world of independent fiduciaries, size does matter, so many smaller firms may not have the same level of access to certain investments and/or competitive pricing.

DIRECTORY OF FEE-BASED ADVISORS

http://findanadvisor.napfa.org/home.aspx

So, if you choose to find your own fiduciary, below are five key initial criteria you may want to consider when selecting an advisor:

1. Make sure the advisor is registered with the state or the SEC as a registered investment advisor or is an *investment advisor representative* (IAR) of a registered investment advisor (RIA).
2. Make sure the registered investment advisor is compensated on a percentage of your assets under management, not for buying mutual funds. Make sure this fee is the *only* fee and is completely transparent. Be sure there are no 12b-1 fees or "pay-to-play" fees being paid as compensation.
3. Make sure the registered investment advisor does *not* receive compensation for trading stocks or bonds.

4. Make sure the registered investment advisor does *not* have an affiliation with a broker-dealer. This is sometimes the worst offense when a fiduciary *also* sells products and gets investment commission as well!

5. With an advisor, you don't want to just give them your money directly. You want to make sure that your money is held with a reputable third-party custodian, such as Fidelity, Schwab, or TD Ameritrade, which offers 24/7 online account access and sends the monthly statements directly to you.

For those who are willing, have the time, and are brushed up on proper asset allocation (more on this in section 4), investing on your own (without a fiduciary) may be a viable option, which could also result in additional cost savings. The added cost of a fiduciary may only be justifiable if they are adding value such as tax-efficient management, retirement income planning, and greater access to alternative investments beyond index funds.

BUY ENRON!

An extremely competent fiduciary in your life will do more than provide transparent advice and investment solutions. They should protect you from the marketing "noise" because history shows us that the noise from a conflicted broker, or the firm he works for, can be extremely dangerous. Let me share an example from recent history.

Remember Enron? The energy giant with $101 billion in annual revenue (in 2000) that decided to cook the books in hopes of keeping shareholders happy. The big brokers and the mutual funds that owned the majority of Enron shares were big fans of the energy giant. My dear friend and business mastermind, Keith Cunningham, is a straight shooter with a classic Texas drawl. When he speaks at my Business Mastery event, he pulls no punches when showing how brokers, with no vested interest in how their clients fare, will pour on bad advice even when the situation is dire. When he shared with me the breakdown of how brokers promoted Enron during its collapse, I was astonished!

In March 2001, just nine months before declaring bankruptcy, Enron signaled that it was having trouble. "Anyone who was willing to look at the cash flow statement could see that they were hemorrhaging cash in spite of what they said its profits were!" Keith shouted to my audience of close to

1,000. "But that didn't stop the big Wall Street firms from recommending the stock." Below is a chart showing the recommendations of the big-brand firms in the nine months leading up to the Enron Chapter 11. **Notice how the recommendation to buy or hold was made until there was literally nothing left to hold—because the stock had no value; the company was bankrupt!**

March 21, 2001	*"Near Term Buy"*	$55.89	Merrill Lynch
March 29, 2001	*"Recommend List"*	$55.31	Goldman Sachs
June 8, 2001	*"Buy"*	$47.26	J.P. Morgan
August 15, 2001	*"Strong Buy"*	$40.25	Bank of America
October 4, 2001	*"Buy"*	$33.10	AG Edwards
October 24, 2001	*"Strong Buy = Attractive"*	$16.41	Lehman Bros
November 12, 2001	*"Hold"*	$9.24	Prudential
November 21, 2001	*"Market Perform"*	$5.01	Goldman Sachs
November 29, 2001	*"Hold"*	$0.36	Credit Suisse First Boston
December 2, 2001	*"Oops = they're bankrupt"*	$0.00	

Needless to say, if you are getting advice from a broker, you can expect that the inherent conflicts will show up in one way or another.

LOBBYING FOR PROFITS

Putting client interests first may seem like a simple
concept, but it's causing an uproar on Wall Street.
—"WHAT'S NO. 1 FOR BROKERS?," *Wall Street Journal*, December 5, 2010

So why hasn't the status quo changed? Under Dodd-Frank, the SEC was required to conduct a study on a "universal fiduciary standard" across all investment firms. **You heard me right. The politicians wanted to conduct a *study* to determine if acting in the client's best interest is a good idea.** It's a tragicomedy played out on Capitol Hill. In my interview with Dr. Jeffrey Brown, I asked about his opinion on fiduciary standards. Who better to ask than the guy who not only advised the Executive Office of the President but was also brought in by China to advise its Social Security program. "I think anybody that is managing money for someone else—it's very, very important that they have a legal and an ethical responsibility for doing the right thing and looking out for other people's money. I mean, these are really people's lives we're talking about here at the end of the day, right?"

The industry backlash has been nothing less than intense. You can hear the gears of the lobbying machine spinning at full speed as it reminds Capitol Hill of the generous campaign contributions.

THE TRUTH AND THE SOLUTION

So now that you know the rules of the game, what's an investor to do?

Above you have the five steps of how to evaluate and find a fiduciary if you choose to find your own. As I mentioned, you can visit Stronghold (www.StrongholdFinancial.com), which has a patented online system which, in just five minutes, will provide you with the following:

- Within seconds, the system will pull in and review your current holdings (stocks, bonds, and mutual funds) from all your accounts, including your 401(k).
- The system will show how much you are *really* paying and how much less you will have at retirement if you don't minimize fees. Remember the effect of compounding fees we reviewed in chapter 2.3!?
- The system will show your risk exposure. In other words, how well did your portfolio hold up in 2008 and other market downturns?
- The system will provide conflict-free advice and introduce you to a number of portfolio options.

- The system will take into account your current tax situation and recommend a more tax-efficient allocation.
- If you decide to move forward, you can quickly and automatically transfer your accounts to one of the recommended third-party custodians (such as TD Ameritrade, Fidelity, or Schwab). From there, the team will implement the recommendations and provide ongoing account management and service.
- If you have more than $1 million in investable assets, you will have access to the Private Wealth Division, which has greater access to investments that are limited to accredited investors.

At any time you can also pick up the phone and speak with a member of the team who is a registered fiduciary advisor to answer any questions regarding your personal situation. Or you can ask to be connected to one of the partners in your local area.

SO WHAT'S THE PLAN?

Wow, we have come a long way! The myths we have already exposed at this point remain unknown by the vast majority of investors. In fact, even many high-net-worth individuals aren't privy to this insider info. And now that we are gaining an unobstructed view, we need to start to look at the actual strategies we are currently using to see if they align with our goals. Let's start with the 401(k). That little piece of tax code that changed the financial world forever! Should we use it or lose it? Let's find out.

> Though the fiduciary issue is hotly contested among some groups, surveys conducted on behalf of the SEC showed a majority of investors don't understand what fiduciary means nor do they realize brokers and investment advisors offer different levels of care.
>
> —"THE BATTLE OVER BROKERS' DUTY TO THEIR CLIENTS REACHES A STANDSTILL," *Wall Street Journal*, January 24, 2012

BROKER	INDEPENDENT FIDUCIARY
Paying commissions for selling funds	Paying flat fee for advice
Nondeductible commissions	Advisory fees (may be deductible)
Paid to sell	Legally bound to provide advice with disclosure of any conflicts
Suitability standard	Fiduciary standard
Offers broad array of products and services that must be approved by the employer and includes those which are proprietary	Ability to access all products and services
Constrained by employer	Independent
Acts as custodian of investments	Uses third-party custodian

MYTH 5: "YOUR RETIREMENT IS JUST A 401(K) AWAY"

Baby boomers have been the primary mice used
in the great 401(k) retirement experiment.
—DOUG WARREN, author of *The Synergy Effect*

Many ideas or inventions start off with great intentions. Nuclear fusion opened the door to free energy for mankind and now can be used to provide electricity to an entire city. By contrast, if stuffed into a warhead, it can level an entire city.

It is often with a dash of man's greed and ingenuity that we can turn something great into something that can cause more damage than good. Such is the 401(k). A great little piece of tax code that, if used right, can power our retirement for years to come. But if used as it is in most of today's plans, it can damage our chances for financial freedom.

And since the 401(k) is the only retirement account most people will ever have, this chapter could be the most important one in this book. In the pages ahead, we will show how to use the 401(k) system and not let the system use you. You will discover how to implement much of what we have learned thus far so that your 401(k) becomes a great retirement plan for *you* (not a retirement plan for the broker or the mutual fund managers). But first a bit of backstory is important.

HOW DID WE GET HERE?

The 401(k), given to us in 1984, gave us the opportunity to participate in the stock market. To own a piece of American capitalism. And we could save on our taxes by making tax-deductible contributions from our paychecks.

But the 401(k) was never meant to be the sole retirement plan for

Americans. I reached out to John Shoven, professor of economics at Stanford. He made it perfectly clear when we spoke by phone: "Tony, you can't save just three percent of your income for thirty years and expect to live another thirty years in retirement with the same income you had when you were working!"

And let's not forget that this social experiment is only a few decades old. We are only now starting to see a generation where the majority will attempt to retire having used only a 401(k) during their lifetime.

When we look back at history, what started out as a loophole for highly paid executives to sock away more cash became a boon for companies that decided to eliminate the cost and obligation of traditional pensions and shift *all* the risk and expense to the employee. That's not to say that pensions didn't have their own problems: for instance, you couldn't move them from job to job.

Interestingly, employees didn't mind taking on this new responsibility because at the time, stocks were soaring. Who wants boring guaranteed pensions when stocks could make us rich?

Money then flowed into the market like never before. All that new money being deposited means lots of *buying*, which is what fueled the bull markets of the '80s and '90s. With trillions up for grabs, mutual fund companies began an unprecedented war to manage your money. The stock market was no longer just a place where companies turned to the public to exchange cash for ownership. It was no longer a place for only high-net-worth investors and sophisticated institutions. It became every man's savings vehicle.

WELCOME, CAPTAIN

When the 401(k) came to be, it represented freedom. Freedom that often gave us the illusion of control. And with markets on the rise, we sometimes mistake luck for being a "good investor."

Dr. Alicia Munnell, the director of the Center for Retirement Research at Boston College, is one of the top retirement experts in the country. We spoke for nearly two hours regarding the retirement crises facing the vast majority of Americans. In her view, "We went from a system of defined benefits—where people had a pension; they had an income for life—to the idea of the 401(k), which was obviously cheaper for employers. And on the surface, it seemed like it was beneficial to individuals because they had more control of their own investment decisions." But even Alicia, a former employee of the Federal Reserve and member of the president's Council of Economic Advisers, made some serious missteps when it came to her own retirement. "So, I have a defined benefit plan [guaranteed lifetime income] from the Federal Reserve Bank of Boston. When I was at the Treasury, one of my colleagues said, 'Oh! Take it early. You can invest that money much better than the Federal Reserve can.' That money is long gone."

Being solely responsible for your investment decisions is a scary thought for most (especially before reading this book). As captain of your financial ship, you must navigate all the available investment choices, generate returns sufficient enough to support your retirement, be a part-time investment expert, and do it all while holding down a full-time job or business and raising a family.

Teresa Ghilarducci of the New School for Social Research authored a brilliant article in the *New York Times* titled "Our Ridiculous Approach to Retirement." In it she managed to pack all the challenges we face into a single paragraph:

> Not yet convinced that failure is baked into the voluntary, self-directed, commercially run retirement plans system? Consider what would have to happen for it to work for you. First, figure out when you and your spouse will be laid off or be too sick to work. Second, figure out when you will die. Third, understand that you need to save 7% of every dollar you earn. (Didn't start doing that when you were 25, and you are 55 now? Just save 30% of every dollar.) Fourth, earn at least 3% above inflation on your investments, every year. (Easy. Just find the best funds for the lowest price and have them optimally allocated.) Fifth, do not withdraw any funds when you lose your job, have a health problem, get divorced, buy a house, or send a kid to college. Sixth, time your retirement account withdrawals so the last cent is spent the day you die.

Yes, the system needs to be fixed, and yes, it will take time and some major progress on both Capitol Hill and Wall Street. But the good news is that for those of you who are informed, you will be able to navigate it. You can use the system as an insider would, and let it work to your advantage.

COME AGAIN?

So let's do a little recap. We now know that actively managed stock-picking mutual funds don't beat the market. And this is exactly what you find in the vast majority of 401(k) plans (but not all). We also know that these expensive funds charge hefty fees, which can erode 50% to 70% of our potential retirement nest egg. Depending on your age today, think of how much you have already left on the table to this point? Is it $10,000? $25,000? $100,000? Scary, huh?

Now, stick those expensive mutual funds inside a name-brand 401(k) plan, usually offered by a payroll or insurance company, and it will charge you a whole host of *additional* costs. (See box on following page.) The sum of all these costs forms an insurmountable headwind. With the vast majority of plans out there, the odds of you winning the 401(k) game are slim to none.

401(k) plans receive the benefit of tax deferral, but most are loaded with up to 17 different fees and costs between the underlying investments and the plan administration.

COMMUNICATION EXPENSES
- Enrollment (materials)
- Ongoing (materials)
- Enrollment (meetings)
- Investment advice

RECORD-KEEPING AND ADMINISTRATIVE EXPENSES
- Base fee
- Per participant fee
- Per-eligible employee fee
- Distributions
- Loans origination
- Loans maintenance
- Semiannual discrimination testing
- 5500 filing package
- Other expenses

INVESTMENT EXPENSES
- Base fee
- Individual (mutual) fund expenses
- Manager/advisor fee
- Other asset fees (revenue sharing, wrap, administration, and so on)

TRUSTEE EXPENSES
- Base fee
- Per-participant fee
- Asset charge

But now the good news! With the right 401(k), one that is lean, mean, and doesn't take your green, you can turn the headwind into a tailwind. You can gain momentum by taking advantage of what the government gave us.

AMERICA'S *"BEST"* 401(K)? OKAY, PROVE IT!

Once I truly grasped what Jack Bogle calls the "tyranny of compounding costs," and realized the destructive power of excessive fees, I immediately called the head of my human resources department to find out the specifics of our own company 401(k) plan. I wanted to know if my employees, who I care about like my own family, were being taken to the cleaners. Sure enough, we were using a high-cost name-brand plan loaded with expensive funds and excessive administration and broker fees. The broker assured me that the plan was top notch, lean on fees, and right on track. Sure it was! Right on track to make his BMW lease payment.

Convinced that there had to be a better plan out there, my team and I began to do some research. After a frustrating process of looking at a bunch of garbage plans, a good friend of mine referred me to a firm called America's Best 401k. That's a bold name. I called the owner, Tom Zgainer, and said, "Prove it!"

In the first five minutes of meeting Tom in person, it's obvious he has immense passion about helping people get free from crappy, fee-loaded 401(k) plans. He calls the 401(k) industry "the largest dark pool of assets where nobody really knows how or whose hands are getting greased." A pretty grim diagnosis of his own industry. "Get this, Tony, the industry has been around for three decades now, and only in 2012 did service providers become required by law to disclose fees on statements. But in spite of the disclosure, **over half of all employees still don't know how much they're paying!"** **In fact, 67% of people enrolled in 401(k)s think there are *no fees*, and, of course, nothing could be further from the truth.**

"How are you different, Tom? How is America's Best truly the 'best,' as you say?" Having been burned once, I felt like Papa Bear looking after his cubs because I knew this decision would directly impact my employees and their kids. They had already been paying excessive fees for years, and I couldn't allow that to happen again. I came to find out that, as the owner of the company, I am also the plan *sponsor*, and I discovered it is my legal duty to make sure they aren't getting taken advantage of. (More in the pages ahead.)

Tom explained, "Tony, America's Best 401(k) only allows extremely low-cost index funds [such as Vanguard and Dimensional Funds], and we don't get paid a dime by mutual funds to sell their products." I had just interviewed Jack

Bogle, and he confirmed that Vanguard does not participate in paying to play, a common practice where mutual funds share in their revenues to get "shelf space" in a 401(k) plan. **By the way, what this means to you is that the so-called choices on your 401(k) plan are not the best available choices. They are the ones that pay the most to be offered up on the menu of available funds.** And guess how they recoup their cost to be on the list? High fees, of course. So not only are you failing to get the best performing funds, but also you are typically paying higher fees for inferior performance.

"Okay, Tom. What about the other plan fees? I want to see full disclosure and transparency on every single possible fee!"

Tom proudly produced an itemized spreadsheet and handed it across the coffee table. "The total cost, including the investment options, investment management services, and record-keeping fees, is only 0.75% annually."

"That's it? No hidden fees or other pop-up-out-of-nowhere fees?"

We cut our total fees from well over 2.5% to just 0.75% (a 70% reduction!). As you recall from earlier in chapter 2, when compounded over time, these fee savings equate to hundreds of thousands of dollars—even millions— that will end up in the hands of my employees and their families. That makes me feel so great! Below is a simple chart showing a sample 401(k), similar to the one my company used to use, versus America's Best 401k, and how those savings compound directly into my employees' accounts.

AMERICA'S BEST 401(K)

	MY OLD PLAN (2.5% TOTAL FEES)	AMERICAS BEST 401K	TOTAL SAVINGS THAT GO BACK TO YOU AND YOUR EMPLOYEES
After Year 1	$15,925,465	$16,006,101	$80,635
After Year 7	$22,265,866	$23,025,978	$760,111
After Year 20	$41,999,917	$45,999,618	$3,999,701

Assumptions: $1 million beginning plan balance, $100,000 in annual contributions, 5% growth rate.

AMERICA'S BEST 401(K)

	MY OLD PLAN (0.75% TOTAL FEES)	AMERICA'S BEST 401K	TOTAL SAVINGS THAT GO BACK TO YOU AND YOUR EMPLOYEES
After Year 1	$14,530,987	$14,582,411	$51,424
After Year 7	$25,077,485	$25,623,385	$545,899
After Year 20	$58,499,799	$61,756,687	$3,355,987

Over $1.2 million going back to my family and my staff by making a simple switch! And by the way, this calculation is based only on fees and doesn't take into account that we are beating 96% of mutual fund managers because we are using low-cost market-mimicking mutual funds.

MEGAPHONE

My staff and I were so impressed that six months after Tom and his team installed my company's plan (and after I had referred him to a ton of my good friends), I decided to partner with America's Best 401k and help it get the word out. I knew this story *had* to be told in this book. And because the company charges so little, it can't afford to run Super Bowl ads or have its sales reps take you golfing. Tom's grassroots efforts are gaining momentum, and I hope to amplify his voice.

NOW IT'S TIME TO PULL BACK THE CURTAIN

Tom and his team have built a powerful online "Fee Checker" that can pull up your company's plan (from the company's tax return filing), and within seconds, it will show how your company's plan stacks up against others and what you are *really* paying in fees. And like the table above, it will show you what the cost savings means to you over time. It's not uncommon to uncover hundreds of thousands of dollars in potential savings! Visit the Fee Checker on the following website: http://americasbest401k.com/401k-fee-checker.

NEED EXTRA MOTIVATION?

As if high fees destroying your retirement weren't enough of a motivation, business owners should be very concerned and employees should be "armed with the truth." Why? Because the US Department of Labor (DOL) is out in full force to defend employees against high-fee plans. And who is liable? *The business owner!* That's right. Not the mutual fund managers. Not the broker. Not the administrator of the crappy 401(k) plan. It's the business owner who can get in serious hot water.

According to the *CFO Daily News*, in 2013 **"[s]eventy-five percent of the 401(k)s audited by the DOL last year resulted in plan sponsors being fined, penalized or forced to make reimbursements for plan errors. And those fines and penalties weren't cheap. In fact, the average fine last year was $600,000 per plan.** That's a jump of nearly $150K from four years ago."

And the DOL just hired another 1,000 enforcement officers in 2014, so we can all expect 401(k) plan audits to increase. I don't know about you, but this certainly got my attention.

Thanks to class action attorneys, numerous corporations are being sued by their own employees. Caterpillar, General Dynamics, and Bank of America, just to name a few. **Even Fidelity, one of the largest 401(k) providers in the industry, recently settled two class-action lawsuits for $12 million after being sued by its own employees over excessive fees in its plan.** Sure, these are big companies with a lot to lose, but it's really the small business owners who are at greater risk because smaller plans (those with less than $10 million in plan assets) have the highest fees of all.

So What Do You Do as a Business Owner? First, *it's the law* that you have your plan "benchmarked" annually against other plans. The new law began in 2012, so it might be news to you. Once a year, the DOL requires that you compare your plan against other "comparable" plans to make sure your plan has reasonable fees. Nearly every business owner I ask has no clue about this! I sure didn't. Do you think the person who sold you that expensive plan is going to call you about it? Of course not!

America's Best 401k will not only provide you with a free fee analysis but

WARNING: DOL FOUND THREE-FOURTHS OF 401(K)S ILLEGAL

Here's a very compelling reason to take a closer look at your 401(k) plan:

SEVENTY-FIVE PERCENT OF THE 401(K)s audited by the DOL last year resulted in plan sponsors being fined, penalized or forced to make reimbursement for plan errors. And those fines and penalties weren't cheap.

In fact, the average fine last year was $600,000 per plan. That's a jump of nearly $150K from four years ago.

Source: CFO Daily News

also provide this complimentary benchmark. If the DOL walks into your office on a Friday afternoon, don't let it ruin your weekend by standing there like a deer in the headlights. You want to be able to confidently hand over your plan benchmark.

WHO TO HOLD TO THE FIRE?

The DOL is on a rampage and can hold the business owner over the fire. I had no idea that as a business owner, and plan sponsor, I am the legal fiduciary for the 401(k) plan. There are numerous cases where business owners have become *personally* liable for an egregious 401(k) plan. By your using a firm like America's Best 401k, it will "install" a professional fiduciary, which will dramatically alleviate your liability (and yes, this is included in the 0.75% annual fee). And it provides ongoing benchmarking as a *free* service.

What to Do If You Are an Employee. First, visit the Fee Checker on the America's Best 401k website (http://americasbest401k.com/401k-fee-checker) and forward the report to the owner (or upper management). Truth is, the highest income earners in any business tend to have the highest account balances, so they too have a lot to lose. You are doing your entire company a wonderful service by educating management on its own plan. High fees are a drain on everyone's hard-earned cash, and a possible change will affect everyone's chances of financial freedom. Remember, we all need a tailwind, not a headwind.

You can also march down to the HR department and make certain they read this chapter. If fees aren't a motivator, remind them that they are the fiduciary to you and your fellow colleagues. They *legally* owe it to you to make sure they have a plan that is competitive and in your best interests. That should grab their attention!

If your employer does not switch to a low-cost option and to the extent that your employer isn't matching your contributions, it may make sense to opt out.

If you decide to opt out but still plan on staying with the company, a good plan will allow for an *in-service distribution*, allowing you to roll your current 401(k) account into an individual retirement account. Just check with your HR department. An IRA is simply a retirement account held in your name alone, but you will have much more freedom to choose the investments. And from there you can implement some of the solutions we will review in section 3. Also, your personal fiduciary can review this account and explain your best options.

Now that we know how to free ourselves from high-cost plans riddled with underperforming mutual funds, how do we best utilize a low-cost plan and the tax benefits that the government gives us?

UNCONVENTIONAL WISDOM

If you haven't noticed, our government has a spending problem. Like an out-of-control teenager with a Platinum Amex, Uncle Sam has racked up over $17.3 trillion in debt and close to $100 trillion in unfunded (not paid for yet!) liabilities with Social Security and Medicare. So do you think taxes will be higher or lower in the future? Did you know that following the Great Depression, the highest income tax bracket was over 90%?! The truth is, you can tax every wealthy individual and corporation at 100% of its income/profits and still fall way short of the government's promises. Take a look at this video I made for an eye-opening presentation: http://training .tonyrobbins.com/exclusive-video-tony-robbins-deconstructs-the-national -debt.

Conventional logic, as most CPAs will attest, is to maximize your 401(k) (or IRA) contributions for tax purposes because each dollar is deductible. Which simply means you don't have to pay tax on that dollar today but will defer the tax to a later day. But here is the problem: *nobody knows what tax rates are going to be in the future, and therefore you have no idea how much of your money will be left over to actually spend.*

I met recently with one of my senior executives on this topic, and I asked him how much he had in his 401(k). He said he was approaching $1 million and felt comfortable that he could live off of this amount if needed. I asked him in a different way:

"How much of the million dollars in your 401(k) is *yours*?"

"All of it, of course," he replied.

"*Half,* my friend! Half! Between state and federal income taxes, you will be spending only half that amount."

The truth sank in. He sat back realizing that $500,000 is *not* his. It's Uncle Sam's. He was simply investing the government's money alongside his own.

But then I asked, "How much is yours if the tax bracket goes up to sixty percent?" A little mental math, and he replied, "Only four hundred thousand dollars, or forty percent, of the million will be mine." Ouch. But that's not possible, is it? If you look at tax rates on the wealthiest Americans over the last 20 years (between 1990 and 2010), they are near the lowest they have ever been. The average for the three decades from the 1930s through the 1950s was 70%! When taxes were raised by Bill Clinton, he raised them on *all* wage earners, not just the wealthy. With the record-breaking levels of debt we have accumulated, many experts say taxes will likely be raised on everyone over the course of time. In short, the percentage of your 401(k) balance that will actually be yours to spend is a *complete unknown*. And if taxes go up from here, the slice of the pie you get to eat gets smaller. And it's a spiraling effect because the less you get to keep and spend, the more you have to withdraw. The more you withdraw, the quicker you run out.

SENATOR WILLIAM ROTH: THE BEST LEGAL TAX HAVEN?

A Roth IRA—and more recently the addition of the **Roth 401(k)**—is often overlooked, but it is one of the best and yet legal "tax havens" in the face of rising future tax rates. And we owe a big tip of the cap to Senator William Roth for their introduction back in 1997. Let's look at how they work.

If you were a farmer, would you rather pay tax on the seed of your crop or on the entire harvest once you have grown it? Most people seem to get this question wrong. We are conditioned to *not* want to pay tax today (and thus defer into the future). They think it's best to pay tax on the harvest. But in reality, if we first pay tax on the seed, that's when the value of what's being taxed is smallest. A big harvest means a big tax! If we pay our taxes now on the seed, then whatever we have come harvest time is ours to keep! A Roth account works this way. We pay our tax today, deposit the after-tax amount, and then never have to pay tax again! Not on the growth and not on the withdrawals. This arrangement protects your pie from the government's insatiable appetite for more tax revenues and, most importantly, allows you to plan with certainty how much you actually have to spend when you take withdrawals.

And here is an incredibly exciting piece of news!

With your 401(k) contributions being Roth-eligible (by checking the box), you can pay tax today and let your growth and withdrawals be free from the IRS's grabby paws. And you can give substantially more because while a **Roth IRA is limited to $5,500 annually, the Roth 401(k) allows for $17,500 per year.** (And you can do both simultaneously).[6]

And for the high-income earner (making more than $122,000 per year), although you can't use a Roth IRA, there are *no income limitations* on the Roth 401(k). Anyone can participate. This is a relatively recent change in our tax code and can provide quite a benefit for higher-income earners.

SAVE MORE TOMORROW

So the secret to the 401(k) is simple: you have to do it. But you have to do it within a cost-efficient plan *and* take advantage of the Roth 401(k) (especially if you believe taxes will go up for you in the future). And if you take advantage of one the greatest breakthroughs in finance: the system we covered earlier called Save More Tomorrow. Most people won't make the commitment to save more today, but they will make the commitment to save more tomorrow. So in essence, you are agreeing in advance that your savings rate will increase each year. For example, let's say today you save 3% of your salary. Then next year you agree to go up 1% (for a total of 4%). And then you keep "auto-escalating" your savings amount until you reach a certain cap. America's Best 401k has this auto-escalation feature built into the system. So not only do you have the lowest possible fees, but you also have an opportunity to set yourself on an accelerated path to financial freedom.

BULL'S-EYE!

Now we have a chance to combine all we have learned! By now you have decided to set aside a percentage of your income, and that may very well be in your 401(k). **You want to make absolutely sure that your 401(k) has the lowest possible fees and low-cost index funds.** You can see how your company plan fares by using the Fee Checker on America's Best 401k

---

6. There are different rules for a Roth IRA and a Roth 401(k). According to the IRS: "If you were age 50 or older before 2014, and contributions on your behalf were made only to Roth IRAs, your contribution limit for 2013 will generally be the lesser of: $6,500, or your taxable compensation for the year." See "Publication 590 (2013), Individual Retirement Arrangements (IRAs)," "Roth IRAs," www.irs.gov/publications/p590/ch02.html#en _US_2013_publink1000253532.

(http://americasbest401k.com/401k-fee-checker). Once again, if you are an employee, you should make the company owner (or management) aware of their legal responsibility to provide the most efficient plan available and that they are at risk of getting into major hot water with the Department of Labor. If you are a business owner, you are legally required to get the plan benchmarked annually, and America's Best will provide a complimentary benchmark; simply take two minutes to fill out this online form: http://americasbest401k.com/request-a-proposal. Here is the great news: the typical small plan will save $20,000 per year in fees alone. Bigger plans will save hundreds of thousands, even millions, over the life of the plan, all of which goes directly back to the employees and the owner's personal retirement plan as well.

SEVEN FREQUENTLY ASKED QUESTIONS

Stick with me here. We're about to start putting ideas into action. These are the seven most common questions that come up in the context of 401(k) plans and IRAs and how to best utilize them. Here we go!

1. SHOULD I PARTICIPATE IN MY 401(k)?
To the extent that your employer matches your contributions, you should certainly take advantage of your 401(k), as the company is essentially covering the taxes for you. **And if you think taxes are going up, checking the box so that your contributions receive Roth tax treatment is the way to go.** (A quick side note: the 401(k) plan itself might be insanely expensive and the investment options poor. If that is the case, you may not want to participate at all! To determine how your company's plan stacks up, go to http://americasbest401k.com/401k-fee-checker and click on Fee Checker to assess your company's plan.)

Just to be clear, if you check the box to make your contributions Roth-eligible, you will still be investing in the same investment options (or list of funds), with the only difference being that you will pay taxes on the income today. But your future nest egg will be completely tax free when you withdraw. Retirement expert Dr. Jeffrey Brown of the University of Illinois gave me his take on his own personal finances. "I'd take advantage of every Roth opportunity I can because . . . I've spent a lot of time looking at the long-term fiscal outlook for the United States, and you know I am a pretty optimistic guy, on the whole. But I have to tell you that **I cannot envision any situation in which our need for tax revenue in the future is not going to be higher than it is today.**"

Taking it one step further, Dr. Brown has personal guidance for his younger students: "Absolutely pour as much money as you can into that Roth because you're going to be paying little or no taxes on it, and then someday you could have the greatest income ever."

If you are one of the few that thinks taxes in future will be lower, you could be in for a huge surprise. "Conventional wisdom" says we *should* be in a lower tax bracket when it comes time to retire, as we won't be earning as much. But in reality, our home is often paid off (so we don't have any mortgage deductions), and the kids are long gone (so we don't have any dependents).

Finally, you might be self-employed and think that all this 401(k) talk is irrelevant. Not so! You can start a Solo 401(k), which is a 401(k) for an individual business owner and his or her spouse.

2. WHAT IS A ROTH 401(k), AND HOW CAN I USE IT TO MY ADVANTAGE?

I said it before, but it's worth repeating: most of today's 401(k) plans allow you to simply "check a box," and your contributions will receive the Roth tax treatment. This decision means you pay tax today, but you never pay tax again!

3. SHOULD I SET UP A ROTH IRA?

Yes!! You can set up a Roth IRA account and contribute $5,500 per year ($6,500 if you're 50 or older). You can even do so if you are already maxing out your 401(k) contributions. Opening a Roth IRA is as simple as opening a bank account. TD Ameritrade, Fidelity, and Schwab are three firms that make the process incredibly simple. You can do it online in less than ten minutes.

4. BUT WHAT IF I MAKE TOO MUCH MONEY FOR A ROTH IRA?

Sadly, you cannot contribute to a Roth IRA if your annual income is over $114,000 as an individual or more than $191,000 for a married couple (for 2014). But don't fret, regardless of how much you make, you can still participate in a Roth 401(k). And if you have an IRA, you might want to consider converting your IRA into a Roth IRA, but know that you will have to pay tax today on all the gains.

5. SHOULD I CONVERT MY TRADITIONAL IRA TO A ROTH IRA?

Let's say you have an IRA with $10,000. The government will allow you to pay the tax today (because it needs the money), and you will never have to pay tax again. This process is called a Roth conversion. So if you are in the 40% bracket, you would pay $4,000 today, and your remaining $6,000 will grow without tax, and all withdrawals will be tax free. Some people cringe at the idea of paying tax today because they view it as "their" money. It's *not*! It's the government's. By paying the tax today, you are giving Uncle Sam his money back earlier. And by doing so, you are protecting yourself and your nest egg from taxes being higher in the future. If you don't think taxes will be higher, you shouldn't convert. You have to decide, but all evidence points to the hard fact that Washington will need more tax revenue, and the biggest well to dip into is the trillions in retirement accounts.

6. WHAT ABOUT MY OLD 401(k) PLAN(S) WITH PAST EMPLOYERS?

Older plans can either be left with a previous employer or "rolled over" into an IRA. One would leave it with an old employer only if the plan itself was low cost and had favorable investment options. By rolling over the plan into an IRA (it takes about ten minutes online to move the funds from your former plan to a third-party IRA custodian like TD Ameritrade, Schwab, or Fidelity), you will have greater control. You can invest in nearly any investment, not just a limited menu it offers. And with this great control, you will be able to hire a fiduciary advisor and implement some exciting strategies and solutions we will review in section 3. With a fiduciary advisor, you don't pay commissions. You pay for advice. And it's typically 1% or less of your invested assets, and remember, you might be able to deduct it from your taxes.

Second, by rolling over your old 401(k) into an IRA, you will then have the option to convert an IRA into a Roth IRA.

7. WHAT ELSE CAN I DO IF I AM MAXING OUT MY PLANS AND WOULD LIKE ADDITIONAL OPTIONS TO SAVE?

Small business owners that are making a lot of money and want to reduce their taxes today can benefit greatly from the addition of a *cash-balance plan* on top of their 401(k) plan. Cash-balance (CB) plans are the fastest growing of the defined benefit pension plans and could overtake 401(k) plans within the next few years, according to researchers at Sage Advisory Services, a registered investment advisory firm headquartered in Austin, Texas. In fact, over one third of Fortune 100 companies have adopted a cash-balance plan. So what is it? A cash-balance plan is basically a pension plan. In other words, the amounts deposited are earmarked to provide the business owner with future retirement income. So what's the biggest draw? For a high-income business owner, not only can she max out her 401(k) *and* a profit-sharing plan, but she can also add a cash-balance plan, which creates some very large, fully deductible contributions. On page 156 is a table showing the possible deductions.

Money Power Principle 2. One of the most important Money Power Principles is "You get what you tolerate." Don't tolerate having your money in a plan that is siphoning off fees to the benefit of someone else. And we have to remember that the 401(k) is only as good as what's inside it. Turn the page and discover the next myth. Because the most popular place for people to put their 401(k) money is one of the most misunderstood investments of our time.

2014 IRS ANNUAL CONTRIBUTION LIMITS			
AGE	401(K) CONTRIBUTION + PROFIT-SHARING PLAN	CASH-BALANCE PLAN CONTRIBUTION	TOTAL
65	$56,000	$237,841	$293,841
60	$56,000	$228,807	$284,807
55	$56,000	$175,068	$231,068
50	$56,000	$133,950	$189,950
45	$51,000	$102,490	$153,490
40	$51,000	$78,419	$129,419
35	$51,000	$60,001	$111,001

MYTH 6:
TARGET-DATE FUNDS:
"JUST SET IT AND FORGET IT"

I am increasingly nervous about target-date funds with each passing day.
—JACK BOGLE, founder of investor-owned Vanguard

When you are looking at your 401(k) investment options, do you ever wonder just how they came up with that list? Or why your spouse or best friend who works across town has an entirely different menu of choices?

As the saying goes, always follow the money.

YOU GOTTA PAY TO PLAY

In the world of mutual funds, the common practice of sharing in revenues is known as pay-to-play fees. According to the Watson Towers worldwide consulting firm, approximately 90% of 401(k) plans require pay-to-play fees in exchange for placing a mutual fund as an available option on your plan's menu. These pay-to-play fees virtually guarantee that the client (you and me) gets a limited selection and will end up owning a fund that proves profitable for the distributors (the broker, the firm, and the mutual fund company). Said another way, the "choices" you have in your 401(k) plan are carefully crafted and selected to maximize profits for the vendors, brokers, and managers. If one has to pay to play, they are going to want to maximize their profits to recoup their cost. And target-date funds, sometimes called *lifecycle funds*, may just be the most expensive and widely marketed creation to make their way into your plan's investment options (with the exception being Vanguard's ultra-low-cost versions).

DO TARGET-DATE FUNDS MISS THE MARK?

Despite being the fastest-growing segment of the mutual fund industry, target-date funds (TDFs) may completely miss the mark.

The pitch goes like this: "Just pick the date/year in which you will retire, and we will allocate your portfolio accordingly [the Golden Years 2035 fund, for example]. The closer you get to retirement, the more conservative the portfolio will become." I am sure you have seen these options in your 401(k), and statistics would say that you are likely invested in one.

Here is a bit more about how they *actually* work.

The fund manager decides upon a "glide path," which is the fancy way of describing its schedule for decreasing the stock holdings (more risky) and ramping up the bond holdings (traditionally less risky) in an attempt to be more conservative as your retirement nears. Never mind that each manager can pick his own "glide path," and there is no uniform standard. Sounds more like a "slippery slope" to me. Then again, this is all built on two giant presuppositions:

1. Bonds are safe.
2. Bonds move in the opposite direction of stocks, so that if stocks fall, your bonds will be there to protect you.

As Warren Buffett says, "Bonds should come with a warning label." And since bond prices fall when interest rates go up, we could see bond prices plummet (and bond mutual fund prices, too) if or when interest rates go up. In addition, numerous independent studies show how bonds have strong "correlation" in bad times. Translation: stocks and bonds don't always move in opposite directions. Just look at 2008, when bonds and stocks both fell hard!

The marketing message for target-date funds is seductive. Pick the date, and you don't have to look at it ever again. "Set it and forget it." Just trust us! We've got you covered. But do they?

ONE GIGANTIC MISUNDERSTANDING

A survey conducted by Behavioral Research Associates for the investment consulting firm Envestnet found that employees who invested in TDFs had some jaw-dropping misconceptions:

- **57% of those surveyed thought they wouldn't lose money over a ten-year period.** There are no facts to support that perception!
- **30% thought a TDF provided a guaranteed rate of return.** TDFs do not give you any guarantee of anything, much less a rate of return!
- **62% thought they would be able to retire when the year, or "target date," of the fund arrives.** Unfortunately, this false perception is the cruelest of all. The date you set is your retirement year "goal." TDFs are not a plan to get you to your goals, but rather just an asset allocation that *should* become less risky as you get closer to retirement.

Considering that there are trillions of dollars in TDFs, a huge percentage of Americans are in for a shocking surprise.

So what are you really buying with a TDF? You are simply buying into a fund that handles your asset allocation for you. It's as simple as that. Instead of picking from the list of fund options, you buy one fund, and voilà! It's "all handled for you."

SORRY, SHE NO LONGER WORKS HERE

After graduating college, David Babbel decided he wanted to work for the World Bank. It would no doubt be an interesting place to work, but for those fortunate enough to be employed there, they also pay no taxes! Smart man. When he applied they turned him away, saying he needed a postgraduate education in one of six categories to land a job. Not one to risk being denied a position, he decided to go get *all* six. He has a degree in economics, an MBA in international finance, a PhD in finance, a PhD minor in food and resource economics, a PhD certificate in tropical agriculture, and a PhD certificate in Latin American studies. When he returned with his fistful of diplomas, they told him they weren't hiring Americans due to the recent reduction of financial support from Washington to the World Bank. It was a punch in the gut for him. Not knowing where to turn, he responded to a newspaper ad from UC Berkeley. After they hired him as a professor, he later found out that they ran the ad to comply with affirmative action, but had no intention of getting qualified candidates to respond.

Years later he moved on to Wharton to teach multiple subjects related to finance. But he isn't just a bookworm. A paper he had written on how to reduce risk in bond portfolios caught the attention of Goldman Sachs. He took a leave of absence and spent seven years running the risk management and insurance division at Goldman Sachs (while still holding down a part-time professorship at Wharton). Later he finally had a chance to work at the World Bank. He has also consulted for both the United States Treasury and the Federal Reserve. But when the Department of Labor asked him to do a counterstudy on whether target-date funds were the best default retirement option, he had no idea the path that lay ahead. On the other side of the pro-verbial aisle was the Investment Company Institute (the lobbying arm for the mutual fund industry), which "had paid two million dollars for a study and got exactly what they wanted. A study that said [TDFs] are the best thing since sliced bread." Keep in mind that at this point, TDFs were just a concept. A glimmer in the eye of the industry.

In his study for the Department of Labor, conducted with two other pro-fessors, one of whom was trained by two Nobel laureates, Babbel compared TDFs to *stable value funds*. Stable value funds are ultraconservative, "don't have losses and historically have yields [returns] at two percent to three per-cent greater than money market funds." According to Babbel, the industry-sponsored study, which painted TDFs in the best possible light, was riddled with flaws. To make TDFs look better than stable value funds, they pumped out more fiction than Walt Disney. For example, they made an assumption that stocks and bonds have *no correlation*. *Wrong*. Bonds and stocks do indeed move in step to a degree and they move even closer during tough times. (Bonds and stocks had 80% correlation in 2008.)

Babbel and his team reviewed the study and picked it apart. They had mathematically dissected the report's fictional findings and were prepared to show its ridiculous assumptions that made TDFs look so superior.

When he showed up on the day to present his conclusion, the economists behind the table, chosen by the Department of Labor to judge both studies, "thought he had some great points that needed further review." But the secretary of labor "had already made her decision and then quit the next day. She didn't even show up at the meeting she had scheduled with him." Dr. Babbel heard that it was prewired. The industry has bought the seal of approval it needed to write its own "fat" check.

Fast-forward, and by the end of 2013, TDFs were used by 41% of 401(k) participants, to the tune of trillions! Not a bad return for the investment community for a $2 million investment in a study Dr. Babbel and his esteemed economist colleagues called "heavily flawed."

A 2006 federal law paved the way for target-date funds to become the "default" retirement option of choice. Employers can't be held liable for sticking employee money in target-date funds. Today well over half of all employers "auto-enroll" their employees into their 401(k). According to research from Fidelity, over 96% of large employers use these target-date mutual funds as the default investment of choice.

YOU NEVER KNOW WHO'S SWIMMING NAKED UNTIL THE TIDE GOES OUT

Imagine that it is early 2008, and you are closing in on your retirement. You have worked the grind for over 40 years to provide for your family; you are looking forward to more time with the grandkids, more time traveling, and just . . . more time. By all accounts your 401(k) balance is looking healthy. Your "2010 target-date funds" are performing nicely, and you trust that since you are only two years away from retirement, your funds are invested very conservatively. Millions of Americans felt this way before 2008 wiped out their hopes for retirement, or at least the quality of retirement they had expected. The list on page 162 shows the top 20 target-date funds (by size) and their gut-wrenching 2008 performances. Remember that these are 2010 target-date funds, so retirement was now only two years away for their investors. Notice the high percentage that certain funds chose to put into stocks (more risky) even though they were supposed to be in the "final stretch" and thus most conservative. To be fair, even if you are retiring, you must have some exposure to stocks, but at the same time, this type of loss could have devastated or at least delayed your plans for retirement.

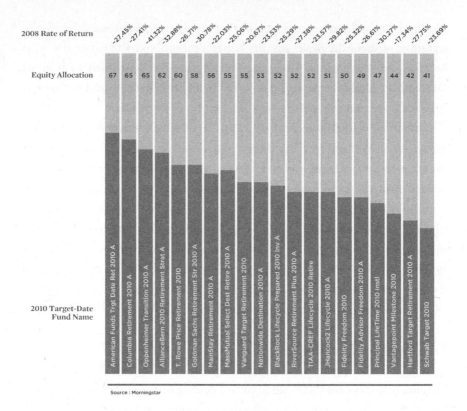

2008 Rate of Return	-27.45%	-27.41%	-41.32%	-32.88%	-26.71%	-30.78%	-22.03%	-25.06%	-20.67%	-23.53%	-25.29%	-27.38%	-23.57%	-29.82%	-25.32%	-26.61%	-30.27%	-17.34%	-27.75%	-23.69%
Equity Allocation	67	65	65	62	60	58	56	55	55	53	52	52	52	51	50	49	47	44	42	41
2010 Target-Date Fund Name	American Funds Trgt Date Ret 2010 A	Columbia Retirement 2010 A	Oppenheimer Transition 2010 A	AllianceBern 2010 Retirement Strat A	T. Rowe Price Retirement 2010	Goldman Sachs Retirement Str 2010 A	MainStay Retirement 2010 A	MassMutual Select Dest Retire 2010 A	Vanguard Target Retirement 2010	Nationwide Destination 2010	BlackRock Lifecycle Prepared 2010 Inv A	RiverSource Retirement Plus 2010 A	TIAA-CREF Lifecycle 2010 Retire	JHancock2 Lifecycle 2010 A	Fidelity Freedom 2010	Fidelity Advisor Freedom 2010 A	Principal LifeTime 2010 Instl	Vantagepoint Milestone 2010	Hartford Target Retirement 2010 A	Schwab Target 2010

Source : Morningstar

LESSER OF TWO EVILS

When I sat down to interview many of the top academic minds in the field of retirement research, I was surprised to learn that they were all in favor of target-date funds.

Wait a second. How could that be!?

I shared with each of them much of what you have just read, and while they didn't disagree that there are issues with TDFs, they pointed to the time before TDFs existed, when people were given the choice to allocate as they wished. This arrangement led to more confusion and, quite frankly, really poor decision making. The data certainly supports their point.

In my interview with Dr. Jeffrey Brown, one of the smartest minds in the country, he explained, "If you go back prior to these things [TDFs], we had a lot of people who were investing in their own employer's stock. Way over-concentrated in their own employer's stock." He reminded me of Enron, where many employees put 100% of their savings in Enron stock, and over-night that money was gone.

When people had 15 different mutual fund options from which to choose, they would divide the money up equally (1/15th in each one), which is not a good strategy. Or they would get nervous if the market dropped (or sell when the market was down) and sit entirely on cash for years on end. Cash isn't always a bad position for a portion of your money, but within a 401(k), when you are paying fees for the plan itself, you are losing money to both fees and inflation when you hold on to cash. In short, I can see Dr. Brown's point.

If the concept of a target-date fund is appealing, Dr. Brown recommends a low-cost target-date fund such as those offered by Vanguard. This could be a good approach for someone with minimal amounts to invest, a very simple situation, and the need for an advisor might be overkill. But if you don't want to use a target-date fund and instead have access to a list of low-cost index funds from which to choose, you might implement one of the asset allocation models you will learn later in this book. **Asset allocation, where to park your money and how to divide it up, is the single most important skill of a successful investor.** And as we will learn from the masters, it's not that complicated! Low-cost TDFs might be great for the average investor, but you are not average if you are reading this book!

If you want to take immediate action to minimize fees and have an advisor assist you in allocating your 401(k) fund choices, you can use the service at Stronghold (www.strongholdfinancial.com), which, with the click of a button will automatically "peer into" your 401(k) and provide a complimentary asset allocation.

In addition, many people think there aren't many alternatives to TDFs, but in section 5, you'll learn a specific asset allocation from hedge fund guru Ray Dalio that has produced extraordinary returns with minimal downside. When a team of analysts back-tested the portfolio, the worst loss was just 3.93% in the last 75 years. In contrast, according to MarketWatch, "the most conservative target-date retirement funds—those designed to produce income—fell on average 17% in 2008, and the riskiest target-date retirement funds—designed for those retiring in 2055—fell on average a whopping 39.8%, according to a recent report from Ibbotson Associates."

ANOTHER ONE BITES THE DUST

We have exposed and conquered yet another myth together. I hope by now you are seeing that ignorance is not bliss. Ignorance is pain and poverty in the financial world. The knowledge you have acquired in these first chapters will be the fuel you will need to say "Never again! Never again will I be taken advantage of."

Soon we will begin to explore the exciting opportunities, strategies, and vehicles for creating financial freedom, but first we have just a couple more myths to free you from.

MYTH 7:
"I HATE ANNUITIES, AND YOU SHOULD TOO"

The Fed chief's largest assets last year were two annuities.

— "Fed Chairman Bernanke's Personal Finances Are No Frills,"
USA Today, July 21, 2008

LOVE 'EM OR HATE 'EM?

I came across an online ad that read "I hate annuities and you should too." The typical internet "hook" promoted a free report on how annuities are terrible investments and that a strategy using stocks and bonds is a much better approach for long-term growth and security. Of course, the advertiser was readily available to sell you his expert stock pickings for a fee. What's not mentioned in the bold print of the ad is that the advertiser is an active-approach stock picker. And as we've already learned from experts Warren Buffett, Jack Bogle, Ray Dalio, and David Swenson—as well as academic research results—active management is ineffective in beating the market on a consistent basis. Their results are inferior to a simple index, which usually has fees that are 500% to 3,000% cheaper, with greater performance. This marketing strategy often works, though, doesn't it? Compare yourself with what's perceived as a terrible product, and suddenly yours doesn't look so bad.

But not everybody hates annuities . . .

On the flip side, I was blown away to find that the former Federal Reserve chairman Ben Bernanke, arguably the most influential man in finance at one point, certainly appreciates the use of annuities in his personal finance plan. Bernanke had to disclose his investments before becoming chairman of the

Fed. The disclosure showed that he held a relatively low amount of stocks and bonds, while his annuities were his *two largest holdings*. My immediate thought was, "What does he know that I don't?"

So which is it?

Are annuities the best thing since sliced bread or just a deal that is good for the insurance company and brokers selling them? The answer? It really depends on the type of annuity you own and the fees the insurance company will charge you. Let's explore.

During the process of writing this book, I was searching for the world's most respected minds to explore the best ways for readers to lock in a guaranteed lifetime income stream; a paycheck for life without having to work. After all, isn't this why we invest in the first place? As I conducted my interviews, Dr. David Babbel was a name that was continually "rising to the top" during my research. If you recall from the last chapter, he is the Wharton professor with multiple PhDs who advised the secretary of labor on two studies on target-date funds.

In early 2013 he presented his own personal story in a report on how he debunked the advice of his Wall Street buddies, who encouraged him to let his investments ride and hope for more growth, and created a lifetime income plan. So instead of risking a penny in stocks or bonds, he used a series of guaranteed *income annuities*, staggered over time, to give him the safe and secure retirement he wants and deserves—a lifetime income plan. The annuities he used also gave him a 100% guarantee of his principal, so he didn't lose in 2000 or in 2008 when the market crashed. Instead, he was comfortably enjoying his life, his wife, and his grandkids with complete peace of mind that he will never run out of money.

I flew to Philadelphia to meet with Dr. Babbel for a "one-hour" interview, which turned into four hours. His strategy, which we will highlight in the "Create an Income for Life" chapter, was powerful yet simple. And the "peace of mind" factor really came through, as I could see the freedom his strategy afforded him. I left with a completely different view on annuities! Or at least certain kinds of annuities.

He was very clear that "not all annuities are created equal." There are many different types, each with its own unique benefits and drawbacks. **There are ones you should indeed "hate," but to lump all annuities** into one category is to thoughtlessly discriminate against the only financial tool that has stood the test of time for over 2,000 years.

THE JULIUS CAESAR INSURANCE COMPANY

The first lifetime income annuities date back 2,000 years to the Roman Empire. Citizens and soldiers would deposit money into a pool. Those who lived longest would get increasing income payments, and those who weren't so lucky passed on; the government would take a small cut, of course. One must render to Caesar what is Caesar's!

The Latin word *annua* is where we get our word *annual*, because the original Romans got their income payment annually. And, of course, that's where the word *annuity* comes from! How's that for "exciting" water cooler trivia?

In the 1600s, European governments used the same annuity concept (called a tontine), to finance wars and public projects (again keeping a cut of the total deposits). In the modern world, the math and underpinnings of these products are still the same, except governments have been replaced by some of the highest-rated insurance companies, including many that have been in business for well over 100 years; insurance companies that stood the test of time through depressions, recessions, world wars, and the latest credit crisis.

But we must be careful when it comes to the different types of annuities. Annuities were pretty much the same over those last 2,000 years. There was just one version: the Coca-Cola Classic of financial solutions. It was a simple contract between you and an insurance company. You gave them your money, and they promised you a guaranteed income or return on your money. And after you made your contribution, you got to decide when to start receiving income payments. The longer you waited, the higher your income payments. And the day you bought it, you had a schedule that showed the exact payment, so there was no guessing.

IS IT PROGRESS OR JUST CHANGE?

Over the last 50 years, annuities have evolved into many different types compared with the original ones offered by Caesar. Sometimes evolution is a good thing. Other times we end up a mutant!

It's safe to say that there are more poor products out there than good ones. As Jack Bogle says, "I remain a recommender of the annuity conceptually, but you'd better look at the details before you do anything." So let's cut to the chase. Which should you avoid?

VARIABLE ANNUITIES ARE INVARIABLY BAD

In 2012 over $150 billion worth of variable annuities were sold. To put that in perspective, $150 billion is just a hair below Apple's gross revenue for 2012. Variable annuities have evolved into the commission darling of many large brokerage firms. So what the heck is a variable annuity? In short, it's an insurance contract where all of the underlying deposits are invested in mutual funds (also known as sub accounts). Yep. The same mutual funds that underperform the market and charge insanely high fees. But this time the investor buys them inside of an annuity "wrapper." Why would anyone want to invest in mutual funds through an annuity? Because annuity products have special tax benefits, and the money inside can grow tax-deferred, just like a 401(k) or IRA. This arrangement is especially attractive, the pitch goes, if you have already maxed out your 401(k) or IRA limits and have extra capital to invest. But now, instead of just paying excessive fees for under-performing mutual funds, there are *additional* fees for the annuity itself.

FEES ON TOP OF FEES

So what's the appeal? Why would someone buy mutual funds wrapped inside an annuity just to avoid taxes? Most variable annuities guarantee that even if the account goes down, your beneficiaries will receive at least the total amount you invested originally. So if you put in $100,000, and the mutual funds drop in value to $20,000, your children would still get $100,000 when you die. That doesn't sound like such a bad deal until you realize that you just bought the most expensive form of life insurance available.

Earlier, in chapter 2.2, we outlined the laundry list of fees you will pay to own an actively managed mutual fund and how these fees can dramatically drag down your performance. To recap, the total of all the fees (expense ratio, transaction costs, soft-dollar costs, cash drag, sales charges) will average **approximately 3.1% per year, according to *Forbes*** (if held in a tax-deferred account such as a 401[k], IRA, or variable annuity).

That's $3,100 per year for every $100,000.

But we ain't done yet.

When you buy a variable annuity, not only are you paying the fees listed above but also you have *additional* fees paid to the insurance company. There is a "mortality expense,"[7] which according to Morningstar averages 1.35% per year, as well as administrative charges that can run somewhere between 0.10% and 0.50% per year.

Let's add 'em up:

Average mutual fund costs = 3.1% (according to *Forbes* article),

Mortality and expense = 1.35% (average),

Administrative cost = 0.25% (average).

A grand total of 4.7% per year, or $4,700 for every $100,000 you invest! And this money comes off the top before you make a dime. **Said another way, if the fund returns 4.7%, you didn't make anything!** All of these additional fees all to avoid tax on the gains? Heck, after all the fees, you probably won't have much gain, if any, to pay taxes on!

PAINTED INTO A CORNER

Even though most people lose money in these variable annuities, they feel locked in and afraid to pull out their money because of the death benefit guarantee (the guarantee that their heirs will get back the original deposit amount). And there are usually heavy surrender charges, so the insurance company might charge you for leaving the party early.

Are there any exceptions to the rule? Only two that experts tell me are worth considering in so far as one needs the tax efficiency. Vanguard and TIAA-CREF both offer extremely low-cost variable annuities with a list of low-cost index funds to choose from. They do not charge commissions, so there are no surrender charges if you want to cash in.

---

7. Fees, included in certain annuity or insurance products, that serve to compensate the insurance company for various risks it assumes under the annuity contract.

NOT YOUR GRANDPA'S ANNUITIES

In chapters 5.3 and 5.4 of this book, "Freedom: Creating Your Lifetime Income Plan" and "Time to Win: Your Income Is the Outcome," we will clearly examine traditional income annuities as well as a relatively new type of annuity (the *fixed indexed annuity*) that provides some of the highest and most compelling income guarantees of any financial product, while also providing 100% principal protection. By the time you are done with this book, you can have the certainty and peace of mind of knowing that every month when you walk to your mailbox, you will be receiving a paycheck (that you won't have to work for). And we can accelerate your path to financial freedom if we can eliminate taxes on your lifetime income payments. How, you ask?

By taking a portion of our money and combining the power of a Roth IRA with the power of a lifetime income annuity. **This means that no matter what the government does with tax rates, you can rest assured that the entire amount you receive is spendable income. That's right: a legal and secure tax-free lifetime income, with no moving parts or worries about market volatility.**

The purpose of this chapter is not only to tell you what to avoid but also to warn you about getting sucked into the marketing myth that *all* annuities are bad. The only reason why I'm not going into more detail on the power of annuities is because you first need to understand where to put your money: asset allocation. And understanding asset allocation will help you know when and where annuities make sense for you.

THE SOLUTION

If you have an annuity, regardless of what type, it's always beneficial to get a review by an annuity specialist. You can reach out to an annuity specialist at Lifetime Income (www.lifetimeincome.com), and he or she will perform a complimentary review, which will help you:

- discover the pros and cons of your current annuity,
- determine the actual fees you are paying,
- assess whether or not the guarantees are the highest available, and

- decide whether to keep it or get out of your current annuity and "exchange" for a different type of annuity.

If you have an annuity that you find is not great, there is a feature called a *1035 exchange*. It requires some simple paperwork to move a cash balance from one insurance company to another **without being hit with a tax penalty.** But you must be aware that your current annuity might have "surrender charges" if you haven't owned the annuity for long enough. It may make sense to postpone an exchange until there are low or no surrender charges. Also, you may be forfeiting the death benefit guarantee.

Stick with me here, as there is just one more truth we must uncover! The last and final illusion is one that insiders are most aware of: the myth that you have to take exorbitant risks to make great returns.

Let's unmask Myth 8. . . .

MYTH 8:
"YOU GOTTA TAKE HUGE RISKS TO GET BIG REWARDS!"

An investment operation is one which, upon thorough
analysis, promises safety of principal and an adequate return.
Operations not meeting these requirements are speculative.
—BENJAMIN GRAHAM, *The Intelligent Investor*

HAVING YOUR CAKE AND EATING IT TOO

Superficially, I think it looks like entrepreneurs have a
high tolerance for risk. But one of the most important
phrases in my life is "protect the downside."
—RICHARD BRANSON, founder of Virgin

My friend Richard Branson, the founder of Virgin and its many incredible brands, decided to launch Virgin Airways in 1984. In true David-versus-Goliath fashion, the master of marketing knew that he could "out market" anyone including the behemoth competitor British Airways. To outsiders, it seemed like a huge gamble. But Richard, like most smart investors, was more concerned about hedging his downside than hitting a home run. So in a brilliant move, he bought his first five planes but managed to negotiate the deal of a lifetime: if it didn't work out, he could give back the planes! A money-back guarantee! If he failed, he didn't lose. But if he won, he won big. The rest is history.

Not unlike the business world, the investment world will tell you, directly or more subtly, that if you want to win big, you've got to take some serious risk. Or more frighteningly, if you ever want financial freedom, you have to risk your freedom to get there.

Nothing could be further from the truth.

If there is one common denominator of successful insiders, it's that they don't speculate with their hard-earned savings, they strategize. **Remember Warren Buffett's top two rules of investing? Rule 1: don't lose money! Rule 2: see rule 1.** Whether it's the world's top hedge fund traders like Ray Dalio and Paul Tudor Jones or entrepreneurs like Salesforce founder Marc Benioff and Richard Branson of Virgin, without exception, these billionaire insiders look for opportunities that provide asymmetric risk/reward. This is a fancy way of saying that the reward is drastically disproportionate to the risk.

Risk a little, make a lot.

The best example of risking very little to make a lot is the high-frequency traders (HFT) who use the latest technologies (yes, even flying robots and microwave towers that are faster than the speed of light) to save 1/1000 of a second! What would you guess is their risk/reward while generating 70% of all trading volume in the stock market? I will give you a clue. Virtu Financial, one of the largest HFT firms, was about to go public, a process that requires it to disclose its business model and profitability. Over the past five years, Virtu has lost money only one day! That's right. One single trading day out of thousands! And what is its risk? Investing in faster computers, I suppose.

TWO NICKELS TO RUB TOGETHER

My friend and hedge fund guru J. Kyle Bass is best known for turning a $30 million investment into $2 billion in just two short years. Conventional wisdom would say that he must have taken a big risk for returns of that magnitude. Not so. Kyle made a very calculated bet against the housing bubble that was expanding like the kid in *Willy Wonka & the Chocolate Factory*. It was bound to burst sooner rather than later. Remember those days? When ravenous, unqualified mortgage shoppers were enticed to buy whatever they could get their hands on. And with no money down or so much as any proof they could afford it. Lenders were lining up to provide loans knowing they could package them up and sell them off to investors who really didn't understand them. This bubble was easy to spot so long as you were on the outside looking in. But Kyle's brilliance, which he reveals in his interview in section 6, is that he only risked 3 cents for every dollar of upside. How's that for taking a tiny risk and reaping giant rewards?

When I spoke with Kyle recently, he shared the details of another asymmetric risk/reward opportunity he had found for himself and his investors. The terms? He had a 95% guarantee of his investment, but if or when the company went public, he had unlimited upside (and he expected massive returns!). But if it all went south, he lost only 5%.

Kyle, like all great investors, takes small risks for big rewards. **Taking a swing for the fence with no downside protection is a recipe for disaster.**

"Kyle, how do I get this point across to my readers?"

"Tony, I will tell you how I taught my two boys: we bought nickels."

"What was that, Kyle?" Maybe the phone was breaking up. "I could have sworn you just said you bought nickels."

"You heard me right. I was literally standing in the shower one day thinking, 'Where can I get a riskless return?'"

Most experts wouldn't even dream to think of such a thing. In their mind, "riskless return" is an oxymoron. Insiders like Kyle think differently from the herd. And by defying conventional wisdom, he always looks for small investments to return disproportionate rewards. The famed hedge fund guru, with one of the biggest wins of the last century, used his hard-earned money to buy . . . well, money: $2 million in nickels— enough to fill up a small room. What gives?

While a nickel's value fluctuates, at the time of this interview Kyle told me, "Tony, the US nickel is worth about 6.8 cents today in its 'melt value.' That means 5 cents is really worth 6.8 cents [36% more] in its true metal value." Crazy to think we live in a world where the government will spend nearly 9 cents in total (including raw materials and manufacturing costs) to make a 5-cent coin. Is anyone paying attention up there on Capitol Hill? Clearly this isn't sustainable, and one day Congress will wake up and change the "ingredients" that make up the nickel. "Maybe the next one will be tin or steel. They did this identical thing with the penny when copper became too expensive in the early eighties." From 1909 to 1982, the penny was made up of 95% copper. Today it's mostly zinc with only 2.5% copper. Today one of those older pennies is worth 2 cents! (Not in melt value; that's the price coin collectors would pay!) That's 100% more than its face value. If you had invested in pennies way back when, you would have doubled your money with no risk, and you didn't even have to melt the pennies!

I admit it sounded gimmicky at first, but Kyle was dead serious. "If I could take my entire cash balance of my net worth and press a button and turn it into nickels, I would do it right this second," he exclaimed. "Because then you don't have to worry about how much money they print. The nickel will always be worth a nickel." And his cash would be worth 36% more— and like pennies, likely 100% more in the future, as soon as the government inevitably cheapens the nickel's recipe.

Kyle was more than an enthusiast. **"Where else can I get a thirty-six-percent risk-free return!** If I am wrong, I still have what I started with." Sure, it's illegal to melt down your nickels (for now), but the point is, "I won't need to melt it down because once they change the way they make the nickel, the old nickels become even more valuable than before because scarcity sets in as they begin to remove them from circulation."

Needless to say, his boys got the lesson as well as a good workout moving boxes of coins into their storage unit!

Now, you might be thinking, "Well, that's great for Kyle Bass, who has millions or even billions just to throw around, but how does that apply to me?" Surely it can't be possible for normal investors to have upside without the downside—to have a protection of principal with major upside potential.

Think again.

The same level of financial creativity that has propelled high-frequency trading (HFT) from nonexistent into a dominant force in just ten years has touched other areas of finance as well. Following the 2008 crash, when people didn't have much of an appetite for stocks, some very innovative minds at the world's largest banks figured out a way to do the seemingly impossible: **allow you and me to participate in the gains of the stock market without risking *any* of our principal!**

Before you write this notion off as crazy, I personally have a *note*, issued and backed by one of the world's largest banks, that gives me 100% principal protection, and if the market goes up, I get to keep a significant chunk of the gains in the market (without dividends). But if the market collapses, I get *all* my money back. I don't know about you, but I am more than happy to give up a percentage of the upside in exchange for protecting myself from stomach-wrenching losses on a portion of my investment portfolio.

But I am getting ahead of myself.

We have come to a point in the United States where most of us feel that the only option for us to grow our wealth involves taking huge risks. That our only available option is to white knuckle it through the rolling waves of the stock market. And we somehow take solace in the fact that everyone is in the same boat. Well, guess what? It's not true! Not everyone is in the same boat!

There are much more comfortable boats out on the water that are anchored in the proverbial safe harbor, while others are getting pounded in the waves of volatility and taking on water quick.

So who owns the boats in the harbor? The insiders. The wealthy. The 1%. Those not willing to speculate with their hard-earned money. But make no mistake: you don't have to be in the .001% to strategize like the .001%.

WHO DOESN'T WANT TO EAT THE CAKE TOO?

In the investment world, having your cake and eating it too would be making money when the market goes up but not losing a dime if the market drops. We get to ride the elevator up but not down. This too-good-to-be-true concept is so important that I have devoted an entire section of this book to it: "Upside Without the Downside: Create a Lifetime Income Plan." But for now, this brief appetizer below is designed to dislodge your preconceived notions that you and all of your money must endure the endless waves of volatility. Below are three proven strategies (explored in more depth in section 5) for achieving strong returns while anchored firmly in calmer waters.

1. **Structured Notes.** These are perhaps one of the more exciting tools available today, but, unfortunately, they are rarely offered to the general public because the high-net-worth investors gobble them up like pigeon seed in Central Park. Luckily, the right fiduciary is able to grant access for individuals even without large sums of investment capital. So listen up.

    A structured note is simply a loan *to* a bank (and typically the largest banks in the world). The bank issues you a note in exchange for lending it your money. At the end of the time period (also called the term), the bank *guarantees* to pay you the *greater* of: 100% of your deposit back *or* a certain percentage of the upside of the market gains (minus the dividends).

That's right. I get *all* my money back if the market is down from the day I bought the note, but if the market goes up during the term, I get to participate in the upside. I call these notes "engineered safety." The catch? I typically don't get to keep *all* of the upside. So you have to ask yourself if you're willing to give up part of the upside for downside protection. Many people would say yes. These solutions become especially valuable when you come to that point in your life, close to or during retirement, where you can't afford to take any big losses. When you can't afford or even survive another 2008.

For those looking to take a bit more risk, some notes will allow for even greater upside if you are willing to take more risk on the downside. **For example, a note available today will give you a 25% downside-protection "airbag." So the market has to go down more than 25% for you to lose. And in exchange for taking more risk, it will give you more than 100% of the upside. One note available right now offers 140% of the upside if you are willing to absorb a loss beyond 25%. So if the market was up 10% over the term, you would get 14% in return.**

So what are the downsides of structured notes? First, a guarantee is only as good as the backer! So it's important to choose one of the strongest/largest banks (issuers) in the world with a very strong balance sheet. (Note: Lehman Brothers was a very strong bank until it wasn't! This is why many experts utilize Canadian banks, since they tend to have the strongest financials.)

Next challenge? Your timing could be way off. Let's say you owned a note with a five-year term, and for the first four years, the market was up. You would be feeling pretty good at that point. But if the market collapses in the fifth year, you will still get your money back, but you didn't get to capture any of those gains. You also might have limited liquidity if you need to sell the note before the end of the term.

It's also important to note that not all structured notes are created equal. Like all financial products, there are good versions and bad versions. Most big retail firms sell you notes that have substantial commissions, underwriting fees, and distributions fees; all of these will take away from your potential upside. Accessing structured notes through a sophisticated, expert fiduciary (a registered investment advisor) will typically have those fees removed because a fiduciary charges a flat advisory fee. And by stripping out those fees, performance goes up. A fiduciary will also help you make sure you own the note in the most tax-efficient way since the tax ramifications can vary.

2. **Market-Linked CDs.** First things first: these are not your grandpa's CDs. In today's day and age, with interest rates so low, traditional CDs can't even keep pace with inflation. This has earned them the nickname "certificates of death" because your purchasing power is being slowly killed. As I write this, the average one-year CD pays 0.23% (or 23 basis points). Can you imagine investing $1,000 dollars for a year and getting back $2.30? The average investor walks into a bank and is willing to lay down and accept 23 bps. But the wealthy investor, an insider, would laugh and tell them to go to hell. That's not enough to buy a latte! Oh, and you still have to pay taxes on that $2.30 return—an even higher ordinary income tax rate (as opposed to the investment tax rate), which historically is significantly lower!

Traditional CDs are very profitable for the banks because they can turn around and lend your money at 10 to 20 times the interest rate they are paying you. Another version of the insider's game.

Market-linked CDs **are similar to structured notes, but they include insurance from the** *Federal Deposit Insurance Corporation* **(FDIC).** Here is how they work.

Market-linked CDs, like traditional versions, give you some small guaranteed return (a coupon) if the market goes up, but you *also* get to participate in the upside. But if the market falls, you get back your investment (plus your small return), and you had FDIC insurance the entire time. Typically, your money is tied up for one or two years (whereas structured notes can be as long as five to seven years). To give you a real-life example, today there is a market-linked CD that pays the exact same interest rate as a traditional CD (0.28%) but also allows you to participate in up to 5% of the market gains. So if the market is up 8% total, you get to keep 5%. In this example, you earned over 20 times the return of a traditional CD with the same FDIC protection! But again, if the market goes down you lose nothing. Keep in mind that rates are constantly changing in this field. Rates may be more attractive at certain times than at others. In 2008, when banks were struggling and looking for deposits, they had a sweetheart deal that my buddy Ajay Gupta, who is also my personal registered investment advisor, couldn't pass up. The note had 100% principal protection with FDIC insurance. The value was linked to a balanced portfolio of stocks and bonds, and when all was said and done, he averaged 8% per year with no risk!

I must warn you again, however, that accessing these directly from a bank will often incur a host of charges and fees. Conversely, accessing these solutions through a fiduciary advisor will typically remove all the commissions and fees that a retail firm may charge, and thus the performance/terms will be better for you.

3. **Fixed Indexed Annuities.** Let me be the first to say that there are a lot of crappy annuity products on the market. But in my research and interviews with some of the top experts in the country, I discovered that other types of annuities are used by insiders as yet another tool to create upside without the downside.

Fixed indexed annuities (FIA) are a type of annuity that has been around since the mid-'90s but have only recently exploded in popularity. A *properly structured* fixed indexed annuity offers the following characteristics:

- 100% principal protection, guaranteed by the insurance company. This is why we have to pick an insurance company with a high rating and a long history of making good on its promises—often a century or more!
- Upside without downside—like structured notes and market-linked CDs, a fixed indexed annuity allows you to participate when the market goes up but not lose if the market goes down. All gains are tax deferred, or if it's owned within a Roth IRA, you won't pay taxes on the returns.
- Lastly, and probably most importantly, some fixed indexed annuities offer the ability to create an income stream that you can't outlive. A paycheck for life! Think of this investment as your own personal pension. For every dollar you deposit, the insurance company guarantees you a certain monthly income payment when you decide to trigger, or turn on, your lifetime income stream. Insurance companies have been doing this work successfully for 200 years. We will explore this strategy in depth in section 5, "Upside Without the Downside: Create a Lifetime Income Plan."

A WORD OF WARNING

Before we move on, let me be very clear on one point: this does not imply that all versions of these products and strategies are great. Some have high fees, high commissions, hidden charges, and on and on. The last thing I want is some salesman using these few pages to sell you something that's not in your best interest. And when we dive into these solutions in section 5, I will give you a specific list of pitfalls you must avoid as well as a list of things you absolutely want to make sure you receive when utilizing these solutions.

YOU GET WHAT YOU TOLERATE

The point of this chapter is to begin to show you ways in which you can have your cake and eat it too. Sometimes, when you have endured the choppy waters for so long, you begin to believe that there is no other option. This tendency is called "learned helplessness." But that's not the way insiders think. From Buffett to Branson, they all look for asymmetric risk/reward. **Insiders are not helpless, nor are you. In every area of life, you get what you tolerate. And it's time to raise the standard.**

HOW FAR WE HAVE COME

We have made some serious progress! Let's recap the myths we have shattered and the truths we have uncovered thus far:

- We have learned that nobody beats the market (except for a handful of "unicorns")! And by using low-cost market-mimicking index funds, we can outperform 96% of mutual funds and nearly as many hedge funds. Welcome to the front of the performance pack!
- Since stock-picking mutual funds are charging us extremely high fees (over 3%, on average), we can drop our investment fees by 80% or even 90%. You could have more than twice as much money when you retire or cut years off the time it will take you to get to financial freedom. Let that soak in for a second!
- We have learned the difference between a butcher and a dietitian—between a broker and a fiduciary. And now we know where to go to get transparent advice (that may also be tax-deductible).

- We learned how to drastically reduce our 401(k) fees by using a low-cost provider like America's Best 401k. You can see how your plan stacks up by using the industry's first fee checker (http://americasbest401k.com/401k-fee -checker). Again, these cost savings will compound our total account balance and put money back in our family's pocket. (For business owners, we showed how you can get yourself compliant with the law and drastically reduce your liability.)

- We learned about the Roth 401(k) and how we can protect against rising taxes by paying the tax today and never paying tax again (not on the growth or the withdrawals).

- We learned that target-date funds (TDFs) are not only expensive but also may be more aggressive or volatile than you think. And if you want to use a TDF, you should stick with a low-cost provider like Vanguard. Later, in the "Billionaire's Playbook," you will also learn how to put together your own asset allocation instead of paying a TDF to do it for you.

- We learned that variable annuities are a mutant evolution of a 2,000-year-old financial product but that other more traditional (fixed) annuities can provide what no other product can: a guaranteed lifetime income stream!

- And finally, we learned that wealth without risk is a possibility. Sure, there is risk in everything, but we learned that certain structures will allow us to participate when the market goes up and not lose when it falls!

Are your eyes beginning to open? Has the blindfold been removed? How will your life be different now that you know the truth? Shattering these myths is the groundwork for creating true financial freedom. I want you to see, hear, feel, and know that *the game is winnable*. If these myths are unsettling, good! They were for me when I first discovered the truth. Let them drive you forward to make financial freedom a *must* in your life, and to declare that you will never be taken advantage of again.

We will take it up a notch and have some fun in section 3. It's here where we will make our dreams become more of a reality by putting in place a plan that is both doable and exciting. And if it's not happening fast enough for you, we will show you how to speed it up and bring it closer into your future.

But first, the last and final myth must be put to death. But unlike the

others, it's not one that someone else has sold you. It's the story you have
sold yourself. It's whatever myth or lie has kept you from taking action in
the past. It's time for a breakthrough! Let's shatter your limits by discovering
the lies we tell ourselves.

THIS "MARKET EKG" CAN KILL YOU!
S&P 500® Yearly Returns (1960-2010)

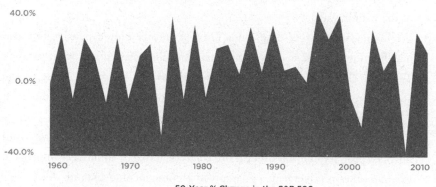

50-Year % Change in the S&P 500

MYTH 9:
"THE LIES WE TELL OURSELVES"

Seek truth and you will find a path.
—FRANK SLAUGHTER

Okay, let's get real here. We've just gone through all of the marketing and investment myths that have been promoted for years, at great expense to us, and to the benefit of big institutions. And my bet is that right now you're probably shocked, but you feel incredibly empowered. You now know what to avoid and what to do to succeed.

But there's one final myth to tackle. The myth that says the reason we're not succeeding, not achieving, not growing is because of someone or something else beyond our control. Or the alternative thought that somehow we just aren't made of the stuff that can help us master this area of our life. **But here's the truth: the ultimate thing that stops most of us from making significant progress in our lives is not somebody else's limitations, but rather our own limiting perceptions or beliefs.** No matter how successful we are as human beings, no matter how high we reach personally, professionally, spiritually, emotionally, there's always another level. And to get there, we have to be honest with ourselves; honest about our unconscious fears. What do I mean?

Everybody has a fear of failure at some level; at times we've all been fearful that perhaps we are not enough. Even when we know what to do, our fear can keep us from executing our plans. As a result, rather than face our natural fears, what do we do? We come up with stories. Stories about why we're not where we want to be. Why we're not smart enough, successful enough, thin enough, rich enough, loved or loving enough. Our stories almost always relate to something outside our control, or our lack of some natural talent or ability. But talent and skill are two key elements to success attainable by anyone who is truly committed. You can get the skill if you can get beyond the mental limits of how hard, difficult, or "impossible" it may be to master something.

You've made the single most important financial decision of your life by deciding precisely how much you're going to save to build your Freedom Fund—so you can tap into that and create a money machine that makes money while you sleep. And we've taken the time to look through all of the marketing myths that can trip you up along the way. So what's left? The last thing out there standing in our way is often our own story, our own limitations, our own fears. The final obstacle to face is ourselves. That's why, for 38 years, my passion has been helping people to break through from what holds them back—to help them get from where they are now to where they want to be, and faster. *My whole life has been committed to helping people create breakthroughs.* And frankly, while lots of people make this step complex, I've found there are only three elements that make the difference between success and failure in the long run—between whether you stay where you are, or you move forward. Whether you make excuses about what you don't have or whether you get to enjoy the life you deserve.

BREAKTHROUGHS

So what is a breakthrough? **A breakthrough is a moment in time when the impossible becomes possible**—when you don't just talk about something, but you finally take massive action and do whatever it takes to make it happen. You make a move to truly change and improve your world.

Often it's frustration, anger, or stress that triggers a breakthrough. We hit our threshold: a point where we say, "Never again and no more." Or inspiration strikes: we meet someone who inspires us and that makes us see how life can be so much greater than we ever dreamed possible. You meet someone who enjoys life fully, has a great relationship, is physically fit or financially free, and you decide, "I'm as smart as he or she is. I'm going to find a way." What was acceptable before no longer is. There's no going back now. It's amazing what you can do when you decide to draw a line in the sand, commit to a new goal, and set a new standard.

Most people say, "It took me ten years to make this change." But the truth is, it didn't take ten years for a breakthrough. True transformation happens in a moment. It may have taken you ten years to *get to the point where you were ready*, or open, or maybe even provoked. But we've all had breakthroughs in our lives, and those breakthroughs happened in a single moment. We struggle with something for years—a job or a career, our weight or a relationship. We're miserable until one day a trigger goes off. Suddenly, "That's it."

"I love you!"

"I quit!"

"I'm in!"

"Let's begin!"

Not within a day or an hour, but in that moment your life changes—and it changes forever.

Have you ever stayed in a relationship way too long, even though you knew you were unhappy, and so was your partner? You came to the edge of dealing with it, and then the fear of the unknown, of change, of being alone, stopped you. The fear of loss and uncertainty kept you from taking action, and you settled.

Whatever you struggle with, I know there's a place where you've had a breakthrough before. Take a moment to think of one. What's an area you used to struggle with—daily, weekly, monthly, for years or even a decade or more, until one day you hit your threshold? You became inspired, or fed up, enough to finally make a real decision to change this area once and for all! And you took massive and immediate action to make a change. You got it done. You finally kicked the habit and quit smoking. Or you left a job that made you miserable and started your own business. Or maybe you finally decided to start exercising and change your body or get yourself out of that bad relationship.

I want you to own that breakthrough. There was a time when things seemed like they couldn't change, but you did it—*you* made it happen. You *do* have the ability to change everything in your life. No matter how long it's been this way, you can change it all in a moment, a moment of real decision, a decision that is acted upon. That's a breakthrough, and one is waiting for you right now.

THREE STEPS TO CREATING
YOUR BREAKTHROUGH

There are three steps to creating a breakthrough: three forces that, together, can massively change any and every aspect of your life. Any one on its own can work, but if you put all three together, you will absolutely change the aspect of your life that you choose to focus on.

What are the three biggest challenges people face in America? What are the three areas that show up over and over again, causing pain in people's lives? Our finances, our relationships, and our bodies. How many people do you know who struggle with money, who can't save, who don't earn enough, who spend too much, or who can't figure out what to do next with their career? And what about relationships? Men and women, we are wired so differently—if we don't understand each other, it can take so much work to maintain healthy intimate relationships, to understand what our partner really needs and wants, to communicate in a loving and supportive way. And then there are our bodies. We live in a time where the majority of people in the Western world are massively overweight. In the United States, nearly seven in ten Americans are either overweight (defined by the Centers for Disease Control and Prevention as having a body mass index of 25.0 to 29.9) or obese (having a BMI of 30.0 or higher). Our struggle with fitness and health has become a national crisis, and it's spreading around the world as developing countries adopt some of our lifestyle and eating patterns.

Why do I bring this all up? What do relationship challenges and unhealthy eating habits have to do with your ability to achieve financial freedom? Well, whatever area you want to create a breakthrough in, whether it's your body, your relationships, or this book's focus, money, there are only three things that you need to look at. And they are the same three things no matter what kind of breakthrough you're hoping to achieve. **If you want to change your life you have to change your *strategy*, you have to change your *story*, and you have to change your *state*.** Let's begin with strategy, because that's where most people start.

THE RIGHT STRATEGY

If you're with me here now, reading this book, you're in search of answers, of strategies, to take control of your money and secure your financial future. I live for finding strategies to improve every area of our lives. I've spent the past 38 years relentlessly focusing on finding strategies and tools to immediately change the quality of people's lives. I've been successful and impacted over 50 million people in 100 countries *because* I'm obsessed with finding simple strategies that quickly lead to breakthroughs—breakthroughs in relationships, in finances, in careers, in growing businesses, in mind, body, and soul.

I've always believed the best way to get a result, the fastest way, is to find someone who has already accomplished what you're after, and model his or her behavior. If you know someone who used to be overweight but has kept himself fit and healthy for a decade, model that person! You have a friend who used to be miserable in her relationship and now is passionate and in love for ten years going? Model her. You meet someone who started with nothing and has developed wealth and sustained it through time? Learn from those strategies! These people aren't lucky. They're simply doing something different than you are in this area of life.

I've spent my entire life as a hunter of human excellence. **So to find a strategy that works, you go to the best; those who have proven results for the long term.** And if you follow their strategies—if you sow the same seeds, then you'll reap the same rewards. This is the essence of what I mean when I say, "*Success leaves clues.*" And this book is filled with strategies modeled from the very best.

The other thing the right strategy can do is save you the most valuable resource of all: time. If you start with *a proven plan, the right strategy,* you can literally convert decades of struggle into days of achievement. You can avoid the inevitable frustration that comes with learning something for the first time by trial and error. Instead, you can get results in days, instead of years, by learning from people who have achieved success already. Why reinvent the wheel?

So now there's the question about the power of strategy. And if you read this book, you'll have the best financial strategies that exist in the world today. I promise you that: because they're not my strategies, they're the strategies of the most successful investors in history. But as obsessed as I am with strategy, I know that strategy alone isn't enough.

Why not? There are two key challenges to thinking that strategy alone can change your life. First, too often people have the *wrong* strategy, which inevitably ends in disappointment. You're trying to lose weight by eating 500 calories a day—which, of course, isn't sustainable. Or you're sure you're going to get rich off one hot stock—highly unlikely.

Where do most people go to learn strategy? Where do we look for advice and guidance? Too often from someone who isn't successful in the very area we want to improve! How often do people get relationship advice from friends who are in lousy relationships themselves? Or fitness advice from a friend who struggles with his weight, too? How many people hear the message reinforced that they can't change their body? Why that message? Because they're surrounded by friends or family who aren't fit. The same is true for financial advice. Looking to someone who has not developed real wealth is a recipe for disaster. It simply reinforces the belief that nothing will work. It's not that nothing will work—it's that *these* strategies won't work.

> However beautiful the strategy, you should
> occasionally look at the results.
> —WINSTON CHURCHILL

THE POWER OF STORY

Let's go back to our biggest challenges: our relationships, our bodies, and our finances. In each of these areas, we get stuck for one of three reasons. First, as we showed above, we lack the right strategy. We all know a couple where the guy doesn't communicate or the woman never stops talking. Neither of them understands the needs of his or her partner, much less meets those needs. And what about the friend who goes on fad diets constantly or is always looking out for a magical way to make a million bucks—telling himself that without it he'll never be financially free. Without the right strategy, you will fail. And when you fail, you develop a lousy story: *"My wife will never be satisfied." "I'll never lose the weight." "The only people who make money are the ones who already have money."* Those limiting stories keep us from finding the right strategies, or, even if we have the right strategies, from executing them.

Do you know anyone like that? You put the answer right in front of their very eyes, and they still say, "No, that will never work because . . ." They'll tell you a million reasons why it won't work—they've got every excuse in the book. So if the right strategies are there in front of us, why aren't people using them? Why are they still not achieving their goals? Why is it so hard to maintain a passionate relationship or lose the weight once and for all? Are 70% of Americans overweight because the strategy for becoming thin, fit, and healthy is really so complex? Is the information hidden and only available to the 1%, or incredibly expensive? Hell, no. The answers are available everywhere: There's a gym with someone who can instruct you within a short drive. (God forbid we were to walk there.) There are trainers all over the world, some of which will coach you online, wherever you are! The web is filled with free advice, and, of course, there are thousands of books on fitness and weight loss available for you to download right now to your iPad or smartphone. You have to work to avoid finding the strategies for becoming fit, strong, and healthy.

So what's the real problem? The answer is: we have to bring in the human factor. **I always say that 80% of success in life is psychology and 20% is mechanics.** How else do you explain how someone can know what he needs to do, wants to do it, has the right strategy to get it done, and still not take action? To solve this riddle we have to delve into the psychology of individuals: the values, beliefs, and emotions that drive us.

When someone has the right strategy in front of her, and she still doesn't succeed, it's because she's missing the second key to a breakthrough: the power of story. If you're not taking action and the answer is sitting there in front of you, there's only one reason: you've created a set of beliefs that you've tied into a story—a story about why it won't work, why it can't work, why it only works for other people. *It's only for the rich, the thin, the lucky, the happy in relationships.* It's easy to come up with a limiting story.

So why bother to take action on a strategy that you "know" will fail? Well, strategy here isn't the problem. Your story is. A half-hearted approach that says, "*It might work, or it might not . . .*"—of course it won't! That belief becomes a self-fulfilling prophecy. **With a disempowering story, failure**

is nothing less than guaranteed. Which, of course, only reinforces your belief that nothing will work. And so the cycle continues.

But the people who make change happen, who get stuff done, who accomplish, who shift, who grow, who learn, they take their strategy and attach a new story to it: a story of empowerment, a story of "I can and I will" instead of "I can't and I won't." **It goes from being a story of limitation to a story of empowerment: "I will not be one of the many who can't, I will be one of the few who do."**

There was a time when I was 38 pounds overweight, and my story was, "I'm big-boned." Which I am. But I was also fat. Stories can be true, but if they don't help us, if they're stopping us from having the life we desire and deserve, we have to change them. We've all had lousy stories in our lives.

I don't make enough.

I can't save more.

I'll never read. I've got dyslexia.

My friend Sir Richard Branson, chairman of the Virgin empire, has dyslexia, but it certainly hasn't limited his life in any way. Why? Because his belief or story about dyslexia was empowering, not limiting. His story wasn't "I'll never read," it was "I have dyslexia, so I have to work harder to make everything happen—and I will." **You can use your story, or your story can use you.** Everybody has got an empowering story if he or she wants to find it. What's wrong with your life is just as easy to find as what's right with your life, when your story changes. If your relationship isn't working out, all the good guys are gone, or they're gay and you're not. Or you're gay and they're not. There's always a story, right? Stories control our emotions, and emotions drive all of our behavior and actions.

Let me ask you a question: Do you worry about money? Does it keep you up at night, stress you out thinking about your next paycheck, your car payment, your kids' college tuition, or whether or not you'll ever have enough money to be able to retire? What's your financial stress really like? According to the American Institute of Certified Public Accountants (AICPA), 44% of Americans, nearly half of us, report "high levels" of financial stress. Have you ever thought to yourself, "All this stress just might kill me?"

Kelly McGonigal, a health psychologist at Stanford University, warned about the dangers of stress for a full decade before she realized that maybe it was her advice, rather than stress itself, that was sending people to their graves faster. "I'm converting a stimulus [stress] that could be strengthening people into a source of disease." With a breakthrough in her thinking, and some powerful new research, McGonigal made a complete turnaround.

Turns out, stress might just be our friend. Just as you put stress on a muscle to make it stronger (by lifting weights or running), emotional stress can make us physically and psychologically stronger too. McGonigal now highlights new research showing that when you change your mind about stress, you can literally change your body's physical reaction to it. In an eight-year study, adults who experienced a "lot of stress" and who believed stress was harmful to their health had a 43% increase in their risk of dying. (That sure stressed *me* out.) **However, people who experienced an equal amount of stress but did not view stress as harmful were no more likely to die!** McGonigal says that physical signs of stress (a pounding heart, faster breathing, breaking out in a sweat) aren't necessarily physical evidence of anxiety or signs that we aren't coping well with pressure. Instead, we can interpret them as indications that our body is energized and preparing us to meet the next challenge. **The bottom line is, science has now proven that how you think about stress matters—the story you attach to stress. Telling yourself it's good for you instead of harmful could mean the difference between a stress-induced heart attack at 50 or living well into your 90s.**

> Success is my only mofo option, failure's not.
> —"LOSE YOURSELF," Eminem

So what story have you been telling yourself about money? What's stopping you from achieving your financial dreams? Are you telling yourself that it's too early to start saving? Or too late to start rebuilding your investments? You're not making enough salary to put anything aside? Or the system is rigged against you, so why bother trying? Maybe your story is, "The government has saddled us with debt, the financial system is in shambles," or "I'm just not good with numbers." Great news: you don't have to be! If you've got a phone and a calculator or can download our app on your phone, to answer six simple questions about where you are today, where you want to go, and what you're willing to do to get a financial plan that you'll clearly understand about how to be financially free.

Maybe your story is "It takes money to make money." One of the first people I shared an early version of this book with had a core belief of "I will never be financially free unless I have a way to make a lot of money. People who start with a lot of money can make millions, but not me." After she read the chapter on building your own money machine with Theodore Johnson—who never made more than $14,000 a year yet turned it into $70 million over his lifetime—her story went out the window. Theodore wasn't lucky. He used a simple system, the same one you're about to learn.

Here's her new story, and it could be yours: "If I just happen to use this simple system of compounding, I can make a lot of money, I can go wherever I want, I can live however I truly want, I can be financially free. There are no limits except the ones I impose on myself."

One of my own financial breakthroughs happened with an important change in story. Growing up poor, I always associated a lack of money with pain for everyone in the family. I swore to myself early on I would never have a child until I was truly financially successful. I swore that someday I would be so successful financially that my family would *never ever* experience the humiliation, frustration, and pain of my childhood years of not being able to pay the bills or put food on the table.

And I made good on my promise. By the time I was 18 years old, I was earning as much as $10,000 a month, which at the time seemed like a huge amount of money. It still is. I was so excited, I ran back to my friends from my community, the guys I had grown up poor with, and said, "Let's go have a blast: let's fly to Egypt and race camels between the pyramids!" I had had this dream as a little boy. And I could now share this dream with my friends. But the response was hardly what I was expecting: "Easy for you, Mr. Rich Man." The level of disdain I got from guys I considered to be friends shook me to my core. I wasn't flaunting my money. I simply wanted to share my abundance with my friends and create an experience of real adventure. But I had to reevaluate. I created a new story: a belief that said you can do well but only *so* well, or else people will judge you. If you stand out and do too well financially, people won't like you.

So for years, I did well in my life and businesses, but my income didn't grow significantly. Until I finally hit a tipping point, a stage in my life where I thought, "This is ridiculous. If I could expand my intelligence, should I?" My answer was, "Of course!" If I could experience and give more love, should I? Of course! If I could expand my ability to give, should I? Of course. If I could earn more and expand my financial wealth, should I? And the answer was, "Of course!" For the first time, I felt hesitancy. Why was it that in every other area of my life it seemed natural to expand and become more, but when the issue came to money, suddenly it was different? Why? It made no sense.

But I knew the truth. I had a deep, unconscious fear that people would judge me because I had expanded in this area as well. I wanted to please everyone, I wanted to be loved so badly that subconsciously I not only made doing well financially something wrong but also subconsciously sabotaged my own success. Like so many people, I told myself that money was not spiritual. How crazy is that? Anyone who's become truly wealthy knows the truth—the only way to become wealthy, and stay wealthy, is to find a way to do more for others than anyone else is doing in an area that people really value. If you become a blessing in other people's lives, you too will be blessed. Money is only one of those blessings, but it *is* a blessing. It's simply another form of freedom and abundance.

Money is nothing more than a reflection of your creativity, your capacity to focus, and your ability to add value and receive back. If you can find a way to create value—that is, add value for a massive number of people—you will have an opportunity to have a massive amount of economic abundance in your life.

I had to hit that threshold where I was tired of living that way and where I saw the absurdity of trying to fit in. It's true: if you do well financially, you may be looked at as "the 1%." In my life, as a kid, being a part of the 1% was something that was aspirational. I came from the 99%, I just wasn't willing to settle for that, for my family or for my life. But staying there just to fit in—well, that didn't make any sense. I decided I was tired of blaming others for my lack of financial progress. The story I had of my financial limitations had to go. I would love others, but I would not spend my life trying to please them—especially knowing that to please them I would have to play small. I don't believe in my heart that our creator made us for that. It was time for me to find a way to earn more in the same way I strove to give more, contribute more, love more, and expand my intellectual, emotional, and spiritual capacity.

With that shift in belief, suddenly—when it was clear that this was not a *should* to conquer this area, but a *must*—along with the relational areas of life, strategies started showing up in front of me; they'd probably been there all along, but because of my mind-set, I was blind to them. Your whole world changes when you change your story.

Change your story, change your life. Divorce the story of limitation and marry the story of the truth, and everything changes. I can tell you: when you get rid of the limiting stories, take massive action, and find the strategies that work, the results you can create are truly miraculous.

Let me give you one final example. A dear friend of mine, Julie, a successful screenwriter who gets paid top dollar for her work, could never seem to make any financial headway. By the time she and her husband were in their 50s, they had a modest mortgage on a nice home, but only about $100,000 in an IRA—way, way short of what they'd need to retire. And their money was invested in a "socially responsible" mutual fund that charged high fees and ate up most of their returns.

Julie's husband, Colin, wanted to invest more aggressively, but Julie wouldn't even talk about finances with him. She told him she hated Wall Street and everything it stood for. In fact, the whole idea of money made her uncomfortable. To her, money was evil.

But then a breakthrough happened. Julie attended my seminar Unleash the Power Within (UPW), where we use the power of Strategy, Story, and changing the State of your mind, body, and emotions to create breakthroughs in every area of people's lives. UPW is intense: I use music, dynamic movement, humor, and a host of other tools to put the audience in a peak state—and that's when breakthroughs happen.

Julie's goal that weekend was to turn her financial life around. How did she do it? First, she recognized that something had to change, or she and Colin were looking forward to some very painful "golden years." It finally hit her that her negative beliefs about money were creating constant pain in her marriage and in her future, and she asked herself, "Where did this story come from?" And then Julie did something really important: she dug down deep and asked herself, "Is this what I really believe? We are not born believing money is good or evil. So where did this belief come from?"

She didn't have to go very far to find the answer. Both of Julie's parents grew up during the Great Depression. Her mother never got the chance to go to college even though her academic scores were off the charts. Instead, she worked as a department store clerk for $9 a week, and didn't dare complain about the low wages or long hours on her feet. Julie grew up hearing the stories over and over: how the rich exploit the poor, how banks and Wall Street stockbrokers destroyed the economy, how you can't trust the stock market. So Julie made the association in her brain: "If I become a wealthy investor, I'll be a bad person, and my mother won't love me."

Julie realized that the story she'd been telling herself about the evils of wealth wasn't her story after all; it was her mother's story. "Money is the root of all evil," was her mother's mantra, not hers. This realization jolted her. The truth set her free, and those words lost all of their power over her. (In fact, when she did her homework on the biblical phrase, she found that it's not "Money is the root of all evil," but "*the love of money*" above all else— love, relationships, contribution—that's the recipe for surefire disaster.)

It was an amazing transformation. Once Julie got past her limiting story, she could sit down with her husband for the first time to talk about their finances. He was thrilled they could be partners in taking back control of their financial life. Imagine how hard it is to build wealth when your core belief is that money is evil. They dumped their high-cost mutual funds and transferred their IRA to a diverse portfolio of index funds with Vanguard. Then they put in place a long-term financial plan, like the one you'll be reading about in these pages, to finally put them on the road to financial freedom.

Julie and Colin shifted their story. And what happened? They learned how to play the game and win, they learned how to create an income for life—just like you're going to do in chapter 5.2. Julie and Colin learned how to put an extra $150,000 to $250,000 into their pockets over their investment lifetime just by getting out of those expensive mutual funds. How great do those golden years look now!

Remember, you know the answer, and the secret is simple: change your story, change your life. Divorce your story of limitation and marry the truth. You can make anything happen.

YOUR STATE

It's hard to change your story when you're in a lousy state. If you feel like hell, you don't think to yourself, "Life is beautiful!" Have you ever been really angry with somebody, and suddenly you remembered every freaking thing that person ever did to irritate or annoy you? When you go into an angry state, it switches on the part of your brain that supports that state, and the story that keeps you there quickly appears.

By contrast, if you've ever fallen head over heels in love, can you remember how the world looked? It was like looking through rose-colored lenses: everything was wonderful, right? Rude clerks didn't bother you; crying babies seemed cute. That's how a positive state can change your outlook—your story.

Your mental and emotional state colors your perception and experience of everything in life. When I work with anyone—from world-class athletes to high-powered executives—**we change his or her state first.** There's a part of you that, when it's turned on, can make anything happen; but when it's turned off, the world is dead. You know what I'm talking about, don't you? You know when you get on a roll, and everything flows just perfectly without your even having to think about it? You ace the tennis shot. You say exactly the right thing in the meeting or walk out of the negotiation with exactly what you wanted. On the other hand, we've also all experienced the opposite: we couldn't remember our home address, the name of our dinner host, or spell the word *the*. I call that the stupid state. But a few minutes later, it comes back to you: you remember the answer because you get in a different state.

The purpose of this book is not to try teaching you how to change your state—that's the basis of many of my other books and audios, programs, and live events. But in a nutshell, you can immediately and radically change how you feel (and not just hope you feel good) by learning that **by changing your body first, you can change your mind.**

I teach many ways to create immediate change in your state, but one of the simplest ways is **to change what I call your physiology.** You can change the way you think by changing the way you move and breathe. Emotion is created by motion. Massive action is the cure to all fear. Think about it, fear is physical. You feel it in your mouth, in your body, in your stomach. So is courage, and you can move from one to another in a matter of milliseconds if you learn to make radical shifts in the way you move, breathe, speak, and use your physical body. I've used these insights for almost four decades to turn around some of the world's greatest peak-performance athletes, financial traders, and business and political leaders. Last year, Harvard University did a scientific study that proved the validity of this approach.

Social psychologist and Harvard professor Amy Cuddy offered a "no-tech life hack" in her famous 2012 TED Talk when she asked the audience to change their posture for two minutes. Cuddy's research showed that just assuming "power poses" or postures of high power (think Wonder Woman with her hands on her hips and legs firmly planted on the ground; or the guy in your office leaning back in his chair, hands clasped behind his head, elbows out wide—you know the one) increased testosterone (the dominance hormone) by 20%, while simultaneously reducing cortisol (the major stress hormone) by 25%. The impact of this biochemical change immediately transforms your willingness to face fears and take risks. All within just two minutes of changing your body. In Cuddy's study, 86 percent of the power posers reported feeling more likely to take chances. But when the second set of volunteers were asked to stand or sit for two minutes in more passive poses, with their legs and arms crossed tightly, their testosterone levels *dropped* by 10 percent, and the stress hormone rose by 15 percent. Far fewer of these men and women, only 60 percent, behaved assertively. Remember, these weren't just psychological changes but actual biochemical changes, hormonal changes. What I have taught for 38 years and what all of my students knew was true through experience was now validated by science. What does this mean? It means, basically, you rock. You've got some swagger in your step, you're ready to put yourself on the line, to take the necessary risks and shape your world. Two minutes of posing can lead to the changes that either configure your brain to be assertive, confident, and comfortable, or really stress reactive. Our bodies are able to change our minds!

There was a time in my life when I was overweight and depressed, living in a studio apartment in Venice, California, staring at the empty furniture and listening to Neil Diamond records. Pretty scary, huh? One day a friend who hadn't seen me in a long time stopped by. He took one look at me and said, "Man, what *happened* to you?" It snapped me out of my trance. I decided then and there to break the pattern.

So I put on my running shoes and grabbed my Sony Walkman. (Yes, I'm ancient enough to have owned one of those.) And in those days, you had to be committed to your music: you had one album to listen to, not 10,000 songs to choose from. I turned to the legendary rock band Heart, put on the song "Barracuda," and let the beat ignite me. I took off running with the determination that I was going to run as hard and as fast as I had ever run in my life, and I wasn't going to stop until I spit up blood. To say I was determined to push myself beyond my limits would be a serious understatement.

I'm sure it must have been a hilarious sight, given my excess 38 pounds and my beer belly flopping back and forth in the wind as I ran like a banshee. When I literally couldn't breathe an ounce more of air, I collapsed on the beach and grabbed a journal I had brought with me. And in that state of absolute conviction, determination, exhilaration, and exhaustion, I sat and wrote down everything in my life I would no longer tolerate. The way my body was, my laziness, my shallow intimate relationship, and my disastrous finances. Right across from it, I wrote what I was now committed to creating in my life—and in that pumped-up, invigorated state, I felt certain I could find the way.

With a strong enough state, you will develop a strong story. My story was: "*This ends here and now; my new life begins today.*" And I meant it with every ounce of my being. I discovered that when you change your state *and* your story, you find or create the right strategy to get what you're absolutely committed to. **That's how you create a real breakthrough—a new state with a new story and a proven strategy.**

I went on to lose 30 pounds in the next 30 days, and 38 pounds total in a little more than six weeks. I was maniacal in my commitment. I set a new standard that day about who I was and what I stood for. It has not waned in the 30-plus years since that day (and my weight has never returned to that level either).

I went from earning less than $38,000 a year to more than $1 million a year just a little more than a year later. It was a level of change I couldn't even imagine creating at the time. More importantly, I regained my emotional and psychological fitness—the two forces that truly change how someone's life turns out. Determination, faith, and courage began to be the forces that guided my every action going forward.

Great strategies can surround you but they will be invisible to you unless you put yourself in a strong, determined, and empowered state. A state that will automatically breed the beliefs and stories that you can, must, and will achieve—and that you are committed to. With state and story combined, you'll not only find the strategies that work, you will execute them and experience the rewards you desire and deserve. Do I have your full attention? If there's any area of your life that you're living that is far less than the life you desire, it's time to change one or more of these elements.

Remember: we all get what we tolerate. So stop tolerating excuses within yourself, limiting beliefs of the past, or half-assed or fearful states. Use your body as a tool to snap yourself into a place of sheer will, determination, and commitment. Face your challenges head on with the core belief that problems are just speed bumps on the road to your dreams. And from that place, when you take massive action—with an effective and proven strategy—you will rewrite your history.

It's time to no longer be one of the many but to become one of the few. One of the few who step up, own your true capability financially and in every area of your life. Most people start out with high aspirations but settle for a life and lifestyle far beneath their true capabilities. They let disappointments destroy them. Disappointment is inevitable when you are attempting to do anything of great scale. **Instead, let your disappointments drive you to find new answers; discipline your disappointments.** Learn from every failure, act on those learnings, and success becomes inevitable.

So next time you come up with a reason why you can't do something, when you know in your heart that your spirit is unlimited, call bullshit on yourself. Change your state. Change your focus. Come back to the truth. Adjust your approach and go after what you really want.

Okay, deep breath. Or loud scream. Get up and shake and move. With these 9 Myths—these past limitations—now out of our way, it's time to move on to Step 3 on our 7-Step path to Financial Freedom. We're going to make the game winnable by coming up with a specific number—a number that reflects your *exact financial dreams realized.* Then we'll create a plan, improve that plan, and find ways to speed it up so you can achieve your financial dreams sooner than you may have ever imagined.

WHAT'S THE PRICE
OF YOUR DREAMS?
MAKE THE GAME WINNABLE

WHAT'S THE PRICE
OF YOUR DREAMS?
MAKE THE GAME WINNABLE

All men dream, but not equally.
—T. E. LAWRENCE

I usually kick off my financial seminars with a question: "What's the price of your dreams?" Then I invite people to stand up and tell me what it's going to take for them to be financially secure, independent, or free. Most of them don't have a clue. There's a lot of shuffling and squirming in the room, and then maybe a few hands shoot up. In hundreds of seminars with hundreds of thousands of people from all walks of life, I've heard just about every number imaginable.

So let me ask you personally now: How much money will *you* need to be financially secure, independent, or free? Just take a guess. You don't have to be right—or even logical. Is it $1 million? $5 million? $500 million? Take a second right now, go with your gut, and write down the number, either in the margin of this book, in a notebook app, or just on a scrap of paper. It's important to write it down, because writing it anchors it and makes it real.

Did you get it done? Soon you'll see why this step is an important first action.

Now, my experience tells me that if you're like most people, that number probably feels a bit large to you right now, doesn't it? Well, keep reading, because we're going to do a few easy exercises to help you tame that number. And I'll bet you'll find out that it can be made much smaller than you ever imagined. **In fact, you're going to learn there's not just one "magic number," because there are five different *levels* of financial dreams that will set you free.** And no matter if you're just starting out or getting ready to retire, no matter how solid or shaky your balance sheet is right now, I guarantee you that at least one or two of those dreams will be within your reach. How? It starts with understanding what you truly need.

Recently, at one of my high-end programs, a young man in the back of the room stood up to name the price of his dreams. He threw back his shoulders and announced, "A billion dollars."

There were a lot of *ooohs* and *aaahs* from the crowd. This person was in his 20s, one of the younger participants at the conference, and he probably hadn't earned his first million yet. So I asked him to consider what that number really meant.

Remember in chapter 1.4, "Money Mastery: It's Time to Break Through," when we talked about how everything people do, they do for a reason? Just as a reminder, there are 6 Basic Human Needs: Certainty, Uncertainty/Variety, Significance, Connection/Love, Growth, and Contribution. So why did this young man want a billion dollars? Which of these needs was he trying to meet? Certainty? You can get Certainty in your life for a lot less than a billion dollars! How about Variety? You can get plenty of Variety with a million dollars, or much less, right? Connection and Love? Hardly. If he gets a billion dollars, there will be a lot of people who want to be in his life, just like lottery winners who suddenly discover dozens of relatives and "friends" they never knew they had. With that kind of money, he'll get connection, all right, but not the connections he wants and needs! Growth and Contribution? By his demeanor, I doubt these were at the top of this young man's list when he named his number.

So when you look at the human needs, which one do you think drives him the most? Clearly, it's Significance. As he said, with a billion dollars, people would take him seriously; he would *matter*. This might be true. But the problem is when he gets a billion, it still won't be enough—because **when you seek Significance, you're always comparing yourself with someone else.** And there's always someone bigger, taller, stronger, faster, richer, funnier, younger, more handsome, more beautiful, with a bigger yacht, a nicer car, a nicer home. So while **there's nothing wrong with significance, if you make it your number one need, you'll never be fulfilled.**

But rather than lecture him, I decided to show him he could feel **significant with a lot less money**—which would make his life a lot easier. After all, he was just picking his number out of the sky. Saying he needed $1 billion made him feel like he was going after an important goal. But the problem is, when you have this huge goal in your head—if in your gut you don't believe it's going to happen—your brain rejects it. It's like living a lie. Have you ever done this? Come up with some ginormous goal, and then a voice in your head pops up to say, "Who are you kidding?" The truth is, you'll never make it happen until it sinks deep into your subconscious—the part of your mind so powerful that it makes your heart beat 100,000 times a day without your ever having to think about it.

Have you ever been driving your car and gotten lost in thought and then suddenly looked up and realized, "Holy sh*t, who's been driving my car for the last five minutes?!" Thankfully, it was the amazing protector of life, your subconscious mind.

To get an idea of how this process works, take a look at the image below. Imagine your brain divided into an upper half and a lower half; the upper half is the conscious mind, while the lower half is your subconscious.

How People Respond in Different Markets

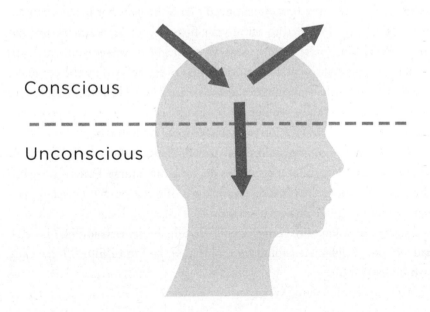

Conscious

Unconscious

Ideas keep trying to lodge in your head, such as "I'm going to make ten million dollars!" or "I'm going to be financially free by the time I'm forty!" But your upper, conscious brain goes, "Screw you! There's no way in hell that will happen!" It quickly rejects the big idea and bounces it back out into space like a tennis ball. But if you resolve within yourself the sense of absolute certainty that "I'm going to do this!" and then **you start to build a plan**—something extraordinary happens. You begin to develop the certainty you can actually achieve it. And with newfound confidence, you suddenly see there is a way to get it done. You'll find a role model who's already achieving what you're after, and you'll take massive action. **The goal seeps down into your subconscious, and it goes to work to make your dream a reality. That's when the magic happens!**

Now, I doubt that you think you need $1 billion to fulfill your financial dreams. But I'd be willing to bet that the number you chose to feel financially secure or independent is pretty intimidating. Almost everybody makes that number bigger than it needs to be, because he or she doesn't take the time to calculate what it really costs to live at different lifestyle levels. And that's why so many never begin to work toward it. They talk a good game, get excited about it, they tell people their big dream, but they never act on it. Why? Because psychologically they don't have *Certainty* that they can do it. And Certainty is the first human need that influences our behavior or actions. Fact. If you've failed to act in your financial world, it's partly because you're uncertain, you're unsure as to what is right or wrong and which approach will succeed or fail. Or you're feeling overwhelmed by the complexity of the system that no one has taken the time to walk you through with clarity. With uncertainty, we default to doing nothing or at least procrastinating. We put off until tomorrow what we need to do today.

To help my would-be billionaire friend identify the real price of his dreams, so that they could lodge in his unconscious and become real, I asked him some questions. They're the same kinds of questions I'll be asking you in a moment to guide you on your path.

I started by asking my young friend what his lifestyle would be like if he had a billion dollars. He thought for a moment and then said, "I'd have my own Gulfstream!"

"Your own jet!" I said. "Where will you fly to?"

He said, "Well, I live in New York. I'd probably fly down to the Bahamas. And I'd probably fly to LA for some meetings."

I had him write down how many times he'd fly in a year, and he figured it was probably a maximum of 12 flights. And how much would a jet cost him? We looked it up, and a long-distance Gulfstream G650 would cost him about $65 million; a slightly used Gulfstream IV would only set him back about $10 million. Not including fuel, maintenance, and crew. Then we looked up the cost of chartering a private jet instead of owning one: a mid-size jet was all he really needed for himself and three family members to fly, and that's around $2,500 an hour. He would be flying for maybe 100 hours a year for a grand total of $250,000 per year, or around $5,000 per hour; or $500,000 if he wanted to fly by Gulfstream on every flight—still far less than the annual price of maintenance on many jets, and at a cost that would be less than 1% of the cost of buying that Gulfstream. Even from the stage, I could see his eyes lighting up and his mind working.

"So what else would you buy with your billion dollars?" I asked.

"A private island!"

That was something I could relate to. I own a small island paradise in the country of Fiji. It was a wild dream I had early in my life to find an escape someday where I could take my family and friends and live. In my early 20s, I traveled to islands all over the world searching for my Shangri-La. When I arrived in Fiji, I found it. A place with not only magnificent beauty but beautiful souls as well. I couldn't afford it at the time, but I bought a piece of a little backpacker resort with 125 acres on the island. I really didn't have the money, and it probably wasn't the best investment at first. But it was part of what I call my Dream Bucket—something you'll learn about later in this book. Still, I made it happen, and I'm proud to say that over the years, I've purchased and converted it into a protected ecological preserve with over 500 acres of land and nearly three miles of ocean frontage. I've turned Namale Resort and Spa into the number one resort in Fiji for the last decade, and it's consistently rated among the top ten resorts in the South Pacific. But how often do I visit this paradise? With my crazy schedule, maybe four to six weeks a year. So my dream has come true: everybody else has a great time there!

I told my young friend, "If you want to enjoy your own island, you might not want to be in the hotel business. And trust me, you're only going to be there a few weeks a year at the most." We looked up the costs and found out he could buy an island in the Bahamas for $10 or so—and then he would have to spend $30 million to $40 million to build a small resort! Or he could rent my friend Richard Branson's Necker Island resort for a week and bring all his friends and family for less than $350,000, with a staff of 50 people to take care of them all. If he did that every year for a decade, it would only cost $3.5 million versus $30 million to $40 million, with no work to maintain the property.

We worked through his list, and guess how much it would take to have the lifestyle he wants for the rest of his life? When we added up the real cost of even his wildest dreams, not just his needs, it came to a grand total of not $1 billion, not $500 million, not $100 million, not $50 million, but *$10 million* to have *everything* he dreamed of having in his lifestyle and never have to work to pay for it—and his dreams were gigantic! The difference between $10 million and $1 billion is astronomical. These numbers exist in different universes.

The challenge is, when we get to really big numbers, people's minds don't fathom what they really mean. There's a radical difference between a million, a billion, and a trillion. Even President Obama uses the terms *millionaires* and *billionaires* in the same breath, as if they're in any way related—they're not. Let me prove it to you. I'm going to give you a little test. I want you to think and make a first guess as to the answer. This exercise will help you gain perspective on a million versus a billion versus the figure the government now uses so often: a trillion. In fact, in Washington, a trillion is the new billion, as they say.

My first question is: How long ago was one million seconds ago? Take a moment, even if you don't know—what do you guess?

The answer is: 12 days ago! How close were you? Don't feel bad, most people have no clue. If you got it, congratulations. Now we're going to up the ante. Since you now have a perspective of what a million is (a million seconds being 12 days ago), how long ago was a billion seconds ago? Stay with me, come on; make a guess, commit to a number. The answer is: 32 years ago! How close were you? For most people, they're pretty far off. **That's the difference between a millionaire and a billionaire: 12 days or 32 years! Do you see what I mean by saying they live in "different universes"?** You can never say "millionaires" and "billionaires" in the same breath and be talking about the same thing.

Just to complete the thought: When you hear the US government has

$17 trillion in debt, how much is a trillion? Well, if a billion seconds was 32 years ago, how long ago was a trillion seconds? The answer: nearly 32,000 years ago (31,689, to be exact)! When humans were not even called humans! **The point of this exercise is to get you to realize that we blur large numbers, and if you get down to the facts, an extraordinary lifestyle probably costs less than you think it does.**

But back to our would-be billionaire. Now, don't get me wrong: $10 million is still a hefty sum but probably within reach for this young entrepreneur over the course of his career. Who knows? He might actually end up with a billion—if he invents the next Instagram. But what if he doesn't? **He could still live the extraordinary life he was dreaming of for 99% less money than he thought he needed.** He wouldn't need to be a billionaire to live like one.

I'll be willing to bet that once you find out the real price of *your* dreams, the number it would take for you to really get where you want to be is a lot less than you think! **And always remember the ultimate truth: life is not about money, it's about emotion.** The real goal is to have the lifestyle you want, not the things. When you die, someone else gets those things anyway. They're not yours. I have no illusions: as much as I cherish and enjoy "my" resort in Fiji, I know I'm just the caretaker. Someday someone else will own this property. But I love that I have nurtured it into a destination where people from all over the world come to experience joy, romance, and adventure. It's part of my legacy—and that's what gives *me* joy. Attaining possessions is not the goal. **Money itself is not the goal.** Our worth is not measured by the weight of our bank accounts but, rather, by the weight of our souls. The path to money, the places money can take us, the time and freedom and opportunity money can bring—these are what we're *really* after.

> You can have it all. Just not all at once.
> —OPRAH WINFREY

Take a moment now and think about what you really want your money to buy. Not everybody wants to live like Donald Trump or Floyd "Money" Mayweather! Is your dream to travel the globe, exploring ancient cities or photographing lions in the Serengeti? Is it owning your own beach house in the Bahamas or a penthouse in New York? Is it starting your own business— the next Snapchat, or creating an extraordinary contribution to humanity like the next Charity Water? Is it something as simple as sending your kids to college and having enough left over for a house in the country with a big vegetable garden? Or is your dream just peace of mind—knowing you can be free forever from debt and worry? Wherever your dreams may take you, I'm going to show you a path to get there. Even if you don't get all the way to the summit, you can reach the dreams that matter most to you and celebrate your victories along the way. Because money is a game of emotions, and we're going to come up with some numbers that will ring your bells and make you say, "I'm certain! I promise myself I can get there!"

Like all journeys, before you get started, you'll need to take stock of where you are. We'll work together on a few simple calculations. If you've never taken the time to figure out exactly what it's going to take to achieve your financial goals, you're not alone. Often, many of those who have earned millions of dollars haven't developed a plan to sustain their lifestyle without having to work at least some of the time. And as we've already said, more than *half* of Americans haven't even tried to calculate how much money they'll need to retire, including 46% of all financial planners! Why don't we know our basic financial picture? The number one reason I've found, after hearing from hundreds of thousands of people from a hundred different countries, is that people are *afraid to know*.

It's like stepping on the scale. You know you've gained weight, but you don't *want* to know how much. It's a form of denial; a way to put off making a change. High school wrestlers and professional boxers step on that thing every day, so that if they're off target on their weight, they'll know right away and can do something about it. **You can't manage your health if you can't measure it. And the same goes for your finances.** You can't reach your financial dreams unless you know precisely how much it will take to get there. I'm here to help you set yourself apart from the masses who hide their heads in the sand when it comes to their money. In a minute, we'll do some quick, easy number crunching to find out where you are and where you need to be. (If adding a few figures is a challenge for you, remember that there's a calculator on your phone! And you can also go to our app, which will ask you the questions and calculate the numbers for you automatically. See www.tonyrobbins.com/masterthegame.)

But first let's look at those five financial dreams. When I say the words "financial security," "financial vitality," "financial independence," "financial freedom," and "absolute financial freedom," do those sound like the exact same thing to you? Do they bring up emotions that feel different in your body when you say them out loud? Give it a try. Which one feels higher: security or vitality? How about vitality or independence? Independence or freedom? What about absolute freedom? Each of these five financial dreams is incrementally bigger, isn't it? And the numbers needed to reach them would be different.

Of these five dreams, you may discover that you are committed to only two or three of them. For some people, financial security alone is life changing and gives them enormous freedom. And so, in designing this exercise, I've included these dreams as steps along the road to absolute financial freedom. Or, if you remember that mountain earlier in this book, as base camps along the climb to the summit. And remember, not all of us need or want to go all the way to the peak of Everest. For some of us, financial vitality would be a blessing, and independence would put us over the moon! Not all of these dreams are "musts" for everybody.

I'm going to invite you to read the five and pick the three that matter to you most—what I call the **Three to Thrive.** You'll have three targets: short-, medium-, and long-term goals. It's set up this way because we don't build on failure; we build only on success. If you're just shooting for the big number in the distance, it might feel too far off, or even overwhelming, and as a result, you may never truly begin the journey. We need a target close enough that we can feel certain it's achievable, and in the relatively near future. That's what gets you to take action and turn a short-term goal into reality. And remember to claim your victories along the way. Why wait until you're financially independent to celebrate? Why not win at different stages? That's what encourages you, excites you, and gives you momentum.

> It takes as much energy to wish as it does to plan.
> —ELEANOR ROOSEVELT

DREAM 1:
FINANCIAL SECURITY

What does security mean? Instead of telling you what it is, let me ask you: How amazing would you feel if these five things were paid for as long as you live, without ever having to work to pay for them again?

1. Your **home mortgage,** for as long as you live—paid forever. *You never have to work again to pay for your house!*
2. Your **utilities** for the home—paid forever. You never have to work to pay your phone bill or to keep the lights on.
3. All the **food** for your family—paid forever.
4. Your basic **transportation** needs,
5. Your basic **insurance** costs—all of them paid for without your ever working another day in your life.

I'd bet that your quality of life would be pretty fulfilling, wouldn't it? You'd feel pretty secure if you knew these things were covered.

Now for some good news: Remember that number you wrote down earlier—the amount you thought it would take to be financially secure and free? It was probably not as extreme as my billion-dollar friend's number but probably felt pretty large, didn't it? Well, I'll bet when you figure these numbers out, you're going to be surprised that the dream of Financial

Security is probably a lot closer than you think. Or if you're one of the rare few who underestimate, you'll have a reality check, and you'll know the precise number it will take to realize your financial dreams.

If you haven't downloaded our free app already, do it now. Or use the worksheet below and jot down what you pay for these five items on a monthly basis. It's really simple: What's your current mortgage payment? (If you're in an early stage of your life where you don't own a home yet, put your monthly rent here. Or you can estimate or check online what your mortgage payment would be on something that may not be your ideal home, but more like a starter home.) If you have your records, great. Next, what's your utility bill each month? Third, what do you spend on food? Keep going, and if you don't have the numbers, take a guess—you can always go back and change them later, but you don't want to lose momentum.

AVERAGE US ANNUAL CONSUMER SPENDING

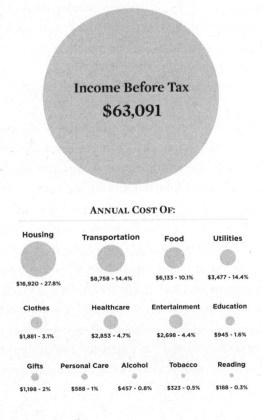

Income Before Tax
$63,091

ANNUAL COST OF:

Housing	Transportation	Food	Utilities
$16,920 - 27.8%	$8,758 - 14.4%	$6,133 - 10.1%	$3,477 - 14.4%

Clothes	Healthcare	Entertainment	Education
$1,881 - 3.1%	$2,853 - 4.7%	$2,698 - 4.4%	$945 - 1.6%

Gifts	Personal Care	Alcohol	Tobacco	Reading
$1,198 - 2%	$588 - 1%	$457 - 0.8%	$323 - 0.5%	$188 - 0.3%

Let's really get a number down that's reasonable. Or pick up your bank book or go online and get your numbers. Just to keep the momentum for you right now in case those aren't easily accessible, let me give you an example.

Do you remember my friend Angela, who I introduced to you in the first chapter? She's 48 years old and single. She's trying to figure out what it would take to be financially secure. Her first guess was $3 million. Could that be right? Or even in the ballpark? So I asked her to go through this exercise, and write down her five basic monthly expenses. As it turned out, her numbers were almost identical to the national averages, which you'll see in the list here.

1. Rent or mortgage payment: $_____ per month (Angela's Average: $1,060)
2. Food, household: $_____ per month (Angela's Average: $511)
3. Gas, electric, water, phone: $_____ per month (Angela's Average: $289)
4. Transportation: $_____ per month (Angela's Average: $729)
5. Insurance payments: $_____ per month (Angela's Average: $300)
                        Total $_____ per month (Angela's Average: $2,889)

Total basic monthly expenses: _____ × 12 = _____ per year
(US average basic annual expenses: $34,668)

When she was done, I had her add it up and multiply the monthly total by 12. That shows the annual income she'll need to cover these items for life—without working—to be financially secure. As you can see, her number of $34,000 is virtually identical to the number for the average American.

Now, how would Angela be able to have $34,000 a year without working? Remember, she's going to build a money machine. She's automated her savings of 10% of her income. She's putting it in a Roth 401(k), where it's being invested in low-fee index funds with an estimated growth rate of 6%. (This is the percent that Jack Bogle estimates the markets will return over the next decade. However, the average stock market return has been 9.2% over the last 20 years.) We ran it through the wealth calculator, which you'll do in the next chapter, and she found out that instead of the $3 million she thought it would take to achieve financial security, she would need to accumulate only $640,000 in her Freedom Fund to have that $34,000 a year for the rest of her life—less than a quarter of the amount she thought she needed!

At first she was shocked. She asked me in disbelief, "That's all it would take for me to have this? I'd still have to work, right?" I told her of course she would, but not to pay for her home, food, utilities, transportation, or basic health care! By the way, these five items, on average, represent 65% of most people's expenses. So Angela now had a way to pay for 65% of her overhead without working. And remember, most of us want to do something meaningful. Without work, we're a little crazy. We just don't want to *have* to work! She could work part-time to pay for the rest of her expenses or full-time and have all that income for other things. I asked her how that would make her feel if everything from her home to transportation was paid for without her working for the rest of her life. "Extraordinary!" she said. "That's an achievable goal. That's something I could figure out how to make happen." I said, "Exactly!" And what you could see in her eyes was a sense of certainty, and because she was certain, she had a reason to act.

I reminded her, "By the way, this doesn't have to be your ultimate goal. It might be your short-term goal." For some people, all they want is financial security, like someone in a later stage of life who may have taken a hit in 2008. For someone who is middle-aged or young, you'll blow through this goal—as long as you know what your number is and you act upon the seven steps of this book.

If you're wondering, by the way, how long it would take to accumulate whatever your security number is, take heart. You don't have to do this calculation. We'll do it in the next chapter, "What's Your Plan?," and if you want, the app will calculate the number for you. Together we'll create three plans: a conservative plan, a moderate plan, and an aggressive plan. And you'll decide which of these plans are most manageable and achievable.

Remember the aspiring billionaire? His annual income for financial security was a mere $79,000. A far cry from the billionaire neighborhood. Your number might be higher or lower. **All you need to know now is the annual income you need to achieve financial security.** If you haven't already done it, calculate the numbers on the app or do it right here now.

1. Rent or mortgage payment: $_____ per month
2. Food, household: $_____ per month
3. Gas, electric, water, phone: $_____ per month
4. Transportation: $_____ per month
5. Insurance payments: $_____ per month
6. Total $_____ per month
7. Total basic monthly expenses: _____ × 12 = _____ per year

By the way, we can't go on to the next goal without talking about something that's a simple requirement, not a dream. And it's something almost everybody should be able to achieve relatively quickly, though few people have it in place: **an emergency/protection fund. According to a Princeton University–University of Chicago study in 2014, 40% of Americans say they couldn't come up with $2,000 if they needed it.** Yikes! That's terrifying! Why do we need to have an emergency supply of cash on hand? What if there's an unexpected interruption in your income flow? It happens in almost everybody's life at some point. An interruption can be a health problem, it can be a problem with your business, it can mean being displaced from a job. So you need some money to cover yourself for somewhere between three to 12 months. But for most people, three months is too short a time, while 12 months may seem like a lot. So perhaps you start by putting aside a few months' overhead, and gradually build toward six or 12 months' worth. Wouldn't it be wonderful to know that if something happened, you had a year to be able to get yourself back on track? You'd still have a roof overhead, food in the cupboard, and the bills would get paid.

Again, this goal is not for an annual income for life. Once you have that, you're set. This goal is just emergency cash to protect you until you develop a large enough nest egg to take care of yourself every year for the rest of your life without working, no matter what happens.

How much do *you* need? Well, you know what your monthly overhead is. So write down that number and memorize it. Again, you can do this exercise on the app, and the number will be saved for you and always available at a glance in your pocket. My friend Angela, who set aside 10% of her salary to build her money machine, started looking into her spending patterns to find more savings. Remember how she realized it was cheaper to buy a brand-new car than to keep fixing her old one? Well, she also found a way to set aside an additional 8% to build her emergency protection fund. She completed her goal, and now she sleeps much better at night! If you haven't already, it's crucial you set up an emergency fund. (And I guarantee you'll have some great new ideas on how to do this after reading chapters 3.3 and 3.4, "Speed It Up.") Keep that amount in cash or in a safe place like an FDIC-insured bank account.

Now let's move on to the next level of dreams. With security achieved, let's look at:

DREAM 2:
FINANCIAL VITALITY

What do I mean by vitality? This goal is a mile marker on your path to Financial Independence and Freedom. You're not all the way there yet, but it's the place where you can be secure and also have some extras thrown in that you can enjoy without having to work.

What do you pay for clothing every month? Is it $100? $500? $1,000? How about for entertainment (cable TV, movies, concert tickets)? How about going out for dinner? Is it Chili's or Nobu tonight? So for food and entertainment, are you shelling out $200 a month or $2,000 plus? How about small indulgences or little luxuries like a gym membership, a manicure or massage, or monthly golf dues? Is it $50, $500, or $1,000 plus? Whatever it is for you, how would it feel if *half* of those costs were already covered **without having to work,** for the rest of your life? That's what happens when you reach Financial Vitality. Sounds like something worth celebrating, doesn't it?

Here's how to calculate your Financial Vitality:

1. *Half* of your current monthly clothing costs $_____ per month
2. *Half* of your current monthly dining and
   entertainment costs $_____ per month
3. *Half* of your current small indulgence or
   little luxury costs $_____ per month

4. Total additional monthly income for vitality $_____ per month

5. You already know your monthly Financial
   Security number (line 6 from page 216),
   so add that here $_____ per month

6. Total monthly income necessary for Vitality $_____ per month

7. Now multiply that by 12 and you'll have
   the annual amount you need for
   financial vitality: $_____ × 12 = _____ per year

Again, just type in these figures, and all of this math will be done for you on the app.

DREAM 3:
FINANCIAL INDEPENDENCE

Pop the champagne, because when you've reached Financial Independence, you no longer have to work to have the same lifestyle you have today! The annual interest earned on the return from your savings and investments (your Freedom Fund) will provide you with the income that you need—while you sleep. You are now truly financially independent; *that is, independent of work.* How amazing would that feel? What kind of peace of mind would that bring you and your family?

Financial Independence means that money is now your slave—you are not the slave to money. Money works for you; you don't work for it. If you don't like your job, you can tell your boss to shove it. Or you can keep right on working with a smile on your face and a song in your heart, knowing that you're working because you *want* to, not because you *have* to.

So let's figure out how much money it would take to maintain your current lifestyle. This number might be really easy to calculate because, unfortunately, most people spend as much as they earn! Or sometimes more than they earn! If you made $100,000 and you spent $100,000 that year (including paying your taxes) just to maintain your lifestyle, your financial independence is $100,000. If you spend less than you earn, congratulations! Unfortunately, you are the exception, not the rule. So if it costs you only $80,000 to live, on a $100,000 salary, then $80,000 a year is what you need to be independent.

So what's your Financial Independence number?
Go to the app or write it here now: $_____.

Remember, clarity is power. When your brain knows a real number, your conscious mind will figure out a way to get there. You now know the income you need to be financially secure, vital, and independent. So let's see what happens when your dreams get bigger.

> Dare to live the dreams you have dreamed for yourself.
> —RALPH WALDO EMERSON

Let me tell you the story of Ron and Michelle, a couple I met at one of the seminars I hold every year at my resort in Fiji. They were in their mid-30s, with two small children. Successful people, they owned a small business in Colorado. Ron was great at running their business, but neither of them paid attention to their household finances. (That's why he was in Fiji attending my Business Mastery event, to grow his business 30% to 130%.) Their accountant drew up personal financial statements for them every month, but they never bothered to look at them! No wonder they were having trouble envisioning the life that they wanted—which turned out to be a life of contribution.

When I asked Ron what he needed to be financially set, as I asked the young would-be billionaire, his number was $20 million. I wanted to prove to him it could be a lot lower than that and still have an extraordinary quality of life for him and his family, so I walked the couple through what they *actually* spent every month. (Bear in mind that, as business owners, Ron and Michelle's annual household income is clearly higher than the average American's.)

First we started with Financial Security, and he told me his five numbers:

Mortgage on their main home	$6,000 per month
Utilities	$1,500 per month
Transportation	$1,200 per month
Food	$2,000 per month
Insurance	$ 750 per month
Total	$11,450 × 12 = $137,400 per year

So for Financial Security, all they needed was $137,400 in income per year. Well within their reach! By the way, if Ron wanted to know how much he would need to accumulate in his nest egg or his Freedom Fund, most financial planners would tell him to multiply his annual income number by 10, or even 15. But today, with such low returns on safe, secure investments, that's not realistic. Remember, on the way up the mountain (the accumulation phase), you might put your investments in an aggressive portfolio that could give you 7% to 10%. On the way back down the mountain (the decumulation phase), you will want your investments in a secure and less volatile environment, where by nature you would likely get smaller returns. So it might be smarter to use 5% as a more conservative assumption. Ten times your income assumes a 10% return. Twenty times your income assumes a 5% return.

Ron discovered that financial security would be within reach—20 × $137,400 = $2,748,000—a number far less than the $20 million he'd projected.

For Financial Independence, they figured they needed $350,000 a year to maintain their lifestyle at the current level, because they had a second home and a lot of toys. Michelle was fond of things with Louis Vuitton labels on them. So, conservatively, they needed $7 million ($350,000 × 20) in their critical mass to live that way without working. Ron was amazed to realize that this number was *almost two-thirds less* than the $20 million he thought it would take! And he's going to get there a lot sooner than he imagined, having to save **$13 million less** than he'd previously estimated!

DREAM 4:
FINANCIAL FREEDOM

Once you've freed yourself from the need to work for the rest of your life, how about freeing up your lifestyle? **Financial Freedom would mean you're independent, you've got everything you have today, plus two or three significant luxuries you want in the future, and you don't have to work to pay for them either.** To get there you need to ask yourself, "What annual income would I need to have the lifestyle I *want and deserve*?" What do you want the money for? Is it for the freedom to travel? To own a bigger home or a second vacation home? Maybe you've always wanted a boat or a luxury car? Or do you want to contribute more to your community or church?

Let's go back to Ron and Michelle. They were already living the lifestyle they wanted for $350,000 a year. So, I asked, what would make them feel financially free? Would it be a bigger home? A condo in Aspen? A boat?

You know what Ron said? He'd feel financially free if he could donate $100,000 a year to their church—and maybe throw in a small Bass fishing boat and a ski vacation condo in Steamboat Springs for his family.

It was an awesome answer. I was so moved by his goal to contribute, I couldn't wait to help them find a way to make it happen. I pointed out that Ron made about $500,000 a year in income, and spent only $350,000—he could already set aside that kind of money for the church if he really wanted to. But how great would it feel if he and Michelle could make that kind of contribution without working? Just from investment income alone?

After adding the costs of financing the boat and condo, along with his contribution, for Financial Freedom they would have to add $165,000 a year to their number for Financial Independence. In other words, they would need $515,000 a year (× 20), or $10.2 million in their money machine. But remember, this number represents an even better lifestyle than he has today! It's a lot, but still roughly *half* of what Ron had thought they needed *just to be independent.*

The world that Ron and Michelle wanted was so close—they just didn't know it. But once you figure out the price of your dreams, there are ways you can get there faster and for less money than you ever imagined.

What would it take for *you* to be financially free?

What items would you add to your total: A sports car? A second home? Or a big donation, like Ron and Michelle? Whatever they are, write them down, and add the cost to your total for Independence. That's the price of Financial Freedom. And if it seems too steep, just wait. You'll learn how to tame that number in the coming chapters.

Here's how Ron calculated his Financial Freedom numbers:

1. Monthly donation to church $8,333 per month
2. 20' Bass fishing boat costing $50,000 financed at 5% =
   monthly payment of $530 per month
3. Family ski condo mortgage costing $800,000 at 4.5% =
   monthly payment of $4,880 per month

4. Monthly income for Financial Independence $29,167 per month

5. Total monthly income number for Freedom $42,910 per month

6. Now multiply that by 12, and you'll have
   the annual amount you need for Financial
   Freedom $42,910 × 12 = $514,920 per year

What are your numbers?

1. Luxury item #1 per month   _____ $_____ per month

2. Luxury item #2 per month   _____ $_____ per month

3. Donation per month   _____ $_____ per month

4. **Monthly** income for Financial Independence
   (Whatever number you calculated
   annually divided by 12) $_____ per month

5. Total monthly income number
   for Financial Freedom $_____ per month

6. Now multiply that by 12, and you'll have the
   annual amount you need for Financial Freedom $_____ per year

DREAM 5:
ABSOLUTE FINANCIAL FREEDOM

How about *Absolute* Financial Freedom? **What would it be like if you could do anything you wanted, anytime you wanted? How would it feel if you and your family never had to want for anything again?** If you were able to give freely and live completely on your own terms—not anybody else's—and all without ever having to work to pay for it. The money you make while you sleep—your investment income—would provide for your unlimited lifestyle. Maybe you would buy your parents the home of their dreams, or set up a foundation to feed the hungry or help clean up the ocean. Just picture what you could do.

I asked Ron and Michelle to tell me the biggest dreams they could dream. What would Absolute Financial Freedom look like for them? Once again, I was deeply moved when Michelle told me her paramount dream was to buy a ranch and turn it into a church camp. What would it cost? Ron figured about $2 million to buy it, and $1 million more for improvements.

I could see the excitement build in them when we ran through the numbers.

If they borrowed the money to buy the ranch, they would need about $120,000 ($3 million at 4%) a year to service the debt. And that was already within reach!

So what else? Ron loved adventure and travel, and owning his own plane was an ultimate dream. So I walked him through the same exercise I did with my young would-be billionaire friend, and convinced him that renting a jet would give him a lot of the same convenience and satisfaction at a fraction of the cost of owning and maintaining a Gulfstream or a Cessna Citation. Do you follow me? You don't have to own the jet to have the lifestyle. You don't have to own the sports team to sit in the sky box. And you don't have to pay for the whole team to be an owner—you can be a partial owner and get all the privileges. That's what my friend Magic Johnson did when he was part of the group that purchased the Los Angeles Dodgers, along with my friend Peter Guber and several other partners in Guggenheim Baseball Management, which spent $2.15 billion to get the team and stadium. I can promise you Magic didn't put in $2.15 billion—but he still gets all the joy, the pride, the excitement, the influence, and the fun of being an owner.

This thinking can create the quality of life you want for yourself and those you love. **What makes most people just dreamers versus those who live the dream is that dreamers have never figured out the price of their dreams.** They make the number so big they never begin the journey. There isn't a dream you can't realize if you're committed enough and creative enough, and if you're willing to find a way to add more value to other people's lives than anybody else.

Now, as you can tell, for most people, this category is mostly for fun. In my seminars, I do this exercise only with people who have really big dreams and want to know the price of them. I understand that most people will never achieve Absolute Financial Freedom, but there's power in dreaming and unleashing your desires. Some of these high-octane dreams might excite you and make you want to earn more, and help you reach your goals faster. But there's another reason to do this exercise. You might achieve financial security without working, and then by working part-time at something you enjoy, you could be financially independent. Or it's possible you could achieve Financial Independence through your investment income and part-time work, allowing yourself to experience the luxuries of Financial Freedom with that income.

So go for it! Write down what you would put on this list or in your app. You never know what you could create if your desires were truly unleashed!

Here's how Ron calculated his Absolute Financial Freedom numbers:

1. A ranch for church camp that costs $3 million, financed at 4% = monthly payment of $10,000 per month
2. A Beechcraft Bonanza plane that costs $300,000 financed at 5% = monthly payment of $3,181 per month
3. Monthly income number for Financial Freedom: $42,910 per month
4. Total monthly income for Absolute Financial Freedom: $56,091 per month
5. Now multiply that by 12, and you'll have the annual amount you need for Absolute Financial Freedom: $673,092 per year.

So for a 20-foot fishing boat, a $100,000 yearly donation to their church, a ski vacation condo, a plane, and turning a ranch into a church camp, plus the lifestyle they have today without having to work, Ron and Michelle would need an income of $673,092 per year. Multiplied by 20, they would need to achieve a critical mass of $13.5 million. Still a third less than the number they thought they needed for mere security or independence!

What are your numbers?

1. Luxury item #1 per month   _____ $_____ per month
2. Luxury item #2 per month   _____ $_____ per month
3. Luxury item #3 per month   _____ $_____ per month
4. **Monthly** income for Financial Freedom
   (page 222) $_____ per month
5. Total monthly income number for
   Absolute Financial Freedom $_____ per month
6. Now multiply that by 12, and you'll have
   the annual amount you need for
   Absolute Financial Freedom $_____ per year

> There is only one thing that makes a dream
> impossible to achieve: the fear of failure.
> —PAULO COELHO

How do all those numbers you've written down look to you now? I hope that you've seen how the price of your financial dreams can be much smaller than you ever thought, and that you've picked out three to aim for, including at least one short-term goal and one long-term goal. **Which of these dreams are your Three to Thrive?** The most important for most people—the most common "musts"—are Security, Vitality, and Independence. Or for those who want to reach higher, it's Security, Independence, and Freedom. If you haven't already done it, pick three and write them down. Make them real and put them in your app; key reminder messages will be sent to keep you on target.

If you're a baby boomer who's had a tough time since the meltdown of 2008, which one of these dreams is the absolute must for you? Security, right? Here's the good news: you may not have as many years to build your savings and investments to a critical mass, but you can absolutely have Financial Security, and I'll show you how. Maybe you'll never get to

Independence, but maybe you will if you make it a "must." If you're starting younger, you're way ahead. You might be able to go for Freedom or even Absolute Freedom and not even be stressed about it. But it's important to decide what matters most to you and know your numbers. Why? Because in a few moments, we're moving on to the next chapter, where you'll be able to calculate how many years it will take for you to achieve these dreams based on how much you are saving at a reasonable average annual rate of return. And then we'll make a plan to get there. This is where the rubber meets the road. I'm going to walk you through each step, and everything will be automated for you. It's absolutely critical that you keep moving forward.

I want you to feel empowered and excited by the journey you're on.

I want you to know that you're the creator of your life, not just a manager. Sometimes we forget how much we've really created in our lives. I don't care who you are, I know there are aspects of your life today that once were just a dream or a goal, or seemed impossible. It could have been a job or higher-level position you wanted that at the time seemed beyond your reach, or a car that you were obsessed with, or a place that you always wanted to visit. Maybe you even live there now. Maybe there was somebody in your life, someone you never thought might even go out with you, and now you're married to them. Instead of being back in those days of dreaming, wondering if this person would ever make love to you, perhaps they are beside you now. If so, reach over and give them a kiss right now and remember this relationship once seemed impossible, and you created it.

What's in your life today that was once a dream? What was a desire you had in the past that at the time seemed difficult or impossible to achieve—but now it's in your life today? If you're going to remember that you're the creator of your life and not just the manager of your life's circumstances, first, you must reconnect to the things you have created consciously. Take a moment and jot down three or four of those things. And take note, your list does not need to be made up of all giant accomplishments. Sometimes the little things that seem difficult or impossible, when conquered or realized, provide us with essential lessons on how to achieve the big things. Also, there may be some things in your life today that once seemed difficult or impossible, and now you have them, but you take them for granted. The law of familiarity says that if we are around anything (or anyone) long enough, we tend to take things just a little bit for granted. So awaken to your appreciation, and jot down your list now.

Second, you have to review what steps you took to turn that dream into your reality. Take a moment right now. Select one of the things you have achieved. What were some of the first actions you took? Jot them down now.

I've interviewed literally tens of thousands of people about how they've taken something that seemed impossible and woven it into their life. How did they create it? How did you? There's a process we all go through. It's a matter of three steps.

Step 1: Unleash Your Hunger and Desire, and Awaken Laser-like Focus. Something happens within you: either you become inspired by something that excites you so much that your desire is completely unleashed—you become completely obsessed with it—and you focus on the object of your desire with laser-like intensity! Your imagination is ignited. Or you hit a wall, a threshold, a place inside yourself, and affirm that you will no longer settle for life as it has been. You make a decision never to go back, and you become ferociously focused on the new life or object you desire. It could be a job change, a relationship change, a lifestyle change. You unleash your hunger for it—and wherever focus goes, energy flows.

Have you ever experienced this? You bought an outfit, or you bought a car, and suddenly you saw that car or outfit everywhere? How did that happen? Because part of your subconscious mind, called the reticular activating system, knows this is important now, so it notices anything that relates to it. Those cars and outfits were always around you, but now you're noticing them because your subconscious makes you aware of the very things you were not seeing before.

That's what's going to happen as you're reading this book. You're going to start noticing the fees charged by mutual funds and hearing about asset allocation. You're going to start hearing things you've never heard before—*high-frequency trading! dollar-cost-averaging!*—and they are going to come to life for you because now your brain knows they're important. Anything that's important, anything that's focused on, energy flows into it. And when you have that level of hunger, desire, and focus, step 2 starts to happen.

Step 2: You Take Massive and Effective Action. If your desire is truly un-leashed and you are obsessively focused on what you want, you will be called to do whatever it takes to make your dream a reality. There are no limits to the energy and flexibility you'll have in the pursuit of what you want. In your heart, you know massive action is the cure-all. If you're willing to put in the effort, you'll get there. You've done it before, right? Maybe there was a time when you just had to see the girl you loved, so you borrowed a car and drove all night through a snowstorm to visit her at college. Maybe you moved heaven and earth to get your child into the best school to suit her needs. If it's a "must" and not just a "should," you'll find a way.

But there's one caveat, of course: you need to put effective execution behind all that effort, right? What if you drove through that snowstorm without a map and ended up in the wrong city? You can throw all your ef-fort into saving for the future, but put your money in a 401(k) loaded with high fees and poorly performing mutual funds, and you'll get nowhere. Or you can invest everything in one company and watch the stock drop 40% in a day. So if you're willing to do whatever it takes, you still have to execute your plan carefully, and keep adapting your approach. Because effort with effective execution creates magic. This book is your map, your blueprint to take you from where you are today to where you want to be financially. By consistently taking massive and effective action, and adapting your approach whenever it doesn't work and trying something new, you will move toward your dream, but there's one final, extraordinary element that plays an impor-tant role in whether your dream becomes a reality or not.

Step 3: Grace! Some call it luck, coincidence, fate, or God's hand. I call it grace: the acknowledgment that there's more in this world than just our-selves, and that perhaps a higher power gives us both the privilege of this life as well as the gifts of insight and guidance when we're open to them. It's amazing how, when you take care of the first two steps, God or the universe or grace—whatever you like to call it—tends to step in and support what you're doing. Things flow to you when you do your part first. We've all experienced the phenomenon of serendipity. Something happens that defies explanation, so we call it a coincidence. We miss a train and meet the person we end up marrying. We fill in for a friend, and it leads us to the job of our dreams. We didn't figure it out in advance, didn't earn it—it just happened. To me, that's grace. And the more you acknowledge and appreciate the grace that's already in your life, the more you experience the gifts that are beyond what you've created. I've had it happen many times in my life, and I know it's real. I also know that gratitude connects you to grace, and when you're grateful, there is no anger. When you are grateful, there is no fear.

So, are you ready to become the creator of your life, not just the manager of your circumstances? Do you know what you're really investing for? An income for life! Are your dreams becoming a part of you, a "must" that your unconscious mind focuses on night and day? Are you willing to do what it takes to make them a reality? Then it's time to turn the page and do what so many others fail to do.

It's time to make a plan. . . .

WHAT'S *YOUR* PLAN?

If you don't know where you are going,
every road will get you nowhere.
—HENRY KISSINGER

Congratulations, you've come a long way! You've taken three huge steps toward Financial Freedom. You've made the most important financial decision of your life. You've become an investor by committing or expanding the percentage of your income that automatically goes into your Freedom Fund, and you've begun to build your money machine that will set you free. You've also learned how to protect yourself from the biggest lies designed to separate you from your money. Finally, you have put a price on your dreams: you know how much income it will take to be financially secure and independent. Now we're going to take what you've learned about the power of compounding and put those **Money Power Principles to work. We're going to work together to create a plan for you and your family that is absolutely attainable and within reach, no matter what level of financial dream you're shooting for: security, vitality, or independence.**

There's one more thing before we start. If you're like most people, you hate talking about money. But hey, it's just us, anyway. No one else will see these numbers unless you decide to share them. What's most important is that you be honest with yourself. No rounding up here. No bending the truth. No looking at your "numbers" with a rosy lens and making your finances look a little better than they are. And by the same token, don't sandbag yourself either by making the plan so conservative that you feel like it's impossible to achieve. Just level with yourself and commit to taking a candid picture of where you are now. That's how to make this plan *really* work.

YOU CAN PLAY ONLY YOUR OWN HAND

A good friend of mine recently had a reunion with a group of his boyhood pals near my home in Palm Beach. They all gathered to celebrate their 50th birthdays. They had gone to nursery school together and lived down the street from one another throughout high school in a Levitt community of tract homes on Long Island, New York. Their fathers were all professionals, or owned their own businesses, their mothers were all housewives; and their household income levels tracked together closely. What struck me most about these lifelong friendships were the demographics. During their formative years, the lives of these friends were in synch, but once they went away to college, the young men splintered in different directions:

One went to work for a leading financial institution on Wall Street.

One became a photographer, opening a frame shop in Manhattan.

One built homes across the mid-Atlantic states.

One started a business as an importer of fine wines and craft beers.

One trained as an engineer and worked on a civil servant's salary in South Florida.

When they got together, these lifelong friends compared notes. Despite the gap in income levels and bank accounts, they were all happy—not happy in precisely the same ways, of course, but happy. Their needs were met. Many of their hopes and dreams as well.

My friend shared the concepts from an early manuscript of this book with his buddies. After a few beers, the conversation turned to money, and they asked one another the same question you answered in the last chapter: How much money would it take to reach financial security or fund their retirements? The Wall Streeter thought he had to save at least $20 million to maintain his present lifestyle without having to work. The Manhattan photographer thought $10 million would do the trick. The real estate developer thought he could manage on $5 million, especially now that his kids were out of college. The wine merchant had recently remarried. In spite of welcoming a new baby, he was counting on a nest egg of $2 million. And the civil servant, the one who'd been conditioned to live within his means and to look ahead to a steady pension for the rest of his life, thought he could live worry free once his pension kicked in and he started collecting Social Security benefits.

Which one of these friends was closest to achieving his goal? Who had the right number and the right plan in place to help him get there? It's a trick question, of course. The answer isn't driven by money. You don't "win" the race of life by amassing the biggest pile of cash or accumulating the most things. And you don't win by grabbing a quick lead and coasting to the finish line.

How do you win? You win by living on your own terms—as well and as fully as you can, for as long as you can.

You create a plan that meets your needs, that works for you, and you stick to it. That's success, plain and simple. If you're scrambling, constantly competing with others' views of success or financial independence and trying to achieve an elusive goal, you're going to fall behind and become frustrated. If you're chasing someone else's goal, you also lose. It doesn't matter how much your neighbor has, what kind of car he or she drives, or the vacation he or she takes. This plan is about you, only you, and no one else.

> The day you stop racing is the day you win the race.
> —BOB MARLEY

THE ILLUSION OF ADVANTAGE

Ever watch track-and-field events in the Olympics? It's easy to stare at the track just before the starting gun fires and wonder how the runner positioned all the way out in front in the outer lane of the track doesn't have a *huge* advantage. Intellectually, we know that all the runners must run the same distance, but visually our eyes seem to deceive us. That so-called lead is called a stagger, and it's meant to even the distance on an oval track. In a 400-meter race, there's a gap of about six meters separating each runner.

But, of course, everyone knows that there's no advantage, physically, to being all the way out in front on the outside of the track, or all the way in the back on the inside. You have to run the same distance either way. Yet the *appearance* of advantage can be a powerful psychological edge. Does the guy out in front think he's got the lead? Does that give him a boost of confidence, or perhaps take away the tiniest fraction of his drive? Does the guy all the way "in back" feel like the underdog—and then run just a little bit faster to compensate?

Let's go back to our five friends, from the outside-looking-in perspective. It might *feel* like the civil servant is all the way in the back, lagging behind the field, and it might *seem* like the Wall Street executive has set himself up for a strong finish, but that's the illusion, not the reality. No one is ahead.

There's no *first place* or *last place* here. Life is not a competition. Often people use money and the acquisition of *things* to measure where they stand: who's got the nicer house, the fancier car, the summer home in the Hamptons. But the truth is, we can't predict how long we'll live or the state of our health as we age. The reality is, **it doesn't matter where we start. It's how we finish that counts.** Here it seemed that all of these lifelong friends were headed in the right direction—*each on his own terms, in his own time. That's one of the reasons they felt so happy with their lives.* With a little discipline and foresight, they all had a shot at winning the race they'd started together, all the way back in nursery school.

The same can happen for you. It doesn't matter where you stand in relation to your friends, your family, your colleagues, or clients. All that matters is your personal journey. It's tempting to look at others as a yardstick and convince yourself that you're all the way out in front, with the appearance of a lead, or resign yourself to the back of the pack. But that's not the point. The **race of life is a marathon, not a sprint.** The only thing to do is focus on the path in front of you. Look ahead. Establish your own pace. Keep moving forward. And then create that plan.

> The only person you should try to be better
> than is the person you were yesterday.
> —ANONYMOUS

YOUR PLAN

Now that you know that your only competition is yourself, it's time to come up with a plan and create a financial blueprint. The good news is, all you have to do is answer six questions in the It's Your Money app. Using this wealth calculator, you'll have a first version of your plan within seconds. If you haven't already downloaded the app, here's the link: www.tonyrobbins .com/masterthegame.

The six questions are related to two areas: where you are now and what you are committed to creating going forward. The few numbers you need to answer you can pull from your records, or perhaps off the top of your head. You may have to do a little bit of homework, but most of these numbers should be close at hand—and, if you can't come up with them right now, it's okay to use a round-number estimate just to get you started to keep the momentum going.

Using these numbers, the app will build a plan tailored just for you, based on variables *you* get to determine: like how much you expect your income to grow, how much you're determined to save, and what rate of return you expect to get on your investments. You can be conservative or aggressive with your estimates—or you can run the numbers both ways and decide on some middle ground. And the beauty here is, once you capture these numbers, the app will do all the work for you. You'll have a true blueprint for your financial future, a clear plan to follow.

CHOOSE YOUR OWN ADVENTURE

The wealth calculator in the app you've just downloaded is a device I've used for more than three decades in my workshops and seminars. It's simple and flexible, and it's helped millions of people create financial plans that work for them. It's built on a series of conservative assumptions, but you're free to go in and change those assumptions if you'd like. **You can make them more conservative or more aggressive. You're in control, so put in numbers that fit with your lifestyle, your current reality, and your future dreams.** If you don't like the picture that comes back to you, you can play with your numbers and choose a different path to financial freedom. In the rest of this section, we'll work together to get you specific steps to speed up your plan and insure its success. The first plan you come up with is just that: your first bite of the apple. Then we're going to take it and improve upon it significantly in the pages ahead . . .

A few things to keep in mind before we start:

One of the biggest factors will be our tax rate, which is radically different for each one of us. This book is read by people all over the world, so rather than make it complex, we've made it very simple. Wherever you live, in the pages ahead you'll learn to utilize the tools in your country that give you the greatest tax efficiency. Wherever possible, you want to use tax-advantaged accounts to accumulate your wealth to generate a greater net rate of return.

This calculator will then show you three potential scenarios, with different annual rates of return for each plan: 4%, 5.5%, and 7%. A conservative plan, a moderate plan, and an aggressive plan. These rates are after-tax rates of return. Some might find these numbers too conservative, or too aggressive; again, you can adjust them to any numbers you like.

How did we get to those numbers? On the high end, if you look at the standard set by the Charles Schwab organization, it will tell you an aggressive return is 10%. Our app's aggressive return is 7%. Why the three-point difference? Schwab has shown that over the past 40 years, from 1972 to 2012, the market has averaged 10%. But our calculator is assuming approximately 30% in taxes, which brings the number to just under 7%. In the United States, long-term investment tax rates are only 20%, not 30%—so our app is being aggressive on the tax side. Also, remember that if you are investing through a tax-deferred vehicle like a 401(k), IRA, or annuity, you are deferring taxes. So if you had a 10% return (as in the Schwab example), you would continue to compound at 10%—with no tax deducted until withdrawal. We are using our lower returns of 4%, 5.5%, and 7% to provide a buffer for mistakes or future returns failing to hit the aggressive mark you had hoped for.[8]

On the low end, or conservative side, if you look at Vanguard, it uses a 4% return after taxes. But we're looking at things a little differently. Most Americans who have money to invest do it through their 401(k), IRA, or 401(k) Roth. What's the best option? We recommend that you go with a Roth (or your country's equivalent), unless you truly are certain your taxes

---

8. At this time of this writing, interest rates have been repressed for an extended period of time. However, the app will be updated if and when interest rates rise. You are also welcome at any time to put in any rate of return that best suits your circumstances and realistic investment return objectives.

are going to be lower in the future. (Lucky you!) Governments all around the world, and especially the United States, have spent money they do not have. How are they going to pay it back? By raising taxes. So while no one knows for certain whether taxes will go up or down, my bet here is they're going up. In a Roth, your returns are 100% yours, meaning that if you've got a 7% return, you keep all 7%—no cut to the tax man ever on the growth of your investments. If you get a 10% return, you keep all 10%.

This is why we built the wealth calculator this way. It gives the flexibility to think about returns in a net (after-tax) approach. You design the plan with what you believe is most appropriate for your planning purposes.

This wealth calculator is designed to quickly give you a sense of how different choices will impact how long it will take you to achieve Financial Security, Vitality, or Independence. After you come up with a basic plan you like, you can also get precision too. As I mentioned earlier, Stronghold (www.StrongholdFinancial.com) has a technology platform to link all of your investment accounts. It will give you immediate feedback on what your actual rate of return has been on your investments in the past. (Most people have no clue!) It will show your best performing years, your worst performing years, and in how many years you have taken a loss. It will also show you how much you are really paying in fees, so you'll know the true impact on your future savings. Go there, if you like, after you have your basic plan completed on the app.

Of course, with the app, the numbers and your plans are completely secure and remain accessible to you wherever you go, on any device. You can change your returns at any time, change how much you're willing to save, and see the impact in moments.

One of the most powerful ways to accelerate the pace at which you achieve your financial goals—and the most painless way I know—is to implement the Save More Tomorrow plan, which has helped over 10 million Americans grow their savings in ways they never thought possible. Do you remember how it works from chapter 7.4, "Your Money Machine"? You commit to automatically taking a percentage of any raise you receive in the future and adding that to your Freedom Fund.

So, for example, let's say you're saving 10% of your current income toward your Freedom Fund: you're investing, but you want to find a way to speed up your plan. By committing to the Save More Tomorrow plan, the next time you get a 10% raise, 3% would go toward your Freedom Fund and the other additional 7% would be available for your improved lifestyle today. Do this three times in the next decade, and you could be saving up to 19%—almost double what you are putting away today—and at no loss to you, because it's all based on additional future income. This will make a huge difference in the speed with which you can achieve your financial dreams.

To take advantage, just click on the Save More Tomorrow option in the app. One final note: I've also taken out the value of your home from the equation. Now, hold on, before you scream and yell. Yes, I know, for many of you, it's the largest investment you have. If you want to add it back in, you can, but I've taken it out so you have yet another conservative cushion. Why? Because you'll always need a home to live in. I don't want you to run these numbers and generate a plan that *relies* on the value of your home to generate income. You may sell your home in ten years and realize a significant gain. Or you may stay in your home for the rest of your life, or you might need to downsize and take some money off the table to help pay off an unanticipated expense. No matter what happens, your plan is designed to keep you afloat no matter what your living situation holds.

Why all these buffers built into the system? Because I want these numbers to be real for you—not just real *in this moment*, but real over time, against any number of real-world events that could set you back. I want to soften the blow in case you veer off course. But I also want you to exceed your own expectations. Most of all, I want you to know with absolute clarity and certainty that the projections we generate together are truly within reach.

Ready to dive in? Open your app!

> When I look into the future, it's so bright it burns my eyes.
> —OPRAH WINFREY

DRUMROLL, PLEASE . . .

Now, I know you are going to want to dive right in, hit Enter, and sit back while the app tells you how the rest of your life will play out. But that's actually not the point. The true value of this next step is to show you what's out there: what's realistic, what's possible, what's worth dreaming and fighting for. It lets you try on different outcomes, and play with some of the variables if you want to create a different picture or produce a different result. In the near term, it gives you a true plan you can follow—a blueprint for your financial future.

Think of it as your personal financial trainer. It takes your "real" numbers—your savings, your income—and calculates what they'll be worth based on a series of anticipated outcomes. Don't worry about *specific* investment strategies just yet. We'll cover these in section 4, but it's important to get some idea of how your money can grow once it starts to work for you.

Remember, **the focus is not on** *where* **or** *how* **you'll invest your money. This exercise is an opportunity to forecast—***to look into the crystal ball of what's possible.* What would your future look like if you could realize a 6% return on your investments? How about 7% or more? How much money would you have after 10 years? After 20? What if you somehow managed to hit the jackpot and found a way to generate gains of 9% or 10%? Remember, just one of the asset allocation portfolios you will learn in chapter 5.1, "Invincible, Unsinkable, Unconquerable: The All Seasons Strategy," has produced an average rate of just under 10% over the last 33 years, and lost money only four times (and one of the losses was only 0.03%)! So there are many possibilities once you educate yourself as to how the top investors on earth conduct themselves.

So play around until you find a number that feels right to you—one that you have a healthy dose of confidence in. **Just a few minutes of your time, and you'll know what your savings, with the power of compounding, at different rates of return, will bring you.**

It is only the first step that is difficult.
—MARIE DE VICHY-CHAMROND

Congratulations on running your first plan. Are you excited about the results? Concerned? Frustrated? Or encouraged? Over the years, working with countless people from all over the world, I've noticed their results tend to place them in roughly one of three categories:

1. Those who are young and in debt, wondering how they're ever going to get to financial security. What's beautiful is that they find out they can!

2. Those who think they are decades away from financial security, and are surprised—or, frankly, shocked—to learn they are only a stone's throw away: five, seven, ten years max. In fact, some are *already* there but had no idea.

3. Those who started late and are fearful of never being able to make up for lost ground.

Let me share with you some examples of other people I've worked with in similar situations and show you how their plans played out—how they achieved Financial Security, Vitality; even Independence and Freedom.

ALL GROWN UP BUT STILL PAYING OFF STUDENT LOANS . . .

Let's start with someone young and in debt. Like a lot of millennials today, Marco graduated with a big chunk of debt. As a 33-year-old engineer earning a respectable $75,000 a year, he was still paying off $20,000 in student loans. Like so many Americans, Marco felt like his debt was consuming his life—he thought he'd be paying it off forever (and probably would be, had he paid only the minimum payments). Marco did, however, expect his salary to grow, slowly but steadily with expected raises of about 3% to 5% per year. After working together on a new plan for Marco, we allocated 5% of his income to paying off his student loans. And Marco committed 3% of any and all future raises to his Freedom Fund.

What did this new plan give him? How about a debt-free life in seven years! On top of that, Marco was going to be able to take that 5%, once he was debt free, and redirect it toward his savings to grow and compound his Freedom Fund. **With this savings and investing plan, Marco could reach Financial Security in 20 years. That may sound like a long time, but he'll still be only 53 years old. And just seven years later, at 60, Marco could reach Financial Independence—a full five years before he'd ever dreamed of retiring,** with more annual income than he ever imagined! Marco went from worrying about *never* paying off his student loans to looking at a future of real financial independence. Even better, within five years, by age 65, with all of his growth and the boost of Social Security added, Marco would actually experience his definition of Financial Freedom—a prospect entirely unfathomable to him before running his new plan. Remember, he began this journey with no assets and nothing but debt!

IF IT LOOKS TOO GOOD TO BE TRUE . . . IT MIGHT ACTUALLY BE TRUE

Then there's our second category of people: those who take a look at their plan and think something must be wrong. Their calculator is not working! They see that Financial Vitality or Independence is popping up far too quickly. "There's no way I can get there that fast," they think. "I can't achieve Financial Independence in five, seven, or eight years. That's crazy!" In their minds, they've got a good 20 or 30 years of hard work and nose-to-the-grindstone days ahead of them.

Where's the disconnect? How is that possible?

It's possible because the number they had in their head—that $10 million or $20 million or $30 million price tag—was totally off base. It had nothing to do with reality. **It was simply a pie-in-the-sky number representing what they *thought* they needed to be financially independent, not what they** actually needed.

Katherine, a woman who attended one of my Wealth Mastery seminars, is a great example. She was a savvy businesswoman who needed $100,000 a year to be financially secure—a large number by many people's standards, but not by her own. To achieve Financial Independence, she'd need $175,000 to maintain her current lifestyle without working. **Katherine assumed it was going to take more than 20 years to get there.**

Want to know what happened when she ran her numbers with my team? The first thing they uncovered was that her current business was earning more than $300,000 a year in net profits and growing at nearly 20% per year. With my team's help and a little bit of research, she found that she could sell her business today for six times her current profits, or a total of $1.8 million. What does this mean?

Well, if she sold her business for $1.8 million and then received a 5% return, her annual investment income would be $90,000 per year. She had other investments already that were providing more than $10,000 per year, **so with a $100,000 annual income, guess what: *Katherine is financially secure right now!***

Katherine was blown away—but also confused. She said, "But Tony, I don't want to sell my business right now!" I told her that I wasn't encouraging her to, nor did she have to. But she should declare victory and realize that she is financially secure today. Why? Because she has the assets to produce the income she needs right now. Even more exciting, at her business's current growth rate of 20% per year, she would double her business in the next three and a half years. And even if her current growth rate was cut in half to only 10% per year, in seven years her business would be worth $3.6 million. If she sells at that point ($3.6 million × 5% = $180,000 per year in income without working), in three and a half to seven years, Katherine will be financially independent. Not 20 years! And this was without making any other investments whatsoever!

By the way, one of the things I show business owners in my Business Mastery program is a little-known set of strategies that allows you to sell a portion (or even a significant majority) of your business and yet still run, control, direct, and profit from it. This allows you to get a large cash-flow bump to secure your Financial Freedom today, while still having the enjoyment and fulfillment of growing the business you love.

YOU CAN BE LATE TO
THE PARTY AND STILL WIN

Let's go back to my friend Angela's story. Angela is anything but average, but from a financial perspective, she represents the average American. Angela is 48 years old. Having lived a free-spirited life, traveling and sailing around the world, she had never saved or invested in her entire life. After finishing section 1, she's now committed to saving 10%, but she's still got a major challenge: she's beginning late in the game. (As she said, "I'm almost fifty!") She has less time to tap into the power of compounding.

When Angela first calculated the amount of income she'd need for Financial Security, **her number came to $34,000 a year. For Financial Independence, she'd need $50,000.** At first glance, her numbers excited her. They didn't have seven zeros, and they were numbers she could get her arms around. However, the timing of those numbers brought her back down to earth. **Starting late in life and saving only 10% of her income was a plan that would take Angela 24 years to get to Financial Security**—if she was 41 years old, that would be a great win. She would achieve it by 65, but since she was starting later, Angela would be 72 years old when she achieved Financial Security. It was certainly a more compelling future than if she hadn't run the plan, and she was glad to know she *could* get there. But she wasn't terribly excited by the long, slow road ahead.

So what could we do to speed up that goal? How could Angela get to Financial Security faster? One way would be to increase her savings and invest it. She was saving 10% already. Never having saved before, 10% seemed like a huge number, but by committing to the Save More Tomorrow plan, she could painlessly save more when she received raises and accelerate her plan. Another way to speed things up was to take a little more risk and increase her rate of return to 7% or more. Of course, that heightened risk could bring about more losses too. But it turned out there was an even simpler insight we had overlooked.

Lucky for Angela, she still had one more round in her arsenal. **She had**

left out a huge piece of future earnings, one that many people neglect to include in their financial planning: Social Security.

Angela, already 48, was only 14 years away from taking Social Security at a reduced rate and 17 years away from capturing her full benefit. She stood to take home $1,250 per month once she turned 62, or about $15,000 a year. So that $34,000 a year in income she needed for Financial Security suddenly dropped down to $19,000. Now when we reviewed the numbers in the app, she shaved a full decade off her timeline. **Instead of getting to Financial Security at 72, she was going to get there at 62!** Angela was going to be financially secure in 14 years, and she was thrilled. She now would have enough income never to have to work again to pay for her mortgage, her utilities, her food, her transportation, and her basic health insurance—a real sense of freedom for Angela.

The impossible became possible. And guess what else happened? Once Angela realized financial security was in view, she took that emotion, that excitement, that momentum, and she said, "Hey, let's kick it up a notch. If I can get to Financial Security by sixty-two, let's take a look at Financial Independence. I'm going to figure out a way to become financially independent, not in my seventies or eighties but in my sixties!" And her number to reach Financial Independence? It was $50,000—only $16,000 more a year in income than she'd need for Financial Security.

Angela took one more step. After reading chapter 3.6, "Get Better Returns and Speed Your Way to Victory," she found yet another way to accelerate her plan. Angela was always extremely interested in owning income-producing real estate, and she learned some simple ways to invest in senior housing (or assisted living facilities) that are available through public and private real estate investment trusts. (These are covered in section 4.) We will highlight more details later in the book, but in short, senior housing facilities are a way to own income-producing real estate that is also tied to what I call a "demographic inevitability": a wave of 76 million baby boomers who are aging and will require the use of these facilities. By investing $438 per month (or $5,265 per year) for the next 20 years, and assuming that she reinvests the income for compound growth, she will have accumulated $228,572. (Note: this assumes a 7% income/dividend payment, which is the current rate on multiple senior housing real estate investment trusts.)

The amount she accumulates will generate $16,000 of income (assuming a 7% income payment), and she won't have to tap into her principal unless she wants to! One last huge benefit? Angela doesn't have to pay income tax on the entire income payment due to the tax deductions for depreciation.

Marco, Katherine, and Angela are real people just like you and me. Your plan is within reach too, and just like them, you might be able to get there sooner than you think. Don't let the first plan you've run on the app be the end-all. Think of it as your starting point to make your dreams happen. In the next chapters, we're going to show you five ways to speed it up and get there even faster.

> Kites rise highest against the wind, not with it.
> —WINSTON CHURCHILL

Whether you're excited about the numbers your plan threw back at you or you're disappointed about the long haul ahead, take heart—disappointment isn't always bad. It often serves as a great kick in the pants that pushes you to create massive change. **Remember, it's not conditions but *decisions*** that determine our lives. Disappointment can drive us, or it can defeat us. I choose to be driven by it—and I'm hoping you take the same view. Most people don't even get to this point in their planning, because they don't want the letdown they're afraid they'll experience once they run their numbers. *But you've taken on the challenge and the promise of this book, so you're not like most people.* You've chosen to be one of the few, not the many.

I vividly remember a Fourth of July trip I took more than 20 years ago with my dear friend Peter Guber and a group of top movie executives through Nantucket and Martha's Vineyard. We were on Peter's private yacht, and a couple of these moguls were throwing around how they had earned $20 million and $25 million on a single film that year. My jaw dropped—that number simply astonished me. Here at 30 years old, I thought I was doing pretty well—that is, until I hung out on deck with a bunch of movie tycoons. These guys had an insane lifestyle, and it didn't take long for me to get seduced by the idea of it all.

This experience jolted me, but it also made me ask a different question: What *did* I really want to create in my life? And could I possibly ever get there? At that time, I didn't see any way I could add enough value to other human beings through my core skill of coaching to ever create that level of Financial Freedom.

Of course, I was being totally unfair, comparing myself and my level of accomplishment to these men. I was 30 years old; Peter and his movie-producing friends were all in their early to late 50s. Peter was in the prime of his career; I was just beginning mine. He had 52 Academy Award nominations and a slew of Hollywood hits to his name. Sure, I was making a name for myself and running a successful business—and changing lives—but financial success for Peter and his friends and financial success for me were light-years apart. And so, as I compared myself to those guys on the boat, I did what so many people do unfairly: I beat myself up for not being at the same level of accomplishment.

But the beauty of that moment, that day, was that it put me in a new and strange environment, and something inside me shifted. I was so far outside of my comfort zone. I felt like I didn't belong—like I didn't deserve to be there. Have you ever felt like this? It's amazing what our minds will do to us if we don't consciously direct them.

And yet contrast is a beautiful thing. When you get around people who are playing the game of life at a higher level, you either get depressed, pissed off, or inspired. That day, I realized I didn't want a yacht, but I was inspired to sharpen my game. I realized there was so much more I could do, give, and be. The best was yet to come. I also realized how incredibly valuable it was for me to get uncomfortable at that point in my life; to put myself in an environment where I didn't feel on top or superior.

Of course, Peter had none of these thoughts. He was just bringing dear friends on a Fourth of July trip as a gift of love! But what he had really done was show me a world of unlimited possibilities. That experience helped awaken the truth in me. It became clear that I did have the capability to create anything I could envision. Maybe I didn't want to have those same grown-up toys, but I sure as hell wanted to have the same types of choices for my family. Today, in my early 50s, those impossible visions have become a simple reflection of the reality I now live. And I *still* don't want a yacht!

Let's be clear. It isn't about the money. It's about choice; about freedom. It's about being able to live life on your terms, not anybody else's.

Don't complain.

Don't say you can't.

Don't make up a story.

Instead, make a decision now!

Find your gift and deliver it to as many people as possible.

If you become stronger, smarter, more compassionate, or more skilled, then your goal is a worthwhile one.

One of my earliest mentors, Jim Rohn, always taught me, "What you get will never make you happy; who you become will make you very happy or very sad." If each day you make just a little progress, you will feel the joy that comes with personal growth. And that leads to perhaps one of the most important lessons I have learned about big goals and achievement.

Most people overestimate what they can do in a year, and they massively underestimate what they can accomplish in a decade or two.

The fact is: you are not a manager of circumstance, you're the architect of your life's experience. Just because something isn't in the foreground or isn't within striking distance, don't underestimate the power of the right actions taken relentlessly.

With the power of compounding, what seems impossible becomes possible. Right now, whether you love your financial plan or hate it, or whether you're excited or afraid, let's make it stronger together. Let's accelerate it by looking at the five elements that can speed it up.

SPEED IT UP:
1. SAVE MORE AND
INVEST THE DIFFERENCE

If everything seems under control, you're not going fast enough.
—MARIO ANDRETTI

Congratulations: you've just taken a huge step toward Financial Freedom! Most people don't take the time to consider their complete financial picture and create a plan. And for those who do, it often stirs up all kinds of emotions. It's big, it's scary. I've been there, I get it. But now that you've done it, take a moment to savor your victory. And ask yourself this: How do you really feel about your plan? Do you feel good about your or your family's future—are you excited to realize that your financial dreams are closer than you imagined? Or is it terrifying to think you might never get to where you'd like to be—are you so deep in debt you're starting to wonder if you'll *ever* dig your way out of the money pit?

Wherever you are, it's okay. You've come a long way, you've made huge strides and there's no turning back now. And now that you've learned to walk, so to speak, let's teach you how to run. **The goal of these next minichapters is to get you thinking about how to make your financial dreams come true faster than you ever thought possible.** Dream big. Make it happen. And then speed it up. Have you ever had a crazy busy day, worked your tail off, raced against the clock, and then, against all odds, finished early? That extra hour or two of life that you reclaim is an absolute gift—a bonus that makes you feel like the world is on your side. You hit the gym and go for a run, head out for cocktails with friends, or race home to tuck the little ones into bed.

I travel like mad; I'm in different countries, on different continents, crossing time zones and flying around the world like the business equivalent of a Harlem Globetrotter. If I arrive somewhere early, if I've got an extra window in my week to refocus my energies or spend time with my wife or my family, I'm energized and excited. I just found some *extra time*!

What if that extra time could last more than just an hour or two? What if you could find not just an extra hour in your day, but, financially, find two years of savings in your life? Or five years? Maybe even a decade of life where you have the freedom of not having to work to support your lifestyle? That's the promise of these pages. Even if your current plan doesn't look like it can get you there, these chapters can show you how to shift your plan and find that opening in your life—that extra money, that extra time, that ultimate freedom.

> He who gains time gains everything.
> —BENJAMIN DISRAELI

If you're going to speed things up, there are five core strategies. You can do any or all of them—it's your choice. Any one of them by itself can significantly speed up the tempo with which you achieve your dreams of financial security, independence, or freedom. Put a couple of them together, and you'll be unstoppable.

> You can be rich by having more than you need,
> or by needing less than you have.
> —JIM MOTT

STRATEGY 1:
SAVE MORE AND INVEST THE DIFFERENCE

The first way to speed up your plan is to save more and invest those savings for compound growth. I know, I know, that's not what you want to hear. Maybe you're even thinking, "Tony, I'm spending every dime I have. There's no way I can possibly save more under any circumstances." If that's true, before we talk about anything else, let's remember the most fundamental strategy you learned back in chapter 2.9, "Myth 9: The Lies We Tell Ourselves": **the best strategy to get around your belief system is to develop a new belief!** You can't squeeze water from a rock, but you can change your story.

Even if you're convinced you have no room to save, Nobel Prize winner Richard Thaler showed us that we can all Save More Tomorrow. Remember those blue-collar workers who said they could never save? And just five years and three pay raises later, they were saving 14%. And 65% of them were saving as much as 19%! You can do this, and you can make it painless if you use that strategy. Let's attack some fresh strategies right now.

What if—in one fell swoop, in one single move—you could save a huge chunk of money toward your Financial Freedom, and it wouldn't cost you a dime more? Do you like that idea? Let's take a look at one of the biggest investments in your life: your home. If you're like millions of Americans, home ownership is important, something you either aspire to or currently take great pride in. Whether you live in Portland, Maine, or Portland, Oregon, your house probably takes the biggest bite out of your monthly apple.

How would you feel if you could save an extra $250,000, $500,000, or even $1 million, from your home? Sound impossible? No, I'm not talking about refinancing your mortgage at a lower rate, although that is one painless way to save hundreds or even thousands of dollars a *month*.

THE BANKER'S SECRET

You don't have to wait for a market downtick to save money on your mortgage. By the time you're reading this, rates may be on their way back up anyway. **You can still cut your mortgage payments in half, however, starting as soon as next month, without involving the bank or changing the terms of your loan.** How? Let me ask you a simple question. Let's say you're applying for a home loan, which would you prefer?

Option 1: 80% of your combined mortgage payments goes toward interest; or
Option 2: a 30-year fixed rate mortgage at 6%.

Go ahead and think about it for a moment. What do you think? Are you tempted by option 2? Does option 1 sound crazy? Did you follow the crowd and choose option 2? Or did you outsmart us all and choose option 1?

The answer: it doesn't matter. They're identical. When you sign your name on the dotted line and take on that 30-year fixed-rate mortgage at 6%, fully 80% of your mortgage payments will go toward interest. Didn't see that one coming, did you? How much does that interest expense wind up costing you over the course of your loan? Is it 30% more? 40% more? 50% more? Life should be so good. **You want to know the banker's secret? Your interest payments will tack on an additional *100% or more* to your loan value.** That half-million-dollar home you buy actually ends up costing you a million dollars after interest payments. If you buy a $1 million home? That costs over $2 million once interest payments are added in! Take a look at the chart below to see the impact of interest expense on your home purchase. The example is a $1 million home, but no matter what price you pay for your home, the ratio of impact is the same. Interest payments will double the cost over time.

$2,160,000
TOTAL PAYMENTS

$1,160,000
INTEREST

$2,500,000

$2,000,000

$1,500,000

$1,000,000

$500,000

$1,000,000 HOME

For most people, their mortgage is the single largest expense, and with the vast majority of your payment going toward interest, I bet you're not surprised to learn that the average American, when you add in credit cards and auto loans, spends 34.5% of every take-home dollar on interest expense. And that's just the average—many people spend more!

So how can you cut down that enormous interest payment? How can you decrease the interest expense you rack up over time—and take that money and funnel it to your Freedom Fund? The answer is so simple it might surprise you.

If you have a traditional fixed-rate mortgage, all you have to do is make early principal payments over the life of the loan. **Prepay your next month's principal, and you could pay off a 30-year mortgage in 15 years in many cases!** Does that mean double your monthly payments? No, not even close! Here's the key:

Money Power Principle 3. Cut your mortgage payments in half! The next time you write your monthly mortgage check, write a second check for the principal-only portion of next month's payment.

It's money you'll have to pay anyway the following month, so why not take it out of your pocket a couple of weeks early and enjoy some serious savings down the road? Fully 80% to 90%, and in some cases even more, of your early payments will be interest expense anyway. And on average, most Americans either move or refinance within five to seven years (and then start the insanity all over again with a new home mortgage).

"It's a pity," mortgage expert Marc Eisenson, author of *The Banker's Secret*, told the *New York Times*. "There are millions of people out there who faithfully make their regular mortgage payments because they don't understand . . . the **benefits of pocket-change prepayments.**"

Let's take a look at an example (in the table on page 252). The average American home is $270,000—but this strategy works whether your home costs $500,000 or $2 million. A 30-year loan on $270,000 at 6% requires an initial monthly payment of $1,618. With this technique, you would also write a second check for an extra $270—next month's principal balance—a very small number, relatively speaking. That second check of $270 is money you'll *never* **pay interest on.** To be clear, you're not paying extra money; you're simply prepaying next month's principal a touch sooner.

Hold yourself to this pay-it-forward strategy each month, and, again, you'll be able to pay off a 30-year mortgage in just 15 years—cutting the total cost of your home by close to 50%. Why not prepay that $270, and cut the life of your mortgage in half? So if you have a million-dollar home, that's a half million dollars back in your pocket! How much would that accelerate your journey to Financial Freedom?!

AVERAGE PRICE OF US HOME: $270,000

Month	Payment	Principal	Interest	Balance
January	$1,618.79	$268.79	$1,350.00	$269,731.21
February	$1,618.79	$270.13	$1,348.66	$269,461.08
March	$1,618.79	$271.48	$1,347.31	$269,189.60
April	$1,618.79	$272.84	$1,345.95	$268,916.76

BABY, YOU CAN DRIVE MY CAR

It's not just our homes where we can save big bucks. One of my sons was dying for a BMW. After years of coveting the "ultimate driving machine," he finally went out and leased a brand-new Beemer with all the performance options. He was thrilled with his purchase. He *loved* that car: he loved the way it drove, what it said about him, what it represented. It was a point of pride and aspiration, and it announced his arrival—in his own mind, at least.

On the flipside, that BMW cost him a *fortune*! He could have made a monthly house payment with what he was paying for that car. A year or two later, the car got a little dinged up, and, no surprise, lost some of its luster. At 30, and newly engaged, he decided he wanted to look for a home for him and his future wife. When he did the math, he almost croaked. That $1,200 payment for his BMW X6 (with a twin turbo V8) could have literally covered an *entire* house payment.

He realized he no longer needed the same ego stroke that came from driving a luxury car. It was just transportation, after all. He saw that he could put himself in a Volkswagen Passat or a Mini Cooper, and it might even be nicer, newer, more fuel efficient.

On top of that, much of the joy that he got from driving that car also disappeared. He found joy elsewhere: in the idea of building a new life, putting down roots with the woman he loved, and buying a home. Getting rid of the BMW was no longer a sacrifice; instead, it became a conscious decision to spend his money elsewhere and start building a financially secure future.

Now, if you're a car aficionado and love cars (as I do), I'm not telling you to go out and drive a Volkswagen. For many guys, that shiny black Ferrari, Porsche, or the new Tesla is just too much to resist. And if your plan is getting you to where you want to be financially, by all means, drive whatever car you want. But if you're *not* getting there, or you're not getting there fast enough, then maybe it's time to rethink your wheels and see if you can find some meaningful savings to put into your Freedom Fund.

Remember Angela? She read an early copy of this manuscript and came home with a new car—her first brand–new car ever! Take a look at her numbers: she was able to trade in her old car and save $400 a month, or almost $5,000 a year, to put toward her savings and start compounding right away.

WHAT ELSE CAN YOU DO?

Houses and cars aren't the only places where we can save. Where else can you work at axing expenses in your life that no longer give you value? I know the idea of living on a budget is totally unappealing to most people. **I don't want to be put on a budget and my guess is you don't either. But what I do believe in is a spending plan. I like the idea of planning how to spend my money so that it gives me the most joy and happiness but also ensures my financial freedom long term.**

Now, to be fair, if you're one of those people who says, "Screw it, I'm not going to save; I'm just going to focus on earning more," then you can just go ahead and skip right over to the next minichapter on earning more and adding value. If the idea of saving just completely exhausts or bores you, you've got four other strategies to help you speed things up, and I don't want you to miss them because saving isn't for you. But if you do, stay with me.

I promise you that little things can make a big difference long term— they add up to surprisingly giant numbers.

To be fair, Amazon and brick-and-mortar bookstores have entire sections filled with books on how to save more money. **Dave Ramsey** is a very caring man with several books in this area, and **Suze Orman** is another author worth investigating if you are looking to find savings. But we're going to take a few pages here to highlight the best simple strategies now.

One thing is for sure: you can create a spending plan that helps you decide in advance *how* and *where* to spend your money to give you the greatest returns today and in the future.

Remember chapter 1.3, "Tap the Power," where we looked at how ordering in pizza with friends instead of going out to dinner could save you $40 a week, or $2,080 a year? At an 8% return, that turns into more than $500,000 over 40 years. A half million dollars! That's a whole different retirement picture than most Americans have today. That kind of money, on its own or added to our 401(k), can certainly help make us rethink our daily Grande skim latte with a shot of vanilla.

Financial expert **David Bach** is a good friend of mine who got his start by attending one of my financial seminars more than 20 years ago. He made a decision to pursue his dream of helping people become financially independent, and just a few years later, I hired him for his first paid speech. Today, through his passion and dedication, he's helped educate over four million people through his bestselling book *The Automatic Millionaire: A Powerful One-Step Plan to Live and Finish Rich*, which includes the concept of creating wealth through finding what he calls your "Latte Factor." And it's not just about coffee: the Latte Factor is simply a metaphor for all those small purchases that we don't even consider—things we wind up wasting our money on without even realizing it. But if you are a coffee fiend, how much is that addiction costing you? Let's say you're a casual "user": at $4 a day, you're effectively giving up almost $56,500 of savings at 6% interest over 20 years. For a single drink! But let's be real: the Starbucks loyalist doesn't go just once a day. What about the real evangelists who are there two or three times a day? **Take your $4 habit and boost it to $10 a day, and now you're drinking away over $141,250 in savings over 20 years. That's the cost of a four-year college education!**

What if you're a purist? You don't binge on caffeine; your body is a temple. But bottled water is your thing. Got any Fiji or Evian enthusiasts out there? Or frankly, even if you just stock up on Poland Spring at Costco, how much are you spending on bottled water every year? A young woman I work with, whom I adore and who considers herself very socially conscious, is about to get married to a guy who regularly buys 12-packs of 1.5-liter bottles of Smartwater. How smart is that? He buys them three at a time, 36 big bottles in total, which lasts him about two weeks and sets him back $75. He's spending $150 a month on water, almost $1,800 a year—on something he could get free from the tap, or filter with a Brita water filter system and a few Nalgene bottles for $50 to $60 a year. Forget that he's killing our planet; he's also killing his wallet. I know her fiancé would be much happier if that $1,800 a year was going into their savings account and compounding annually. At 8% over 40 years, that's $503,605 being pissed away—literally.

I'm not saying you have to give up bottled water or stop getting coffee, but the savings are there somewhere. Isn't it time to find them?

And finally, let's not forget about our impulse purchases: you know, the ones that feel great in the moment, like the pricey work bag or the beautiful Hermès tie. Lisa, a young mom from Nashville, has a taste for the finer things in life. She drives her husband batty with her impulse purchases. She'll come home with a great new dress or an amazing pair of boots, and her husband will invariably ask, "Were they on sale?" or "Did you check online to see if you could get them cheaper?" After several spats, Lisa and her husband agreed on a new plan. When Lisa found herself unexpectedly at Saks Fifth Avenue or Jimmy Choo, she'd take a photo of her next "must-have" and send it to her husband. He had two weeks to find her a better price online; otherwise she'd order her purchase over the phone at full retail. But as Lisa sheepishly admitted to me, over 80% of the time, he did find whatever she was looking for—at often at 20% or 30% cheaper.

So take a page from Lisa and her husband and check out all the online rewards programs that can save you real money. **Upromise.com** helps you earn cash back for college from your everyday spending, from online purchases to dining out and booking travel. You can put those savings toward a student loan, savings account, or 529 college savings plan, a tax-deferred savings plan set up by parents for their kids' college tuition. And if college has passed or it's not a priority, but cash is, there are hundreds of other cash-back websites out there—Extrabux, Ebates, Mr. Rebates—all of which can save you 10% to 30% on purchases at thousands of online stores. As for Lisa and her husband, they put all their savings back into their Upromise account, and now everyone feels better about that pair of stilettos.

At the end of the day, the question to ask yourself is this: Do my expenses, big and small, bring me the thrill they once did? It's not about depriving yourself; it's about adjusting your spending habits to mirror your core values and indulge only the experiences that truly matter to you. *That* deliberate spending allows you to invest in a quality of life that is sustainable and brings you joy. Whether you've got 20, 30, or 40 years to invest, no matter where you are, how much you can save, or how many years you've got to do it, **you can take advantage of the unparalleled power of compounding.** Financial security, financial independence—whatever your goals, you will get there a whole lot faster when you put your money to work for you.

It's not about lifestyle, it's about *timing*. Why not make simple changes today to insure you have more than enough down the road to continue to fund your lifestyle *and* your dreams? You can still enjoy life's finer pleasures—but you're in control now. You get to choose how to allocate your funds and where to get the biggest bang for your buck. Whether you're going to tackle your mortgage expense or trade in those fancy wheels, make your online purchases work for you or do a little better on your everyday expenses—it's in there. Real, meaningful savings, to the tune of *hundreds of thousands* of dollars to a million dollars or more are there for you to find and to reinvest.

Now let's turn the page and uncover the fastest way I know to speed up your plan and achieve financial independence faster. Let's learn to earn more.

MINDFUL SAVINGS

Here's a quick-and-easy six-step exercise to get you thinking more aggressively—more *purposefully*—about saving:

1. Brainstorm about all the recurring expenditures that you could eliminate or reduce to cut your expenses. Car insurance, cell-phone bills, lunch money, movie tickets. Think about where you can make changes.

THE EARLIER YOUR START, THE BIGGER YOUR NEST EGG
(Assumes 10% Annual Rate of Return)

DAILY INVESTMENT	MONTHLY INVESTMENT	10 YEARS	20 YEARS	30 YEARS	40 YEARS	50 YEARS
$5	$150	$30,727	$113,905	$339,073	$948,612	$2,598,659
$10	$300	$61,453	$227,811	$678,146	$1,897,224	$5,197,317
$15	$450	$92,180	$341,716	$1,017,220	$2,845,836	$7,795,976
$20	$600	$122,907	$455,621	$1,356,293	$3,794,448	$10,394,634
$30	$900	$184,360	$683,432	$2,034,439	$5,691,672	$15,591,952
$40	$1,200	$245,814	$911,243	$2,712,586	$7,588,895	$20,789,269
$50	$1,500	$307,267	$1,139,053	$3,390,732	$9,486,119	$25,986,586

2. How much do these items or activities cost? Highlight the most significant of these expenditures and make a note of the associated costs. Next, calculate how many times per week you indulge in this expense and take a reality-check snapshot.

3. Now, on a scale from 0 to 10 (with 0 representing *none* and 10 representing *extremely pleasurable*), how much joy do you get from each of the items above? Attach a number to each activity or item to help you associate these costs to your life.

4. Next, think of what it would feel like to have Absolute Financial Freedom. Remember how you responded to that concept back in chapter 3.1: "What's the Price of Your Dreams? Make the Game Winnable"? Remember how it made you *feel*? But at the same time, remember that this was a feeling you experienced in the abstract, in theory. Here it's close enough to taste. What would you be able to enjoy, have, do, be, or *give* if you were absolutely financially free?

5. Decide which is more important to you: the joy you receive from the recurring expenditures on your list or the feeling of Absolute Financial Freedom. Remember that life is a balance. You don't have to cut out *everything* from your list to move the needle on that feeling of freedom.
6. Write down at least three expenditures you are resolved to eliminate. Calculate how much money this will save you over the course of the next year.

TAKE CONTROL: A QUICK EXERCISE IN MINDFUL SAVINGS

#	ITEM / ACTIVITY	COST OF ITEM / ACTIVITY	# TIMES / WEEK	TOTAL COST (COST OF ITEM X TIMES PER WEEK)	LEVEL OF ENJOYMENT (1-10)
1					
2					
3					
4					
5					
6					
Grand Total of Cost per Week					
Grand Total of Cost per Year					

SPEED IT UP:
2. EARN MORE AND
INVEST THE DIFFERENCE

Try not to become a man of success,
but rather try to become a man of value.
—ALBERT EINSTEIN

Okay, let's kick into second gear. If saving is one way to speed up your plan, there is an even faster way that literally has no limits—*if* you unleash your creativity and focus, and become obsessed with finding a way to do more for others than anyone else. That's how you earn more and shift into the fast lane to freedom.

DRIVING A TRUCK TO FINANCIAL FREEDOM?

When I was growing up, my mother had a great plan for me. She wanted me to become a truck driver. She had seen these ads on television, over and over, for Truckmaster truck driving education school. She told me that with a little training, I could qualify as a truck driver and make up to $24,000 a year. Wow, $24,000! That was twice what my dad was earning as a parking attendant in downtown LA. She thought that this would provide a great future for me. She worked into her sales pitch that I'd have the freedom to be on the open road and drive. It actually appealed to me on a certain level: the idea that I could just turn on my music and go—kind of a cool thought for a 14-year-old kid who wasn't even driving yet. I'd have the opportunity to get up and go instead of being stuck in an underground parking garage for 30-plus years.

But after all of the misery I had witnessed, all of the shame associated with four different fathers, of never having enough money for clothing or food, I realized I could never drive a truck long enough or far enough to allow me to escape the pain of that situation. In my head, I decided that there was no way in my lifetime I would have a family that would suffer this way. On top of that, I wanted to use my mind and my heart. I wanted to get in the game of life at a different level.

I looked around and wondered how other people's lives could be so vastly different from my own. Why were we struggling constantly to make ends meet, to stay ahead of the bill collector—choosing between canned beans or spaghetti with ketchup because we couldn't afford tomato sauce? And yet, in the same city, not far from us, kids I went to high school with were taking fancy vacations and studying on picture-perfect college campuses—living a life well beyond my wildest dreams—a life so obviously different from the one we would ever experience. What did they know that we didn't know? What were they doing differently from my father and mother?

I became obsessed. How was it possible that someone could earn twice as much money in the same amount of time? Three times as much? Ten times as much? It seemed crazy! From my perspective, it was an unsolvable riddle.

INVEST IN YOURSELF

I was working as a janitor, and I needed extra money. A man my parents knew, and whom my father had called a "loser," had become quite successful in a short period of time, at least in financial terms. He was buying, fixing, and flipping real estate in Southern California and needed a kid on the weekend to help him move furniture. That chance encounter, that fateful weekend of working my tail off, led to an opening that would change my life forever. His name was Jim Hannah. He took notice of my hustle and drive. When I had a moment, I asked him, "How did you turn your life around? How did you become so successful?"

"I did it," he said, "by going to a seminar by a man named Jim Rohn." "What's a seminar?" I asked. "It's a place where a man takes ten or twenty years of his life and all he's learned and he condenses it into a few hours so that you can compress years of learning into days," he answered. Wow, that sounded pretty awesome. "How much does it cost?" "Thirty-five dollars," he told me. *What!?* I was making $40 a week as a part-time janitor while going to high school. "Can you get me in?" I asked. "Sure!" he said. "But I won't—because you wouldn't value it if you didn't pay for it." I stood there, disheartened. How could I ever afford $35 for three hours with this expert? "Well, if you don't think you're worth the investment, don't make it," he finally shrugged. I struggled and struggled with that one—but ultimately decided to go for it. It turned out to be one of the most important investments of my life. I took a week's pay and went to a seminar where I met Jim Rohn—the man who became my life's first mentor.

I sat in an Irvine, California, hotel ballroom listening to Jim, riveted. This silver-haired man literally echoed the questions that had been burning in my mind. He, too, had grown up poor, wondering, even though his father was a good man, why his father struggled so hard only to suffer while others around him prospered. And then, suddenly, he answered the question I had been asking myself literally for years.

"What's the secret to economic success? The key," he said, "is to understand how to become more **valuable** in the marketplace.

"To have more, you simply have to become more.

"Don't wish it was easier; wish **you** were better.

"For things to change, **you** have to change.

"For things to get better, **you** have to get better!

"We get paid for bringing value to the marketplace. It takes time . . . but we don't get paid for time, we get paid for value. America is unique. It's a ladder to climb. It starts down here, at what? About $2.30 an hour. What was the top income last year? The guy who runs Disney—$52 million! Would a company pay somebody $52 million a year? The answer is: of course! If you help a company make a billion dollars, would they pay you $52 million? Of course! It's chicken feed! It's not that much money.

"Is it really possible to become that valuable? The answer is: *of course!*" And then he let me in on the ultimate secret. "How do you truly become more valuable? **Learn to work harder on yourself than you do on your job.**

"So can you personally become twice as valuable and make twice as much money in the same time? Is it possible to become ten times as valuable and make ten times as much money in the same time? Is that possible? Of course!" And then he paused and looked directly in my eyes and said, *"All*

you have to do to earn more money in the same amount of time is simply
become more valuable."

And there it was! There was my answer. Once I got that, it turned my life around. That clarity, that simplicity, the wisdom of those words—they hit me like a 100-pound brick. Those are the exact words I've heard Jim Rohn speak probably a hundred times. I have carried them in my heart every day since, including the day that I spoke at his funeral in 2009.

That man, that seminar, that day—what Jim Rohn did was put me back in control of my own future. He made me stop focusing on what was outside of my control—my past, the poverty, other people's expectations, the state of the economy—and taught me to focus instead on what I could control. I could improve myself; I could find a way to serve, a way to do more, a way to become better, a way to add value to the marketplace. I became obsessed with finding ways to do more for others than anyone else was doing, in less time. That began a never-ending process that continues to this day! At its most basic level, it provided a pathway to progress that continues to drive and lead every single decision I make and action I take.

In the Bible, there is a simple tenet that says there's nothing wrong with wanting to be great.[9] **If you wish to become great, learn to become the servant of many.** If you can find a way to serve many people, you can earn more. Find a way to serve millions of people, you can earn millions. It's the law of added value.

And if the gospel of **Warren Buffett** is more your thing than biblical verse, **the Oracle of Omaha is famous for saying that the most powerful investment he ever made in his life, and that anyone can make, is an investment in himself.** He talks about investing in personal development books, in educating himself, and how a Dale Carnegie course completely changed his life. Buffett once told me this story himself when we were on the *Today* show together. I laughed and asked him to keep telling that story. "It's good for business," I said, grinning.

I took Jim Rohn's message to heart and became obsessed—I would never stop growing, never stop giving, never stop trying to expand my influence or

---

9. "Instead, whoever wants to become great among you, must be your servant," Matthew 20:26, New International Version.

my capacity to give and do good. And as a result, over the years, I've become more valuable in the marketplace. To the point that I'm extremely fortunate enough today that finances are no longer an issue in my life. I'm not unique. Anyone can do the same—if you let go of your stories about the past, and break through your stories about the present and its limits. Problems are always available, but so is opportunity.

What does the American income ladder look like today? My bet is Jim Rohn couldn't have imagined that **in 2013, the low end of the ladder would be $7.25 an hour ($15,080 annually) and that the high-end earner of the year would be Appaloosa Management founder and hedge fund leader David Tepper, who earned $3.5 billion in personal income.** How could any human being make even $1 billion a year, much less $3.5 billion? Why such an incredibly low income for some people and such a high-income opportunity for others? The answer is the marketplace puts very little value on being a cashier at McDonald's ($7.77 an hour) because it requires a skill that can be learned in a few hours by almost anyone. However, successfully expanding people's financial returns in a significant way is a much more rare and valued set of skills. When most Americans are getting less than 33 basis points (a third of 1%) annually as a return on their money from the bank, David Tepper delivered a 42% return for his investors in the same time! How valuable were his contributions to their economic lives? If he got them a 1% return, he would have been 300% more valuable. A 42% return means he added 12,627% more economic value to their lives!

So how about you? What are you going to do to add more value to the marketplace? How are you going to ensure abundance rather than struggle? **If we're going to make a radical shift and take you from where you are today to where you want be—to financial freedom—then this path is the most powerful one I know to get you there.**

Now, before you start your rallying cry of objections, let me just say: I know that things are different today. I know it's a challenging time for the economy. I know we've lost two million jobs since 2008, and the ones that are coming back are mostly service or low-paying jobs. And yes, I realize that incomes have been stagnant since the 1990s.

Guess what interest rates and unemployment looked like in 1978, when I started my career? Within two years, interest rates had skyrocketed! My first investment, a fourplex in Long Beach, California, had an 18% mortgage. Can you imagine interest rates at 18% today to buy a home? We'd have a revolt on the White House lawn. But history is circular—always has been, always will be. Yes, incomes are stagnant, if you don't find a way to geometrically add more value. But if you find a way to add value, incomes move in one direction, and that's always up.

During the Great Recession, 8.8 million jobs were lost. In 2008, 2.3 million jobs were lost in that year alone! Unemployment peaked at 10%. But remember, that 10% unemployment rate is an average. Some portions of the population had unemployment levels over 25%, but for those making $100,000 per year or more, what would you guess was their unemployment rate? The answer: close to 1%! The lesson? If you truly develop skills that are needed in the current marketplace—if you constantly improve and become more valuable—someone will employ you or you'll employ yourself, regardless of the economy. And if you employ yourself, your raise becomes effective when you are!

Even today, it's a totally different story in Silicon Valley, where jobs are for the taking. Technology companies can't fill their openings fast enough; they can't find enough qualified people. Jobs are out there, but you and I need to retool our skill sets—retool ourselves—so that we become valuable in the new marketplace. I can promise you this: most of those "old jobs" aren't coming back.

Let's look at history. In the 1860s, 80% of Americans were farmers. Today 2% of the US population work in farming and agriculture, and we feed the entire world. New technology disrupted everything—suddenly one farmer could do the work of 500. Many people struggled, many lost their jobs. For those who didn't adapt, the industrial revolution was an incredibly painful time. But that very same technology that brought along steam power and machine tools, which displaced people in the short term, made the quality of life of everyone around them exponentially better and provided more jobs at a higher level of income.

Today's new technologies are causing massive disruption once again. Oxford researchers say that almost half of America's occupations are at risk of becoming automated (translation: replaced) within the next 20 years! You and I have to retool to a different level. I promise you, 150 years ago, no one could have fathomed a day when there would be jobs called social media marketer, stem cell scientist, and robotics engineer. No one could imagine that an electrician or a plumber would make $150,000 a year, or that a factory worker could learn how to use a computer to automate a machine and earn $100,000 in the process. But just because people couldn't imagine it, didn't mean it wouldn't happen.

I meet people everyday who tell me the job market is frozen, or they've been laid off and fear they'll never find work again. But I'm here to tell you it's not the market, it's you. You can increase your earnings potential—anyone can. You can add value to the marketplace. You can learn new skills, you can master your own mind-set, you can grow and change and develop, and you can find the job and economic opportunity that you need and deserve.

But if your job is going to be obsolete in the next five or ten years, it's time to think about making a pivot and trying something new. A pivot is what Silicon Valley calls it when you go from one business to another, usually after a colossal failure.

If you're reading this book right now, **you're a person who looks for answers, for solutions, for a better way.** There are hundreds of ways you can retool your skill set. You can do it by going after a college education, a trade education, or self-education. **You can earn $100,000 to millions a year, and not by just going and spending a boatload of money on a four-year college degree** (that can put you $100,000 or more in debt). Millions of jobs are available in this country, but there is also a major skills gap. According to Mike Rowe, host of Discovery Channel's *Dirty Jobs*, there are about 3.5 million jobs available right now, and only 10% of them require a four-year degree. That means that the other 90% of them require something else: training, skill, or a willingness to get dirty, perhaps, but mostly a willingness to learn a new and useful trade. According to Rowe, "That's always been for sale, but it's kind of fallen out of [our country's] narrative."

Retooling is both exciting and scary. Exciting because of the opportunity to learn, grow, create, and change. Exciting once you realize "I'm valuable; I have a contribution to make; I'm worth more." Scary because you think, "How am

I going to do this?" Remember Jim Rohn's words: "For things to change, you have to change. **For things to get better, you have to get better.**" Retool or be the fool. Get rid of your story of limitation and shift into high gear.

People often say to me, "Tony, that's great if you have your own business or you work in a company where it's growing. But what if you're in a traditionally low-paying job, and you love what you do? What if you're a teacher, what then?" Let's step outside our own limiting thinking, and let me give you a perfect example of a schoolteacher who used to struggle, but because of his passion and his desire to help more students, he found a way to add more value and earn more than most teachers ever dream about. The real limitation in our earnings is never our job—it's our creativity, our focus, and our contribution.

CREATIVITY, CONTRIBUTION, AND THE KOREAN ROCK STAR

If you ever had a third-grade teacher who inspired you to try something new, or an eighth-grade teacher who believed in your own child beyond measure, you know the power of a single role model in the life of a child. Our teachers are one of our greatest yet most underappreciated and underpaid assets. So what do you do if you're a teacher, or you have a similar job where your upside potential seems to be limited? As a teacher, how can one think about adding value to more than just 30 students in the classroom? Is there a way you might be able to add value to hundreds of students, thousands of students, even millions?

There are plenty of schoolteachers who think, "I'll never make enough money doing what I love." There is broad agreement that we as society don't value teachers in the way that we should. But as we now know, that limiting belief holds people back. Kim Ki-hoon is a teacher in South Korea who refused to buy into that story.

Unlike most teachers, Kim Ki-hoon is known as a "rock star" in South Korea. Kim is one of the most successful teachers in his country. How did he become so successful? He worked harder on himself, on his ability to teach, than he did on his job.

Sixty years ago, according to the *Wall Street Journal*, the majority of South Koreans were illiterate. The country realized it needed to take massive and dramatic action. Today teachers there are constantly encouraged to study, to innovate, to teach the same class in a new way every day. They're taught to learn from one another, mentor one another—find the best techniques to add more value. The result? Today 15-year-olds in South Korea rank second in reading, and with a 93% graduation rate—compared with just 77% in the United States.

Ki-hoon took that model and ran with it. He put enormous time into finding the best teachers, studying their patterns, learning how to create breakthroughs. He found a way to help his students learn faster, better, smarter—and not just his students but also students all across the country. Why focus on just helping 30 students? he thought, Why not help as many as I can? With the advent of technology, he realized he could put his classes online and make his passion for teaching and learning available to everyone.

Today Ki-hoon works about 60 hours a week, but only three hours of those are for giving lectures. **The other 57 hours are spent researching, innovating, developing curriculum, and responding to students.** "The harder I work, the more I make," he says. And he works hardest to become better for the people he serves. Ki-hoon records his classes on video, and circulates them on the internet, where students log on at the rate of $4 an hour. How does he know it works? How does he know he's adding more value than anyone else? The marketplace always tells you your true worth or value. Guess how many people buy his classes? **Last year, his annual earnings topped $4 million!** The more value Ki-hoon offers via online classes and tutorials, the more students sign up. And, it follows, more students means more money—in this case, *a lot more.*

A teacher earning $4 million. How does that compare to the best schoolteacher you know? Ki-hoon's story shatters the belief that our profession limits us. He's part of the 1% not because he's lucky, not because he was in the right place at the right time, not because he chose a lucrative profession. No, Ki-hoon is a wealthy man, part of the 1%, because he has never stopped learning, never stopped growing, never stopped investing in himself.

THE ULTIMATE MULTITASKER

But what if you're not an entrepreneur? What if you have absolutely no interest in hanging up your own shingle? What if you work in corporate

America or even for a small business? Can you still figure out a way to add more value and increase your earning potential? Let me tell you about a young woman. Daniela worked in a marketing department doing art design and didn't see any clear path toward moving up in her company. She was extremely talented, but more importantly, she was hungry. She was constantly looking to do more and give more; it was just her nature. And so she often helped her colleagues with visual arts. And then she wanted to learn about marketing, so she started studying marketing and offered to help. And then, of course, she realized she didn't really know anything about social media— but the opportunities there seemed huge, so she decided to educate herself on social media as well.

After a few years, Daniela was doing many of the jobs of her coworkers. And they forgot that she was offering a gift, and they started to take her for granted. A new pattern emerged where, at five o'clock, when jobs with key deadlines were still not done, she worked alone at her desk as her associates slipped out the door. She didn't want to stay late, but she wasn't going to let the company and their clients down. When it was clear her colleagues were actually taking advantage of her drive and ambition, she reached her limit. "I'm doing three people's jobs plus my own!" But instead of getting angry, Daniela decided it was an opportunity.

What did she do? Daniela approached her CEO and laid it on the line: "Right now I'm doing the work of four people. I've gone to courses, I've learned and taught myself about visual arts, marketing, and social media. I'm not here to throw anybody under the bus, but I can save you fifty percent of your marketing cost right now and eliminate three people by taking on their jobs myself. And I'll do a better job, too. I don't need you to trust me on this: let me prove myself to you. Let them keep doing their jobs for six months, and I'll do my assignments *and* theirs, so you'll have two different examples to pick from. You decide what's best."

All Daniela asked was that if she did a better job, after six months, her boss would give her more responsibility and double her pay. And guess what? She did it: she proved herself on the visual art and marketing fronts, with great copywriting and a successful social media campaign. Daniela showed that not only could she handle the extra work, but also she could run circles around the competition—she could outperform them all. She added enough value that the company realized it could pay one person twice as much money, and still cut its costs in half. The marketplace had spoken.

> Happiness is not in the mere possession of money;
> it lies in the joy of achievement, in the thrill of creative effort.
> —FRANKLIN D. ROOSEVELT

OPPORTUNITY IS EVERYWHERE

How are you going to add more value to the world? How are you going to contribute more, earn more, and increase your impact? There are hundreds, if not thousands, of stories of average individuals who saw a problem, looked at things just a little bit differently, and went on to transform entire industries or create entirely new markets. They weren't entrepreneurs; they were just people like you and me, people who wouldn't settle. In the world we live in today, no industry or product is immune: the intersection of all things digital—the internet, social media, and technology—the interconnectedness of every person and everything on earth. That means that even the biggest companies and the most mature or stable businesses are ripe for disruption. Enter Nick Woodman.

RIDING THE WAVE

Who would have predicted that Kodak, the corporate titan that dominated the world of photography in the 20th century, would be caught flatfooted when digital imaging came on the scene? Kodak *invented* digital photography. And yet after 124 years in business, the company filed for bankruptcy in 2012—a move that had a disastrous ripple effect on the economy in and around Rochester, New York, where over 50,000 jobs were lost.

But those same massive technological and cultural changes that killed Kodak provided a huge opportunity for a California surfer named Nick Woodman. Woodman was obsessed with surfing. His absolute love of and devotion to the sport, along with his drive and his hunger, enabled him to find a way to add value.

Chances are you've never heard of Woodman, but he had the brilliant idea to strap a waterproof camera to his wrist while riding the waves. All

Woodman set out to do was find a way to enjoy his surfing after it happened. With digital photography coming out, he started to tinker with cameras to see if he could make them more waterproof and capture better-quality video. And as technology changed, he continued to tinker. And tinker. He ended up inventing the GoPro, a tiny, broadcast-quality, clip-on-and-take-anywhere digital camera.

This cool little device is now on the head of every extreme sports person in the world. Whether you're riding a bike, paddling through rapids, snow-boarding, or catching the waves, the GoPro allows you to capture the magic of your adrenaline rush and share it with everyone you love. Woodman's timing couldn't have been better: he began marketing the GoPro just as people started uploading their videos to YouTube and Facebook. He created a product *he* wanted to use and figured he couldn't be the only guy needing one. Woodman figured out how to add value to millions of lives by making the new technology convenient, fun, and affordable. Ultimately, Woodman got in front of a trend. That trend was actively sharing digitally whatever was there. **One of the key secrets if you really want to become wealthy: get in front of a trend. Today the surfer from San Diego, California, is worth over $1 billion.**

A NEW "CATEGORY" IS BORN

Back in 2010, Matt Lauer invited me to join him for a special roundtable discussion about where the economy was headed. I was joining Warren Buffett and the world's youngest female self-made billionaire: a woman named **Sara Blakely.** Any opportunity to discuss the economy with Warren Buffett was a huge privilege, but what I didn't bank on was being totally blown away by Sara's story.

Blakely didn't disrupt an industry so much as create an entirely new one. A former Walt Disney World employee, Sara was getting ready for a party when she realized she didn't have the right underwear for a pair of fitted white pants. Rather than go commando, she decided to take matters into her own hands. Armed with nothing more than a pair of scissors and a whole lot of sass, she cut the feet off her control-top pantyhose, and, voila, a new industry was born.

Of course, it didn't happen overnight, and it didn't happen easily. Sara shared with me that one of the most important secrets to her success was that from an early age, **her father actually encouraged her to "fail!"** But he defined failure not as failure to achieve a result . . . but failure to try. Around the dinner table, he would ask if she had failed today, and he was truly excited if she had—because he knew that meant she was on the path to success. "Tony, it just took away my fear of trying," she told me.

Down and out in a dead-end office-products sales job, Blakely invested all the money she had in the world, $5,000, and set out to create body wear that would work for her. "I must have heard 'no' a thousand times," she said. But she didn't listen. In addition to the $5,000 she invested, she saved $3,000 (which she didn't have) on legal fees by writing her own patent from a textbook.

Ultimately, the company she founded, Spanx, created an entirely new category of products called "shapewear" and has inspired a cultlike following among women worldwide. According to my wife, put on a pair to pull in all your "its and bits," and you'll take three inches off your waistline immediately.

With Oprah Winfrey's blessing, Spanx turned from a small business into a worldwide sensation. **Today Spanx is worth over a billion dollars, and the brand now includes over 200 products** that help women look and feel great. Ever the optimist, Sara tried to work her magic on me: she tried to get me to wear a pair of her new Spanx for men when we were together on the *Today* show. I thanked her and mentioned gently that perhaps she didn't understand the male market as well as the female market. But I remain inspired by her example. In the end, Spanx for men has also taken off—no thanks to me. **Today Blakely owns 100% of her company, has zero debt, and has never taken on outside investment. In 2012 *Time* magazine named her one of its "100 Most Influential People in the World."**

Like Nick Woodman, she saw a need and moved to fill it. She refused to be limited by her own story and found a way to add value.

You can too! You don't have to start a billion-dollar company, disrupt an entire category, or make $4 million as a teacher online. You don't even have to take on four jobs at once. But if these people are capable of doing that, couldn't you find a way to make an extra $500 or $1,000 a month? Or maybe even an extra $20,000, $50,000, or even $100,000 or more a year? Couldn't you figure out how to unleash *your own* creativity, contribution, and focus to add more value to the marketplace and put that money in your Freedom Fund? You can. The time to begin is now. . . .

Find a way to earn or save an extra $500 per month, or $6,000 a year. If it is invested at an 8% return over 40 years, it is worth $1.5 million—remember our pizza example. If you find a way to earn $1,000 per month, or $12,000 a year, that's worth $3 million in your nest egg. If you find a way to earn $3,000 per month, or $36,000 a year, that's worth $9 million in your nest egg. What's the lesson? Go add value, earn more, and invest your earnings, and you can create any level of financial freedom you truly desire.

SPEED IT UP:
3. REDUCE FEES AND TAXES
(AND INVEST THE DIFFERENCE)

We have what it takes to take what you have.
—SUGGESTED IRS MOTTO

"You must pay taxes. But there's no law that says you gotta leave a tip."
—MORGAN STANLEY ADVERTISEMENT

So now you're rocking and rolling—you're speeding up your path to financial freedom by *saving* more and *earning* more! What's left? Doesn't that cover it? Actually, no. You now know as an insider that **it's not what you earn that matters, it's what you keep.** Our third strategy for speeding things up is to get more money out of your investments by reducing your fees and taxes, and reinvesting the difference.

Remember our three childhood friends from chapter 2.2, "Myth 2: 'Our Fees? They're a Small Price to Pay!' "? They all invested $100,000 at the age of 35 and earned a 7% return on their investment. But each one was subject to a different set of fees—and the difference between the 1%, 2%, and 3% fees came out to hundreds of thousands of dollars. **Taylor, who paid just 1% in fees, accumulated almost *twice as much* money as her friend Jason, who paid 3% in fees.** Her investment grew to $574,349, while he was left with only $324,340!

Remember, those hidden fees on mutual funds average an astronomical 3.17%. The difference between owning high-cost, fee-laden mutual funds versus low-cost index funds could literally cost you a decade's worth of your life's work—talk about slowing you down on your path to Financial

"Those are fees incurred for requesting an explanation of your fees."

Freedom! And to add insult to injury, studies show that the high fees that come along with those mutual funds almost never lead to increased performance.

So stay away from excessive fees. Run for the hills. Find low-cost index funds to invest in and heed the warning of Jack Bogle, who showed us that paying through-the-nose fees can eat up as much as 50% to 70% of your future nest egg! The mantra is simple: take the money you save on fees and reinvest it for compounded growth. This strategy is another fast lane to freedom.

And what about an even bigger bite of your savings? Do you know what the *single largest* bite to come out of your nest egg is? Survey says: taxes!

Over the course of our lives, the **average American pays more than half of his or her income to an assortment of taxes: income tax, property tax, sales tax, tax at the pump, and so on. (According to what many experts estimate, currently, that's 54.25 cents per dollar.)** Good ol' Uncle Sam. And we're not done yet.

After 54.25% has been lopped off for the tax man, you can also say goodbye to another 17.25% of each dollar you earn in interest and fees. Got a car, a house, any credit card or student loan debt? In April 2014 the average

THE GOLDEN EGG
ACTUAL INCOME FOR LIFE

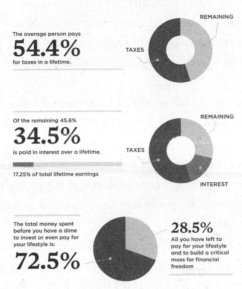

The average person pays
54.4%
for taxes in a lifetime.

TAXES

REMAINING

Of the remaining 45.6%
34.5%
is paid in interest over a lifetime.

17.25% of total lifetime earnings

TAXES

REMAINING

INTEREST

The total money spent before you have a dime to invest or even pay for your lifestyle is:
72.5%

28.5%
All you have left to pay for your lifestyle and to build a critical mass for financial freedom

US household had credit card debt of over $15,000; student loan debt of over $33,000; and mortgage debt of over $150,000. As a nation, we are up to our eyeballs in debt.

The fact is, on average, approximately one-third of the income you have left after taxes will be spent on paying down interest!

That leaves you with (drumroll, please) a whopping 28.5% of your hard-earned income left over to pay for everything else in life: food, clothing, shelter, education, health care, travel, entertainment, and anything else you happen to stumble upon at the mall or on Amazon! **Plus, out of this same number, you have to find a way to save and invest for Financial Freedom,** or at least some form of retirement income!

Becoming more efficient with your taxes is one way to get back some of that 54% you've given away. Keep more of your hard-earned income, and that's money that you could invest and compound to achieve your vision of Financial Freedom quicker.

In fact, if you're a high-income earner, living in a high-income state like California (as I used to), your total tax bill **(including income, investment, payroll, Obamacare, and Social Security) clocks in at 62%.** Which means that unless you have an efficient tax strategy, you get to keep only 38 cents out of every dollar you earn.

There's no good reason to pay more than you have to—in fact, it's your right as an American *not* to pay more than you have to. As Billings Learned Hand, one of the most influential judges of all time, stated:

> Anyone may arrange his affairs so that his taxes shall be as low as possible; he is not bound to choose that pattern which best pays the Treasury. There is not even a patriotic duty to increase one's taxes. Over and over again the Courts have said that there is nothing sinister in so arranging affairs as to keep taxes as low as possible. Everyone does it, rich and poor alike and all do right, for nobody owes any public duty to pay more than the law demands.

I follow Judge Hand's wisdom. I don't believe in paying any more than I absolutely have to, and neither should you. I continually look for legal, ethical ways to lower my tax bill, and I do my best to make use of government initiatives that allow me to build my nest egg in a tax-free environment. **I learned from those I interviewed that tax efficiency is one of the most direct pathways to shorten the time it takes to get from where you are now to where you want to be financially.**

> I am proud to be paying taxes in the United States. The only
> thing is, I could be just as proud for half of the money.
> —ARTHUR GODFREY

Let's be clear: I'm a patriot. I love America. I am one of millions of examples of the American Dream, and I'm happy (well, perhaps not happy, but proud) to pay my taxes. Yet I pay millions of dollars in taxes every year. My tax bill is more than I ever thought I'd earn in a lifetime, much less in a year. But I know from Yale's David Swensen that there are only three forces that can help you achieve the greatest returns:

1. Asset allocation,
2. Diversification,
3. Tax efficiency.

It helps, of course, that David runs a nonprofit organization, but for the rest of us, even with current tax laws, there are ways to maximize investment returns and minimize your tax bill.

Money Power Principle 4. *Tax efficiency is one of the simplest ways to continuously increase the real returns on your portfolio. Tax efficiency equals faster financial freedom.*

(Reader alert: If your brain is going to blur as I talk about taxes, I get it! Then simply jump immediately to the next chapter so you don't lose momentum. *But* be sure to schedule a time to sit down with your fiduciary and/or a tax expert to learn how to be most tax efficient with your investments. If you're willing to go for it, the next four pages offer some simple tax distinctions that, when understood, will allow you to keep more of your invested income and achieve your financial dreams faster.)

PICK YOUR TAX!

What if you realized that a small amount of tax knowledge could save you from needlessly paying 30% of what you earned to the tax man? How much faster could you achieve your financial goals?

You need to pay close attention to three types of taxes as an investor:

1. Ordinary Income Tax.
   As stated, if you're a high-income earner, your combined federal and state income taxes are nearing or exceeding 50%.
2. Long-Term Capital Gains.
   This is a tax on investments, which is only 20% *if* you hold your investment for longer than one year before you sell.
3. Short-Term Capital Gains.
   This is a tax on investment gains if the investment is sold before you have held it for a minimum of one year. Today the rates are currently the same as ordinary income taxes. Ouch!

Now that you know the power of compounding, I'm sure you realize how compounding your growth after taking a 50% tax bite as opposed

to a 20% tax bite can mean the difference between arriving at your financial goals a decade early or never getting there at all.

Want to understand the real impact of this?

- If you're getting an 8% gross return on your mutual fund, you're paying as much as 3% in fees on average—let's call it 2%, conservatively.
- So now your 8% return nets you 6% after fees. But we're not done yet.
- If you're a high-income earner from California or New York with a 50% federal and state ordinary income tax, you're left with closer to 3% on your investment after all these fees and taxes.

Remember you get to spend only what you keep; if you invest with a 3% net return, it takes 24 years to double your money.

If you made the same investment in an index fund, your 8% return would have fees in the range of 10 to 50 basis points (or 0.10% to 0.50%). We'll go for the larger number just to be conservative. That means you have a 7.5% return (8% - 0.5% = 7.5%), but since the index is not trading constantly, you defer all tax, and so your net return for the year is 7.5%. That means you can reinvest those returns and tap into the incredible power of compounding without the tax man interfering.

If you conscientiously manage your investments for tax efficiency, your 7.5% allows you to double your investments in 9.6 years instead of 24 years! Now do you see the importance of both tax and fee efficiency?

So how do you lower your tax bill and keep more of your earnings so you can compound your investments and achieve your idea of Financial Freedom faster?

- Make sure that wherever possible, you invest in a way that allows you to defer your taxes (401[k], IRA, annuity, defined benefit plan) so that you compound tax free and pay tax only at the time you sell the investment. Or set up a future tax-free environment by growing your investments in a Roth.
- When you do sell any investment held outside of a tax-deferred account (like an IRA), make sure you hold for a minimum of a year and a day in order to qualify for the lower long-term capital gains rate (again, at the time of this writing the rate is 20%).

ONE MORE THING:
BEWARE OF MUTUAL FUNDS

For most people, a home sale is usually a once- or twice-a-decade thing, and your accountant or tax expert can easily explain how to do this most tax-efficiently. But let's take a look at mutual funds. Do you know what those mutual fund managers of yours are doing every day? They're trading. They are buying and selling stocks and bonds on a daily, monthly, or quarterly basis. This is what the industry calls "turnover."

According to Charlie Farrell of CBS MarketWatch, "So although their marketing material encourages investors to buy and hold, the managers certainly don't practice what they preach. What they really mean is buy and hold their mutual fund, while they trade your retirement savings like crazy."

Experts say that the vast majority of mutual funds do not hold on to their investments for a full year. Why else would you buy them other than hoping they can trade their way to better performance? And you know what that means? Unless you're holding all of your mutual funds inside your 401(k), you're typically paying ordinary income taxes on any gains.[10]

In short, there's a good chance you're being charged 35%, 45%, or up to 50% or more in income tax, depending on what state you live in and your income level. All this tax, and you didn't even sell your mutual fund! So instead of keeping all your gains and having them continue to compound tax deferred, you are taking a devastating hit to your compounding ability that is completely avoidable if you understand tax efficiency.

Even if you've maxed out your 401(k) and IRA, you can still make investments in a form that allows you to defer taxes. Index funds do not constantly trade individual companies; they usually hold a fixed basket of companies that changes only if the index that the fund tracks actually changes—which is rare.

As a result, if you're investing in an index long term, you're not taking the tax bite each year; instead, you're deferring the taxes, since you haven't sold

---

10. However, in certain situations, the gains may be long-term if the fund held the position for an extended period.

anything. That money can remain in the fund and continue to compound earnings to its owner: you!

Your fiduciary or a great tax expert can help you understand all the ways you can produce more net growth in your Freedom Fund so that your compounding process is maximized. Remember, this can save you years or even decades!

And finally, in section 5, there is a strategy that you'll learn about in the "Secrets of the Ultrawealthy" chapter that you can use, too: an IRS-approved method that will make a huge difference by allowing you to compound your investments and help you keep your nest egg tax free. This could allow you to achieve your financial goals up to 25% to 50% faster without taking any greater investment risks!

Have I got your attention? I hope so. **Because it's your money and it's your life! Don't let anyone take it or waste it!** So you now have three fast-track strategies to speed up the pace and win the money game:

1. Save more and invest the difference.
2. Earn more (add value) and invest the difference.
3. Reduce fees and taxes and invest the difference.

Now it's time to turn on the juice and take a quick look at some of the ways you can increase what your investments earn....

SPEED IT UP:
4. GET BETTER RETURNS AND
SPEED YOUR WAY TO VICTORY

If you're prepared, and you know what it takes, it's not a risk.
You just have to figure out how to get there.
There is always a way to get there.
—MARK CUBAN

How do you get a greater return while still reducing risk? Most people think that in order to get high returns, you have to take huge risks. But the greatest investors know that's simply not the case. Remember Kyle Bass from chapter 2.8, "You Gotta Take Huge Risks to Get Big Rewards"? **He blew the high-risk, high-return myth out of the water with something called asymmetric risk/reward.**

That's a fancy term for a pretty simple concept. How do you explain it? Kyle turned $30 million into $2 billion by finding an investment opportunity where he risked only 3 cents for the opportunity to make $1—more accurately, $3 million for a $100 million upside—and expanded that risk/reward ratio into billions. Remember how he taught his sons to make "riskless" investments with significant upside by buying nickels? The upside (reward) is way bigger than the downside (risk) on this deal, which makes it asymmetric.

One of Paul Tudor Jones's greatest successes is that he knows he can be wrong and still be successful, because he uses asymmetric risk/reward to guide his investment decisions. He's always looking for what he calls a 5:1 investment—where if he risks $1, he believes he can make $5.

Jones is willing to risk $1 million when his research shows he's likely to make $5 million. Of course, he could be wrong. But if he uses the same 5:1 formula on his next investment, and he's successful, he will have made

$5 million, minus the first investment loss of $1 million, for a net investment gain of $4 million.

Using this formula of constantly investing where he has the opportunity for asymmetric rewards for the risk he's taking, Paul could be wrong four out of five times and break even. If he loses $1 million four times in a row trying to make $5 million, he'll have lost a total of $4 million. But when the fifth decision is a success, with a single home run he's earned back his total $5 million investment. The greatest investors in history know how to maximize their returns—they know how to set the game up to win.

You'll learn more about what Paul teaches in section 6, "Invest Like the .001%: The Billionaire's Playbook," and in my interview with him. He is going to share with you his "$100,000 MBA," or the most important things he's learned about investing—one of which is how to be wrong and still win!

So asymmetric risk/reward is the first way to get higher returns. The second way? You'll learn more about this in chapter 4.1 on asset allocation, but for now, just know that if real estate's mantra is "Location! Location! Location!" then the mantra for getting better returns while reducing risk is "Diversification! Diversification! Diversification!" Effective diversification not only reduces your risk but also offers you the opportunity to maximize your returns.

Asset allocation is the *one thing* that every investment professional I've talked to, the best in the world, has said is the key factor in where you end up financially. It's the most important skill, and it's the one most investors know little about. So in chapter 4.1, "The Ultimate Bucket List: Asset Allocation," you're going to learn the power of asset allocation and be able to implement its gifts to benefit you and your family for the rest of your life. On top of that, you're going to see in section 6 the exact asset allocation of some of the most successful investors in the world who have consistently produced the highest returns.

Yes, you read that right: you'll be able to model the *exact* strategies of the best investors on the planet. You'll have Ray Dalio's asset allocation! Obviously, past performance doesn't guarantee future performance, but in the case of Ray Dalio, your strategy is coming from one of the greatest investors of all time, and his focus is getting you the greatest return with the least amount of risk. Dalio has been estimating every type of market and finding what the best ratio is through asset allocation for over 20 years. He has more than $160 billion in assets under management and a record of only three losing years out of the last 22. After reading this book, you will learn a strategy that is based on Ray's groundbreaking approach for the world's wealthiest individuals, institutions, and governments.

HOW FAST CAN YOU GO?

It's probably pretty obvious that we'd all like better returns. But what's less obvious is the massive impact that better returns have on your time horizon for investing. The "rule of 72" says that it takes 72 years to double your money at a 1% compounded rate. So if you've got $10,000 to invest at 1% compounded, you may not be around to see that money double. You can cut that timeline *in half* by doubling your rate to 2%, and *in half* again by doubling that rate to 4%! So what's the difference between a 10% return and a 4% return? **A 10% return doubles every 7.2 years; a 4% return doubles every 18 years!** If you want to radically change your plan and get to financial freedom in seven years versus 18 years, you can. Or 14 years instead of 36! Those are the types of differences that are possible when you learn how to get better returns. And the most important thing is to get these greater returns without taking significantly greater risks wherever possible. You're looking for that asymmetric risk/reward that all great investors seek. **It's elusive, but it's out there, and this is just one more way that you can speed up your approach to realizing your dreams.** (Take a look at the table on page 284 to see how fast—or slow—your money will double.)

Your next question is likely, "Where do I start looking for my own asymmetric risk/reward opportunities?" Sometimes they turn up in the unlikeliest places. For me—maybe because I grew up in Southern California—I've always believed in including real estate as a key component of my portfolio. If you ever turn on the news, it's hard not to notice the demographic shift that's taking place in this country right now, with 10,000 people turning 65 every day. The boomers are hitting retirement in droves. In the back of my mind, I always knew there had to be a way to provide some of my capital to help expand quality facilities for people entering this stage of life, while providing a profit for me. But it wasn't until I visited my wife's grandmother in

NUMBER OF YEARS TO DOUBLE YOUR INVESTMENT VALUE
BASED ON RATE OF RETURN

RATE OF RETURN	YEARS TO DOUBLE $$
25%	2.88
20%	3.60
19%	3.80
18%	4.00
17%	4.20
16%	4.50
15%	4.80
14%	5.10
13%	5.50
12%	6.00
11%	6.50
10%	7.20
9%	8.00
8%	9.00
7%	10.20
6%	12.00
5%	14.40
4%	18.00
3%	24.00
2%	36.00
1%	72.00

Vancouver, British Columbia, that I connected the dots for a future investment in retirement communities.

My wife, my Bonnie Pearl—my "Sage"—is the love of my life. Her family
is my family. Her grandma Hilda was my grandma. I loved her dearly. After
being married for 58 years, her husband died, and we all watched as she suffered. For ten years, Hilda cried herself to sleep at night. She was living on
her own, proud and independent, but heart-achingly lonely, missing her life
partner. We didn't have the heart to put her in a home, yet with Hilda's dementia worsening, Bonnie Pearl's mom, Sharon, was determined to find her
a home with the best possible care.

We had heard that some retirement communities were pretty spectacular, and after weeks of looking, Sharon finally found a community that gave the Four Seasons a run for its money—this place is amazing. I always said *I'd* stay there, and I don't say that about many places.

So guess what happened to Grandmom after moving into her new digs? Forget that she traded up to a beautiful new apartment with modern amenities and 24-hour care. That was just the tip of the iceberg. More amazing than that, she began a second life! At 88 years old, she transformed into a new woman and fell in love again. A 92-year-old Italian captured her heart. ("I don't let him under my shirt yet, but he tries all the time," she said with a grin.) They had four beautiful years together before he passed away, and I kid you not, at his funeral, she met her next beau. Her last decade was filled with a quality of life she never could have envisioned. She found happiness, joy, love, and friendship again. It was an unexpected last chapter of her life and a reminder that love is the ultimate wealth. It can show up unexpected anytime, anywhere—and it is never too late.

Grandmom's story opened up the realization that there was a real need for retirement communities that were effectively staffed and beautiful just like hers. How could I find a way to invest in an opportunity like that? Obviously just walking into a home and asking to invest is probably not the most effective strategy. So I went to my personal advisor, Ajay Gupta at Stronghold, and told him what I believed in and what I was looking for. He found an opportunity where my investment not only stood to make a great return but also aligned with my values and beliefs and with a broader trend in the market. Many experts look at this category as a "demographic inevitability" because the 75-year-old age segment will grow by 84% between 2010 and 2030. Demand will be greater than supply!

Ajay found an investment company run by an amazing entrepreneur who builds, invests, and manages high-end senior living facilities. He started with nothing and has built it into a $3 billion enterprise. He finds the sites, puts up as much as half the money himself, and then rounds up a small group of investors to put up the rest. Here's what I get in exchange: I get a preferred return on my money (which are income payments each month) based on the profitability of the facility. This can range 6% to 8% per year, and because it's real estate, I also get the tax benefit of *depreciation*, which means I don't have to pay income tax on the entire income payment. Plus, I own a piece of the real estate, which, over the long term, I believe will increase in value. I get to participate in the exit strategy when the investor group eventually sells the facility. To be clear, this specific investment is limited to investors who are accredited[11] and meet certain net worth/income requirements. But don't fret! For those who are nonaccredited, there are publicly traded REITs (real estate investment trusts) that focus solely on owning a basket of properties around the country. These can be purchased for as little as $25 a share at the time of this writing and offer dividend (income) payments each quarter. Do your homework and/or have a fiduciary advisor help you find the best available.

If senior housing seems out of reach, another strategy in real estate is lending your money with a first trust deed as security. In the chapter on asset allocation, I'll describe to you an example of how investors who need money will take short-term loans at high rates—for example, a one-year loan for 8% or 10%, and you get the first trust deed as collateral. When done effectively, you can loan, say, $50,000 on a $100,000 home, or $500,000 on a $1 million home, and the property could drop 50%, and you'd still be in good shape. While others are collecting 3% and 4% returns, you're getting 8% to 10%.

Once you start focusing passionately on ways to save more, earn more, reduce fees and taxes, and find better returns with even less risk, you'll be amazed at how many new opportunities you'll discover. Again, a great fiduciary advisor won't just guide you; he or she can also help you to find investment opportunities with that magical asymmetric risk/reward that all successful investors seek.

Okay, we're coming to the home stretch of this section. This final step can massively increase the speed at which you achieve your most important financial goals. Plus, it's fun to dream and explore. You're going to love the journey of this next chapter. Let's discover . . .

---

11. For an individual to be considered an accredited investor, he must have a net worth of at least US$1 million, not including the value of his *primary* residence; or have income of at least $200,000 each year for the last two years (or $300,000 together with a spouse if married).

SPEED IT UP:
5. CHANGE YOUR LIFE—
AND LIFESTYLE—FOR THE BETTER

My favorite things in life don't cost any money.
It's really clear that the most precious resource we all have is time.
—STEVE JOBS

What would happen if, for just a moment, you considered making a change? A big change, like picking up and moving to another city? You could be living large in Boulder, Colorado, for what you're paying just in rent in New York City or San Francisco. The cost of homes, food, taxes, and so on differ wildly depending on where you live. Our country—our *world*—is one of boundless opportunity waiting for you to explore. So why not take off the blinders just for a moment to consider what life could be like if you lived in a new city or town?

Are you freezing your butt off in the Midwest winters, or battling the heat of the summer in Atlanta, wondering year after year why you don't hoof it to a better climate? As a native son of Southern California, I'm always amazed by people who spend their lives freezing to death in the Arctic tundra of Minneapolis or Chicago. And even if you don't care about the weather, you've got to care about your cost of living. A million-dollar home in Washington, DC, costs a fraction of that in Raleigh, North Carolina—a city rated as the third best place for business and careers by *Forbes*, not to mention a high-tech and educational hub (that also has great weather). Or what about something more local: a move from San Francisco to San Diego? You can stay in the great state of California and *still* cut your housing costs by 32%.

It's one thing to be tax-efficient in your investments; it's another to be tax-efficient in your *life*. You're trying to save 5% here, 10% there. What about saving 10% or 15% or more in *everything* you do by moving to a less expensive city or a tax-friendly state? Think about all the additional money you'd have to invest, share, donate if it didn't go straight to rent, food, or transportation. **One single move could give you a 10% to 30% increase in your income.** If you're already saving 10%, with a move you now can save 20% to 40% without spending an additional dime. **This change in your savings rate will put some rocket fuel in your money machine that will massively improve the pace at which you achieve financial freedom.**

I know what you're going to say: "Move to a new city? You've got to be crazy, Tony. I can't just pick up and move! I have a job, I have family, I have friends; I've lived my whole life in Dallas." (Or Seattle or Miami or Denver.) But if you saw that you could save ten years of your investing life, reach your Financial Freedom goals a decade sooner or even more, might it be worth it?

Generations of Americans have looked at retirement as a time to pick up and move to a warmer climate, a less expensive city, or to a beautiful, low-key place like Boise, Idaho, or Greenville, South Carolina, to breathe clean air and enjoy the outdoors. **But why wait until retirement? Why not change your zip code today? Why not find a place to raise your family that allows you to reduce your cost of living *and* elevate your quality of life at the same time, while you're young enough for both you and your children to reap the rewards?**

If you're still shaking your head no, I get it. I was with you on this one, actually—until recently. I grew up in California and never imagined living anywhere else. Even when I started traveling extensively and buying homes and properties all over the world, California was always my home base.

Then in 2012 California raised taxes on the highest income earners by more than 30%, to 13.3%. After a lifetime of paying through the nose on state income taxes (historically among the most punishing in the country), the tax situation got even worse. My effective tax rate—after federal and state income taxes, Social Security, investment taxes, payroll taxes, and the Obamacare tax—shot up to 62%. That meant I was left with 38 cents on every dollar. Just 38 cents! And on top of that, the new state income tax increase was made *retroactive*, meaning that I was going to have to pay additional tax on income I had already earned that year. They changed the rules of the game after the fact! I had reached my limit—this was outrageous. Because of my travel and the time I spent in my other homes, I was living in California for only 90 days out of the year! Just 90 days for literally a multimillion-dollar state tax bill? California was no longer sustainable for me—I'd had enough!

I had played by the rules, and the rules had come back to bite me. But instead of feeling sorry for myself, I voted with my conscience—or with my feet, I should say. Along with thousands of others, Sage and I realized we were no longer welcome in California. So we decided to take the plunge and look for a new place to live. (In fact, California has lost over $30 billion in annual income tax revenue over the last two decades to states such as Nevada, Arizona, Texas, and Wisconsin. If you want to see how big this trend is and how many people are moving from high-tax to low-tax states, go to www.howmoneywalks.com.)

We turned it into a kind of treasure hunt. We looked at places like Lake Tahoe, where we really liked the mountains, the mix of seasons, and the small-town vibe; and Austin, Texas, where music, energy, and high tech come together to create the fabric of an innovative and connected community.

We looked at Florida too, reluctantly. All I knew of Florida were alligators and old people. But that's the stereotype, not the reality. What we found instead was a paradise in Palm Beach. After looking at 88 properties in three states in just three weeks (I told you I'm a massive-action guy), we found the only brand-new home on the water in Palm Beach. Two acres, nearly 200 feet of ocean frontage on one side, and the Atlantic Intracoastal Waterway on the other, with a 50-foot boat dock. I feel like I'm back in my home in Fiji—it's extraordinary. Sage has everything she wants close by: world-class restaurants, shopping, easy access to the entire East Coast, and all the privacy and serenity of living on an island right here in the United States.

Of course, the price tag was way higher than I ever wanted or imagined paying for a home. But Florida has no state income tax. We went from 13.3% state income tax in California to nothing—nada, zip. So here's the kicker: with the state taxes we're saving every year, we are literally paying off our entire new home in six years! Did you catch that? We're paying for our *entire home* out of the tax savings we now get as residents of the Sunshine

State instead of the Golden State. Kind of makes you think we should have done it sooner, huh? Better late than never.

And if that weren't enough (which it is!), we've massively improved our quality of life in the bargain. Every day we pinch ourselves as we wake up with magnificent weather: 78 degrees with a cool breeze off the ocean and water you can melt into, it's so warm. In fact, Sage and I have become almost evangelical in our enthusiasm for our new home; we tell friends and family to think about moving down to Palm Beach to join us. My youngest son has already moved here. Two of my dearest friends in the world are on their way down from Connecticut and New York, and they're here to stay. And, of course, even if they'd decided not to move here, we would have happily taken our tax savings and flown them all out here to visit us in paradise anyway!

So whether or not *you* decide to join us in Palm Beach, there's a new zip code out there that might be just right for you. You don't have to wait for retirement to get there. From Nashville, Tennessee, to Portland, Oregon, and from Augusta, Maine, to Ann Arbor, Michigan, there are hundreds of affordable havens for young and old alike: retirees looking to stretch their savings and continue to enjoy a rich, rewarding lifestyle; and young professionals looking to jump-start or reimagine their careers. Check out *U.S. News & World Report*'s feature on the best places to live for as little as $75 a day (http://money.usnews.com/money/retirement/articles/2013/10/15/the -best-places-to-retire-on-75-a-day). Also seriously consider the seven states where there's no state income tax at all: Alaska, Florida, Nevada, South Dakota, Texas, Washington, and Wyoming. Or try Tennessee and New Hampshire, where only your dividend and interest income are taxed at the state level. The Memphis and Nashville music scenes *and* more money in your pocket—how bad does that sound?

GIVE YOUR GLOBE A SPIN

And while we're at it, why not think *all the way outside the box* on this one? Forget just a 10% to 20% increase in your spending power, how about cutting your cost of living by a third, or in half? Get out your globe and give it a spin—and think about some of the beautiful (and beautifully *affordable*) places you could live if only you expanded your horizons.

There are huge opportunities all over the world to improve your lifestyle and lower your expenses, in places such as Bali, Fiji, Uruguay, Costa Rica—*if* you have the courage and the freedom to *go for it*! You can rent an extraordinary apartment in the mountains outside of Buenos Aires, Argentina, for a fraction of what it would cost for a studio walk-up in a major US city. You can move to the Czech Republic and find a room just off Wenceslas Square in Prague's New Town area, the heart of the city's cultural community.

Remember my BMW-loving son? After he traded in his fancy wheels for a chance at a better lifestyle, he decided to think really big. He went down to Costa Rica for a couple of days and was completely blown away by the extraordinary culture. Turns out there is a huge English-speaking community in Costa Rica—tons of ex-pats who discovered their money went a lot further down there, their days were a little richer, their nights more exciting. And Costa Rica isn't just a place to relax and unwind. Some of our leading companies have established important bases of operations there. Procter & Gamble, Heinz, Microsoft, Intel—the list goes on and on, which means there are countless career opportunities available.

Life can be an adventure. Take a trip and explore a foreign city with an eye toward moving there. Turn your next vacation into a fact-finding expedition, where the endgame is to try on a whole new way of life. You don't have to live in a box and go through the same motions each and every day. You don't have to worry about making your rent or covering your basic expenses if you open yourself up to the idea of massive change. Lift yourself from your comfort zone and spend 60%, 70%, even *80%* less money, getting you to your goal of financial freedom that much faster. And while you're at it, improve the quality of your life in an exponential way.

Even if a move across the world seems too radical now, think about this option over the long term—a five-year plan or a ten-year plan, or maybe a retirement plan. Why not at least open yourself to the idea that there's a beautiful and affordable place out there waiting to be discovered? Our world is dynamic—it's changing constantly. The idea that a move would be bad for your kids is a thing of the past. We live in a global economy; what an amazing experience to give your kids an opportunity to see the world, learn a new language, adapt to a new culture. You can make a family decision about creating a better quality of life for everyone.

Life is like a bicycle. To keep your balance, you must keep moving.
—ALBERT EINSTEIN

At the end of the day, it's all about being more efficient and more effective with your earnings and your savings and speeding up your path to Financial Freedom. You can find a way to improve the quality of your life while reducing your cost of living simultaneously. It's the ultimate win-win. At the end of the day, the best investment you can make is the one you make in yourself and your lifestyle.

Wow, you've taken three giant steps toward Financial Freedom:

Step 1. You've made the most important financial decision of your life.
You've decided to become an investor, not merely a consumer. You've committed a percentage of your income to save and invest in your Freedom Fund, and you've automated it.

Step 2. You've become an insider who knows the rules of the game.
You've debunked the 9 Myths, and you'll never be taken advantage of again.

Step 3. You've made the game winnable.
- **You know exactly how much money it will take for you to achieve Financial Security, Independence, or Freedom.** You know your Three to Thrive: your short-term, medium-term, and long-term goals.
- **You've come up with an initial financial plan and a timeline for achievement.** You've used the app to calculate approximately how long it will take you to meet financial goals you're most committed to.
- **You've reviewed the five ways to speed up your plan.** Ideally, you've begun to brainstorm ways to apply these insights to sock away more money or keep more money in your financial Freedom Fund. This can help you reach your cherished financial goals even quicker.

So what's next? **Step 4 answers the obvious question that's probably burning in your mind: "Where do I put my money? What specific investments will maximize my upside and protect me against the downside?" It's time to make the most important *investment* decision of your life. It's time to learn the power of asset allocation . . .**

MAKE THE MOST IMPORTANT *INVESTMENT* DECISION OF YOUR LIFE

THE ULTIMATE BUCKET LIST: ASSET ALLOCATION

Never test the depth of the river with both feet.
—WARREN BUFFETT

Say you've got your money machine cranking: your boss just gave you an unexpected $10,000 bonus, or perhaps you suddenly came into a $100,000 inheritance. What would you do with it? Would you put it in your savings account or your IRA? Invest in a virtual pocketful of Bitcoin? Bid on a case of vintage wine on eBay? Fly to Vegas and bet it all on a roll of the dice? Or maybe buy 100 shares of Apple stock? Would you put it all in one place or spread it around?

The answer to that last question is the key to your financial future.

Asset allocation is the most important *investment* decision of your lifetime, more important than any single investment you're going to make in stocks, bonds, real estate, or anything else. What's the difference? Well, the *financial* decisions you've already made—to automatically invest a percentage of your income for compound returns—gets you in the game. But once you decide to get in the game, now you've got to stay in the game—for the long term! You can lose it all if you aren't careful about *where* you put your money. **Anybody can *become* wealthy; asset allocation is how you *stay* wealthy.**

But don't just take it from me. Listen to David Swensen, the rock star of institutional investing. Remember, he's the guy who grew Yale's portfolio from $1 billion to more than $23.9 billion by achieving a 13.9% average annual return across three decades of bear and bull markets. Nobody does it better. When I sat down with him in his office in New Haven, Connecticut, I asked, "What are the most important insights investors must have to achieve financial freedom?" **He told me that there are only three tools for reducing your risk and increasing your potential for financial success:**

1. **Security selection—stock picking;**
2. **Market timing—short-term bets on the direction of the market; and**
3. **Asset allocation—your long-term strategy for diversified investing.**

Before I could even ask about the first two, he made one thing perfectly clear: "Overwhelmingly, the most important of the three is asset allocation," he said. "It actually explains more than a hundred percent of returns in the investment world." Wait a second: How could it be *more* than 100%? Because those fees, taxes, and losses that come along with stock picking and market timing put a drag on your profits.

Asset allocation is more than diversification. **It means dividing up your money among different classes, or types, of investments (such as stocks, bonds, commodities, or real estate) and in specific proportions that you decide in advance, according to your goals or needs, risk tolerance, and stage of life.**

Wow, that's a mouthful, isn't it?

Yet it's the key to success or failure for the world's best financial players, including every single one of the investors and traders I interviewed for this book. Paul Tudor Jones swears by it. Mary Callahan Erdoes, perhaps the most powerful woman on Wall Street, leads 22,000 financial professionals whose livelihoods depends on it. Ray Dalio, who founded the largest hedge fund in the world and is now worth $14 billion personally, lives it.

This chapter takes a complex subject and makes it simple enough for you to act on and positively affect your investment returns for the rest of your life, so give it your full commitment and focus! It doesn't matter if you have only $1,000 that you're going to save and invest or $1 million. The principles you're about to learn are *critical* to start applying immediately. If you think you know them already, it's time to take them to the next level.

Let's talk about why asset allocation is so crucial to *your* investment plan, and how you can start making it work for you today.

Anyone who thinks there's safety in numbers
hasn't looked at the stock market pages.
—IRENE PETER

How many times have you picked what looks like the fastest line at the grocery store, but it turns out to be the slowest? Or how often do you switch
to the fast lane in a traffic jam and watch the cars in the slow lane whiz past
you? You think you're getting there faster, and then you're wrong. And what
about intimate relationships? In spite of how much you know about yourself
and what you believe and value, have you ever chosen the "wrong" partner?
We all know *that* decision can have an extraordinary impact on the quality
of your life!

The same thing can happen with your investments. Except that when
you make mistakes with your nest egg, if it's too big a mistake, it's all over.
It can mean losing your home. Or still looking for work when you're 70. Or
having no money for your children's education. That's why this chapter is so
important.

Asset allocation is the one key skill that can set you apart from 99% of all
investors. And guess what? It won't cost you a dime. David Swensen likes to
quote Harry Markowitz, the Nobel Prize–winning father of modern portfolio theory, to whom I also reached out to interview for this book. He said
famously, "Diversification is the only free lunch." Why? Because spreading
your money across different investments decreases your risk, increases your
upside returns over time, and doesn't cost you anything.

We've all heard the old adage "Don't put all your eggs in one basket."
Well, asset allocation protects you from making that financial mistake. It
sounds like such a basic rule, but how many people do you know who vio-
late it?

I have a friend who got so excited about Apple that he put all his money
in the company. For a while, it was the most successful stock in the world—
until it dropped by 40% in a matter of weeks. *Ouch.* Then there's another
friend who was in her 30s when she quit her job as a television executive, sold
her house in Los Angeles at the height of the real estate market boom, and
used the money to open a rustic diner in Wyoming. She invested what was

left in high-risk stocks and junk bonds, thinking the interest would provide enough income to support her. And it did for a while. But the stock market crash of 2008 wiped out her entire savings. She had to fold up her teepee and go back to work as a freelancer for a fraction of what she used to make.

We've all heard horror stories from the economic meltdown. Maybe you know some baby boomers who had all their money tied up in real estate before the bottom fell out. Or a couple who were ready to retire with their 401(k) full and their target-date funds about to mature. They had the RV picked out, the boat in the driveway, the itinerary drawn up with visits to the grandkids marked out. Then the financial world unraveled. Their net worth was cut nearly in half, and their dream of retirement turned into 20 more years of work.

These stories are heartbreaking, and I want to make sure nothing like that ever happens to you. And the good news is, it never has to. That's why I wrote this chapter: so that you'll not only be protected but also can grow your nest egg faster.

What's the simple and core investment lesson here? **What goes up will come down!** Ray Dalio told me point-blank that in your lifetime "it's almost certain that whatever you're going to put your money in, there will come a day when you will lose fifty percent to seventy percent." Yikes! That means any investment you pick is going to lose half to two-thirds or more of its value! And don't most people typically favor one type of investment because they feel they "know" more about that area, or because it's currently providing a "hot" return? Some people tend to put all their money in real estate, others in stocks, bonds, or commodities. If you don't diversify enough, you stand to lose your shirt! Are you hearing me? No matter how well you plan, there will be a day of reckoning for every type of asset. **So, diversify or die. But if you diversify *well*, you'll win!**

By now I'm sure you're crystal clear about the consequences of not diversifying! Now would you like to hear about the incredible impact of the *right* diversification? It's almost like having a license to print money. I know that's an exaggeration, but imagine what it would feel like if you knew you were making money while you sleep, and that your diversification gave you true peace of mind regardless of the economic climate.

Here's a real example. How would you feel if, in that Defcon environment of 2008, when stock markets were losing more than $2 trillion, bonds were tanking, and real estate was falling through the floor, you could have had an asset allocation where your maximum loss was just 3.93%? This example is not a fantasy. This is the power of asset allocation that I've mentioned several times in this book, and I'm going to demonstrate it to you shortly. Better yet, what if in the last 30 years of your life (between 1984 and 2013), your asset allocation was so powerful that you lost money only four times, with an average loss of just 1.9%, and never more than 3.93%? Remember, everyone else during those three decades was riding the wild wave of inflation and deflation. In the last decade alone, we had two market drops of nearly 50%, yet you would have coasted through the storm without a single gut check and still averaged a compounded annual return of just under 10%. I'm not describing a hypothetical situation. What I'm describing to you is an actual portfolio, a specific asset allocation, designed by Ray Dalio. Soon I'll show you the exact formula that has produced these mind-blowing results. But before you can use it, **you have to understand the core principles laid out in this chapter.**

Rule 1: don't lose money.

Rule 2: see Rule 1.

I can't say it enough: *good people often fail because they do the right thing at the wrong time.* Buying a house—is it the right thing to do? Most experts would say yes. But in 2006, it was the wrong time! **So the question is: If we're all going to be wrong some of the time, where do we put our money?** That's where asset allocation comes in.

Here's another way to think about it: when you're trying to build a winning team in sports, you have to know the capabilities of each player. You have to know his strengths and weaknesses. You have to decide who you can count on in different situations. Now, say your portfolio is the team, and your investment choices are the players. Asset allocation helps you choose who starts and at which positions. **Ultimately, it's the right mix at the right time that brings you victory.**

Asset allocation offers you a set of guiding principles: a philosophy of investing to help you decide where to put Freedom Fund money or your nest egg and in what proportions.

Think of it as taking chunks of your money and putting them into two separate investment buckets with different levels of risk and reward. One of these first two buckets is a safe environment for your money, but it's not going to grow very fast there. You might get bored with it, but it's secure, so that when you need it, it's there. The second bucket is sexier because it can give you the opportunity for much quicker growth, but it's risky. **In fact, you have to be prepared to lose everything you put in here!**

So how much goes in each bucket? It depends on how much time you've got to grow your investments and how much risk you're willing to take. You've got to ask yourself, "How much risk can I *afford* to take at my stage in life?" But remember, you're not diversifying just to protect yourself. You want to enhance your results: to find the ideal blend of investments that will make you thrive, not just survive!

But, hey, if we're willing to admit it, many people have more than enough stress in their daily lives without adding a ton of anxiety worrying about their investments day and night. A significant part of financial security or even freedom is peace of mind, that feeling that you don't have to think about money. The first bucket will give you certainty in your life, which, after all, is the first basic human need. And that's why I call it the **Security/ Peace of Mind Bucket.** It's where you want to keep the part of your nest egg you can't afford to lose—or even *imagine* losing without waking up in a cold sweat! **It's a sanctuary of safe investments that you lock up tight— and then hide the key.**

> I don't gamble, because winning a hundred dollars doesn't give
> me great pleasure. But losing a hundred dollars pisses me off.
> —ALEX TREBEK, host of *Jeopardy!*

Taking a financial hit not only lightens our wallets but also can steal the joy from our lives. Remember that behavioral economics study with the monkeys and the apples? A monkey was happy if he was given an apple. But if he was given two apples, and then one was taken away, he freaked out—even though, in the end, he still had an apple. Humans are the same way. Research on human emotion shows that the majority of people around the world underestimate how badly they feel when they lose. The pleasure of our victories is dwarfed by the pain of our failures and our losses. So we all have to set up a Security/Peace of Mind Bucket to protect ourselves from taking the kind of hits that will not only set us back financially but also will make us miserable.

To familiarize you with the kind of investments that are considered a bit more secure, let's look at eight basic types of assets (investment options or resources) that might belong in this Security Bucket. This is just a sampling. It's not meant to be everything that would fit in this bucket. But as you read, you will notice a pattern: none of these types of investments tends to have extreme volatility—meaning that its value doesn't tend to fluctuate much— especially compared with things you'll see later in the Risk/Growth Bucket. (Although, as we've all experienced, there are short periods in history where virtually all investments have increased volatility. Later Ray Dalio will show us how to prepare for this as well!) But this quick list is designed to get you to think about your investments in the future, and give you a feel for what might go here. **Ask yourself, "Before I invest, is this putting me at risk?**

Is this something I'd be better off having in my Risk/Growth Bucket or in my Security Bucket?"

So let's take a look at what this is all about, starting with the first and perhaps the most important place to put a portion of your money: the **Security/Peace of Mind Bucket.** What assets would you want to put in here? Remember, this bucket is the slow but steady contender, like the turtle in the race to financial freedom. Because the turtle often wins! And you have to treat it like your sacred temple of savings and investments—because what goes in here doesn't come out.

And before you go on, bear in mind that the beginning of this chapter has some fundamentals: the blocking and tackling of asset allocation. If you're a sophisticated investor, you can scan through the list of investment options because you probably already know what they are, and you can save yourself some time. But I didn't want to leave out anyone. Besides, you might find a distinction or two that you'll find valuable.

So let's dive in.

1. **Cash/Cash Equivalents.** At some time in our lives, every one of us will need a cushion to cover our needs in case of an emergency or a sudden loss of income. No matter your income level, you need some liquidity—or instant access to cash. Is it possible to be rich in assets and feel poor because you don't have cash or liquidity? A lot of people were caught short in 2008 when the banks froze up and stopped lending (even to one another), and real estate seemed impossible to sell. In fact, according to a 2011 study, *half* of all Americans would struggle to come up with $2,000 in a crisis such as an unexpected medical bill, legal cost, or home or car repair. So you need some cash to make sure that doesn't happen to you. Think about it: it wouldn't take a lot of focus or a lot of savings for you to be better off than more than half of America!

   But once you've decided how much cash you need to have on hand, where do you keep it? Most of us choose bank accounts that are insured by the FDIC for balances of up to $250,000. Unfortunately, brick-and-mortar banks pay almost no interest these days—the last time I checked, some were as low as 0.01%!—while online banks have been offering slightly higher rates. Maybe not ideal, but at least we know the money is safe and available. You also may want to keep some of that cash in a safe place or for safety near your home—you know, "under your mattress"—in a hidden safe in case there's an earthquake or hurricane or some other kind of emergency, and the ATMs stop working.

Other tools for cash equivalents include *money market funds*—there are three types, and if you want to learn more, see the box for details.

For larger amounts of money that we need to keep safe and liquid, **you can buy into ultra-short-term investments called *cash equivalents*. The most well-known are good old money market funds.** You may even already own one. These are basically mutual funds made up of low-risk, extremely short-term bonds and other kinds of debt (which you'll learn more about in a moment). They can be great because you get a somewhat higher rate of return than a boring old bank account, but you still get immediate access to your cash 24 hours a day—and there are some that even let you write checks.

By the way, most banks offer *money market deposit accounts*, which are *not* the same as money market funds. These are like savings accounts where the *banks* are allowed to invest your money in short-term debt, and they pay you a slightly better interest rate in return. There's usually a minimum deposit required or other restrictions, low rates, and penalties if your balance falls too low. But they are insured by the FDIC, which is a good thing. And that sets them apart from money market *funds*, which are *not* guaranteed and could potentially drop in value.

But if you want to keep your money safe, liquid, and earning interest, one option is a **US Treasury money market fund with checking privileges.** True, these funds aren't insured by the FDIC, but because they are tied only to US government debt and not to any corporations or banks that might default, the only way you can lose your money is if the government fails to pay its short-term obligations. If that happens, there is no US government, and all bets are off anyway!

---

2. **Bonds.** We all know what a bond is, right? When I give you my bond, I give you my word. My promise. When I buy a bond, you give me your word—your promise—to return my money with a specific rate of interest after

X period of time (the maturity date). That's why bonds are called **"fixed-income investments."** The income—or return—you'll get from them is fixed at the time you buy them, depending on the length of time you agree to hold them. And sometimes you can use those regular interest payments (dividends) as income while the bond matures. So it's like a simple IOU with benefits, right? But there are zillions of bonds and bond funds out there; not all but many are rated by various agencies according to their levels of risk. **At the end of this chapter, you'll find a quick bond briefing** to find out when they can be hazardous to your financial health, and when they can be useful—even great!—investments.

Bonds can also be kind of confusing. Like a seesaw, they *increase in value* when interest rates go *down*, and *decrease in value* when rates go *up*.

THE BOND SEESAW

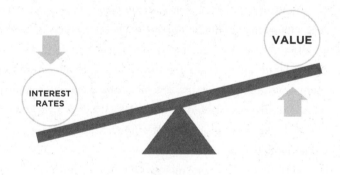

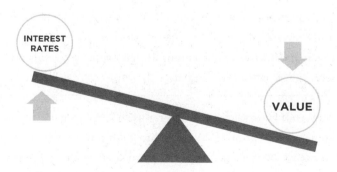

After all, who wants to buy an old low-interest-rate bond when a shiny new bond with a higher interest rate comes on the market? But one way to avoid worrying so much about price fluctuations in bonds is to diversify and buy into a low-cost bond index fund.

And just remember, not all bonds are equal. Greece's bonds are not going to be as strong as Germany's. Detroit's municipal bonds are not going to be as strong as the US Treasury's. In fact, some investment advisors say the only completely safe bond is one backed by the full faith and credit of the United States. And you can actually buy US bonds called *Treasury inflation-protected securities*, or TIPS, that rise in value to keep up with inflation through the consumer price index. Again, we'll cover all of this in the bond briefing. And later I'll be showing you an amazing portfolio that uses bond funds in a totally unique way. But meanwhile, let's consider another fixed-income investment that might belong in your Security Bucket.

3. **CDs.** Remember them? With certificates of deposit, *you're* the one loaning the money to the bank. It takes your cash for a fixed rate of interest, and then returns it—along with your earnings—after a set amount of time. Because CDs are insured by the FDIC, they're as safe as savings accounts, and—at the time of this writing—just about as exciting. But I wrote this book for every season, and seasons keep changing. I don't know what season you're in now, but I can tell you this story: in 1981, when I was 21 years old, you could buy a six-month CD for . . . wait for it . . . 17% interest! But you don't have to go that far back to see how some types of CDs, in the right environment, can give you quality returns. Remember the story of how my Stronghold advisor **got a small fixed rate on a CD in 2009,** but it was a **market-linked CD,** which was attached to the growth of the stock market, and **he *averaged 8% interest over time*!** That was an unusually good deal, but there are still ways to get more bang for your buck (without risking your principal) by investing in these **market-linked CDs.** (You can go back to chapter 2.8 for a recap about how they work.)

So how's our team of assets doing so far? CDs, cash, money market funds, and bonds would be obvious players for your Security Bucket. But when do you put them in the game? Some players will do well in some environments and poorly in others. What's the advantage of the cash player? The cash player can jump into the game any time. You can keep your money safe and ready to deploy when the right investment comes along. On the other hand, if you hold too much money in cash, your spending power is not growing. In fact, it's shrinking due to inflation each year. But in deflationary times, like 2008, your cash will buy you more. If you had cash in 2008 and had the stomach to do it, you could have bought a home for almost 40% less than that same house cost the year before. (By the way, that's what many hedge funds did. They bought tens of thousands of homes during the down time, fixed them up and rented them, and then sold them between 2011 and 2014 for a big profit.) Many stocks could be bought at a similar or even greater discount in 2008.

What's the advantage of the bond player? Depending on the type of bond, you've got a guaranteed rate of return that gives you security when other asset class prices might be dropping. Regular CDs, as I'm writing this in 2014, probably don't interest you at all, and they don't interest me either. But that player can do well in high-interest-rate environments. And while market-linked CDs excel when the stock indexes are hot, they're rock solid in every environment because you don't lose principal. Here is the downside of bonds: if you want to sell bonds before their maturity date (when you receive your full investment plus interest), and interest rates have risen significantly and new bonds provide a higher rate of return, you will have to unload them at a discount.

If all this seems incredibly complex, here's the good news. Ray Dalio has created a strategy called All Seasons, which will show you how to succeed with the right mix of bonds, equities, commodities, and gold in any economic season. We'll learn more about that later.

First, understand that because secure bonds offer a promised or stated rate of return and a return of principal, they are more secure than investments that do not guarantee either the rate of return or the principal. But the promise is only as good as the bond issuer. The point here is that you need the right player for the right season in the right proportions and at the right time.

Now let's take a look at a few other assets for your Security Bucket team you might not have thought of:

4. **Your home** goes in here, too. Why? Because it's a sacred sanctuary. We shouldn't be "spending our home"! Americans have learned a hard lesson in

recent years about the dangers of house flipping and using their homes like ATMs. A home, if it's your primary residence, shouldn't be seen as an investment to leverage, and it shouldn't be counted on to produce a gigantic return. But wait, haven't we always been told that your home is your best investment because it always goes up in value?

In my search for answers, I sat down with the **Nobel Prize–winning economist Robert Shiller,** the leading expert on real estate markets, and creator of the Case-Shiller home price index of housing prices. His breakthrough insights were used to create the following chart. Shiller found that when he adjusted for inflation, US housing prices have been nearly flat for a century! He exploded one of the biggest myths of our time: that home prices keep going up and up. "Unless there's a bubble," he told me. And we all know what eventually happens to bubbles.

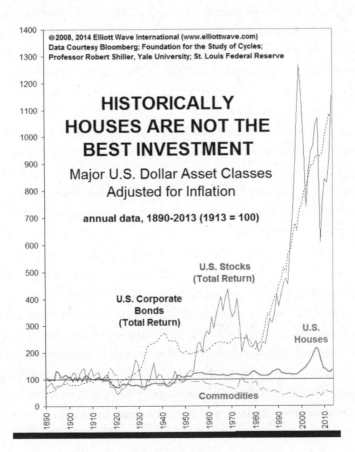

© 2008, 2014 Elliott Wave International (www.elliottwave.com)
Data Courtesy Bloomberg; Foundation for the Study of Cycles;
Professor Robert Shiller, Yale University; St. Louis Federal Reserve

HISTORICALLY HOUSES ARE NOT THE BEST INVESTMENT

Major U.S. Dollar Asset Classes Adjusted for Inflation

annual data, 1890-2013 (1913 = 100)

U.S. Stocks (Total Return)

U.S. Corporate Bonds (Total Return)

U.S. Houses

Commodities

On the other hand, owning your home with a fixed-rate mortgage is a hedge against inflation, and there's a tax advantage. What's more, if you own a home outright, and you rent out all or part of it, it can be a safe way to earn some income. Also, as you'll soon learn, there are some great ways to invest in real estate—like *first trust deeds*, REITs (real estate investment trusts), senior housing, income-producing properties, and so on. So nobody's suggesting that you give up on real estate investments if that's what you like to do! But it's probably a good rule of thumb to put them in the next bucket we're going to talk about: the Risk/Growth Bucket.

Meanwhile, what other assets might belong in Security?

5. **Your Pension.** Got one? This bucket is the place to keep it if you're one of the lucky few. Remember the example of Dr. Alicia Munnell, director of the Center of Retirement Research at Boston College? She liquidated her pension and took an early payout, thinking she could invest and get a higher return than her past employer, the Federal Reserve. She learned the hard way that you don't want to risk your lifetime income plan, and now she shares her story as a warning to others.

6. **Annuities.** If you're young, and you hear this word, you may think this doesn't have any value for you. In the past, they took a lot of money, and you had to be a certain age in order to tap into these investment tools. But as you'll learn in chapter 5.3, "Freedom: Creating Your Lifetime Income Plan," there are some new tools you can arm yourself with. Remember, these investments are insurance products that can give you a **guaranteed income for life. They're like private pensions if they're done right.** But as we've discussed, most annuities out there are terrible investments with high fees and ridiculous penalties. Most variable annuities should come with more warnings than a Viagra commercial! But you can find a few select annuities— which you will learn about in section 5—that are so safe and affordable that many experts call them the Holy Grail of retirement income solutions. How's that? **They can give the kind of returns you enjoy in your Risk/Growth Bucket within the safety of your Security Bucket. A guaranteed income that will last your lifetime and never go down in value!**

7. **At least one life insurance policy belongs in your Security Bucket, and you don't mess with it.** Why? Got a family? If you die, your family will be taken care of. Term life will suffice for most people. However, another type of life insurance policy, **described in section 5, can provide you with an income for life, tax free, while you're still alive!** And if structured correctly, it can also provide enormous tax efficiency. The largest corporations and the ultrawealthy have been using this IRS-sanctioned approach for decades. Be sure to check out chapter 5.5 for details on how to use this tool to perhaps cut the time it takes to get to your financial goals by 25% to 50% depending on your tax bracket.

8. **Structured Notes.** These products have been called "engineered safety" for investors. Structured notes are like market-linked CDs, but they aren't covered by FDIC insurance. How do they work? You lend money to a bank—usually one of the biggest banks in the world—and the bank promises to give you back the money after a specified period of time, *plus* a percentage of whatever gains accumulate in a particular index (say, the S&P 500—minus the dividends—commodities, gold, REITs, or a combination). For example, at the time of this writing, **J.P. Morgan has a seven-year structured note with 100% downside protection, meaning you'll never lose your original investment, plus it gives you 90% of the upside gain of the S&P 500.** No wonder, as you learned in chapter 2.8, the ultrawealthy often use this tool to invest. The right kind of structured note can be a great way to participate in the upside of the market without worrying about the downside—especially at a stage of life when you can't afford to take such volatility risks.

When I sat down with **Mary Callahan Erdoes, CEO of J.P. Morgan Asset Management,** with $2.5 trillion under management, she told me structured notes can be good investment choices, particularly for people afraid to put their money in *anything* after the financial meltdown of 2008. And they're *not* a gimmick. "A lot of times, people will look at a structured note and say, 'That looks too good to be true,'" she told me. "But you need to understand the product from start to finish. **There are no gimmicks, there are no gadgets; it's just math in the markets . . . The longer you don't need liquidity, the more the market will pay you for that.** If you're going to put your money away for seven years, you should be able to get that much upside."

So do structured notes belong in *your* Security Bucket? The structured note is only as secure as the bank that issues it. Erdoes made it clear that J.P. Morgan was the largest bank in the world. Some fiduciaries will recommend the Royal Bank of Canada or other Canadian banks, since they have been rated as some of the best and safest in the world. (The United States saw more than 9,400 banks collapse during the Great Depression and almost 500 in the recent Great Recession. *Not one bank failed in Canada!*) So, as always, you have to weigh the benefits against the risk and make your own decision. Also, watch out for fees and complicated contracts. As we said in chapter 2.8, structured notes can be a terrible product, just like mutual funds, if there are too many fees attached. If the issuer is fiscally strong, you won't lose your money. But if the timing is off, you won't make any money in that time period. So this is more of a secure protection strategy. It's best to talk over this investment with your fiduciary advisor before jumping in.

TIME IS ON YOUR SIDE

Whew! That was a lot. But remember, if your head is exploding with all these choices, you're not in this alone. You can have your complimentary asset allocation (and full portfolio review) done for you online at www.strongholdfinancial.com or by your own fiduciary advisor.

But it's important to understand the concept of asset allocation and which investments are available for each of these buckets so that your overall portfolio—your group of investments—reflects your goals and level of risk tolerance. That way you're still running the show! At every decision point, you'll be thinking, "How much am I risking and how much am I keeping secure?" That's where the game is won or lost!

And, as you've already seen, the biggest challenge for your Security Bucket today is: *What is really secure?* We know the world has changed, and even conservative savers have been forced into riskier and riskier investments by crazy-low interest rates. It's tempting to shoot for bigger returns, especially when the stock market is galloping. You may start thinking, "I'll never get where I need to go from here." But you can if you're willing to play the long game. (And especially if you find some investments that guarantee returns without risking principal—which you'll learn about soon.)

Just like in that old Rolling Stones song, time is on your side when it comes to growing your wealth. And time is certainly the greatest asset for the Security Bucket—even if you start later in life. After all, more and more of us are living into our 80s and 90s, so our investments can mature along with us. And if you're Generation X, Y, or Z—yes, there is a Generation Z, the postmillennials!—you're way ahead of the game! You can start with a tiny amount and let the magic of compounding get you where you want to go so much easier.

What happens to the money in your Security Bucket reminds me of an old gambler's trick on the golf course. The gambler tells his mark, "You play golf? I just started playing, and I'm no good. You want to play ten cents a hole?" So the guy says, "Sure, great!" On the way to the first hole, the gambler says, "You know, ten cents is kind of boring. Just to make it more fun, why don't we just double the bet every hole?" The first hole is 10 cents, the second hole is 20 cents, the third hole is 40. By the time they get to the fifth hole, it's $1.60. The sixth hole is $3.20, and they're only one-third of the way through 18 holes. By the time they get to the 18th hole, how much are they playing for? How about $13,107! That's a steep golf bet, even for Donald Trump. And that's the magic of compounding in action.

It's also what happens when you're investing in your Security Bucket over the long haul. You reinvest the interest you make, and, for a long time, there seems to be no progress at all. But you get to the 13th hole, and then the 14th, and then the 16th, and then it explodes. Take a look at the chart on page 312. That's the exponential progression that will work for you.

Of course, sitting tight is a challenge for this generation! As a society, we're wired for instant rewards, and waiting for the assets in our Security Bucket to increase in value can initially feel like watching grass grow. And that's why we get tempted into putting too much of our money into the next bucket, Risk/Growth. But not everything in your Security Bucket has to be dull as dishwater. If you have a talented and connected fiduciary advisor, he or she can show you how to take some of these boring security tools and eke out a more reasonable return, or even a significant return if you find the right environment.

GAME OF GOLF

HOLE	$
1ST	.10
2ND	.20
3RD	.40
4TH	.80
5TH	1.60
6TH	3.20
7TH	6.40
8TH	12.80
9TH	25.60
10TH	51.20
11TH	102.40
12TH	204.80
13TH	409.60
14TH	819.20
15TH	1,638.40
16TH	3,276.80
17TH	6,553.60

LET'S PLAY

$.10
Per Hole

18TH HOLE

13,107.20
Dollars

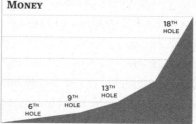

MONEY

Here's just one example of what my Stronghold advisor found for me—and it's an asset that most people wouldn't normally put in their Security Bucket: a residential real estate loan!

It starts with a guy building a house in Indian Wells, California, who ran into some financial trouble and had to sell it to a group of investors. Ever hear of Indian Wells? It's like the Beverly Hills of Palm Springs, which is one of the highest-income environments per capita in the United States. The city is beautiful, with extraordinary weather, surrounded by golf courses and resorts—an amazing place to own a home or a vacation home. The investment company that bought the guy's house buys up dozens of properties, so it needs a lot of cash—but the company doesn't need it for long because it fixes up and resells the houses quickly. To keep the money flowing, the company needs investors to give it short-term loans in exchange for first deeds of trust on the properties it holds.

Ever hear about first trust deeds? If you own a home and have a mortgage, a financial institution loaned you the money to buy your house, and you gave it your bond to pay it back at a certain rate of return. However, if you don't keep your word and fail to keep up the payments, the entity that owns the mortgage, *or trust deed*, has the right to force you to sell—and it continues to receive interest until a new owner takes over. As an investor, I look for ways to get maximum rewards in a secure environment—a first trust deed structured properly can be perfect for this purpose.

My advisor and I found out that the real estate investment company was offering the first deed of trust on that house in Indian Wells as collateral on a $1 million loan, which would pay 10% interest for one year. It was willing to have one investor take this on, or as many as 25, each contributing $40,000. In the end, I decided to invest in the full $1 million myself. You might say, "Wow, that's a great deal! You get a hundred-thousand-dollar profit to tie up your money for just one year. But Tony, what's your risk?" That's exactly why we did a lot of research. The home, we learned after two qualified appraisals, was worth $2 million in its current state. So if I'm loaning $1 million, that loan has a 50% loan-to-value ratio, right? Even if the company defaults, my $1 million is secure because the value of the property is $2 million.

This was a pretty great deal, but I've also bought deeds of trust on smaller homes. Say I'd found a starter home in the Midwest that was worth $80,000. If I could get the mortgage for $40,000, at 50% loan to value, I might make the loan. The Indian Wells deal was similar, only on a larger scale. So I decided to go for it, and I put that investment in my Security Bucket.

Okay, I can already hear you saying, "Wait a minute, Tony! What if the market drops? Doesn't that investment belong in your Risk/Growth Bucket?"

That's a great question, because we've just been through one of the worst real estate crashes in history! And on the surface, it looks like you'd probably put this in your Risk Bucket. But here's why I think it's a safe investment: in 2008, when the real estate market just went through the floor, and the world was upside down, the prices of houses in most parts of the United States dropped 30% to 40%, max. There were a few exceptions, such as some parts of Las Vegas, Phoenix, and Miami, where the prices dropped more than 50%. But all of those places had massive price growth right before the bubble burst. The Indian Wells area didn't experience that size of bubble— and while prices dropped 31% from 2008 to 2010 (far below the 50% mark), the biggest loss in a single year was only 13.6% (from 2008 to 2009). And remember, we're loaning for only one year. So if residential real estate didn't take anything close to a 50% hit in Indian Wells in 2008, it's not likely to happen this year.

That's why I decided to move forward with this as the investment to put in my Security Bucket. **It's the place where you have to be cautious.** But it doesn't have to be totally boring. And sometimes the returns can be very nice (8% to 10%, whereas many people typically settle for 1% to 4% returns in the Security Bucket) if you do your homework!

It is my contention that Aesop was writing for the tortoise market.
Hares have no time to read.
—ANITA BROOKNER

Boredom comes from a boring mind.
—"THE STRUGGLE WITHIN," Metallica

Now, what if that same company offered me a 12% return to invest in that $2 million property—but for the better rate, it wanted me to loan it $1.5 million instead of $1 million? That would make the loan-to-value ratio 75%—obviously I'd get a greater return by taking a greater risk. It means if the market dropped by 25% or more, I might lose some of my investment. Not likely, but possible. So if I was willing to take the extra risk for an increase in returns, it might be something I'd consider. But I would not put this investment in my Security Bucket. It belongs in the next bucket you're about to discover: the one that should be wrapped in yellow caution tape and handled with oven mitts, because if you approach it the wrong way, I guarantee you're going to get burned! But handled effectively, it can speed up your journey to Financial Freedom.

By now you can see why asset allocation is an art, not a science. The idea of security is totally subjective. Some people think nothing is safe! Others can live with a tiny bit of risk and still feel secure. So you've got to look at each investment on an individual basis.

The real payoff of asset allocation comes when you figure out the right mix of how much of your money you keep safe and how much you're willing to risk to get greater rewards and have the potential to grow faster. In investing, that's where you live or die, succeed or fail. So what percentage do you think you should put in your Security Bucket—in safe investments? One-third? Half? Two-thirds? Failure to secure a significant portion of your hard-earned money in safe investments can spell financial disaster. Conversely, putting too much in this bucket can significantly slow your growth. How do we find the right balance? That's what we've been working toward. And now that we've locked down the foundation for security, it's time to *really* get in the game. It's time to play to win.

As a quick note, bonds can be such a potentially important investment for your Security Bucket that I wanted to give you a quick bond briefing that might be well worth your review. If now's not the right time, remember this is here as a reference for you, and skip over to the next chapter. Keep up the momentum! We're on our way to bigger risks and potentially bigger rewards.

A FEW WORDS ABOUT BONDS

Gentlemen prefer bonds.

—ANDREW MELLON, founder of the Bank of New York Mellon

Not that long ago, bonds were supposed to be the safest, most reliable form of investment. They were the big guns in the portfolios of the ultrawealthy, and the bedrock of your Security/Peace of Mind Bucket for the average investor. But bonds have taken a bad rap in recent years, and for good reason. With the US government keeping interest rates insanely low, and some of the companies, cities, and even nations that issue bonds teetering on the brink—or even going bankrupt—they don't seem like such a great deal to everyone anymore.

But most experts still think bonds are an important part of your investment mix. (In fact, they're the foundation of the mind-blowing portfolio that works in all economic climates, which you'll learn about in chapter 5.1.) So let's look at the basic kinds of bonds out there to see what can be great about them—and also what to watch out for.

- **US Treasury Bonds.** Many investment experts, including Yale's asset allocation wizard David Swensen, feel that the safest bonds are good old US Treasuries, because they are backed by the full faith and credit of the government. David told me, "Treasury bonds are really there as an anchor for the portfolio." But because these bonds are so safe from default, they have smaller returns. And like other, less secure bonds, they can fluctuate in price based on outside events—particularly how much inflation or deflation is happening at the moment. So suddenly what you thought was a bomb-proof investment can blow up in your face!

  Treasuries come in four different types (and they have different names for how long they last to maturity).

  1. **T-bills:** These Treasury bills are government debt obligations that come due in less than 12 months. They are the basis for most short-term bond index funds and money market funds.
  2. **T-notes:** Treasury notes mature in one to ten years, and offer a fixed interest rate (known as "the coupon"). You get interest payments on these every six months.
  3. **T-bonds:** Same as T-notes, but Treasury bonds mature in ten to 30 years.
  4. **TIPS:** First created in 1997, these Treasury inflation-protected securities protect you against spikes in inflation. When you buy TIPS, the principal (or "par value") of your bond goes up or down when the consumer price index on inflation changes—and so does your semiannual interest payment. So if you buy $10,000 worth of TIPS at 1.5% interest, and the CPI doesn't change in six months, the "par value" of your bond stays the same, and you get a $150 interest payment. But—and here's the beauty of TIPS!—if the cost of living goes up 2%, your bond is now worth $10,200, and your semiannual payment is $153. If you own a lot of TIPS, and there's a lot of inflation, that money can add up! Here's a chart that shows you how it works:

RAYMOND JAMES TIPS CHART

YEAR	COUPON	PAR VALUE	INFLATION PERIOD	CHANGE IN CPI	ADJUSTED PRINCIPAL VALUE	INTEREST PAYMENT
1	1.5%	$1,000	Inflationary	+2%	$1,020	$15.30
2	1.5%	$1,020	Deflationary	-1%	$1,010	$15.15
3	1.5%	$1,010	Inflationary	+3%	$1,040	$15.60
4	1.5%	$1,040	Inflationary	+2%	$1,060	$15.90
5	1.5%	$1,060	Inflationary	+1%	$1,070	$16.05

Notice that the value of the bond can be adjusted down, too. So if we go into another economic recession or depression, you could potentially lose some of your principal if you need to liquidate and get the value of your bond today.

Basically, if you buy TIPS, you're betting that we're heading into a period of inflation. Does that seem likely? If you're not sure (and, really, nobody ever knows for sure), you may want to do what David Swensen recommends in his ideal portfolio: because TIPS go *up* in price when interest rates rise (which usually happens during inflationary times), balance them with an equal amount of traditional Treasuries that go *down* in price when interest rates rise. That way, you're protected in any situation!

Of course, the US government isn't the only country that issues bonds to pay for its operations. And in the good old days of a few years ago, a bond backed by the full faith and credit of a sovereign nation used to be considered a fairly safe bet. But now that we've had Greece, Spain, and other nations teetering on default—or, like Argentina, plunging over the edge—foreign government bonds have become a riskier deal. Foreign bonds are also more vulnerable to inflation risks, and if you buy bonds in an unstable currency, you might run into big trouble exchanging them back into dollars. Most advisors say to leave these investments to expert traders and hedge funds.

But what about some other bonds that can bring in better returns than plain old Treasuries? Some of the types listed below are safer than others.

You can find out what others think about their prospects through a rating system that categorizes bonds by the level of risk to investors.

There are several internationally recognized bond rating agencies, such as Moody's, Fitch Ratings, and Standard & Poor's, that use special formulas to come up with credit ratings for different issuers—kind of like the way your credit is rated when you apply for a car loan or Visa card. For S&P, the grades range from AAA (the highest level of confidence that a company or country won't default on its debts) to BBB (adequate for "investment grade" bonds), and all the way down to D (which means the bond issuer is already in default). The lower the rating, the more interest the issuer usually has to pay to bond holders for the risk that they're taking. The expertly renamed **high-yield bonds,** formerly known as junk bonds, have a rating of lower than BBB, which makes them "subinvestment grade."

- **Corporate Bonds.** Corporations issue bonds when they want to raise money to expand, make acquisitions, pay dividends, fund a loss, or any number of reasons. Should you buy corporate bonds? It depends on the risk. If you pick the wrong bond, you could lose most or all of your money. Even iconic companies such as TWA and Kodak have gone bankrupt. A year after it declared Chapter 11, Kodak's unsecured bonds were selling for 14 cents on the dollar. But bonds from most giant US corporations are still considered safe bets. Apple (with an AA+ rating) has been selling high-grade bonds to eager buyers—but the interest those bonds earn is only about 1% higher than comparable US Treasuries! Some investors, like David Swensen, say, "Why bother with corporate bonds when you can get a better return just buying stock in the company?"

  But if you're looking for higher yields in bonds, you have lots of options—as long as these investments go into your Risk/Growth Bucket and not your Security Bucket! For instance, not everybody shies away from so-called junk bonds. You have to look at each one and decide if it's worth the risk. In May 2014 Australia's largest airline, Qantas, offered a subinvestment-grade eight-year bond in Australian dollars for a 7.75% interest rate. The company had its credit rating downgraded because of recent losses and debt problems, but would you count it out? Or at a more extreme level, in January 2013 in the midst of chaos, there were people who were **buying one-year Egyptian Treasury bills with a "guaranteed" (a guarantee only as strong as you think an unstable government can make) return of 14.4%.** Those who did this were betting that the US government and the Saudi Arabian government would keep Egypt stable and solvent.

Would the rewards be worth the risk of default? That's the kind of decision you'd have to make before buying the junk bond.

Of course, not many of us have the experience or time to do this level of research. That's where a talented fiduciary advisor who's an expert in the area might come in handy. But there are also domestic and international high-yield bond index funds that can give you good returns while spreading the risk among many bonds.

- **Municipal Bonds.** How about munis? When a state, city, or county needs to raise funds for a big public works project (sewer systems, hospitals, mass transit), it borrows money by issuing a bond. In the past, these municipal bonds were considered a win-win deal for everybody, because the interest they paid was usually exempt from federal and possibly state taxes. But what's been happening to cities and counties all over the United States? San Bernardino and Stockton, California? Jefferson County, Alabama? Detroit? Chicago? All bankrupt or on the verge, and their bondholders potentially left holding the bag. Doesn't sound like such a sure thing anymore. Also, when interest rates drop, sometimes the issuer of the bond can "call" it in and pay back your principal before the bond matures. You lose that guaranteed rate of return you were counting on. **But once you acknowledge the risks, there can be some great opportunities in municipal bonds if you know where to look.** And the tax advantages can be outstanding.

  Here's an example that might prove valuable to you: a friend of mine recently bought a New York City bond where he's getting a 4% return *tax free*—which, for someone in a high tax bracket, is the equivalent of an approximately 7% return in a taxable bond! Why isn't he worried about the risk? These bonds are secured by a lien on future tax revenues. So if New York City gets into trouble, it has the ability to tax its way out of it

and pay him back! He feels so good about this bond that he's putting it
in his Security Bucket!

   The point is, there are plenty of municipal bonds that could be valuable for you—but you have to educate yourself and sit down with a
registered investment advisor or some other knowledgeable investment
expert who knows his or her munis.

Want to take the guesswork out of choosing the right bond mix for your
portfolio? Vanguard founder Jack Bogle suggests buying into **low-cost,
low-fee bond index funds that spread out your risk because you'll own
every part of the bond market.** You can see how Bogle puts this concept
to work in his own portfolio in section 6, "Invest Like the .001%: The Billionaire's Playbook."

   Now onward to greater risk and potentially greater reward.

PLAYING TO WIN:
THE RISK/GROWTH BUCKET

The winner ain't the one with the fastest car.
It's the one who refuses to lose.
—DALE EARNHARDT SR.

The **Risk/Growth Bucket** is where everybody wants to be. Why? Because it's sexy! It's exciting! You can get a much higher return in here—but the key word is *can*. **You *can* also lose everything you've saved and invested. So whatever you put in your Risk/Growth Bucket, you have to be prepared to lose a portion or even all of it if you don't have protective measures in place.** How do we know this? Because everything in life, including markets, runs in cycles. There are going to be up times and down times. And anybody who invests in one particular kind of asset while it's on a roll—be it real estate, stocks, bonds, commodities, or whatever—and thinks the party will last forever because "this time will be different" should get ready for a rude awakening. When I interviewed Jack Bogle for this book, he repeated one of his mantras: "Markets always revert to the mean." (That means what goes up is going to come down, and vice versa.) And I'm sure Ray Dalio got your attention when he said that whatever your favorite investment might be, at some point in your life, you can count on it *dropping 50% to 70% in value.* **While there's unlimited potential for upside in this bucket, never forget that you could lose it all (or at least a significant portion).** That's why I call this the Risk/Growth Bucket and not the Growth/Risk Bucket, because growth is not guaranteed, but risk is!

So what investments would you put in here?

Here's a sampling of seven main asset classes to consider:

1. **Equities.** Another word for stocks, or ownership shares of individual companies or vehicles for owning many of them at once, like mutual funds, indexes,
   and *exchange-traded funds* (ETFs).

Exchange-traded funds (ETFs) have been called the "It" girl of the stock
market, ballooning in popularity by more than 2,000% from 2001 to 2014,
and holding more than $2 trillion in investments. But what exactly are they?
ETFs are built like mutual funds or index funds, because they contain a
diversified collection of assets, but you can trade them just like individual
stocks. Most of them follow a theme (small-cap stocks, municipal bonds,
gold) and/or trace an index. But with an index or mutual fund, you have to
wait until the end of the trading day to buy or sell; ETFs can be traded all
day long. Experts say that if you like the idea of an index fund, but you want
to buy when you see the price is low and sell when the price is high during a
trading session, an ETF might be for you. But that's trading, not investing,
and trying to time a market brings very intense and special risks.

But there's another difference: **when you buy shares of an ETF, you
are not buying the actual stocks, bonds, commodities, or whatever else
is bundled in the fund—you are buying shares in an *investment fund*
that owns those assets.** That company *promises* that you'll receive the same
financial outcome as if you'd owned them yourself. But don't worry, it sounds
more complicated than it is.

A lot of people like ETFs because they give you a tremendous amount of
diversity at a low cost. In fact, many ETFs have lower fees than even comparable traditional index funds, and sometimes lower minimum investment
requirements. And because they don't engage in a lot of the kind of trading
that produces capital gains, they can be tax efficient (although there is a move
toward more actively managed ETFs coming to the market, which makes
them less tax efficient).

Should you invest in ETFs? Jack Bogle, founder of Vanguard (which,
incidentally, offers many ETF funds), told me he sees nothing wrong with
owning broad-spectrum index ETFs, but he warns that some are too special-
ized for individual investors. "You can not only bet on the market," he told
me, "but on countries, on industry sectors. And you may be right and you
may be wrong." David Swensen wonders why individual investors should

bother with ETFs at all. "I'm a big believer in buying and holding for the long run," he told me. "The main reason you'd go into an ETF is to trade. And so I'm not a big fan."

2. **High-Yield Bonds.** You might also know these as junk bonds, and there's a reason they call them junk. These are bonds with the lowest safety ratings, and you get a high-yield coupon (higher rate of return than a more secure bond) only because you're taking a big risk. For a refresher, go back and read the bond briefing at the end of the last chapter.

3. **Real Estate.** We all know real estate can have tremendous returns. You probably already know a lot about this category, but there are many ways to invest in property. You can invest in a home that you rent out for an income. You can buy property, fix it up, and then flip it in the short term. You can invest in first trust deeds. You can buy commercial real estate or an apartment. One of my favorites that I mentioned to you already is investing in senior housing, where you get both the income and the potential growth in appreciation as well. Or you can buy REITs: real estate investment trusts. These are trusts that own big chunks of commercial real estate (or mortgages) and sell shares to small investors, like mutual funds. REITs trade like stocks, and you can also buy shares of a REIT index fund, which gives you a diversity of many different REITs.

For growth, the Nobel economist Robert Shiller told me that you're better off investing in REITs than owning your own home (which belongs in the Security Bucket, anyway). "Buying an apartment REIT sounds to me like maybe a better investment than buying your own house," he said, "because there seems to be a tilt toward renting now." That could change, of course. And, as with any investment, you've got to pause and think, "What am I betting on?" You're betting that the price of property is going to go up over time. But there's no guarantee, so that's why it's in the Risk/Growth Bucket. If it goes up, it could have a nice rate of return; if it doesn't, you get nothing—or you could lose it all. When you buy your own home, you're betting that the price of your home will go up. When you're buying real estate that has income associated with it (a rental unit, an apartment building, commercial real estate, an REIT, or an index that holds these), Shiller points out you have two ways to win. You make income along the way and if the property increases in value, you also have the opportunity to make money when you sell on the appreciation.

4. **Commodities.** This category includes gold, silver, oil, coffee, cotton, and so on. Over the years, gold has been considered the ultimate safe haven for many people, a staple of their Security Bucket, and conventional wisdom said it would only go up in value during uncertain times. Then its price dropped more than 25% in 2013! Why would you invest in gold? You could keep a small amount in your portfolio that says, "In case paper money disappears, then this is a little portion of my security." You know, if all hell breaks loose, and the government collapses under a zombie invasion, at least you've got some gold (or silver) coins to buy yourself a houseboat and head to sea. (On second thought, can zombies swim?) Otherwise gold probably belongs in your Risk/Growth Bucket. You'd invest in it as protection against inflation or as part of a balanced portfolio, as we will learn later on, but you have to accept the risk. So don't kid yourself: if you buy gold, you're betting it will go up in price. Unlike many other investments, there's no income from this investment like you might get in stocks from dividends or from income-producing real estate or bonds. So gold could be a good risk or a bad one, but it goes in your Risk/Growth Bucket for sure. This is not an attack on gold. In fact, in the right economic season, gold is a superstar performer! That's why in chapter 5.1, "Invincible, Unsinkable, Unconquerable: The All Seasons Strategy," you'll see why it can be invaluable to have a small portion of gold in your portfolio.

5. **Currencies.** Got a yen to buy some yen? Since all currency is just "paper," currency investing is pure speculation. There are people who make a fortune in it and even more who lose a fortune. Currency trading is not for the faint of heart.

6. **Collectibles.** Art, wine, coins, automobiles, and antiques, to name a few. Once again, this asset class requires very special knowledge or a lot of time on eBay.

7. **Structured Notes.** What are these doing in *both* buckets? Because there are different types of structured notes. Some have 100% principal protection, and those can go in your Security Bucket, as long as the issuing bank is financially solid. Then there are other kinds of notes that give you higher potential returns, but only partial protection if the index drops. Say you buy a note with 25% protection. That means if the stock market drops up to 25%, you don't lose a dime. If it goes down 35%, you lose 10%. But for taking more

risk, you get more upside: sometimes as much as 150% of the index to which it's tied. In other words, if the market went up 10%, you'd receive a 15% return. So there's potential for greater gains, but there's definitely increased risk. Remember once again, structured notes should be purchased through an RIA, who will work to strip out all excess fees and deliver them to you in the form of an even greater return.

> Safety doesn't happen by accident.
> —FLORIDA HIGHWAY SIGN

We've now covered a sample of some of the investment vehicles/assets that you might find in a diversified Risk/Growth Bucket. You may be wondering why I haven't included some of the more daring investment vehicles of our time: call and put options, *credit-default obligations* (CDOs), and a whole host of exotic financial instruments available to traders these days. If you build up a lot of wealth, you may want to have your fiduciary look into some of these vehicles. **But just realize that if you're playing this game, you're most likely no longer just an investor, you've become a speculator as well.** It's what's called *momentum trading*, and you have to realize you can lose everything *and more* if you play the game wrong. And because the mantra of this book is that the road to financial freedom is through saving and *investing* for compounded growth, I'll leave a discussion of these momentum assets for another day.

IT'S TIME TO GET IN THE GAME

Okay, now you know the players that belong in your allocation buckets, and you know the key to building a winning team: **diversify, diversify, diversify!** But there's more. You not only have to diversify *between* your Security and your Risk/Growth Buckets, but *within* them as well. As Burton Malkiel shared with me, you should **"diversify across securities, across asset classes, across markets—and across time."** That's how you truly get a portfolio for all seasons! For example, he says you want to invest not only in both stocks and bonds but also in different *types* of stocks and bonds, many of them from different markets in different parts of the world. (We'll talk about diversifying across time in chapter 4.4, "Timing Is Everything?")

And, most experts agree, the ultimate diversification tool for individual investors is the low-fee index fund, which gives you the broadest exposure to the largest numbers of securities for the lowest cost. "The best way to diversify is to **own the index,** because you don't have to pay all these fees," David Swensen told me. "And you get tax efficiency." Meaning that if you're investing outside of your IRA- or 401(k)-type account, you don't get taxed for all that constant buying and selling that goes on in most mutual funds.

HAVE SOME FUN!

Of course, **if you have your money machine in full gear, and you have the desire, there's nothing wrong with setting aside a tiny percent of your Risk/Growth Bucket to pick some stocks and do some day trading.** "Index your important money, then go have fun," Burton Malkiel told me. "It's better than going to the racetrack." But, he said, limit yourself to 5% or less of your total assets or portfolio.

Is all of this giving you an idea of what kind of portfolio mix would be best for you? Before you decide, just remember that we all have a tendency to pile up on the investments that we think will give us our greatest victories. And everybody gets victories. You know why? Different environments reward different investments. So let's say real estate is hot. You've invested in real estate, so now you're a genius. Stock market is hot? If you have stocks, you're a genius. Bonds are doing great? If you have bonds, once again you're an investment master. Or maybe you just landed in the right place at the right time, right? So you don't want to get overconfident. That's why asset allocation is so important. What do all the smartest people in the world say? "I'm going to be wrong." So they design their asset allocation ideally to make money in the long term even if they're wrong in the short term.

LET'S TEST YOUR KNOWLEDGE

In the coming pages, I'll be showing you the portfolios, or the asset allocations, designed by some of the greatest investors of all time. Let's start with a sample from someone you've been hearing from throughout this book: **David Swensen, Yale's $23.9 billion–plus man,** a true master of asset allocation. Would you be interested in seeing his personal portfolio recommendations? Me too! So when we sat down together in his office at Yale,

I asked him the key question: **"If you couldn't leave any money to your kids, only a portfolio and a set of investment principles, what would they be?"**

He showed me the asset allocation that he recommends for individual investors—one he thinks will hold up against the test of time. He also recommends this portfolio for all institutions other than Yale, Stanford, Harvard, and Princeton. Why? Because these four institutions employ an army of full-time top analysts.

When I saw his list, I was amazed by how elegant and simple it was. I've shown you 15 types of assets to choose from; he uses only six categories, all in index funds. I was also surprised by how much weight he gave to one particular bucket. Can you guess which one? Let's activate some of what we've learned thus far about the division between the Security and Risk/Growth Buckets.

Have a look at the box below and jot down where each asset class belongs. Check which ones you think belong in the Security Bucket, where you put things that are going to give you modest returns in exchange for lower risk; and then check which belong in the Risk/Growth Bucket, where there's greater upside potential but also greater downside.

David Swensen Portfolio		Which Bucket?	
Asset Class (Index Funds)	*Portfolio Weight*	*Risk/Growth*	*Security*
Domestic stock	20%	❑	❑
International stock	20%	❑	❑
Emerging stock markets	10%	❑	❑
REITs (real estate investment trusts)	20%	❑	❑
Long-term US Treasuries	15%	❑	❑
TIPS (Treasury inflation-protected securities)	15%	❑	❑

Let's start with the top four. The first is a broad domestic stock index, something like the Vanguard 500 Index or the Wilshire 5000 Total Market Index. Where would you put it? Does it come with risk? Absolutely. Have you got a guaranteed return? Absolutely not. Could you lose it all? Unlikely—but it could drop significantly—and it has at times! Over the long term, US stocks certainly have a great track record. Remember how they compare to owning your own personal real estate? Equities have done well over time, but they are one of the most volatile asset classes in the short run. In the last 86 years (through 2013), the S&P lost money 24 times. So stock index funds belong in which bucket? That's right: Risk/Growth.

How about international stocks? David Swensen puts a lot of weight in foreign stocks because of the diversity they bring to the portfolio. If there's a slump in America, business may be booming in Europe or Asia. But not everybody agrees with David. Foreign currencies aren't as stable as good old US greenbacks, so there's a "currency risk" in investing in foreign stocks. And Jack Bogle, the founder of Vanguard, with 64 years of success, says that owning American companies *is* global. "Tony, the reality is that among the big corporations in America, none are domestic," he told me. "They're all over the world: McDonald's, IBM, Microsoft, General Motors. So you own an international portfolio anyway." Where do foreign stocks belong? I think we can agree on the *Risk/Growth Bucket,* no?

Emerging markets? David Swensen likes to put some money into the volatile stocks of developing nations, like Brazil, Vietnam, South Africa, and Indonesia. You can get spectacular returns, but you can also lose everything. *Risk/Growth Bucket?* You bet!

How about REITs? David told me he likes "real estate investment trusts that own big central business district office buildings and big regional malls and industrial buildings. They generally throw off a high-income component." So these index funds can generate great returns, but they rise and fall with the American commercial real estate market. Which bucket? You've got it: *Risk/Growth.*

What about the last two on the list: long-term US Treasuries and TIPS? Do they offer lower returns in exchange for more safety? Spot on! So which bucket do they belong in? You've got it: *Security.*

Congratulations! You've just assigned six major asset classes to their proper allocation buckets, which is something 99.9% of the people you pass on the street wouldn't be able to do! Pretty cool thing, isn't it? But let's dig a little deeper here to understand why David chose this mix, and why it may or may not be right for you.

First let's look at the Security Bucket. David said he chose only US

Treasury bonds "because there's a purity there in having the full faith and credit of the US government backing them." But why did he pick this particular combination of bond funds? Half are traditional long-term Treasury bonds, and half are inflation-protected securities.

I said to David, **"You're basically saying if I'm going to be secure, I'm going to protect myself against both inflation and deflation."**

"That's absolutely right," he said. "I can't believe you saw that! A lot of people who put together bond indexes lump the two together. The Treasuries are for deflation, like we had in 2008. But if you buy regular Treasury bonds, and inflation takes off, you're going to end up having losses in your portfolio. If you buy the TIPS, and inflation takes off, you're going to be protected."

I want you to notice that David Swensen, like all the best, doesn't know which is going to happen: inflation or deflation. So he plans for both scenarios. You might say as you look at this, "Well, yes, fifty percent for inflation and fifty percent for deflation. Doesn't he just break even?" It's not that simple, but your thinking is quality. He is using his Security Bucket investment as protection that if his equity investments or real estate go down, he's lowering his downside by having something to offset some of those investment risks. So he's certain to make some money in his Security Bucket. And he doesn't lose his principal, so he's practicing smart Security Bucket usage. He won't lose money, but he'll make some additional money if things inflate or deflate. A *very* smart approach.

But I was a bit surprised that only 30% of his asset allocation goes into the Security Bucket, while 70% of his assets go into the Risk/Growth Bucket! That seemed pretty aggressive to me for some investors, so I asked David how it would work for the average investor.

"That's a good question, Tony," he said. **"Equities are the core for portfolios that have a long time horizon.** I mean, if you look at recent long periods of time—ten, twenty, fifty, one hundred years—you see that the equity returns are superior to those that you get in fixed income."

Historical data certainly back him up. Have a look at the visual below that traces the returns of stocks and bonds for periods of 100 and 200 years. It shows that US stocks have historically outperformed bonds in compounded annual returns. In fact, **$1 invested in 1802 at 8.3% per annum would have grown to $8.8 million by the turn of the new millennium.**

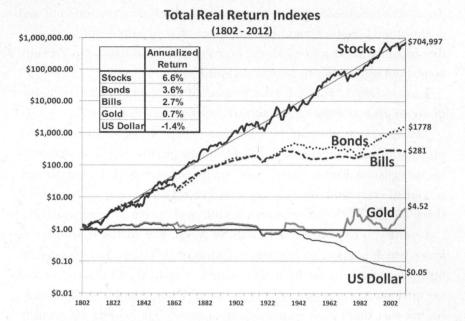

Total Real Return Indexes
(1802 - 2012)

	Annualized Return
Stocks	6.6%
Bonds	3.6%
Bills	2.7%
Gold	0.7%
US Dollar	-1.4%

So David Swensen designed his ideal portfolio to be a wealth-generating machine that offers some stability through its tremendous diversity. And because it takes a long-term view of investing, it has the time to ride out periodic drops in the stock market.

I was curious to see how this asset allocation mix would have fared in the past: those volatile 17 years from April 1, 1997, when TIPS first became available, to March 31, 2014. It was during those years when the Standard & Poor's index performed like a rodeo bull, yet it dropped 51%. So I had a team of financial experts test its performance against the index during those years. Guess what? **The Swensen portfolio outperformed the stock market with an annual return of 7.86%!** During the bear market of 2000 through 2002, when the S&P 500 dropped almost 50%, Swensen's portfolio stayed relatively stable, with a total loss of only 4.572% over those three terrible years! Like other portfolios heavy in equities, Swensen's took a hit in the massive crash of 2008, but it still did better than the S&P 500 by more than 6%, (losing 31% as opposed to 37%) and then bounced back. (Note: see the end of this chapter for the specific methodology to calculate the returns. Past performance does not guarantee future results.)

So, ladies and gentleman, it's safe to say that **David Swensen is one of** those rare unicorns who can actually beat the stock market on a consistent basis—and in this portfolio, he does it with the power of asset allocation alone! And you have access to his best advice, right here, right now. If that was all you got out of this chapter, I think you'd agree it's been worth the time! However, the most important thing to understand is this: even though this portfolio might do better and be more stable than the general market, it is still an aggressive portfolio that takes a strong gut because few people can take a 35% loss of their lifetime savings and not buckle and sell. So is it right for you? If you're a young person, you might be very interested in this kind of mix, because you've got more time to recover from any losses. If you're getting ready to retire, this portfolio might be too risky for you.

But not to worry. I'm going to give you several other examples of portfolios in the coming pages, including that one particular allocation mix Ray Dalio shared with me that practically knocked me off my chair! It was so spectacular that I've devoted a whole chapter to it in the next section. But here's a hint: its mix was much less aggressive than Swensen's, but when we tested it over the same time frame, the Dalio portfolio **had a higher average annual return and significantly less volatility—it's a smooth ride. It may be the Holy Grail of portfolio construction, one that gives you substantial growth with the lowest ratio of risk I've seen!**

> In any moment of decision, the best thing you can do is
> the right thing, the next best thing is the wrong thing,
> and the worst thing you can do is nothing.
> —THEODORE ROOSEVELT

But for now, let's get back to the big picture and look at how you'll decide your own basic numbers: What percentage of your assets are you going to put at risk, and what percentage are you going to secure? Before you make the choice, you have to consider three factors:

- your stage in life,
- your risk tolerance, and
- your available liquidity.

First, how much time do you have ahead of you to build wealth and make mistakes with your investments along the way before you need to tap into them? If you're younger, once again, you can be much more aggressive because you'll have longer to recover your losses. (Although nobody wants to get in the habit of losing!)

Your percentages also depend on **how much access to income** you have. If you earn a lot of money, you can afford to make more mistakes and still make up for it, right?

GAME SHOW TIME:
WHAT ARE YOU WILLING TO RISK?

And when it comes to risk, everyone has radically different ideas about what's tolerable. Some of us are very security driven. Remember the 6 Human Needs? Certainty is the number one need. But some of us crave Uncertainty and Variety; we love to live on the edge. You have to know your personality before you dive in here. So let's say you're on a game show; which of the following would you take?

- $1,000 in cash
- A 50% chance at winning $5,000
- A 25% chance at winning $10,000
- A 5% chance at winning $100,000

Here's another: you have just finished saving for a once-in-a-lifetime vacation. Three weeks before you plan to leave, you lose your job. Would you:

- cancel the vacation;
- take a much more modest vacation;
- go as scheduled, reasoning that you need the time to prepare for a job search; or
- extend your vacation, because this might be your last chance to go first class?

Rutgers University has developed a twenty-question, five-minute online quiz (http://njaes.rutgers.edu/money/riskquiz) that can help you identify where you fit on the risk-tolerance scale. But the real answer is in your gut.

For the past 30 years, I've been putting on my **Wealth Mastery**

seminars, where I've worked with people from more than 100 countries to transform their financial lives by putting them in a total-immersion four-day wealth-mastery process. In it, I like to play a little game with them called "the money pass." From the stage, I tell the audience to "trade money" with one another. That's all I say. There's usually a few moments of silent confusion, and then they start trading. Some people pull out a dollar, some take out a twenty, some people a hundred. You can guess what happens. People are moving around, they're looking at one another, they decide how to exchange. Some negotiate, some give away all their money, and some take another person's $100 bill and give them $1. You can imagine the astonished look on that individual's face. After three or four minutes of this type of trading, I say, "Okay, grab a seat." And I move on to the next subject.

Invariably, some guy will shout, "Hey! I want my hundred dollars back!"

I'll say, "Who said it was your hundred?" And he says, "Well, we're playing a game." And I say, "Yeah. What made you think the game was over?" Usually I get a confused look as the person sits down, still frustrated over the lost $100. Eventually they get the insight: their perception of their risk tolerance and the reality are in different universes. This guy thinks he has a high tolerance for risk, but he can get pissed off over the loss of $100. It always amazes me. Imagine if you were to lose $10,000, $100,000, or $500,000. That's what aggressive investors can lose in a relatively short period of time. People don't know their true tolerance for risk until they've had a real-life experience taking a significant loss.

I've taken God-awful losses—multimillion-dollar hits at a stage in my life when I didn't have that much to lose, when the losses equaled more than all that I owned. Those gut checks will wake you up! But the numbers don't matter. You can get thrown by losing $100 or $1,000. The pain of losing far exceeds the joy of winning. And that's why it's great to have something like the All Seasons portfolio in your investment arsenal, because, through asset allocation alone, you can significantly reduce the risk of sizeable losses.

Just as science shows us that we're hardwired to hate losing, it also shows that humans are not good at assessing our potential to win. Sometimes after you've made a few successful investments, you start thinking, "Hey, I'm good at this; I can do anything!" It's just human nature to think you can beat the system. It's what psychologists call motivational bias. Most of us think we're better than we really are at predicting patterns and luckier than we really are when there's a jackpot at stake. What else can explain why so many people play the lottery?! A famous 1981 study at Stockholm University found that 93% of US drivers think their skills are above average. There's even a name for this phenomenon: "the Lake Wobegon Effect," referring to author Garrison Keillor's mythical town where "all the children are above average." Hey, who *doesn't* think they're above average! But when it comes to money, delusions that you're better than everybody else can kill you.

If you're a man, you're guilty of this bias by biochemistry. Testosterone equals overconfidence. Study after study show that women tend to be better investors because they don't overestimate their abilities to anticipate the future accurately. Sometimes confidence works against you. Just watch little boys. "I'm Superman! I'm going to fly! Watch me jump off this roof!" Suffice it to say, if you're a woman reading this book, you have a built-in advantage!

When the markets are going up and up and up, investors can be mesmerized by their returns. Everybody's seduced by the *possibility* of growth, thinking it's the *probability* of growth. That's where they get into trouble. As a result, they pour the majority or all of their money into investments that fit into the Risk/Growth Bucket—not just 70% but sometimes 80%, 90%, or 100%. Some even borrow money to make investments that they believe are going to go up forever, until they don't. And because of poor asset allocation, with too much of their money riding on one horse, they lose it all or even end up in debt. And the reason people get screwed is that by the time they hear that the stock market (or gold, or the real estate market, or commodities, or any other type of investment) is a great place to go, very often the bubble is just about to end. So you need to put in place a system to make sure you don't get seduced into putting too much of your money in any one market or asset class or too much in your Risk/Growth Bucket.

All of this may sound pretty basic, especially to sophisticated investors who feel like they've got everything covered. But sometimes it's high-level investors whose strings of successes send them veering off course. They forget the fundamentals.

Naturally, there will always be investors who can't listen to reason, whose "irrational exuberance" runs away with them. They talk themselves into

believing the biggest myth of investing: **"This time will be different."**
I know dozens of these stories, all with unhappy endings. Take Jonathan,
a friend who made a fortune in business (and whose real name will remain
anonymous for his privacy) and then liquidated everything to invest in
the booming Las Vegas real estate market. He had some early wins, so he
doubled down and borrowed like crazy to keep building condos. Every time
Jonathan came to my financial programs, he heard about the importance
of putting some of your wins into your Security Bucket and not putting all
your eggs into any one basket no matter how compelling the returns might
be today. Jonathan gave credit to me and my Business Mastery programs for
the more than 1,000% increase in his business that made all these investments possible. He made more than $150 million selling his company. But
he didn't listen when it came to taking money off the table and putting it in
the Security Bucket, and, boy, did he pay a price. Today he acknowledges
that he let his ego get in the way of his eardrums. He wanted to be a billionaire, and he knew he was on target to become one. But then, do you remember what happened when the real estate market in Las Vegas collapsed?
How far did housing prices go down? How about 61% between 2007 and
2012. Jonathan didn't just lose everything—he lost a half billion dollars
more than he had.

© MARK ANDERSON, WWW.ANDERTOONS.COM

"What's interesting is the rate at which they part."

I sincerely hope all this is sinking in. If there's anything you should take away from this chapter, it's this: putting all of your money in the Risk/Growth Bucket is the kiss of death. It's why many experts estimate that 95% of investors lose money over virtually any decade. Typically they ride the wave up (in real estate, stocks, gold), and when the wave disappears, they sink like a rock, and they're pounded by financial losses during the inevitable crash.

Some people just won't listen to advice. They have to learn the hard way, if at all. But to avoid those kinds of painful lessons, and to help you decide which options are right for *you*, I have to remind you that a conflict-free, independent investment manager can be the right choice. Notice how professional athletes, men and women at the top of their sport, always have coaches to keep them at peak performance? Why is that? Because a coach will notice when their game is off, and can help them make small adjustments that can result in huge payoffs. The same thing applies to your finances. Great fiduciary advisors will keep you on course when you're starting to act like a teenager and chasing returns. They can talk you off the ledge when you're about to make a fateful investment decision.

PICK A NUMBER, ANY NUMBER . . .

Okay, the moment of reckoning has arrived! Say you've still got that $10,000 bonus in your hand (or you've accumulated $100,000, $200,000, $500,000, or $1 million or more), and you've decided to invest it all. Knowing what you know so far, how would you divide it up? What's your *new* philosophy of investing? What percentage of your money are you going to keep growing in a secure environment and what percentage are you willing to risk for potentially greater growth?

You've probably heard that old rule of thumb (or what Jack Bogle calls a "crude method"): invest your age in bonds. In other words, subtract your age from 100, and that would be the percentage you should keep in stocks. So if you were 40 years old, 60% should go to equities in your Risk/Growth Bucket and 40% in your Security Bucket as bonds. At age 60, the ratio should be 40% stocks and 60% bonds. But those ratios are out of whack with today's reality. The volatility of both stocks and bonds has increased, and people live a lot longer.

So what should it be for you? Would you like to be more aggressive with your risk, like David Swensen? With a 30% security and 70% risk? That would mean putting 30% of your $10,000 windfall—$3,000—in Security and 70%—or $7,000—into your Risk/Growth Bucket. (If you had $1 million, you would be putting $300,000 in Security and $700,000 in Risk/Growth.) Can you really afford that kind of split? Do you have enough cash? Do you have enough time? Are you young enough? Or do you need to be a little bit more conservative, like most pensions are, at 60/40? Or is 50/50 right for you? Are you close enough to retirement that you'd want to have 80% in a secure place, and only 20% in riskier investments? What matters is not what most people do. What matters is what will meet both your financial and emotional needs.

I know, it's such a personal choice, and even the brightest stars in finance sometimes have to think long and hard about what's right for them and their families. When I interviewed J.P. Morgan's Mary Callahan Erdoes, I asked her, "What criteria would you use in building an asset allocation? And if you have to build one for your kids, what would that look like?"

"I have three daughters," she told me. "They're three different ages. They have three different skill sets, and those are going to change over time, and I'm not going to know what they are. One might spend more money than another. One may want to work in an environment where she can earn a lot of money. Another may be more philanthropic in nature. One may have something that happens to her in life, a health issue. One may get married, one may not; one may have children, one may not. **Every single permutation will vary over time,** which is why even if I started all of them the first day they were born and set out an asset allocation, it would have to change.

"And that has to change based on their risk profile, **because over time, you can't have someone in a perfect asset allocation unless it's perfect for them.** And if, at the end of the day, someone comes to me and says, 'All I want is Treasury bills to sleep well at night,' that may be the best answer for them."

I said to her, "Because it's about meeting their emotional needs, right? It's not about the money in the end."

"Exactly, Tony," she said. "Because if I cause more stress by taking half that portfolio and putting it in a stock market, but that leads to a deterioration of the happiness in their lives—why am I doing that?"

"What is the purpose of investing?" I asked. "Isn't it about making sure that we have that economic freedom for ourselves and for our families?"

"That's right, to be able to do the things you want to do," she said. "But not at the expense of the stress, the strains, and the discomfort that goes along with a bad market environment."

So what's the lesson here from one of the best financial minds in the world? What's more important even than building wealth is doing it in a way that will give you peace of mind.

So what will it be? Write down your numbers and make them real! Are those percentages a comfortable fit? Walk around in them. Live in them. Own them! Because those percentages are the key to your peace of mind as well as your financial future.

Done?

Okay! **You've just made the most important *investment* decision of your life. And once you know what your percentage is, you don't want to alter it until you enter a new stage of life, or your circumstances change dramatically. You've got to stick with it and keep the portfolio in balance. I'll show you how later in this section.**

Are you still concerned about making the right choice? Just remember, you've got a fiduciary to help you. And you don't need tens of thousands, hundreds of thousands, or millions of dollars to get started—you could get started with next to nothing for free with today's online services.

By the way, I'm not done with you yet! There are ways to increase your returns within these buckets, and we're going to get to that.

Now that you understand these principles, and you've made this decision about how much you want to put in your Risk Bucket versus your Security Bucket, let me tell you the best news of all: after interviewing 50 of the most successful investors in the world, the smartest financial minds, **I've uncovered the ways in which you can get Growth-like returns with Security Bucket protections.** The most important piece of advice every investor I talked to echoed was, "Don't lose money!" But for many investors, that means having to settle for mediocre returns in the Security Bucket. In just a couple of chapters, I'm going to share with you how to have the upside without the downside. How to have significant growth without significant risk. I know it sounds crazy, but it's real, and it's exciting.

As hard as we've worked here, I'm happy to tell you that the next chapter is easy and pure pleasure. Now I'm going to reveal a third bucket that we haven't talked about yet, but you're going to love it because it's fun, inspiring, and can give you a greater quality of life today, not decades in the future. Let's discover what's going to go in your Dream Bucket.

David Swensen provided the specific percentage for each asset class, but he did not provide the specific indices to represent each asset class. Independent analysts used the following indices to represent each asset class, and it is assumed that the portfolio would be rebalanced quarterly. **Note that past results do not guarantee future performance. Instead, I am providing you the historical data here to discuss and illustrate the underlying principles.**

20%	Wilshire 5000 Total Mkt TR USD
20%	FTSE NAREIT All REITs TR
20%	MSCI ACWI Ex USA GR USD
15%	Barclays US Long Credit TR USD
15%	Barclays US Treasury US TIPS TR USD
10%	MSCI EM PR USD

THE DREAM BUCKET

When you cease to dream, you cease to live.
—MALCOLM FORBES

What's a Dream Bucket? It's where you set aside something for yourself and those you love so that all of you can enjoy life while you're building your wealth. It's something for today, not tomorrow! Your Dream Bucket is meant to excite you, to put some juice in your life so you want to earn and contribute even more. Think of the items you're saving for in your Dream Bucket as *strategic splurges.*

What would float your boat right now? Maybe you'd buy yourself that pair of Manolo Blahniks you've always wanted, or a floor-side seat at a Miami Heat game. Or a VIP tour of Disneyland for the kids. Or you could start filling that bucket for a bigger reward: season tickets. A trip to the mountains in the summer or a ski or snowboarding vacation in the winter. A new car—maybe one that isn't so practical, like a Mini Cooper or a Mustang. A vacation condo or home.

I know a millionaire who always flew coach because he liked to save a dollar, but his wife complained about it constantly. "We have plenty of money. Why don't we enjoy it?" she said. It was a constant source of strife between them because they traveled so much for business. After attending my Wealth Mastery seminar, he decided to use his Dream Bucket to upgrade to business class when he flew with his family. He discovered it not only made his travel life more comfortable but also (even more importantly) his home life as well. Way to flame out, dude! Maybe someday he'd like to consider chartering a private jet instead of flying commercial—and it might not be as expensive as he thinks.

Many people have a lot of money but not much lifestyle. They spend their lives watching numbers accumulate in a bank account and miss out on the joy and enjoyment they can create and share along the way.

I remember that when I made my first Growth Bucket hits early in my career, my idea of a jackpot was to buy two new suits because they were on sale at a Men's Warehouse–like store. Or maybe take a vacation in Hawaii. That was a big deal for me back then!

My resort in Fiji was a much bigger dream that came true. As I shared with you, when I was 24 years old, I fell in love with the turquoise waters of the South Pacific islands. It was like my heart had found a home. I wanted a refuge for myself and my friends and family. Now, over the years, Namale Resort and Spa has become a pretty sizeable asset because I built it up and turned it into one of the top destinations in the South Pacific. But that's just a bonus. In fact, it's the number one resort in Fiji for more than ten years, and Oprah selected it as her favorite place to go last year. A jackpot on top of the dream that created it.

Your dreams are not designed to give you a financial payoff, they are designed to give you a greater quality of life. And isn't that why you've filled the first two buckets in the first place? But you've got to practice some restraint here, too. If you take all your money and put it only in the Dream Bucket, you're likely to end up going broke like Willie Nelson. So it's a matter of balance. And the jackpots in your Dream Bucket don't have to be just for yourself. The best jackpots are the ones you give to others.

> Dreams are the touchstones of our character.
> —HENRY DAVID THOREAU

Maybe you're like me, and you just love giving gifts. And the best gifts are the ones that are unexpected.

My mother never had money when she was young, and we always struggled as a family, living in cheap housing east of LA, where the nearly daily smog alerts announced on the news let us know it wasn't safe to walk outside.

And so one day, after my business started taking off, I asked my mom to help me check out a condo I was thinking of buying on the water in Huntington Beach. I walked her through it and showed her the magnificent ocean views. Then we stepped out on the beach and breathed the salt air.

"I really love this place, but I want your final word," I told her. "What do you think?"

"Are you kidding?" she said. "This is incredible! Can you imagine coming from where we came from, and now you're going to live here?"

"So you think it's the right place, Mom?"

"Oh, it's unbelievable!"

Then I handed her the keys.

"What's this?" she asked.

"It's yours, Mom."

I'll never forget the look of astonishment on her face and then tears of joy. My mom has passed away now, but I still remember those moments so vividly as some of the favorite of my life.

You don't have to wait. You could do this, too. **You can fulfill your dreams. If you want it badly enough, you'll find a way.**

Not long after I gave my mother that condo, I met with a group of a hundred or so fifth graders from a poor neighborhood at a school in Houston, Texas. Most of them were on a track that would never get them to college. So I decided then and there to make a contract with them. I would pay for their four-year college education if they kept a B average and stayed out of trouble. I made it clear that with focus, anyone could be above average, and I would provide mentoring to support them. I had a couple of key criteria: They had to stay out of jail. They couldn't get pregnant before graduating high school. Most importantly, they needed to contribute 20 hours of service per year to some organization in their community. Why did I add this? College is wonderful, but what was even more important to me was to teach them they had something to give, not just something to get in life. I had no idea how I was going to pay for it in the long run, but I was completely committed, and I signed a legally binding contract requiring me to deliver the funds. It's funny how motivating it can be when you have no choice but to move forward. I always say, **if you want to take the island, you have to burn your boats!** So I signed those contracts. Twenty-three of those kids worked with me from the fifth grade all the way to college. Several went on to graduate school, including law school! I call them my champions. Today they are social workers, business owners, and parents. Just a few years ago, we had a reunion, and I got to hear the magnificent stories of how early-in-life giving to others had become a lifelong pattern. How it caused them to believe they had real worth in life. How it gave them such joy to give, and how many of them now are teaching this to their own children.

I'm telling you this because you don't need to wait until you're absolutely ready to fulfill your dream. You just do it, and you find a way, and grace will find you. **Grace comes when you commit to doing something that will serve more than just yourself—some would call it luck or coincidence. I leave it to you to decide what to believe. Just know that when you give your all, the rewards are infinite.** I really believe motive does matter. But it doesn't mean that it can't benefit you too, right?

Jackpots can help you create more wealth, because **the key to creating wealth is to unleash your creativity** and find a way to do more for others than anyone else is doing. **If you find a way to add more value than anyone else, you can also find a way to prosper personally.** That can apply to your own life as well as the lives of others. Remember when we talked about speeding up your plan, how if you wish to be great, learn to become the servant of many? We already know that life supports what supports more life. And by supporting life, you lift yourself up as well, and more bounty comes to you.

> Give yourself peace of mind.
> You deserve to be happy. You deserve delight.
> —HANNAH ARENDT

So how do you fill your Dream Bucket? Let's talk about three ways. First, when you score a big hit, like that $10,000 bonus we were talking about earlier in the last chapter. Or, second, if your Risk/Growth Bucket gets a positive hit, and you score big. Just like in Vegas, it might be time to take some of the risk off the table. An approach many of my students use is to take those profits, divide them up, and invest them back in a fixed proportion: say, one-third in Security, one-third in Risk/Growth, and one-third in Dream. In the case of that bonus, that would be about $3,333 for your Dream Bucket.

By putting one-third of your Risk/Growth Bucket money into Security, it's like taking money off the table to help speed the growth of your most secure investments, and with it your peace of mind. By leaving one-third in Growth, you continue to take risks with a potential larger upside, but you're doing it with your winnings. By putting one-third in your Dream Bucket, you're creating a jackpot that you can enjoy today. This will stimulate and excite you in ways that will likely cause you to want to earn more, save more, and invest even more effectively—because of the rewards today, not just some day in the future.

The third way to fill your Dream Bucket is to save a set percentage of your income and sock it away, building it up until you're able to purchase your dreams—whether that be your first home, a car, a vacation, or those fun little items that will light you up today. But keep in mind, this is not taking any money out of what you are already saving for your Freedom Fund. That's sacred and untouchable money! But you can find ways to increase the amounts you can put in your Freedom Fund *and* your Dream Bucket. Here's a quick reminder from the "Speed It Up!" chapters:

- Save more and invest the difference.
- Earn more and invest the difference.
- Reduce fees and taxes and invest the difference.
- Get better returns.
- Change your lifestyle.

So you can take some of those savings to invest, and some of those savings to make your dreams a reality today or in the near future.

What will be your strategy to fill this bucket? Will you wait for a bonus or a stock market score, or will you set aside a percentage like my friend Angela? At first she thought she had no money she could possibly save even toward her financial freedom.

But by the time she went through the process of this book, she saw that relocating to Florida would save her enough money in state income tax that she could now set aside 10% of her income for her Freedom Fund and still earmark an additional 8% for her Dream Bucket. **The tax man was now filling her Dream Bucket.** How cool is that? Plus, she's got better weather, too! She went through her accounts and figured out a way to become even more tax efficient to be able to put an additional 2% into her Freedom Fund for a total of 12%, on top of the 8% she was saving toward her dreams.

If you would have told her in the beginning that she would have found a way to save 20%, she would have said you were absolutely crazy. But today she not only has her future secured but also is saving for some important dreams in the short term that excite her. Hiking in the Himalayas and rowing across the ocean. Her degree is in anthropology, and she's always dreamed of spending time with famed paleontologist Louise Leakey at her institute in Kenya. She was even invited. She just doesn't have the money right now. But if she sticks to her fiscally sound plan, she will. How cool to be able to be financially secure and independent, and, at the same time, live this life of adventure? Remember the strategy of Save More Tomorrow? You can decide that in your next salary increase, maybe 3% could go to your Freedom Fund, and maybe 1.5% or 2% could go to your Dream Fund— especially if there are some dreams that are important to you now, like saving for the down payment on your first home or a vacation getaway. There are so many ways to do it!

But let me tell you the secret: the most important thing is to make a list of your dreams. Put them in order of importance, big and small, short term and long term. Write down why you must achieve them or experience them. I've found that if you try to figure out a percentage to save without really knowing what you're saving for, it's not going to happen. The secret is to know what you truly want and why you want it, and make it a burning passion. Suddenly your creativity will be unleashed, and you'll find new ways to earn more, to save more, to add more value, to become more tax efficient, to become a better investor, or to make a lifestyle change that improves your life and gives you some of your dreams today, and not in the future. That's the key to it all.

But decide today! Take a moment now and make a list of your dreams. Write them down so they become real to you. How much would you be willing to save for them? Get excited, and get started!

> Every great dream begins with a dreamer.
> —HARRIET TUBMAN

In the end, what percentage of your total assets do you think should go in your Dream Bucket? It doesn't have to be much—maybe as little as 5% or 10%. But please don't forget to reward yourself. While it's important to keep your money safe and growing, never forget to have fun, to give, and to live your life fully on your path to financial freedom. That's what it's all about. Don't save your Dream Bucket for "a rainy day." Why not get out and soak up the sunshine?

If you don't, you could end up like a couple that a friend of mine told me about. They scrimped and saved their whole lives, and then finally decided they had enough to afford a fantastic Caribbean cruise. It was a weeklong trip on one of those giant cruise liners, hopping around the islands. You can picture it: the ship had swimming pools, a climbing rock, dozens of restaurants and discos. The couple was so excited, but they still wanted to be prudent with their capital, since they'd worked so hard to save for their retirement. They didn't want to spend extra money on the lavish meals. The trip by itself was a big enough splurge for them. So to save money, they loaded their suitcases with boxes of cheese and crackers to snack on during the cruise and vowed to avoid those expensive dinners.

The weather was perfect, and the couple had a great time with all the activities on board. But every lunch and dinner, when everybody else was eating incredible feasts served up on huge buffet tables—shrimp, lobster, prime rib, mountains of desserts, and fine wines from around the world—the two of them went back to their room and ate the cheese and crackers. They didn't mind. They were enjoying the trip of a lifetime, and they were proud of themselves for being frugal. But on the last day, they finally broke down and decided to splurge and have a magnificent final dinner upstairs! So they tucked into one of those amazing buffets and piled their plates with the best food they'd had in their lives.

After having multiple desserts and drinking wine, they asked the waiter for the bill. And with an astonished look on his face, he said, "What bill?" They said, "The bill for this magnificent dinner. The wine, desserts, everything."

The waiter turned to them with shock and said, "Didn't you know the meals come with the trip?"

The meals came with the trip. How's that for a metaphor? So don't settle for cheese and crackers on this journey; enjoy everything that comes with it.

And one more reminder: so much of what makes us wealthy is free. Remember what Sir John Templeton told us earlier: the secret to wealth is gratitude. It's not just what we achieve or accomplish. It's what we appreciate. It's not just the adventure of a cruise. It's what we take the time to enjoy. You can find an adventure and joy in those you love, in the dancing eyes of your children, or the joyous faces of those you love. There are jackpots everywhere if you wake up to the beauty of your life today. So don't vow to someday get beyond scarcity; start beyond it. Realize how lucky you are and all the wealth you possess in love, joy, opportunities, health, friends, and family. Don't get rich. Start rich.

So far we've learned how to allocate our investments among different types and classes of assets, and to put chunks of money in separate buckets for Security/Peace of Mind and for Risk/Growth. We've learned we also need to set aside another chunk of money for a Dream Bucket that will add juice to our lives as we build our wealth, and incentives to do better for ourselves and others. So now we have one final, brief chapter to teach you a set of three simple skills that can increase your returns 1% to 2% per year and, more importantly, make certain you avoid the mistakes so many people make by trying to time the market. Let's learn how from the power of knowing . . .

TIMING IS EVERYTHING?

We have met the enemy, and he is us.

—POGO

What's the secret of success for investors and stand-up comedians . . . ?

Timing. It's everything.

The best comics know exactly when to deliver a punch line. **And the smartest investors know just when to enter the market—*except for when they don't*!** Even the best of the best fail to hit every beat every single time. For a comedian, a mistake in timing results in an embarrassing, deathly silence in the house—and maybe a few thrown objects. **But if you're an investor, a mistake in timing can destroy your nest egg. So we need a solution that doesn't require us to be a psychic.**

We've already seen how diversifying your portfolio across different asset classes and across different markets can protect you in a volatile economy. **But haven't we all had the experience of being at the right place or doing exactly the right thing . . . but at the wrong time?** So by now you might be thinking, "Okay, Tony, so now I know how to diversify my investments—but what if my timing is off?"

I've asked myself the same question. **What if I put my money in the stock market at its peak, and it starts dropping? Or if I buy into a bond fund, and the interest rates begin to spike? Markets are always going to fluctuate, and we've learned that nobody, I mean *nobody*, can consistently and successfully predict when it's going to happen.**

So how do we protect ourselves from all the ups and downs and really succeed?

Most investors get caught up in a kind of mob mentality that has them chasing winners and running away from losers. Mutual fund managers do the same thing. It's human nature to want to follow the pack and not to miss out on anything. "Emotions get ahold of us and we, as investors, tend to do very stupid things," the Princeton economist Burton Malkiel told me. **We tend to put money into the market and take it out at exactly the wrong time."**

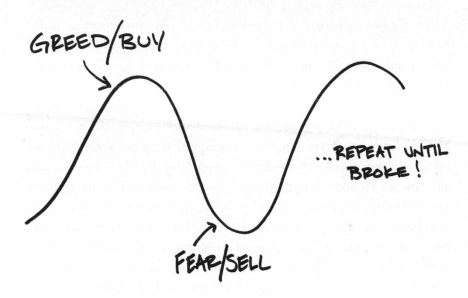

He reminded me of what happened during the tech bubble at the turn of the 21st century: **"More money went into the market in the first quarter of 2000, which turned out to be the top of the internet bubble, than ever before,"** he said. **"Then by the third quarter of 2002, when the market was way down, the money came pouring out."** Those investors who bailed instead of riding out the slump missed out on one of the greatest upturns of the decade! "Then in the third quarter of 2008, which happened to coincide with the peak of the financial crisis," said Malkiel, "more money went out of the market than ever, ever, ever before. So our emotions get ahold of us. We get scared."

And who could blame anyone for being scared during that epic crash! In October 2009, after the stock market had lost more than $2 trillion in value, and when hundreds of thousands of Americans were losing their jobs every month, Matt Lauer at NBC's *Today* show called my office. He asked me to come on the air the next morning to talk about what viewers could do to cope with the crisis. I'd known Matt for years and had been on his show a number of times, so of course I agreed. When I arrived on the set, his producer told me, "Okay, you've got four minutes to pump the country up."

I thought, "Are you kidding me?"

"Well, pumping people up is not what I do," I said. "I tell them the truth." And that's what I did. I warned the *Today* show audience in two different segments that the stock market meltdown was not over, that the worst could still be coming. How's that for pumping them up?

"Many stocks that were selling for fifty dollars not long ago are selling for ten dollars or five dollars, and here's the truth: some may go down to a dollar," I said, as news anchor Ann Curry's eyes grew wider and wider. But I also told the viewers that, instead of freaking out, they should fight their fears and educate themselves about people who had done well in tough times. Like Sir John Templeton, who had made all his money when markets were crashing during the Great Depression. I said that if you studied history, you knew there was a great chance, based on what happened in the '70s and even in the '30s, that in a short period stocks that had gone down to $1 would go up again. They might not get back to $50 for a long time, but, historically, many would jump to $5 in a few months. That's a 400% return, and it could happen in six months! "If you stay strong and smart, and the market continues to recover, you could make a thousand percent or more! This could be the greatest investment opportunity since you've been alive!" I said.

It was not exactly the message the *Today* show expected to hear, but it turned out to be dead-on. **How did I know the market was going to keep dropping? Because I was so brilliant?** Hardly. I wish I could say that. The reality was that my friend and client Paul Tudor Jones had been warning me about what was happening in the markets almost a year in advance of the crisis. He is one of those unicorns who can actually time the markets on a fairly consistent basis. It's part of what made him not only one of the most successful investors in history but a legendary figure. He predicted the Black Monday crash of 1987, and when everyone else was freaking out, he helped his clients make a 60% monthly return and 200% for the year.

So you can bet I was grateful for Paul's insights! In early 2008 he told me a stock market and real estate crash was coming, and soon. I was so concerned that I reached out to my **Platinum Partners,** an exclusive group of my clients who I work with three to four times a year in intimate, intensive sessions to transform their relationships, businesses, and finances. I called a surprise meeting and asked them all to fly and meet me in Dubai in April 2008 to warn them about the coming crisis and help them prepare for it. Remember, anticipation is power. With a four- to six-month jump, many of my clients were able to actually profit from one of the worst economic times in history.

Yes, sure enough, stock prices plummeted throughout the last quarter of 2008. **By March 2009, the market was so bad, Citigroup bank shares had dropped from a high of $57 to—you guessed it!—as I had warned, $0.97. You could literally own the stock for less than it cost you to take your money out of one of its ATMs!**

So what should an investor do in this extraordinary kind of situation? If you believe Sir John Templeton's motto, "The best opportunities come in times of maximum pessimism," or Warren Buffett's mantra, "Be fearful when others are greedy, and be greedy when others are fearful," it was a great time to scoop up bargains. Why? Because smart, long-term investors know that seasons always change. They'll tell you that winter is the time to buy—and the early months of 2009 were definitely winter! It's the time when fortunes can be made, because even though it may take awhile, spring always comes.

But what if you got scared or felt you had to sell when the markets collapsed? You might say, "Tony, what if I lost my job in 2008 and had no other source of income? Or my kid's tuition was due and the banks wouldn't loan me any money?" If you sold your stocks in 2008, all I can say is, I feel your pain, but I wish you could have found another way to make ends meet. Individual investors who liquidated their funds when the market plunged learned an agonizing lesson. Instead of riding the tide back up, they locked in their losses—permanently. If and when they got back into stocks, they had to pay a much higher price, because as you know, the market roared back to life.

Seeing so many people lose so much in such a short time, and feeling the suffering that all this created, is what started my obsession with wanting to bring the most important investment insights to the general public. It literally was the trigger for the birth of this book.

It also made me search to see if the same level of financial intelligence that created high-frequency trading (where the HFT investors truly have the upside without the downside) could be harnessed in some way for the good of the average investor. Remember, the HFT investors make money and virtually never lose.

So what's the good news? In the upcoming section of this book, "Upside Without the Downside: Create a Lifetime Income Plan," you're going to learn there's a way for you to never leave the market yet never take a loss. Why? Because there are financial tools—insurance products, to be specific—where you don't have to worry about timing at all. You make money when the market goes up, and when it goes down 10%, 20%, 30%, or even 50%, you don't lose a dime (according to the guarantees of the issuing insurance company). It sounds too good to be true, but in reality, it's the ultimate in creating a portfolio that truly offers you peace of mind. For now let me show you three tools that can help you limit many of your investment risks and maximize your investment returns in a traditional investing format.

> The future ain't what it used to be.
>
> —YOGI BERRA

> Prediction is very difficult, especially about the future.
>
> —NIELS BOHR

On March 2, 2009, Paul Tudor Jones told me that the market was hitting its absolute bottom. Prices would start rising again. Spring was coming. So I tweeted:

4:01 PM Mar 2nd from web

"Gratitude is the mother of all feelings. It is the highest expression of emotion within human consciousness."amma In tuff times gratitudeis
4:00 PM Mar 2nd from web

"the key to managing Crisis is to keep an eye on the long term while you're dancing in the flames!" Sir Philip Hangden
3:52 PM Mar 2nd from web

"Markets are never wrong; opinions are." The infamous trader Jesse Livermore-- I am not a market timer! ;-) best of luck! tony
3:50 PM Mar 2nd from web

Educate yourself.make your own decisions & only on investments you could afford to make.. I am not dispensing advice only advocate be aware
3:48 PM Mar 2nd from web

I coach one of top financial traders in world (for 17years now) Not giving trading advice but do watch for possible bottom coming. educate..
3:46 PM Mar 2nd from web

For those who asked...I would die in heart beat to protect my wife Sage, & I would give my life for my children. Love is worth dying for!
3:28 PM Mar 2nd from web

By the way, it was the first time I ever tweeted any information on the potential direction of the stock market! As it **turned out, only seven days later, the US stock exchange indexes did exactly that: bottomed out on March 9.** Prices started rising gradually and then took off. And sure enough, Citigroup stocks, which were $1.05 on March 9, 2009, closed on August 27, 2009, at $5 a share—a 400% increase![12] What an incredible return you could have had if you'd managed your fear and bought when everyone else was selling!

Now, I'd love to be able to say that past market behavior can predict the future, or that Paul Tudor Jones or anyone else I know could continuously successfully forecast these market swings, but it isn't possible. Based on analysis from those "in the know," I put out another heads-up warning for potential challenges in 2010, this time on video, when it looked like the market was overextended and heading for another correction. I wanted people to make a conscious decision whether they wanted to protect themselves from the potential of another huge hit. But this time we were wrong. **Nobody could guess that the US government would do something that no government has ever done in human history—it decided to prop up the markets by "printing" $4 trillion, while telling the world that it would continue to do so indefinitely, literally until the economy recovered!**

By magically adding zeroes to its balance sheet, the Federal Reserve was able to pump cash into the system by buying back bonds (both mortgage-backed bonds and Treasuries) from the big banks. This keeps interest rates unnaturally low and forces savers and anyone looking for some sort of return into the stock market. And the Fed kept doing it year after year. No wonder US stocks never came down from that sugar high!

---

12. If you look on most of today's stock charts, you may see that Citigroup was selling for $10.50 on March 9, 2009, and $50.50 on August 27, 2009. This is not accurate. These charts have been reformatted to reflect the fact that on May 6, 2011, Citigroup did a reverse stock split. Every ten shares of stock that was selling for $4.48 on May 5 were combined into one share of stock worth $44.80 a share, which ended the day at $45.20, for a small gain per share. Thus 29 billion shares of Citigroup were converted into just 2.9 billion shares in order to raise the price per share. Or as the *Wall Street Journal* stated on May 10, 2011, "Citigroup became a $40 stock the first time since 2007, as its share price appeared to rise more than 850% from Friday's close. One catch: Investors didn't earn a dime."

FEDERAL RESERVE TOTAL ASSETS (US$ MIL) AND S&P500 INDEX WEEKLY

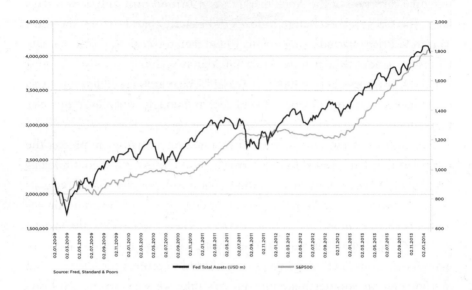

Source: Fred, Standard & Poors

Fed Total Assets (USD m)   S&P500

So if you think you can time the markets, you're wrong. Even the best in the world can't do it every time because there will always be factors they can't predict. Like stock picking, it's best to leave market timing to the masterminds who employ large staffs of analysts—ones like Paul, who can also afford to be wrong because of the many different bets they place on the direction of the markets. But this does not mean you can't take advantage of the *concept* behind market timing—the opportunities of rising and falling markets—by applying a couple of simple but powerful principles that you're about to learn here. Both involve taking yourself out of the picture and automating your investment schedule. "You can't control the market, but you can control what you pay," Burt Malkiel told me. "You have to try to get yourself on automatic pilot so your emotions don't kill you."

> Far more money has been lost by investors preparing
> for corrections, or trying to anticipate corrections,
> than has been lost in corrections themselves.
> —PETER LYNCH

SO WHAT'S AN ANSWER TO
THE DILEMMA OF TIMING?

One of these techniques is as old as Warren Buffett's original teacher, **Benjamin Graham,** the dean of modern investing. Graham, who taught at Columbia Business School in the mid–20th century, championed a gutsy technique with a boring name: *dollar-cost averaging.* (In fact, Buffett credits Graham with first coming up with the famous top rule of investing: "Don't lose money!") It's a system designed to reduce your chances of making the big investment mistakes we all fear: buying something right before it drops in price, or pulling out of an investment right before its price goes up.

We've already learned the first two keys of asset allocation: diversify across *asset classes* and diversify across *markets*. But remember, there's a third key: **diversify across *time*. And that's what dollar-cost averaging does for you.** Think of it as the way you activate your asset allocation plan. **Asset allocation is the theory; dollar-cost averaging is how you execute it.** It's how you avoid letting your emotions screw up the great asset allocation plan you've just put together by either delaying investing—because you think the market's too high and you hope it will drop before you get in—or by ignoring or selling off the funds that aren't producing great returns at the moment.

According to the many fans of dollar-cost averaging—and that includes powerhouses like Jack Bogle and Burt Malkiel—it's the key to sleeping better at night, knowing your investments will not only survive unstable markets but also continue to grow in the long term, no matter what the economic conditions. Sound great? All you need to do is make equal contributions to all of your investments on a set time schedule, either monthly or quarterly.

Easy, right?

But there are two challenges I have to warn you about. First, dollar-cost averaging is going to seem counterintuitive, and you might feel like you're going to be making less money using it. But I'll show in just a moment that what's counterintuitive is actually to your advantage. **Remember, the goal is to take emotion out of investing because emotion is what so often destroys investing success,** whether it's greed or fear. Second, there's been some recent debate about the long-term effectiveness of dollar-cost averaging, and I'll show what both sides are saying. But first, let's talk about the most common way investors use it and its potential impact.

When you invest on a set schedule, with the same amount of money invested each month or week in exact accordance with your asset allocation plan, the fluctuations of the market work to *increase* your gains, not decrease them. If you have $1,000 to invest each month, and you have a 60% Risk/Growth and 40% Security asset allocation, you're going to put $600 in your Risk/Growth Bucket and $400 in your Security Bucket regardless of what's happened to prices. **Volatility through time can become your friend.** This part might seem counterintuitive. But Burt Malkiel gave me a great example of how it works:

Here's a great test. Take a moment and give me your best answer to this question: Suppose you're putting $1,000 a year into an index fund for five years. Which of these two indexes do you think would be better for you?

Example 1
- The index stays at **$100** per share for the first year.
- It goes down to **$60** the next year.
- It stays at **$60** the third year.
- Then in the fourth year, it shoots up to **$140.**
- In the fifth year, it ends up at **$100,** the same place where you started.

Example 2
- The market is at **$100** the first year.
- **$110** the second year.
- **$120** the third.
- **$130** the fourth, and
- **$140** the fifth year.

So, which index do you think ends up making you the *most* money after five years? **Your instincts might tell you that you'd do better in the second scenario, with steady gains, but you'd be wrong. You can actually make higher returns by investing regularly in a volatile stock market.**

Think about it for a moment: in example 1, by investing the same amount of dollars, you actually get to buy *more* shares when the index was cheaper at $60, so you owned more of the market when the price went back up!

Here's Burt Malkiel's chart that shows how it happens:

Mutually Beneficial

Broadly diversified portfolio of mutual funds (with annual rebalancing) vs. portfolio containing U.S. stocks only

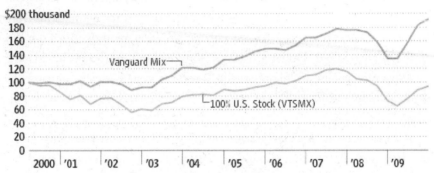

*33% fixed income (VBMFX), 27% U.S. stock (VTSMX), 14% developed foreign markets (VDMIX), 14% emerging markets (VEIEX), 12 % real-estate investment trust (VGSIX)
Sources: Vanguard and Morningstar

After five years of a steadily rising market, your $5,000 turns into $5,915. Not bad.

But in that volatile market, you make *14.5% more in profit*, winding up with $6,048! The problem, Malkiel told me, is that most people don't let the first scenario work for them. "When the market falls, they say, 'Oh my God! I'm going to sell!' So you have to keep your head and keep a steady course."

Investors learned a hard lesson during the first ten years of the 2000s, or what's known in financial circles as the lost decade. If you put all your money into the US stock market at the beginning of 2000, you got killed. **One dollar invested in the S&P 500 on December 31, 1999, was worth 90 cents by the end of 2009.** But according to Burt Malkiel, **if you had spread out your investments through dollar-cost averaging during the same time period, you would have made money!**

Malkiel authored a *Wall Street Journal* article titled " 'Buy and Hold' Is Still a Winner," in which he explained that if you were diversified among a basket of index funds, including US stocks, foreign stocks, and *emerging-market* stocks, bonds, and real estate, between the beginning of 2000 and the end of 2009, a $100,000 initial investment would have grown to $191,859. That's over 6.7% annually during a lost decade.

"Dollar-cost averaging is how you make the volatility of the market work for you," he told me.

Everyone from Warren Buffett's mentor Benjamin Graham to Burt Malkiel and many of the most respected academics certainly make a case for using dollar-cost averaging when you're investing a percentage of your steady stream of income. But if you have a lump sum to invest, it may not be the best approach. If this is your current situation, read the breakout box in this chapter titled "Dollar-Cost Averaging Versus Lump-Sum Investing."

What dollar-cost averaging really means is systematically putting the same amount of money across your full portfolio—not just the stock portion.

Remember, volatility can be your friend with dollar-cost averaging, and it can also allow for another technique that will keep you on track, "rebalancing," which we'll address in a moment.

So what's the best way to put dollar-cost averaging to work for you? Luckily, most people who have 401(k)s or 403(b)s that automatically invest the same amount on a fixed time schedule already reap the benefits of dollar-cost averaging. But if you don't have an automated system, it's easy to set one up. I have a self-employed friend who set up her own tax-advantaged retirement account with Vanguard, and she's instructed it to automatically deduct $1,000 from her bank account every month to distribute among her diversified index funds. She knows she might not always have the discipline to buy when one market feels too high or another drops too low, so she takes herself out of the picture. She's a long-term investor who doesn't worry about timing anymore, because her system is automated, and the decision is out of her hands.

There's a way to make dollar-cost averaging even easier, and that's by setting up an account with Stronghold, where it will do this for you automatically.

Also, remember, in the next section I'll show you an extraordinary tool that can protect you from losing your principal in these volatile times. Where, even if your timing is all wrong, you don't lose a dime in the stock market. And if you're right, you win even bigger. But before we get there, let's have a look at a second time-tested *pattern of investing* that will protect your savings and help you maximize your Freedom Fund as you build true wealth.

THE PATTERN TO AVOID:
THE AVERAGE PERSON'S
APPROACH TO INVESTING!
A REBALANCING ACT

David Swensen and Burt Malkiel sometimes take different approaches to finance. But there's one lesson they both told me, and all the other experts I've interviewed agree on this: **to be a successful investor, you need to rebalance your portfolio at regular intervals.**

You have to take a look at your buckets and make sure your asset allocations are still in the right ratio. From time to time, a particular part of one of your buckets may grow significantly and disproportionally to the rest of your portfolio and throw you out of balance.

Say you started out with 60% of your money in your Risk/Growth Bucket and 40% of your money in your Security Bucket. Six months later, you check your account balances and find out that your Risk/Growth investments have taken off, and they no longer represent 60% of your total assets—it's more like 75%. And now your Security Bucket holds only 25% instead of 40%. You need to rebalance!

Like dollar-cost averaging, rebalancing is a technique that seems simple at first, but it can take a lot of discipline. And unless you remember how important and effective rebalancing is in maximizing your profits and protecting against your losses, you'll find yourself getting caught up in the momentum of what seems to be working in the moment. You'll be hypnotized into the illusion that your current investment successes will continue forever, or that the current market (stock market, real estate market, bond market, commodity market) can go only in one direction: up.

This pattern of emotion and psychology is what causes people to stay with an investment too long and end up losing the very gains they were so proud of originally. It takes discipline to sell something when it's still growing and invest that money into something that's down in price or growing more slowly, but this willpower is what makes someone a great investor.

A powerful example of this principle was the day I was visiting with investment icon **Carl Icahn.** It was just announced that he had made a profit of nearly $800 million on his **Netflix** stocks. He'd bought the majority of his shares at $58 the previous year and was now selling them for $341 a share. His son, Brett, who works with Carl and who originally brought this investment opportunity to him, protested the selling of the stock. He was certain that Netflix had more growth ahead of it. Carl said he agreed, but their portfolio needed to be rebalanced. If they didn't rebalance, they could find themselves losing some of the extraordinary profits that they gained. Carl took his 487% profit and reinvested those profits into other assets in his portfolio, while keeping 2% of his Netflix shares to take advantage of any potential growth. Some of that money he used to buy $2.38 trillion in a little company called Apple, which he believed was undervalued at the time. He sold high and bought low. And rebalancing was a key part of that process.

IF BILLIONAIRES DO IT,
MAYBE YOU SHOULD TOO!

So what do you do if you find that you're out of balance? You were 60% Risk/Growth and 40% Security, but as we described above, your stocks have soared, and you're now 75%/25% as a result. In this case, your rebalancing action plan requires you to shift your regular contributions to the Risk/Growth Bucket into Security until the 25% is back up to 40%. Or you have to divert the profits or even sell some of the Growth/Risk investments that are booming and reinvest them back into bonds or first trust deeds or whatever combination of assets you're keeping in your Security Bucket. But this can be agonizing, especially if, say, REITs are roaring, or international stocks are suddenly going through the roof. Who wants to jump off when you're riding a rocket? All you want is more! But you have to take some of those assets off the table to reduce your exposure to risk and make certain that you keep some of the gains or profits you've made.

Just like dollar-cost averaging, you've got to take your emotions out of the picture. Portfolio rebalancing makes you do the opposite of what you want to do. In investing, that's usually the right thing to do.

Let's take a real-world example: say it's the summer of 2013, and the S&P 500 index is lurching back to record-breaking levels, while bonds are still coughing up meager returns. Do you want to sell your stocks and buy bonds? No way! But the rules of rebalancing say that's exactly what you have to do to keep your original ratio—even though a voice inside you is shouting, "Hey, stupid! Why are you putting money into those dogs?!"

The rules of rebalancing don't guarantee you're going to win every time. But rebalancing means you're going to win more often. It increases your probabilities of success. **And probabilities through time are what dominate the success or failure of your investment life.**

Sophisticated investors also rebalance *within* markets and asset classes, and that can be even more painful.

Say you owned a lot of Apple stock back in July 2012. It would have seemed insane to sell those shares, which had been surging—up 44% in the previous two quarters—and were worth more than $614 per share. But if Apple stock is dominating your portfolio (remember, it has grown 44%, and it's put you out of balance, likely significantly), the rules of rebalancing say that you have to sell some Apple to get your ratio right. Ouch. But you would have thanked yourself the same time next year. Why? Apple stocks took a roller coaster ride, plummeting from a high of $705 per share in September 2012, to a low of $385 the following April, and ending at $414 in July 2013—a 41% loss that you avoided because you rebalanced.

How often should you rebalance? Most investors rebalance once or twice a year. Mary Callahan Erdoes of J.P. Morgan told me she believes rebalancing is such a powerful tool that she does it "constantly." What does that mean? "That's as often as your portfolio gets out of whack with the plan that you originally put in place, or the adjusted plan based on what's happened in the world. And that shouldn't be set. **It should be a constant evaluation, but not an obsessive evaluation.**"

Burt Malkiel, on the other hand, likes to ride the momentum of bull markets. **He advises rebalancing only once a year. "I don't want to just be trigger-happy and sell something because it's going up," he said. "I like to give my good asset class at least a year in the run."**

However often you do it, rebalancing can not only protect you from too much risk—it can dramatically increase your returns. Just like dollar-cost averaging, the discipline once again makes you invest in underperforming assets when their prices are low, so that you own lots of them when their prices go up. Your profits get passed along to the other players on your team, like the ball in an LA Lakers motion offense, or relay runners passing the baton on the way to victory at the finish line.

The number of times you rebalance does have an impact on your taxes, however. If your investments are not in a tax-deferred environment, and you rebalance an asset you have owned less than a year, you'll typically pay ordinary income taxes instead of the lower long-term investment tax rate!

If rebalancing seems a little intimidating, the good news is this work can be done for you automatically by Stronghold or any other fiduciary advisor you choose. He or she will guide you on being tax-efficient while still tapping into the power of rebalancing.

So now you've learned two time-tested ways to reduce your risk and increase your returns just through asset allocation. But there's still one final trick that can take the sting out of your losses—and your taxes!

IT'S HARVEST TIME

So what happens when it's portfolio-rebalancing time, and you have to sell some stocks that aren't in your 401(k) or other tax-advantaged account? Uncle Sam will have his hand out for part of your profits. Are the capital gains taxes making you crazy? Listen, **there's a perfectly legal way for you to lower those taxes while keeping your portfolio balanced: tax-loss harvesting.** The benefit you get by tax-loss harvesting is that **you reduce your taxes, and that increases your net return!** In essence, you use some of your inevitable losses to maximize your net gains.

Burt Malkiel believes that tax-loss harvesting can increase your annual rate of return by as much as 1% per year, so it's certainly worth investigating.

Billionaires and big institutions increase their returns this way, although few ordinary investors take advantage of these powerful techniques. Few know of them, and even those who do may think rebalancing and tax harvesting sound too complicated to try on their own. Not to worry! You can get access to your own fiduciary advisor or access to software that will make it as easy as ordering a pizza online, or at least updating your Facebook security settings.

Now, bear in mind, my goal is to make investing simple for everyone, and this section is probably the one that tested your brain the most! So first, congratulations on sticking with me. This stuff feels very technical, and most people avoid it like the plague. If you feel a bit overwhelmed by asset allocation and the idea of dollar-cost averaging, rebalancing, and tax-loss harvesting, I want you to know all of this can be automated for you. But it's still helpful to understand what these strategies are and the principle reasons why they're effective.

Just remember four things from this section of the book:

1. **Asset allocation is everything!** So you want to diversify between your Security Bucket and your Risk/Growth Bucket. You want to diversify across asset classes, markets, and time.
2. **You don't want to hesitate to get in the market trying to have perfect timing; instead, use dollar-cost averaging and know that volatility can be your friend,** providing opportunities to buy investments cheaply when the market is down. This technique will increase your portfolio's value when the markets come back up.
3. **Have a Dream Bucket that gives you emotional juice and excitement so you can experience the benefits of your investing prowess in the short term** and midterm instead of just someday far in the future.
4. **Use rebalancing and tax harvesting to maximize your returns and minimize losses.**

When I first brought up that I was going to teach asset allocation and these additional refining strategies in this book, many of my friends in the financial world said, "You're crazy! It's just too complex. The average person won't understand it, and few will even take the time to read it." My answer was simple: "I'm here for the few who do versus the many who talk." It takes hunger to push yourself to master something new. But in the case of mastering investment principles, it truly is worth the effort. Even if you have to read something a couple of times to get it down, the rewards can be immense—it could mean saving years of your life without having to work. More importantly, mastering these will give you a greater sense of empowerment and peace of mind today.

Mastering this section is a lot like trying to learn to drive a stick-shift car for the first time. What?! I'm supposed to figure out how to use the accelerator, the brake, the clutch, the stick, the rearview mirror, the steering wheel, *and* watch the road too? Are you kidding me?! But after awhile, you're driving the car without thinking about it.

Well, we've already come a long way together on the 7 Simple Steps to Financial Freedom. **Let's check in where we are now:**

1. **You've made the most important financial decision of your life by deciding to save a percentage of your income—your Freedom Fund—and invest it automatically for compounded interest.** Have you acted on this yet by setting up an auto-deduct account? If not, do it today!
2. **You've learned the rules of investing and how to avoid Wall Street's nine biggest marketing/investment myths.** You're becoming the chess player, not the chess piece.
3. **You've taken the third step on your path to financial freedom by making the game winnable.** There are three stages within this step: Number one, you've calculated your top three financial goals, which for many people are financial security, vitality, and independence. Number two, you have a plan with real numbers. And number three, you've looked for and are implementing ways to speed it up so you can enjoy your rewards even sooner.
4. **In this section, you've made the most important *investment* decision of your life by allocating your assets into a portfolio with a specific percentage into different buckets (Security, Risk/Growth, Dream). You've diversified, and you have a plan that will fuel your financial dreams.**

You're already light-years ahead of other Americans (or investors anywhere in the world) when it comes to understanding your finances and managing your money. And if you're anything like the men and women who have been gracious enough to read this book in manuscript form, you might already be so excited by what you've learned that you're jumping up and down and grabbing your friends by the collars to show them some of the ways you've learned that they can add hundreds of thousands of dollars, or even millions, to their lifetime investment earnings. **So you might be surprised to learn: you ain't seen nothin' yet! I promise you, the best is still to come. And everything from here on out is much easier than this section!**

Now that you're thinking and acting like an insider, I'll show you how to truly invest like one. Let's find out how you can be successful in any financial environment and how you can tap into the power of the upside without the downside, creating a lifetime income stream.

DOLLAR-COST AVERAGING VERSUS LUMP-SUM INVESTING

But is it the best approach if you have a lump sum to invest?

What do you do if you have a sudden windfall, like that $10,000 bonus we talked about earlier in this section? Or what if you got a $50,000 insurance payout? Do you use dollar-cost averaging to invest it over a set time schedule of months or even years, or do you invest in a lump sum?

Here's where the controversy comes in. Some investment advisors have turned against dollar-cost averaging because, as even Burt Malkiel admits, it's not the most productive strategy for investing in the stock market when it keeps going straight up—like it's been doing in the years following the recent Great Recession.

You would have made more money by investing "everything" at the beginning of the bull market than if you had doled out your money over five years. That's obvious, right? And there have been recent studies, including one by Vanguard in 2012, showing that in rolling ten-year periods over the past 80 years in the US, UK, and Australian stock markets, lump-sum investing has outperformed dollar-cost averaging more than two-thirds of the time.

Why is this true? Because you're putting more of your money to work sooner and over a longer period of time, and limiting your trading fees. Onetime lump-sum investing gives you the opportunity for greater potential growth but also greater overall loss when markets drop. Research shows that lump-sum investing over the long term, when diversified successfully, is more profitable. But by how much? In the end, the average increased returns were no more than 2.3% more. And remember the statistics that Burt Malkiel shared with us for the 2000-to-2010 lost decade period—in that case, if you had invested $1 in the S&P 500 on December 31, 1999, ten years later it was worth only 90 cents. But if you did dollar-cost averaging, you made money during that same period. What would you do? Would you plunk down the whole ten grand as soon as you got it? Or would you keep it in a more secure place and invest $1,000 a month over ten months? Or $50,000 over two years? If the market keeps going up and up, you might lose out on some gains. But behavioral economics tells us you won't have as much regret as you would if the market crashed two days after you'd invested it all!

So it's totally up to you. Once again, I'm not here to give you my opinion, just the best insights available from the best experts. For most people, lump-sum investing is not an issue because they don't have a significant sum to invest! If that's your situation, you'll still maximize your returns by investing in a diversified portfolio with dollar-cost averaging.

UPSIDE WITHOUT THE DOWNSIDE: CREATE A LIFETIME INCOME PLAN

INVINCIBLE, UNSINKABLE, UNCONQUERABLE: THE ALL SEASONS STRATEGY

Invincibility lies in the defense.

—SUN TZU, *The Art of War*

There are events in our lives that forever shape our view of the world. Mile markers on our journey that, whether we knew it or not, have given us the lens through which we now see the world. And what we choose to allow those events to mean to us will ripple through our behavior and decision making for the rest of our lives.

If you grew up in the Roaring Twenties, your life was shaped by prosperity and grandeur. It was the days of the Great Gatsby. But if you grew up during the Great Depression, your life was shaped by struggle and anxiety. Growing up in a severe economic "winter" forced you to become a survivor.

Today's generations have a completely different experience of the world. They have grown up in incredible prosperity, even if their incomes don't land them in the 1%. We all get the benefits of living in an on-demand world. We can have groceries delivered to our door, deposit checks from the comfort of our pajamas, and watch thousands of television channels whenever and wherever we choose. My granddaughter hasn't learned to tie her shoes, but at age four she can navigate an iPad as well as I can, and she already knows that Google can answer any question she has on a moment's notice! This is also the era of possibility, where a start-up like WhatsApp, with only 50 or so employees, can disrupt an industry and sell for $19 billion!

Without a doubt, our lives are shaped by the seasons and events through which we live, but more importantly, it's the meaning we give those events that will determine our ultimate trajectory.

THE 1970S

Ray Dalio, now 65, came of age in the 1970s. It was a time of violent change in seasons and arguably the worst economic environment since the Great Depression. High unemployment was accompanied by massive inflation, causing interest rates to skyrocket into the high teens. Remember I shared with you that my first mortgage coming out of the inflation of the 1970s was a whopping 18% interest! There was also an "oil shock" in 1973, as an embargo caught the United States off guard, causing oil prices to rise from $2.10 a barrel to $10.40. No one was prepared for this. Just a few years later, the government imposed odd-even rationing, where people were forced not only to wait in line at the pump for hours but also were allowed to gas up only on odd or even days of the month! It was a season of political strife as faith in our government dwindled after Vietnam and Watergate. In 1974 President Nixon was forced to resign and was later pardoned by his successor, former vice president Gerald Ford, for any wrongdoing (wink, wink).

In 1971 Ray Dalio was fresh out of college and a clerk on the New York Stock Exchange. He saw bull and bear markets come in short bursts and create massive volatility in different asset classes. Tides changed quickly and unexpectedly. Ray saw the huge opportunity but was equally or even more aware of the enormous risks that came with the territory. As a result, he became ferociously committed to understanding how all these scenarios and movements were intertwined. By understanding how the bigger economic "machine" worked, he would ultimately figure out how to avoid those cataclysmic losses that doom so many investors.

All of these events shaped young Ray Dalio to ultimately become the world's largest hedge fund manager. But the seminal moment that most shaped Ray's investment philosophy happened on a hot night in August 1971, when a surprise address from President Nixon would change the financial world as we know it.

A NIXON NIGHT

All three major networks had their broadcasting interrupted unexpectedly as the president of the United States suddenly appeared in living rooms across America. In a serious and agitated state, he declared, "I directed Secretary

[John] Connally to suspend temporarily the convertibility of the dollar to gold." In one brief sentence, just 14 words, President Nixon announced to the world that the dollar as we knew it would never be the same again. No longer would the dollar's value be tied directly to gold. Remember Fort Knox? It used to be that for every paper dollar, the government would have the equivalent value of physical gold stocked away safely. And with Nixon's declaration, the dollar was now just paper. Imagine you had a treasure chest filled with gold, only to open it one day and find a yellow paper sticky note that said simply "IOU."

Nixon was saying that the dollar's value would now be determined by whatever we (the market) deemed its worth. This news also shocked foreign governments that had held huge sums of dollars, believing that they had the option to convert to gold at any time. Overnight, Nixon removed that option from the table (once again living up to his nickname "Tricky Dick"). Oh, he also issued a 10% surcharge on all imports to keep the United States competitive. And like a blizzard in late October, Nixon's address signified a change in seasons of epic proportions.

Ray was watching the president's address from his apartment and couldn't believe what he was hearing. What were the implications of Nixon's decision to take the United States off the gold standard? What did it mean for markets? What did this mean for the US dollar and its position in the world?

One thing Ray thought for sure: "It means the definition of money is different. I would have thought maybe it's a crisis!" He was certain that when he walked onto the trading floor the next morning, the market was sure to plummet.

He was wrong.

To his amazement, the Dow Jones was up nearly 4% that next day, as stocks soared to the highest single-day gain in history. Gold also skyrocketed as well! It was completely counterintuitive to what most experts would expect. After all, we had just broken our sacred promise to the world that these pieces of paper with dead presidents on them were actually worth something of value. Surely this change wouldn't inspire confidence in the US economy or government. This was a head scratcher. This market boom eventually became known as the "Nixon rally."

But it wasn't all great news. By letting the value of the dollar be

determined by "whatever we all think it's worth," an inflationary storm
brewed on the horizon. Ray elaborates: "But then in 1973, it set up the ingredients for the first oil shock. We never had an oil shock before. We never
had inflation to worry about before. And all of those things became, in a
sense, surprises. And I developed a modus operandi to expect surprises." It's
the surprises that we can't afford, or stomach. It's the next 2008. It's the next
shock wave sure to rumble through our markets.

The Nixon rally was a catalyst for Ray: the beginning of a lifelong obsession to prepare for anything—the unknown around every corner. His
mission was to study every conceivable market environment and what that
meant for certain investments. This is his core operating principle that allows him to manage the world's largest hedge fund. Not espousing that he
knows all. Quite the opposite. He is insatiably hungry to continually discover what he doesn't yet know. Because what's obvious is obviously wrong.
The prevailing thought is usually the wrong thought. And since the world is
continually changing and evolving, Ray's journey to uncover the unknown is
a never-ending endeavor.

ULTIMATE INVESTOR NIRVANA

What you are about to read could very well be the most important chapter
in the entire book. Yes, yes, I know, I said that before. And it's true that if
you don't know the rules of the game, you will get crushed. And if you don't
think like an insider, conventional wisdom will lead you to accept the fate of
the herd. And if you don't decide on a percentage and automate your savings, you will never get the rocket off the ground. Yet I wholeheartedly believe that there is nothing in this book that tops Ray's strategy for the largest
returns possible with the least amount of risk. This is Ray's specialty. This is
what Ray is known for throughout the world.

**The portfolio you are going to learn about in the pages ahead
would have provided you with:**

1. **Extraordinary returns—nearly 10% annually (9.88% to be exact, net of
   fees) for the last 40 years (1974 through 2013)!**
2. **Extraordinary safety—you would have made money exactly 85% of the
   time over the last 40 years! There were only six losses during those 40**

years, and the average loss was only 1.47%. Two of the six losses were breakeven, for all intents and purposes, as they were 0.03% or less. So from a practical perspective, you would have lost money four times in 40 years.

3. **Extraordinary low volatility—the worst loss you would have experienced during those 40 years was only –3.93%!**

Remember Warren Buffett's ultimate laws of investing? Rule 1: don't lose money. Rule 2: see rule 1. The application of this rule is Ray's greatest genius. This is why he is the Leonardo da Vinci of investing.

Anybody can show you a portfolio (in hindsight) where you could have taken gigantic risks and received big rewards. And if you didn't fold like a paper bag when the portfolio was down 50% or 60%, you would have ended up with big returns. This advice is good marketing, but it's not reality for most people.

I couldn't fathom that there was a way for the individual investor (like you and me) to have stock market–like gains, yet simultaneously have a strategy that would greatly limit both the frequency and size of the losses in nearly every conceivable economic environment. Can you imagine a portfolio model that declined just 3.93% in 2008, when the world was melting down and the market was down 50% from its peak? A portfolio where you can more than likely be safe and secure when the next gut-wrenching crash wipes out trillions in America's 401(k) accounts? This is the gift that lies in the pages ahead. (Note that past performance does not guarantee future results. Instead, I am providing you the historical data here to discuss and illustrate the underlying principles.)

But before we dive in, and before you can appreciate the beauty and power of Ray's guidance, let's understand the backstory of one of the most incredible investors and asset allocators to walk the planet. Let's learn why governments and the world's largest corporations have Ray on speed dial so they can maximize their returns and limit their losses.

I'M LOVIN' IT

Nineteen eighty-three was a bad year for chickens. It was the year that McDonald's decided to launch the wildly successful "Chicken McNugget."

They were such a hit that it took a few years to work out supply-chain issues because they couldn't get their hands on enough birds. But if it wasn't for the genius of Ray Dalio, the Chicken McNugget wouldn't even exist.

How does the world of high finance intersect with the fast-food-selling clown? Because when McDonald's wanted to launch the new food, it was nervous about the rising cost of chicken and having to up its prices—not an option for its budget-conscious clientele. But the suppliers weren't willing to give a fixed price for its chickens because they knew that it wasn't the chickens that are expensive. It's the cost of feeding them all that corn and soymeal. And if the feed costs rose, the suppliers would have to eat the losses.

McDonald's called Ray, knowing that he is one of the world's most gifted minds when it comes to eliminating or minimizing risk while maximizing upside—and he rang up a solution. He put together a custom futures contract (translation: a guarantee against future rising prices of corn and soymeal) that allowed suppliers to be comfortable selling their chickens for a fixed price. Bon appétit!

Ray's expertise extends far beyond the boardrooms of major corporations. Just how far does his wisdom reverberate throughout the world? **In 1997, when the US Treasury decided to issue inflation-protected bonds (today, they are commonly known as TIPS), officials came to Ray's firm, Bridgewater, to seek advice on how to structure them.** Bridgewater's recommendations led to the current design of TIPS.

Ray is more than just a money manager. He is a master of markets and risk. He knows how to put together the pieces to tilt the odds of winning drastically in favor of him and his clients.

So how does Ray do it? What's his secret? Let's sit at the feet of this economic master and let him take us on a journey!

INTELLECTUAL NAVY SEALS

Remember the jungle metaphor Ray gave us way back in chapter 1? As Ray sees it, to get what we really want in life, we have to go through the jungle to get to the other side. The jungle is dangerous because of the unknowns. It's the challenges lurking around the next bend that can hurt you. So, in order to get to where you want to go, you have to surround yourself with the smartest minds that you also respect. Ray's firm, Bridgewater, is his personal team of "jungle masters." He has more than 1,500 employees who are almost as obsessed as Ray with figuring out how to maximize returns and minimize risk.

As I mentioned early on, Bridgewater is the world's largest hedge fund, with nearly $160 billion under its watch. This amount is astonishing, considering most "big" hedge funds these days hover around $15 billion. Although the average investor has never heard of Ray, his name echoes in the halls of the highest places. His observations, a daily report, are read by the most powerful figures in finance, from the heads of central banks to those in foreign governments, and even the president of the United States.

There is a reason why the world's biggest players, from the largest pension funds to the sovereign wealth funds of foreign countries, invest with Ray. And here is a clue: it's not "conventional wisdom." He thinks way outside the box. Heck, he shatters the box. And his voracious appetite to continually learn and challenge the conventional and find "the truth" is what propelled Ray from his first office (his apartment) to a sprawling campus in Connecticut. His jungle team at Bridgewater has been called a group of intellectual Navy SEALS. Why? Because by working at Bridgewater, you are going through the jungle with Ray, arm in arm. The culture requires you to be creative, insightful, and courageous—always able to defend your position or views. But Ray also requires that you have the willingness to question or even attack anything you consider faulty. The mission is to find out what is true and then figure out the best way to deal with it. This approach requires "radical openness, radical truth, and radical transparency." The survival (and success) of the entire firm depends on it.

ALPHA DOG

Ray Dalio put himself on the map with the extraordinary (and continual) success of **his Pure Alpha strategy. Launched in 1991, the strategy now has $80 billion and has produced a mind-boggling 21% annualized return** (before fees were taken out), and with relatively low risk. The fund's investors include the world's wealthiest individuals, governments, and pension funds. It's the 1% of the 1% of the 1%, and the "club" has been closed to new investors for many years. The Pure Alpha strategy is actively managed, meaning that Ray and his team are continuously looking for opportunistic investments. They want to get in at the right time and get out at the right time. **They aren't just riding the markets, which was evidenced by a 17% gain (before fees) in 2008 while many hedge fund managers were closing their doors or begging investors not to pull out.** The investors in the Pure Alpha strategy want big rewards and are willing to take risks—albeit still limiting their risk as much as humanly possible.

CHILDREN AND CHARITY

With incredible success managing the Pure Alpha strategy, Ray has built up quite a sizeable personal nest egg. Back in the mid-'90s, he began to think about his legacy and the funds he wanted to leave behind, but he wondered, "What type of portfolio would I use if I wasn't around to actively manage the money any longer?" What type of portfolio would outlive his own decision making and continue to support his children and philanthropic efforts decades from now?

Ray knew that conventional wisdom and conventional portfolio management would leave him in the hands of a model that continually shows that it can't survive when times get tough. So he began to explore whether or not he could put together a portfolio—an asset allocation—that would do well in any economic environment in the future. Whether it's another brutal winter like 2008, a depression, a recession, or so on. Because nobody knows what will happen five years from now, let alone 20 or 30 years out.

The results?

A completely new way to look at asset allocation. A new set of rules. And **only after the portfolio had been tested all the way back to 1925, and only after it produced stellar results for Ray's personal family trust, in a variety of economic conditions, did he begin to offer it to a select group. So long as they had the minimum $100 million investment, of course.** The new strategy, known as the **All Weather** strategy, made its public debut in 1996, just four years before a massive market correction put it to the test. It passed with flying colors.

QUESTIONS ARE THE ANSWER

We've all heard the maxim "Ask and you shall receive!" But if you ask better questions, you'll get better answers! It's the common denominator of all highly successful people. Bill Gates didn't ask, "How do I build the best software in the world?" He asked, "How can I create the intelligence [the operating system] that will control all computers?" This distinction is one core reason why Microsoft became not just a successful software company but also the dominant force in computing—still controlling nearly 90% of the world's personal computer market! However, Gates was slow to master the web because his focus was on what was inside the computer, but the "Google Boys," Larry Page and Sergey Brin, asked, "How do we organize the entire world's information and make it accessible and useful?" As a result, they focused on an even more powerful force in technology, life, and business. A higher-level question gave them a higher-level answer and the rewards that come with it. To get results, you can't just ask the question once, you have to become obsessed with finding its greatest answer(s).

The average person asks questions such as "How do I get by?" or "Why is this happening to me?" Some even ask questions that disempower them, causing their minds to focus on and find roadblocks instead of solutions. Questions like "How come I can never lose weight?" or "Why can't I ever hang on to my money?" only move them farther down the path of limitation.

I have been obsessed with the question of how do I make things better? How do I help people to significantly improve the quality of their lives now? This focus has driven me for 38 years to find or create strategies and tools that can make an immediate difference. What about you? What question(s) do you ask more than any other? **What do you focus on most often? What's your life's obsession? Finding love? Making a difference? Learning? Earning? Pleasing everyone? Avoiding pain? Changing the world? Are you aware of what you focus on most; your primary question in life? Whatever it is, it will shape, mold, and direct your life.** This book answers the question, "What do the most effective investors do to consistently succeed?" What are the decisions and actions of those who start with nothing but manage to create wealth and financial freedom for their families?

In the financial world, Ray Dalio became obsessed with a series of better-quality questions. Questions that led him to ultimately create the All Weather portfolio. It's the approach you are about to learn here and has the potential to change your financial life for the better forever.

"What kind of investment portfolio would one need to have to be absolutely certain that it would perform well in good times and in bad—across all economic environments?"

This might sound like an obvious question, and, in fact, many "experts" and financial advisors would say that the diversified asset allocation they are using is designed to do just that. But the conventional answer to this question is why so many professionals were down 30% to 50% in 2008. We saw how many target-date funds got slaughtered when they were supposed to be set up to be more conservative as their owners neared retirement age. We saw Lehman Brothers, a 158-year-old bedrock institution, collapse within days. It was a time when most financial advisors were hiding under their desks and dodging client phone calls. One friend of mine joked painfully, "My 401(k) is now a 201(k)." All the fancy software that the industry uses— the "Monte Carlo" simulations that calculate all sorts of potential scenarios in the future—didn't predict or protect investors from the crash of 1987, the collapse of 2000, the destruction of 2008—the list goes on.

If you remember those days back in 2008, the standard answers were "This just hasn't happened before," "We are in uncharted waters," "It's different this time." Ray doesn't buy those answers **(which is why he predicted the 2008 global financial crisis and made money in 2008).**

Make no mistake, what Ray calls "surprises" will always look different from the time before. The Great Depression, the 1973 oil crisis, the rapid inflation of the late '70s, the British sterling crisis of 1976, Black Monday in 1987, the dot-com bubble of 2000, the housing bust in 2008, the 28% drop in gold prices in 2013—all of these surprises caught most investments professionals *way* off guard. And the next surprise will have them on their heels again. That we can be sure of.

But in 2009, once the smoke had cleared and the market started to bounce back, very few money managers stopped to ask if their conventional approach to asset allocation and risk management might have been wrong to begin with. Many of them dusted themselves off, got back in the selling saddle, and prayed that things would just get back to "normal." **But remember Ray's mantra, "Expect surprises," and his core operating question, "What *don't* I know?" It's not a question of whether or not there will be another crash, it is a question of when.**

MARKOWITZ:
THE SECRET TO MAXIMIZING RETURNS

Harry Markowitz is known as the father of modern portfolio theory. He explains the fundamental concept behind the work that won him the Nobel Prize. In short, investments in a portfolio should not just be looked at individually, but rather as a group. There is a trade-off for risk and return, so don't just listen to one instrument, listen to the entire orchestra. And how your investments perform together, how well they are diversified, will ultimately determine your reward. This advice might sound simple now, but in 1952 this thinking was groundbreaking. At some level, this understanding has influenced virtually every portfolio manager from New York to Hong Kong.

Like all great investors, Ray stood on Markowitz's shoulders, using his core insights as a basis for thinking about the design of any portfolio or asset allocation. But he wanted to take it to another level. He was sure that he could add a couple more key distinctions—pull a couple key levers—and create his own groundbreaking discovery. He took his four decades of investing experience and rounded up his troops to focus their brainpower on this project. Ray literally spent years refining his research until he had arrived at a completely new way to look at asset allocation. The ultimate in maximizing returns and minimizing risk. And his discoveries have given him a new level of competitive advantage—an advantage that will soon become yours.

Up until this book's publication, Ray's life-altering, game-changing approach has been for the exclusive benefit of his clients. Governments, pension plans, billionaires—all get the extraordinary investment advantages you are about to learn—through Ray's All Weather strategy. As I mentioned, it's where Ray has serious skin in the game. It's where he invests all of his family and legacy money alongside the "Security Buckets" of the most conservative and sophisticated institutions in the world. Like Ray, I also now invest a portion of my family's money in this approach, as well as my foundation's money, because as you'll begin to see, it has produced results in every economic environment over the last 85 years. From depressions and recessions, to times of inflation or deflation; in good times and in bad, this strategy has found a way to maximize opportunity. Historically it appears to be one of the best approaches possible to achieving my wishes long after I am gone.

GAME DAY

To be able to sit with yet another of the great investment legends of our time was truly a gift. I spent close to 15 hours studying and preparing for my time with Ray, combing over every resource I could get my hands on (which was tough, because he typically avoids media and publicity). I dug up some rare speeches he gave to world leaders at Davos and the Council on Foreign Relations. I watched his interview with Charlie Rose of *60 Minutes* (one of his only major media appearances). I watched his instructional animated video *How the Economic Machine Works—In Thirty Minutes* (www.economicprinciples.org). It's a brilliant video I highly encourage you to watch to really understand how the world economy works. I combed through every white paper and article I could find. I read and highlighted virtually every page of his famous text *Principles*, which covers both his life and management guiding principles. This was an opportunity of a lifetime, and I wasn't going to walk in without being completely prepared.

What was supposed to be a one-hour interview quickly turned into nearly three. Little did I know Ray was a fan of my work and had been listening to my audio programs for almost 20 years. What an honor! We went deep. We were pitching and catching on everything from investing to how the world economic machine really works. I began with a simple question: **"Is the game still winnable for the individual investor?"**

"Yes!" he said emphatically. But you certainly aren't going to do it listening to your broker buddy. And you certainly aren't going to do it by trying to time the market. **Timing the market is basically playing poker with the best players in the world who play round the clock with nearly unlimited resources.** There are only so many poker chips on the table. "It's a zero-sum game." So to think you are going to take chips from guys like Ray is more than wishful thinking. It's delusional. "There is a world game going on, and only a handful actually make money, and they make a lot by taking chips from the players who aren't as good!" As the old saying goes, if you have been at a poker table for a while, and you still don't know who the sucker is: it's you!

Ray put the final warning stamp on trying to beat/time the market: *"You don't want to be in that game!"*

"Okay, Ray, so we know we shouldn't try to beat the best players in the world. So let me ask you what I have asked every person I have interviewed for this book: If you couldn't leave any of your financial wealth to your children but only a portfolio, a specific asset allocation with a list of principles to guide them, what would it be?"

Ray sat back, and I could see his hesitancy for a moment. Not because he didn't want to share, but because we live in an incredibly complex world of risk and opportunity. "Tony, that's just too complex. It's very hard for me to convey to the average individual in a short amount of time, and things are constantly changing." Fair enough. You can't cram 47 years of experience into a three-hour interview. But I pressed him a bit . . .

"Yeah, I agree, Ray. But you also just told me how the individual investor is not going to succeed by using a traditional wealth manager. So help us understand what we *can* do to succeed. We all know that asset allocation is the most important part of our success, so **what are some of the *principles* that you would use to create maximum reward with minimal risk?"**

And that's when Ray began to open up and share some amazing secrets and insights. His first step was to shatter my "conventional wisdom" and show me that conventional wisdom on what is a "balanced" portfolio is not balanced at all.

> The secret of all victory lies in the organization of the nonobvious.
> —MARCUS AURELIUS

UNBALANCED

Most advisors (and advertisements) will encourage you to have a "balanced portfolio." Balance sounds like a good thing, right? Balance tells us that we aren't taking too much risk. And that our more risky investments are offset by our more conservative ones. But the question lingers:

Why did most conventional balanced portfolios drop 25% to 40% when the bottom fell out of the market?

The conventional balanced portfolios are divided up between 50% stocks and 50% bonds (or maybe 60/40 if you are a bit more aggressive, or 70/30 if you are even more aggressive). But let's stick with 50/50 for the sake of this example. That would mean if someone has $10,000, he would invest $5,000 in stocks and $5,000 in bonds (or similarly, $100,000 would mean $50,000 in bonds and $50,000 in stocks—you get the idea).

By using this typical balanced approach, we are hoping for three things:

1. We *hope* stocks will do well.
2. We *hope* bonds will do well.
3. We *hope* both don't go down at the same time when the next crash comes.

It's hard not to notice that *hope* is the foundation of this typical approach. But insiders like Ray Dalio don't rely on hope. Hope is not a strategy when it comes to your family's well-being.

RISKY BUSINESS

By dividing up your money in 50% stocks and 50% bonds (or some general variation thereof), many would think that they are diversified and spreading out their risk. **But in reality, you really are taking much more risk than you think.** Why? Because, as Ray pointed out emphatically multiple times during our conversation, **stocks are *three times* more risky (aka volatile) than bonds.**

"Tony, by having a fifty-fifty portfolio, you really have more like ninety-five percent of your risk in stocks!" Below is a pie chart of the 50/50 portfolio. The left side shows how the money is divided up between stocks and bonds *in percentage terms*. But the right side shows how the same portfolio is divided up *in terms of risk*.

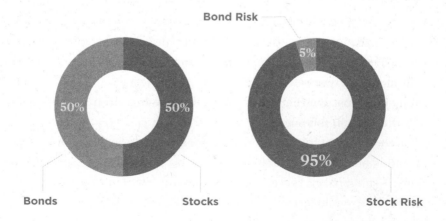

So with 50% of your "money" in stocks, it *seems* relatively balanced at first glance. But as shown here, you would have closer to 95% or more at "risk" because of the size and volatility of your stock holdings. Thus, if stocks tank, the whole portfolio tanks. So much for balance!

How does this concept translate to real life?

From 1973 through 2013, the S&P 500 has lost money nine times, and the cumulative losses totaled 134%! During the same period, bonds (represented by the Barclays Aggregate Bond index) lost money just three times, and the cumulative losses were just 6%. So if you had a 50/50 portfolio, the S&P 500 accounted for over 95% of your losses!

"*Tony*," Ray said, "*when you look at most portfolios, they have a very strong bias to do well in good times and bad in bad times.*" And thus your de facto strategy is simply *hoping* that stocks go up. This conventional approach to diversifying investments isn't diversifying at all.

I had never heard this concept of balance versus risk explained so simply. As I sat there, I started to think back to my own investments and where I may have made some wrong assumptions.

So let me ask you, how does this understanding make you feel about your "balanced" portfolio now?

Does this change your view as to what it means to be diversified? I sure hope so! Most people try to protect themselves by diversifying the *amount of money* they put into certain investment assets. One might say, "Fifty percent of my money is in 'risky' stocks (with perhaps greater upside potential if things go well) and fifty percent of my money is going in 'secure' bonds to protect me." Ray is showing us that if your money is divided equally, yet your investments are not equal in their risk, you are not balanced! You are really still putting most of your money at risk! You have to divide up your money based on how much risk/reward there is—not just in equal amounts of dollars in each type of investment.

You now know something that 99% of investors don't know and that most professionals don't know or implement! But don't feel bad. Ray says most of the big institutions, with hundreds of billions of dollars, are making the same mistake!

RAINMAKER

Ray was now on a roll and was systematically dissecting everything I had been taught or sold over the years!

"Tony, there is another major problem with the balanced portfolio 'theory.' It's based around a giant and, unfortunately, inaccurate assumption. It's the difference between correlation and causation."

Correlation is a fancy investment word for when things move together. In primitive cultures, they would dance in an attempt to make it rain. Sometimes it actually worked! Or so they thought. They confused *causation* with *correlation*. In other words, they thought their jumping up and down *caused* the rain, but it was actually just coincidence. And if it happened more and more often, they would build some false confidence around their ability to predict the *correlation* between their dancing and the rain.

Investment professionals often buy into the same mythology. They say that certain investments are either correlated (move together) or uncorrelated (have no predictable relationship). And yes, at times they might be correlated, but like the rainmaker, it's often just happenstance.

Ray and his team have shown that all historical data point to the fact that many investments have completely random correlations. The 2008 economic collapse destroyed this glaring assumption when almost all asset classes plummeted in unison. The truth is, sometimes they move together, sometimes they don't. So when the professionals try to create balance, hoping stocks move in the opposite direction of bonds, for example, it's a complete crapshoot. But this faulty logic is the underpinning of what most financial professionals use as their "true north."

Ray has clearly uncovered some glaring holes in the traditional asset allocation model. If he were a professor at an Ivy League school and had published this work, he probably would have been nominated for a Nobel Prize! But in the trenches—in the jungle—is where Ray would rather live.

THE FOUR SEASONS

When I talked with David Swensen, Yale's chief investment officer, he told me that **"unconventional wisdom is the only way you can succeed."** Follow the herd, and you don't have a chance. Oftentimes people hear the same advice or thinking over and over again and mistake it for the truth. But it's unconventional wisdom that usually leads to the truth and more often leads to a competitive advantage.

And here is where Ray's second piece of unconventional wisdom came crashing in. "Tony, when looking back through history, **there is one thing we can see with absolute certainty: every investment has an ideal environment in which it flourishes. In other words, there's a season for everything.**"

Take real estate, for example. Look back to the early 2000s, when Americans were buying whatever they could get their hands on (including people with little money!). But they weren't just buying homes because "interest rates were low." Interest rates were even lower in 2009, and they couldn't give houses away. People were buying during the boom because prices were inflating rapidly. Home prices were rising every single month, and they didn't want to miss out. Billionaire investing icon George Soros pointed out that "Americans have added more household mortgage debt in the last six years [by 2007] than in the prior life of the mortgage market." That's right, more loans were issued in six years than in the entire history of home loans.

In Miami and many parts of South Florida, you could put down a deposit, and because of inflationary prices, before the condo was even finished being built, you could sell it for a sizeable profit. And what did people do with that home equity? They used their home like an ATM and spent it, and that massive spending stimulated the profitability of corporations and the growth of the economy. Soros cited some staggering numbers: "Martin Feldstein, a former chairman of the Council of Economic Advisers, **estimated that from 1997 through 2006, consumers drew more than $9 trillion in cash out of their home equity.**" To put this in perspective, in just six years (from 2001 to 2007), Americans added more household mortgage debt (*about $5.5 trillion*) than in the prior life of the mortgage market, which is more than a century old. Of course, this national behavior is not a sustainable way to live. When home prices dropped like a rock, so did spending and the economy.

In summary, which season or environment can powerfully drive home prices? Inflation. But in 2009 we experienced *de*flation, when prices sank, and many mortgage holders were left with a home underwater—worth less than what they owed. Deflation drops the price of this investment class.

How about stocks? They too perform well during inflation. With inflation comes rising prices. Higher prices mean that companies have the opportunity to make more money. And rising revenues mean growth in stock prices. This has proven true over time.

Bonds are a different animal. Take US Treasury bonds, for example. If we have a season of deflation, which is accompanied by falling interest rates, bond prices will rise.

Ray then revealed the most simple and important distinction of all. There are only four things that move the price of assets:

1. inflation,
2. deflation,
3. rising economic growth, and
4. declining economic growth.

	GROWTH	**INFLATION**
RISING ⬆	Higher than expected economic growth	Higher than expected inflation
FALLING ⬇	Lower than expected economic growth	Lower than expected inflation

Ray's view boils it down to only four different possible environments, or economic seasons, that will ultimately affect whether investments (asset prices) go up or down. (Except unlike nature, there is not a predetermined order in which the seasons will arrive.) They are:

1. higher than expected inflation (rising prices),
2. lower than expected inflation (or deflation),
3. higher than expected economic growth, and
4. lower than expected economic growth.

When you look at a stock (or bond) price today, the price already incorporates what we (the market) "expect" about the future. Ray said to me, "Tony, there is a literal picture of the future when you look at prices today." In other words, the price of Apple's stock today incorporates the *expectations* of investors who believe the company will continue to grow at a certain pace. This is why you may have heard that a stock will fall when a company says that its future growth (earnings) will be lower than it had initially expected.

"It's the *surprises* that will ultimately determine which asset class will do well. If we have a real good growth surprise, that would be very good for stocks and not great for bonds. For bonds, if we have a surprise drop in inflation, it would be good for bonds."

If there are only four potential economic environments or seasons, Ray says you should have 25% of your *risk* in each of these four categories. He explains: "I know that there are good and bad environments for all asset classes. And I know that in one's lifetime, there will be a ruinous environment for one of those asset classes. That's been true throughout history."

This is why he calls this approach All Weather: because there are four possible seasons in the financial world, and nobody really knows which season will come next. With this approach, each season, each quadrant, is covered all the time, so you're always protected. Ray elaborates: **"I imagine four portfolios, each with an equal amount of risk in them. That means I would not have an exposure to any particular environment."** How cool is that? We aren't trying to predict the future, because nobody knows what the future holds. What we do know is that there only four potential seasons we will all face. By using this investment strategy, we can know that we are protected—not merely hoping—and that our investments are sheltered and will do well in any season that comes our way.

Bob Prince, the co-chief investment officer at Bridgewater, describes the uniqueness of the All Weather approach: **"Today we can structure a portfolio that will do well in 2022, even though we can't possibly know what the world will look like in 2022."**

I honestly sat there with my jaw open because nobody had ever described to me such a simple yet elegant solution. It makes perfect sense to have investments, divided up equally by risk, that will do well in all seasons but *how* you actually accomplish this is the golden ticket.

"So we know the four potential seasons, but which type of investment will perform well in each of these environments?" Ray responded by categorizing them into each season. Below is a chart that makes it easy to break down visually.

		GROWTH	INFLATION
RISING ⬆		Stocks Corporate Bonds Commodities/Gold	Commodities/Gold Inflation Linked Bonds (TIPS)
FALLING ⬇		Treasury Bonds Inflation Linked Bonds (TIPS)	Treasury Bonds Stocks

TWO DOWN, ONE TO GO

On the surface, asset allocation might sometimes feel complex, even when you understand the principles that Ray has laid out. But there's one thing I know for sure: **complexity is the enemy of execution.** If you and I are *actually* going to get ourselves to follow through with this process and receive the rewards, I had to find a way to make this advice *even* simpler.

So I said to Ray, "What you have shared with us here is invaluable. A completely different way of looking at asset allocation. By now we all know asset allocation is one of the single most important keys to all successful investing. But the challenge for the average investor—and even for the sophisticated investor—is how to take these principles and translate them into an actual portfolio with the most effective percentages of each asset class. It will be too complex for ninety-nine percent of us to figure out. So it would be a huge gift if you could share the specific percentages that people would invest in each asset class so that their risk would be divided equally among seasons!"

Ray looked at me, and I could see the wheels turning. "Tony, it's not really that simple." Ray explained that in his All Weather strategy, they use very sophisticated investment instruments, and they also use leverage to maximize returns.

I understood where Ray was coming from, so I asked him for a more simplified version: "Can you give me the percentages that the average person can do, without any leverage, to get the best returns with the least amount of risk? I know it's not going to be your absolute perfect asset allocation because I'm putting you on the spot to create it right here and now. But Ray, your best estimate will certainly be greater than most people's best plan. Could you give a version of the All Weather portfolio that readers could do on their own or with the help of a fiduciary advisor?"

Ray has taken on very few investors in the last ten years, and the last time he did, you had to be an institutional investor with $5 billion in investable assets, and your initial investment needed to be a minimum of $100 million just to get Ray's advice. This helps you understand what a big ask I was making. But I know how much he cares about the little guy. He certainly hasn't forgotten his roots as a self-made man from humble beginnings in Queens, New York.

"Ray, I know you've got a huge heart to help, so let's give folks a recipe for success. You won't take anybody's money, even if they are worth five billion dollars today. Help your brothers and sisters out!" I said with a big smile.

And then something magical happened.

I looked in Ray's eyes, and a smile came across his face. "All right, Tony. It wouldn't be exact or perfect, but let me give you a sample portfolio that the average person could implement." And then slowly he began to unfold the exact sequence for what his experience shows will give you and me the increased probability of the highest return in any market environment, as long as we live, with the least amount of risk.

DRUMROLL, PLEASE

You are about to see the exact asset allocation built by a man whom many call the best asset allocator to walk the planet. A self-made man who built himself from nothing financially to a net worth of over $14 billion, and who manages $160 billion a year and produces annual returns of more than

21% for his investors (before fees). Here he shares not only which type of investment but also what percentage of each asset class you need to win! In fact, if you look online, many people have tried to replicate a version of this based upon Ray's previous interviews. In fact, there is a whole new category of investment products now called "Risk Parity," based on Ray's innovations. Many funds or strategies say they were "inspired" by Ray's approach, but nobody received the specific allocation like Ray provided here. Many of the replicas were down as much as 30% or more in 2008. More like "some weather" than "All Weather," if you ask me. A fake Rolex will never be a Rolex. (A quick note: the strategy below is *not* the same as Ray's All Weather strategy, of course. As he said, his fund uses more sophisticated investments and also uses leverage. But the core principles are the same, and the specific percentages are designed directly by Ray, and no one else, **so let's call this portfolio herein the "All Seasons" portfolio.**)

GIVE ME THE NUMBERS

"So tell me, Ray, what are the percentages you would put in stocks? What percentage in gold? And so on." He graciously proceeded to sketch out the following breakdown:

First, he said, **we need 30% in stocks (for instance, the S&P 500 or other indexes for further diversification in this basket).** Initially that sounded low to me, but remember, stocks are three times more risky than bonds. And who am I to second-guess the Yoda of asset allocation!?

"Then you need long-term government bonds. **Fifteen percent in intermediate term [seven- to ten-year Treasuries] and forty percent in long-term bonds [20- to 25-year Treasuries]."**

"Why such a large percentage?" I asked.

"Because this counters the volatility of the stocks." I remembered quickly it's about balancing risk, not the dollar amounts. And by going out to longer-term (duration) bonds, this allocation will bring a potential for higher returns.

He rounded out the portfolio with 7.5% in gold and 7.5% in commodities. "You need to have a piece of that portfolio that will do well with accelerated inflation, so you would want a percentage in gold and commodities. These have high volatility. Because there are environments where rapid inflation can hurt both stocks and bonds."

Lastly, the portfolio must be rebalanced. Meaning, when one segment does well, you must sell a portion and reallocate back to the original allocation. This should be done at least annually, and, if done properly, it can actually increase the tax efficiency. This is part of the reason why I recommend having a fiduciary implement and manage this crucial, ongoing process.

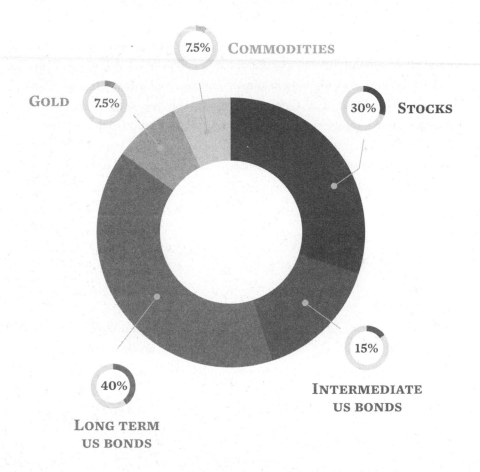

GRATITUDE

Wow! There it was in black and white. Ray had masterfully and graciously provided a game-changing recipe that would impact the lives of millions of

Americans. Do you realize the level of generosity this man provided both you and me that wonderful day? Giving from the heart is at the core of who Ray is. Which is why I wasn't the least bit surprised to learn later that he and his wife, Barbara, have signed the Giving Pledge—a commitment by the world's wealthiest individuals, from Bill Gates to Warren Buffett, to give away the majority of their wealth through philanthropy.

DO I HAVE YOUR ATTENTION NOW?

When my own investment team showed me the back-tested performance numbers of this All Seasons portfolio, I was astonished. I will never forget it. I was sitting with my wife at dinner and received a text message from my personal advisor, Ajay Gupta, that read, "Did you see the email with the back-tested numbers on the portfolio that Ray Dalio shared with you? Unbelievable!" Ajay normally doesn't text me at night, so I knew he couldn't wait to share. As soon as our dinner date was over I grabbed my phone and opened the email . . .

IT'S TIME TO THRIVE: STORM-PROOF RETURNS AND UNRIVALED RESULTS

If no mistake have you made, yet losing you are . . .
a different game you should play.

—YODA

THE PROOF IS IN THE PUDDING

It's safe to say that in the past 80-plus years, we have experienced every possible economic season and more than a handful of surprises, from the Great Depression to the Great Recession and everything in between. So how did the All Seasons portfolio perform? As I mentioned, I took it to a team of analysts to have it tested extensively all the way back to 1925! The results astonished everyone.

We already saw in the previous chapter how the All Seasons approach did over 40 years, so let's dig a little deeper. But **let's take a look at how it did during what I call the "modern period"—the 30 years from 1984 through 2013. The portfolio was rock solid:** [13]

- **Just under 10% (precisely 9.72%, net of fees) average annualized return.** (It's important to note that this is the actual return, not an inflated average return.)
- **You would have made money just over 86% of the time.** That's only four down/negative years. The average loss was just 1.9%, and one of the four

---

13. This assumes the portfolio was rebalanced annually. Past performance does not guarantee future results. Instead, as I mentioned prior, I am providing you the historical data here to discuss and illustrate the underlying principles.

losses was just 0.03% (essentially a break-even year)—so **effectively you would have lost money only three out of 30 years.**

- **The worst down year was −3.93% in 2008 (when the S&P 500 was down 37%!).**
- Investor nerd alert! Standard deviation was just 7.63%. (This means extremely low risk and low volatility.)

Why did we select the modern period from 1984? This time frame marks the beginning of the 401(k) plan, when every American became an investor and no longer was the stock market just for the sophisticated. For some perspective, 30 years ago, there was no World Wide Web. Heck, the first "portable" handheld cell phones came out in 1984. The Motorola DynaTac was a beige brick that cost nearly $4,000. The plan itself also cost $50 a month and 50 cents per minute, but you could talk only for 30 minutes before the battery died. I know because I'm ancient enough to be one of the first proud owners.

But let's not point out just the positives. **Let's look at how the portfolio held up in the worst times: the economic winters.** This analysis is what the industry calls stress testing.

If you look at what I call the "historical period," from 1939 to 2013 (75 years), consider these startling stats. (Please note that in order to go back further in time, we had to use different "indexes" to represent the asset allocation because certain indexes didn't exist prior to 1983. See the end of the chapter for a full explanation on the methodology used.)

S&P vs. All Seasons (75-Year History)

S&P	All Seasons
In 75 years, the S&P lost money 18 times*	In the same time period, the All Seasons portfolio lost money just ten times (slightly more than once a decade, on average).**
It's largest single loss was -43.3%	The largest single loss was just -3.93%.
The average loss was -11.40%.	The average loss was only -1.63%.

* Includes dividend reinvestment.
**Two of the ten loss years were only 0.03% (essentially break-even years; thus from a practical perspective, there were only 8 years of loss in a 75-year track record).

Let's go back even further, all the way to 1927, which includes the worst decade in our economic history, the Great Depression:

S&P vs. ALL SEASONS (SINCE 1928)

S&P	ALL SEASONS
In 87 years (through 2013), the S&P lost money 24 times (roughly 27% of the time).	The All Seasons portfolio lost money only 14 times during the same period (which means 73 years of positive returns).
In the heart of the depression, the four consecutive losing years (1929-1932) the S&P lost 64.40%.	During the same four-year period, 1929-1932, the All Seasons portfolio had a total loss of 20.55% (59% better than the S&P).
The average loss was 13.66%.	The average loss was just 3.65%.

* includes dividend reinvestment

If a house is deemed storm-proof, the only way to know for sure is to endure the test of time and the worst of storms. Below is a chart showing the seven worst drops since 1935. As you will see, the All Seasons portfolio was

WORST DROPS SINCE 1935

YEAR	S&P*	ALL SEASONS
1937	-35.03%	-9.00%
1941	-11.59%	-1.69%
1973	-14.69%	3.67%
1974	-26.47%	-1.16%
2001	-11.89%	-1.91%
2002	-22.10%	7.87%
2008	-37%	-3.93%

*includes dividend reinvestment

Source: Jemstep

actually *up* in two out of seven of those "winters"! And the losses it did sustain were relatively small in comparison with the US stock market. Talk about bucking the trend. While winter was kicking everyone's butt, this portfolio would have allowed you to spend the winter skiing or snowboarding and enjoying your hot chocolate!

If you look at how the All Seasons portfolio would have performed against the market in more recent years, the difference is even greater! **From January 1, 2000, through March 31, 2014, the All Seasons portfolio destroyed the returns of the market (the S&P 500).** During this time frame, we endured all kinds of what Ray calls "surprises": the tech crash, the credit crisis, the European debt crisis, and the largest single-year drop in gold (down 28% in 2013) in more than a decade. This time frame includes what experts call the lost decade, in which the S&P 500 was flat for ten years, from the beginning of 2000 to the end of 2009. Take a look at the difference in how his design performed:

% GROWTH

BURN 'EM DOWN

It's fascinating and quite sad that we live in a time where the media is salivating to take down anyone considered to be "best in class." Culture seems to lift them onto a pedestal of perfection only to hope they come crashing down. Whether it's an athlete, a CEO, or a money manager, any false move or seemingly slight crack in the armor is exploited to the fullest. Stone them in the town square of television and the internet.

I found it mind boggling that with more than 30 years of stellar returns, Ray's All Weather strategy received intense criticism when he was down approximately 4% in 2013. A whopping 4%. Not the whopping 37% hit that the S&P took just a few years earlier. Remember, based on history, the All Seasons approach will take losses, but the goal is to minimize those dramatic drops. Let's be honest: you could buy into this portfolio and see a loss the first year. This portfolio is not meant to shoot out the lights. It's a long-term approach for the smoothest possible ride. It would be a mistake to judge it by any single year, rather we need to evaluate its overall long-term performance—like any other investment opportunity. At the time of this writing (mid-2014), the media is back on the Dalio bandwagon, as his All Weather fund was up 11% through June.

Imagine, all this media attention over a 4% loss? Never mind that over the last five years, between 2009 and 2013, the All Weather has averaged over 11% per year, even including this single down year! But the fact he lost even a small amount when the market was up and that he received big media attention shows how his incredible performance has become expected. You are only as good as your last "at bat" when it comes to the financial media. How ridiculous. Never mind the fact that Ray's clients have enjoyed incredible returns year after year, decade after decade, as the *New Yorker* reported in a 2011 article on Bridgewater called "Mastering the Machine":

"In 2007, Dalio predicted that the housing-and-lending boom would end badly. Later that year, he warned the Bush Administration that many of the world's largest banks were on the verge of insolvency. In 2008, a disastrous year for many of Bridgewater's rivals, the firm's flagship Pure Alpha fund rose in value by 9.5% after accounting for fees. Last year, the Pure Alpha fund rose 45%, the highest return of any big hedge fund."

The point is, there are a number of pundits who will sit back and criticize *any* strategy you may deploy. To echo my favorite quote from Dr. David Babbel, "Let them criticize; let us sleep."

GOOD QUESTIONS

When it comes to the All Weather approach, the biggest question from the bloggers is: What happens when interest rates go up? Won't the government bonds go down and cause a loss to the portfolio because of the large percentage allocated to bonds?

It's a fair question, but deserves more than a sound bite from an armchair quarterback. First, remember that by having a large allocation to bonds, it's not a bet on bonds alone. This portfolio spreads your risk among the four potential economic seasons.

Ray showed us that the point is not to plan for a specific season or pretend to know what season is coming next. Remember, it's the surprises that will catch most off guard.

In fact, many have been trying to proselytize and predict the next season by calling for interest rates to rise quickly. After all, we are at all-time lows. Yet Michael O'Higgins, author of the famous book *Beating the Dow*, says that people may be waiting quite some time for any significant interest rate increases, since the Fed has a history of suppressing interest rates for long periods to keep costs of borrowing low: "To the great number of investors who believe interest rates will inevitability go higher in the coming year (2014), **remember that the US Fed kept long (duration) rates below 3% for 22 years from 1934 to 1956.**"

The Fed has kept rates low since 2008, so who knows how long interest rates will remain low. Nobody can tell you with certainty. In early 2014, when everyone was expecting rates to rise, they dropped yet again and caused a spike in US bond prices. (Remember, as rates go down, prices go up.)

HOW DID THE ALL SEASONS PERFORM IN A RISING-INTEREST RATE MARKET?

A revealing exercise is to look back in history at what happened to the All Seasons portfolio during a season when interest rates rose like a hot air balloon. After interest rates declined for many decades, the 1970s brought rapid inflation. **Despite skyrocketing interest rates, the All Seasons portfolio**

had just a single losing year in the 1970s and had an annualized return of 9.68% during the decade. This includes enduring the back-to-back drops of 1973 and 1974, when the S&P lost 14.31% and then another 25.90% loss, for a cumulative loss of 40.21%.

So let's not let the talking heads persuade us to believe that they know what season is coming next. But let's certainly prepare for all seasons and the series of surprises that lay ahead.

LET'S GET REAL

One final and crucial advantage of the All Seasons portfolio has a much more human element. Many critics will point out that if you could stomach more risk, you might have been able to beat this All Seasons approach. And they would be right. But the point of the All Seasons portfolio is to reduce volatility/risk while still maximizing gains!

If you are younger and have a longer time horizon, or you are willing to stomach more risk, you could still take advantage of the All Seasons foundation but make a small adjustment in the stocks versus bonds to, hopefully, produce a greater return. But keep in mind, by adding more stocks and decreasing your bonds, this change will increase risk/volatility and have you betting more on one season (in which you hope stocks will go up). In the past, this has worked quite well. If you visit the Stronghold website, you can see how, over time, by adding more stocks, the portfolio would have produced a greater returns but also produced greater downside in certain years. But here is what's incredibly interesting. When compared with a standard 60%/40% balanced portfolio (60% in the S&P 500 and 40% in the Barclays Aggregate Bond index), **the All Seasons approach, with more stock exposure, outperformed handily—and you would have to have accepted nearly 80% more risk (standard deviation) with the traditional 60/40 portfolio to still achieve results that would still fall slightly short of the All Seasons with increased equity focus.**

But let's be honest with ourselves. Our stomach lining is much weaker than we let on. The research firm Dalbar revealed the truth about our appetite for risk. **For the 20-year period from December 31, 1993, to December 31, 2013, the S&P 500 returned 9.2% annually, but the**

average mutual fund investor averaged just over 2.5%, barely beating inflation.[14] To put this in perspective, you would have received a better return by investing in three-month US Treasuries (which is nearly a cash equivalent) and avoided the stomach-turning drops.

Why did the average investor leave so much on the table?

Dalbar president Louis Harvey says investors "move their money in and out of the market at the wrong times. They get excited or they panic, and they hurt themselves."

One of the more startling examples is a study conducted by Fidelity on the performance of its flagship Magellan mutual fund. **The fund was run by investment legend Peter Lynch,[15] who delivered an astonishing 29% average annual return between 1977 and 1990. But Fidelity found that the average Magellan investor actually lost money!!!** How in the world? Fidelity showed that when the fund was down, people would cash in— scared of the possibility of losing more. And when the fund was up again, they would come running back like the prodigal investor.

Here is the reality: most people couldn't stomach another 2008 without selling some or all of their investments. It's human nature. So when people talk about better performance, for the most part they are talking about a fictitious investor; one with nerves of steel and a drawer full of Tums. Case in point: I was reading MarketWatch recently and came across an article by Mark Hulbert. Mark's financial publication tracks the performance of subscription newsletters that tell investors exactly how to trade the markets. The best performing newsletter over 20 years was up 16.3% annually! Outstanding performance, to say the least. But with the ups come major downs. As Mark explains, "[T]hat high-flying performance can be stomach churning, with his performance during the downturns of the last three market cycles—since 2000—among the very worst of his peers. During the 2007–09 bear market, for example, the service's average model portfolio lost nearly two-thirds of its value." Two-thirds?! That's 66%! Can you

14. Source: Richard Bernstein Advisors LLC, Bloomberg, MSCI, Standard & Poor's, Russell, HFRI, BofA Merrill Lynch, Dalbar, FHFA, FRB, FTSE. Total Returns in USD.
15. I had the privilege to interview Peter Lynch on his core investing principles while he was on his great winning streak, when he spoke at my Wealth Mastery program in the early 1990s.

imagine investing $100,000 and now seeing only $33,000 on your monthly statement? Or $1 million of your life savings reduced to just $333,000? Would you have white knuckled it and held on?

When Mark asked the newsletter publisher about whether or not investors could actually hang on during the roller coaster ride, he provided quite the understatement by saying, in an email, that his approach isn't for an investor who "bails out of his/her broadly diversified portfolio the first time a worry arises."

I would call a 66% drop more than "a worry." He makes it sound like us mere mortals are prone to overreaction, as though I jumped out of a moving car when the check engine light came on. **Remember, a 66% loss would require nearly 200% gains just to get back to even—just to recoup the portion of your nest egg that it may have taken your entire life to save!**

If You Lose	Gain Required to Break Even
5%	5%
10%	11%
15%	18%
20%	25%
25%	33%
30%	43%
35%	54%
40%	67%
45%	82%
50%	100%
75%	300%
90%	900%

> Without exception, the "money masters" I interviewed for this book are obsessed with not losing their money. They understand that when you lose, you have to make significantly more to get back to where you started—to get back to breakeven.

The *reality* is, if we are being honest with ourselves, we all make emotional decisions about our investments. We are all emotional creatures, and even the best traders in the world are always fighting the inner fear. This All Seasons portfolio protects you not only from any potential environment but also from yourself!!! It provides "emotional scaffolding" to keep you from making poor decisions. If your worst down year in the last 75 years was 3.93%, what is the likelihood that you would have freaked out and sold everything? And in 2008, when the world was burning down but your All Seasons portfolio was down just 3.93% while everyone else seemed to be melting down, how peaceful would have you felt?

So there you have it! The All Seasons recipe from the master chef Ray Dalio. And rather than wait until you have a $5 billion net worth, you get access here, for the few dollars you invested in this book! He has simplified it by taking out the leverage and also making it a more passive approach (not trying to beat the market by being the best picker or predictor of what's coming next). You are welcome to implement this portfolio yourself, but if you do, let me just add a few points of caution:

- The low-cost index funds or ETFs you choose will change the performance. It's crucial to find the most efficient and cost-effective representations for each percentage.
- The portfolio will need to be monitored continually and rebalanced annually.
- The portfolio is *not* tax efficient at times. It's important to use your qualified accounts (IRAs/401[k]s) or other tax-efficient structures to maximize tax efficiency appropriately. You could also use a low-cost variable annuity like the ones offered by TIAA-CREF or Vanguard. (However, those are the only two that experts seem to agree are worth the cost.)

ALL SEASONS + LIFETIME INCOME

The team at Stronghold (www.strongholdfinancial.com) currently uses the All Seasons portfolio as one of the many options available to their clients. Some readers will want to implement this on their own, while others will be better served using the expertise and assistance of a fiduciary advisor like Stronghold. Please take action in whatever form supports you most.

TAKE MASSIVE ACTION

The ball is now in your court. If you have a better strategy that has proven effective to minimize downside and maximize upside, maybe you should be running your own hedge fund. You now are armed with info to do this on your own, or if you choose, you can have a fiduciary implement and monitor this for you as part of a comprehensive plan.

If you want to create your own personal plan in less than five minutes, go to the website now (www.strongholdfinancial.com) to see how your current portfolio approach stacks up against a variety of strategies, including the All Seasons approach provided here.

LET'S TAKE YOUR BROKER FOR A TEST DRIVE

Stronghold's complimentary analysis allows you to "look under the hood" and find out how much you are *really* paying in fees and how your current investments are *really* performing. It will also highlight how much risk you're currently taking as well as your true performance over the past 15 years, during which we have seen two near 50% declines (2000–02 and 2008–09)!

If you choose to take action, you can transfer your accounts online and begin the process today. If not, you'll have all the information you need for free.

WHAT ABOUT MY 401(K)?

The All Seasons approach can be implemented in your existing 401(k) plan so long as there are fund choices available that represent the recommended investments. This you can do on your own or with the help of an advisor. If you use Stronghold, it will automatically link your 401(k) account to your overall plan and make sure that the 401(k) portfolio is set up correctly. Again, **America's Best 401k** can provide you with the All Seasons strategy as well.

INCOME IS THE OUTCOME

Whew! Wow, we covered a ton of territory in these last two chapters. But by now I think you can see why. What you hold in your hands is an investment plan with a track record of "smooth" returns that is second to none! You can implement it in a few minutes, and you no longer have to live with the worry about the ups and downs of the market. Of course, nobody knows what the future holds, but history would tell us that by doing so, you will be set up to do well and be protected in any environment.

So now let's go back to our "personal Everest" metaphor of investing. By using the All Seasons strategy, you have the best odds of having a smooth and steady climb to the top. Yes there will be surprises, but you will be set up to succeed over the long term. Now remember, once you have built up the value of your investments to a critical mass where you have enough to be financially free, you will need to ultimately turn your nest egg (those investments) into a guaranteed income stream—your own lifetime income plan. A paycheck for life without ever having to work again. That's ultimately where financial freedom comes from. Let's turn the page now and learn why "All Seasons + Income for Life Can = Real Financial Freedom." Let's learn how to create an income for life!

HOW DOES HE DO IT?

How does Ray Dalio keep generating such extraordinarily consistent returns? He has learned that this giant economy is one big machine, and everything is linked together in some way. Sometimes it's obvious, many times not. He can look at the machine and know that there are predictable patterns he can take advantage of. In fact, the culmination of his findings on the economic machine is packed into a brilliant 30-minute video that, in my opinion, should be required viewing for every American! Ray decided to produce the video only to make an impact on society and help demystify the economics that make our world go round. Take the time to watch it, and you will be glad you did: www.economicprinciples.org.

HOW DID WE CALCULATE THE RETURNS?

In order to insure the accuracy and credibility of the results produced by the All Seasons portfolio shared here, a team of analysts tested this portfolio using the annual historic returns of low-cost, broadly diversified index funds where possible. Why is this important to you? By using real fund data as opposed to theoretical data from a constructed index, all the returns listed in this chapter are fully inclusive of annual fund fees and any tracking error present in the underlying funds. This has the benefit of showing you realistic historic returns for the All Seasons portfolio (as opposed to theoretical returns that are sometimes used in back-testing). This insures that the investment holdings and numbers used in back-testing this portfolio were and are accessible to the everyday man on the street and not only available to multibillion-dollar Wall Street institutions. Where they were unable to use actual index fund data because the funds didn't exist at that time, they used broadly diversified index data for each asset class and adjusted the returns for fund fees. Note that they used annual rebalancing in the calculations and assumed that the investments were held in a tax-free account with no transaction costs. Finally, I would like to thank Cliff Schoeman, Simon Roy, and the entire Jemstep team for their in-depth analysis and coordination with Ajay Gupta at Stronghold Wealth Management in this effort. (Past performance does not guarantee future results.)

FREEDOM: CREATING YOUR LIFETIME INCOME PLAN

Lifetime Income Stream Key to Retirement Happiness
—*TIME*, July 30, 2012

I have enough money to retire comfortably for the rest
of my life. Problem is, I have to die next week.
—ANONYMOUS

In 1952 Edmund Hillary led the first expedition to successfully climb Mount Everest, a feat once thought to be impossible. The Queen of England promptly knighted him, making him "Sir" Edmund Hillary for his amazing trek.

Despite his accomplishment, many people believe Sir Edmund Hillary may not have been the first person to reach the peak of Everest. In fact, it is widely believed that George Mallory may have been the first person to reach the peak, nearly 30 years prior!

So, if George Mallory reached the peak of Mount Everest in 1924, why did Edmund Hillary receive all the fame—including being knighted by the Queen?

Because Edmund Hillary didn't just make it to the peak, he also successfully made it *back down* the mountain. George Mallory was not so lucky. Like the vast majority of those who have died on Everest, it was coming down that proved fatal.

INVESTING FOR WHAT, EXACTLY?

I often ask people, "What are you investing for?"

The responses are wide and diverse:

"Returns."

"Growth."

"Assets."

"Freedom."

"Fun."

Rarely do I hear the answer that matters most: *Income!!!!!*

We all need an income that we can count on. Consistent cash flow that shows up in our account every single month, like clockwork. **Can you imagine never worrying again about how you will pay your bills or whether your money will run out?** Or having the joy and freedom of traveling without a care in the world? Not having to worry about opening your monthly statements and praying the market holds up? Having the peace of mind to give generously to your church or favorite charity and not wonder if there will be more where that came from? We all know intuitively: *income is freedom!*

Shout it from the hilltops like Mel Gibson in the movie *Braveheart*: "Income is freedom!!!"

And *lack* of income is stress. Lack of income is struggle. Lack of income is not an acceptable outcome for you and your family. Make this your declaration.

Dr. Jeffrey Brown, retirement expert and advisor to the White House, said it best in a recent *Forbes* article: "[I]ncome is the outcome that matters most for retirement security."

The wealthy know that their assets (stocks, bonds, gold, and so on) will always fluctuate in value. But you can't "spend" assets. You can only spend cash. The year 2008 was a time when there were lots of people with assets (real estate, in particular) that were plummeting in price, and they couldn't sell. They were asset "rich" and cash "poor." This equation often leads to bankruptcy. **Always remember that income is the outcome.**

By the end of this section, you will have the certainty and the tools you need to lock down exactly the income you desire. This is what I call **"income insurance." A guaranteed way to know for certain that you will have a paycheck for life without having to work for it in the future—to be absolutely certain that you will *never* run out of money.** And guess what? You get to decide when you want your income checks to begin.

There are many ways to skin the proverbial cat, so we will review a couple of different methods for getting the income insurance that makes sense for you.

One of the more exciting structures for locking down income has other powerful benefits as well. **It is the *only* financial vehicle on the planet that can give you the following:**

- **100% guarantee on your deposits.**[16] **(You can't lose your money, and you keep total control.)**
- **Upside without the downside: your account value growth will be tied to the market, so if the market goes up, you get to participate in the gains. But if the market goes down, you *don't lose* a dime.**
- **Tax deferral on your growth.** (Remember the dollar-doubling example? Tax efficiency was the difference between having $28,466 or more than $1 million!)
- **A guaranteed lifetime income stream where *you* have control and get to decide when to turn it on.**
- **Get this: the income payments can be made *tax-free* if structured correctly.**
- **No annual management fees.**

You get all of these benefits by using a modern version of a 2000-year-old financial tool! How is this possible? I am sure it sounds too good to be true, but stick with me. It's not! I use this approach, and I am excited to share the details with you.

As we have highlighted throughout the book, the financial future that you envision is very much like climbing Mount Everest. You will work for decades to accumulate your critical mass (climbing to the top), but that's only half the story. **Achieving critical mass without having a plan and**

---

16. Insurance guaranty associations provide protection to insurance policy holders and beneficiaries of policies issued by an insurance company that has become insolvent and is no longer able to meet its obligations. **All states, the District of Columbia, and Puerto Rico have insurance guaranty associations.** Insurance companies are required by law to be members of the guaranty association in states in which they are licensed to do business. Each state has its own maximum amount that you are covered up to, and in most states, that varies per person up to $300,000 to $500,000.

strategy for how to turn it into income that will last the rest of your lifetime will leave you like George Mallory: dead on the back side of a mountain.

A NEW AGE

We are, without a doubt, in uncharted waters. In the past 30 years, the concept of retirement has transformed radically. Heck, even as recently as the late '80s, over 62% of workers had a pension plan. Remember those? On your last day of work, you got a gold watch and the first of your guaranteed lifetime income checks. Today, unless you work for the government, a pension is a relic; a financial dinosaur. Now, for better or worse, you are captain of your own ship. You are ultimately responsible for whether or not your money will last. That's quite a burden to bear. Throw in market volatility, excessive fees, inflation, and medical "surprises," and you quickly start to understand why so many are facing a massive retirement crisis. Many people, including your neighbors and colleagues, are going to face the real likelihood of outliving their money. Especially with the prospect of living longer than ever before.

IS 80 THE NEW 50?

A long, fruitful retirement is a concept that's only a few generations old. If you recall from our discussion earlier, when President Franklin Roosevelt created Social Security in 1935, the average life expectancy was just 62. And the payments wouldn't kick in until age 65, so only a small percentage would actually receive Social Security benefits to begin with.

At the time, the Social Security system made financial sense because there were 40 workers (contributors) for every retiree collecting benefits. That means there were 40 people pulling the wagon, with only 1 sitting in the back. By 2010, the ratio had dropped to only 2.9 wagon pullers for every retiree. The math doesn't pencil out, but since when has that stopped Washington?

Today the average life expectancy for a male is 79, while the average female will live to 81. For a married couple, at least one spouse has a 25% chance of reaching age 97.

BUT WAIT, THERE'S MORE!

You could be living *way* longer than even these estimates. Think how far we have come in the past 30 years with technology. From the floppy disk to nanotechnology. Today scientists are using 3-D printing to generate new organs out of thin air. Researchers can use human cells, scraped gently from your skin, to "print" an entirely new ear, bladder, or windpipe![17] Science fiction has become reality. Later we'll hear directly from my friend Ray Kurzweil, the Thomas Edison of our age and currently the head of engineering at Google. When asked how advances in life sciences will affect life expectancies, he said:

"During the 2020s, humans will have the means of changing their genes; not just 'designer babies' will be feasible, but designer baby boomers through the rejuvenation of all of one's body's tissues and organs by transforming one's skin cells into youthful versions of every other cell type. People will be able to 'reprogram' their own biochemistry away from disease and aging, radically extending life expectancy."

Those are exciting words for us boomers!!! Wrinkles be damned! We may all soon be drinking from the proverbial fountain of youth.

But the implications for our retirement are clear. Our money has to last even longer that we may think. Can you imagine if Ray is right, and us boomers live until we are 110 or 120? Imagine the type of technology that will alter the lifespan of millennials. What if 110 or 115 is in your future? Nothing will be more important than guaranteed lifetime income. A paycheck that you can't outlive will be the best asset you own.

> When I was young, I thought that money was the most
> important thing in life; now that I am old, I know that it is.
> —OSCAR WILDE

---

17. Dr. Anthony Atala, director of the Wake Forest Institute for Regenerative Medicine, has been creating and implanting organs like this for more than a decade.

THE 4% RULE IS DEAD

In the early 1990s, a California financial planner came up with what he called **the "4% rule."** The gist is that if you wanted your money to last your entire life, you could take out 4% per year if you had a "balanced portfolio" invested in 60% stocks and 40% bonds. And you could increase the amount each year to account for inflation.

"Well, it was beautiful while it lasted," recounts a 2013 *Wall Street Journal* article entitled "Say Goodbye to the 4% Rule." Why the sudden death? Because when the rule came into existence, government bonds were paying over 4%, and stocks were riding the bull! If you retired in January 2000, and you followed the traditional 4% rule, you would have lost 33% of your money by 2010, and, according to T. Rowe Price Group, you would now have only a 29% chance that your money would last your lifetime. Or spoken in a more direct way, you'd have a 71% chance of living beyond your income. Broke and old are not two things that most of us would like to experience together.

Today we are living in a world of globally suppressed interest rates, which is, in effect, a war on savers. And most certainly a war on seniors. How can one retire safely when interest rates are near 0%? They must venture out into unsafe territory to try to find returns for their money. Like the story of the thirst-stricken wildebeest that must venture down to the crocodile-infested waters to seek out a drink. Danger lurks, and those who need positive returns to live, to pay their bills, become increasingly vulnerable.

CRITICAL MASS DESTRUCTION

No matter what anyone tells you, or sells you, there isn't a single portfolio manager, broker, or financial advisor who can control the primary factor that will determine if our money will last. It's the financial world's dirty little secret that very few professionals know. And of those who do, very few will ever dare bring it up. In my usual direct fashion, I put it smack dab in the middle of the table when I sat down with legend Jack Bogle.

Remember Jack Bogle? He is the founder of the world's largest mutual fund, Vanguard, and about as straightforward as a man could be. When we spoke for four hours in his Pennsylvania office, I brought up the dirty little secret, and he certainly didn't sugarcoat his opinion or thoughts. "Some things don't make me happy to say, but there is a lottery aspect to all of this: when you were born, when you retire, and when your children go to college. And you have no control over that."

What lottery is he talking about?

It's the big luck of the draw: What will the market be doing when *you* retire? **If someone retired in the mid-1990s, he was a "happy camper." If he retired in the mid-2000s, he was a "homeless camper."** Bogle himself said in an early 2013 CNBC interview that, over the next decade, we should prepare for *two* declines of up to 50%. Holy sh*t! But maybe we shouldn't be surprised by his prediction. **In the 2000s, we have already experienced two drawdowns of nearly 50%. And let's not forget that if you lose 50%, you have to make 100% just to get back to even.**

The risk we all face, the dirty little secret, is the devastating concept of *sequence of returns*. Sounds complicated, but it's not. In essence, **the earliest years of your retirement will define your later years.** If you suffer investment losses in your early years of retirement, which is entirely a matter of luck, your odds of making it the distance have fallen off the cliff.

You can do everything right: find a fiduciary advisor, reduce your fees, invest tax efficiently, and build up a Freedom Fund.

But when it's time to ski down the backside of the mountain, when it's time for you to take income from your portfolio, if you have one bad year early on, your plan could easily go into a tailspin. A few bad years, and you will find yourself back at work and selling that vacation home. Sound overly dramatic? Let's look at a hypothetical example of how the sequence of returns risk plays out over time.

JOHN BIT THE DOG

John bit the dog. The dog bit John. Same four words, but when arranged in a different sequence, they have an entirely different meaning. Especially for John!

John is now 65 and has accumulated $500,000 (far more than the average American) and is ready to retire. Like most Americans nearing retirement, John is in a "balanced" portfolio (60% stocks, 40% bonds), which, as we learned from Ray Dalio, isn't balanced at all! Since interest rates are so low, the 4% rule won't cut it. John decides that he will need to take out 5%, or $25,000, of his nest egg/Freedom Fund each year to meet his income needs for his most basic standard of living. When added to his Social Security payments, he "should" be just fine. And he must also increase his withdrawal each year (by 3%) to adjust for inflation because each year the same amount of money will buy fewer goods and services.

As John's luck would have it, he experiences some market losses early on. In fact, three bad years kick off the beginning of his so-called golden years. Not such a shiny start.

JOHN

Age	Hypothatical stock market gains or losses	Withdrawal at start of year	Nest egg at start of year
64			$500,000
65	-10.14%	$25,000	$500,000
66	-13.04%	$25,750	$426,839
67	-23.37%	$26,523	$348,766
68	14.62%	$27,318	$246,956
69	2.03%	$28,318	$251,750
70	12.40%	$28,982	$228,146
71	27.25%	$29,851	$223.862
72	-6.56%	$30,747	$246,879
73	26.31%	$31,669	$201,956
74	4.46%	$32,619	$215,084
75	7.06%	$33,598	$190,084
76	-1.54%	$34,606	$168,090
77	34.11%	$35,644	$131,429
78	20.26%	$36,713	$128,458
79	31.01%	$37,815	$110,335
80	26.67%	$38,949	$95,008
81	19.53%	$40,118	$71,009
82	26.38%	$36,923	$36,923
83	-38.49%	$0	$0
84	3.00%		
85	13.62%		
86	3.53%		
87	26.38%		
88	23.45%		
89	12.78%		
	Average return 8.03%	Total withdrawal $580,963	

Average return **8.03%** **Total withdrawal** **$580,963**

In five short years, John's $500,000 has been cut in half. And withdrawing money when the market is down makes it worse, as there is less in the account to grow if or when the market comes back. But life goes on, and bills must be paid.

From age 70 onward, John has many solid positive/up years in the market, but the damage has already been done. The road to recovery is just too steep. By his late 70s, he sees the writing on the wall and knows that he will run out. By age 83, his account value has collapsed. In the end, he can withdraw just $580,963 from his original $500,000 retirement account. In other words, **after 18 years of continued investing during retirement, he has just an additional $80,000 to show for it.**

But here is the crazy thing: **during John's tumble down the mountain, the market averaged over 8% annual growth.** That's a pretty great return, by anyone's standards!

Here's the problem: the market doesn't give you *average* annual returns each year. It gives you *actual* returns that work out to an average. (Remember our discussions about the difference between real and average returns in chapter 2.3, "Myth 3: 'Our Returns? What You See Is What You Get' "?) And "hoping" you don't suffer losses in years in which you can't afford them is *not* an effective strategy for securing your financial future.

FLIP-FLOP

Susan is also age 65, and she too has $500,000. And like John, she will withdraw 5%, or $25,000 per year, for her income, and she too will increase her withdrawal slightly each year to adjust for inflation. And to truly illustrate the concept, we used the exact same investment returns, but we simply **flipped the sequence of those returns.** We reversed the order so that the first year becomes the last year and vice versa.

By merely reversing the order of the returns, Susan has an entirely different retirement experience. In fact, **by the time she is 89, she has withdrawn over $900,000 in income payments and still has an additional $1,677,975 left in her account! She never had a care in the world.**

Two folks, same amount for retirement, same withdrawal strategy: one is destitute, while the other is absolutely free financially.

		SUSAN	
Age	Hypothetical stock market gains or losses	Withdrawal at start of year	Nest egg at start of year
64			$500,000
65	12.78%	$25,000	$500,000
66	23.45%	$25,750	$535,716
67	26.38%	$26,523	$629,575
68	3.53%	$27,318	$762,140
69	13.62%	$28,318	$760,755
70	3.00%	$28,982	$832,396
71	-38.49%	$29,851	$827,324
72	26.38%	$30,747	$490,684
73	19.53%	$31,669	$581,270
74	26.67%	$32,619	$656,916
75	31.01%	$33,598	$790,788
76	20.26%	$34,606	$991,981
77	34.11%	$35,644	$1,151,375
78	-1.54%	$36,713	$1,496,314
79	7.06%	$37,815	$1,437,133
80	4.46%	$38,949	$1,498,042
81	26.31%	$40,118	$1,524,231
82	-6.56%	$41,321	$1,874,535
83	27.25%	$42,561	$1,712,970
84	12.40%	$48,383	$2,125,604
85	2.03%	$45,153	$2,339,923
86	14.62%	$46,507	$2,341,297
87	-23.37%	$47,903	$2,630,297
88	-13.04%	$49,340	$1,978,993
89	-10.14%	$50,820	$1,677,975

Average return	Total withdrawal
8.03%	$911,482

And what's even more mind boggling: **they both had the same average return (8.03% annually) over the 25-year period!**

How is this possible? Because the "average" is the total returns divided by the number of years.

Nobody can predict what will happen around the next corner. Nobody knows when the market will be up and when it will be down.

Now, imagine if John and Susan both had income insurance. John would have avoided an ulcer, knowing that as his account dwindled, he had a guaranteed income check at the end of the rainbow. Susan would have simply had more money to do with as she pleases. Maybe take an extra vacation, give more to her grandkids, or contribute to her favorite charity. The value of income insurance cannot be overstated! And when coupled with the All Seasons portfolio, you have quite a powerful combination.

6 DEGREES OF SEPARATION

You might recall from earlier in the book when I introduced Wharton professor Dr. David Babbel. He is not only one of the most well-educated men I have ever met but also a gentle and caring soul with a grounding faith. And he prefers David over "Doctor" or "Professor."

Here is a quick refresher on David's accomplished background. He has six degrees! A degree in economics, an MBA in international finance, a PhD in finance, a PhD minor in food and resource economics, a PhD certificate on tropical agriculture, and a PhD certificate in Latin American studies. He has taught investment at Berkeley and the Wharton School for over 30 years. He was the director of research in the pension and insurance division for Goldman Sachs. He has worked for the World Bank and consulted for the US Treasury, the Federal Reserve, and the Department of Labor. To say he knows his stuff is to say Michael Jordan knows how to play basketball.

David is also the author of a polarizing report in which he lays out his own personal retirement plan. When it came time for David to retire, he wanted a strategy that would give him peace of mind and a guaranteed income for life. He remembered that *income is the outcome*. And he also wisely took into consideration other factors such as not wanting to make complex investment decisions in his older years. He considered all his options and drew upon his vast knowledge of risk and markets. He even consulted with his friends and former colleagues on Wall Street to compare strategies. In the end, David decided that the best place for his hard-earned retirement money was *annuities*!

Whoa! Wait a second.

How could Babbel commit what his Wall Street buddies call "annuicide"? *Annuicide* being the term that brokers first coined for a client who withdraws money from the stock market and uses age-old insurance companies to guarantee a lifetime income. Brokers see it as an irreversible decision that no longer allows them to generate revenues from your investment. The death of *their* profits.

Come to think of it, **when was the last time your broker talked to you about creating a lifetime income plan?** Probably never. Wall Street typically has no interest in promoting concepts related to withdrawal. To them, *withdrawal* is a four-letter word. Here is the irony: you represent a lifetime of income for the broker so long as you never leave.

> Americans should convert at least half of their
> retirement savings into an annuity.
> —US TREASURY DEPARTMENT

Dr. Jeffrey Brown knows a thing or two when it comes to creating a lifetime income plan. He is an advisor to the US Treasury and the World Bank, and is one of the people called on by China to help evaluate its future Social Security strategy. He was also one of only seven individuals appointed by the president of the United States to the Social Security Advisory Board.

Jeff has spent most of his professional career studying how to provide people an income for life. **What did he resolve? That annuities are one of the most important investment vehicles we have.**

Jeff and I had a fascinating three-hour interview around income planning and how baffling it is to him that income is omitted from most financial planning conversations. How is it possible that income insurance is barely discussed in the offices of most financial planners, nor is it included as an option inside 401(k) plans, the primary retirement vehicle for Americans?

I asked him, "How do people find a way to protect themselves so they really have an income for life when they are living longer than ever before? They're retiring at sixty-five, and today they've got twenty or thirty years of retirement income needs ahead of them, but their financial plan won't last that long. What's the solution?"

"The good news, Tony, is we actually do know how to address this problem," he said. "We've just got to get people to change the way they are thinking about funding their retirement. There are products out there in 'economist land' that we call annuities, which basically allow you to go to an insurance company and say, 'You know what? I am going to take my money and put it with you, you're going to manage it, grow it, and you're going to pay me back income every month for as long as I live.' **The easiest way to understand this is, it's exactly what Social Security does. With Social Security, you know, you're paying in over your lifetime while you're working, and then when you retire, you get paid back income every month for as long as you live.** You don't have to be limited by Social Security; you can expand your lifetime income by doing this on your own as well."

Jeff and his team performed a study where they compared how annuities were described, or "framed," and how the shaping of that conversation completely changed people's perceptions of their need or desire for an annuity.

First, they portrayed them the way stockbrokers do: as a "savings" account or investment with relatively low levels of return. Not surprisingly, only 20% of people found them attractive. Sound familiar? You can hear the broker saying, "Annuities are a bad investment!"

But when they changed just a handful of words and described the *actual* and *real* benefits of an annuity, the tide changed. By describing the annuity as a tool that gives you a guaranteed income for the rest of your life, more than 70% found them attractive! Who doesn't want income insurance that kicks in if you have burned through your savings? Maybe your cost of living was greater than you expected. Maybe you had an unexpected medical emergency. Or maybe the market didn't cooperate with its timing of returns. What a gift to know that your future income checks are just a phone call away.

And today a revolutionized financial industry has created a whole new set of annuity opportunities. Many of these pay you returns that mimic the performance of the stock market but carry none of its downside losses. Annuities aren't just for your grandpa anymore. **Turn the page, and let me show you the five types of annuities that could change your life.**

TIME TO WIN:
YOUR INCOME IS THE OUTCOME

The question isn't at what age I want to retire, it's at what income.
—GEORGE FOREMAN

Annuities have long been the whipping boy of the financial industry. When I first heard the concept of using an annuity a few years ago, I scoffed. I had been conditioned to believe that annuities are bad news. But when challenged, I didn't really have a solid reason why I thought they were bad. I was simply picking up my torch and pitchfork like the rest of the mob.

But the conversation has been shifting. Imagine my surprise when I was handed a 2011 issue of *Barron's* with this cover line:

"Best Annuities—Special Report—Retirement: With Their Steady Income Payments, Annuities Are Suddenly Hot."

Barron's? The classic investment magazine, with an annuity cover story! Is the sky falling? I flipped open the pages, and there it was in black and white:

"Now, as baby boomers approach retirement with fresh memories of big market losses, many sharp financial advisors are recommending an annuity as an important part of an income plan."

Wow. Annuities have been given quite the promotion lately. From your grandpa's annuity stuffed away in a dusty drawer to the hottest product recommended by sharp financial advisors. But guess what? **Annuities are not just for retirees any longer. More often, younger individuals are starting to use annuities, specifically those where the growth is tied to a market index (such as the S&P 500), as a "safe-money" alternative.**

To be clear, they are *not* an alternative to investing in the stock market, or a way to try to beat the market. We already made it quite clear that nobody beats the market over time, and as Jack Bogle and so many others have echoed, using a low-cost index fund is the best approach to investing in the markets. But certain annuities, specifically those "linked" to market returns, can replace other safe-money alternatives such as CDs, bonds, Treasuries, and so on—and **offer superior returns.**

But I am getting ahead of myself! Let's take a moment to do a quick overview as to what's available today and what's coming soon.

First, let's be clear: there are really only two general categories of annuities: *immediate annuities* **and** *deferred annuities.*

IMMEDIATE ANNUITIES

Immediate annuities are best used for those at retirement age or beyond. If you aren't there yet, you can skip over this page and go right to deferred annuities, or you can keep reading because this might be applicable for some special people in your life, such as your parents or grandparents.

Simply put, **immediate annuities beat every other potential vehicle for providing a guaranteed lifetime income** for one reason: a concept called *mortality credits.* I know it sounds gruesome, but it's really not. Remember how annuities got their start 2000 years ago in the time of Caesar? For hundreds of years, insurance companies have successfully guaranteed lifetime incomes for millions of people because when a bunch of people buy an immediate annuity, some people will die early, while others will live a long time. By "pooling" the risk, **the annuity buyer who lives a long time gets the benefit,** while those who die early leave some money on the table. But before we shun the potential of leaving some money on the table, let's look at the power of annuities when wielded appropriately.

2,750% MORE INCOME

My son Josh has been in the financial services industry his entire adult life. He was telling me a story about a client of his who came to him ready to retire. He had just turned 65, and over his lifetime he had managed to sock away about $500,000. He needed a secure income stream, and he felt taking risks in the market was not an option. Sadly, his former broker had him allocated to a very aggressive portfolio, which resulted in a near 50% drawdown in the 2008 crash. It wiped out hundreds of thousands of dollars that had taken him a full decade of hard work to sock away. And like so many other people, he'd barely gotten back to even, and now he was more afraid than ever of running out of money.

He wanted his income checks to start immediately. So Josh began to walk him through his limited options.

- He could go to a bank, and a CD would pay him 0.23% (or 23 basis points) per year. This arrangement would give him $95.80 per month in fully taxable income for a $500,000 deposit. That's a whopping **$1,149 a year**—before taxes. Don't spend it all in one place!
- Bonds would pay him closer to 3% per year, or about **$15,000 a year** before taxes, but the risk that option would entail would be if interest rates rise. This would cause the value of his bonds (his principal) to shrink.
- Josh showed him that a $500,000 deposit into an immediate lifetime income annuity, as of today would pay him $2,725 per month or **$32,700 per year,** guaranteed for life![18] That's a 2,750% increase over CDs and an 118% increase over bonds, without their risk.

At today's life expectancies, this man has at least 14 more years to live, and if Ray Kurzweil is right, he could live well beyond that! When he added this guaranteed income to his Social Security payments, he had more than enough to maintain his standard of living and could spend his time focused on what mattered most to him: his grandchildren and fishing.

Do you see the power here? When compared with any other type of "sure thing" investment, he will certainly run out of money. But with an immediate annuity, which is really a form of income insurance, he has protection for life.

Critics will say, "Yes, but if you die early, they keep your money! You will have left that money on the table." When I asked David Babbel about this concern, his response was swift and blunt: **"If you are dead, who cares?! What's painful is if you live too long with no income—that's when you'll really suffer."** And if you are really worried about premature

---

18. The effective tax on income from immediate annuities is dependent on what the IRS calls the *exclusion ratio*. A portion of your income payments are deemed a return of your principal and thus "excluded" from tax.

death, you can select an option where the insurance company will refund your heirs the same amount you put in. (This arrangement, however, will decrease the size of your income payments, so there is a trade-off.) Or as David recommends, use an inexpensive term life insurance policy. So if you live a long fruitful life, you win because you have income insurance. Or God forbid, if you pass early, with a life insurance policy, your heirs win as well.

CONTROL IS AN ILLUSION

We all love control. But control is often an illusion. We think we have control over our health, our finances, our kids—okay, maybe not our kids. But we all know that things can change in the blink of an eye. A storm can cause your house to flood (as it did to my brand-new home in Florida after a torrential rain had my wife and I wading through 12 inches of water at three in the morning). Or you could get a callback from the doctor after a supposedly routine checkup. The point is, control is often more of an illusion than a reality.

Stockbrokers will tell you that by handing your money to an insurance company in exchange for a lifetime income, you are "losing control" of your principal. Let's look at this a little more thoughtfully. Say you are 60 years old and have accumulated a $1 million nest egg. Your broker advises the traditional approach of stocks and bonds, and you apply the 4% rule for your income (which means you'll be able to take out $40,000 per year). The reality is you will need every bit of that $40,000 to pay your bills. You know your money needs to be invested, so you really can't afford to touch your principal. **And what happens if the market drops?** You don't want to sell at the bottom, but at the same time, you may also feel that you can't afford more losses at this stage of life. You are between a rock and a hard place. **This so-called control is an illusion. Floating with the whims of the market waves and hoping the tide turns in your favor can be a recipe for disaster.**

Remember, our focus is not just on asset growth. Our theme is: **guaranteed income for life!**

> It is better to have a permanent income than to be fascinating.
> —OSCAR WILDE

DEFERRED ANNUITIES

Okay, so we said there are two general types of annuities. You now know what an immediate annuity is: you give your money to an insurance company, and it immediately starts to provide you with an income for life.

The other type of annuity is called a deferred annuity. This simply means you give the insurance company money either in one lump sum or over a period of years, and instead of receiving an immediate income, your returns are reinvested in a tax-deferred environment so that when you're ready you can, at will, turn on the income stream you want for the rest of your life. You literally have a schedule for what your income will be when you're 40, 50, 60—for every year of your life.

While there are many different versions of immediate annuities, with different terms and rewards that vary by the company that puts them out, similarly, there are a variety of types of deferred annuities. **Here's the good news, though: there are roughly only three primary types of deferred annuities.** Once you know these three different types, along with your understanding of immediate annuities, you will fundamentally understand what your options are, and you will be able to **tap into the power of this safe-money vehicle.**

So let's make it as simple as 1, 2, 3. There are three types of deferred annuities. They are:

1. **Fixed annuity**: This is where you get a fixed, guaranteed rate of return every year (independent of any stock market ups or downs), very much like you would receive with a CD or bond, but the rates are different.
2. **Indexed annuity:** This is where your rate of return is tied to how the stock market does, but you get a percentage of the upside of the market (not all) with no downside and no possibility of loss.
3. **Hybrid "indexed" annuity:** This is where you get the benefits of an indexed annuity with the addition of a "lifetime income" rider. **This lifetime income feature gives you the ability to turn on a paycheck for life!** (Note: technically speaking, there isn't a product called a "hybrid." However, it has become a common name among professionals to describe the category, which includes the lifetime income feature.)

HOW SAFE ARE ANNUITIES? THE POWER OF INCOME INSURANCE

A guarantee is only as good as the insurance company that issues it, so highly rated insurance companies are key. Many of the top companies have over 100 years in the business, succeeding in spite of depressions, recessions, and world wars. But with over 1,000 insurance companies in the United States, it's really only a handful that command the top ratings. I asked Dr. Jeffrey Brown about the safety of annuities and people's concern that the insurance company could go under.

"Yes, this is a concern that a lot of people have," he acknowledged. "I start by reassuring the people that to my knowledge—and I've been studying this for, you know, fifteen years or more—I don't know of anyone who's ever actually lost money in an annuity product, and there are a lot of reasons for that. Depending on what state you're in, there are **insurance guaranty associations** run by the state insurance departments that will guarantee up to a certain amount/deposit of the product you buy. And the way these work is essentially every insurance company that operates in that state is basically agreeing to insure all the other ones."

Each state has its own limits, but **the guarantee can be as high as $500,000,** for which you are insured against loss in the rare event of an insurance company failure. How rare? According to the FDIC (Federal Deposit Insurance Corporation), there were 140 bank closures in 2009 alone, yet not a single major insurance company went under.

VARIABLE ANNUITIES

There is one type of deferred annuity I deliberately didn't mention above, and that is the variable annuity. The reason for that is, **nearly every expert I interviewed for this book agreed that variable annuities should be avoided.** They are extremely expensive, and the underlying deposits are invested in mutual funds (also known as sub accounts).

So not only are you paying fees for stock-picking mutual funds (which don't beat the market and can average upward of 3% in annual fees), you are also paying the insurance company (between 1% and 2% annually). These

INVESTMENTS AND
RETIREMENT PLANNING

**"If you work hard and invest wisely, you can
afford to turn 65 on your 80th birthday."**

products can be toxic, and yet brokers manage to sell about $150 billion in new deposits each year. I spent more time addressing variable annuities in chapter 2.7, "Myth 7: 'I Hate Annuities, and You Should Too.'" Feel free to flip back for a refresher.

So let's take a few moments and go a little deeper with each of these three options.

FIXED ANNUITIES

A *fixed deferred annuity* offers a specific guaranteed rate of return (for instance, 3% or 4%) for a specific period of time (such as five or ten years). The money grows tax deferred, and at the end of the term, you have a few options. You can walk away with your money, you can "roll your money" into a new annuity and keep the tax protection, or you can convert your account balance into a guaranteed lifetime income. There are no annual fees in a fixed deferred annuity. You will know in advance what your growth will be at the end of the term.

Pretty simple, right? These rates of return might not be terribly exciting in today's market, but they change with interest rates. And at least this type of annuity has tax efficiency, so handled properly, this can increase your net rate of return significantly.

But let me share with you something quite a bit more interesting:

THE LONGER YOU WAIT, THE MORE YOU GET

What if you're young and just getting started building your financial future, or you're at a stage of life where you don't need income today but you're concerned that your investment income may not last as long as you live? Remember, if someone retires today at 65, he or she may have 20 or 30 years of income needs. Trying to figure out how to make your money last that long is a fairly daunting task. So a new approach called *longevity insurance* has become increasingly popular. These products allow you to create income insurance so that you have guaranteed rates of income from, for example, age 80 or 85 until your passing. Knowing you have an income starting at that later stage gives you the freedom to have to plan for only 15 years of retirement instead of 20 or 30. Let me give you an example:

In a 2012 *Wall Street Journal* article titled "How to Create a Pension (with a Few Catches)," writer Anne Tergesen highlights the benefits of putting away $100,000 today (for a male age 65) into a *deferred fixed-income annuity*. This man has other savings and investments, which he thinks will last him to age 85 and get him down the mountain safely. *But* if he lives past 85, his income insurance payments will begin, and the amounts he receives will be staggeringly large compared with how much he put in.

"Currently, a 65-year-old man paying $100,000 for an immediate fixed annuity can get about $7,600 a year for life . . . But with a longevity policy [a long-term deferred fixed-income annuity—I know the language is long] that starts issuing payments at age 85, his annual payout will be $63,990, New York Life says."

Wow. **At age 65, if he makes a onetime deposit of just $100,000, his payments at age 85 are close to $64,000 per year! Why is this so valuable? Because at age 85, if he lives another ten or 15 years, he will get $64,000 *every* year, dwarfing his initial investment.** But the best part is that he has to make his initial savings and investments last only 20 years, not 30 or 35. And with the volatility of markets and the inevitable challenge of sequence of returns, this task can be challenging for almost anyone.

I ran these numbers myself, and since I am only 54, my payments at age 85 would be $83,000 per year for the same onetime $100,000 deposit today! (And you don't have to have a $100,000 lump-sum payment. It can be sizably smaller, which would also provide a smaller income.) That means if I live until I am 95, I would receive $830,000 in payments (10 years × $83,000) for my $100,000 deposit. And I don't have to wait until age 85 to turn on the income. The day I make the deposit, I'm given a schedule of what the annual income payments will be at any age I want to begin taking income. If I felt I needed or wanted money at age 65 or 75, I know exactly how much that's worth to me.[19]

Income insurance, when structured correctly and as part of an overall plan, is an incredible tool that reverses or eliminates the risk of living too long and becoming a burden on your family members. When I met with Alicia Munnell, director of the Center for Retirement Research at Boston College, she echoed my enthusiasm: "So many people that I work with are very excited about and positive about the advanced-life deferred annuity, which is essentially longevity insurance."

At my annual financial event in Sun Valley, Idaho, I interviewed famed publisher Steve Forbes. I asked him about his own approach to personal finance, and even he said that he has longevity insurance in place!

One more very cool thing? The IRS looks very favorably on these deferred income annuities, so you don't have to pay tax on the entire income payment (because a good chunk of the payment is considered a return of your original deposit).

THE ULTIMATE INCOME SOLUTION

It's been said that if you give a man a hammer, everything becomes a nail. This is to say that the solution outlined below, as exciting as it is, is not the be-all and end-all solution, nor is it for everyone or every situation. It's part of an overall asset allocation. My objective here is to outline a powerful financial product, a hybrid annuity, that gives us great upside potential during its growth phase but also provides a guaranteed lifetime income down the road, when we crest the top of the mountain and begin the "second act" of our lives. It's called a **fixed indexed annuity (FIA).**

---

19. Obviously, if I start the annuity income sooner, at 65 or 70, the income I receive will be less than at 85.

To be clear, there are two relatively new types of deferred annuities that have surged in popularity since they were introduced in the early 1990s:

1. the indexed annuity, where the rate of your return is tied to a stock index, and . . .
2. **the even more popular hybrid version, where you get both a fixed rate of return and the option of a return tied to the growth of the stock market index as well as a guaranteed lifetime income feature.** These hybrid annuities are more commonly known as fixed indexed annuities, with a lifetime income rider or a guaranteed minimum withdrawal benefit. (I told you we'd make sense of this alphabet soup of financial terms.)

In 2013 alone, these annuities collected over $35 billion in deposits. In fact, as we were wrapping up this book, fixed indexed annuity deposits were at record levels through the first half of 2014, with over $24 billion in new deposits, a 41% growth over 2013. **Why this record growth?**

- **In a fixed indexed annuity, your deposits remain entirely in your control. You are *not* giving up access to your cash.**
- **It offers the potential for significantly higher annual returns than other safe-money solutions such as CDs or bonds.**
- **It provides a 100% guarantee**[20] **of your principal—you can't lose money.**
- **The growth is tax-deferred, providing maximum compounded growth for the expansion of your Freedom Fund.**
- **It provides income insurance, or a guaranteed income for life, when you select an optional income rider.**

As I alluded to earlier, these structures offer upside without the downside. Gains with no losses. In many ways, they are an antidote to the problem of sequence of returns.

How do they work?

First of all, a fixed indexed annuity is **fixed, which means your account is guaranteed never to go down. No matter what happens, you will not**

---

20. Remember, there are state insurance guarantees as well as corporate guarantees.

lose your original deposit. That's half the battle! However, instead of getting a small guaranteed rate of return like a traditional fixed annuity, your "base account" growth is determined by tracking the gains of a stock market index such as the S&P 500. As an example, if the S&P 500 goes up 8% in a given year, you would get to keep (or "participate in") a certain **percentage of that gain, which is typically subject to a cap. For example, if your cap was 5%, you would receive a 5% credit to your base account value.**[21] In other words, there is a "cap" or a "ceiling" in most annuities on how much of the gain you get to keep. **But conversely, if the market goes down in that year, you don't lose a dime!**

In recent years, there have been a few unique products that allow you to keep 100% of the market/index gains and, yes, still avoid the down years! There is no cap on your upside. What's the catch? Instead of putting a cap on your annual gains, the insurance company will share in a small portion of your gains (1.5%, in many cases). So let's say the index/market was up 8% in a given year; you would receive 6.5% added to your account, and the insurance company keeps 1.5%. Or if the market has a stronger year, with gains of 14%, you get to keep 12.5%. Many experts I spoke with anticipate that these uncapped annuities may be the future.

Okay, but what happens if the market goes down?

If the market index drops, even if it's one of those nasty 20%, 30%, or 50% drawdown years, you don't lose a dime. You get to avoid all the bad years and only participate in the up years of the market index.

Now, I know what you are thinking. It's exactly what I was thinking when I first heard of these products: **"How in the world can insurance companies give you the upside with no downside?"**

"There is no magic here," said Dr. Babbel when I asked him the same question. He explained that the insurance company parks the bulk of your money safely in its cash reserves, never actually investing it in the stock market. This is how it guarantees your principal. The remainder is used to buy "options" on the stock market index and to cover expenses. So if the market is up, you receive your portion of that gain. If it goes down, the options "expire," but you don't lose—and neither does the insurance company. Win, win.

---

21. Participation rates and caps will depend on the individual products.

LOCK IN YOUR GAINS

In addition to having the upside without the downside, these FIAs have another special benefit. Look, we all love opening our stock account statements and seeing our account balance on the rise. But we never *really* know if those dollars will truly be ours to spend one day or if another market drop could wash away those gains. **One of the huge benefits of an FIA is that each and every year, any gains or upside are locked in,** and now this becomes our new floor. For example, if I earn 6.5% on my $100,000 account, I now have $106,500 locked in. Never can I lose that $6,500 in growth. Each and every year, the account will be either flat, because I am guaranteed not to partake in market losses, or the account will be up. Like an elevator that only goes up, this unique feature of locking in gains each year is a powerful tool for our safe money.

INCOME! INCOME! INCOME!

As powerful a tool as these FIAs can be for a safe-money return, **it's their ability to simultaneously provide you a guaranteed lifetime income stream** that makes make them so darn attractive. And while I *like* fixed indexed annuities for the reasons above (principal guarantees, tax efficiency, upside without downside), I have come to *love* them for the guaranteed income aspects. This is what happens when we elect to add a *guaranteed lifetime income rider.* Let me translate into English.

No matter how your account performs, even if it is flat or up moderately over many years, the addition of a guaranteed lifetime income rider ensures that you will receive a guaranteed annual income stream when you decide to turn it on, regardless of what happens to your base account.

Get this: **I have an annuity in which the income account is *guaranteed* to grow at 7% per year for 20 years with no market risk.** The day I went to buy it, I received an income schedule, so that whenever I decide to turn it on, **I will know exactly how much income I am guaranteed for the rest of my life (no matter how long I live).** And the longer I wait, the more my income account will grow, and thus, the higher the income payments will be. This account has become an important part of my Security

Bucket. Again, sounds too good to be true, right? I had my fiduciary advisor dig beneath the surface, and he discovered that not only was it legit, but also it was attracting billions in annual deposits from baby boomers like me.

After all, who wouldn't want a product with a 7% guaranteed return in their income account while simultaneously avoiding market risk, sequence-of-returns risk, and so on? Remember, this was early 2009, when the market was melting down. There was seemingly no such thing as a safe place. And other guaranteed vehicles like CDs came with tiny returns. As you probably recall, there was a panic in the air, and people were scouring the world for financial safety. I found out later that this specific product became the fastest-selling annuity on the planet at the time.

After I made the investment, my next thought was, "How do I set this up for my kids and grandkids? This is too good to be true."

So what's the catch? I came to find out that the insurance companies offer this product only if you are in your mid-50s or older. They can't offer 7% forever, so they give a maximum of 20 years. If you are younger, the insurance company obviously can't afford to give you a 7% return in your income account forever. Also, this annuity requires a sizeable lump-sum deposit up front. I was baffled and frustrated. If this product is this powerful for someone my age, it would be even more powerful for someone in his 20s, 30s, or 40s who has so much time to allow his deposits to compound. **That day, I made it my mission to create an affordable solution for younger people.** Where else could they build a secure lifetime income plan that would allow them to carve a clear path to financial freedom without all the stress and volatility of the market?

YOUR PERSONAL JACKPOT

Cody Foster and his two partners, David Callanan and Derek Thompson, are living Horatio Alger stories. In 2005 these three buddies sat around Cody's kitchen table in sleepy Topeka, Kansas. They had pooled their life savings, and with $135,000 in the bank, they decided to launch Advisors Excel. You might never have heard of Advisors Excel, because it doesn't service the end consumer. The firm services only top-tier financial advisors. And "service" is the understatement of the year. Advisors Excel works with the top insurance companies to give financial advisors access to the most in-novative and secure annuities in the country. You could think of their com-pany as the advisor to the advisors.

Fast-forward just nine short years. **Advisors Excel is now the largest annuity wholesaler in the country, with nearly $5 billion in annual deposits.** In an industry of firms that have been around for decades, Advi-sors Excel dominates. In the company's short existence, it's grown so quickly that the three founders have outgrown their office space five separate times! Their first location was in the basement of a dentist's office (where they used boxes as a makeshift desk for their first employee). Today they are in an 80,000-square-foot state-of-the-art facility. Who knows how long until they outgrow that space!

When you meet Cody, you would never know that this humble man from Topeka owns a multibillion-dollar company. He is salt of the earth and hasn't forgotten his roots, or the grace of God that he credits for his success. I met Cody for the first time in my hotel in San Jose, California, the morning after he attended a 6,000-person Unleash the Power Within event. We had been brought together for this meeting by my son Josh. The meeting was scheduled for an hour but ended up going three hours (not uncommon in my world!).

I dove in . . .

"Cody, I have an idea that I believe can transform the lives of millions of people by helping them reach their financial goals sooner and with a whole lot less stress and risk."

"Okay, shoot," he said and inched to the end of his chair in anticipation.

"I want to see if we can take what's available for wealthy older folks and give the same opportunity to younger people who may or may not have a lot to invest. A fixed indexed annuity where younger people could contribute monthly, similar to how they would a 401(k), and know that for every dollar they contribute, they are guaranteed a lifetime income stream. A personal pension plan."

Cody sat back. He seemed slightly skeptical.

This was outside the box by a mile.

I went into full-on "seminar-style" assault mode. I gave him my most pas-sionate plea as to why this solution could be a game changer. Engaging with the millennials is the Holy Grail for the financial services industry, as they are independent self-thinkers and notoriously tough to reach. And studies show that they aren't huge fans of the stock market. Just as they were getting their feet wet, the crash of 2008 wiped out the little they had saved. Even worse, one study by LIMRA, the largest trade association for the life insurance and financial services industry, found that Gen Xers lost 55% of their median net worth between 2005 and 2010! Ouch. Now they want guarantees! They want protection. They want income. And they want it to be easy.

Cody began to nod. He understood what I was thinking, but he also knew the challenges. After all, he has been in this industry since graduating college and knows intimately the limitations and strengths of each of the biggest insurance companies in the world.

"Tony, I can see what you're going after, but you need to understand the business. Insurance companies can't do this for somebody younger because what makes lifetime income annuities work, and what makes the insurance numbers work, is that they are driven by understanding mortality rates. And at fifty-five, they know your lifespan, on average, and they can make financial decisions based on that. It's harder to do it at forty-five or thirty-five or, heck, twenty-five."

I had anticipated this answer and had an idea:

"What if you gave them a guarantee that they won't lose their money, first and foremost? And since it costs more to insure their future income, why not give them a smaller annual growth guarantee and then **add to it** whatever upside the index in the stock market brings? That could end up being more than seven percent, especially for younger people in their twenties, thirties, or forties, because they have so much time for their investments to compound. Most people know that, over time, the stock market has produced the greatest growth, but the problem is the risk of those nasty market drops! **You could give them upside without the downside on their deposits and a guaranteed income for life.**

"You still have to **make it affordable** by not requiring a lump-sum payment up front, **but instead, only small monthly payments in the amount they choose.** With this approach, the insurance company won't have to worry about superlong life expectancies, and the client has the potential for a much higher income stream since the majority of the income is tied to the market upside."

Cody liked the idea because over long periods of time, the market will perform for investors, especially when you are participating only in the up years. But one major hurdle remained:

"Tony, the way I see it, this product would need to be efficient and lean. But traditionally, the most expensive aspect when pricing an annuity is the commission. Insurance companies pay commissions up front from their own pocket so they aren't deducted from the customer's account. So for this to work, insurance companies can't afford to pay large amounts of compensation to sell this, which means it is tough to get traditional agents to sell it. It's a catch-22."

Again, I had a counter prepared.

"What if they don't pay any up-front commissions?" I asked. "Think outside the box in terms of sales. Fifty years ago, life insurance was sold door to door. Today you can do it online and never speak to a salesman—and as a result, it's now ultraconvenient and cheaper than ever before. This new annuity should follow suit. Younger ages actually prefer *not* to talk to anyone! *Cut out the middleman!*

"This should be as simple as going online, deciding how much money you want to invest per month, and having it deducted automatically from your checking account. Set it and forget it. The site could project exactly how much income it will provide for you at any future age—fifty, fifty-five, sixty—depending on how much you can afford to set aside. With just a few clicks, a person could be set up with an income plan for life. They don't have to be rich or old to take advantage. Heck, they could even track it with an app on their iPhone."

Cody was catching the vision. So I asked him, "Cody, how many lives do you think this could impact? How many lives could be touched if you guys used your sway with the insurance companies to create a product that anyone could access and would provide them with a more secure financial future?"

Cody smiled. "Over the years? *Millions! Tens of millions! The vast majority of America!*" My words had struck a chord with this small-town farm boy who grew up on the lower end of the middle class. Cody is incredibly benevolent with his wealth and wants everyone to get a fair shot. Especially a fair shot at financial freedom.

Cody left the hotel. He was on fire. He left on a mission: to see if he could use his influence to convince the world's largest insurance companies to build a "lifetime income plan" solution for younger ages and with smaller deposit requirements.

FAST-FORWARD

Just a few years back, the minimum age for most fixed indexed annuities was 50 or 55, depending on the company, and most required a minimum $20,000 to $50,000 deposit. And finding a guaranteed lifetime income rider for the younger marketplace (below 50) was virtually impossible. But the game has now officially changed. I'm proud to report to you that through the efforts of my partnership with Advisors Excel, we have managed to get some of the largest insurance companies in the world to begin to set up and build new, revolutionary products for you, regardless of your age or income level.

These new FIAs provide benefits such as:

- **Guarantee of your principal:** whatever money you've invested, you'll never lose.
- **The upside without the downside:** you participate in 100% of the stock market index growth. That's right: 100% of the upside with no downside, no chance of loss, and no cap on your winnings. The insurance company simply shares in your profits by taking a small "spread" (ranging between 1.25% to 1.75%). If the market is up 10%, and it keeps 1.5%, you get 8.5% credited to your account value. **Conversely, if the market is down in a given year, the insurance company does not keep anything, and you don't lose a dime or pay any fees!** You pay the spread only if you make money.

To understand how powerful this arrangement really is, I came up with a metaphor when I was having dinner with a buddy at the Wynn Encore in Las Vegas. I looked out over the casino floor and said to my friend, "Imagine if this casino had a special gaming table reserved only for VIPs. The rules would be that you could gamble all night, and you would never lose a dollar. No matter what happened, Steve Wynn would guarantee that you would leave with what you started—a guarantee of your principal.

"If you win, you get to keep all your gains with the exception that the house gets to keep 1.5% of your winnings. How much would you bet? **How long would you play for if you knew you couldn't lose, and if you won, you just had to pay a small portion of your upside?"**

He smiled and said, "As much I could, for as long as I could!" I laughed. "Me too!" That's exactly what this fixed indexed annuity does, and now it's no longer limited to older people with lots of money.

- **There are also no annual management fees or sales charges that come out of your account.**
- **If you'd like to have a guaranteed income for life, you can select that optional income rider as well.** When you do this, you'll have two accounts that compete with each other: (1) a base account that accumulates as the stock market grows and locks in its returns each year, as we described earlier; and (2) an income account where, depending upon the issuing insurance company, you'll have a guaranteed rate of return or a combination of a guarantee and market performance. To your benefit, the income you'll receive will be based on whichever account is larger at the time you decide you want the income.

Most importantly, on top of all this, Cody was able to influence the insurance companies to eliminate the lump-sum payment and make this financial vehicle available to almost anyone. The days of needing $25,000 to $50,000 to get started are gone. Now you can start with a small initial deposit as low as $300. You can even set up the convenience of a monthly auto-deduction program from a checking account so that your Freedom Fund is growing every month into a "personal pension"—an income for life.

Even if you have a very small amount or no amount in other investments, this product can be a phenomenal place to start. Why? Because it gives you the upside of the stock market index without the downside. **Imagine knowing that for every dollar you contribute, you are guaranteeing yourself a lifetime income stream.** The more you save, the higher your income will be. And you are guaranteed not to lose your deposits!

Since there are thousands of income annuity products with a wide range of income payouts, Cody and his team have established a website to educate and empower you when it comes to finding and selecting the right annuity products for your specific situation: **www.lifetimeincome.com.**

By visiting LifetimeIncome, just a few simple steps will allow you to quickly and easily set up your lifetime income plan. **Within seconds, you can calculate your potential future income based on how much you can afford to contribute. Regardless of your age, the system will reveal the best approach for you and show you the most competitive income payouts available.** So whether you are younger and want a flexible, smaller monthly contribution, or if you are over 50 and have a lump sum and are looking for longevity insurance, the system will guide you to the best income solution. You have the option to set it up online, over the phone with a specialist, or be connected to an annuity advisor in your hometown. **Lifetime Income has a network of over 500 annuity specialists in all 50 states.** It will also provide a free review and analysis of any existing annuities you might have to see if you should hang on to the one you have or transfer your account value to a different insurance company in a tax-free exchange.

As I mentioned, when coupled with the All Seasons portfolio, the right lifetime income product is a powerful tool! Lifetime Income is the exclusive annuity provider for Stronghold. So if an annuity is just a portion of your overall asset allocation (and just part of your Security Bucket), you can also access these same products through Stronghold. It will connect you to an annuity specialist.

TOOLS OF THE .001%

We have come a long way! Not only do we have the mind-set of an insider, we have the tools of the insiders! In this section alone, we have learned a powerful portfolio model from icon Ray Dalio that has proven resilient throughout every economic season since 1925. And most people have to invest $100 million to get his insights! We can be confident that his portfolio model will survive and over the long term thrive in all environments.

We have also learned how correctly structured income insurance, an annuity, can give us a paycheck for life without having to work for it. And not only that, but with the right fixed indexed annuity, our deposits can participate in 100% of the upside of the market/index but avoid losses when the market goes down! A Security Bucket with some excitement. Although there are many approaches to achieve financial freedom, the one-two punch of an All Seasons portfolio and the certainty of a guaranteed lifetime income stream is a powerful combination for peace of mind.

But once you build your wealth, you also must protect it for you and your children. The ultrawealthy protect their wealth with an entourage of extremely sophisticated advisors. So who or what do they protect it from? **Let's find out the secrets of the ultrawealthy in chapter 5.5!**

FREQUENTLY ASKED QUESTIONS

Here are a handful of common questions that seem to come up when people learn about fixed indexed annuities:

What happens if I die "early"?

If you die before turning on your income stream, your entire account balance is left to your heirs. This is a *huge* benefit over a traditional income annuity. When you do decide to eventually turn on your lifetime income stream (with a simple phone call), you *do not* forfeit your entire account to the insurance company. Your heirs would still get your account balance minus any income payments you had taken to that point.

Can I take out money in case of an emergency?

Most FIAs allow you to withdraw up to 10% to 15% of your account without any penalty or surrender charge. Keep in mind, if you make this withdrawal prior to age 59½, you will be charged a 10% penalty by the IRS, which is standard for any investment that gives you tax deferral on the growth. If you need all your money back, you can surrender your annuity and get your money out (plus any growth). However, this withdrawal may incur a surrender charge, depending on how long you have owned the annuity. A surrender charge is really a self-imposed penalty because you are taking back your money early. The typical schedule will start at 10% and go down by 1% per year until you reach 0%. So if you have held the annuity for five years, you would have a 5% charge if you surrender the contract and get back all your money. Any money invested in this vehicle should be considered money invested for the long term.

What are the fees within an FIA?

There are no annual management fees withdrawn from your account. However, if you select the guaranteed lifetime income rider, the annual fee for this ranges between 0.75% and 1.25% annually, depending on each company's individual offerings.

Can I put my IRA money into an annuity?

Yes, you can use money from your IRA (or Roth IRA), or you can also use after-tax dollars (money you have already paid tax on) to fund an annuity. This scenario is also known as qualified or nonqualified dollars, both of which can be used.

What is the cap on my account growth, and how is it determined?

The cap, the ceiling on how much of the market growth you get to keep, is typically tied to interest rates. If interest rates are higher, the cap is high (and vice versa). Some newer products offer 100% upside with no cap, *but* they take a small spread, which is a share of your upside/profits. If the market is up 10%, you might get 8.75% credited to your account (which means the insurer kept a 1.25% spread). But if the market goes down, it doesn't take anything, and you don't lose a dime. I like these uncapped strategies because they give the highest upside potential in a given year.

To what underlying markets will my account be "linked"?

The most popular index is the S&P 500. But newer indexes are being added quite frequently. For example, some accounts can be linked to the Barclays Dynamic Balanced Index (a mix of stocks and bonds) or the Morgan Stanley Dynamic Allocation Index (a mix of 12 different sectors). Some indexes are even tied to commodities.

What factors will determine how much income I get?

The amount that you contribute to the annuity, the length of time before you decide to access your income stream, and your age at the time your income begins are the primary factors that will ultimately contribute to the amount of income you'll receive. However, the biggest factor is the product you select. Every annuity contract is different in the amount of contractually guaranteed income it will provide, so it's important you understand this before you pull the trigger.

What is the tax treatment of an FIA?

The growth within your FIA is tax deferred. When you turn on the income stream, you will be paying ordinary income tax rates on the lifetime income payments. Because the government is giving you tax deferral, it will penalize you if you take money out before you reach age 59. If you own the FIA within a Roth IRA, there no will be no tax on either the gains or the lifetime income stream.

Here's what you can avoid with a fixed index annuity: the benefits of getting the upside without the downside becomes incredibly powerful when you look back at the history of Wall Street crashes. What's astonishing is just how long it took for the market to recover—for investors to get back to breakeven. Just for fun, take a look at some of the history of the stock market crashes—and remember, with this type of investment, you can avoid all of these.

1901–1903

- The Dow fell 46 percent.
- Recovered by July 1905.
- Total time to recovery: two years.

1906–1907

- The Dow fell 49 percent.
- Recovered by September 1916.
- Total time to recovery: nine years.

1916–1917
- The Dow fell 40 percent.
- Recovered by November 1919.
- Total time to recovery: two years.

1919–1921
- The Dow fell 47 percent.
- Recovered by November 1924.
- Total time to recovery: three years.

1929–1932
- The Dow fell 89 percent.
- Recovered by November 1954.
- Total time to recovery: 22 years.

1939–1942
- The Dow fell 40 percent.
- Recovered by January 1945.
- Total time to recovery: three years.

1973–1974
- The Dow fell 45 percent.
- Recovered by December 1982.
- Total time to recovery: eight years.

2000–2002
- The Dow fell 36 percent.
- Recovered by September 2006.
- Total time to recovery: four years.

2008–2009
- The Dow fell 52 percent.
- Recovered by April 2011.
- Total time to recovery: two years.

SECRETS OF THE ULTRAWEALTHY (THAT YOU CAN USE TOO!)

*It's viewed as an insider's secret for the affluent: a legal way
to invest . . . all without paying taxes on the gains.*
—*NEW YORK TIMES*, February 9, 2011

A NEW WORLD RECORD

In early 2014 the *Guinness Book of World Records* announced that a new world record had been established. No, it wasn't for the Tallest Man in the World, or the World's Longest Fingernails. It was a record that went largely unnoticed:

"Mystery Billionaire Buys Record-Breaking $201 Million Life Insurance Policy."

Why in the world would a billionaire buy life insurance? Won't his kids be just fine if he passes away prematurely? Or was the media missing the point? Believe it or not, the ultrawealthy do indeed buy astronomical amounts of life insurance, but it's not the billionaires who buy the most. The biggest buyers are banks and large corporations, from **Wal-Mart** to **Wells Fargo.** As an example, Wells Fargo's balance sheet shows $18.7 billion of its Tier 1 capital deposited in life insurance cash value (as of May 27, 2014). By the way, Tier 1 capital is the core measure of a bank's financial strength! Contrary to what the media says, corporations and the ultrawealthy are not looking to benefit from anyone's death. **What they really want is a place to park their cash in an IRS-sanctioned vehicle that allows them to grow their investments tax free.** Sound too good to be true? In fact, it's very much like a Roth IRA in terms of tax treatment. You pay taxes when you earn your money (income), but once you deposit your after-tax dollars within a specific type of life insurance policy, the IRS says you aren't required to pay taxes as it grows; and if structured correctly (more below), you aren't required to pay taxes when you pull out money. So while it *is* life insurance, it's *really* designed to benefit you while you are alive!

If it's good enough for billionaires and the world's largest corporations, it's probably good enough for us! Let's dive in and figure out how to take this powerful tax-planning tool and accelerate our path toward financial freedom.

RICH MAN'S ROTH

The strategy in the pages ahead, known as *private placement life insurance* (*PPLI*), has been called "the secret of the affluent" by the *New York Times*—and for good reason. I was introduced to this tool by two of the wealthiest individuals I know. But you don't have to be ultrawealthy to take advantage. Many high-income earners, such as doctors, lawyers, and small business owners will find tremendous value in the pages ahead, but those with as little as a few thousand to invest will learn how to create a version of the structure that will provide all the same benefits. Here are the astounding benefits available to all:

- **unlimited deposit amounts (with no income limitations)**
- **no tax on the growth of your investments**
- **no tax when accessed (if structured correctly) and**
- **any money left over for your heirs cannot be taxed.**

Let's not just breeze over this as a pretty cool strategy. This is essentially removing part or all your nest egg from the tax system entirely! **Never again will you pay tax on growth of your investments or the money you access within this structure. This is why the media sometimes calls PPLI the "rich man's Roth."** Consider this quote from the *Wall Street Journal*:

The main attraction: Because the investments are held within an insurance wrapper, gains inside the policy are shielded from income taxes—as is the payout upon death. What's more, policyholders may be able to access their money during their lifetimes by withdrawing or borrowing funds, tax-free, from the policy, depending on how it's set up . . . One big reason for the growth: In recent years, the Internal Revenue Service has issued a series of rulings and regulations that have laid out more clearly what's allowable and what's not in private-placement life insurance and annuities. That, in turn, has removed uncertainty among insurance and investors.

By taking taxes out of the equation, the time it takes to reach your critical mass and financial independence will be massively accelerated. No longer do you have to worry about how much of your money will actually be yours to spend after the tax man takes his bite of your apple. In fact, one of the biggest challenges in knowing how much money you will really need in the future is the unknown of what tax rates will be for you in the future. Remember, taxes can easily be raised, and suddenly the amount of spendable income you have shrinks. If you're planning on a 50% tax rate, but in the future taxes on the wealthy increase to 70%, or you're currently at 30% and taxes grow to 50% for your income class, the amount of money you thought would get you to financial freedom will no longer get you there.

Let's look at an example of how you can use this tool to achieve financial security or independence in less than half the time. Or double the amount of spendable cash you have if you keep the same investment horizon.

If you're a high-end earner, like a doctor, dentist, lawyer, or small business owner, you may be fortunate enough to earn $250,000 per year of pretax income. As a high-income earner, that means that after tax (assuming a 50% combined federal and state rate), you will net approximately $125,000. This is the amount you need today to support your current lifestyle. It's your total spendable income. **Traditional financial planning would say you need to accumulate 20 times your current income, or $5 million in critical mass, to generate $250,000 of pretax income (assuming a 5% withdrawal rate). But if you aren't required to pay tax, and the actual income you need is $125,000 without taxes,** you really need to accumulate only 20 times $125,000, or a total critical mass of just $2.5 million within this structure. **That means you get to your goal 50% faster *or* you**

get twice the spendable income if you reach your original goal of critical mass in the same time.

Now, if you make $50,000 a year, you may be saying, "So what? Isn't that nice for the rich man or woman?" Stay with me here while I explain how this works for the rich, and then **I'll show you how to make this work for anyone who wants to get to his or her financial goals 30% to 50% faster—and all with the total support of the IRS, just as it supports 401(k)s or Roths.**

ISN'T LIFE INSURANCE EXPENSIVE?

When my attorney initially told me about PPLI, I had an immediate aversion to the words *life insurance*. Like most, I had been sold expensive "retail" life insurance in the past and wasn't going to be taken again.

She went on to explain, "Tony, this is not your typical retail life insurance. You can't buy this off the shelf from a salesman with well-coiffed hair and a gold Rolex. This is an institutionally priced policy with no commissions, no surrender charges, or other nonsense you encounter from retail agents. Think of it as an 'insurance wrapper' you are buying to place around your investments. And because of the specific tax code, which has been around for many decades, all of your deposits will be legally sheltered from tax in this insurance wrapper. They can be invested in a variety of different funds, and you will not pay tax on the growth or when you access your cash if we do it right."

TAX-FREE COMPOUNDING

Compounded over time, the advantage of private placement life insurance is astounding. Let's look at an example of how the identical investment compares when wrapped inside of PPLI versus taking the standard approach of paying tax each year.

Let's take a healthy male, age 45, and assume he makes four annual deposits of $250,000 (for a total contribution of $1 million over four years). If he makes a 10% return and has to pay tax each and every year, after 40 years, his total account balance will be $7 million. Not bad, right? But if he wraps the investment within private placement life insurance and pays a relatively small amount for the cost of insurance, his ending balance (cash value) is just over $30 million! **Same investment strategy, but he is left with more than four times (or 400%) as much money for him and his family simply by using the tax code to his advantage.** (Please note that there are very strict rules around the investment management, which must be done by a third-party investment professional, not the policy owner.)

By the way, this same powerful advantage applies even to smaller investment amounts. This is compounding without taxes! But then I wanted to know, **"What about when I want to access my money?"**

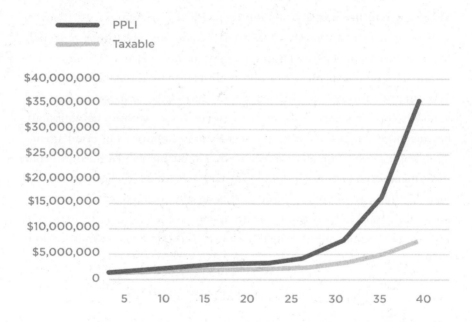

TAKING OUT MONEY

The power of PPLI is that you don't have to worry about what tax rates are in the future. During the course of your investment lifetime, you will never again pay taxes on the gains that are within this policy. But what if you need the cash? Well, like any vehicle in which the government grants the benefit of tax deferral, you will have to pay tax if you take a withdrawal. *But*—and it's a *huge but*—you also have the ability to "borrow" from your policy. In other words, you can call the insurance company and access your cash value, but it's legally deemed and actually is a loan—and loans are not taxable. You can repay the loans at a future date of your choosing or allow the life insurance proceeds to pay off the loans when you pass away. **It's a legitimate loan, and it does get paid off.** One more huge benefit to stack on? Life insurance death benefit proceeds are income tax free when your kids receive the benefit.

DO YOU QUALIFY?

In order to access PPLI, you must be what's called an accredited investor[22] and the typical minimum annual deposits are $250,000 for a minimum of four years. However, **there is a "version" of PPLI that is now available to nonaccredited investors with as little as a few thousand to invest.** Founded in 1918 by visionary Andrew Carnegie to serve teachers, TIAA-CREF "functions without profit to the corporation or its shareholders." It now offers financial services to the general public, but TIAA-CREF's unique not-for-profit structure allows it to offer a life insurance product with no sales or surrender charges. The underlying investment options within the policy include low-cost index funds (such as Dimensional Fund Advisors), which is in keeping with what we have learned from many experts in the book. And the tax benefits are no different from what we have learned regarding PPLI. Remember, being a no-load product with no commission, there won't be insurance agents knocking down your door to sell you this product, so you will need to visit its website (www.tiaa-cref.org/public) and acquire it on your own or ask a fiduciary advisor to help guide you in setting up a policy.

As a fiduciary, your representative cannot take commissions. If she is skilled in this area and has a full understanding of how to set up this tax-efficient strategy, she will be doing you a great service. Depending on your

22. In order to qualify for private placement life insurance, you must be an accredited investor. This means you must have a net worth of at least $1 million (not including the value of your primary residence), *or* you have an income of at least $200,000 each year for the last two years (or $300,000 combined with your spouse).

current tax rate, it could help you achieve your goals 30% to 50% faster with no additional risk. Of course, if you are a Stronghold client, we have a team that can arrange all these details for you.

THE "BILLIONAIRE'S PLAYBOOK"

What a journey we have been on! We conquered the jungle with Ray Dalio and learned how a portfolio designed for all seasons has provided a smooth ride for nearly 75 years. We learned how to create a guaranteed lifetime income plan and achieve upside without downside with income insurance. And finally, we learned how a rare no-load life insurance policy can give us the equivalent of a Roth IRA without income or deposit limitations. Now it's time for the opportunity—the gift—to sit down and learn directly from some of the most brilliant minds in the financial universe; to hear what has shaped them into who they are today and what they would teach their children on how to be successful investors. So let's turn the page and meet the masters.

LIVING TRUST

One more quick but important note about protecting your family: the wealthy are diligent about planning to protect their families. **One of the simplest things you can do to protect your family is to establish a living revocable trust.** The key benefit to using a living trust to own your core assets (your home, brokerage account, and so on) is that if you pass away, those assets will **avoid probate**—a costly and lengthy procedure of allowing the courts to sort through your assets (and make everything public record). **But unlike a will, a living trust can also protect you and your family while you are alive.** If you become ill or incapacitated, you can include an incapacity clause that allows someone to step in and handle your bills and other affairs. Don't let experts tell you that a living trust costs thousands. You can get a template document for free by visiting http://getyourshittogether.org. Chanel Reynolds started this nonprofit site after her husband was killed in a bike accident, and she wanted to make sure that nobody else went through the same experience of being unprepared. If you want to understand more about how simple and important living trusts are, go to her site.

In addition, if you want assistance, you can always find an expensive attorney, but you can also use LegalZoom and set up one for as little as $250 with the help of its attorneys (www.legalzoom.com/living-trusts/living-trusts-overview.html).

I'm including this reminder for you here because even though this book is not designed to be an estate-planning tool, **one important responsibility we all have is to make sure that whatever wealth we build, however large or small it may be, our families benefit from it and don't get stuck in a legal process that drains the gift from our heirs.** As you begin to succeed, please seek out quality assistance when thinking about estate planning, but in the meantime, don't wait to set up a living trust. **Everyone needs one.**

INVEST LIKE THE .001%: THE BILLIONAIRE'S PLAYBOOK

MEET THE MASTERS

There are not more than five primary colors,
yet in combination they produce more hues than can ever be seen.
SUN TZU, *The Art of War*

Four years ago, I began an amazing journey to find a way for individual investors like you to take control of your money in a system that seems rigged against you. I vowed to bring you the best possible information from the most knowledgeable and influential experts in the world. What a trip it's been! Since then, I've interviewed **more than 50** self-made billionaires, Nobel Prize winners, investment titans, bestselling authors, professors, and financial legends, asking them some of the same questions you'd ask if you were in the room with me. Here's a sampling:

"What is your competitive advantage in investing? What sets you apart? What insights have allowed you to dominate the markets decade after decade?"

"Is the game still winnable? How can individual investors thrive in the volatility of today's economy?"

"What are the biggest challenges around the world and what are the biggest opportunities for investors today?"

And, perhaps the most important of all, "If you couldn't leave any of your money to your children, but only a portfolio or a set of financial principles to pass on to help them thrive, what would it be?"

Their answers excited me, shocked me, sometimes made me laugh. Other times they moved me to tears. It was beyond any university education one could imagine. It was the ultimate PhD in investing, straight from the trenches. Where my "professors" were moving markets and shaping the world economy *while* they were coaching me one-on-one.

My mission has been to synthesize the best of all they've shared into an integrated, simple 7-step financial blueprint. One that you could use in a practical way to move from where you are now to where you truly want to be.

I wish I could bring them all to you, but their voices are all captured in these pages, whether quoted directly or not. The amount of time I've spent with each of them ranged from the more than 20 years I've counted Paul Tudor Jones as my dear friend and client, to an informal 20 minutes with Warren Buffett, whom I grabbed for a short conversation in the greenroom while we were filming a series of segments together for the *Today* show.

Most of the interviews were scheduled for an hour or less but turned into three- and four-hour sessions. Why? Because each of these financial giants was interested in going deep when he or she saw that I wasn't there just for some shallow questions. My mission to serve you, the individual investor, moved them. They were all incredibly generous with their precious time.

The diversity of conversation was extraordinary. I had the privilege of bringing together some of the most brilliant financial minds in the world. One of the more interesting encounters occurred at my financial conference in Sun Valley, Idaho. I interviewed Larry Summers, formerly the US secretary of the Treasury, director of the National Economic Council, and advisor to President Obama in the midst of the world economic crisis. We talked about what was done and what *needs* to be done to turn around the US economy. Publisher and former Republican presidential candidate Steve Forbes was listening to Summers and raised his hand with a question. You can only imagine the respectful "sparks" that flew.

Another moment: when I learned that Carl Icahn had been a fan of Jack Bogle's for years, but they had never met. I had the privilege of introducing these two titans. Between them, they have more than a century of investing experience. Jack invited me to join them for the meeting, but I was out of the country. Wouldn't it have been amazing to be a fly on that wall when they finally met?

The crazy part is, after all the time I've spent with each of these experts, you'll see only five to ten pages for each interview as opposed to the average 75-page transcript. To keep this section under 9,000 pages, I'm including highlights from just 11 of the interviews. Well, 11 plus one bonus. Even though he's passed away, I couldn't leave out the interview I conducted with Sir John Templeton, one of the greatest investors of all time and an extraordinary soul.

Like all experts, the money masters you'll be hearing from in these pages have different views of what the near-term future might hold, and they have different opinions on which investment vehicles they favor most. Some are short-term traders; some like to hold long term. Some think the index is the way to go, while others swear you can make more money in arbitrage. So even though they disagree sometimes on tactics, we can applaud how often these money masters take different paths to the same goals.

And one thing is for certain: all of them are great leaders. Take the exceptional Mary Callahan Erdoes, who leads 22,000 financial professionals, including some of the finest portfolio managers in the world, overseeing an astonishing $2.5 trillion in assets for J.P. Morgan Asset Management. Or Chuck Schwab, who transformed an industry with his obsession to serve and protect the individual investor—building a company with 8.2 million client brokerage accounts and $2.38 trillion in assets served by 300 offices around the world.

The pages ahead will show you that there are many ways to win—many ways to succeed financially and become wealthy in the world we live in today. Even though each of these financial legends has a distinct approach, I found that they share at least four common obsessions:

1. **Don't Lose.** All of these masters, while driven to deliver extraordinary returns, are *even more* obsessed with making sure they *don't* lose money. Even the world's greatest hedge fund managers, who you'd think would be comfortable taking huge risks, are actually laser focused on protecting their downside. From Ray Dalio to Kyle Bass to Paul Tudor Jones—if you don't lose, you live to fight another day. As Paul said, "I care deeply about making money. I want to know I'm not losing it . . . The most important thing for me is that defense is ten times more important than offense . . . You have to be very focused on the downside at all times." And this statement comes from a guy who's made money for his clients for 28 consecutive years. It's so simple, but I can't emphasize it enough. Why? **If you lose 50%, it takes 100% to**

get back to where you started—and that takes something you can never get back: *time.*

2. **Risk a Little to Make a Lot.** While most investors are trying to find a way to make a "good" return, each of these hall of famers, without exception, looks for something completely different: home runs! They live to uncover investments where they can risk a little and make a lot. They call it asymmetric risk/reward.

    You'll note how Sir John Templeton's path to great gains with the least risk was *not* by buying the market but by waiting until—as the 18th-century English nobleman Baron Rothschild put it—there is "blood in the streets," and everybody is desperate to sell. That's when you pick up the best bargains. Paul Tudor Jones, on the other hand, follows trends in the market. But, as he says in his interview, he doesn't make an investment until he can potentially get a return of at least $5 for every $1 he risks. And that, he says, is a $100,000 MBA in a nutshell! In Kyle Bass's interview, you'll learn how he figured out how to risk just 3% to make 100% returns. And how he parlayed that victory into more than a 600% return!

3. **Anticipate and Diversify.** The best of the best anticipate; they find the opportunity for asymmetric risk/reward. They really do their homework until they know in their gut that they are right—unless they're not! And to protect themselves, they anticipate failure by diversifying. Because in the end, all great investors have to make decisions with limited information. When I interviewed Kyle Bass's former partner Mark Hart, he told me, **"A lot of brilliant people are terrible investors. The reason is that they don't have the ability to make decisions with limited information. By the time you get all the information, everyone else knows it, and you no longer have the edge."** T. Boone Pickens says it this way: "Most people say, 'Ready? Aim! Aim! . . .' But they never fire."

4. **You're Never Done.** Contrary to what most people would expect, this group of achievers is never done! They're never done learning, they're never done earning, they're never done growing, they're never done giving! No matter how well they've done or how well they've continued to do, they never lose their hunger—the force that unleashes human genius. Most people would think, "If I had all this money, I would just stop. Why keep working?"

Because each believes, somewhere in his or her soul, that "to whom much is given, much is expected." Their labor is their love.

Just like these money masters invest in different ways, they give back in different ways. They share their time, they share their money, they create foundations, they invest in others. Each of them has come to realize that true meaning in life comes from giving. They feel a responsibility to use their gifts to serve others. As Winston Churchill said, "We make a living by what we get. We make a life by what we give." What unites them is the ultimate truth that life is about *more* than what you have. It's really about what you have to give.

So how will the Billionaire's Playbook serve you as an investor? It means that you can sit by my side as I ask 12 of the greatest minds in finance how you can uncover your own path to financial freedom. You'll gain insight into how they became the titleholders in the field of finance, and how you too have to stay alert and be ready for anything that happens. **You'll learn investment strategies that will prepare you for all seasons, for times of inflation and deflation, of war and peace, and, as Jack Bogle puts it, "times of sorrow and joy."**

CARL ICAHN:
MASTER OF THE UNIVERSE

The Most Feared Man on Wall Street

Question: When is a single tweet worth $17 billion?

Answer: When Carl Icahn says Apple is undervalued and announces he's buying the stock.

Within an hour of Icahn's tweet in the summer of 2013, Apple stock had jumped 19 points. The market got the message: whenever the billionaire businessman takes an interest in a company, it's time to buy. Four months later, *Time* magazine put his face on the cover with the headline "Master of the Universe." It went on to say that he's "the most important investor in America." That's right. In the past four decades, Icahn's ventures have earned 50% more than that other investment icon, Warren Buffett. A recent analysis by *Kiplinger's Personal Finance* shows that while most people think of Buffett as providing the greatest returns through time, if you'd invested with Icahn in 1968, in 2013 you would have had a compounded return of 31% versus Berkshire Hathaway—Buffett's company—with "only" a 20% return.

Icahn's business skills have made him one of the richest men in the world—at last check of the *Forbes* list, he was 27th, with a net worth of more than $23 billion—and he's made billions more for ordinary shareholders who invest in his diversified holding company, Icahn Enterprises LP (NASDAQ: IEP), or own stock in the companies he targets. The secret to his success? Even his critics will tell you **Carl Icahn doesn't just look for opportunities in business—he makes them.**

But most outsiders still think of him as a Wall Street caricature, a ruthless vulture capitalist who pillages companies for personal gain. When you Google the term *corporate raider,* Icahn's name autofills in the search bar.

But Carl Icahn is challenging that creaky old stereotype. Icahn thinks of himself as a "shareholder activist." What does that mean? "We go in and shine a light on public companies that are not giving shareholders the value they deserve," he told me. His obsession, he says, is to stop the abuse of stockholders by improving corporate governance and accountability—which makes American companies stronger and therefore the American economy stronger.

The *New York Times* describes him this way: "By rattling corporate boards, mounting takeover efforts and loudly jostling for change at companies, he has built a multibillion-dollar fortune, inspiring fear among chief executives and admiration among his fellow investors in the process."

Icahn buys up shares of top-heavy or underperforming companies and then puts them on notice that it's time to step up their game—or face a proxy fight for control of the board.

He sees himself in a battle with those who use the coffers of public companies to enrich themselves at the expense of the shareholders. "Tony, people have no idea how they're getting screwed," he said, adding that average investors aren't aware of the abuses that go on behind the closed doors of boardrooms. But part of the problem is that shareholders don't believe they have the power to change things because they don't think like owners. Icahn, however, knows the power of leverage—and he's not afraid to use it.

$24 BILLION FOR COCA-COLA MANAGEMENT INCENTIVES?

An example of the kind of action that public company boards take that outrage Icahn can be found in his recent criticism of Coca-Cola. Coke was planning to dilute the company's stock value by issuing $24 billion in new, discounted shares. The reason? To finance huge compensation packages for top management. This would weaken the retirement investments of ordinary investors, including teachers and firefighters, because so many people have Coke stock in their retirement portfolios.

Icahn wrote an editorial in *Barron's* blasting the company for the scheme, and calling out Warren Buffett—Coca-Cola's single largest shareholder and a board member—for not voting against the move. "Too many board members think of the board as a fraternity or club where you must not ruffle feathers," Icahn wrote. "This attitude serves to entrench mediocre management."

Buffett responded that he had abstained from the vote but was opposed to the plan, and that he had been quietly talking to management about reducing its excessive pay proposal—but he didn't want to "go to war" with Coke over the issue.

In contrast, Carl Icahn is always ready for war. He's been in the trenches many times before, making runs on companies as diverse as US Steel, Clorox, eBay, Dell, and Yahoo. But this time was different: instead of Icahn, a younger fund manager named David Winters was buying stock and leading the charge against Coke's management. To the dismay of overpaid CEOs everywhere, a new generation of "activist investors" is taking up the fight Icahn started decades ago.

Naturally, Carl Icahn has ticked off a lot of corporate dynamos, enemies with big clout in the media. So you'll often hear his critics saying that he's only in it for the money, or that he "pumps and dumps" stocks, sacrificing long-term corporate goals for short-term profits. But Icahn points out that this is ridiculous, in that he often holds his positions for much longer than people realize—sometimes 10, 15, even 30 years. And when he does take control of a company, its value continues to rise for years, even after he's left. This claim has been borne out by a study conducted by Harvard Law School professor Lucian Bebchuk, who analyzed 2,000 activist campaigns from 1994 to 2007. It concluded that "operating performance improves following activist interventions." The study also found that not only were there no detrimental long-term effects, but instead, five years later these firms continued to outperform.

Carl Icahn isn't after the head of every CEO in America. He's often acknowledged that there are some extraordinary leadership teams out there, and executives who maximize company resources and make the economy more resilient. But he's always looking for ways to make the management—even of the most popular and well-run corporations—more responsive to shareholders.

Take that Apple tweet, for example. He told me he wasn't trying to drive up the price and sell his stock. (In fact, on the day of our interview, he bought a large amount of Apple stock.) And he wasn't trying to interfere with the company's management—which he thinks is solid. The tweet was just part of a campaign to pressure Apple to return $150 billion of its cash reserves to its shareholders as dividends. The company eventually expanded its capital return program to over $130 billion in April 2014, including an increase in its share repurchase authorization to $90 billion from the previously announced $60 billion level. At the same time, Apple announced an increase to its quarterly dividend and a seven-for-one stock split. Today it is 50% higher than the day he did the tweet.

Icahn is a CEO himself, owning 88% of a public company, Icahn Enterprises. The company's stock has done amazingly well, even during the so-called lost decade. **If you'd invested in Icahn Enterprises from January 1, 2000, to July 31, 2014, you would have made a total return of 1,622%, compared with 73% on the S&P 500 index!**

Carl Icahn wasn't born into this life. He says he grew up "in the streets" of Far Rockaway, New York. His mother was a teacher; his father, a former law student and a frustrated opera singer who worked as a cantor at a local synagogue. Carl played poker to pay for his expenses at Princeton, where he majored in philosophy. After a brief attempt at medical school and a stint in the army (and more poker), he realized that his greatest talent was for making money. Corporate America has never been the same.

Icahn is now 78 years old and thinking about his legacy. He's been busy writing op-ed pieces and giving select interviews about the rights of investors and shareholders. But, frankly, he's sick of being misunderstood and quoted out of context. Which is why, not knowing who I was or my true intent, he asked that my video crew not film our interview and stated, "I'll give you a few minutes."

To my great relief, Icahn warmed up after those first awkward moments, and two and a half hours later I was lingering with him in the hallway and being introduced to Gail, his extraordinary wife of 15 years. Carl is very different from his public persona. He's funny and curious, even grandfatherly. His friends say he's mellowed a bit. But he still talks with a Queens accent, and he still has the sharp edge of a New York street brawler. Icahn says he's not the kind of guy who gives up. Especially when he's found something worth fighting for.

TR: You come from a family of modest means, and you went to public schools in a rough part of Queens. Did you have a goal when you started out, that you were going to become one of the best investors of all time?

CI: I'm a very competitive guy. Passionate or obsessive, whatever you want to call it. And it's my nature that whatever I do, I try to be the best. When I was applying to colleges, my teachers told me, "Don't even bother with the Ivy League. They don't take kids from this area." I took the boards anyway and got into all of them. I chose Princeton. My father had offered to pay for everything, then he backed out and would only pay tuition, which—if you believe it—was $750 a year back then. I said, "So where do I sleep? How do I eat?" My parents said, "You're so smart, you'll figure it out."

TR: So what did you do?

CI: I got a job as a beach boy at a club in the Rockaways. I was a good beach boy! The cabana owners used to say, "Hey kid, join our poker game and lose your tips for the week." At first I didn't even know how to play, and they cleaned me out. So I read three books on poker in two weeks, and after that I was ten times better than any of them. To me it was a big game, big stakes. Every summer I won about $2,000, which was like $50,000 back in the '50s.

TR: How did you get started in business?

CI: After college I joined the army, where I kept playing poker. I came out with maybe $20,000 saved up and I started investing it on Wall Street in 1961. I was living good, had this gorgeous model girlfriend and I bought a white Galaxie convertible. Then the market crashed in 1962, and I lost everything. I don't know what went first, the girlfriend or the car!

TR: I read that you got back in the market, selling options, then going into arbitrage.

CI: I borrowed money to buy a seat on the New York Stock Exchange. I was a hotshot guy. My experience taught me that trading the market is dangerous, and it was far better to use my mathematical ability to become an expert in certain areas. Banks would loan me 90% of the money I needed for arbitrage, because back then, in riskless arbitrage, if you were good, you literally couldn't lose. And I was starting to make *big* money, $1.5 to $2 million a year.

TR: I'd love to talk to you about asymmetric returns. Were you also looking for those when you began taking over undervalued companies?

CI: I started looking at these companies and really analyzing them. I tell you, it's sort of like arbitrage, but nobody appreciates that. When you buy a company, what you're really buying are its assets. So you've got to look at those assets and ask yourself, "Why aren't they doing as well as they should be?" Fully 90% of the time, the reason is management. So we would find companies that weren't well run, and I had enough money that I could come in and say: "I'm taking you over unless you change, or unless the board does X, Y, or Z." A lot of times the board said, "Okay." But sometimes the management would fight us and perhaps go to court. Very few people had the tenacity I had—or were willing to risk the money. If you looked at it, it appeared that we were risking a lot of money, but we weren't.

TR: But you didn't see it as risky because you knew the asset's real value?

CI: You look for risk/reward in the world, right? Everything is risk and reward. But you've got to understand what the risk is, and also understand what the reward is. Most people saw much more risk than I did. But math doesn't lie, and they simply didn't understand it.

TR: Why not?

CI: Because there were too many variables and too many analysts that could sway your opinion.

TR: They're making it harder for you to beat them these days.

CI: Not really. The system is so flawed that you can't get mediocre managers out. Here's an example: let's say I inherit a nice vineyard on beautiful land. Six months later I want to sell it, because it's not making any money. But I've got a problem: the guy who manages the vineyard is never there. He's playing golf all day. But he won't give up his job running the vineyard. And he won't let anybody look at the vineyard because he doesn't want to see it sold. You might say to me, "What are you, crazy? Get the police, kick him out!" But that's the trouble with public companies: you can't do it without a very difficult fight.

TR: The rules make it hard to kick the CEO off your property.

CI: That's the trouble: the shareholders of corporations have great difficulty being heard, but at IEP we fight and often win. Once in power, sometimes we find the CEO is not so bad. But the bottom line is: the way public companies are governed is really bad for this country. There are so many rules that keep you from being an activist. There are many barriers to getting control, but when we do, all shareholders, as the record shows, generally do very well. Additionally, what we do is also very good for the economy, because it makes these companies more productive, and this is not just short term. Sometimes we don't sell for 15 to 20 years!

TR: What's the solution?

CI: Get rid of the poison pills [that issue more stock at a discount if any one shareholder buys too much] and get rid of the staggered board elections so the shareholders can decide how they want the company run. We should make these companies be accountable and have true elections. Even in politics, as bad as it is, you can get rid of the president if you wanted to. He's only there for four years at a time. But at our companies, it is very hard to get rid of a CEO even if he or she is doing a terrible job. Often CEOs get that top job because they're like the guy in college who was the head of the fraternity. He wasn't the smartest guy, but he was the best social guy and a very likeable guy, and so he moved up through the ranks.

Investment Highlights

- IEP stock performance has meaningfully outpaced all its peers

	Time Period	IEP	Berkshire	Leucadia	Loews	S&P 500	Dow Jones	Russell 2000
Gross Return on Investment in Stock	3 Years ended July 31, 2014	104%	69%	-22%	8%	59%	47%	47%
	5 Years ended July 31, 2014	215%	94%	8%	45%	117%	100%	114%
	7 Years ended July 31, 2014	37%	71%	-29%	-7%	55%	52%	59%
	April 1, 2009(1) through July 31, 2014	382%	117%	78%	97%	171%	161%	184%
	January 1, 2000 through July 31, 2014	1622%	235%	264%	372%	73%	104%	168%
Annualized Return	April 1, 2009(1) through July 31, 2014	34.3%	15.6%	11.5%	13.6%	20.5%	18.8%	21.6%
	January 1, 2000 through July 31, 2014	21.5%	8.7%	9.3%	11.2%	3.8%	5.0%	7.0%

(1) April 1, 2009 is the approximate beginning of the economic recovery.

Source: Bloomberg. Includes reinvestment of distributions. Based on the share price as of July 31, 2014.

3

TR: Sometimes you don't need a proxy fight to change the direction of a company. You bought a lot of stock in Netflix recently, almost 10%, and you made $2 billion in two years.

CI: That was my son, Brett, and his partner who did it. I don't know much about technology, but he showed me in 20 minutes why it was a great deal. And I just said, "Buy everything you can!" It wasn't really an activist play.

TR: What did you see? What did he show you in those 20 minutes that made you know that the stock was that undervalued?

CI: Simple: most of the great experts were worried about the wrong thing. At that moment, Netflix had $2 billion in fees coming in every year. But those fees aren't on their balance sheet. And so, all these experts were saying, "How are they going to get money to pay for content?" Well, they've got the $2 billion coming in! And generally subscribers are loyal for longer than you would imagine! It would take much longer than most people thought to put the huge cash flow in jeopardy, no matter what happened.

TR: But you never tried to take over Netflix?

CI: They thought they were going to have a proxy fight. But I said, "Reed [Hastings, Netflix cofounder and CEO], I'm not going to have a proxy fight with you. You just got a hundred-point move!" Then I asked them if they knew the Icahn rule. They said, "What's that, Carl?" I said, "Anybody who makes me eight hundred million in three months, I don't punch them in the mouth."

TR: [*Laughs.*] You cashed out a portion of the stock toward the end of 2013.

CI: When the stock got to $350, I decided to take some off the table. But I didn't sell it all.

TR: What is the biggest misconception about you?

CI: I think people don't understand, or maybe I don't understand, my own motivations. While it may sound corny, I really do think that at this point in my life, I am trying to do something to keep our country great. I want my legacy to be that I changed the way business is done. It bothers me that so many of our great companies are so badly managed. I want to change the rules so that the CEO and boards are truly accountable to their shareholders.

TR: You and your wife have signed the Giving Pledge. What other types of philanthropy are you most passionate about?

CI: I give a lot, but I like doing my own thing. I just put $30 million into charter schools because in charter schools the principal and teachers are

Investment Highlights

- Mr. Icahn believes there has never been a better time for activist investing, if practiced properly, than today.
  - Several factors are responsible for this:
    1) low interest rates, which make acquisitions much less costly and therefore much more attractive,
    2) abundance of cash-rich companies that would benefit from making synergistic acquisitions, and
    3) the current awareness of many institutional investors that the prevalence of mediocre top management and non-caring boards at many of America's companies must be dealt with if we are ever going to end high unemployment and be able to compete in world mark
  - **But an activist catalyst is often needed to make an acqustion happen**
  - We, at IEP, have spent years engaging in the activist model and believe it is the catalyst needed to drive highly accretive M&A and consolidation activity
  - As a corollary, low interest rates will greatly increase the ability of the companies IEP controls to make judicious, friendly, or not-so-friendly acquisitions using our activist expertise
- Proven track record of delivering superior returns
  - **IEP total stock return of *1,622%*[1] since January 1, 2000**
    - S&P 500, Dow Jones Industrial, and Russell 2000 indices returns of approximately 73%, 104%, and 168% respectively over th same period
  - **Icahn Investment Funds performance since inception in November 2004**
    - Total return of approximately 293%[2] and compounded average annual return of approximately 15%[2]
    - Returns of 33.3%, 15.2%, 34.5%, 20.2%[3], 30.8%, and 10.2% in 2009, 2010, 2011, 2012, 2013, and YTD 2014[4] respectively
- Recent Financial Results
  - Adjusted Net Income attributable to Icahn Enterprises of $612 million[5] for the six months ended June 30, 201·
  - Indicative Net Asset Value of approximately $10.2 billion as of June 30, 2014
  - LTM June 30, 2014 adjusted EBITDA attributable to Icahn Enterprises of approximately $2.2 billion
- $6.00 annual distribution (5.8% yield as of July 31, 2014)

(1)   Source: Bloomberg. Includes reinvestment of distributions. Based on the share price as of July 31, 2014.
(2)   Returns calculated as of June 30, 2014.
(3)   Return assumes that IEP's holdings in CVR Energy remained in the Investment Funds for the entire period. IEP obtained a majority stake in CVR Energy in May 2012. Investment Funds returns were approximately 6.6% when excluding returns on CVR Energy after it became a consolidated entity.
(4)   For the six months ended June 30, 2014.

accountable. As a result, a charter school run correctly gives our children a much better education than they generally get in public schools. We are a great country, but, sadly, the way we run our companies and our educational system, for the most part, is dysfunctional. I hope to use my wealth to aid me in being a force in changing this. Sadly, if we don't, we are on the road to becoming a second-rate country or even worse.

THE VALUE OF ACTIVIST BOARD MEMBERSHIP

The following chart has been prepared by Icahn Enterprises and responds to those that question the efficacy of including activists' designees on public company boards of directors.

From January 1, 2009 to June 30, 2014 (a 5½ year period) Icahn designees have joined the boards of the 23 companies listed in the chart. As reflected in the chart, a person that invested in each company on the date that the Icahn designee joined the board, and that sold on the date that the Icahn designee left the board (or continued to hold through June 30, 2014, if the designee did not leave the board) would have obtained an annualized return of 27%.

#	COMPANY NAME	DATE JOINED BOARD	DATE EXITED BOARD (OR 6/30/2014 IF STILL ON BOARD)	HYPOTHETICAL INVESTOR ANNUALIZED RETURN DURING BOARD TENURE
1	Amylin Pharmaceuticals, Inc.	6/9/2009	8/8/2012	38%
2	Biogen Idec, Inc.	6/10/2009	6/30/2014	43%
3	Chesapeake Energy Corp.	6/21/2012	6/30/2014	33%
4	CIT Group, Inc.	12/18/2009	5/10/2011	38%
5	Dynegy, Inc.	3/9/2011	10/1/2012	-81%
6	Ebay, Inc.	6/17/2014	6/30/2014	76%
7	Enzon Pharmaceuticals, Inc.	5/21/2009	6/30/2014	-10%
8	Forest Laboratories, Inc.	8/5/2012	6/30/2014	77%
9	Genzyme Corp.	6/16/2010	4/11/2011	61%
10	Herbalife International, Ltd.	4/25/2013	6/30/2014	60%
11	Hologic, Inc.	12/9/2013	6/30/2014	28%
12	Mentor Graphics Corp.	5/18/2011	6/30/2014	13%
13	MGM Studios	4/25/2012	8/15/2012	96%
14	Motorola Mobility, Inc.	1/3/2011	5/22/2012	22%
15	Motorola Solutions, Inc.	1/4/2011	3/1/2012	23%
16	Navistar International Corp.	10/8/2012	6/30/2014	33%
17	Nuance Communications, Inc.	10/7/2013	6/30/2014	2%
18	Talisman Energy, Inc.	12/1/2013	6/30/2014	-15%
19	Take-Two Interactive Software, Inc.	4/15/2010	11/26/2013	12%
20	The Hain Celestial Group, Inc.	7/7/2010	11/19/2013	52%
21	Transocean, Ltd.	5/17/2013	6/30/2014	-10%
22	Voltari Corp.	6/17/2010	6/30/2014	-62%
23	WebMD Health Corp.	7/24/2012	8/5/2013	124%

TOTAL: 27%

Returns assume equal weighting in each investment.

Source of return data = Bloomberg Total Return function, including dividends reinvested.

The chart does not reflect the actual results of IEP's investment segment, nor is it necessarily indicative of future results of IEP's investment segment.

DAVID SWENSEN:
A $23.9 BILLION LABOR OF LOVE

Chief Investment Officer, Yale University, and Author of
Unconventional Success: A Fundamental Approach to Personal Investment

David Swensen is probably the best-known investor you've never heard of. He's been described as the Warren Buffett of institutional investing. Over the course of his celebrated tenure as Yale's chief investment officer, he's turned $1 billion in assets into more than $23.9 billion, boasting 13.9% annual returns along the way—a record unmatched by many of the high-flying hedge funds that have tried to lure him away over the last 27 years.

As soon as you meet Swensen, you realize that he's not in it for the money—he's in it for the love of the game and a sense of service to a great university. And he's got the paycheck to prove it: his worth in the private sector would be exponentially higher than what he earns at Yale.

At his core, Swensen is an inventor and a disruptor. His Yale model, also known as the endowment model, was developed with his colleague and former student Dean Takahashi, and is an application of modern portfolio theory. The idea is to divide a portfolio into five or six roughly equal parts and invest each in a different asset class. The Yale model is a long-term strategy that favors broad diversification and a bias toward equities, with less emphasis on lower-return asset classes such as bonds or commodities. Swensen's position on liquidity has also been called revolutionary—he avoids rather than chases liquidity, arguing that it leads to lower returns on assets that could otherwise be invested more efficiently.

Before his days as the rock star of institutional investing, Swensen worked on Wall Street for bond powerhouse Salomon Brothers. Many credit him with structuring the world's first currency swap, a trade between IBM and the World Bank, which in effect led to the creation of the interest rate and ultimately credit-default swap markets, representing over $1 trillion in assets today. But don't hold that against him!

I had the privilege of sitting down with Swensen at his Yale office, and before I ventured up the hallowed halls of that storied institution, I did what any good student would do: I spent the night before cramming. Not wanting to be anything less than prepared, I absorbed 400 pages of *Unconventional Success*, Swensen's manifesto on personal investing and diversification, before the meeting. What follows is an edited and abridged version of our nearly four-hour interview.

TR: You work on behalf of one of the largest institutions in this country, yet you have a deep interest in and commitment to the individual investor. Talk to me about that.

DS: I'm basically an optimistic person, but when it comes to the world that individual investors face, it's a mess.

TR: Why is that?

DS: The fundamental reason that individuals don't have the types of choices they should have is because of the profit orientation in the mutual fund industry. Don't get me wrong, I'm a capitalist, and I believe in profits. But there's a fundamental conflict between the profit motive and fiduciary responsibility—because the greater the profits for the service provider, the lower the returns for the investor.

TR: When we're talking about fiduciary responsibility, not all investors even know what that means. What we're really talking about is: you have to put investors' interests ahead of your own.

DS: The problem is that the managers of the mutual funds make more money when they gather huge piles of assets and charge high fees. The high fees are in direct conflict with the goal of producing high returns. And so what happens over and over again is the profits win and the investor seeking returns loses. There are only two organizations where that conflict doesn't exist, and they're Vanguard and TIAA-CREF. Both operate on a not-for-profit basis—they're looking out for the investors' interests, and they're strong fiduciaries. And fiduciary responsibility always wins.

TR: Because mutual funds spectacularly underperform the market. I've read that from 1984 to 1998, only about 4% of funds [with over $100 million in assets under management (AUM)] beat the Vanguard 500. And that 4% isn't the same every year—a more simple way of saying that is that 96% of all mutual funds fail to beat the market.

DS: Those statistics are only the tip of the iceberg. The reality is even worse. When you look at past performance, you can only look at the funds in existence today.

TR: Survivors.

DS: Exactly. Those statistics suffer from survivorship bias. Over the last ten years, hundreds of mutual funds have gone out of business because they performed poorly. Of course, they don't take the funds with great returns and merge them into funds with lousy returns. They take the funds with lousy returns and merge them into funds with great returns.

TR: So the 96% isn't accurate?

DS: It's worse.

TR: Wow.

DS: There's another reason the investor's reality is worse than the numbers you cite, and that's because of our own behavioral mistakes we make as individual investors. Individuals tend to buy funds that have good performance. And they chase returns. And then when funds perform poorly, they sell. And so they end up buying high and selling low. And that's a bad way to make money.

TR: What's the reality of chasing returns?

DS: A lot of it has to do with marketing. Nobody wants to say, "I own a bunch of one- and two-star funds." They want to own four-star funds. And five-star funds. And brag about it at the office.

TR: Of course.

DS: But the four- and five-star funds are the ones that *have* performed well, not the ones that *will* perform well. If you systematically buy the ones that have performed well and sell the ones that have performed poorly, you're going to end up underperforming. So add to your statistics that more than 90% of funds fail to match the market, and then add in the way people behave—they further depress their returns below the market.

TR: So chasing returns is a guaranteed way to have a lower return or lose money?

DS: Those factors that randomly cause something to perform well are just as likely to reverse themselves and cause what had performed well to perform poorly—it's called reversion to the mean.

TR: Okay, so what can investors do to help their cause?

DS: There are only three tools, or levers, that investors have to [increase] returns. The first is asset allocation: What assets are you going to hold in your portfolio? And in which proportions are you going to hold them? The second is market timing. Are you going to try to bet on whether one asset class is going to perform better in the short run relative to the other asset classes you hold?

TR: Are you going to be in bonds, or stocks, or real estate?

DS: Yes, those short-term market-timing bets. And the third tool is security selection. How are you going to structure your bond portfolio or stock portfolio? And that's it. Those are the only three tools we have. The overwhelmingly most important [as you figured out] is asset allocation.

TR: I read that in your book, and it blew me away.

DS: One of the things I love teaching my students at Yale is that **asset allocation actually explains more than 100% of returns in investing!** How can that be true? The reason is, when you engage in market timing, it costs you money; it's not something you can play for free. Every time you buy or sell, you pay a broker. So there's a leakage in fees and commissions paid—which reduces overall returns. And the same is true for security selection.

TR: So this takes us back to index funds and a passive approach to investing.

DS: Right. The active managers charge higher fees with promises of beating the market, but we've seen it's a false promise more often than not. You can take a passive approach and own the whole market. **And you can buy the entire market for a very, very low fee.**

TR: How low?

DS: Less than 20 basis points. And you can get it through a mutual fund offered by Vanguard. So if you can implement your investment with low-cost, passively managed indexed funds, you're going to be a winner.

TR: You're not paying fees, and you're not trying to beat the market.

DS: Plus, you get another benefit: **your tax bill is going to be lower.** This is huge. One of the most serious problems in the mutual fund industry, which is full of serious problems, is that almost all mutual fund managers behave as if taxes don't matter. But taxes matter. Taxes matter a lot.

TR: Is there any bigger bill we face in our lives?

DS: No. **And this speaks to the importance of taking advantage of every tax-advantaged investment opportunity that you can.** You should maximize your contributions if you've got a 401(k), or a 403(b) if you work for a nonprofit. You should take every opportunity to invest in a tax-deferred way.

TR: How do we set up the most efficient asset allocation?

DS: Anybody who's taken freshman economics has probably heard "There ain't no such thing as a free lunch." But Harry Markowitz, whom people call the father of modern portfolio theory, says that "diversification is a free lunch."

TR: Why is that?

DS: Because for any given level of return, if you diversify, you can generate that return with a lower risk; or for any given level of risk, if you diversify, you can generate a higher return. So it's a free lunch. Diversification makes your portfolio better.

TR: What's the minimum diversification you need?

DS: There are two levels of diversification. One is related to security selection. If you decide to buy an index fund, you are diversified to the maximum extent possible because you own the whole market. That's one of the beauties of the index fund, and it's one of the wonderful things Jack Bogle did for investors in America. He gave them the opportunity in a low-cost way to buy the whole market. But from an asset-allocation perspective, when we talk about diversification, we're talking about investing in multiple asset classes. There are six that I think are really important and they are US stocks, US Treasury bonds, US Treasury inflation-protected securities [TIPS], foreign developed equities, foreign emerging-market equities, and real estate investment trusts [REITs].

TR: Why do you pick those six versus others? And what's your portfolio allocation?

DS: Equities are the core for portfolios that have a long time horizon. Equities are obviously riskier than bonds. If the world works the way it's supposed to work, equities will produce superior returns. It's not true day in and day out, or week in and week out, or even year in and year out, but over reasonably long periods of time, equities should generate higher returns. I have a straw-man portfolio in my book, and 70% of the assets in there are equities [or equity-like], and 30% are fixed income.

TR: Let's start with the equity side of the portfolio: the 70%. One of your rules for diversification is to never have anything weighted more than 30%, is that correct?

DS: Yes.

TR: And so you put the first 30% where?

DS: US stocks. One of the things I think that's really important is **we should never underestimate the resilience of the US economy. It's very powerful.** And no matter how much the politicians try and screw it up, there's an underlying strength there. And I never want to bet against that.

TR: And that's why you're so heavily weighted, 70%, toward growth. Not just in the US economy but in overall business around the world.

DS: And then I probably put 10% in emerging markets, 15% in foreign development, and 15% in real estate investment trusts.

TR: Tell me about the 30% fixed-income securities.

DS: I've got all of them in Treasury securities. Half of them are traditional bonds. The other half are in inflation-protected TIPS. If you buy regular Treasury bonds, and inflation takes off, you're going to end up with losses.

TR: People get confused by that, unfortunately.

DS: When I first started on Wall Street, I remember going to my first client meetings and whispering to myself over and over again, "Interest rates up, prices down." I didn't want to get that wrong. That would have been really embarrassing.

TR: Can an individual investor make money in today's market?

DS: That's the beauty of having a long-term buy-and-hold strategy. **That's why you diversify. I'm not smart enough to know where the markets are going to go.** In the late '90s, people said, "Why did you take all this trouble to diversify your portfolio? All you needed to do was own the S&P 500." And what they were doing was, they were looking at the best asset class, and it just happened to be our equity market. And they said, "Everything you did was a waste of time." But that was the American experience. And that's not the only experience in the world. And if, at the beginning of the 1990s, you were a Japanese investor who put all your money in the Japanese market, at the end of the '90s, you'd be miserable. You're never going to have the return that's equal to the best individual asset class return, and you never know what that asset class is going to be before the fact.

TR: What do you say to the baby boomers out there, the ones who are facing retirement in the not-too-distant future?

DS: Unfortunately, I think most individuals don't have any idea how much money they need to save for their retirement. I really worry that a lot of people will look at their 401(k) account and say, "I have fifty thousand dollars or a hundred thousand—that's a lot of money." But if you're talking about financing a retirement, it's not a lot of money.

TR: A lot of people aren't going to be able to retire when they want to retire.

DS: The only way people can get to the right place is to educate themselves. And I'm thrilled you're trying to help people get the knowledge that they need in order to make intelligent decisions.

TR: I understand that you went through a tough health time. What's next for you?

DS: About a year ago, I was diagnosed with cancer. I didn't have a bucket list. I didn't want to quit and travel around the world. I wanted to keep on doing what I could to support the university. Manage Yale's portfolio as long as I could do it. And that's what I'm doing. I love my job.

TR: That's awesome.

DS: I think Yale is one of the world's great institutions. And if I can do anything to make it a stronger place and a better place, then maybe I will have made a difference.

TR: David, thank you, this has been extraordinary. I feel like I went to Yale and took a class on portfolio construction.

DS: Well, you did.

JOHN C. BOGLE:
THE VANGUARD OF INVESTING

Creator of the Index Fund; Founder
and former CEO of the Vanguard Group

If you haven't read any of Jack Bogle's books or listened to his no-nonsense commentary on TV, then you've been missing out on an American treasure. ***Fortune* magazine named Bogle one of the four investment giants of the 20th century.** He's been compared with Benjamin Franklin for his inventiveness and civic spirit. Some say he's done more for the individual investor than anyone in the history of business.

How did he do it? When Jack Bogle founded the Vanguard Group in 1974, index funds were just an academic theory. But Bogle was willing to bet his company on the idea that low-cost, low-fee mutual funds that tracked the performance of the whole stock market would outperform most managed funds year after year. Why? **Because investors as a group can't *beat* the market, because they *are* the market.** Talk about a disrupter! At first, his index funds were mocked as "Bogle's Folly." A competitor even called the idea un-American.

But Bogle brushed off his critics and went on to build Vanguard into the largest mutual fund management firm in the world, with $2.86 trillion in assets under management. How big is that? If Vanguard were a country, its economy would be the same size as Great Britain's! And now, according to Morningstar, US index funds represent **more than a third** of all equity mutual fund investments.

Jack Bogle was born in New Jersey in 1929, right at the start of the Great Depression. His family wasn't wealthy, but Bogle was smart enough to get a scholarship to Princeton, where he served meals to other students to help pay his way. He wrote his senior thesis in economics about mutual funds, hinting at the path he would later carve in the industry. And he never forgot what a friend told him during a summer job as a stock runner: **"Bogle, I'm going to tell you everything you need to know about the stock market: *nobody knows nothin'*."**

After graduating magna cum laude, in 1951 he joined the Wellington Management Company in Philadelphia, where he rose to become president. But during the "go-go" years of the mid-1960s, Bogle merged with a management group he hoped would pump up his business. "It was the worst mistake of my life," he told me. The new partners ran the mutual funds into the ground and then used their seats on the board to fire Bogle.

So what did he do? Instead of accepting defeat, Bogle turned that failure into his greatest victory, one that changed the face of investing. Because of the legal structure of mutual funds, Bogle was still in charge of Wellington's *funds*, which were separate from the management company, with a somewhat different board of directors. He stayed on as the funds' chairman, but he wasn't allowed to *manage* them. "So how do I get into investment management without being an investment manager?" he said during our interview. "You've already figured out the answer. Start an unmanaged fund. **We called it an index fund; I named it Vanguard. At first everybody**

thought it was a joke." Incredible! If Jack Bogle hadn't made that mistake, he would never have founded Vanguard, and millions and millions of individual investors might never have had the chance to avoid excessive fees and add billions of dollars to their collective returns.

I sat down with this living legend in his office on the Vanguard campus in Malvern, Pennsylvania, as a winter storm bore down on the East Coast. He still goes to work every day at the Vanguard research center that he's headed since stepping down as senior chairman in 2000. Jack shook my hand with the grip of a man half his age. Maybe that's because a 1996 heart transplant gave him a new lease on life to continue what he calls a "crusade to give investors a fair shake."

What follows is an edited and abridged version of our four-hour conversation.

TR: Tell me, Jack, where does your drive come from?

JB: **From my earliest memories of my youth, I had to work.** I started working at nine delivering newspapers around the block. I always loved it. I'm something of an introvert, and after working all the time, you don't have to make a lot of idle conversation. And I have a competitive streak. That kind of spoiling for a good fight—even when you don't need one—makes up for a lot.

TR: You started your career at a traditional mutual fund management company.

JB: I was young, I was not wise enough to learn the lessons of history that I should have known, or to act on them. **I thought there was such a thing as a permanently good investment manager; there is not. They come and go.**

TR: Why is that?

JB: There's an awful lot of luck relative to skill. Investing is 95% luck and 5% skill. And maybe if I'm wrong, it's 98 and 2.

TR: Not to insult any active managers!

JB: Look, you put around 1,024 people flipping coins in a room. You tell them all to flip, and one of those 1,024 is going to flip heads ten times in a row. And you'd say, "What a lucky guy." Right? But in the fund business, you'd say, "What a genius." [*Laughs.*] You can even have gorillas do it, and the outcome is exactly the same!

TR: What did you mean when you said, "There's a big difference between a smart guy and a good investor"?

JB: Well, first of all, investors are average. Let's start with that. Very simple. **And most individual investors pay too much for the privilege of being average.**

TR: How's that?

JB: Active management is going to cost you around 2% all-in for the average fund (including the 1.2% average expense ratio, transaction costs, cash drag, and sales charges). So that means in a 7% market, they'll get 5. [An index fund that costs 0.05% means that you get a 6.95% return.] **At 6.95%, you turn $1 into about $30 over 50 years. But at 5%, you get $10 instead of $30. And what does that mean? It means you put up 100% of the cash, you took 100% of the risk, and you got 30% of the reward.** That's what happens when you look at returns over the long term. People don't, but they're going to have to learn to do that.

TR: They don't see the compounding of costs and compounding of fees.

JB: People out there really should understand why they're buying stocks. It's for the dividend yield, and it's for the earnings growth. **The fact is that over the long term, half of the return in the stock market has come from dividends.** And that's where all the fund's expenses come from. So think about this for a minute, Tony: The gross yield of the average equity fund is 2%. The average equity fund has an expense ratio of 1.2%. They're going to take that out of that yield. So you're getting a yield of 0.8%. **The manager is taking half of your dividends to pay himself!** And this industry is consuming every bit of 60% of dividends. And sometimes 100% and sometimes more than 100%. You can see why I'm such a pain in the tail to the industry.

TR: Yet there are still 100 million people invested in actively managed mutual funds. How is that humanly possible?

JB: Well, never underestimate the power of marketing. Back in 2000, we checked, and the average fund that was advertised in *Money* magazine then had an annual return of 41%. Many of these funds—perhaps most—are no longer around. **Investors expect their smart manager will be smart forever, but it won't happen.** They expect that he's generated 20% returns, he'll continue to generate 20%. And that's just ridiculous; it can't happen, it won't happen.

TR: Vanguard is managed only to benefit its fund shareholders, who actually own the company. Are you a supporter of the universal fiduciary standard?

JB: I'm a demander, and I may be one of the very first. The Investment Company Institute [the mutual fund industry's lobbying organization] says, "We don't need a federal standard of fiduciary duty. We are a fiduciary." Well, number one, then why do they object to it? That's an interesting question.

But number two, they don't understand we have this conflict of fiduciary duties. The manager of a publicly held firm like, say, BlackRock has two sets of fiduciary duties. One is fiduciary duty to the shareholders of the BlackRock mutual funds, to maximize their returns. And the other is the fiduciary duty to earn the most money they possibly can for the public owners of BlackRock. And so BlackRock CEO Laurence D. Fink has the consummate dilemma. To maximize the return to mutual fund shareholders, he must lower fees. But to maximize the return to the owners of BlackRock, he must increase fees. So they're trying to do both. And the company is making more money than ever.

TR: How ironic.

JB: Is this a great country, or what?

TR: What's next, in your mind, over the next ten years that is compelling and/or challenging?

JB: I see corporate America continuing to grow. And, remember, the stock market is a derivative. It's a derivative of the value created by our corporations. They earn money, and they're going to continue to earn money. They may earn a little less, but they will still get bigger and bigger, more and more efficient. **So they'll continue growing, probably at a slower rate than we're accustomed to, but still a healthy rate.**

TR: Primarily because spending will decrease based on demographics, or because we've just borrowed so much that we have to still get our house in order?

JB: We still have to deleverage. **There's too much borrowing in the country.** There's not really too much leverage on the corporate side. Corporate balance sheets are in pretty good shape. But government balance
sheets, including federal, state, and local, are all overextended. And we've
got to do something about that.

One of the big risks—one of the big questions, really—is the Federal
Reserve now has in round numbers $4 trillion in reserves. That's $3 trillion more than usual, with about $3 trillion having been acquired in the
last five, six years. And that has to be unwound. And it's not clear to anybody exactly how that's going to happen. But everybody knows it has to
happen sooner or later.

TR: How concerned should we be about another financial crisis?

JB: If you're thinking not as an average investor but as someone who is thinking about the big picture, never lose your sense of history. Don't think it
won't repeat itself. As Mark Twain says, "History may not repeat itself,
but it rhymes." So we do face the possibility of a serious world financial
crisis. Even a world depression. **What are the chances of a world depression? I'd say maybe one in ten.** But it's not one in a thousand. So
I don't look at it as likely, but anyone that says "It can't happen here" is
wrong—

TR: —is not paying attention to history.

JB: Yes. So, basically, use your God-given common sense. Not getting
carried away by the fads and fashions of the moment. And not getting
carried away by the momentary gyrations in the markets, stocks or
bond.

TR: In your 64 years in the business, you've gone through every type of
market. How do you take the human emotional element out of investing?

JB: None of us can, including me. I'm trying to. **People say, "How do you
feel when the market goes down 50%?" I say, honestly, I feel miserable.** I get knots in my stomach. So what do I do? I get out a couple of
my books on "staying the course" and reread them!

TR: If you couldn't pass on any money to your kids or grandkids, but you
could pass on some principles, what would they be?

JB: I would say, to begin with, pay attention to where your assets are invested. Choose your asset allocation in accordance with your risk tolerance and your objectives. Number two would be, diversify. And be sure and diversify through low-cost index funds. There are a lot of high-cost ones out there. We shouldn't forget that. And don't trade. **Don't do something— just stand there**! No matter what! And you'll be able to resist that temptation more easily if you had a little bit more of your assets allocated to bonds than you think you should.

TR: What other advice do you have for investors?

JB: Don't open the *Wall Street Journal*! Don't watch CNBC! We kid about it. I do interviews on CNBC a lot, and I keep wondering why they keep asking me back. I can handle somewhere between 40 seconds and 50 seconds of Jim Cramer. **All the yelling and screaming and buy this and sell that. That's a distraction to the business of investing.** We spend too much time, focus too much of our energy on all these things to do with investing, when you know what the outcome's going to be. You're going to get the market return plus or minus something. Mostly minus. And so why spend all this time trying to trade the Standard & Poor's 500 all day long in real time, as an early marketing campaign for the first ETF [exchange-traded fund] suggested?

Anybody who is doing that should get a life. Take the kids out to the park. Take your wife out to dinner. If all else fails, read a good book.

TR: What does money mean to you?

JB: **I look at money not as an end but a means to an end.** There's a great story about the two writers Kurt Vonnegut and Joe Heller. They meet at a party on Shelter Island. Kurt looks at Joe and says, "That guy, our host over there, he made a billion dollars today. He's made more money in one day than you made on every single copy of *Catch-22*." And Heller looks at Vonnegut and says, "That's okay, because I have something he, our host, will never have. Enough."

I'm leaving my kids enough so they can do anything that they want, but not so much they can do nothing. I often say to them, "Sometimes I wish that you would have grown up with all the advantages I had." And their first reaction was, "Don't you mean disadvantages?" "No, kid, I don't. I mean advantages. Getting along in the world, working your way through it all."

TR: It took years for the concept of indexing to take hold, and now index funds are taking the industry by storm. **How's it feel to be right?**

JB: Well, people say, you must be very proud. Look at what you built. And I tell them, there will be time for that, I think, someday. But not yet. I think it's Sophocles who said, "One must wait until the evening to enjoy the splendor of the day." And my evening isn't here yet.

You know, I've got to confess to you, I should have been dead a long, long time ago. I had eight heart attacks before I got the heart [transplant]. **My heart stopped. And I have no right to be around. But it is absolutely fabulous to be alive.** I don't spend a lot of time thinking about this. But I realize that I am seeing what I believe is the triumph of indexing. And really a revolution in investor preferences. There's not any question about that. It's going to change Wall Street. Wall Street's getting a lot smaller. I'm not sure I understand the thing fully, but I'm guessing if I were dead, I wouldn't be seeing it.

TR: Will you ever retire, by the way?

JB: Probably more likely to be in God's hands than mine. I'm enjoying myself, and thriving on my mission to give investors a fair shake.

Jack Bogle Portfolio Core Principles

1. **Asset allocation in accordance with your risk tolerance and your objectives.**
2. Diversify through low-cost index funds.
3. Have as much in bond funds as your age. A "crude" benchmark, he says.

Jack is in his 80s and has 40% of his total portfolio invested in bonds. But a very young person could be 100% equities.

So in my total portfolio, including both my personal and retirement accounts, about 60% of my assets are in stocks, mostly in Vanguard's stock index funds. The rest is split between Vanguard's Total Bond Market Index Fund and tax-exempt [municipal bond] funds. My municipal bond holdings are split about two-thirds in Vanguard's

Intermediate-Term Tax-Exempt Fund and about one-third in Vanguard's Limited-Term Tax-Exempt Fund [limited being somewhere between short and intermediate; a little bit longer for the extra yield].

I won't need to draw on the money, I hope, in my taxable portfolio. And those are still nice tax-exempt yields, around 3% or so, which is the equivalent of 5% for someone in my tax bracket, and I don't need any more than that. I'm happy to get it.

I worry a little bit, of course, about the solidity of the municipal bond market, but I've decided that with our top-notch analysts here at Vanguard, they should be okay. **In my tax-deferred portfolio, which is my largest asset, my bond assets are largely in Vanguard's Total Bond Market Index Fund.** That includes long-, intermediate-, and short-term bonds. It holds Treasury, mortgage, and corporate bonds.

I'm very satisfied with the returns on my total portfolio. After an awful 17% decline in 2008 [the S&P 500 was down 37% that year, more than twice as much], my returns have been consistently positive, averaging almost 10% per year. I'm happy to simply "stay the course" and ride it all out.

WARREN BUFFETT: THE ORACLE OF OMAHA

The Legend Who's Said It All; CEO, Berkshire Hathaway

I was in the greenroom of the *Today* show, waiting to go on the air, when in walked *the man* himself: Warren Buffett, one of the greatest investors of the 20th century and, with $67.6 billion to his name, the third wealthiest man in the world. We were scheduled to appear (together with Spanx founder Sara Blakely and future secretary of Housing and Urban Development Julian Castro) in a roundtable discussion with Matt Lauer about economic success and our views on the direction of the US economy. I've always been a huge fan of Buffett's. Like millions of investors around the world, I've been inspired by the story of how a humble stockbroker from Nebraska turned a failing New England textile business called Berkshire Hathaway into the fifth largest publicly held company in the world, with assets of nearly a half trillion dollars and holdings in everything from Geico insurance to See's Candies. His not-so-secret to success has been "value investing": a system he learned and perfected from his mentor Ben Graham. It revolves around looking for undervalued companies and buying stock with the expectation it will rise in price over the long term. It's one of the simplest forms of asymmetric risk/reward, and one that requires a tremendous amount of research, skill, and cash—which is one of the reasons Buffett pursued insurance holdings that throw off great cash flow and thus investment opportunities.

Not only has Buffett been phenomenally successful in business, but also he's become one of the most generous philanthropists in history, pledging 99% of his vast personal fortune to charity through the Bill and Melinda Gates Foundation. He's also probably the most quotable—and quoted— business leader ever, and you've already read some priceless nuggets of his wisdom sprinkled throughout these pages.

When I finally had him in the same room with me, I couldn't resist the opportunity to tell him about this book project. Perhaps we could sit down for an interview about how the individual investor can win in this volatile economy?

He looked up at me with a twinkle in his eye. "Tony," he said, "I'd love to help you, but I'm afraid I've already said everything a person can say on the subject."

It was hard to argue with that. Since 1970, he's been putting out an eagerly awaited annual letter to his shareholders filled with plain-spoken investing advice and commentary. Plus, there have already been nearly 50 books published with his name on the jacket—even a few of them written by Buffett himself!

Still, I pressed ahead.

"But now that you've announced you're leaving almost all of your wealth to charity, what kind of portfolio would you recommend for your family to protect and grow their own investments?"

He smiled again and grabbed my arm. "It so simple," he said. Indexing is the way to go. Invest in great American businesses without paying all the fees of a mutual fund manager and hang on to those companies, and you will win over the long term!"

Wow! The most famous stock picker in the world has embraced index funds as the best and most cost-effective investment vehicles.

Later, even after Steve Forbes and Ray Dalio reached out on my behalf to encourage Warren to have a more detailed interview with me, he let me know there was no need. Warren told me that everything he had to say about investing that's important is already published. All he would tell an individual investor today is to invest in index funds that give you exposure to the broad market of the best companies in the world and hold on to them for the long term. I guess repetition *is* the mother of skill. I got it, Warren! In this year's letter to the shareholders, Warren emphasized the same advice to all investors once again! What's his asset allocation? Below are the instructions he has left for his wife and their trust after he has passed:

"Put 10% . . . in short-term government bonds and 90% in a very low-cost S&P 500 index fund. (I suggest Vanguard's.) I believe the trust's long-term results from this policy will be superior to those attained by most investors—whether pension funds, institutions, or individuals—who employ high-fee managers."

Jack Bogle is very happy about this advice! America's most respected investor is endorsing the strategy Jack has promoted for almost 40 years!

Remember, Buffett made a $1 million wager against New York–based Protégé Partners betting that Protégé could *not* pick five top hedge fund managers who will collectively beat the S&P 500 index over a ten-year period? Again, as of February 2014, the S&P 500 was up 43.8%, while the five hedge funds were up 12.5%.

The Oracle of Omaha has spoken!

CHAPTER 6.5

PAUL TUDOR JONES:
A MODERN-DAY ROBIN HOOD

Founder, Tudor Investment Corporation;
Founder, Robin Hood Foundation

One of the most successful traders of all times, Paul Tudor Jones started his own firm at the age of 26, after cutting his teeth trading cotton in the commodity "pits."

Paul has defied gravity, having produced 28 straight full years of wins. He is legendary for predicting Black Monday, the 1987 stock market crash that saw a 22% drop in a single day (still the largest percentage stock market drop in any day in history). At a time when the rest of the world was experiencing a meltdown, Paul and his clients captured a 60% monthly return and a nearly 200% return for the year!

Paul is one of my closest friends and personal heroes. I've been privileged to be his peak-performance coach since 1993—21 of his 28 full consecutive years of wins and the majority of his trading career. What's even more impressive to me than Paul's stunning financial success is his heartfelt obsession to constantly find ways to give back and make a difference. As the founder of the iconic Robin Hood Foundation, Jones has inspired and enrolled some of the smartest and wealthiest investors in the world to attack poverty in New York City. Paul and the Robin Hood team do this work with the same analytical rigor that hedge fund billionaires typically reserve for financial investments. Since 1988, Robin Hood has invested over $1.45 billion in city programs. And just like Jones's relentless pursuit of asymmetric returns in his financial life (he'll share his rule of 5 to 1 in a moment), his foundation work is no different. Robin Hood's operating and administrative costs are covered 100% by board participation, so donors earn a 15-to-1 return on their investment in their community! As Eric Schmidt, executive chairman of Google, says, "There is literally no foundation, no activity, that is more effective!"

Jones himself will tell you he's a trader, not a traditional investor, but like his former employer, E. F. Hutton, when Jones talks, people listen. As a macro trader, he studies the impact of fundamentals, psychology, technical analysis, flows of funds, and world events and their impact on asset prices. Instead of focusing on individual stocks, he bets on trends that are shaping the world—from the United States to China; from currencies to commodities to interest rates. He is sought out by some of the most influential financial leaders on the planet: finance ministers, central bank officials, and think tanks around the world.

I met Paul for this interview at the magnificent campus in Greenwich, Connecticut, for his Tudor Investment family. During the interview, we dug down for the most valuable investment principles he has to share to benefit you, the individual investor. As a result, Paul is about to give us his "$100,000 business education," the one he shares with his own family of traders and a few university students fortunate enough to hear his message each year. All this wisdom in just six pages.

TR: Paul, what you've done in investing, in trading, is extraordinary: 28 consecutive wins—28 years without a loss. How does a mortal do that?

PTJ: We're all products of our environment. I started out as a commodity trader in 1976. The great thing about being a commodity trader—trading cotton, soybeans, orange juice—is that [those] markets are hugely impacted by weather. In a space of three or four years, you'd have huge bull markets and huge bear markets. I very quickly learned the psychology of the bull market *and* the bear market, and how quickly they could change. What the emotions were like when there were lows. I saw fortunes made and lost. I sat there and watched Bunker Hunt take a $400 million position in silver to $10 billion in 1980, which made him the richest man on earth. Then he went from $10 billion back down to $400 million in five weeks.

TR: Wow!

PTJ: So I learned how quickly it can all go away; how precious it is when you have it. The most important thing for me from that is that defense is ten times more important than offense. The wealth you have can be so ephemeral; you have to be very focused on the downside at all times.

TR: Absolutely.

PTJ: When you have a good position in something, you don't need to look at it; it will take care of itself. Where you need to be focused is where you're losing money, and that's actually when people generally don't want to look: "My account's going down. I don't even want to open it." **So I've created a process over time whereby risk control is the number one single most important focus that I have, every day walking in.** I want to know I'm not losing it.

TR: What do you think are the biggest myths that the general population has about investing? What hurts them?

PTJ: You can invest for the long term, but you're not going to necessarily be wealthy for the long term—because everything has a price and a central value over time. But it's asking a lot, I think, of an average investor to understand valuation metrics all the time. The way that you guard against that—guard against the fact that maybe you're not the most informed person of every asset class—is you run a diversified portfolio.

TR: Of course.

PTJ: Here's a story I'll never forget. It was 1976, I'd been working for six months, and I went to my boss, cotton trader Eli Tullis, and said, "I've got to trade, I've got to trade." And he said, "Son, you're not going to trade right now. Maybe in another six months I'll let you." I said, "No, no, no — I've got to trade right now." He goes, "Now, listen, the markets are going to be here in thirty years. The question is, are you?"

TR: How perfect.

PTJ: So the turtle wins the race, right? I think the single most important thing that you can do is diversify your portfolio. Diversification is key, playing defense is key, and, again, just staying in the game for as long as you can.

TR: Following up on diversification, how do you think about asset allocation in terms of playing defense?

PTJ: There's never going to be a time where you can say with [absolute] certainty that this is the mix I should have for the next five or ten years. The world changes so fast. If you go and look right now, the valuations of both stocks and bonds in the United States are both ridiculously overvalued. And cash is worthless, so what do you do with your money? Well, there's a time when to hold 'em and a time when to fold 'em. You're not going to necessarily always be in a situation to make a lot of money, where the opportunities are great.

TR: So what do you do?

PTJ: Sometimes you just have to say, "Gee! There's no value here, there's nothing compelling. I'm going to be defensive and run a portfolio where I don't have any great expectations. I'm going to be in a position where I don't get hurt, and if and when values do rise, I'll have some firepower to do something."

TR: Okay, any specific strategies for protecting your portfolio?

PTJ: I teach an undergrad class at the University of Virginia, and I tell my students, "I'm going to save you from going to business school. Here, you're getting a hundred-grand class, and I'm going to give it to you in two thoughts, okay? **You don't need to go to business school; you've only got to remember two things. The first is, you always want to be with whatever the predominant trend is.** You don't ever want to be a contrarian investor. The two wealthiest guys in the United States—Warren Buffett and Bill Gates—how did they get their money? Bill Gates got his money because he owned a stock, Microsoft, and it went up eight hundred times, and he stayed with the trend. And Warren Buffett, he said, 'Okay. I'm going to buy great companies. I'm going to hold these companies, and I'm not going to sell them because—correctly and astutely—compound interest or the law of compounding works in my favor if I don't sell.' "

TR: And so he made his money from the cash flow of all his insurance companies.

PTJ: He sat through one of the greatest bull runs in the history of civilization. He withstood the pain of gain.

TR: Amazing. So my next question is, how do you determine the trend?

PTJ: **My metric for everything I look at is the 200-day moving average of closing prices.** I've seen too many things go to zero, stocks and commodities. The whole trick in investing is: "How do I keep from losing everything?" If you use the 200-day moving average rule, then you get out. You play defense, and you get out. I go through this exercise when I'm teaching a class on technical analysis. I'll draw a hypothetical chart like the one below—it will go all the way to the top on a clean sheet of paper on a white board.

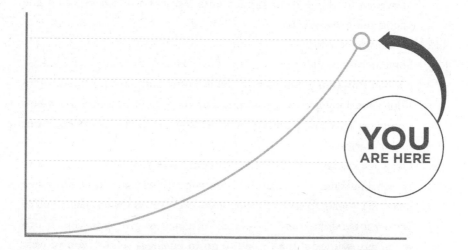

And then I ask, "Okay, all you know is what you see right here. How many people want to be long and stay long on this chart?" And about 60% will raise their hands, yes. And how many want to get off this investment and sell it? Then 40% or so will say get out. And I say, **"You 40%**

should never ever invest your own money in your entire life! Because you've got this contrarian bug, and it's the greatest way to ruin that there possibly is. It means you're going to buy every brand—you're going to buy things that go to zero and sell things that go to infinity, and one day, you're going to die."

TR: That's great, makes total sense. In fact, you say some of your greatest victories have been turning points, right? That's what's been different about you.

PTJ: Right, the crash of 1987. I made my money on the day of the crash.

TR: Okay, you have to tell me about that. **That's considered one of the top three trades of all time, in all history!** Most people would be thrilled with a 20% annual return; you made 60% on that trade alone that month. Did your theory about the 200-day moving average alert you to that one?

PTJ: You got it. It had gone under the 200-day moving target. At the very top of the crash, I was flat.

TR: So you waited until it turned?

PTJ: Yes, absolutely.

TR: That's amazing! I'm blown away by that one. So you don't consider yourself to be a risk taker, and you focus on how to protect constantly and how to align with the trend. What's the second thought for students?

PTJ: Five to one.

TR: Asymmetric risk/reward?

PTJ: Exactly. **Five to one means I'm risking one dollar to make five.** What five to one does is allow you to have a hit rate of 20%. **I can actually be a complete imbecile. I can be wrong 80% of the time, and I'm still not going to lose**—assuming my risk control is good. All you've got to do is just be right one time out of five. The hard part is that that's not how we invest. The way that human nature is, we're never really calculated about our entry points. We're never really thoughtful about where we give in and what are we really risking.

TR: And Paul, you are not wrong 80% of the time! Since asset allocation is so important, let me ask you: If you couldn't pass on any of your money to your kids but only a specific portfolio and a set of principles to guide them, what would it be? I'm asking this to help people get a model of how the average person can look at investing through your eyes.

PTJ: I get very nervous about the retail investor, the average investor, because it's really, really hard. If this was easy, if there was one formula, one way to do it, we'd all be zillionaires. One principle for sure would be get out of anything that falls below the 200-day moving average. Investing with a five-to-one focus and discipline would be another. But here's what I do know. You've got to go interview Ray Dalio. He knows better than anybody. If you're looking for asset allocation, he's the one guy who does it better than anybody.

TR: He's next on my list, thanks! Okay, let's shift gears. You've had this phenomenal success in your life, you're legendary, and you're so humble about it. Tell me about giving back: What's driven all of the amazing philanthropic work that you do? What continues to drive you to make a difference in so many people's lives?

PTJ: As a young child, I'd gone to this huge outdoor vegetable market in Memphis, and I remember all of a sudden looking up, and my mommy was gone. And when you're four years old, your mother is everything. And this extraordinarily kind, very old, very tall black man came over and said, "Don't worry. We're going to find your mama. Don't cry, we're going to find her. You're going to be happy in a minute." He took my hand and walked me down those roads until, finally, he saw my mother, and she started laughing because she could see I was crying.

TR: Wow.

PTJ: You never forget stuff like that. God's every action, those little actions become so much bigger, and then they become multiplicative. **We forget how important the smallest action can be. For me, I think, it kind of spawned a lifetime of trying to always repay that kindness.**

TR: That's so beautiful, Paul; I see and feel the depth of impact of that moment on your life even now. You got us both on the edge of tears. Thank you. Last question for you: most people have an illusion that if they have enough money, stress goes away. Is it true? Does financial stress ever go away?

PTJ: That day still has not come.

TR: Okay. That's what I wanted to hear.

PTJ: The problem is, like anything, it's never enough. Financial stress right now for me is that there are so many causes that I believe in. My financial stress relates to being able to give to the things that make me happy, that create passion in my life, and that are really exciting. There's a huge conservation project that I've just discovered about a month ago that I probably can't afford. The time frame on this is 100 years, at least. And I'm thinking, "Oh my God! If I went and bought this timber operation, and let that land heal, and restored it. One hundred years from that day—it's going to be one of the most breathtakingly beautiful places! This is where God would have spoken to Adam; it has to be the Garden of Eden." And I'm thinking, **"Okay, I can't afford it, but I really want to do it. I better go out there and work my ass off, because it will be the best contribution I can make to someone one hundred years from now.** They won't know who did it, but they'll love that spot and they'll be so happy."

TR: Thank you, Paul. I love you, brother.

RAY DALIO:
A MAN FOR ALL SEASONS

Founder and Co-Chief Investment Officer, Bridgewater Associates

Ray Dalio has been part of the DNA of this book from the moment I first sat down to interview him at his Connecticut home. Our initial meeting went on for nearly three hours of pitching and catching ideas about everything from the benefits of meditation ("It gives me equanimity," said Ray) to the workings of the economy ("It's a simple machine"). I already knew the astounding track record of his $160 billion hedge fund, Bridgewater

Associates, the biggest in the world. I knew that Ray manages risk better than anyone else on the planet, and that he's the go-to guy for world leaders and huge financial institutions when they need a safe harbor in the volatile marketplace. But I had no idea that when I asked him the same question that I asked every financial superstar in this book—What portfolio would you leave your children if you couldn't leave them money?—that Ray's answer would turn out to be the Holy Grail I was seeking when I first began this quest. What was it? Nothing less than an investment plan for individual investors like you to grow your nest egg, and one that would work in all seasons and without risking your life savings. Until now, only Ray Dalio's clients had access to his magic formula for investing success in every season. His generosity in choosing this time and place for sharing it with the world leaves me astonished and grateful.

I don't need to go into Ray's background here. You've been on this journey with him from the first pages of this book, and if you've gotten this far, you've already read chapters 5.1 and 5.2, "Invincible, Unsinkable, Unconquerable: The All Seasons Strategy" and "It's Time to Thrive: Storm-Proof Returns and Unrivaled Results," which tell his story and lay out the basis for his entire portfolio. I was going to list it here, but it's not as powerful without the context. If you jumped ahead, don't cheat! Go back and read those chapters. They will blow your mind and change your life! If you've read them already, it's time to implement. Ray Dalio is the master of All Seasons.

MARY CALLAHAN ERDOES: THE TRILLION-DOLLAR WOMAN

CEO, J.P. Morgan Asset Management Division

Mary Callahan Erdoes may only be five foot two, but she casts a long shadow as CEO of one of the largest asset management groups in the world, at the biggest bank in the United States. *Forbes* magazine has called her "the rare female comet in the male-dominated firmament of Wall Street" and listed her among the 100 Most Powerful Women in the World. Since 2009, when she took over J.P. Morgan's Asset Management Division, it's grown by *more than half-a-trillion-with-a-T* dollars—more than a 30% increase! Today

Erdoes oversees the management of $2.5 trillion invested by foundations, central banks, pension funds, and some of the world's wealthiest individuals. She's often mentioned in the media as being on the short list to succeed JPMorgan Chase CEO Jamie Dimon.

While most of the voices in this book advocate that passive, low-fee money management brings the best results for individual investors over time, Erdoes makes a case that funds that are actively managed by the best minds in the business are worth the fees they charge. She says the proof is in the loyalty of their satisfied clients, as well as the new business they continue to attract.

Money management is in Erdoes's blood. She was the firstborn child and only girl in a large Irish Catholic family in Winnetka, Illinois. Her father, Patrick Callahan, was an investment banker with Lazard Freres in Chicago. Mary excelled at math in high school—while also winning equestrian medals—and went on to become the only female math major in her class at Georgetown University. She met her husband, Philip Erdoes, while they were both earning MBAs at Harvard Business School.

As a financial services executive, Erdoes has broken the mold in more ways than one: in a business famous for aggressive management, her colleagues describe her style with words such as "loyal," "team-oriented," and "caring." When she was coming up at J.P. Morgan, she was known for flying across the country to meet with clients who needed extra help in managing their assets. Now 47 years old and part of the highest level of management in a firm with 260,000 employees, she is honored as much for her extraordinary leadership as for her financial brilliance.

Our meeting took place at J.P. Morgan's world headquarters in the classic Union Carbide Building, overlooking Park Avenue and the skyscrapers of Manhattan. As I rode the elevator to the conference room, J.P. Morgan Asset Management's communications director, Darin Oduyoye, told me a story that touched me deeply, and illustrated the kind of person I was about to meet. Oduyoye had always wanted to be a broadcaster but took a job in J.P. Morgan's mutual fund division before transferring to public relations. When Erdoes asked him to be a producer of a daily morning meeting broadcast for wealth management employees all over the world, he was shocked.

"I don't know enough about investing!" he objected.

"Well, you told me you always wanted to be in broadcasting," she said. "Now you get to be a talk-show producer!"

"She saw more in me than I saw in myself," Darin told me.

It doesn't matter what they do for the company, Erdoes goes out of her way to know each of her employees. But she still carves out the time period-ically to have lunch with her three young daughters and pick them up from school most days. That's the way she rolls, and it makes her the extraordi-nary leader—and human being—that she is.

TR: You lead one of the largest management groups in the world. Tell me a little about your journey, the challenges you faced, and the principles that guide you.

ME: I don't think you can lay out a path in life to get exactly where you want to go. A lot of it happens by accident or circumstance.

I remember when I was given my first stock: Union Carbide. It was a birthday gift from my grandmother. I think I was seven or eight—old enough to remember and young enough not to know what to do with it.

The first thing she told me was, "You don't sell this." I'm not sure if I agree with that now! But she said, "This is the value of compound-ing. If you keep this, it will hopefully grow over time, and you will have something much larger." That also ingrained in me at an early age the importance of saving and started me thinking about money management. I already knew I had a knack for numbers, so the concept of saving versus spending was a powerful one for me.

It helped that my father worked in the industry, and I spent a lot of weekends with him at work playing "office." I sat at his desk, and I had my brothers at his assistant's desk! We had good fun growing up, and I think that showed me how interesting and exciting financial services could be, and that it wasn't something to be fearful of. That was very helpful early in life.

TR: You work in a business that has been dominated by men. What were some of the biggest challenges that you've faced along the way?

ME: Money management is an industry where results speak for themselves. It's a virtuous cycle: if you perform for your clients, they'll invest more money with you, and their money will make money—again, the idea of compounding that I learned from my grandmother. So because of the focus on performance, money management is a business that fosters equality. If you perform, you will succeed.

TR: What's leadership? How do you define it?

ME: It's important not to confuse management with leadership. For me, leadership means not asking anyone to do anything I wouldn't do myself. It's waking up every morning trying to make your organization a better place. I truly believe that I work for the people of J.P. Morgan Asset Management, not the other way around, and because of that, I try to see beyond what people even see themselves.

Having been a portfolio manager, client advisor, and business leader, I know what we're capable of achieving for clients. So I consider it my job not just to lead our teams but to get in the trenches alongside them and join them on the journey.

I think in many ways you're either born with leadership or not, but that doesn't mean you're not constantly working at it, honing it, and figuring out what works and what doesn't. The style of leadership will change with different people or different situations, but the basic tenets of leadership are consistent.

TR: I recently interviewed Dr. Robert Shiller, who just won the Nobel Prize in economics, and he was talking about all the good that financial institutions do in the world that people take for granted. Why do you think their reputations have shifted, and what can be done to turn it around?

ME: Following the financial crisis, it's easy to understand why some people lost trust in the industry. In hindsight, there were some things that needed to change—products that were too complex or confusing. But overall, the financial services industry contributes a lot to the world. We provide companies with capital to grow, which ultimately fuels employment. We help individuals save and invest their hard-earned money so they can do things like buy a house, pay for college, or retire more comfortably. We support local communities both financially and through the intellectual and physical capital of our people.

I'm incredibly proud to be part of the industry and even prouder to be part of J.P. Morgan. We have 260,000 people who work hard for clients every day and always strive to do the right thing. We have a saying that if you wouldn't let your grandmother buy a product, then it's probably not a business we should be in. It's a simplistic yet important way to look at things.

TR: It's a sensitive issue, I'm sure, but if you listen to Ray Dalio, you listen to Jack Bogle, David Swensen, Warren Buffett—they all say active management doesn't work over the long term. That 96% of active managers don't beat the index. I wanted to get your view on it because your performance has been extraordinary.

ME: One of the biggest challenges about successful investing is there's no such thing as a one-size-fits-all approach. But if you look at the world's most successful portfolio managers, you'll find that many of them manage money actively, buying and selling companies in which they think that they have added insight. Their track records have proven that active management, compounded over long periods of time, makes a very large difference in your portfolio. What an active manager can do is look at two seemingly similar companies and make a judgment, based on extensive research, about which is the better long-term investment. We've surrounded ourselves at J.P. Morgan Asset Management with managers who have done that successfully for a sustained period of time, and that's why we have $2.5 trillion in assets that people ask us to help them manage.

TR: Great investors are invariably looking for asymmetric risk/reward, right? And the ultrawealthy have always done this. But tell me, how does the average investor today get wealth without risk, or at least wealth with little risk, if they're not already ultrawealthy?

ME: It is not about a wealth level, it's about being well rounded, well advised, and sticking to a plan. What happens too often is people start with a diversified plan, but as market conditions change, they try to time the markets so they are getting either more upside opportunities or better protection in unfavorable conditions. But that's a very dangerous thing to do because it's impossible to predict every scenario.

What a well-diversified portfolio does is help you capture those tail risks [risks that can bring great rewards], and if you stick to that plan, you can create a tremendous amount of wealth over the long term.

TR: What are some of the biggest opportunities for investors today and the largest challenges that they need to prepare for?

ME: I think that we will look back at the time that we're living in right now and say, "That was a great time to have invested." We have so much liquidity in the system to take care of a lot of the things that went wrong. But investing over the next five years—particularly those with long-term growth prospects—are opportunities to consider right now. Most investors today want income, tempered volatility, and liquidity. There's still the hangover effects of 2008, where many are concerned about, "If I need my money right away, can I get it?" If you don't need it right away, get it invested. It will serve you very well over the coming years, and you will look back and be incredibly thankful that you did it.

In addition, the industry has made a lot of changes in rules and regulations to attempt to insure better conditions for the future. That's not to say there won't be market anomalies, but the system is better, and so it should be safer.

TR: I've asked this of every multibillionaire that I've spoken with who started with nothing: Does financial stress ever go away for you?

ME: Financial stress never goes away for people regardless of the level of their wealth or success.

TR: Why is that?

ME: Because no matter what stage you're in, you want to make sure you are using your money most effectively, whether that's paying for health care and your family's well-being, or insuring you are investing your money properly for future generations or to fulfill philanthropic goals.

TR: Is there an antidote to that stress? What is it for you?

ME: For me, it's all about keeping things in perspective and focusing on the things you can control, like insuring that you're doing as much as you can every day and giving it your all. You can never be out of balance in taking care of yourself as a person, taking care of your work as a professional, taking care of your family, taking care of your friends, your mind, your body. It's okay for things to get out of whack every once in a while, but they can't *stay* out of whack.

TR: If all you could pass on to your children was a set of rules and/or a portfolio strategy or an asset allocation strategy, what would it be?

ME: Invest for the long term and only take money out when you truly need
      it. Specific portfolio construction will be different for different people.
      For example, I have three daughters. They're three different ages. They
      have three different skill sets that will change over time. One might spend
      more money than another. One might be more frugal. One may want to
      work in an environment where she can earn a lot of money. Another may
      be more philanthropic in nature. One may get married, one may not;
      one may have children, one may not—so they'll have different depen-
      dents. Every single permutation will vary over time, which is why even
      if I started all of them the first day they were born and set out an asset
      allocation, it would have to change.

TR: How old are your girls?

ME: Eleven, ten, and seven. They're lots of fun.

TR: From my understanding of what I've read, you believe in "work-life inte-
      gration." Tell me a little bit about that.

ME: I have the great fortune of working at a company that is very supportive
      of families and gives people a lot of flexibility to do what works best
      for them. So whether that means logging off a little early to catch your
      child's soccer game but then reconnecting later in the evening to finish
      a project, or bringing the kids to the office on the weekends like my dad
      used to with me, you have the option to do what's best for you and your
      family.

TR: Like you did at your father's office! And they're sitting behind your desk,
      preparing for the future.

ME: Exactly. My work life and family life are all one thing, and I'm always
      determined to get the most out of both of them.

T. BOONE PICKENS:
MADE TO BE RICH, MADE TO GIVE

Chairman and CEO of BP Capital Management

T. Boone Pickens, dubbed the "Oil Oracle" by CNBC, has always been ahead of his time. In the early 1980s, he was the original corporate raider—although "shareholder activist" has always been the term he's preferred. His early focus on maximizing shareholder value, virtually unheard of at the time, has long since become a standard of American corporate culture. As *Fortune* magazine declared, "Boone's once revolutionary ideas [are] so completely taken for granted that they have become linchpins of the economy."

By the early 2000s, Pickens had become a hedge fund manager, **making his first billion *after* turning seventy—with a second career investing in energy assets.** In the next decade and a half, he'd turn that billion into $4 billion—$2 billion of which he'd lose again, and $1 billion of which he'd give away.

Ever the optimist, Boone recently married for the fifth time, and at 86, he's got a huge social media presence and shows no signs of slowing down. After falling off the *Forbes* 400 list last year, he sent a famous tweet declaring, "Don't worry. At $950 million, I'm doing fine. Funny, my $1 billion charitable giving exceeds my net worth." When I spoke to him regarding his net worth, he said, "Tony, you know me; I'm going to get the other two billion back in the next couple of years."

Boone, a Depression-era baby, started with nothing. At 12, he delivered papers and quickly expanded his route from 28 to 156 papers, later citing his boyhood job as an early introduction to "growing by acquisition." After graduating from Oklahoma State University (then known as Oklahoma A&M) in 1951 with a degree in geology, Pickens built an energy empire in Texas. By 1981, his Mesa Petroleum Corporation had become one of the largest independent oil companies in the world. His corporate takeovers of the 1980s were the stuff of legend, with Gulf Oil, Phillips Petroleum, and Unocal being some of his most famous takeover targets.

But Pickens's fortunes (and fortune) were always shifting. When he left Mesa in 1996, after a downward spiral in the company's profits, many counted him out—he would soon lose 90% of his investing capital. But Pickens went on to stage one of the greatest comebacks in his industry, **turning his investment fund's last $3 million into billions.**

While almost everyone we hear from these days is focused primarily on two asset classes, stocks and bonds, Boone's BP Capital fund is different: he's betting on the direction of the energy futures and derivatives markets. And while this book is devoted to helping you achieve financial independence, **Boone says our dependence on foreign oil is the single greatest threat not only to national security but also to our economic well-being.** Always one to be ahead of the curve, Boone is on a crusade today to free this country from our dependence on OPEC oil and usher in a new wave of energy policy with his Pickens Plan.

I've been a fan of Boone's for as long as I can remember, and I'm now privileged to call him a friend. He's been gracious enough to speak at many of my wealth events. What follows below is an excerpt of our latest conversations around building wealth, protecting America's energy future, and his humble beginnings.

TR: The first thing I have to start with is the incredible story of your birth. You often say you're the "luckiest guy in the world," and you really mean it. Tell me about that.

TBP: My mom got pregnant in 1927, and I showed up in May 1928, in a small town in rural Oklahoma. And the doctor said to my father, "Tom, you're going to have to make a tough decision here—whether your wife or your child survives." And my dad said, "You can't do that. Surely you can figure out how to get the baby without losing either one of them." And the lucky thing was, that of two doctors in that small town, my mom's doctor was a surgeon. And he said, "Well, Tom, what you're asking me to do is a Caesarean section. I've never done it. I've seen it. I've read about it, and I'll show you how much I've read." So he took him across the room and showed him a page and a half he had on Caesarean sections. "Tom, this is all I have to go on," he said. My dad read it and looked at him. "I think you can do it." They knelt down and prayed. **And then he talked that doctor into delivering me that day, in 1928, via Caesarean.**

TR: Wow!

TBP: It was 30 years later before they did another Caesarean in that hospital.

TR: **How incredible that your father had the courage not to accept what other people told him when it came to the life and death of those he loved.** He had the courage to say there is another way, and he wouldn't bend. That certainly has influenced your life, hasn't it, Boone? You don't take no for an answer, do you?

TBP: No, I don't.

TR: Well, your father is the ultimate role model of somebody who had the power to make a tough decision. You're here, and your mama lived as well. What a beautiful story. I now understand the reference to "Luckiest Guy in the World."

TBP: Yep.

TR: You've also been deeply impacted by the concept of honesty, which for many people, unfortunately, in the financial industry, isn't a core principle. Talk to me about that.

TBP: Tony, I was on my paper route [as a boy] when I looked down, and something caught my eye, and it was a billfold in the grass. And I recognized it as a neighbor's of someone on my paper route, so I knocked on the door of his house, and I said, "Mr. White, I've found your billfold." And he said, "Oh my gosh, this is very important to me, thank you. I want to reward you." And he gave me a dollar, which I couldn't believe. I mean, a dollar was a lot of money back then.

TR: Of course.

TBP: It was 1940. I was 11 years old.

TR: Wow.

TBP: So I went home, and I was very happy, and I started to tell my mom and my aunt and my grandma my story—that Mr. White had given me a dollar. And they were all shaking their heads. I could tell they didn't like the story, and I said, "Don't you understand? He was happy that I found his billfold and took it to him." And my grandmother looked at me and said, "Son, you're not going to be rewarded for honesty." So it was decided for me to take the dollar back to Mr. White.

TR: That's awesome! So making tough decisions and honesty—those two values have really shaped you. I remember reading a quote from you that inspired me as a kid. I've always been fascinated by what makes someone a leader versus a follower, and you said you always lived your life on your own terms. And I think I remember you saying that the secret to leadership was being decisive.

TBP: We tried to take over Gulf Oil in 1984, and I thought it was a very weak management team. And I said, "These guys can't even pull the trigger. They just aim, aim, aim, and they never fire!"

TR: That's great. So you're able to fire more quickly?

TBP: A lot of people get put in leadership positions, and it drives me crazy because they don't make decisions. They don't want to make decisions; they would like somebody to do it for them. I feel like the decisions I make will be good, and I'll see good results.

TR: Well, that theory has certainly proven itself true. You became a billionaire by understanding energy and taking advantage of it.

TBP: I'm 19 of 21 accurate predictions on oil prices.

TR: Wow, 19 out of 21?

TBP: On CNBC, yes.

TR: That's absolutely incredible. And you got $4-a-gallon gasoline right, yes? No one thought it would go that high back in 2011.

TBP: When I spoke at your event, Tony, back in 2011 in Sun Valley, I stuck my neck out and said we were going to see $120 a barrel by Fourth of July weekend, which we did. I remember saying global demand was going to hit 90 billion barrels a day, and the price was going to have to go up to meet that level of demand.

TR: Many of my Platinum Partners made a lot of money betting on that prediction, Boone. You gave them a synthetic option for taking advantage of that run-up. It was spot-on, thank you. So given your track record: one of the themes I've seen over and over with many of the greatest investors has been a focus on asymmetric risk/reward. How do you think about reducing your risk or making sure it's worth the reward? What's your philosophy on that?

TBP: You get an MBA, that's what they'll teach you: cut your downside and give yourself a greater upside, and the payoff will come. I never approach investing that way.

TR: Really?

TBP: Listen, some deals are better than others, and I think we do a good job analyzing risk. But I can't tell you specifically how I arrive at a decision. I know if I hit it, I'm going to knock it out of the park. And on the same one, maybe I strike out. I am willing to take big risks to make big rewards.

TR: Okay, understood. So let me ask you this: If you couldn't pass on any of your financial wealth, but all you could pass on to your children was an investment philosophy, or a portfolio strategy, what would it be? How would you encourage them so that they could have wealth long term?

TBP: I really believe that if you've got a good work ethic, you probably pass it on. And if you have a good education to go along with a good work ethic, if you're willing to work hard; I believe you can get there. I think the good

work ethic came to me from a small town in Oklahoma. I saw my grandmother and mother and father all work hard; I saw people all around me
work hard. I saw those who got a good education make more money.

TR: It sounds like rather than teach them a portfolio you want to teach them
a mind-set, a work ethic.

TBP: That's right.

TR: You've made and lost billions. What is money to you? What is wealth?

TBP: Well, I can tell you when I knew I was wealthy.

TR: When was that?

TBP: When I had 12 bird dogs.

TR: And how old were you?

TBP: I was 50.

TR: Really!

TBP: I was hunting one day. I'd always had bird dogs, and I'd always been a
quail hunter. My dad was, and I was too. But I had one bird dog in the
backyard, and when I did better, I had two. When I got 12 bird dogs,
I had a kennel. And one day I said, "You know, I'm a rich guy. I've got 12
bird dogs!"

TR: And you've used that wealth to do so much good for this country. I know
that you are one of the most generous university benefactors of all time,
having given over $500 million to your alma mater, Oklahoma State Uni-
versity, which is absolutely incredible.

TBP: My goal has always been to make OSU more competitive, in athletics and
academics. I am privileged to give to my alma mater.

TR: Wasn't your 2005 gift to OSU athletics the single largest in NCAA history?

TBP: That's correct.

TR: That's just amazing. And I know that's just part of your contribution and
giving, which I so admire. Let's switch gears and talk about energy independence. You made your fortune in the oil industry. You're not the most
likely candidate to be preaching oil independence for this country, and
yet that's been your mission for the past seven years. Tell me about the
Pickens Plan.

TBP: Here's the thing, Tony. **America is addicted to oil. And that addiction
threatens our economy, our environment, and our national security.**

It's been getting worse every decade. In 1970 we imported 24% of our oil. Today it's nearly 70%, and growing.

TR: Wow. So you're trying to move us away from that.

TBP: Well, we've put our security in the hands of potentially unfriendly and unstable foreign nations. If we are depending on foreign sources for nearly 70% of our oil, we are in a precarious position in an unpredictable world. And over the next ten years, the cost will be $10 trillion—**it will be the greatest transfer of wealth in the history of mankind.**

TR: That's incredible. So what's the solution?

TBP: We can make huge gains by upgrading to renewable sources of energy, but that doesn't solve our OPEC[23] problem. OPEC actually has nothing to do with renewables; wind and solar are not transportation fuels. That's where natural gas comes in. Seventy percent of all the oil used every day in the world goes for transportation use. The only thing that we've got to take out OPEC is natural gas or our own oil.

TR: So what do we do?

TBP: We import about 12 million barrels a day, five of which come from OPEC. We need to produce more natural gas here in the United States to get rid of the OPEC oil. And we have the resources to do it. **Tony, we're sitting on a hundred-year supply of natural gas here in America.** We've got at least 4 trillion barrels of oil equivalent (BOE). That's three times the amount of the oil reserves that Saudi Arabia has. If we don't capitalize on that, we're going to go down as the dumbest crab that ever came to town.

TR: That's incredible.

TBP: And natural gas is so cheap right now. A $100-barrel of oil is equivalent to [about] $16 of natural gas—we've never seen $16 natural gas. Whether it's for trucking, or power generation, anybody that uses energy today has to consider natural gas.

TR: I know you've spent a ton of your own time, energy, and money on the Pickens Plan. You've taken your case to the American public and

23. Organization of the Petroleum Exporting Countries, which include Saudi Arabia, Iran, Iraq, Kuwait, and others.

bankrolled a national campaign and media blitz. What do you think—is it going to work?

TBP: I launched this plan in Washington, DC, in 2008, and I've spent $100 million of my own money on this. I feel like I've done everything I could on this, and yes, we're going to get an energy plan for America.

TR: I talk a lot about asset allocation in this book. Virtually all of your assets are in energy; that's been most of your life, correct?

TBP: That's right, but in energy you have lots of different sectors. We invest across the energy spectrum but don't go beyond that.

TR: So that's your version of asset allocation. If you were an individual investor today, and you had, let's say, $50,000 to invest, where would you put it?

TBP: Downstream, you have exploration companies and refineries and all. Most of my time has been spent upstream, on the exploring and producing side of the equation. But right now, natural gas is so cheap. It's very interesting; that's the place to be. Overall, I think the oil and gas industry has a fabulous future, because of technology. The advancements we've made in technology have been unbelievable. **Our country today looks a lot better from a standpoint of natural resources than we did ten years ago.** I didn't feel this way ten years ago. I didn't feel near as confident as I do today.

TR: Tell me what drives you, Boone?

TBP: You know, Tony, what drives me at this point is that I like to make money. I like giving it away—not as much as making it, but it's a close second. I firmly believe that one of the reasons I was put here on this earth was to be successful, to make money, and be generous with it.

TR: Be generous?

TBP: One of my goals is to give away $1 billion before I die. You know Warren Buffett's and Bill Gates's Giving Pledge? They called me up and asked me to join. And I said, "If you look at *Fortune* magazine from 1983, **why don't you join** *my club***, where I said I was going to give ninety percent away?"**

TR: That's spectacular.

TBP: Every day I go to the office, and I look forward to going to the office. That's the way it has been throughout my life. And so, my work is everything to me. But you say that, "No, my family is everything to me. You can't say that." It's just all fun. When I'm with my family, it's fun. When I'm working, it's fun. The results aren't perfect, but they're good enough to make you think the next day is going to be a home run. They may not be, but I still think every day will be.

TR: You inspire me, like you inspire so many people around the world. I'm inspired by your passion and intensity. At 86, Boone, with so many extraordinary accomplishments, you just keep on growing and giving.

TBP: Thank you, Tony, you've been a successful man too, and helped so many people—probably helped a lot more than I have.

TR: Oh, I don't know.

TBP: But we're both winners because we do give.

TR: Yes, I agree. I love you dearly, my friend. Thank you.

KYLE BASS:
THE MASTER OF RISK

Founder, Hayman Capital Management

As a competitive diver, Kyle Bass understands the basic law of physics. He knows well that what goes up must come down. That's why in 2005 he began to ask questions about the booming US housing market—questions no one else thought to ask, like, "What happens if housing prices don't keep going up [forever]?" Those questions led him to make one of the biggest bets in the world on the impending housing crash of 2008 and the economic meltdown that followed. That trade would earn him his first billion. Bass would go on to make a 600% return on his money in just 18 months and secure his place as one of the brightest, most thoughtful hedge fund managers of his time.

Kyle does very few interviews, but it turned out my work had inspired him while he was still in college, so I had the privilege of flying out to Texas to sit down with him in his skyscraper building overlooking the great city of Dallas. Bass is one of the few financial powerhouses who views his distance from New York City as a competitive advantage. "We don't get bogged down by the noise," he says.

Bass is humble and approachable. When I asked him about the questioning that led him to bet against the housing market, he replied, "Tony, this isn't rocket science, this is just some idiot from Dallas asking questions."

Bass lives with his wife and family and serves on the board of trustees of the University of Texas Investment Management Co., helping to oversee one of the largest public endowments in the country, with over $26 billion in assets. You've already learned about Bass and his nickels: he's the guy who taught his children the lesson of asymmetric risk/reward by buying up $2 million worth of nickels and earning a 25% return on Day One of his investment. In fact, Bass says he'd put his entire net worth in nickels if he could find that many coins on the market to buy!

Nickels aside, Bass's relentless focus on asymmetric risk/reward has led to two of the biggest return bets of the century: in both the housing market and the European debt crisis that began in 2008. And he's got a third bet under way that he says is even bigger. What follows is an excerpt of our two-and-a-half-hour conversation in his downtown office.

TR: Tell me a little about yourself.

KB: I was a springboard and platform diver, which people think is intensely physical. But it's 90% mental. It's basically you versus yourself. For me, it was very rewarding. It taught me how to be disciplined and how to learn from my failures. It's really how you deal with failure that defines you as a person. I have a loving mother and a loving father, but they never saved any money. I swore I would never be like that. My parents both smoked; I swore I would never smoke. For me, I've always been driven harder by the negative things in my life versus the positive—there are many congruencies in my life and your teachings.

TR: Absolutely. When I look at the one common denominator that makes somebody succeed, beyond education or talent, it's hunger.

KB: Hunger and pain.

TR: The hunger comes from the pain. You don't get really hungry when it's been easy.

KB: That's right.

TR: So your hunger drove you to start your own fund. It was 2006, right?

KB: Correct.

TR: The thing that's so amazing to me is the speed at which you started producing returns.

KB: That was lucky.

TR: You had 20% the first year and, like, 216% the next year, right?

KB: That's right. It was just fortuitous that early on I saw what was going on in the mortgage market. I believe in the saying "Luck is where preparation meets opportunity." I think I might have read that in one of your books when I was in college. Well, I was prepared. I like to think that I was lucky and in the right place at the right time because I had all my resources dedicated to that in the moment.

TR: A lot of people knew about [the housing] problem and didn't act on it. What was different about you? What really made you succeed in that area?

KB: If you remember back then, money was basically "free." In 2005 and 2006, you could get a LIBOR-plus-250 term loan [meaning, a very cheap loan], and you and I could go buy any company we wanted with a little bit of equity and a ton of debt. I was on the phone with my friend and colleague Alan Fournier at the time, and we were trying to figure out how *not* to lose betting against housing. And the pundits kept saying, "Housing is a product of job growth and income growth," so as long as you had income growth and job growth, home prices would keep going up. That, of course, was flawed thinking.

TR: Yes, as we all found out.

KB: I had a meeting at the Federal Reserve in September of 2006, and they said, "Look, Kyle, you're new to this. You have to realize that income growth drives housing." And I said, "But wait, housing has moved in perfect tandem with median income for fifty years. But in the last four years, housing has gone up 8% a year, and incomes have moved only 1.5%, so we're five or six standard deviations[24] from the mean." To bring those relationships back in line again, incomes would have to go up almost 35%, or housing had to drop 30%. So I called around all the desks on Wall Street, and I said, "I want to see your model. **Show me what happens if home prices go up only four percent a year, two percent a year, or zero percent." There wasn't one Wall Street firm, not one, in June of 2006 that had a model that contemplated housing being flat.**

TR: Are you serious?

KB: Not one.

TR: These guys just drank their own Kool-Aid.

KB: So in November of 2006, I asked UBS to put forth a model that had flat home prices. And their model said that losses to the mortgage pool would be 9%. [A mortgage pool is a group of mortgages with similar maturities and interest rates that were lumped together into a single package, or security, called a *mortgage-backed security*. These securities were assigned a high credit rating and then sold to investors—for an expected return. Assuming house prices continued to go up, the pool would deliver high returns.] But if home prices didn't go up, if they just sat still, these things were going to lose 9%. I called Alan Fournier of Pennant Capital Management [he formerly worked for David Tepper's Appaloosa Management], and I said, "This is it." And when I formed the general partner of my subprime funds, I named it AF GP—after Alan Fournier, because of the phone call we had. Because for me, that phone call flipped the switch.

TR: Wow. And can you tell me what the risk-reward ratio of that bet for you and Alan was?

KB: Basically, I could bet against housing and only pay 3% a year. If I bet a dollar, and home prices went up, all I could lose was three cents!

TR: Amazing. So the risk—the price to bet against housing—was totally out of whack.

KB: Yep. It only cost me 3%.

24. In finance, standard deviation is applied to the annual rate of return of an investment to measure the investment's volatility. Standard deviation is also known as historical volatility and is used by investors as a gauge for the amount of expected volatility.

TR: Because everyone thought the market would go up forever. And the up-side?

KB: If housing stayed flat or went down, I'd make the whole dollar.

TR: So 3% downside if you were wrong, 100% upside if you were right.

KB: Yes. And it's a good thing I didn't listen to every mortgage expert I met with. They all said, "Kyle, you have no idea what you're talking about. This isn't your market. This can't happen." I said, "Okay. Well, that's not a good enough reason for me, because I've done a lot of work on this, and I may not understand everything you understand." But I could see the forest for the trees. And the people that live in that market, all they could see were the trees.

TR: You understood the core of risk/reward.

KB: I also heard this a lot: "Well, that can't happen because the whole financial system would crash." That still wasn't good enough for me either. That bias—the positive bias that we all have is built in; it's innate in human nature. You wouldn't get out of bed if you weren't positive about your life, right? It's a bias we have as humans to be optimistic.

TR: It works for us everywhere but in the financial world.

KB: That's exactly right.

TR: What's even more amazing is that after calling the housing bust, you were also right about Europe and Greece. How did you do that? Again, I'm trying to understand the psychology of how you think.

KB: In mid-2008, post–Bear Stearns, right before Lehman went bankrupt, we sat in here with my team and said, "Okay, what's going on throughout this crisis is that the risk in the world—that used to be on private balance sheets—is moving to the public balance sheets. So let's get a white board and let's reconstruct the public [government] balance sheets of the nations. Let's look at Europe, let's look at Japan, let's look at the United States. Let's look everywhere there's a lot of debt, and let's try to understand." So I thought, "If I'm Ben Bernanke [head of the Fed at the time] or Jean-Claude Trichet, president of the European Central Bank, and I want to get my arms around this problem, what do I do? How do I do it? Well, here's what I'd do: I'd look at my own balance-sheet debts as a country. And then I need to know how big my banking system is in relation to two things: my GDP [gross domestic product], and to my government revenue."

TR: Makes sense.

KB: So we basically looked at a bunch of different countries and asked, "How big is the banking system? How many loans are out there?" Then we tried to figure out how many of them were going to go bad, and then back-solved for how bad it was going to be for us as a country. So I told my team to go call some firms and find out how big those countries' banking systems were. Guess how many firms had a handle on that mid-2008?

TR: How many?

KB: Zero. Not one. And we called everybody.

TR: Wow!

KB: So I dug into the white papers on sovereign [country] debt and read them all. They are mostly focused on emerging economies, because historically, it was emerging nations that restructured their sovereign balance sheets.

TR: Developed nations only restructured postwar.

KB: Right. Two countries spend a fortune to go to war; they run up debts, and to the victor go the spoils and to the loser went defeat, every time. That's how the world works. **In this case, it was the largest accumulation of debt in peacetime in world history.**

TR: Amazing.

KB: So how big is the banking system? We went out there and gathered the data and used two denominators: GDP and central government tax revenue. And this was a huge learning process because we had never done it before.

TR: It sounds like nobody else had.

KB: This isn't rocket science, Tony. This is some idiot in Dallas saying, "How do I get my arms around the problem?" And so we did the work, and I came up with charts, and I said, "Rank them worst to best." Who is the single worst entry on that sheet?

TR: Iceland?

KB: Right, Iceland went first. Who was next? It wasn't rocket science.

TR: Greece?!

[*Kyle nods yes.*]

TR: Wow.

KB: So we did all this work, and I looked at the analysis, and I said, "This can't be right." I was being hyperbolic to my team. I was saying, "If this is right, you know what's going to happen next."

TR: Correct.

KB: So then I asked, "Where are the insurance contracts trading on Ireland and Greece?" and my team said, "Greece is eleven basis points." Eleven basis points! That's 11/100ths of 1%. And I said, "Well, we need to go buy a billion of that one."

TR: Wow, that's incredible.

KB: Mind you, this is third-quarter 2008.

TR: The writing was on the wall at that stage.

KB: I called Professor Kenneth Rogoff at Harvard University, who didn't know me from Adam. And I said, "I've spent several months constructing a world balance sheet and trying to understand this." I said, "The results of our construct, they're too negative for me." I literally said, "I think I must be misinterpreting these. Could I come sit down and share with you the results of my work?" and he said, "By all means."

TR: That's great.

KB: So I spent two and a half hours with him in February of 2009. And I'll never forget: he got to the summary page, with a chart of all the data, and he sat back in his chair, put his glasses up, and said, "Kyle, I can hardly believe it's this bad." And I'm immediately thinking, "Oh shit! All of my fears are being confirmed by the father of sovereign balance sheet analysis." So if he wasn't thinking about it, do you think Bernanke and Trichet were? No one was thinking about this; there was no cohesive plan.

TR: None?

KB: He was dealing with curveballs as they were being thrown.

TR: That's just unbelievable. So I have to ask about Japan, because I know that's what you're focused on now.

KB: Right now, the biggest opportunity in the world is in Japan, and it's way better than subprime was. The timing is less certain, but the payoff is multiples of what the subprime market was. **I believe the world's stress point is Japan. And it's [about] the cheapest it's ever been right now—meaning, [to buy] a kind of insurance policy.**

TR: Yes, and what is it costing you?

KB: Well, the two things to take into account for the options pricing model are (1) the risk-free rate and the (2) volatility of the underlying asset.

So imagine if the turkey used this theory. If he were gauging his risk [of being killed] based upon the historical volatility of his life, it would be zero risk.

TR: Right.

KB: Until Thanksgiving Day.

TR: Until it's too late.

KB: When you think about Japan, there's been ten years of suppressed prices and subdued volatility. The volatility is mid-single digits. **It's as low as any asset class in the world. The risk-free rate is one-tenth of 1%.** So when you ask the price on an option, the formula basically tells you it should be free.

TR: Right.

KB: So if the Japanese bonds move up 150 basis points to 200 basis points [1.5% to 2%], it's over. The whole system detonates, in my opinion.

TR: Wow.

KB: But my theory is, I have always said to our investors, "If it moves two hundred basis points, it's going to move fifteen hundred."

TR: Right.

KB: It's either going to sit still and do nothing, or it's going to blow apart.

TR: This all plays into your idea of "tail risk." Tell me what tail risk is; not many investors focus on it.

KB: If you look at what I'm doing, I'm spending three or four basis points a year on Japan. That's four-hundredths of 1%, okay? If I'm right about the binary nature of the potential outcome of the situation there, these bonds are going to trade at 20% yields or higher. So I'm paying four-tenths of 1% for an option that could be worth 2,000%! **Tony, there has never been a more missed-price option that's existed in the world's history.** Now, that's my opinion. I could be wrong. So far I am, by the way.

TR: You're wrong on timing.

KB: I'll tell you what. I can be wrong for ten years, and if I'm right ten years from now, it was still 100% odds on that to be there before it happened. And people say to me, "How you can bet on that, because it's never happened before?" And I say, "Well, how can you be a prudent fiduciary if I give you the scenario I just laid out, and not do this? Forget whether you think I'm right or wrong. When I show you the cost, how do you not do that? If your home is in an area that is prone to fire, and 200 years ago there was a big fire that wiped everything out, how do you not pay for home owner's insurance?"

TR: Got it, that's awesome. So let me ask you this: Do you consider yourself to be a significant risk taker?

KB: No.

TR: I didn't think so; that's why I asked. Why do you say you're not a risk taker?

KB: Let me rephrase that. Significant risk taker means we can lose all of our money. I never set myself up for the knockout punch.

TR: Tell me this: If you could not pass on any of your money to your children, but you can only pass on a portfolio and a set of rules, what would that look like for your kids?

KB: I'd give them a couple hundred million dollars' worth of nickels because then they wouldn't have to worry about anything.

TR: They're done, their investment portfolio is done. Oh my God, that's wild. What gives you the most joy in life?

KB: I have my kids.

TR: That's awesome!

KB: A hundred percent.

TR: Kyle, thank you. I so enjoyed this, and I learned a lot!

MARC FABER:
THE BILLIONAIRE
THEY CALL DR. DOOM

Director of Marc Faber Limited;
Publisher of *Gloom, Boom & Doom* report

The fact that Marc Faber's investment newsletter is called the *Gloom, Boom & Doom* report should give you a hint about his outlook on markets! But this Swiss billionaire isn't your average bear. Marc, who's been a friend of mine for many years, is a colorful, outspoken contrarian who follows the advice of the 18th-century investor Baron Rothschild: "The best time to buy is when there's blood in the streets." And like Sir John Templeton, he hunts for bargains that everybody else ignores or avoids. That's why, while so many are focused on the US stock market, Marc Faber looks almost exclusively to Asia for his growth investments. He's also a blunt critic of all central banks, particularly the US Federal Reserve, which he blames for destabilizing the world's economy by flooding it with trillions of dollars, virtually "printed" out of thin air.

Marc has earned the nickname "Dr. Doom" by continually predicting that the most popular assets are overpriced and headed for collapse. As the *Sunday Times* of London wrote, "Marc Faber says the things nobody wants to hear." But he's often been right, especially in 1987, when he made a huge fortune anticipating the US stock market crash.

Faber's father was an orthopedic surgeon, and his mother came from a family of Swiss hoteliers. He earned a PhD in economics at the University of Zurich, and started his financial career with the global investment firm White Weld & Company. By 1973, he had transferred to Asia, and never looked back. From his office in Hong Kong and his villa in Chiang Mai, Thailand, Marc has had a front row seat to the incredible transformation of China from a communist quagmire to the growth engine that drives the whole region. He's now considered one of the leading experts in Asian markets.

Marc is known for his eccentricity—he gleefully acknowledges his reputation as a "connoisseur of the world's nightlife"—and is a popular speaker at financial forums and on cable news shows. **He's a member of the prestigious Barron's Roundtable, where, according to independent observers, his recommendations have had the highest returns, almost 23% per annum, for 12 years in a row.** Marc is also the author of several books on Asia, and the director of Marc Faber Limited, a Hong Kong–based advisory and investment fund. Marc speaks English with a gravelly Swiss accent and never takes himself too seriously. Here's an excerpt from my onstage interview with him at my Sun Valley economic conference in 2014.

TR: What would you say are the three biggest investment lies that are still promoted in the world today?

MF: Well, I think everything is a lie! It's always very simple! But, I mean, look: I've met a lot of very honest people and so forth, but unfortunately, in your lifetime, you will come across more salesman-type financial advisors. You should really have people that are very honest. But I can tell you this from experience: everybody will always sell your dream investments, and my experience has been, being the chairman of many different investment funds, usually the clients make very little money. But the managers of the fund and the promoters, they all walk away with a lot of money. All of them.

TR: Where should investors turn?

MF: There are different theories in the investment world. There are essentially the efficient-market theory proponents. They say that markets are efficient. In other words, when you invest, the best is just to buy an index. And the individual selection of securities is basically useless. But I can tell you, I know many fund managers that have actually significantly outperformed the markets over time, significantly. I believe that some people have some skills at analyzing companies because they're either good accountants or they have skills.

TR: What do you think of the markets these days?

MF: I think there's still risk in the emerging world, and it's still too early to buy their currencies and stocks—and it's too late to buy the US. I don't want to buy the S&P index after it reaches 1,800. I don't see any value. So best is to go drinking and dancing and do nothing! Do you understand? It was Jesse Livermore [a famous early-20th-century trader] who said, "The most money made is by doing nothing, sitting tight." Sitting tight means you have cash.

In your life, the important thing is not to lose money. If you don't see really good opportunities, why take big risks? Some great opportunities will occur every three, four, or five years, and then you want to have money. There was a huge opportunity in US housing prices at the end of 2011. Actually, I wrote about this. I went to Atlanta to look at homes, and then Phoenix. I don't want to live there, but there was an opportunity. But the opportunity closed very quickly, and the individuals were at a disadvantage because the hedge funds came in [with cash]—the private equity guys, they just bought thousands of homes away.

TR: Do you see deflation or inflation coming?

MF: The inflation-deflation debate is misplaced, in my view, in the sense that inflation should be defined as an increase in the quantity of money. If the money in circulation increases, as a result credit increases, we have monetary inflation. This is the important point: monetary inflation. Then we have the symptoms of this monetary inflation, and these symptoms can be very diverse. It can be an increase in consumer prices, it can be an increase in wages, but again, it's not as simple as that because in the US, we have, in many sectors actually, a decline in wages in real terms over the last 20 or 30 years already, inflation adjusted. But what about the wages in Vietnam and in China? In China, wages have been going up at the rate of something like 20% or 25% per annum and also elsewhere in emerging economies.

So to answer your question, in a system, we can have deflation in certain things, and assets and goods and prices and even services and inflation in others. It's very seldom that in the world everything will go up in price at the same rate or everything will collapse in price at the same rate. Usually, if you especially have a fiat currency system, those who can print money, and what you will have is the money doesn't really disappear. It just goes into something else. What can disappear is credit—that's why you could have an overall price level that would be declining.

But for us investors, we essentially want to know which prices will go up. Like, "Is the price of oil going to go up or down?" Because if it goes up, then maybe I want to own some oil shares; and if it goes down, I may want to own something else.

TR: What would you suggest would be the asset allocation to take advantage of in the environment we're in right now and to protect yourself?

MF: Well, my asset allocation used to be 25% shares [stocks], 25% gold, 25% cash and bonds, and 25% real estate. Now I have reduced my stock positions as a percentage of the total assets. I have more cash than I would normally have. I increased the real estate in Vietnam, and I increased the equity portfolio in Vietnam.

TR: So what might that look like today then, percentage-wise, out of curiosity?

MF: Well, I mean, it's difficult to tell because it's so big.

TR: Are you talking about portfolio or something else?

MF: [*Laughs.*] No, the thing is this: I don't know! I mean, I'm not counting everything every day.

TR: Well, what would it look like roughly?

MF: Roughly, I think bonds and cash would be now something like 30%, 35%. And then stocks maybe 20%; then real estate, I don't know, 30%; and gold 25%. It's more than 100%, but who cares? I'm the US Treasury!

TR: We know why you like cash. What about bonds, when many people are afraid they're at the lowest level they can be?

MF: The bonds I traditionally hold are emerging-market bonds. The corporate bonds are also mostly in dollars and euros. But I want to explain this very clearly. These emerging-market bonds have a very high equity character. If the stock markets go down, the value of these bonds also decline. Like, in 2008, they tumbled like junk bonds. So they're more like equities than Treasuries. I own some of these. That's why when I say I've a low equity exposure of 20%, my equity exposure through these bonds is probably more than 20%—maybe 30%.

I think sometimes as an investor, we make a mistake that we have too much confidence in our view, because my view is irrelevant for the whole marketplace, do you understand? The market will move independently of my view, so I may not be optimistic about Treasuries, but I could see a condition under which Treasuries would actually be quite a good investment even for a few years. You will only earn your 2.5% or 3%. But that may be a higher return in a world where asset prices go down. Do you understand? If the stock market goes down for the next three years by, say, 5% per annum or 10% per annum, and you have this yield of 2.5% to 3%, then you'll be the king.

TR: What about other asset classes?

MF: There's a lot of speculation for high-end real estate; high-end real estate is at an incredibly inflated level. I believe all these inflated levels—I'm not saying they can't go any higher, but I am suggesting that one day they'll come down meaningfully. And that in that condition, you want to have something that is a hedge.

TR: You have a quarter of your assets in gold. Why?

MF: Actually, what is interesting is when I told this to audiences before 2011 [when prices started dropping], people said, "Marc, if you're so positive about gold, why would you only have 25% of your money in gold?" I said, "Well, maybe I'm wrong, and I want to be diversified because the gold price has already had a big move and is due for consolidation." Gold is probably to some extent a hedge, but not a perfect hedge in an asset-deflation scenario if you have it in physical form. But it's probably a better investment than a lot of other illiquid assets. It will probably also go down in price, but less than other stuff. Treasury bonds, for a few years at least, should do okay in a deflation scenario for asset prices—at least until the government goes bankrupt!

TR: Last question. If you couldn't pass on money to your kids, only a set of principles to build a portfolio, what would they be?

MF: I think the most important lesson I would give a child or anyone is: it's not important what you buy; it's the price at which you pay for something. You have to be very careful about buying things at a high price. Because then they drop, and you're discouraged. You have to keep cool and have money when your neighbors and everybody else is depressed. You don't want to have money when everybody else has money, because then everybody else also competes for assets, and they are expensive.

I would also say, look, I personally think we have in general no clue about what will happen in five or ten minutes' time, let alone in a year's time or ten years' time. We can make certain assumptions, and sometimes they look fine and sometimes they're bad and so forth, but we really don't know for sure. That's why as an investor, I would say you should be diversified.

Now, not every investor can do that because some investors, they invest in their own business. If I have a business like I'm Bill Gates, then I put all my money in Microsoft—and that was, for a while, at least, a very good investment. Probably for most people, the best is to have their own business and to invest in something where they have a special edge compared with the rest of the market; where they have an insider's knowledge. That's what I would do. Or give money to a portfolio manager. If you're very lucky, he will not lose your money, but you have to be very lucky.

CHARLES SCHWAB: TALKING TO CHUCK, THE PEOPLE'S BROKER

Founder and Chairman of Charles Schwab Corporation

You've seen the ads: a handsome, white-haired man looks directly at you through the camera and urges you to "own your tomorrow." Or maybe you remember the ones where cartoon people ask questions about their investments, and a balloon pops up encouraging them to **"Talk to Chuck." That's the style of personal engagement and openness that's kept Charles Schwab at the pinnacle of the discount brokerage industry for the past 40 years, and has helped build a financial empire with $2.38 trillion in client assets under management,** 9.3 million brokerage accounts, 1.4 million corporate retirement plan participants, 956,000 banking accounts, and a network serving 7,000 registered investment advisors.

Before Chuck Schwab came along, if you wanted to buy some stocks, you had to go through a cartel of traditional brokers or brokerage firms that charged exorbitant fees for every trade. But in 1975, when the Securities and Exchange Commission forced the industry to deregulate, Schwab created one of the first discount brokerages and pioneered a whole new way of doing business that shook Wall Street to its core. He led an investor revolution, where suddenly individuals could participate fully in the markets without costly middlemen. While clubby brokerages like Merrill Lynch raised their trading fees, Charles Schwab slashed—or even eliminated—his fees and offered an array of no-frills services that put the clients' interests first and established the model for a new industry. Later he led the charge into electronic trading, and he continues to pioneer innovations that educate and empower investors to make their own decisions.

At age 76, Chuck Schwab comes across with tremendous humility and integrity. "People seem to have confidence in us," he told me. "We try to treat everyone with the sense that we are trustworthy and we need to take care of their assets in a very cautious way."

It's possible that Chuck's modesty and quiet confidence come from a life spent overcoming a series of challenges, beginning with a struggle with dyslexia—a learning disability he shares with a surprising number of ultra-successful business leaders, from Richard Branson of the Virgin Group to John Chambers of Cisco Systems. Despite his reading difficulties, Chuck graduated from Stanford University and earned an MBA from Stanford Business School. He launched his career in finance in 1963 with an investment newsletter. Chuck embraced his status as a Wall Street outsider and planted his flag in his native California, establishing his brokerage firm in San Francisco in 1973. Since then, the Charles Schwab Corporation has ridden the wild bull and bear markets of the past four decades, bouncing back from the crashes of 1987, 2001, and 2008 that wiped out lesser firms, taking on the slew of copycat companies that eroded its market share, always finding ways to innovate and grow in every environment.

Although he turned over the reins as CEO in 2008, Chuck stays active in the company as its chairman and largest single shareholder. According to

Forbes, **Chuck Schwab has a personal fortune of $6.4 billion.** With his wife and his daughter, Carrie Schwab-Pomerantz, he's been incredibly involved in the family's private foundations, which support entrepreneurial organizations working in education, poverty prevention, human services, and health. He's also chairman of the San Francisco Museum of Modern Art.

Chuck Schwab and I both have crazy schedules, but we were finally able to meet in his San Francisco offices just as this book was about to go to press. Here are some excerpts from that conversation:

TR: Everyone knows the name **Charles Schwab.** They know the institution. But most people don't really know your story. I wonder if you would just share a few highlights? I understand you started becoming interested in investing as early as thirteen?

CS: That's right. When I was thirteen, it was right after World War II, and the world wasn't too rich. My dad was a small-town lawyer in California's Sacramento Valley, and certainly our family wasn't very rich. I thought I'd be better off in life if I had more money, so I had to figure out how to make money. I talked to my dad about it, and he encouraged me to read biographies of the famous people in America. And they all seemed to do something about investing. So I said, "Man, that's for me!"

    So when I was 13, I started a chicken company. Raised chickens and all that. And then I did a bunch of other little business kinds of things. So I knew a lot about business and started thinking about how businesses function and operate.

TR: What was your original vision? And what were your first real practical steps? Give me highlights, if you would, to give people a sense of your journey.

CS: Well, I was quite lucky early in the journey. I started out as a financial analyst, and I had some ups and downs along the way. I was about 35, and I had a lot of experience before I really started the company in 1973. And as a result, I knew some of the handicaps of the financial business. Including why they didn't treat people well enough. It was because they were really focused on making *themselves* money—but not on giving the investor a fair shake. They always thought about their institution and making money first. I said, "*Aha!* There's gonna be a different way!"

TR: What has been the **competitive advantage at Charles Schwab** over the years? I mean, if you look at the size of the North American investment market, I think it's about $32 trillion. And you guys have to represent a sizeable amount.

CS: We're probably 5% to 10% of the retail market. Something like that. But you know, as I got into business, **I wanted to look at every product, every service that we offer clients,** *through clients' eyes*. We would design a product like a no-load mutual fund. We did it in a big way. We made it **free** for people to buy no-load funds through us, years ago.

People would say, "Well, how are you gonna make money at that?" So we figured out a way to make some money at it. We worked with the mutual fund companies and convinced them to pay us a little fee out of their management fees. And our clients would benefit from it. And it flourished. So the individual got a great advantage by buying a plethora of no-load mutual funds for no fee. We did the same kind of analysis along the way for other things that we did. We looked at it first through the clients' eyes.

But **Wall Street did just the reverse.** They always made a decision: "How much money can we make on this first? Okay, let's do it. Let's go sell it, boys." That's the way they made decisions. We were completely the opposite.

TR: Has that shifted? Or is it still the same?

CS: It's still the same. And that's why it's a pretty interesting market for us. You know, we have sort of an unlimited destiny, I think, to continue to treat the client as the king. And make sure we do everything that's in *their* interests first. Yes, we will make a little bit of money. Which we do, of course. We're a profit-making organization. But first, we think about the client.

TR: What do you think are the two or three myths that you try to point out to them to pay attention to so they don't get sucked in when they think about investing?

CS: Well, it's so easy. I've watched it in Wall Street so many times. You see the abuses that come about. Some really fancy broker comes along and says, "Ma'am, would you like to make some money?" Of course, we all say, "*Yes!*" And then you get engaged in the conversation. "These guys have the best widget you've *ever seen in your life*. And it's gonna be just like another Apple." So we all, naturally, sort of listen to the story, then say, "Okay, I'll put some money into that."

Well, the probability of that working out is about 1 in 10,000. It's like, why don't you just go to the horses? Or buy a lottery ticket that day? That'll satisfy your speculative thing. Put the real money you have into an index fund, where you know the outcome is going to be highly predictable and returns will be really quite good.

TR: So many people will get hurt because they don't know things and they don't ask questions. And you're one of the first people to say, "Ask questions."

CS: Right.

TR: But very few people know the questions to ask. You know, they see a mutual fund, and they see its return. And they think that's the return they receive. And as you and I both know, that's just not true.

CS: It's just not true. It's never. Anything of the past is never promised for the future. But there are reasons why we put out a pamphlet, a white paper on index funds. We talk about the reason why stocks are the greatest place, really, to have long-term investments. And the reason why is that companies are in business to grow. Every board I've ever been on—and I've done six or seven different Fortune 500 boards—every conversation at the board meeting is about growth. How can we grow this company? If you don't grow, you fire the management. Get a *new management team in.*

Now, that building over there is a beautiful building. But you come back 100 years from now. That building would still be the same size. Or be knocked down. But it doesn't grow. Only companies grow. And that's why it's a fantastic thing to go to stocks. And, of course, in our case, we try to encourage people to go into index funds, so they get a broad blend of industries and stocks and so forth. Then they have—

TR: —the lowest costs.

CS: The lowest costs, and they get a high degree of certainty that they're going to do as well as the index will do. And if you look at any industries over the last 100 years, they've done extraordinarily well over time and brought great returns to clients.

TR: If you listen to Vanguard's Jack Bogle or somebody like David Swensen from Yale, they all say passive management is the way to go. Because 96%

of all mutual funds do not match the index over a ten-year period of time. But how do you feel about it for the average investor: passive versus active?

CS: Well, I'm a mixed investor. I invest in a lot of individual stocks. But I have the time. I have the expertise. I have the education. But 98% of people *don't focus on that.* They have other things in life to do, rather than fuss around with investments as I have done, or Warren Buffett has. You know, they are professionals, and they're doctors. Or lawyers. They're whatever. We need all those people to make a successful society. And maybe 2% of us really know about investing. So the rest of the people need some help and advice. That's what I learned early on, and that's what we do today. **And the 98% should really predominantly go into index funds, in my view. They have the most predictable outcomes.** Better than they would ever do by trying to pick different things, which is very difficult to do. And *then* do their other job too. You can't do both.

TR: The other part is, people just don't realize what the cost is, as Jack Bogle points out. For every 1% over the lifetime of investing, it's 20% of your money you're giving up.

CS: Yeah. It's over.

TR: Give up 2%, that's 40%. Give up 3%, that's 60%.

CS: That's a whole lot. And on an after-tax basis, it really mounts up.

TR: Every major investor that I spoke to talks of the fact that **asset allocation is the single most important investment decision a person can make.** You deal with so many different *types of investors.* What philosophy do you try to have your team apply to help people understand what their asset allocation should be?

CS: Well, it's actually pretty easy today. It wasn't that true 40 years ago. Now we have index funds that we mentioned. And ETFs. So you can get different slices of the market so you can have plenty of diversification. You want energy stocks? You can get an energy ETF. You want medical devices? You can do that. And, of course, I tend to believe you should be diversified among the very biggest and ten biggest industry groupings. And that's what you generally get in a general index fund. You get all of them, because you never know. Sometimes electronic equipment will be going, zooming right up. Oil might not be doing so well. But next year? Oil is in demand, so oil prices are going up. And that does well. And so on and so forth. But it allows you to get the balance of the benefits of each of these sectors.

TR: How do you feel about investing in America versus international, when you're trying to create that asset allocation?

CS: That's another level of sophistication, which I think everybody should have in their portfolio. Some chunk devoted to international, because the very simple fact is, America is growing at about 2% to 3% per annum now. There are many other countries that are beginning to, from China to Indonesia to Japan, have better growth than America. So that's where you're gonna get your returns, where there is better growth, frankly.

But even though the American economy is only growing 2%, there are some parts of our economy that are really growing quite fast. So obviously you want to be attracted to them too.

TR: Where do you see the **world going in the next ten years**? What do you think those opportunities and challenges are for investors?

CS: I think there are enormous opportunities ahead of us still. Despite how slow things are going right now. It will explode once we get the kind of policies I think will eventually get back in. Because there's no way you're gonna take the growth component out of America. The innovation going on in this country is profound. I mean, I live in the San Francisco area, where it's just going, busting at the seams wherever you walk. It's there.

TR: Are we in a market bubble with the Fed controlling rates the way they are? Where you would have to take significant risk to see rewards? The market seems to be the only place for the money to go. How long does that last?

CS: Well, I'm not a great fan of the present policy of the Federal Reserve. I think manipulating rates, as long as they have, is really not the right decision. And I guess it does create the potential and the possibility of some kind of bubble. It won't be forever. We will probably pay a price for it. But it's not a permanent issue. And so there'll be some high inflation or down markets. There will be a consequence for what we're doing now. But we'll get through it. As we do every time there're bad decisions made by policymakers.

TR: They all have a different language for it, but for every single major investor in the world, one of their competitive advantages is asymmetric risk/

reward. They take a little risk to try to get a big reward. How does the average investor do that today? Is there any insight you can give them?

CS: Well, I think it's all coming back to the answer: **Where can you get the best growth? Understanding the fundamentals of growth is crucially important to get long-term returns.** Now, in the case of Warren Buffett, he learned that at a young age. He just buys companies, and he never sells. Why? Companies keep growing. They just keep growing. And he gets richer and richer.

TR: He doesn't pay taxes.

CS: And he doesn't pay taxes. If you don't sell, you don't pay taxes!

TR: That's pretty awesome.

CS: That's his mystery. The myth has been solved! *He doesn't sell!*

TR: I believe you have five children.

CS: And twelve grandkids.

TR: Twelve grandkids! Tell me: If you could leave none of your money to your children, but you could only leave a set of investment principles and maybe a portfolio, what would be your advice to them?

CS: Well, I think it really starts with earning your own money. Having success in that. And the concept of putting some money aside.

- Make sure you get the right education. And hopefully it fits into the marketplace, where jobs are being created.
- You've got to have a well-paying job, which are not that plentiful today.
- And then putting the money aside in your 401(k) or IRA. It takes giving up things. Not buying that car. Giving up that vacation. Having something set aside.
- And then you could begin doing the proper investing.

It's a pretty simple formula. Lots of people don't realize it, but hopefully you can teach people to do that.

TR: [*Laughs.*] Hopefully I can!

CS: You know, I believe in leaving something. Making sure the kids are educated, but not sizeable sums of money. Don't take away their sense of their own opportunity, their own ego development. Their own kinds of things that will fulfill them. You have to be a really curious person. Make sure every one of your kids is really curious. And it's not necessarily about making money.

Having come from a background of no money and no wealth, I clearly know the difference. And of course, in the last 20 years, I've had the benefit of success, which allows me incredible choices. For my wife and me, we take a vacation without worrying about the cost of it. Having a good time. I enjoy my sports. I love my golf. And it goes on and on and on. And so we want to perpetuate this success. We want our next generations to have what we had, and then some.

TR: You've dealt with so many successful people. You've studied successful companies and the individuals who drive their growth. What do you think is the single most important factor?

CS: You know, maybe it's 99% necessity. But lots of people out there in the world really do need more resources. But they don't have the education. Somehow they didn't have the motivation. Maybe they don't sense opportunity in front of them. How to perceive the opportunity that is right there? You look around at these other guys who have been successful, and you think, "I can do that too." How do you sense that? I don't know.

TR: You're 76 now, and you didn't find out you were dyslexic until you were in your 40s, right?

CS: Right.

TR: A lot of people think of that as a limit on their life. How come it was never a limit to you?

CS: Maybe, thank God, that I didn't know when I was a kid! But my son was just starting school when we took him for testing [and found out he was dyslexic]. I said, "Oh my God. All the things that I had to deal with at age seven, eight, and nine, he's dealing with now!" And it was very clear that I was also dyslexic, so that solved a lot of my issues when I thought back about my early schooling. The alphabet was impossible for me. My reading—even to this day, I don't read novels. I read nothing but nonfiction.

TR: Wow. So what allowed you to succeed in the financial business, then?

CS: Well, I was pretty good at math. And I was pretty good with people. I wasn't a great writer, but I had people around me who were great writers. So you learn very quickly: *you can't do it all yourself.* You need to have people around you who are better than you are at most other things. But you have to be able to inspire the people around you to work together for whatever your common purpose is. And that's what I've been able to do all these years.

TR: What's your passion?

CS: I'm totally passionate about the necessity for people to earn and save and grow because of the responsibility we all have for our own retirements. And goodness gracious, we're gonna live, you know. I'm in my seventies. But the probability now is living to 90, 95. It's a *long time* to be in retirement. And so you've got to put aside a lot of assets, I think, in order to live comfortably.

TR: People I talked to who knew you 20 years ago say your passion is as great or greater than it ever was.

CS: Probably greater. [*Laughs.*]

TR: Wow. Why is that? How have you maintained that? How has that continued to expand?

CS: Well, I have seen, for instance, what you can do with philanthropy. And how you can really help people. By being successful. Well, I couldn't do it if I was *not successful*. I wouldn't have the resources to do it with. But I can make things happen in different ways. Whether it's issues around dyslexia. I can help kids. Or in charter schools, we can help kids. Or if it's in museums, help build better and bigger places for people to come and see and view art.

I think one of the great fulfillments of achieving great success is being able to, in your lifetime, give back to things; that it really enhances many, many times, you know, what people can really enjoy, and yourself.

TR: If someone was starting out brand new, what would be the advantage you would try to give them, looking to start a business? How do you go from the vision of a young man that you were, who said, "I want to really help people look out for the customer," to building a multitrillion-dollar business? What would you tell people they should really focus on?

CS: Well, getting all the education and the practical experience. And then having the patience to do it day in and day out. Day in and day out. It's not easy, let me tell you that. It's like the restaurateur serving great food every meal. It's not easy. But that's how you make a great restaurant. That's how you make a great car dealership. Service every day. You can't miss the ball. You've gotta hit the ball out of the park every day. With service. And the same with technology. In our lifetime, we've seen many companies go in the tank because they weren't able to innovate. Or actually, they didn't figure out a product or service that really served the customer well. They lost their customers. *Never lose a customer.* Figure that one out.

TR: Last question. I'm sure it will be 20 or 30 years from now, because you're taking care of yourself and your health, and you're so passionate, but how do you want to be remembered? What's your legacy for you and what you've built over this lifetime?

CS: Well, I [have] a variety of them, of course. For my family and so forth. In terms of the professional side, **I feel really proud about the fact that I really made a huge change to the practice of Wall Street.** This is an institution that's been around for a couple hundred years. And we, this little company on the West Coast, took them on in different ways. And really made a change in the character of how they treat clients. And they're doing a much better job. Not as good as we are! [*Laughs.*] But they're doing a much better job and are much more thoughtful about how they treat their clients.

TR: You led by example.

CS: Thanks very much.

TR: Blessings to you. Thank you for your time.

SIR JOHN TEMPLETON: THE GREATEST INVESTOR OF THE 20TH CENTURY?

Founder of Templeton Mutual Funds; Philanthropist;
Creator of the £1 Million Templeton Prize

Sir John Templeton wasn't just one of the greatest money masters of all time, he was one of the greatest human beings who ever lived. And I had the honor of counting him as one of my mentors. His motto, "How little we know, how eager to learn," guided his long and dazzling life as an investment pioneer, iconoclast, spiritual seeker, and philanthropist. **Sir John was known for his ability to look at the most difficult situations in the world and find a way to take advantage of them for the greater good.**

John Templeton was not always known as "Sir John." He came from humble beginnings in a small town in Tennessee, where he was reared to value thrift, self-sufficiency, and personal discipline. He worked his way through Yale and Oxford, and got his first job on Wall Street in 1937, in the depths of the Great Depression. He was the original contrarian, who believed in buying shares at "the point of maximum pessimism." **When everyone else thought the world was going to end, John thought it was the right time to invest.** When everyone else thought, "Oh my God! These are the greatest times in history!"—that was when it was time to sell.

He first put his theory to the test in the fall of 1939. With the Depression still raging and Hitler's troops rolling into Poland at the start of World War II, John Templeton decided to take all the money he had saved and borrow some additional money as well and buy $100 worth of every stock valued at $1 or less on the New York exchanges. That portfolio became the basis of a vast personal fortune and asset management empire. He also became a pioneer in international investing. While the rest of Americans refused to look beyond US borders, John was scouring the world for opportunities.

And as his fortune grew, so did his commitment to giving back. **In 1972 he established the world's largest annual award given to an individual, bigger than the Nobel Prize, honoring spiritual achievements.** Mother Teresa was the first recipient of the Templeton Prize. His foundation also funded research in science and technology, and in 1987 Queen Elizabeth knighted him for his enormous contributions to humanity.

Sir John continued to speak and write and inspire millions with his humble message of integrity, entrepreneurship, and faith, right up to the time of his death in 2008 at the age of 95. (Incidentally, he had accurately predicted the collapse of the housing bubble that year.) The following is an excerpt from an interview I conducted with him just months before his passing. His kindness shines through in every answer, as he shares his philosophy that the same qualities that make you a great investor can also make you a great human being.

TR: Sir John, most people seem to be either money oriented or spiritually oriented—they have to be one or the other—but you seem to have found a way to integrate these two in a truly natural and real way in your life. Can people integrate both in their lives?

JT: Definitely! There is no disparity. Would you want to deal with a business-
        man you could not trust? No! If a man has a reputation for not being
        trustworthy, people will run away from him. His business will fail. But if
        another man has high ethical principles, high spiritual principles, he will
        try to give to his customers and his employees more than they expect. If
        so, he will be popular. He will have more customers. He will make more
        profit. He will do more good in the world, and thereby he will prosper
        himself and have more friends and be more respected.

        So always start out to give more than is expected from you, to treat the
        other person more than fairly, and that is the secret of success. Never try
        to take advantage of anyone or to hold anyone back in their own prog-
        ress. **The more you help others, the more prosperous you will be
        personally.**

TR: What was your first investment? What drew you to it, and how did it
        turn out?

JT: I was just getting started when it was the beginning of the Second World
        War in September 1939. We had just finished the world's greatest de-
        pression and there were many bankrupt companies. But a war causes a
        demand for almost every product, so during a war almost every company
        will prosper again. So I gave a stockbroker an order to buy $100 worth of
        every stock on both exchanges selling for $1 or less, and there were 104
        of them. And out of those, I made a profit on 100 and lost money on only
        four.

        So three years later, when my wife and I had an opportunity to take
        over this small practice of a retiring investment counselor, we had the
        savings needed to do that! We began with no clients in Radio City in
        New York and worked there for 25 years, **continuing to save 50 cents
        out of every dollar so that we could build up our assets for our re-
        tirement and for charity.**

TR: Wow! And you got quite a bit of a return saving 50 cents out of every
        dollar, Sir John. Most people today would say "That's impossible! I can't
        save fifty percent of my money and invest it." But that's how you built
        from nothing, and you did this during the Depression! I've also read that
        if someone invested $100,000 dollars with you [in 1940], never put

**another dime in, and forgot about the money, by 1999, that would
have been worth $55 million! Is that the accurate number?**

JT: Yes, provided they reinvested their distributions.

TR: Let me ask about your investing philosophy: in the past, you've said to
        me, "Not only do you buy at maximum pessimism, but you want to sell at
        the peak of optimism." Is that correct?

JT: That's correct. There's a good saying there, Tony. **"Bear markets start
        on the time of pessimism. They rise on the time of skepticism.
        They mature on the time of optimism, and they end on the time of
        euphoria!"** That always happens in every bull market, and it helps you
        determine where you are. If you just talk with enough investors to find
        their psychology, you can tell whether the market is still safe at a low level
        or high at a dangerous level.

TR: What do you think is the single biggest mistake investors make?

JT: The great majority of people do not build up any wealth because they
        do not practice the self-discipline of saving some of their income every
        month. But beyond that, once you've saved that money, then you have
        to invest it wisely in good bargains, and it's not easy. It's very rare for any
        one person, particularly any one person working in just their spare time,
        to select the right investments. **Any more than you would want to be
        your own medical doctor or your own lawyer, it's not wise to try to
        be your own investment manager.** It's better to find the best profes-
        sionals; the wisest security analyst to help you.

TR: When I was talking to some of your associates down in the Bahamas,
        I was asking them, "What does he invest in?" and they said, "Anything!
        He'll buy a tree if he thinks he can get a good deal on it." Then I said,
        "How long will he hang on to it?" and they said, "Forever! Basically until
        it's worth more!" Sir John, how long do you hang on to an investment be-
        fore you know to let it go? How do you know if you've made a mistake?
        How do you know when it's time to actually liquidate?

JT: That is one of the most important questions! Many people will say,
        "I know when to buy, but I don't know when to sell." But over these 54
        years that I've been helping investors, I think I have the answer, and that
        is: you sell an asset only when you think you have found a different asset

that's a 50% better bargain. You search all the time for a bargain, and then you look at what you now own. If there's something in your present list that is a 50% less good bargain than the one you found, you sell the old one and buy the new one. But even then, you're not right all the time.

TR: Sir John, why should Americans feel good about investing outside their own country?

JT: Think about this: if our job is to find the best opportunities, surely we will find more opportunities if we do not limit ourselves to just any one nation. Likewise, perhaps we will find better opportunities if we are able to look everywhere rather than just one nation. But most important is that it does reduce your risk because every nation has bear markets. **Usually twice every 12 years, there's a severe bear market in a major nation, but they do not occur at the same time.** So if you are diversified, having your assets in many nations, you do not have to suffer through the bear market in one nation as a person who had all of his eggs in one basket would.

He have always advised our investors to be diversified—not only diversified into more than one corporation and diversified into more than one industry, but also diversified into more than one nation in order that they will get greater safety and greater potential profit.

TR: What do you think it is that has separated you from all the other investors out there? What's made you one of the greatest investors of all time?

JT: Thank you. I do not regard myself as that. We've not always been right. No one is, but we have tried to be a little better than the other competitors and to give more than is expected from us and always to try to improve our methods, to use new methods in order to stay ahead of the competition. If there's any secret in it at all it is this: **do not try to be a go-getter. Try to be a go-giver!**

TR: Sir John, there's so much fear out there today on so many levels of society. How do we deal with fear?

JT: To overcome fear, the best thing is to be overwhelmingly grateful. If you wake up each morning and think of five new things for which you're overwhelmingly grateful, you're not likely to be fearful, you're likely to radiate your optimism, your attitude of gratitude, you're likely to do things in a better way, draw more people to you. **So I would think an attitude of gratitude will prevent a life of fear.**

TR: I would love to hear through your own perception: Who is Sir John Templeton? What is your life really about? In the end, how do you want to be remembered?

JT: I am a student, always trying to learn. I am a sinner. All of us are. I've tried to be better day by day, and particularly I try to keep asking myself, "What are the purposes of God? Why did God create the universe? What does God expect of his children here?" And the closest you can come in just a few words is: **He expects us to grow spiritually.** He gives us trials and tribulations just like you have examinations in school, because it may help you to grow into a greater soul than you would have otherwise. So life is a challenge. Life is an adventure. It's a marvelous, exciting adventure. All of us should do the very best we can as long as the Lord allows us to be on this planet.

JUST DO IT, ENJOY IT, AND SHARE IT!

THE FUTURE IS BRIGHTER THAN YOU THINK

The point of living is to believe the best is yet to come.
—PETER USTINOV

Why do most people pursue wealth? It's because they're after a greater quality of life. And one thing I know beyond a shadow of a doubt is that anybody can deal with a tough today if he or she feels certain that tomorrow has greater promise.

We all need a compelling future.

So if you're wondering why we would take time to talk about the future and technological breakthroughs in a financial book, it's **because technology is a *hidden asset* that every day is compounding its capacity to enrich your life.**

There are breakthroughs occurring today and in the months and short years to come that will revolutionize the quality of your life and the lives of everyone else on earth. This tide of technology will offer the opportunity for all boats to rise.

And in financial terms, you know what's really great? The cost of technology is decreasing while its capacity is geometrically expanding! What does that mean for you? It means that even if you start building wealth late in life, you will likely still have a great quality of life in the future, for even less money than you might think.

Also, **learning about these trends in technologies can awaken you to some of the greatest investment opportunities of your lifetime. These technologies are growing exponentially. The time to pay attention to them is right now.**

My hope is that this chapter will also inspire you to take greater care of yourself and your family, not only financially but also perhaps physically as well. Without physical health, there is no wealth. Being around long enough to take advantage of some of these huge advances in technology should be a priority—especially after you hear about some of the changes that are unfolding as we speak.

So let's take a brief journey together and explore the cutting edge of our technological future. I'll say in advance: this chapter takes an unabashedly positive view. But it's not just based on my enthusiasm—but rather reflects the work of some of the greatest scientists on the face of the earth. Not those who just predict, but those who deliver what they predict. Individuals who have done everything from decode the human genome, to design the first digital voice recognition system, to develop commercial space shuttles that fly people back and forth to the International Space Station.

Now, I acknowledge that many people have a different, more skeptical view of technology. And perhaps they'll be right. Some look into the future and see a *Terminator*-style dystopia of killer robots and genetically altered Frankenfoods. Others look forward to a world of flying cars, like they had in *The Jetsons*; or android helpers, like *Star Wars*'s C-3PO; or meat and vegetables that can be grown from single cells to feed the world's hungry. None of these extreme scenarios has come to pass yet. I choose to look at how technology will be used to make a massive difference in the quality of our lives. I also understand that people often fear new technologies and worry that we're going too fast.

After all, there has always been a "dark side" to these advances—often because these technologies initially put people out of jobs until they adapt to new forms of employment. As Steven Rattner, the influential financier and columnist, pointed out in the *New York Times*, even Queen Elizabeth I of England refused to patent a 16th-century knitting machine because it would put her "poor subjects" out of work. But according to Rattner, "The trick is not to protect old jobs . . . but to create new ones. And since the invention of the wheel, that's what has occurred."

Most of the time, these new tools have been used to enhance human life. And today some of the biggest challenges in the world, from too much carbon dioxide in the air, to a lack of fresh water, to a scarcity of farmland, are being solved by new technologies. And all this seems to be happening overnight. But throughout history, there has also been a minority who will take any tool or technology and use it as a weapon. Electricity can light up a city or kill someone. But there are millions more streetlights than electric chairs. A Boeing jetliner can carry us across oceans or be used as a bomb to murder thousands—but there are millions more flights than hijackings.

It's natural for human beings to fear the new and unknown, and to focus on worst-case scenarios. Our brains are wired for survival, and that's how we've made it as a species. But our imaginations can also hold us back. Science fiction has made many fear futuristic technologies, like artificial intelligence. But actual scientists and futurists such as Ray Kurzweil, Peter Diamandis, and Juan Enriquez see advanced technologies as an opportunity for humanity to evolve and transform into something better.

So if you're irritated by an optimistic future, you should move on to the next chapter! But if you're a person who is truly interested in knowing how technology is shaping our lives, I think this will help you understand what's available and what's coming. The way I look at it, you can choose to be fearful about the future, or you can embrace it. But nothing is going to change it.

Why? **Because the future is already here.**

> The best way to predict the future is to invent it.
> —ALAN KAY

Every ten minutes in America someone is horribly burned. They're rushed to the hospital in searing pain—one of the most intense pains a human body can suffer. The nurses scrub away the blistered and charred flesh and cover the wound with cadaver skin to keep the person from dying of infection. Can you imagine the skin off a dead body put on top of your own?! If the patient survives, the scarring can be brutal. I'm sure you've seen faces, arms, and legs scarred beyond recognition. Sometimes there are multiple surgeries, and healing can take years.

So imagine how one night Matt Uram, a 40-year-old state trooper, finds himself about to become another one of those grim statistics. His life altered forever.

How? He's next to a bonfire when someone throws a cup of gasoline on the flames, and the burns cover his right arm and the right side of his head and face. The doctors and nurses move fast, cleaning off the blistered skin, disinfecting Matt's wounds, applying salves. Normally he would be in the burn unit for weeks or months, going through the same agonizing process twice a day. Instead, a team of specialists goes to work with a new technique. They harvest a layer of healthy cells from unburned patches of his own skin. No cadaver skin for Matt! These cells are cultured, and before long, a spray gun is gently painting the wounds with a solution of Matt's own stem cells.

Three days later, his arms and face are completely healed. (And this miracle has to be seen to be believed! Go to www.youtube.com/watch?v=eXO _ApjKPaI and see the difference.) There's barely a scar visible on him. I know it sounds like a scene from a sci-fi film. But it's a real story that took place in Pittsburgh just a few years ago.

While the technique that healed Matt Uram is still in clinical trials in the United States, a similar stem cell procedure has already been used on hundreds of burn victims in Europe and Australia. Amazing, isn't it?! Now there's even a "bio-pen" that allows surgeons to draw healthy cells on layers of bone and cartilage. The cells multiply and grow into nerves, muscle, and bones, healing the damaged section. The technology allows the surgeon to place cells wherever he or she wants them, in an instant. And this is just another one of the incredible new therapies coming online and becoming more affordable for everyone.

If you hadn't already noticed: **the world we live in today is a place of everyday miracles, and change is happening so fast that sometimes we don't even notice it.** Or maybe we just take it for granted.

But if you were to describe the world of 2015 to a person back in 1980, just 35 years ago, he would think what you're doing is magic! Spraying on stem cells? Hell, it would be a miracle just to talk to someone on the phone while you were driving in your car, right?

We're used to the idea that we can predict tomorrow by looking at what happened today or yesterday. But that can't be done anymore. Until very "recently," change was very rare, and so slow that it was measured in eras: the Bronze Age, the Iron Age, and so on. Now change is exponential. That means it's speeding up, making huge leaps forward in shorter periods of time. It means we're making tools that can transform the quality of our lives faster and better, and they're available to just about everyone.

The average person today already has options the richest pharaoh in Egypt never dreamed of. Imagine what he would have given to be able to fly in the sky in a chair or in a bed to another part of the world in a few hours, instead of months fighting the oceans? Now you can do that for $494 on Virgin Atlantic Airways.

Even a pharaoh couldn't spend $200 million to make a movie to entertain himself for two hours. And yet every week, multiple new films are coming out that we can enjoy in the theater for $10 (or $9.99 per month on Netflix).

Let's face it, we're living in one of the most extraordinary times on earth. We've seen the lifespan of human beings in the last 100 years go from 31 years old to 67 years old—more than doubling. In the same time, the average per capita income (adjusted for inflation) of every person on this planet tripled. One hundred years ago, the majority of Americans used to spend 43% of each day working just to get food. Now, because of advances in agriculture and distribution, it's 7%.

YOU'VE GOT MAIL!

The first time I met President Bill Clinton back in the early 1990s, I vividly remember sitting down with him and saying, "You know, Mr. President, maybe there's a way we could communicate electronically." He looked puzzled, so I said, "I've started using this new thing called email. I've got an account on AOL. Do you have one?" And the president said, "Oh, I've heard about that!" But there was no email account for the president of the United States back then. Now the phone that an Amazonian tribesman carries around the jungle has more instant computing power than Clinton had at his disposal as leader of the free world. He can go online to buy supplies for his cows or pay his child's school fees. He can translate languages. If he wants, he can access free courses in economics from Yale and math from MIT. We're living in a whole different universe now, and we're just at the beginning of the beginning.

"It keeps me from looking at my phone every two seconds."

And things are getting better, faster, every day. "The future is going to be a whole lot better than you think," says my dear friend Peter Diamandis, founder of the X Prize Foundation, aerospace engineer, medical doctor, entrepreneur, and all-around great human being. "Humanity is now entering a period of radical transformation, in which technology has the potential to significantly raise the basic standards of living for every man, woman, and child on the planet."

What does this mean for you? It means that even if you screw up and don't follow through on anything you've learned in these pages, in the future you'll still be able to enjoy a better quality of life than you ever imagined, even if you don't have a large income. And for those who do, the possibilities are limitless.

> The key to abundance is meeting limited
> circumstances with unlimited thoughts.
> —MARIANNE WILLIAMSON

Technology is going to change what we think of as scarcity. It's the common denominator that makes us fearful. The idea that there won't be enough of what we need and what we value: water, food, money, resources, time, space, joy, and love. Why do people want to be wealthy? They believe if they are, they'll always have enough, that they'll never have to go without. It's a fear that's hardwired into our brains.

But scarcity doesn't have to be a permanent condition. Technology can change it. Did you know that there was a time when the rarest, most precious metal on Earth was . . . aluminum? That's right! Separating the element from clay used to be incredibly difficult and expensive. Aluminum was the ultimate status symbol in 19th-century France. At an imperial banquet, Napoléon III served the king of Siam with aluminum utensils instead of the usual gold. But by the end of the century, scientists figured out how to process aluminum on a mass scale, and the light, inexpensive metal suddenly flooded the market.

Peter Diamandis likes to use the story of aluminum to point out that scarcity is a function of our ability—or lack of ability—to access resources. He wrote an extraordinary book, *Abundance: The Future Is Better Than You Think*, which covers in 300 or so pages the concepts that this chapter is trying to capture in just a few. Here's a great metaphor from the book about how technology can overcome scarcity: "Imagine a giant orange tree packed with fruit," Peter writes. "If I pluck all of the oranges from the lower branches, I am effectively out of accessible fruit—oranges are now scarce. But once someone invents a piece of technology called a ladder, I've suddenly got new reach. Problem solved. Technology is a resource-liberating mechanism."

Given the way our world population is growing, we'll need to be liberating those resources faster than ever. That exponential change we were talking about? Here's an example:

- It took a little more than **200,000 years**—or until the year **1804**—for the population of human beings to multiply to a total of **1 billion people**.
- It took only **123 years (1927)** for the human population to double to **2 billion people**.
- But it took just **33 years (1960)** before there were **3 billion people** on the planet!

- It took a mere **14 years (1974)** for another billion to be added, for a total of **4 billion people.**

This growth has not stopped. In spite of China's one-child-per-family policy for its 1.3 billion population, and all the other efforts to stop world population growth, in the last 40 **years** alone, we've added more than **3 billion more people!** That's 300% more people in these four decades than it originally took 200,000 years to achieve! Today there are **7.2 billion people on the planet!** If we keep going at our current pace of growth, scientists estimate, the population will be **9.6 billion by 2050.**

How can the Earth sustain so many people? If we keep consuming our natural resources at the current rate, according to Jim Leape of the World Wide Fund for Nature International, as quoted in the *Wall Street Journal,* "We are using 50% more resources than the Earth can sustainably produce, and unless we change course, that number will grow fast—by 2030, even two planets will not be enough."

Human ingenuity and technology together have a way of keeping up with our needs.

I remember a time when we thought we were running out of oil. In the early 1970s, when I was a junior in high school, there was an oil crisis in the Middle East. If you recall, gas was rationed on odd or even days. I was wondering if we'd run out of fuel before I even got my license! Then one day in school, my engineering teacher said, "Let me read you an article." I had already seen the *Time* magazine with a report from the Club of Rome, scaring the daylights out of everybody with predictions that our oil supply would last only a few more years, and the whole economy would collapse. This article sounded just like that, using the same language of gloom and doom. Then he showed us what he'd been reading: a newspaper article from the 1850s about an oil crisis. And the oil they were talking about was . . . whale oil!

In the 19th century, whale blubber was the main source of lamp oil. You couldn't light your home without it. But whales were being overfished, people were worried about shortages of oil, and prices were going through the roof. But what happened in 1859? Crude oil was discovered in Pennsylvania. A whole new source became available. Before long, we had kerosene lamps and then internal combustion engines. The oil crisis of 1973?

Technology had already eased that scarcity. New exploration and extraction techniques were opening up vast quantities of fossil fuels. And now with sideways drilling technologies, we have more gas than Saudi Arabia has oil! Such technologies change not only an economy but can also have an impact on geopolitical power. For the first time in almost a decade, in 2013 the United States produced more domestic oil than it imported from the Middle East.

The future is in alternatives such as wind power, biofuels, and—the grand-slam winner—solar energy. According to the inventor and futurist Ray Kurzweil, all of the world's energy needs can be met with 1/10,000th of the sunlight that falls on the Earth each day. The challenge has been to capture and store that power for a competitive cost. Ray predicts that the cost per watt of solar energy will be less than oil and coal in just a few years.

> What we need is more people who specialize in the impossible.
> —THEODORE ROETHKE

Let's pause for a moment and think: Where will all this new technology come from? It's already been bubbling out of the usual places: Silicon Valley, NASA, the Defense Advanced Research Projects Agency (DARPA), and the world's great universities and laboratories. But more and more, do-it-yourself inventors are using the vast resources of the internet to find ways to do things faster and better and cheaper.

Let me tell you about a teenager I met who is revolutionizing the world of prosthetics from a lab—in his bedroom! Easton LaChappelle was running a robotics program for NASA when he was 17, and he didn't have to go to a major university to learn engineering—he had the internet.

Easton grew up in a tiny town in southwestern Colorado where there wasn't much for a kid to do, so he entertained himself by tearing up and reassembling household gadgets. When he was 14, he decided to build his own robotic hand. Hey, why not? There was no big library in town, no university nearby, so he scoured websites like Instructables and Hack It! to teach himself electronics, programming, and mechanics. Then he used objects he had lying around—Legos, fishing line, electrical tape, small hobby motors, and a Nintendo Power Glove—to build a prototype.

By the time he was 16, he had refined his design by getting access to a

3-D printer and creating a mechanical hand out of layers of plastic. He entered his invention at the state science fair, and it was there that Easton had what he calls his "aha!" moment. He met a seven-year-old girl with a prosthetic arm that cost her parents $80,000. She would need two more over her lifetime. Easton thought, "Who can afford that?" Besides, the mechanical hand attached to the arm had only one sensor and one motion. His device was much more sophisticated, with five flexible fingers. Then and there, he decided to create a simple, functional, and affordable prosthetic to help amputees like this little girl.

Easton went back to his bedroom lab and built a full robotic limb that replicated the motion and strength of a human arm. Even more amazing, he came up with an EEG headset that converts electronic brainwaves into Bluetooth signals that control it. (Yes, these things don't just exist in sci-fi movies.) The arm weighs one-third less than the $80,000 version, and it's much stronger. In fact, a person using this arm can curl more than 300 pounds! A giant improvement on the past technology. So what do you think his new invention costs to make as opposed to the $80,000 limb? $20,000? $5,000? $1,500? How about *$250*?!

After meeting President Obama in the summer before his 18th birthday, Easton interned with NASA at Houston's Johnson Space Center, where he led a team working on robotics for the International Space Station. By the end of August, Easton was already thinking, "I'm out of here. These guys are too slow!" He missed building the things he designed, and there were too many layers of bureaucracy. He went back home to work on building a robotic exoskeleton for a boy in his high school who was paralyzed from the waist down after an accident. Easton wanted him to walk at his graduation.

When I read about Easton's exoskeleton project, I knew I had to contact him. I've been working with the survivors of recent mass shootings, including the massacres at Newtown, Connecticut, and Aurora, Colorado. I've helped many of them work to turn their lives around in the aftermath of such unimaginable loss, including Ashley Moser, a pregnant mother who watched the insane killer murder her six-year-old daughter before he turned the gun on her. The two bullets he pumped into Ashley's body killed her unborn baby and left her paralyzed from the waist down. When I met her, she was filled with suicidal thoughts. I flew her family and medical team to our Unleash the Power Within event, and together we worked to create an environment where this remarkable young woman could begin her emotional healing.

I want Ashley to walk again! So I reached out to Easton and offered to fund his project. **Since then we've gone into business together to create low-cost prosthetic devices that can be used all over the world and make a massive difference in people's lives.** No matter where they live, no matter how much money they have. That's Easton's mission. (And by the way, Easton's high school friend is scheduled to graduate in 2015, and Easton reports that he is currently on track to make sure he walks to the podium. Easton's goal is an exoskeleton so thin and flexible that it can be worn under clothing! You might not know someone is wearing one.)

Easton's other mission is to spread the word to young people all over the world that they too can become the makers of technology instead of just consumers. "Everyone can be a creator," Easton told me. "With access to the internet and 3-D technology, kids can do anything they want. They don't have to restrict themselves by thinking, 'I have to go to college to be successful, there's really no other way.' You really do have other options."

There's no doubt that Easton LaChappelle is an extraordinary person. It would be safe to call him a genius. But how many other Eastons do you think are out there—in places like India, Tanzania, Australia, Dagestan, Uruguay, Singapore—logging on to their computers and dreaming up ways to improve the world we live in? Easton used open-source technology to share his first robotic hand design, so people all over the world could copy it and improve it if they wanted. **Now all of us can be our own publishers and creators and share our ideas with anyone with an internet connection.**

The floodgates have been opened, ushering in one of the greatest revolutions of our time—what people are calling the MakerBot Era or the Maker Revolution. Easton LaChappelle is simply one of the many people at the forefront of an explosion of do-it-yourself (DIY) innovation fueled by the wild growth in technology. Chris Anderson, CEO of 3-D Robotics, calls it the "New Industrial Revolution." Now the whole world can learn what students learn at Harvard, MIT, and Stanford. They can interact with the very best teachers—and one another—sharing ideas and techniques, and making devices and supplying services that used to cost millions of dollars for hundreds of dollars.

Each year, Maker Faires are held all around America, bringing together inventors, hobbyists, engineers, students, teachers, artists, and entrepreneurs in what's called "the Greatest Show (and Tell) on Earth." In 2013 over 540,000 people attended 100 Maker Faires globally, and in 2014 Maker Media, creator of the faires, is expecting that number to climb to 140 Maker Faires. President Obama recently hosted a Maker Faire at the White House, where a 17-foot robotic giraffe named Russell greeted him, and the president toured a tiny portable house and played a keyboard made of bananas. **He also met Marc Roth, from San Francisco, who was living in a homeless shelter when he started going to a local "TechShop" to learn how to use 3-D printers and laser cutters. Sixteen months later he had started his own laser-cutting business, and now runs a program to teach high-tech skills to others who need a fresh start.**

Obama also gave a shout-out to two tween-age girls from North Carolina who started a robotics company instead of getting a paper route. Their motto: "If you can imagine it, then you can do it—whatever it is."

"And that's a pretty good motto for America," Obama told the crowd. "This is a country that imagined a railroad connecting a continent, imagined electricity powering our cities and towns, imagined skyscrapers reaching into the heavens and an internet that brings us closer together." He challenged every company, college, and community to support these Makers. "If we do, I know we're going to be able to create more good jobs in the years to come. We're going to create entire new industries that we can't yet imagine."

This Maker Revolution is being made possible by the explosion of new technologies and the massive expansion of the internet. **Ten years ago, the internet connected 500 million people; today it connects 2 billion people. Within six years, experts estimate another 3 billion will be joining the web, for a total of 5 billion people. Imagine the power of that much connected and unleashed creativity across the planet!** The first internet was the internet of military agencies and colleges. Then it was the dot-com internet of companies; then it was the internet of ideas; then, with social media, it was the internet of relationships. Now it's the internet of things, of all things. Computers and sensors are embedded in everyday objects, transmitting messages back and forth to one another. Machines are connecting to other machines, which are in turn connecting to us and uniting everything in one powerful global network. And 3-D printing is how this internet will be transformed and expanded beyond our craziest dreams.

3-D PRINTING:
SCIENCE FICTION TO SCIENCE FACT

You know the "replicators" they use in those *Star Trek* movies to synthesize hamburgers and hot coffee out of thin air on the starship *Enterprise*? Well, scientists say we're not that far from creating the real thing! We've already been talking a lot about 3-D printing, but it's hard to grasp what a powerful technology it can become until you've seen it in action. 3-D printing is really a catchall phrase for digital manufacturing, and the "printers" are actually minifactories that use computer files as blueprints to create three-dimensional objects layer by layer. **The printers can use at least 200 different liquefied or powdered materials, including plastic, glass, ceramic, titanium, nylon, chocolate—and even living cells. What *can* you make with them? A better question is: What *can't* you make with them?!** So far 3-D printers have been used to create running shoes, gold bracelets, airplane parts, tableware, bikinis, guitars, and solar panels—not to mention human tracheas, ears, and teeth. As you've already learned, there are 3-D printers, small enough to fit into a teenager's bedroom, that are capable of turning layers of synthetic goop into a functioning prosthetic limb. And there are hangar-sized 3-D printers in China that can print out ten houses a day using layers of concrete mixed with recycled construction waste. The cost? Just $5,000 per home, and there's almost no labor required!

Perhaps even more importantly, NASA has partnered with America Makes, a network of 3-D printing companies, to sponsor a worldwide competition to address one of humanity's greatest challenges: the need for shelter, especially emergency shelter, in times of natural disaster such as hurricanes, tsunamis, and earthquakes. Imagine 3-D printers printing out homes on the spot, using local materials in hours, not months. The impact of this technology, effectively used, is limitless.

Someday you might be able to print your own custom-fit blue jeans without leaving your house, **while remote villages in the Himalayas will**

be able to download patterns from the cloud and print tools, water pumps, school supplies—anything they need. So will space travelers. Of course, as new technologies like 3-D printing come online, old ones will be disrupted, and some businesses may disappear. There won't be much need for spare-parts warehouses anymore, will there? And much less need for shipping. Great for the planet—but not so good if you're a truck driver. Experts project that 3.5 million truck drivers will be without a job in the United States alone because there will be robotic self-driving trucks that can operate 24 hours a day versus the eight hours a human can drive before having to take a break. Also, there's no salary to pay after you make your initial investment in the self-driving truck.

As old industries fall away, new ones will arise. We just need the education and training and mind-set to embrace change and meet the demands of the new, emerging economy.

But 3-D printing is only one technology that's part of the extraordinary growth that's going to change the quality of *your* life. Nanotechnology, robotics, and tissue regeneration are three others to watch. And if you're wondering why we're talking about all this—we know that technological advances that offer solutions for our most pressing problems will keep happening no matter what the economic season may be, whether we're experiencing inflation or deflation, or whether we're at war or at peace.

Heard about the demographic wave? The consumer spending of 77 million baby boomers has been driving the US economy for decades. But now 10,000 boomers are turning 65 every single day. And that's morphed into a potential retirement crisis wave, as most have not saved their money and have no pensions.

We have a debt wave building in this country that's larger than anything in the history of the world: $17 trillion in debt and a $100 trillion worth of unfunded liabilities, between Medicare, Medicaid, Social Security, and other commitments.

There's an environmental wave, even if you don't believe in climate change. And clearly we're overfarming our land. **But however big these waves may be, the technology wave is even bigger.** The technology wave promises to lift all boats and carry the whole world into a more abundant future.

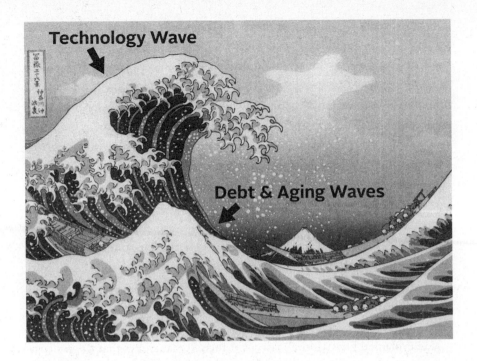

"I think those trends of technology tend to be bigger than any crisis," the futurist and venture capitalist Juan Enriquez said at one of my recent economic conferences. "While everybody was worried about the Korean War and the Cold War, people were building transistors. While everybody was worried about World War II, people were making antibiotics. Most of those advancements have had more of an impact on your life and my life than the wars or the ups or the downs."

Our problems come in waves, but so do the solutions.

I'm surfing the giant life wave.
—WILLIAM SHATNER

Nobody understands this idea better than my friend Ray Kurzweil, the inventor, author, and entrepreneur. One of the most brilliant minds on the planet, he's been called the Thomas Edison of our age. Yet you've probably never heard his name unless you're a TED Talk junkie, or if you study the lineup at Google, where Ray is head of engineering. But Ray Kurzweil has affected your life in more ways than you could ever imagine. If you listen to tunes on your phone, on the internet—anywhere—he's the guy you can thank. He created the first digital music. If you've ever dictated an email to Siri or other voice-to-text systems, that's because of Ray.

I remember meeting Ray Kurzweil nearly 20 years ago and listening with amazement as he described the future. It seemed like magic then, but it's all real now. Self-driving cars. A computer that could beat the world's greatest chess master. He had already invented an optical character-recognition system to create the first reading machine for the blind—Stevie Wonder was his first customer. Now he wanted to help blind people read street signs and navigate cities without help, and go into restaurants and order off the menu using a little device the size of a pack of cigarettes. He told me the year it was going to happen: 2005.

"How do you know, Ray?" I asked.

"You don't understand, Tony. Technology feeds on itself, and it gets faster and faster. It grows exponentially."

He explained how Moore's law—a principle that shows that the processing power of computers doubles every two years, while its cost decreases at the same rate—doesn't work just with microchips. It can be applied to all information technologies—and eventually all aspects of our lives.

What does that mean? When things grow exponentially, instead of increasing in a linear or arithmetic pattern (1, 2, 3, 4, 5, 6 . . .) they are continuously doubling: 1, 2, 4, 8, 16, 32, and so on. So their *rate* of growth gets faster and faster. But as we've discovered, this concept is hard for us to grasp. It's not the way humans were built to think.

"First of all, exponential growth is radically different from our intuition," Ray says. "We have an intuition about the future hardwired in our brains. A thousand years ago, when we walked through the savannah and we saw an animal coming at us out of the corner of our eye, we made a linear prediction of where that animal would be in twenty seconds and what to do about it." But with an exponential progression, the animal would take a few slow steps, speed up, and then suddenly be on the next continent.

Peter Diamandis offers another metaphor: "If I say to you, 'Take thirty linear steps,' normally you're going to end up about 30 meters away. But if I say to you, 'Instead of taking thirty linear steps, take thirty exponential steps.' How far will you go? How about **a billion meters**? That's twenty-six times around the planet!"

Once you understand exponential growth, says Ray, its trajectory is predictable. **He knows when the technology will catch up with his vision.** He predicted the launch date for his first pocket-sized reader for the blind, and other products. Ray often speaks at my seminars, and he told us recently how he accurately predicted one of the most incredible discoveries of our time: the mapping of the human genome.

"I predicted that the genome project would finish within fifteen years when it was started in 1990 because I realized the progress would be exponential," he said. But skeptics thought it would take a century to break the complex human code. **After seven and a half years, only 1% of the project was finished. According to Ray, "The skeptics were still going strong, saying, 'I told you this wasn't going to work. You're halfway through the project, and you've only finished one percent of it. This is a failure.' " But Ray pointed out that wasn't a failure: it was right on schedule! "Exponential growth is not dramatic at first. You're doubling these tiny little numbers. It looks like nothing is happening. But by the time you get to one percent, you're only seven doublings away from one hundred percent." The genome was successfully sequenced in 2003, ahead of schedule.**

So, what's next? We've already seen how stem cells can regrow human skin without the pain and scars of skin grafts, and how the abundant energy of the sun and wind can be harnessed to fuel our future. But what about other great challenges?

Lack of fresh water is one of the biggest concerns for populations growing like crazy in dry regions of the planet, and shortages are everywhere, from Los Angeles, California, to Lagos, Nigeria. According to the UN, more than 3.4 million people die each year because of water-borne diseases. But new desalinization technologies are turning seawater into tap water from Australia to Saudi Arabia. Already an Israeli company called Water-Gen is manufacturing a machine that extracts clean water out of air, and it uses only two cents' worth of electricity to produce each liter of water. And in remote villages that have no electricity, there's **a new kind of water tower that uses only its shape and natural materials to pull moisture out of the air and turn it into drinking water.**

The amazing inventor Dean Kamen (best known for the Segway scooter) has partnered with Coca-Cola to bring the world an energy-efficient machine the size of a dorm-room refrigerator that vaporizes dirty water and makes it clean and safe. It's called the Slingshot—as in a David-sized solution to a Goliath of a problem. With innovations such as these, before long the problem of water scarcity will be solved, period.

How about food? Ray Kurzweil says new food technologies are emerging that will overcome the twin challenges of too little arable land *and* agricultural pollution. How? By farming vertically instead of horizontally. Ray envisions a world in the next 15 years "where we grow plants vertically, and also grow meat without the slaughtering of animals, by using in-vitro cloning of muscle tissue in computerized factories—all at very low costs, with high nutritional qualities and without environmental impact." No insecticides. No more nitrogen pollution. No more need to kill animals for protein. Wow! That sounds impossible, but Ray says it's real and it's coming.

With these basic needs under control, humans will have the chance to live more fulfilling lives—especially if we meet the other challenges that Ray Kurzweil believes we can solve: health and aging.

> Age is an issue of mind over matter. If you don't mind, it doesn't matter.
> —MARK TWAIN

All these changes we've talked about are revolutionary, but according to Juan Enriquez, the changes that technology will bring to the future of health care will blow your mind more than anything else. Life, as it turns out, is an information technology. How can that be? Well, we know that our DNA is made up of a sequence of chemical bases labeled (if you remember your life science homework) A, C, T, and G. In other words, the building blocks of life itself can be expressed as a code. And codes can be altered. Or created. As in making artificial life. Which is what Craig Venter, the human genome pioneer, was able to do in 2010. Juan Enriquez was part of his team.

When Juan spoke at one of my recent seminars, I asked, "How did you and Craig Venter first come up with this idea of creating artificial life?"

He chuckled and said, "A bunch of us were having drinks at a bar in Virginia, and after the fourth scotch, somebody said, 'Wouldn't it be cool if you could program a cell from scratch, just in the same way as you program a computer chip from scratch? What would happen?' " He paused. "That only took five years and thirty million bucks to find out!" First, they took all the gene code out of a microbe. Then they inserted a new gene code, and it became a different species. Incidentally, it's the first life-form with a website embedded in its genetic code. As Craig Venter put it when he announced the breakthrough: **"This is the first self-replicating species that we've had on the planet whose parent is a computer."**

As Ray Kurzweil explains, our genes are like software programs that can be changed to switch behaviors on and off. What does that mean? It means that we can use cells as little machines and program them to build other things—including more of themselves. "This software makes its own hardware. No matter how I program a ThinkPad, I will only have one ThinkPad tomorrow morning, not a thousand ThinkPads. But if I program a bacteria, I will have a billion bacteria tomorrow," Juan said.

It sounds insane, like something out of a movie, but—as I keep reminding myself—this isn't science fiction. The technique is already being used to produce clothing. "All the stuff you are now wearing—that breathable, stretchable stuff like Under Armour?" Juan said. "All that is now being made from bacteria, not out of petrochemicals." In Japan, bacteria is growing synthetic silk that's stronger than steel. And genetically altered farm animals are already being used as medical factories. In New England, there's a dairy where cows produce milk that may be able to treat cancer.

> Whatever the mind of man can conceive and believe, it can achieve.
> —NAPOLEON HILL

I told you, it's a whole new world, and it's going to be a wild ride. Advances in nanotechnology and 3-D printing mean that medical devices the size of blood cells may someday be traveling through your body, fighting conditions like Parkinson's disease and dementia. Nanoscale computerized implants will replace the biological nerve cells destroyed by disease. And microscopic cochlear implants will not only restore hearing but also improve it, so that humans will hear as many notes as whales can sing. **According to Ray, work is already being done to create genetically enhanced**

**red blood cells that may one day carry enough oxygen to allow a diver
to last 40 minutes underwater on one breath—or to save a soldier's life
on the battlefield.**

Scientists are working on ways to use 3-D printers to create custom
organs and other body parts for you when you need them, eliminating the
need for dangerous, expensive donor transplants. Dr. Anthony Atala, director of the Wake Forest Institute for Regenerative Medicine, says, "In theory,
anything that is grown inside the body can be grown outside the body." Dr.
Atala has already created fully functioning human bladders in the lab and
completed the transplants. **In the last 15 years, none of the tissues made
from stem cells has ever been rejected by the body.** He and others are
already working on more complex organs, like hearts, kidneys, and livers. So
someday, if a heart attack or virus damages your heart valves, your doctors
will be able to order you up some new ones. Or maybe they'll just grow you
a new heart from a few of your skin cells!

If you have means, some of these miraculous cures are available already.
There's something called "extracellular matrix," or ECM, made of cells from
a pig's bladder. When you apply it to injured human tissue, the matrix coaxes
our own stem cells to regrow muscles, tendons, even bone. It's been used
already to regrow fingertips! This extraordinary substance exists right now.
It's not available to everyone yet, but it will be soon.

The concept behind regenerative therapies is simple: our body already
knows how to regrow its parts; we just have to learn how to turn on the stem
cells that already live inside us. We already know that when we lose our baby
teeth, another set grows in. But did you realize that, according to Dr. Ste-
phen Badylak from the University of Pittsburgh, if a newborn loses a finger,
another one can grow in its place up to the age of two? We lose that ability
as we grow older, so the question is: How do we stimulate it? **Salamanders
grow back their tails—why not human limbs or spinal cords?** When we
figure out how to harness the full power of stem cells, the medical and cos-
metic applications are limitless.

Ray Kurzweil says that if we're going to take advantage of these medical
breakthroughs and extend our lives, we'd better start taking care of ourselves right now. The idea is to live long enough for the technology to catch
up. If you're a millennial, you might experience it. If you're a baby boomer,

it's time to get on the elliptical machine and start eating right. Ray has even teamed up with a medical doctor to write a book titled *Transcend: Nine Steps to Living Well Forever*, with strategies to optimize your health and keep yourself alive long enough to tap into the technology that will further extend your lifespan.

His immediate goal is to stick around long enough to see the day when computers become smarter than humans. That day is coming soon.

COMPUTERS "R" US

What takes us hours to absorb, computers can already do in seconds. But by 2020, says Ray, a $1,000 computer will have the full capacity of a human mind. By 2030, it will be able to process the knowledge of all human minds *combined*.

By then, we won't be able to recognize the difference between human and artificial intelligence, he says, but we won't have anything to fear. Why? Because computers will have become a part of us, making us smarter, more powerful, healthier, and happier. Don't think that can happen? How do you feel when you don't have your smartphone nearby? A little lost? It's because **that technology and all that connectivity have already become parts of our lives.** The smartphone has become an "outboard brain"—it's our portable memory center, storing so much of our personal information as to be indispensable. And we'll be moving from mobile phones, to wearables, to implantables over the next 20 years.

So think a little further ahead. Imagine a world where you won't have to read this book—you can just upload its content into your brain. (And I suspect that by now you are wishing the future was here already. Especially with this monster-sized book!) Or imagine a world where you can upload your mind, your thoughts, and your personality to the cloud to be preserved forever? That's roughly the time when Ray Kurzweil and other great thinkers and futurists believe that humans and machines will merge. This epic moment is called "the Singularity" (aka "the Rapture for nerds"). When will it happen—if it does? Ray predicts the Singularity will be here by 2045.

> Those who have a "why" to live, can bear with almost any "how."
> —VICTOR FRANKL

If technology solves the problems that make our resources scarce, will we be safer, freer, happier? You bet. Scarcity brings out the survival instincts in human beings; it activates that deep part of the reptilian brain that makes you believe *it's you* or *me*. That fight-or-flight mechanism can help us survive, but it often can bring out the worst side of people in a "civilized" society. The brain we have is two million years old. It hasn't evolved that much. So aggression and war will always be a big challenge. But with less scarcity, perhaps there's less of a trigger to spark violence.

There's statistical evidence to show that more access to technology can make people happier. The World Values Survey has shown that from 1981 to 2007, happiness rose in 45 of the 52 countries studied. And what was going on during those years? That's right. The digital revolution. The technology wave was spreading across the globe—or what the report calls "the transition from industrial to knowledge societies." Social scientists have interpreted this index to mean that "economic development, democratization, and rising social tolerance have increased the extent to which people perceive that they have free choice, which in turn has led to higher levels of happiness around the world." The same survey said that more money doesn't make people happier. Some of the happiest people came from the poorest countries; citizens of the Philippines consider themselves happier than people in the United States. **Happiness has more to do with values than with GDP.**

We all know that subsistence labor robs us of our most precious commodity: time. Remember when I mentioned that not too long ago most Americans were farmers, and spent 80% of their time digging in the ground for food; now we spend about 7% of every day earning money for food? With more technology, there's more time on our hands, and that means there's more opportunity to learn, to grow, to connect with others, and to give—all pursuits that fulfill us as human beings.

But there's also a dark side to the gift of time.

Artificial intelligence and robotic devices are going to be taking on more and more of the tasks humans now perform. A study by Oxford University found that 47% of the current US labor market is at risk of being mechanized in the future. In essence, Oxford's experts are saying that half of all workers might one day be replaced by robots! That means society will have to reboot to create meaningful work for everybody, and we are all going to have to step up to learn new skills. It's going to be a difficult transition, no question about it.

But what happens in the future if work itself disappears, and computers do all the labor and most of the thinking? When all there is for us to do is ride around in self-driving vehicles and wait for drones to deliver the groceries? When there's nothing to push back against to give us strength? That's an interesting question.

More than a decade ago, I discussed this question with Ray Kurzweil, and he told me the story about a *Twilight Zone* episode that he'd seen as a child. I don't know if you're old enough to remember *The Twilight Zone*, but it was a very interesting series, and the shows always had a creepy twist at the end. In this episode, a guy who loves to gamble dies and wakes up with a friendly "guide" in a white suit at his side. This guide, this angel, who's more like a butler, takes him to a luxurious casino—which is this gambler's idea of heaven. He's ushered into an amazing suite, and he opens the closet to find it overflowing with incredible suits and fancy shoes. They all fit him perfectly. His guide opens a drawer, and it's stuffed with cash, more than he's ever seen before. So the gambler gets dressed, goes downstairs to the gaming tables, and everybody knows his name. Everybody smiles at him. He's surrounded by gorgeous women. It's his ultimate fantasy! He plays blackjack, and hits 21 the first time. He wins. This is great! He rakes in the chips. The next time: 21. Next time: 21. Ten times in a row. It's extraordinary! He turns around and plays craps, and he wins, wins, wins. He has huge piles of chips. All he has to do is ask for drinks, steaks, women, and they appear. Everything he's ever wanted, he gets. He goes to sleep that night . . . we'll just say, not alone, and very happy.

This goes on day after day after day. After a few months, he's playing at the blackjack table, and the dealer says, "Blackjack!"

The gambler screams, "Of course it's blackjack!"

The dealer says, "Twenty-one! You win!"

"Of course! I always win! I'm sick of this! I win every time, no matter what happens!" He looks at his guide in the white suit and asks to speak to the head angel.

When the head angel appears, the man unleashes a tirade: "I'm so bored

I'm going out of my mind! You know what? There must be some mistake. I'm not that good a person. I'm in the wrong place. I don't deserve to be in heaven!"

And the angel's smile suddenly curdles as he says, "What makes you think you're in heaven . . . ?"

So what happens when we get everything we want with little effort? After a while, it would be like hell, wouldn't it? Then we'd have a new problem: **Where will we find meaning in a world of abundance?** So maybe in the future, your problem won't be scarcity. And the solution won't just be an abundance of material things. As Peter Diamandis says, "Abundance isn't about providing everyone on the planet with a life of luxury—rather, it's about providing all with a life of possibility."

So in our final chapters together, let's look at the core of what is going to give your life lasting meaning. Something that can give you joy whether you're facing enormous challenges or extraordinary opportunities; a source of strength in difficult economic times or abundant ones. Let's uncover the ultimate wealth of fulfillment and meaning. Let's learn to tap into the wealth of passion.

THE WEALTH OF PASSION

Man is only great when he acts from passion.
—BENJAMIN DISRAELI

We've come a long way together, haven't we? It's been an incredible adventure, and I'm honored and grateful that you've chosen to make this journey with me.

By now you've navigated the money myths that block your way to financial freedom; climbed the mountain of successful saving and investing on the way to achieving your financial dreams; and learned new ways to safely glide to a secure future where you can work only because you want to work, not because you have to work.

You've met some remarkable financial geniuses and incredible human beings, such as Ray Dalio, Paul Tudor Jones, Mary Callahan Erdoes, Carl Icahn, David Swensen, Jack Bogle, Charles Schwab, and dozens of others to help guide you on your path. I'm hoping you'll return to the 7 Simple Steps you've learned in this book again and again throughout your life, to keep yourself on target. Also, I'm providing an action list at the end of this section to help you track and sustain your progress. In addition, you'll find a simple reminder system built into our app to keep you on target. Use these as a way to insure that you remain committed to the simple principles that will secure your freedom. Picking up this book and reviewing it in the future might be a useful way to remind yourself that you are not a creature of circumstance but a creator of your life. Remember, knowledge is not power—action is! Execution trumps knowledge every day of the week!

For me, this journey has been the culmination of decades of learning and teaching, and this book is truly a labor of love. It is my heartfelt gift to you. My hope is that you do so well that you can also pass on this gift to others.

Because the greatest gift of life is to live it for something that outlasts it: a legacy that continues to grow beyond our years.

And as we begin to complete this journey together, I want to make sure that I don't leave you without reminding you of what this all has really been about.

> Happiness is not something ready-made. It comes from your own actions.
> —DALAI LAMA XIV

It has been my great privilege to work with people from every walk of life: leaders in politics, finance, entertainment, and sports, but also in the religious and spiritual world. I've worked in the Middle East, where I brought young Israelis and Palestinians together in a leadership program in the West Bank. At first they expressed a seething hatred for one another—but within a week, they'd become great friends (and in nine years have continued to work on various peace projects in support of one another).

As a result, the Dalai Lama came to visit our Sun Valley home and later invited me to an interfaith peace conference in San Francisco in 2006. It took place during a week in April when three great religious faiths observed one of their high holidays: Easter for Christians, Passover for Jews, and, for Muslims, Mawlid an-Nabi, the birthday of Muhammed. The timing was significant, as the conference aimed to promote compassion and better understanding among all the great religions.

The Dalai Lama, draped in deep red and saffron robes, greeted me in the ballroom of the Mark Hopkins Hotel with a warm embrace and a belly laugh. He radiated warmth and joy—like a walking, breathing embodiment of the "art of happiness" he teaches. There were about 1,000 people attending the conference, but I had the honor of sitting in an intimate meeting he hosted with about 25 of the world's top theologians and spiritual leaders: Hindus, Buddhists, Episcopalians, Native Americans, Catholics, Jews, Sunnis, and Shiites—the list went on.

It was a fascinating experience because it started out as most of these conferences do, with everybody being wonderful and kind and gracious. But then we got into the nitty-gritty of human lives and age-old conflicts—and ideology and dogma started boiling up from beneath the surface. The conversation got a little heated, with everybody talking at once and nobody really listening.

Finally, the Dalai Lama raised his hand like a little boy in class. He wasn't upset at all, but he just kept waving his hand with a serene, amused smile on his face. Gradually, people saw him, and you could tell they were a little embarrassed for arguing and ignoring their host. When they finally became quiet, he dropped his arm.

"Ladies and gentlemen, one thing we can all agree upon in this room," the Dalai Lama said. "The great faiths of the world are represented here, and many of us are considered to be leaders of those faiths. We all have great pride in our individual traditions. But I think we don't want to lose sight of what the purpose of our religions is, and what the people we represent really want." He paused for effect and said, "What they all want is to be happy!" What's the common denominator, he asked, between the goat herder in Afghanistan and the financial trader in New York City; the tribal chief in Africa and the mother of ten in Argentina; the fashion designer in Paris and the weaver in Peru? *"They all want to be happy."*

"That's the essence of everything," His Holiness said. "If what we do creates more unhappiness, then we've truly failed."

But what is it that creates happiness?

I've always taught that success without fulfillment is the ultimate failure.

It's important to remember what you're really, truly after: that sense of joy, freedom, security, or love—whatever you want to call it. Each one of us finds a pathway we believe will lead to happiness, fulfillment, or meaning. And there are so many paths. Some look for happiness through religion, or nature, or relationships. Others think a great body, money, prominent degrees, children, or business accomplishments will make them happy. But true wealth, as you and I know deep in our souls, cannot be measured only by the size of your bank account or the number of assets you have acquired or grown.

So what's the final secret, the key to a rich life? Enjoy it and share it! But first you must take action. As the saying goes, if what you learn leads to knowledge, you become a fool; but if what you learn leads to action, you can become wealthy. Remember: rewards come in action, not in discussion.

So before you put down this book, go over the final checklist and make sure you've nailed those 7 Simple Steps and are on your way to building the life you desire and deserve.

Then take a breath and remember what it's all about.

> Wealth is the ability to fully experience life.
> —HENRY DAVID THOREAU

We all know there are many kinds of wealth: emotional wealth; relationship wealth; intellectual wealth; physical wealth, in the form of energy, strength, and vitality; and, of course, spiritual wealth: the sense that our life has a deeper meaning, a higher calling beyond ourselves. One of the biggest mistakes we human beings make is when we focus on mastering one form of wealth at the expense of all the rest.

This book has never really been just about money. What it's really about is creating an extraordinary quality of life—life on your terms. Until now we've zeroed in on how to master the game of money and financial independence because money can have a significant effect on everything from our psychology, to our health, to our intimate relationships. But it's important to remember that it's impossible to live an extraordinary life if you don't also master the game of relationships, the game of fulfillment, and the game of health.

Being the richest man in the graveyard is not the goal.

I will never forget taking my children to see Cirque du Soleil when the troupe came to our hometown in Del Mar, California, almost three decades ago. We were fortunate enough to get VIP tickets with floor seats right next to the stage. You could almost reach out and touch the performers.

Just before the show began, I noticed three prime seats were still open beside us, and I thought, "Wow, someone is going to miss out on an amazing show." But a minute or two later, a giant man, walking with the help of a cane and two assistants, came down the stairs. He must have weighed at least 400 pounds. When he sat down, he took up the three empty seats and was wheezing and sweating from the short walk to the front row. I felt so bad for this man—and for my daughter, who was being crushed by his body spilling over that third seat and onto her! I overheard a person behind me whispering that he was the richest man in Canada. It turns out he was *one* of the richest men in Canada—financially. A billionaire, no less! Yet in that moment, I couldn't help thinking about the pain he must live in—all because he put so much of his focus into money while neglecting his health and the physical wealth of his body. He was literally killing himself! And by failing to master more than one aspect of his life, he couldn't enjoy what he had—not even a simple, magical evening at the theater.

> We can only be said to be alive in those moments
> when our hearts are conscious of our treasures.
> —THORNTON WILDER

What's the point of massive achievement if your life has no balance? And what's the point of winning the game if you never take the time to celebrate and appreciate the life you have? There's nothing worse than a rich person who's chronically angry or unhappy. There's really no excuse for it, yet I see this phenomenon so often. It's the result of an extremely unbalanced life—one with too much expectation and not enough appreciation for what's already here. Without gratitude and appreciation for what we already have, we'll never know true fulfillment. As Sir John Templeton said, **"If you've got a billion dollars and you're ungrateful, you're a poor man. If you have very little but you're grateful for what you have, you're truly rich."**

How do you cultivate gratitude? Start by looking at the force that controls your mind and emotions.

Our decisions ultimately control the quality of our lives. In all the years I've worked with people, I've found that **there are three key decisions that we make every moment of our lives.** If we make these decisions unconsciously, we end up with lives like the majority of people, who tend to be out of shape physically, exhausted emotionally, and often bored with or too comfortable in their intimate relationships—not to mention financially stressed.

But if you make these decisions consciously, you literally can change your life in an instant! What are the three decisions that determine the quality of your life? That determine whether you feel rich or poor in any given moment? The first one is:

DECISION 1:
WHAT ARE YOU GOING TO FOCUS ON?

In every moment of our lives, there are millions of things we can focus on. We can focus on the things that are happening right here, right now, or on what we want to create in the future, or we can put our focus back on the past. We can direct our focus to solving a big challenge or to appreciating the beauty of this moment, or to feeling sorry for ourselves about some disappointing experience. If we don't direct our focus consciously, the environment we're in tends to make constant demands to get our attention.

There are hundreds of billions of dollars spent on advertising, trying to get this precious commodity of yours. The news tries to get your focus by telling you the scariest story: "Your child could *die* from drinking fruit juice! Film at eleven!" or some other ridiculous claim. Why? Because as they say in the media, "If it bleeds, it leads." If that's not enough, we live in a social media world where the buzz in your pocket is constantly calling to you. But here is the key: **where focus goes, energy flows.** What you focus on, and your pattern of focus, shape your whole life.

Let's look at two of these patterns that control and can immediately shift your level of joy, happiness, frustration, anger, stress, or fulfillment.

The first question is: **Which do you tend to focus on more—what you have or what's missing from your life?** I'm sure you think about both sides of this coin, but if you had to look at your habitual thoughts, where do you tend to spend most of your time?

Even those of us who are in the most difficult situations have plenty in our lives that we can appreciate. **If you're struggling financially, might it be worthwhile to remember that if you make an income of just $34,000 a year, you are actually in the top 1% of all wage earners in the world? Yes, the average annual income on the planet is only $1,480 a month. In fact, almost half the world, or more than 3 billion people, live on less than $2.50 per day, which is a little more than $900 per year. The average drink at Starbucks is $3.25. If you can afford that, you're spending more with one purchase of a cup of coffee than what half the planet has to live on for one day.**

That puts things in perspective, doesn't it? So if you want to occupy Wall

Street because you resent the so-called 1%, you might stop to consider that 99% of the rest of the world might want to occupy *your* "terrible" life!

But in all seriousness, rather than focusing on what we don't have and begrudging those who are better off financially, perhaps we should acknowledge that there's so much to be grateful for in our lives that has nothing to do with money. **We can be grateful for our health, our friends, our opportunities, our minds, and the fact that we get to drive on roads that we didn't have to build, read books we didn't have to take years to write, and tap into the internet that we didn't have to create.**

Where do you tend to put your focus? On what you have or on what's missing?

A pattern of appreciating what you have will create a new level of emotional well-being and wealth. And my guess is that if you're reading this book, you may be one of those people who already notices what you have. But the real question is, do you take time to deeply *feel* grateful in your mind, body, heart, and soul? That's where the joy and the gifts will be found. Not with just intellectual appreciation or by the acquisition of another dollar, or another $10 million.

Now let's consider a second pattern of focus that impacts the quality of your life: **Do you tend to focus more on what you *can control* or what you *can't control*?** I know the answer will be contextual, as it could change from moment to moment, but I'm asking you overall: What do you tend to do more often? Be honest.

If you focus on what you *can't* control, there's no question you're going to have more stress in your life. You can influence many aspects of your life, but you can't control the markets, the health of those you care about, or the attitudes of your children—as anyone who has lived with a two-year-old or a 16-year-old knows!

Yes, we can influence many things, but we can't control them. The more we feel out of control, the more frustrated we become. In fact, **self-esteem can be measured by how much we feel we control the events in our life versus feeling that life's events are controlling us.**

Now, as soon as you begin to focus on something, your brain has to make a second decision, which is:

DECISION 2:
WHAT DOES THIS MEAN?

What does this mean? Ultimately, how we feel about our lives has nothing to do with the events of our lives, or with our financial condition, or what has or has not happened to us. The quality of our lives is controlled by the meanings we give these things. Most of the time we're unaware of the impact of these quick meaning decisions that are often made in our unconscious mind.

When something happens that disrupts your life—a car accident, a health issue, a lost job—do you tend to think it's the end or the beginning? If someone confronts you, is he or she "insulting" you, "coaching" you, or truly "caring" for you? Does this "devastating" problem mean that God is punishing you, or challenging you, or is it possible this problem is a gift from God? Your life becomes whatever meaning you give it. Because with each meaning comes a unique feeling or emotion, and the quality of our lives is where we live emotionally.

Meanings don't just affect the way we feel; they affect all of our relationships and interactions. Some people think the first ten years of a relationship is just the beginning; that they're just now getting to know each other, and it's really exciting. It's an opportunity to go deeper. Other people could be ten days into a relationship, and the first time they have an argument, they think it's the end.

Now tell me, if you think this is the beginning of a relationship, are you going to behave the same way as if it were the end? That one slight shift in perception, in meaning, can change your whole life in a moment. In the beginning of a relationship, if you're totally in love and attracted, what will you do for the other person? The answer is: *anything*! If he or she asks you to take out the trash, you might leap to your feet and say, "Anything that lights you up, sweetheart!" But after seven days, seven years, or seventy years, people say things like, "What the hell do you think I am, your janitor?!" And they wonder what happened to the passion in their life. I've often shared with couples having trouble in their relationships that if you do what you did in the beginning of the relationship, there won't *be* an end! Because in the beginning of the relationship you were a giver, not an accountant. You weren't weighing constantly the meaning of who was giving more. Your entire focus was just lighting up that person, and his or her happiness made you feel like your life was filled with joy.

Let's look at how these first two decisions, focus and meaning, often combine to create one of modern society's biggest afflictions: depression. I'm sure you must wonder how it's possible that so many people who are "rich" and famous—with every resource you could ever desire—could ever be depressed. How is it that so many of those who were beloved by millions of people, and have tens of millions of dollars or more, have even taken their own lives? We've seen it over and over again with extraordinarily intelligent individuals, from businessmen to entertainers to comedians. How is this possible, especially with all of the modern treatments and medications available today?

In my seminars, **I always ask, "How many of you know someone who is on antidepressants and is still depressed?" Everywhere around the world, in rooms of 5,000 to 10,000 people, I'll see about 85% to 90% of the room raise their hands. How is that possible?** After all, you're giving them a drug that should make them better.

Well, these antidepressants do come with labels warning that suicidal thoughts are a possible side effect. But perhaps the real challenge is, no matter how much you drug yourself, if you focus constantly on what you can't control in your life and what's missing, it's not hard to find yourself in despair. If you add to that a meaning like "life is not worth living," you have an emotional cocktail that no antidepressant will be able to overcome consistently.

But I can tell you beyond a shadow of a doubt that if that same person can come up with a new meaning—a reason to live or a belief that all of this was meant to be—then he will be stronger than anything that has ever happened to him. If she can focus consistently on who needs her, wants her, loves her, what she still wants to give to this world, then anyone can be shifted. How do I know? Because in 38 years of working with people, I've never lost one to suicide out of the thousands I've dealt with. And knock on wood—there are no guarantees—hopefully I never will. But when you can get people to shift their habitual focus and meanings, there's no longer a limit on what a person's life can become.[25]

A change of focus and a change in meaning can literally change your biochemistry in a matter of minutes. Learning to master this becomes an emotional game changer. How else can you explain the power and beauty of people like the great therapist and thinker Victor Frankl and so many others who made it through the horrors of Auschwitz? They found meaning even in their extreme suffering. It was a higher meaning, a deeper meaning that kept them going—not only to survive but also to save the lives of so many others in the future by saying, "This will never happen again." We can all find meaning, even in our pain. And when we do, we may still experience pain, but the suffering is gone.

So take control, and always remember: **meaning equals emotion, and emotion equals life.** Choose consciously and wisely. Find the empowering meaning in anything, and wealth in its deepest sense will be yours today.

DECISION 3:
WHAT AM I GOING TO DO?

Once we create a meaning in our minds, it creates an emotion, and that emotion leads to a state in which we make our third decision: **What am**

---

25. If you'd like, you can go online to www.tonyrobbins.com and see some of these interventions. We've even followed people three and five years later to show that the changes lasted. It will give you an idea of how you can master the meaning in your own life.

I going to do? The actions we take are powerfully shaped by the emotional states we're in. If we're angry, we're going to behave quite differently than if we're feeling playful or outrageous.

If you want to shape your actions, the fastest way is to change what you focus on and change the meanings to something more empowering. But even two people who get in an angry state will behave differently. Some will pull back when they're angry; others push through. Some people express anger quietly or loudly or violently. Some suppress it only to look for a passive-aggressive opportunity to regain the upper hand, or even exact revenge. Some people confront their anger by going to the gym and working out.

Where do these patterns come from? We tend to model our behavior on the people in our lives whom we respect, enjoy, and love. The people who frustrated or angered us? We often reject their approaches, but far too often find ourselves falling back into the pattern that we witnessed over and over again and were so displeased by in our youth.

It's very useful to become aware of what your patterns are when you get frustrated or angry or sad or feel lonely—because you can't change your pattern if you're not aware of it. In addition, now that you're aware of the power of these three decisions, you might start looking for role models who are experiencing what you want out of life. I promise you, those who have passionate relationships have a totally different focus and come up with to- tally different meanings for challenges in the relationship than people who are constantly bickering or fighting. Or those who judge each other con- stantly. It's not rocket science. If you become aware of the differences in how people make these three decisions, you'll have a pathway that can help you create a permanent positive change in any area of your life.

> At the age of 18, I made up my mind to never have
> another bad day in my life. I dove into an endless sea
> of gratitude from which I've never emerged.
> —DR. PATCH ADAMS

How can you use these three decisions to enhance the quality of your life? It turns out that what we focus on, what emotional states we tend to live in, and what we do can all be conditioned, or "primed," into our lives with a simple routine. After all, you don't want to merely hope that positive emotions just show up; you want to condition yourself to live in them. It's like an athlete developing a muscle. You must train yourself if you want to have an extraordinary quality of fulfillment, enjoyment, happiness, and achievement in your personal, professional, and intimate lives. You must train yourself to focus, feel, and find the most empowering meanings.

This practice is rooted in a concept in psychology called **priming**, in which words, ideas, and sensory experiences color our perceptions of the world and affect our emotions, motivations, and actions.

What if you were to discover that many of the thoughts that you think are *your* thoughts are simply conditioned by environmental triggers, or in some cases manipulated consciously by others who understand the power of priming? Let me give you an example.

Two psychologists conducted a study[26] in which a stranger handed the subjects either a mug of hot coffee or a cup of iced coffee. The subjects were asked to read about a hypothetical character and asked to describe the character's true nature. The results were astonishing! Those who were given the hot coffee described the character as "warm" and "generous," while the iced-coffee holders described him as "cold" and "selfish."

In another study at the University of Washington, women of Asian descent were given a mathematics test. Before the test, they took a brief questionnaire. If they were asked to list their ethnicity, the women scored 20% higher on the math test. But for those who were asked to fill in gender instead of ethnicity, the simple act of writing that they were female produced significantly lower scores. That's the power of priming in the form of cultural conditioning. It affects our unconscious patterns—shrinking or unleashing our true potential.

We can make use of this phenomenon by developing a simple ten-minute daily practice to prime our minds and hearts for gratitude—the emotion that eliminates anger and fear. Remember, if you're grateful, you can't be angry simultaneously. You can't be fearful and grateful simultaneously. It's impossible!

26. The study was funded by the National Institutes of Health, and coauthored by John A. Bargh (Yale) and Lawrence Williams (University of Colorado).

I begin every day with a minimum of ten minutes. I stop, close my eyes, and for approximately three minutes reflect on what I'm grateful for: the wind on my face, the love in my life, the opportunities and the blessings I experience. I don't focus just on big things; I make a point not only to notice, but also to deeply feel an appreciation for the little things that make life rich. For the next three minutes, I ask for health and blessings for all those I love, know, and have the privilege to touch: my family, friends, clients, and the stranger I may meet today. Sending love, blessings, gratitude, and wishes for abundance to all people. As corny as it sounds, it's the real circle of life.

I spend the remaining time on what I call my "Three to Thrive": three things that I want to accomplish. I envision them as if they were already achieved and feel a sense of celebration and gratitude for them. Priming is an important gift to yourself—if you did it for ten days, you'd be hooked. (Here's a link to get you started: www.tonyrobbins.com.)

This simple practice is important because a lot of people say they're grateful, but they don't take time to *be* grateful. It's so easy in life to lose track of the beauty and grace of what we already have! If we don't consciously do something each day to plant the right seeds in our mind, then the "weeds of life"—frustration, anger, stress, loneliness—tend to creep in. You don't have to plant weeds; they grow automatically. My teacher Jim Rohn taught me a simple principle: every day, stand guard at the door of your mind, and you alone decide what thoughts and beliefs you let into your life. For they will shape whether you feel rich or poor, cursed or blessed.

In the end, if we're going to truly be happy, we have to get outside of ourselves.

The human mind is an amazing thing. It's a survival mechanism, so it tends to look for what's wrong, what to avoid, what to look out for. You may have evolved, but your brain is still a 2-million-year-old structure, and if you want to be fulfilled and happy, that's not its first priority. You have to take control of it. And the fastest way to do that— besides priming—is to step into the highest of the 6 Human Needs, the two spiritual needs that fulfill human beings: Growth and Contribution.

The core reason that I believe we all have a desire to grow is because when we do, we have something to give. That's where life has its deepest meaning. "Getting" might make you feel good for a moment, but nothing beats the nirvana of having something to give that you know deeply touches someone or something beyond yourself.

> Everyone can be great, because everyone can serve.
> —DR. MARTIN LUTHER KING JR.

If it's really true that giving is what makes us feel fully alive, then perhaps the ultimate test of this theory is what life is like for those willing to give their lives for something they believe in. One of my greatest heroes of the last century was civil rights leader Martin Luther King Jr. Recently his eldest son and namesake, Martin Luther King III, was in Fiji for my Date with Destiny event. I had the opportunity of sharing with him how much his dad inspired me because he lived his life on pure passion—he knew what he was made for. Even as a child, I remember hearing his words: **"A man who has not found something he will die for is not fit to live."**

Real wealth is unleashed in your life the moment you find something you care so deeply for you will give it your all—even your life, if necessary. This is the moment in which you will have truly escaped the tyranny of your own mind, your own fears, your own sense of limitation. A big order, I know. But I also know that most of us would give our lives for our children, our parents, or our spouses. Those who have found a mission that possesses them have discovered a wealth of energy and meaning that has no match.

THE WEALTH OF PASSION

You've probably heard of the Pakistani teenager Malala Yousafzai. She was shot in the head by Taliban terrorists because she had the audacity to insist that girls have the right to go to school. A bullet pierced her eye socket and bounced around her skull, nearly killing her. Miraculously it missed her brain. Malala survived her horrific injuries and has become an international activist for the empowerment of girls and women. The man who shot her remains free, and the Taliban still threatens to kill her. But she openly defies them. In a speech before the United Nations on her 16th birthday, Malala said she has no fear. "They thought that the bullet would silence us, but they failed. And out of this silence came thousands of voices. The terrorists thought that they would change my aim and stop my ambitions, but nothing changed in my life, except this: **weakness, fear, and hopelessness died. Strength, fervor, and courage was born."**

In an interview with Malala, CNN's Christiane Amanpour asked the young woman if she feared for her life. Malala replied, "The thing is, they can kill me. They can only kill Malala. But it does not mean that they can kill my cause as well; my cause of education, my cause of peace, and my cause of human rights. My cause of equality will still be surviving . . . **They only can shoot a body, but they cannot shoot my dreams."**

This 16-year-old young woman has mastered those three decisions. She's focused on what matters. She's found a mission beyond herself that gives her life meaning. And her actions are fearless.

While we might not be called to put our lives on the line like Malala, we can all choose to live fearlessly, passionately, and with boundless gratitude. So let's turn the page and finish our wealth-building journey together with the most important lesson of all: the final secret.

THE FINAL SECRET

We make a living by what we get. We make a life by what we give.
—WINSTON CHURCHILL

As we take these final steps of our journey together, I want to invite you to think about **what you are most passionate about in this world. What do you care for most deeply? What excites you? What legacy would light you up? What could you do today that would make you proud?** What action could you take that would be a signal to your own spirit that your life is being lived well? And if you were truly inspired, what would you like to create or give?

All these questions bring us closer to **the final secret of true wealth.** But—and here's the deal—part of the key may seem counterintuitive. We've spent a lot of time talking about how to master money, save, invest, and build a critical mass that can ultimately create freedom and increase the quality of your life. But at the same time, **we've all been taught that money cannot buy happiness.** As one study attests, most people believe that if their income doubled, their happiness would also double. But the study's findings proved that, in reality, people who went from earning $25,000 per year to $55,000 per year reported only a 9% increase in happiness. Additionally, one of the most widely quoted studies on the subject tells us that once you make a solid middle-class salary—about $75,000 per year in America—earning more money doesn't make any measureable difference in a person's level of happiness.

"So, what's the point?" you might ask.

The truth is: **more recent studies have proven that money *can* make us happier.** Scientists have shown that "spending as little as five dollars a day can significantly change your happiness." How so? **Well, it's not the amount of money you spend, but how you decide to spend it that** matters. **"Every day spending choices unleash a cascade of biological and emotional effects that are detectable right down to saliva,"** reports Harvard's Elizabeth Dunn and Michael Norton in their brilliant 2013 book, *Happy Money: The Science of Smarter Spending.* "While having more money can provide all kinds of wonderful things—from tastier food to safer neighborhoods—its real power comes not in the amount but how we spend it."

They have scientifically proven that there are many different ways you can spend your money that will actually increase your happiness significantly. I won't reveal them all here and will leave it to you to pick up their book, but three of the most important are:

1. **Investing in experiences**—such as travel, learning a new skill, or taking some courses, rather than acquiring more possessions.
2. **Buying time for yourself**—"Whenever we can outsource our most dreaded tasks (from scrubbing toilets to cleaning gutters), money can transform the way we spend our time, freeing us to pursue our passions!"

But can you guess the greatest thing you can do with your money that will bring you massively increased happiness?

3. **Investing in others**—That's right. Giving our money away actually makes us really happy!

Research shows that the more you give to others, the happier you are. And the more you have, the more you are able to give. It's a virtuous cycle. Dunn and Norton demonstrate through their own scientific studies that **people get more satisfaction spending money on others than they do spending it on themselves.** And the benefits "extend to not only subjective well-being, but also objective health."

In other words, giving makes you both happier and healthier.

According to the authors, this phenomenon spans continents and cultures, rich countries and poor, people in the highest and lowest income groups, young and old, "from a Canadian college student purchasing a scarf for her mother, to a Ugandan woman buying lifesaving malaria medication for a friend." Again, the data shows that the size of the gift doesn't really matter.

In one of their studies, the authors handed participants either $5 or $20 to spend by the end of the day. Half were told to buy something for themselves; the others were instructed to use the money to help somebody else. "That evening, people who had been assigned to spend the money on someone else reported [significantly] happier moods over the course of the day than did those people assigned to spend the money on themselves," they wrote.

The authors' colleague, psychologist Lara Aknin of Simon Fraser University, conducted another study in which she handed out $10 Starbucks gift cards to her subjects.

- Some were instructed to go into Starbucks alone and **use the gift card on themselves.**
- Some were told to **use the gift card to take another person out for coffee.**
- Some were told to **give the gift card away to someone else,** but they weren't allowed to go to Starbucks with that person.
- Some were told to **take another person with them to Starbucks but to use the card only for themselves,** not the person with them.

At the end of the day, which subjects do you think reported being happiest? You're right if you picked the ones who were there in Starbucks when they treated someone else to a cup of coffee. According to the authors, people are happiest when they connect with those they help, and "see how their generous actions have made a difference."

The happiness we feel from helping others is not only more intense, but it lasts longer too. When I brought up the topic of money and happiness in my interview with renowned behavioral economics expert Dan Ariely, he told me, "If you ask people, 'What would make you happy: buying something for yourself, or buying something for somebody else?' they say, 'Oh, something for myself.' But that's not true. Research shows that when people buy something for themselves, they get happy for a few minutes or usually a few hours. But if they buy even a small gift for somebody else, the giver's happiness lasts a minimum to the end of the day, but often the happiness can carry over for days or even weeks on end."

Dan also told me about a **"beautiful experiment"** in which employees of a certain company were given bonuses in the $3,000 range. Some people got the bonuses to spend on themselves. And some were instructed to give the money away. Guess who was happier?

"Six months down the line, the people who gave it away reported being much happier than the group that kept it for themselves," Dan said. "I mean, think about what giving is all about, right? It's an amazing thing that connects you to other people . . . and there's a cycle of benefits that comes from that."

When you give away money, especially if you do something for a stranger versus if you do something for someone you love, the level of multiplied happiness is geometric. It's the equivalent of doubling or tripling your salary.

In my own experience, I've witnessed so many amazing things that happen when you give. When you get beyond your own survival and success mechanisms to a world where you're living for more than just yourself, suddenly your fear, your frustration, your pain and unhappiness disappear. I truly believe that when we give of ourselves, then life, God, grace— whatever you want to call it—steps in and guides us. Remember, *life supports whatever supports more of life.*

Let me give you an example of how a young boy's life was reignited after his heart and soul were nearly crushed in the aftermath of the horrific school shooting in Newtown, Connecticut. His is a story of finding purpose and inspiration and a release from pain through the act of giving.

A POWER BEYOND PAIN

JT Lewis will never forget December 14, 2012. That morning a deranged shooter broke into **Sandy Hook Elementary School** with a death wish for himself and 26 others, including 20 children ranging from ages five to ten. At one point during the rampage, JT's six-year-old brother, Jesse, noticed the shooter's weapon had jammed and shouted for his classmates to run. That brave little boy saved many lives that morning, but, unfortunately, not his own. The gunman turned on Jesse and shot him dead.

Imagine the devastation if Jesse were your son. Or brother. I had the privilege of meeting 13-year-old JT, and his and Jesse's mother, Scarlett, when I flew to Newtown on the first anniversary of the massacre to help a group of survivors cope with the ongoing impact of this devastating tragedy. As I expected, so many of these families were tortured with grief. But I was astonished to talk to JT and learn how his pain and suffering had been transformed through a single interaction with a group of extraordinary Rwandan orphans. These young boys and girls had heard about JT's loss and wanted to reach out across the globe to share a message of healing.

These orphans had all survived one of the worst tragedies in history. In 1994, mass genocide in Rwanda led to the death of as many as 1 million Tutsis, who were killed by their Hutu neighbors in roughly 100 days. During a Skype call, one of the girls, Chantal, told JT how sorry she was for the loss of his brother. **But she wanted him to know that no one can take away joy and happiness from your life, only you;** *the shooter does not have that power.*

She then went on to share her own story of how she was only eight years old when she had been forced to witness the horrendous sight of her parents being hacked to death by men with machetes. Next the killers turned on her, slashing her neck and throwing her tiny body in a mass grave. Buried beneath the ground, bleeding profusely and terrified, but filled with a will to survive, Chantal clawed her way out of that shallow grave and made her way to freedom in the mountains above her village. Hiding in the dark forest, she could look down on the community she once called home, as flames swallowed house after house, and the air echoed with screams of the people she loved. She lived on grass for a month while she waited for the killing to stop.

Certainly you would expect a child forced to witness the murder of her own parents would be emotionally scarred for life. One would expect her to live in anger and fear, but she doesn't. She is a master of the three decisions that shape our lives.

As she told JT, "I know you don't believe it now, but you can heal immediately and live a happy and beautiful life. It simply requires training yourself to, every day, be grateful, forgiving, and compassionate. Grateful for what you do have, instead of focusing on what you don't. You must forgive the shooter and his family and find a way to serve others, and you will be freed from your pain." **Her face was filled with a joy greater than JT could have ever imagined. As bad as his life was, the horror she described was more intense than anything he could conceive. If she could be free of her pain, then so could he. And now was the time.**

But how would he do it? He decided he must find a way to give back to this young soul who had reached across thousands of miles to send him love on his day of need. Chantal found her reason to live, her passion and sense of purpose, in deciding to protect, love, and raise some of the other younger orphans of the genocide. This became her mission, and it freed her from focusing on herself or any sense of loss.

Her example of service to others touched JT deeply, and he became obsessed with the idea of giving. He decided that helping to create a better future for this extraordinary girl was his mission. He began to work day and night to raise money to put her through college. Within several months, this 13-year-old boy was able to Skype back and announce that he had raised $2,100—enough money to send Chantal to college for a year! She was incredibly touched. But like many young people, especially in the third world, university was simply not a practical option for her, especially as she had already started her own small business as a shopkeeper. (And as you might imagine from a woman with her spirit, she is quite a successful entrepreneur!) So, in the continued spirit of giving, Chantal passed this amazing gift on to her best friend, Betty, another orphan who had also been on the call to encourage JT.

I was so moved by JT's commitment that I decided on the spot to provide the additional three years of college for Betty, and support Chantal by providing her the funding to build a new shop and a permanent residence for the rest of her adopted orphan family.

Today we're all working together to expand the resources available for many more of the 75,000 orphaned children who survived the genocide.[27]

The lesson here is this: human beings can overcome our pain when we choose to see life's beauty and find a way to give of ourselves. That is where the healing gift comes from. The key is finding something that will inspire you to *want* to give. That sense of mission—that's the ultimate power in life. That's when you truly become wealthy—that is when you move from a mere life of enjoyment to a life of joy and meaning.

---

27. We train psychologists and professional coaches who learn core practical and psychological skills to make a difference during these crises. If you are qualified and would like to volunteer during a time of crisis, reach out to the Anthony Robbins Foundation (www .anthonyrobbinsfoundation.org).

GIVING IS HEALING

Of course, giving means more than just giving money. It's also giving your time, it's giving your emotion, it's giving your presence to your kids, to your family, to your husband or your wife, to your friends, to your associates. Our work is also our gift. Whether that gift is a song, a poem, building a multinational business, serving as a counselor, a healthcare provider, or a teacher, *we all have something to give*. In fact, after love, one of the most sacred gifts we can give is our labor. And volunteering your time, giving your unique level of caring, and sharing your skills will also give you significant "returns."

My friend Arianna Huffington cites studies in her brilliant book *Thrive* that show how the act of giving actually improves your physical and mental health. One example I love in particular is the 2013 study from Britain's University of Exeter Medical School that reveals how volunteering is associated with lower rates of depression, higher reports of well-being, and a 22% reduction in death rates! She also writes, "Volunteering at least once a week yields improvements to well-being tantamount to your salary increasing from $20,000 to $75,000!"

So what's the final secret to wealth? **It's that *giving* in any form builds wealth faster than *getting* ever will.** I don't care how powerful any of us are as individuals, whether you're a business titan, political leader, financial mogul, or entertainment icon—the secret to a fulfilled life is not only to do well but also to do good. After all, we all know the story of how society has been transformed by magnificently wealthy individuals who woke up one morning and realized, "Life is about more than just me."

> Being the richest man in the cemetery doesn't matter
> to me. Going to bed at night saying we've done
> something wonderful, that's what matters to me.
> —STEVE JOBS

Before the 19th century, most charity was handled by religious organizations—until steel magnate Andrew Carnegie came along. Kings and nobles and the wealthiest families weren't interested in giving back to their communities; for the most part, they just wanted to hang on to their money for themselves and their heirs. Many businessmen shared the same belief.

But Carnegie led the other "robber barons" of his era to create philanthropy as we've come to know it today.

Carnegie was a ruthless businessman, but he made the steel that built the railroads and skyscrapers that transformed America. He had to add value to be profitable, so society benefitted, and so did he. In his lifetime, he became the richest man in the world. But there came a stage in his life where he had gotten all the things that he wanted and then some. He had so much money that he began to realize that it had very little meaning—unless he used it for something beyond himself. So Carnegie spent the first half of his life accumulating money and the second half giving it away. He described his personal transformation in an essay (and later a book) that's still worth reading called *The Gospel of Wealth*. My friend, Nobel Prize winner and Yale economics professor Robert Shiller, insists that all of his students read it because he wants them to know that capitalism can be a force for good. Carnegie's essay changed society, influenced his peers, and even challenged the incomprehensible wealth of his greatest rival, John D. Rockefeller. Inspired by a fierce competitive spirit, Rockefeller began shoveling mountains of money into some of the nation's greatest foundations. Carnegie created a new standard: a standard of measuring your significance not by what you have but by what you give. His focus was education. In fact, during his lifetime, Carnegie's contributions doubled the number of libraries in the United States, and provided so much of the intellectual growth and capital of our society before the internet came into being.

Our friend Chuck Feeney became a modern Carnegie, giving away almost all of his $7.5 billion fortune—except *he* chose to keep quiet about it until recently!

By the time I came to meet Chuck, he was 83 and in the final stage of his life. He had difficulty speaking for extended periods of time, but in his presence is found an experience more profound than words. In his presence, you feel the power of a life well lived. You can see it in the joy in his eyes, in the smile that flashes so easily for him, in the kindness that emanates from his heart.

Chuck Feeney, in turn, inspired another generation. Many say Ted Turner was the next to reignite this form of large-scale philanthropy with his $1 billion pledge to the United Nations. Since then, Bill Gates and Warren Buffett have joined forces to create the Giving Pledge to inspire the world's wealthy to leave at least half of their fortunes to charity. At last count, more than 120 billionaires had signed up, including some of the ultrawealthy individuals in this book, such as Ray Dalio, T. Boone Pickens, Sara Blakely, Carl Icahn, and Paul Tudor Jones. (See the website, at http://givingpledge.org, to read some of the moving letters they wrote to accompany their gifts.)

T. Boone Pickens told me he's gotten a bit carried away with his philanthropy. He'd recently given nearly a half billion dollars to his alma mater, Oklahoma State University, bringing his total charitable gifts to over $1 billion. However, he recently took some losses that lowered his net worth to $950 million—just shy of that billion he gave away! But Boone is not concerned. After all, he's only 86 years old. "Don't worry, Tony," he said. "I'm planning on earning another two billion in the next few years." He feels no sense of loss, because the joy he's received in giving is priceless.

In modern times, the richest and the most influential men and women in the world have tackled the world's big problems. Carnegie took on education. Bill and Melinda Gates take on scholarship and preventable epidemics. Bono's passion is forgiving the debt that enslaves third world countries. But do you have to be a billionaire or a rock star to solve the world's greatest problems? Not in today's interconnected world. If we work together through the use of technology, we can each do a little bit and still have a huge impact.

SWIPEOUT HUNGER, SWIPEOUT DISEASE, SWIPEOUT SLAVERY

I'm not sure what your passion is, but one area I personally feel deep empathy for is children and families in need. You need to have ice in your veins not to feel for a child who is suffering. So let's take a minute to look at three of the biggest problems affecting children and their families today, and what immediate, concrete steps we could easily take to make a difference.

The first is hunger. **Who do you think goes to bed hungry each night in the richest country in the world? According to the US Census Bureau, as staggering as it sounds, one in four American children under the age of five lives in poverty, and almost one in ten lives in *extreme* poverty (which is defined as an annual income below $11,746, or $32 a day, for a family of four to live on).**

Fifty million Americans, including nearly 17 million children, live in food-insecure homes—or as Joel Berg of New York's Coalition Against Hunger told Theresa Riley of *Moyers & Company*, homes that "don't have enough money to regularly obtain the food they need"; that "are rationing food and skipping meals. Where parents are going without food to feed their children." At the same time, **Congress has cut $8.7 billion of annual SNAP benefits—what used to be called food stamps—eliminating** *more than a week's worth of meals every month* **for a half million American families.**

I lived in one of those homes; ours was one of those families. That's where my passion to make a difference in this area comes from. I know those aren't just statistics; those are human beings who are suffering.

I've already shared with you how my life was transformed one Thanksgiving Day when I was 11 years old. Again, it wasn't just receiving food that changed my life, it was the fact that a stranger cared. That simple act has had an exponential effect. I've continued to pay that gift forward by feeding 42 million people over the last 38 years. The key is I didn't wait until I could handle this huge problem on a large scale. I didn't wait until I became wealthy. I started to attack the problem where I was, with what little I had.

At first it was a financial stretch to feed just two families, but then I became inspired and I doubled my goal—to feed four. The next year it was eight, then 16. As my companies and influence grew, it became a million a year, then 2 million. Just like investments compound, so do investments in giving—and they provide an even greater reward. The privilege of being in a place where today I am able to donate 50 million meals, and in partnership with you and others, provide more than 100 million meals, is beyond description. I was the guy who had to *be* fed, and now through grace and commitment, it's my honor to feed others and to multiply the good that was done for me and my family.

There's nothing like the power of the human soul on fire. Along the way, caring touched me, and so did books. They transported me from a world of limitation to a life of possibility as I entered the minds of authors who had already transformed their lives. In that tradition, I approached my publisher, Simon & Schuster, and let them know that I wanted to feed not just bodies but also minds. They have joined me in this mission by donating my simple change-your-life book called *Notes from a Friend*, which I wrote to help someone in a tough place to turn his or her life around with practical advice, strategies, and inspirational stories. To match the investment you've made in buying *this* book, my publisher has pledged to provide a copy of *Notes from a Friend* to a person in need through my partners at Feeding America. They are the nation's largest network of food banks and considered to be the most effective charity in the United States for feeding the homeless.

But now I'd like to ask you to consider partnering with me in a way that would continue to do these good works for years to come. It's a simple strategy that can provide 100 million meals not only this year but also every year for those hungry families in need. It doesn't require a substantial donation. **The plan I'm proposing offers you the opportunity to change and save lives by effortlessly giving away your spare change.** How? Join me in the campaign to SwipeOut hunger, SwipeOut disease, and SwipeOut slavery!

USE YOUR SPARE CHANGE TO CHANGE THE WORLD

So I have an offer for you. My goal in this book was to help you understand the distinctions, insights, skills—and give you a plan—that can truly empower you to create lasting financial security, independence, or freedom for you and your family. I'm obsessed with finding ways to add more value to your life than you could ever imagine with one book (although a big one, I must admit). I want it to inspire you to get beyond scarcity and become a wealthy man or woman right now! And that occurs the day that you start giving with joy in your heart—*wherever you are financially*—**not because you have to, not out of guilt or demand, but because it excites some part of you.**

According to the Bureau of Labor Statistics of the US Department of Labor, there are 124 million households in the US that spend an average of $2,604 per year on entertainment—that's more than $320 billion a year just on entertainment. Imagine if just some of this money went to solving previously intractable problems like hunger, human trafficking, and access to clean water? In the US, it takes one dollar to provide ten meals to needy individuals. Imagine helping to provide 100,000,000 meals a year! That's only a little over $10 million—just .0034% of what we spend on entertainment! It's pennies on the dollar—America's pocket change! So I partnered with some great minds in business and marketing, including Bob Caruso (social capitalist and former managing partner and COO of one of the top 100 hedge funds in the world, Highbridge Capital Management) and my dear friend Marc Benioff (philanthropist, founder, and CEO of Salesforce.com) to build the technology that allows you to easily and painlessly put those pennies to work to save lives.

In less than a minute, you can go online and opt in to SwipeOut (**www.swipeout.com**), so that every time you use your credit cards anywhere in the world, the price of your purchase will automatically round up to the nearest dollar.[28] That amount will go directly to an approved and effective charity that will report back to you with stories of the lives you have touched. Here's how it works: if you paid $3.75 for your Starbucks, $0.25 would be routed to preselected charities. For an average consumer, this change adds up to just under $20 a month. You can put a limit on what you give, but we do ask that you keep it at a minimum of $10.

Want to know what your impact would be? For about $20 a month:

- **you could provide 200 meals for hungry Americans (that's 2,400 meals per year!); or**
- **you could provide a clean, sustainable source of water for ten children in India each month—that's 120 children per year that you personally protect from a waterborne illness; or**
- **you could make a down payment on rescuing and rehabilitating a young Cambodian girl trafficked into slavery.**

These are the three big issues facing children and families. In America, it's hunger. Which is why our focus is on swiping out hunger with our partner Feeding America.

But the biggest challenge for children in the world is disease. Did you know that disease caused by contaminated water is the world's leading killer, accounting for 3.4 million deaths per year, according to the World Health Organization (WHO)? **In fact, every 20 seconds, another child dies from a waterborne disease—and more have perished than the total number of people who've died in all the armed conflicts since World War II.**

This is why the second commitment of SwipeOut is to swipe out

28. Using patented technology with bank-level security.

waterborne disease and provide clean water for as many children as possible worldwide. There are a variety of organizations with sustainable solutions out there, and some require as little as $2 a person to provide these children and their families with a reliable supply of clean water.

WHAT'S THE PRICE OF FREEDOM?

Throughout this book, we've been working to make sure that you can achieve financial freedom. What about investing a tiny fraction of what you spend each month to help secure freedom for one of the 8.4 million children in the world trapped in slavery? In 2008 ABC News correspondent Dan Harris went undercover to see how long and how much it would take to buy a child slave. He left New York and ten hours later was in Haiti negotiating to buy a child for $150. As he said, in the modern world, it costs less to buy a child than an iPod.

It's unimaginable to even consider this happening to our own children or anyone we love. **But try to imagine the impact of your actions freeing a human life, a soul that has been enslaved for years.** There are no words. And once again, you can know that as you sleep, your contribution is empowering those who are winning this fight every day.

So how do we tackle these huge challenges? Each of us together, a little bit at a time. This year, you and I and a few of our friends are going to feed 100 million people. But wouldn't it be incredible to feed 100 million people *each* year in a sustainable way? I provide fresh water for 100,000 people a day in India—it's one of my passions. Wouldn't it be amazing for us together to provide 3 million people with clean water a day and grow it from there? Or how about together freeing 5,000 children who had been enslaved, and supporting their education and a path to a healthy life?

That's what the power of just 100,000 of us can do. Just as I built my foundation, this mission could grow geometrically. If over a decade or more we could find a way to grow to a million members, that would be a billion meals provided each year, 30 million people with clean water, or 50,000 children freed from slavery. These figures would be extraordinary, but in truth, even one child's life saved would be worth all the effort.

So what's *your* vision? Most people overestimate what they can do in a year and often underestimate what they can do in a decade or two.

I can tell you that when I started on my own mission and fed two families, I was excited. My goal was to feed 100 families in need. Then it grew to 1,000. Then 100,000. Then 1 million. The more we grow, the more we see what's possible. It's up to us. Will you join me? Put your change to work, and let's change the world.

> I have found that among its other benefits,
> giving liberates the soul of the giver.
> —MAYA ANGELOU

Whether you sign up with SwipeOut or another organization, make a decision to take a small portion of the money you earn, or of your time, and consciously choose to invest it in something that doesn't benefit you directly, but rather goes to someone in need. This decision is not about being right or wrong, it's not about looking good, it's about real wealth—truly feeling more alive and genuinely fulfilled.

In *Happy Money*, Dunn and Norton wrote that when giving outside of ourselves is done right, **"when it feels like a choice, when it connects us with others, and when it makes a clear impact—even small gifts can increase happiness, potentially stirring a domino effect of generosity."**

Moved by this potency of "prosocial spending" (that is, gifts for others and donations to charity) Dan Ariely and his wife were inspired to put into practice a simple system that they and their two sons could adhere to together as a family. When the kids get their allowances, they have to divide the money among three jars.

Jar 1 is for **themselves.**

Jar 2 is for **somebody they know.**

Jar 3 is for **somebody they don't know.**

Notice that two-thirds of those jars are for prosocial spending, because that's what will make the kids happy. All three jars are great, but the Arielys were careful to set aside an equal portion for people they don't know. Spending on friends and family is beautiful, because it's giving to people you love, but philanthropy is the third jar, and that can be the most satisfying and important form of giving.

I can also tell you there are extraordinary positive consequences for those who give when it isn't easy. It primes our brain; it trains and conditions us to know that there's more than enough. And when our brain believes it, we experience it.

Sir John Templeton, not only the world's greatest investor but also one of the greatest human beings, shared something with me almost 30 years ago: he said that he's never known anyone who tithed—meaning the person gave 8% or 10% of what he earned to religious or charitable organizations over a ten-year period—who didn't massively grow his financial wealth. But here's the problem: everybody says, "I'll give when I'm doing better." And I used to think that way too. But I'll testify to this: you deserve to start wherever you are today. You've got to start the habit of giving even if you think you're not ready; even if you think you don't have anything to spare. Why? Because, as I said to you in the very first chapter of this book, if you don't give a dime out of a dollar, you're not going to give $1 million out of $10 million, or $10 million out of $100 million.

How will you *fuel* your legacy of giving? Will you give your time and energy? Will you tithe a portion of your earnings? Or will you start by taking a minute to go online and sign up with SwipeOut and **have your change become invested in changing lives?** If you're inspired, **please do this now while you are connected to the impact you can have.** And remember: the person you will be giving the most to might very well be yourself. A life as a philanthropist begins with a single small step. Let's take it together.

> I don't think of all the misery, but of the beauty that still remains.
> —ANNE FRANK

By the way, I wasn't always as conscious of the meaning of gratitude and giving. I used to live in scarcity. Looking back, my life hasn't always been easy, but it's always been blessed. I just didn't recognize it at the time. Because I grew up financially poor, I was always working to make sure I could achieve at the highest level. But I didn't realize that achievement comes in spurts.

It takes a long time not only to learn something but also to truly master it—to where it becomes so ingrained that it becomes a part of your life. So when I was just starting out, I suffered a series of setbacks. How did I react? Let's just say not with the grace of an enlightened soul! I was constantly angry, frustrated—pissed off! Because nothing was going my way. And I was running out of money!

Then one night around midnight, I was driving on the 57 Freeway near the Temple Avenue off-ramp near Pomona, California, wondering, "What's wrong? I'm working so hard. What's missing? Why am I failing so miserably in getting what I want? Why isn't this working?" Suddenly tears started to well in my eyes, and I pulled over to the side of the road. I dug out the journal I always carried with me—I still have it to this day—and started scribbling furiously by the dashboard light. I wrote in giant letters on a full page this message to myself: **"THE SECRET TO LIVING IS GIVING."**

Yes! I realized I'd forgotten that's what life was about. I'd forgotten that this is where all the joy is found—that life isn't just about me. It's about *we*.

When I pulled back on the freeway, I was inspired and refocused and re-ignited with a renewed sense of mission. I started doing well for a while. But, unfortunately, what I had written that night was just a concept, really—an insight that I hadn't yet fully embodied. Then I started running into more challenges, and six months later, I had lost everything financially. Before long, I found myself at what I thought was the lowest point of my life, living on the floor of a 400-square-foot bachelor apartment in Venice, California, seething with resentment. I had fallen into the trap of blaming everyone else for the natural challenges that show up whenever you go after reasonably large goals. I decided that I had been manipulated by a variety of people who had taken advantage of me. "If it wasn't for them," my ego said, "I'd be in great shape!" So I threw myself a pity party. And the angrier and more frustrated I became, the less productive I became.

Then I started to eat as my way of escaping—all this crappy and ridiculous fast food. I gained over 38 pounds in just a few months; that's not easy to do. You have to eat tons of food and not move much to pull that off! I found myself doing things I used to make fun of in other people—like watching daytime television. If I wasn't eating, I was watching soap operas. I got pulled into the show *General Hospital*—if you're old enough to remember when Luke and Laura got married, I was there!

It's humorous (and a bit humiliating!) to look back and see how far down I had dropped. I was down to my last $19 and some change, and I didn't have any prospects. And I was particularly pissed off at a friend who had borrowed $1,200 from me when I was doing well, but never paid it back. Now I was broke, but when I asked for the money, he'd turned his back on me. He wasn't answering my calls! I was furious, thinking, "What the hell am I going to do! How am I even going to eat?"

But I was always pragmatic. I thought, "Okay, when I was seventeen and homeless, how did I get by?" I'd go to a smorgasbord and load up on the all-you-can-eat buffet for as little money as possible. That gave me an idea.

My apartment wasn't that far from a beautiful place called Marina del Rey, where LA's wealthy dock their yachts. There was a restaurant called El Torito that had a fabulous buffet for about $6. I didn't want to waste any money on gas or parking, so I walked the three miles to the restaurant, which sat right on the marina. I took a seat by the window and loaded up plate after plate of food, eating like there was no tomorrow—which might have been the case!

While I ate, I was watching the boats going by and dreaming about what life could be like. My state started to change, and I could feel layers of anger melting off me. As I finished my meal, I noticed a small boy dressed up in a little suit—he couldn't have been more than seven or eight years old—opening the door for his young mother. Then he proudly led her to their table and held out her chair. He had a special *presence*. This kid seemed so pure and so good. He was such a giver—you could tell by the respectful, loving way he treated his mom. I was deeply moved.

After I paid my check, I walked over to their table and said to the boy, "Excuse me, I just want to acknowledge you for being such an extraordinary gentleman. It's amazing how you're treating your lady like this."

"She's my mom," he confided.

"Oh my God!" I said. "That's even cooler! And it's great that you're taking her to lunch!"

He paused and in a quiet voice said, "Well, I really can't, because I'm only eight years old—and I don't have a job yet."

"Yes, you are taking her to lunch," I said. And in that moment, I reached into my pocket, took all the money I had left—maybe a grand total of $13 and some change—and put it down on the table.

He looked up at me and said, "I can't take that."

"Of course you can," I told him.

"Why?"

I looked at him with a big smile and said, "Because I'm bigger than you are."

He stared up at me, shocked, and then he started to giggle. I just turned and walked out the door.

I didn't just walk out of that door, I *flew* home! I should have been freaking out, because I didn't have a dime to my name, but instead I felt totally free!

That was the day my life changed forever.

That was the moment I became a wealthy man.

Something inside of me finally got past the feeling of scarcity. I was finally free of this thing called money that I had let terrorize me. I was able to give everything without any fear. Something beyond my mind, something deep in my spirit knew that I—as we all are—was guided. And this moment was meant to be. Just as you're meant to be reading these words right now.

I realized I had been so busy trying to *get* that I had forgotten to *give*. But now I had recovered myself; I had recovered my soul.

I gave away my excuses, the blaming others, and suddenly I wasn't angry anymore. I wasn't frustrated. You might also have said I wasn't very smart! Because I had no idea in hell where I was going to get my next meal. But that thought wasn't even in my head. Instead, I felt an overwhelming sense of joy that I was released from a nightmare—the nightmare of thinking my life was doomed because of what other people had "done" to me.

That night, I committed to a plan of massive action. I decided exactly what I was going to do and how to get myself employed. I felt certain I'd make it happen—but I still didn't know when my next paycheck would arrive or, even more urgently, my next meal.

And then a miracle happened. The next morning, the old traditional snail mail arrived, and I found a special letter in my mailbox. In it was a handwritten note from my friend saying he was so sorry he'd been avoiding my calls. I had been there for him when he needed me, and he knew that I was in trouble. So he was paying me back everything he owed. Plus a little more.

I looked inside the envelope, and there was a check for $1,300. It was enough to last me a month or more! I cried, I was so relieved. ***And then I thought, "What does this mean?"***

I don't know if it was coincidence, but I chose to believe that those two events were connected, and that I had been rewarded because not only had I given but I had also wanted to give. Not out of obligation or fear—it was just an offering from my heart and soul to another young soul on the path.

And I can tell you honestly, I've had many tough days in my life, economically and emotionally—as we all have—but I've never gone back to that feeling of scarcity, and I never will.

The ultimate message of this book is very simple. It's the sentence I wrote down in my journal on the side of the freeway. The final secret of wealth is: *the secret to living is giving*.

Give freely, openly, easily, and enjoyably. Give even when you think you have nothing to give, and you'll discover there is an ocean of abundance inside of you and around you. Life is always happening for you, not to you. Appreciate that gift, and you are wealthy, now and forever.

Understanding this truth brought me back to what I'm made for, what we're all made for: to be a force for good. I was brought back to a life of deep meaning, constantly looking to fulfill my prayer—and that is **each day to be a blessing in the lives of all those people I meet and have the privilege to connect with.**

Even though I may not have met you personally, I wrote this book from that same state, asking and praying that each chapter, each page, each concept, would be a deeper step in helping you to experience more of the blessings of who you are, and more of the blessings in what you are able to create and give in this life.

My heartfelt wish and the purpose of this book is to give you yet another way to expand and deepen the quality of your life and the lives of all those *you* have the blessing to love and touch. In this, it's been a privilege to serve you.

And I look forward to someday, hopefully, crossing paths—either being able to meet you and serve you at one of my events somewhere in the world, or just meeting you on the street. I will be excited to hear how you used these principles to enhance your life.

And so, as we part, I want to leave you with a blessing, and a wish that your life will forever be filled with abundance. I wish for you a life of joy, passion, challenge, opportunity, growth, and giving. I wish for you an extraordinary life.

With love and blessings,
TONY ROBBINS

Live life fully while you're here. Experience everything. Take care of yourself and your friends. Have fun, be crazy, be weird. Go out and screw up! You're going to anyway, so you might as well enjoy the process. Take the opportunity to learn from your mistakes: find the cause of your problem and eliminate it. Don't try to be perfect; just be an excellent example of being human.

—TONY ROBBINS

7 SIMPLE STEPS: YOUR CHECKLIST FOR SUCCESS

Here's a quick checklist for you to use anytime you want to see where you are and what still needs to be done to move you along the path to financial freedom. Take a look at the 7 Simple Steps and make sure that you not only understand them but have also activated them.

Step 1: Make the Most Important *Financial* Decision of Your Life
1. Did you make the decision to become an investor, not just a consumer?
2. Have you committed a specific percentage of savings that always goes toward your Freedom Fund?
3. Have you automated it? If not, do it now: www.tdameritrade.com or www.schwab.com.
4. If the amount you're committing now is small, have you committed to your employer to use the Save More Tomorrow program? See http://befi.allianzgi.com/en/befi-tv/pages/save-more-tomorrow.aspx.

Step 2: Become the Insider: Know the Rules Before You Get in the Game
1. Do you know the 9 Myths, and are you now protected? Here's a mini-test:
   a. What percentage of mutual funds beat the market (or their benchmark) over any ten years?
   b. Do fees matter, and what's the average mutual fund fee?
   c. If you pay 1% versus 3% in fees, how much of a difference does it make to your final nest egg?
   d. Have you taken your broker for a test drive? Have you gone online and seen what your current costs are, how much risk you have in

your current investments, and how your current investment strategy has compared over the last 15 years with other simple, inexpensive options?

e. Do you know the difference between advertised returns and what you actually earn?

f. Do you know the difference between a broker and a fiduciary?

g. Are target-date funds your best option?

h. How do you maximize your 401(k), and should you elect to use a Roth 401(k)?

i. Do you have to take huge risks to make big rewards? What are some of the tools that will allow you to get the upside of the market without the downside losses?

j. Have you identified any of the limiting stories or emotions that have held you back or sabotaged you in the past, and have you broken their pattern of control in your life?

2. Do you have a fiduciary now representing and guiding you? If not, go online and find one at http://findanadvisor.napfa.org/home.aspx or go to Stronghold and review its services approach (www.Stronghold Financial.com).

3. If you own a company, or you're an employee with a 401(k) plan, have you taken 30 seconds to check how your fees compare with the rest of the market? Go to http://americasbest401k.com/401k-fee-checker.

4. If you're a business owner, have you met your legal requirement to benchmark your 401(k) against other comparable plans? Remember, the Department of Labor has reported that 75% of the 401(k)s it audited resulted in an average penalty of $600,000 (www.americasbest401k .com).

Step 3: Make the Game Winnable

1. Have you made the game winnable?

a. Have you found out what your real numbers are? Have you figured out what it's really going to take for you to achieve financial security, vitality, and independence? Have you calculated it?

b. If not, go back and do that right now. Or if you want to revisit them, go back and do the numbers now or go to your app, where you can keep the numbers in your pocket, and it will be calculated in a few minutes. You can do it in just a few minutes.

   c. Remember, **clarity is power.** See www.tonyrobbins.com/masterthe game.

2. Once you've got the numbers, did you use your wealth calculator and come up with a plan that shows you how many years it will take in a conservative, moderate, or an aggressive plan to achieve financial security or independence? If not, give yourself the gift. Go to the app and do this now.

3. Have you looked over and made any decisions about the five elements of how you can speed up your plan and achieve financial security or independence even faster?

   a. Save more:

- Have you looked at the places you could save? Your mortgage? Daily purchases?

- Have you implemented a Save More Tomorrow plan so that you don't have to give up anything today, but when you get additional income in the future, you'll save more? Go to http://befi.allianzgi .com/en/befi-tv/pages/save-more-tomorrow.aspx.

- Have you found something that you could cut down easily in order to increase your savings? Is it the $40 pizza? Is it the water bottle? Is it Starbucks? And have you calculated how much more money you'll have in your Freedom Fund and how much faster you can achieve your goals by doing this? Remember, $40 a week can equal $500,000 over an investment lifetime. You don't have to do any of these if you're already on target, but these are options if you're not yet on target to achieve your financial goals.

   b. Earn more. Have you found ways to increase the value you can add to others? Do you need to retool yourself and switch to a different industry? What are the ways you can add more value and grow more so you can give more?

   c. Save in fees and taxes. Have you come up with a way to apply what we've taught you to reduce your fees and/or reduce your taxes?

   d. Get better returns. Have you found a way to invest with greater returns without undue risk? Have you reviewed any of the portfolios that are here that might enhance your earnings and protect you from those gut-wrenching downturns in the market?

e. Change your life—and improve your lifestyle. Have you considered a new location with an even better lifestyle? Have you considered putting yourself in a place where you reduce or eliminate state taxes and then put all of that money toward building wealth and your family's financial security and freedom?

Step 4: Make the Most Important *Investment* Decision of Your Life

1. Have you decided on asset allocation so that you never put yourself in a position to lose too much? (Not all your eggs are in one basket, right?)

2. Have you decided what percentage belongs in your Security Bucket and what specific types of investment you'll use to be safe and still maximize returns? Are you diversifying with different types of investments within the Security Bucket? Have you decided what percentage of your savings or investment capital will go in the Security Bucket?

3. Have you decided what percentage belongs in your Risk/Growth Bucket and what specific types of investments you'll use to maximize returns yet still limit your downside as best as possible? Are you diversified with your Risk/Growth Bucket?

4. Have you evaluated your actual risk tolerance effectively? Did you take the test developed by Rutgers (http://njaes.rutgers.edu/money /riskquiz)?

5. Have you considered your stage of life and whether you should be more or less aggressive based on the length of time you have to save and invest? (If you're young, you can lose a bit more because you have more time to recover; if you're closer to retirement, you have less time to recover, and perhaps you need more in your Security Bucket.)

6. Have you evaluated the amount and size of your cash flow and whether that will play a role in your level of conservativeness or aggressiveness in your asset allocation?

7. Have you resolved the ratio of Security versus Risk/Growth as a percentage of your overall investments? 50/50? 60/40? 70/30? 30/70? 40/60? 80/20?

8. Have you come up with a list of short-term and long-term goals for your Dream Bucket that excite you? Do you have to wait until someday in the future, or do you have some things you're going to make happen right away?

9. Have you established a way to fund your Dream Bucket with either a small amount of savings or a portion of the profits of windfalls from successes in your Risk/Growth Bucket?

10. Rebalancing and dollar-cost averaging:

   a. Are you consistently committing the same amount of money to investments regardless of whether the market is moving up or down? Remember, timing the market never works.

   b. Are you continually rebalancing your portfolio, or do you have a fiduciary doing this for you? Either way, this is crucial to optimizing returns and minimizing volatility.

Step 5: Create a Lifetime Income Plan

1. The power of All Seasons:

   a. Have you taken the time to read, understand, and take action on the powerful insights that Ray Dalio gave us with his All Seasons approach? He has brought successful investment returns 85% of the time and lost money only four times in 30 years, but never more than 3.93% to date!

   b. Have you gone to Stronghold and taken five minutes to see what kind of returns you're getting on your current investments compared with All Seasons (and other portfolios) or to see what it would take to set up an All Seasons portfolio in minutes?

2. Income Insurance:

   a. Have you done the most important thing of all? Have you made sure that you will not run out of income as long as you live? Have you established a guaranteed lifetime income plan?

   b. Do you know the difference between an **immediate annuity** and a **deferred annuity,** and have you selected which might be right for you depending on your stage in life?

   c. Have you reviewed and initiated a hybrid annuity or tapped into the **upside-without-the-downside** strategy that's now available to anyone regardless of age and without any lump-sum payment whatsoever?

    d. Have you gone online and found out how much future income you could have for as little as $300 a month or more? If not, go to www.lifetimeincome.com or call an annuity specialist at Stronghold.

3. Secrets of the Ultrawealthy:

    a. Have you investigated how to drastically cut the amount of time it will take you to achieve financial freedom by 30% to 50% through the use of tax-efficient life insurance strategies? Remember, PPLI (private placement life insurance) is great for high net worth, but anyone can use the policies offered through TIAA-CREF with minimal deposit amounts. If you haven't yet explored these tools, reach out to a qualified, expert fiduciary today or contact Stronghold for a free analysis.

    b. Have you invested the $250 to set up a living trust so that your family is protected and your assets will go to them without going through a year of probate? Have you protected your wealth not only for your current generation but also your grandchildren and your great grandchildren?

Step 6: Invest Like the .001%

1. Have you taken the time to absorb some of the short interviews with 12 of the smartest financial people on earth, the greatest investors in history?
2. Who is the "Master of the Universe" in the financial world? What kind of returns has he gotten compared with anyone else, including Warren Buffett, and how could you invest with him if you wanted to?
3. What did you learn about asset allocation from Yale's David Swensen? Or J.P. Morgan's Mary Callahan Erdoes?
4. What did you learn from the indexing master Jack Bogle? Or from Dr. Doom, Marc Faber?
5. Did you capture the simple strategy that Warren Buffett now recommends for everyone, including his wife and her legacy trust?
6. Did you absorb the importance of how to get asymmetric returns?

7. Did you absorb the $100,000 MBA that Paul Tudor Jones gave you by never making an investment of less than five to one and always tapping into the power of the trend?

8. Did you check out Ray Dalio's *How the Economic Machine Works—In Thirty Minutes* video? If not, watch it now at www.economicprinciples.org.

9. Did you soak in the concepts of Kyle Bass's solution on investing where you cannot lose money? Remember the power of nickels? Where investments are guaranteed forever by the US government, and you'll have a potential upside of anywhere from 20% to 30%?

10. Did you take in the core lessons from Charles Schwab, and Sir John Templeton's gift that continues to give of being able to know that the worst environment is your greatest opportunity—to be most optimistic when the world is "ending" like it did in World War II, like it did in inflation in South America, like it did in the Depression, like it did in Japan after World War II? Did you absorb his true core strategic philosophy that made him the first international investment billionaire in history?

11. What actions can you take today to start investing like the .001%?

Step 7: Just Do It, Enjoy It, and Share It!

1. Your Hidden Asset:
   a. Have you connected to the truth that the future is a magnificent place?
   b. It will be filled with exciting challenges. Opportunities and problems are always there, but are you clear that there is a wave of technology that is going to continue to innovate and empower us as individuals and enhance the quality of life for human beings all over the earth?

2. Have you given yourself the ultimate gift—the commitment to be wealthy now, not someday in the future—by appreciating and developing the daily habit of priming your appreciation of what you already have and building on that success?

3. Would you trade expectation for appreciation? And have you committed to a life of progress? **Progress equals happiness. Life is about growing and giving.**

4. Have you figured out what you're here to serve and what the higher purpose is for your life? Have you begun to think about your legacy?

5. Have you decided to convert your pocket change into massive change in the world? If so, **go to www.swipeout.com now, take one minute, and start the process of saving lives while you enjoy your own.**

6. Are you embodying the truth that makes you wealthy in this moment: the secret to living is giving?

This is a quick overview checklist for maximizing the pages you've read. If there's anything you've missed, give yourself the gift of going back and absorbing it and also remember, **repetition is the mother of skill. Action is where all your power is found.**

So, my dear friend, come here and know that you're not alone. You can tap into your own resources, or I've also made a ton of support resources available here as well: the website, the app, Stronghold, Lifetime Income, and America's Best 401k. But whatever you do, make sure you take action and make sure that the people guiding you have your best interests in mind. Finding the right fiduciary is the place to start. The right one can help you create or refine your plan.

This list is not everything; it's just a great checklist to trigger you to keep growing and keep implementing. Remember that **knowledge is not power, execution is.** Just make a little bit of progress each day or each week, and before you know it, your path to financial freedom will be realized.

I look forward to meeting you in person someday soon. Until then, step up, keep moving forward, master the game, and live with passion.

ACKNOWLEDGMENTS

When I sat down to make note of all the individuals for whom I am so grateful, I was completely overwhelmed. I had just finished writing a 600-plus-page book! But acknowledging everyone who had helped get me here still stood as a daunting task. Where would I ever begin? Sitting here, this undertaking feels most like something you would see at the end of a movie: hundreds of names scrolling and key scenes flashing in tribute to the superstars. So many people have played so many roles to get me to this deeply fulfilling moment.

As I review the 4-year journey—and, frankly, the 30 years that led me here—I see the faces and feel the grace of so many extraordinary individuals. I won't be able to acknowledge them all, but I'd like to start close to home with the people who have touched my life most deeply.

First, my family. Of course, this begins with the love of my life, my magnificent wife, Bonnie Pearl—my Sage. "My girl." She's the never-ending source of the joy and happiness in my life. I feel that SHE is the ultimate reward for the "good karma" that has come from serving tens of millions of people over the decades. She tells me she was born to love me, and all I can say is that God has truly blessed me with the love of this beautiful soul. To her parents, Bill and Sharon—Mom and Dad—thank you for creating and raising this amazing woman. You have provided me with the greatest gift of my life: your daughter, the greatest source of love I've ever known or could ever even imagine. Thank you for all the love you poured into her, and for loving me as your own. You both live lives of such real true contribution, and you both inspire me every single day. My dear brother-in-law Scotty (who is really my brother) for his warrior-like courage and his constant focus on raising standards and making sure that we're able to reach out and serve more souls. And to each of my four children, Jairek, Josh, Jolie, and Tyler, who in every stage in my life have brought me inspiration, love, and a reason to be more. I also give thanks to the grace of our creator. And for my passionately intense mother, who imparted extraordinary standards, and the four fathers who each impacted my life uniquely. To my brother and sister, Marcus and Tara, and all of my extended family, I love you.

To my core team at Robbins Research International that allows me each day the privilege to explore, integrate, constantly create, test, and retest new insights, tools, strategies, and pathways to improving the quality of people's lives worldwide. To Sam Georges and Yogesh Babla—my confidants who look out for me and all of our companies while I'm traveling the globe. To my dear friends and protectors Mike Melio and "General Jay" Garrity. To Shari, Rich, Marc, Brook, Terri, and all the rest of our amazing, loyal, and mission-driven executive staff. To my outstanding creative team—especially the remarkable manager and creative partner Diane Adcock—you are amazing, and our bright light Katie Austin, I love you. To all personnel at San Diego HQ and far beyond who work with me every day across departments at RRI and all our partners that make up the Anthony Robbins Companies. Thank you to each of you for all that you do in our quest to constantly work to create breakthroughs for people in their business, finances, health, emotions, time management, and personal relationships. We are here together to change lives. We are called to rise up. We drive Financial, Business, and ultimately Human Elevation. We are catalysts of the spirit—this is the gift we are all made for. I feel so fortunate to work with you as we help make a difference in people's lives all over the world! Extra special thanks to our volunteer staff and all of our crew—and especially our road warriors, who travel the earth making everything happen behind the scenes. Our events could not happen without you, and our entire team is grateful for the gifts you give. Also thanks to all the wives and husbands who loan out their family to us as we span the globe and to Joseph McLendon III, Scott Harris, Joe Williams, Michael Burnett, Richard and Veronica Tan, and Salim for providing the leverage to touch even more lives worldwide.

My life has been powerfully shaped by deep friendships with four brilliant men. To my dear friend and brother Paul Tudor Jones, I thank you for more than 21 years of being a role model of how to find your way to victory no matter how big the challenge! The only thing greater than Paul's legendary trading ability is the depth of his love and generosity. He is a soul driven completely to make a difference in the world; and he does every day. To Peter Guber, who has been one of my dearest friends in life, and a creative force of nature whose generosity also knows no limits. Peter, you constantly inspire me to see what's possible! Thank you for all the laughter, your coaching, your love, and the privilege to be your friend throughout the decades. To Marc Benioff, my brother on the path. Your amazing mind, you unconquerable heart, your constant innovation in business, and your remarkable philanthropic efforts excite me and millions of others entrusted to uphold the standard you've set so successfully and continue to sustain at Salesforce .com. I'm proud to partner with you in changing lives. I love you, man. To Steve Wynn, thank you for your love and for being an impeccable, brilliant creator that nothing on earth can stop! You truly are a genius, and yet so humble. You're always looking out for those you love. The way you take a vision and turn it into reality excites everyone around you. To be your friend is such a gift. Each day I spend with you is another day I am inspired to take my game to another level.

Through my events and appearances, I am afforded the opportunity to meet hundreds of thousands of people each year who have touched my life. But this book, at its core, was uniquely shaped by a group of more than 50 extraordinary souls whose insights and strategies have touched me and all those who will read these pages. To those who shared their time and life's work in our interview sessions, I am eternally grateful. To Ray Dalio, for the unique gift you gave in this book by providing the average investor with an "all-seasons" investment approach based on the insights of the genius of your famous "All Weather" strategy. Ray gave us the gift of a simplified system that creates what, at least historically, has provided investors the smoothest possible ride over the long-term financial path. The value of Ray's "secret sauce" is beyond measure, but just one reflection of his inherent generosity.

To Jack Bogle, for investing 64 years of his life and having a relentless focus on what's right for the investor: your commitment to create index funds has changed investing as we know it for everyone in the world. Thank you for giving me four hours in what proved to be one of the most raw, honest, and insightful interviews that I've had the privilege to participate in. To T. Boone Pickens, for being the absolute epitome of honest American individualism and cowboy courage. To Kyle Bass, for showing us all that massive rewards do not require massive risks. To Sir John Templeton, bless his soul, for the many decades he inspired me with his insights that in times of "maximum pessimism" we are offered our greatest opportunities. To Marc Faber, for his always-innovative investing advice and, most of all, his exuberance. To the fearless Carl Icahn, for his unbridled boldness, courage, and passion—for challenging the status quo and bringing extraordinary returns for your investors. To Mary Callahan Erdoes, the trillion-dollar woman from J.P. Morgan, for being such an extraordinary example of the power of servant leadership, and for modeling how we can all be extraordinary in business and yet still so connected to what really matters most.

To all the extraordinary, insightful academics and businessmen and businesswomen. From Nobel laureates like Robert Schiller and Harry Markowitz to Dan Ariely (MIT) and the tandem of Shlomo Benartzi and Richard Thaler, whose Save More Tomorrow allows individuals to get around the cognitive and emotional limitations that most human beings find themselves entrapped by. To Dr. David Babbel, your focus on lifetime income and your living example helped shape a big part of this book. Burton Malkiel, you are a treasure to this country. Your original focus on indexing set the stage for a world of financial choice, and your straight talk is a bright spot in a sometimes dark and murky financial world. To Alicia Munnell (Boston College), Teresa Ghilarducci (New School), Dr. Jeffrey Brown, and Dr. David Babbel (Wharton): thank you for your astute insights into our retirement system—you are revolutionaries. To Steve Forbes and to Harvard professor and former secretary of the Treasury Larry Summers, for giving us two hours of extraordinary and lively debate—showing us all an "across-the-aisle" look at how we got here and what America needs to do to turn things around. To David Swensen—the rock star of institutional investing—for opening Yale's sacred doors and allowing me to share in his extraordinarily effective investment approach, but, more importantly, for standing as a shining example of how our labor is a reflection of our love. His work is a gift and his constant personal focus on what he can give touches me to this day.

To Warren Buffett, for forging the way for us all. Thank you for being such a straight shooter. While I would have loved to have spent more time with you, the brief meeting we shared on the *Today* show struck a chord deep within. When the Oracle of Omaha says that indexing is the way, it leaves very little room for argument!

To Elliot Weissbluth, for his willingness to take on this challenge far before the subject was ever breached. You've worked to bring true transparency and conflict-free advice to the wealthy, and now you shoulder a crusade to democratize opportunities for the average individual investor regardless of his or her economic capabilities. Elliot is a real example of integrity, courage, and intrinsic commitment to do what is right. Thank you for your partnership.

Thanks to all those who provided interviews, or who gave of their time at my Platinum Partnership Wealth Events, and for those who have shared your insights over the years and who have served as examples of what is possible—you all inspire me, and your wisdom is echoed in these pages in so many different ways.

Thanks and gratitude to my dear friend John Paul DeJoria (who once lived out of his car, too!). Thanks to the maverick Marc Cuban, to Charles Schwab, Sara Blakely, Reid Hoffman, Sir Richard Branson, Chuck Feeney, Evan Williams, Peter Lynch, Ray Chambers, David Walker, Eddie Lampert, Tony Hsieh, Tony Tan, Michael Milken, Mark Hart, Mitch Kaplan, Luca Padulli, Harry Dent, Robert Prechter, Michael O'Higgins, Jim Rodgers, James Grant, Eric Sprout, Mike Novogratz, Stanley Druckenmiller, George Soros, Sir Roger Douglass, Domingo Cavallo, Daniel Cloud, Geoffrey Batt, Joshua Copper Ramo, Russel Napier, Emad Mostaque, Dr. Donny Epstein, Tom Zgainer, and, of course, Ajay Gupta! Special thanks to Adam Davidson, Alex Blumberg, and Helen Olin for the insightful views of what is unjust and what can be done with the crazy, connected, and volatile financial world that now dominates all our lives.

My deepest thanks to my partners at Simon & Schuster, who moved heaven and earth to meet this insane timeline. I was so committed to getting this book out, and the size of it grew geometrically as I interviewed more and more of the world's greatest financial minds. First to Jonathan Karp, president and publisher, for his vision and willingness to support me on this endeavor, and for spearheading the Simon & Schuster team that helped us edit and publish this beast in record time—we must have broken some kind of record. And it could only have been done with the help of the editors: Ben Loehnen and Phil Bashe.

Thanks to all who have helped us spread the word about this labor of love. From Heidi Krupp, to Jenifer Connelly, to Jan Miller and Shannon Marven, to Suzanne Donahue and Larry Hughes, to Mark Thompson, Mat Miller, to Frank Luntz and his amazing team, David Bach, and my dear friend Dean Graziosi, in addition to all of my marketing partners like Brendon Burchard, Jeff Walker, Frank Kern, Joe Polish, Brett Ratner, Mike Koenigs, Tim Ferriss, GaryVaynerchuck, Eben Pagan, Russell Brunson, Dean Jackson, Marie Forleo, Chris Brogan, Jay Abraham, Jason Binn, David Meerman Scott, Scott Klososky, and so many others. My deepest thanks to Praveen Narra, Cliff Wilson, and all the partners at app development for building our amazing smartphone app.

To the media icons who have so lovingly spread the message, especially Oprah Winfrey, Ellen DeGeneres, and Dr. Oz. To my dear partners—who feel more like my family—at Impact Republic, for the all-night marathons on book covers and the like; a special shout-out to Kwaku, and my dear brothers "PMF" Chris Jennings and Bob Caruso. Thank you Jarrin Kirksey, Sybil Amuti, and the entire Impact Republic team not only for your dedication to this book but also for helping us refine our ability to rise up and reach millions more people every passing year. I love and appreciate you all!

And, of course, the mission of this book is to serve not only those who will be reading it but also the many that society has forgotten. And so my deepest thanks to everyone at the Anthony Robbins Foundation and our strategic partners—most importantly Brian Berkopec and all our partners at SwipeOut, and Dan Nesbit at Feeding America for helping us coordinate this never-before-attempted approach to provide 100 million meals: the distribution of my initial donation of 50 million meals and the efforts of all those working tirelessly to secure matching funds that will enable the delivery of 50 million more. Deep thanks to my partner Cody Foster, and the whole Advisors Excel team, for being one of the first to step up—not only to create distinct, new income solutions for people but also for their trailblazing commitment to provide 10 million meals before anyone else did.

For insights into technology and the future, my deep thanks to my dear visionary friends Peter Diamandis and Ray Kurzweil. It's always a privilege to spend time with either of these extraordinary men. They provide a window into a future reality that few on earth can even bear to imagine, and they work every day to make that world a reality. Ray and Peter, you absolutely blow me away, and it's been a privilege to partner with you at Singularity University and in the new Global Learning X Prize. I'm excited about what we'll create together. Thanks again for the insights we were able to share in this book. Thanks also to Easton LaChappelle for brimming with creative ambition for the greater good, and to Juan Enriquez for showing us how even what we call "life" is being redesigned and refashioned into fresh opportunity as we speak.

To those around me doing all the little things that make the biggest difference: Dear Ms. Sarah, Steph, and Stephanie. *Bula vinaka* to my Fijian family. And to Andrea, Maria, and Tony, for helping preserve a sacred sanctuary amid a crazy life.

Finally, and most importantly, I thank my core research team, without whom there is no way this book would have been written:

Starting with my son Josh, whose lifetime in the financial business has provided invaluable insights. I have delighted in our middle-of-the-night brainstorming sessions trying to figure out how to bring more value to individual investors. Our time has brought me more joy and excitement than I could have imagined—not only in what we've been able to create together but also in the beautiful time that we've shared throughout this project.

And to the four other people this book could not have been written without: Jenn Dawes, whose inhuman capacity to capture my thoughts, almost at the speed I speak them, is what keeps the structure organized, connected, communicated, and from splitting at the seams! I'm eternally indebted to you, and I love you.

Finally to Maryanne Vollers and Jodi Glickman, for caring so deeply and for your willingness to work with me through many a sleepless night, refining and editing this manuscript.

And to Mary Buckheit, whose dedication and love kept me going in some of the most exhausting moments of this long, arduous process, giving birth to the "treasures" we both know will touch lives for decades to come. I love you and give you my eternal appreciation.

To the grace that has guided this entire process, and to whatever God unleashed inside me at an early stage of my life that has made me never satisfied with what is, and to be so insanely obsessed with a hunger and a drive to serve at the highest level possible. To that which is always reminding me that it's not only the big things but also the little things that matter. And for the privilege of my readers and all those who have ever put their faith in me by making an investment in a product, or a service, or taking that leap of faith to come attend an event where they gave me the most valuable resource they have: their faith, their trust, and their time. To partner with them, taking back control of their lives; taking it to whatever level it was, and to whatever level it deserves to be.

And to all those friends and teachers along the path of my life—too many to mention, some famed and some unknown, whose insights, strategies, example, love, and caring are the shoulders I have had the honor to stand on. On this day, I give thanks to you all, and I continue my never-ending quest to each day be a blessing in the lives of all those I have the privilege to meet, love, and serve.

ANTHONY ROBBINS COMPANIES

ANTHONY ROBBINS FOUNDATION

The Anthony Robbins Foundation is a nonprofit organization created to empower individuals and organizations to make a significant difference in the quality of life for people often forgotten by society: our youth, the homeless and hungry, prisoners, and the elderly. Its international coalition of caring volunteers provides the vision, inspiration, cutting-edge resources, and specific strategies needed to empower these important members of society.

What began nearly 40 years ago as one man's individual effort to feed two families has now grown into a movement. **The foundation was built upon the belief system that regardless of stature, only those who have learned the power of sincere and selfless contribution will experience life's deepest joy: true fulfillment.** Connecting, inspiring, and demonstrating true leadership throughout the world, the foundation's global impact is provided through an international coalition of caring donors and volunteers.

All of the author's profits from *Money: Master the Game* have been donated in advance to the Tony Robbins 100 Million Meal Challenge, where individuals, corporations, and philanthropists alike are invited to participate in matching Tony Robbins's donation of 50 million meals to feed hungry families in need. For over 38 years, Tony has committed his time and resources to feeding 42 million people across the nation and around the world. Inspired by a stranger's generosity to feed his own family years ago, Tony has now partnered with **Feeding America** in conjunction with **SwipeOut (www.swipeout.com),** and Salesforce.com to donate over 100 million meals within a year; the first program of its kind.

www.moneymasterthegame.com

SWIPEOUT

Let your spare change change the world. What if every time we made a purchase, it helped someone? What if our small, ordinary daily transactions helped make an extraordinary impact across the globe? **What if your credit card was a weapon against global injustice?** In less than a minute, the SwipeOut app allows consumers to connect their credit/debit cards to the patented system that will automatically round up each consumer purchase to the nearest dollar. All of the spare change—100%—will be channeled to the world's most pressing problems facing children and those affected by extreme poverty: hunger, disease, and slavery. Our partners include Tony Robbins as well as Marc Benioff, founder of Salesforce.com.

www.swipeout.com

INTERNATIONAL BASKET BRIGADE

The International Basket Brigade is built on a simple notion: "one small act of generosity on the part of one caring person can transform the lives of hundreds." What began as Tony's individual effort to feed families in need has now grown into the Anthony Robbins Foundation's International Basket Brigade, providing baskets of food and household items for more than 2 million people annually in countries all over the world.

GLOBAL YOUTH LEADERSHIP SUMMIT

The Anthony Robbins Foundation Global Youth Leadership Summit is a five-day program that provides participants aged 14 to 17 with an environment designed to boost them into leadership roles that will change their lives and communities. Global Youth Leadership Summit's format includes small-group discussions, hands-on service learning experiences, leadership simulation games, and exercises designed to enable summit participants to identify their own particular leadership strengths.

THE CHALLENGE

Life is a gift, and all of us who have the ability must remember that we have the responsibility to give something back. Contributions can truly make a difference. Please join us now and commit to helping those less fortunate enjoy a greater quality of life.

The Anthony Robbins Foundation's charter is fulfilled through these programs and others like them. People interested in more information may call 1-800-554-0619 or visit us online at www.anthonyrobbinsfoundation.org.

STRONGHOLD WEALTH MANAGEMENT

Stronghold Wealth Management LLC and Stronghold Financial LLC are both SEC-registered investment advisors firms. They provide fiduciary advisory services with complete transparency as the core operating principle. **They do not charge commissions. Combined with extraordinary service, a personal touch, and unparalleled solutions, Stronghold seeks to help people across a wide spectrum of investable assets, and it also provides complimentary portfolio analysis through its proprietary web platform. Stronghold can be reached at**

www.StrongholdFinancial.com.

ANTHONY ROBBINS

ABOUT THE ANTHONY ROBBINS COMPANIES

The Anthony Robbins Companies (ARC) is an alliance of diversified "impact-focused" organizations dedicated to providing extraordinary world-class events, programs, products, and services that improve the quality of life for individuals and organizations worldwide. Founded by America's number one life and business strategist, Tony Robbins, ARC is composed of more than a dozen companies with combined revenue exceeding $5 billion a year. While diverse in characterization and business lines, all ARC companies are aligned in the mission of human, business, and financial elevation.

HUMAN ELEVATION COMPANIES

ROBBINS RESEARCH INTERNATIONAL (RRI)

Reaching into more than 100 countries, RRI conducts public and corporate seminars all over the world on topics ranging from peak performance and life transformation to business growth and financial mastery. Tony Robbins conducts his live **Unleash the Power Within** events with translation in seven languages. One of the most sought-after experiences offered by RRI is Robbins's year-round **Mastery University, Business Mastery, and Platinum Partner** programs. Based on 38 years of modeling the most successful individuals in the world of business and peak performance, these courses offer specific breakthrough strategies and a course of work that help individuals transform their lives and help business owners to grow their companies 30% to 130% within the first 12 months. RRI offers a variety of individual and total-immersion coaching experiences that help individuals and organizations create breakthrough results. RRI has been honored to engage with some of the world's most extraordinary individuals through its events, programs, and coaching: President Bill Clinton, Serena Williams, Hugh Jackman, Oprah Winfrey, Melissa Etheridge, Quincy Jones, Anthony Hopkins, Pat Riley, Usher, Pitbull, Mark Burnett, Brett Ratner, Derek Hough, and Donna Karan, and many professional sports teams, ranging from the NBA to the NFL, have enjoyed the impact of Tony Robbins's work.

NAMALE RESORT AND SPA

This exclusive South Pacific resort and spa has served as Tony Robbins's personal escape for more than 25 years. Encircled by a natural coral reef and crystal-clear turquoise waters, the idyllic destination promises to relax and romance its guests, who flock from around the world. In 2013 **Oprah selected Namale as the number one place to go in the world. Visitors choose this 500-acre private island paradise to escape and de-stress, pampered by the unique combination of serenity and excitement. Namale is consistently ranked among the top ten resort spas in the entire South Pacific, and its intimate charm places it among the top five honeymoon resorts in the world.** A tropical paradise with three miles of ocean frontage, tropical rainforests, waterfalls, and extraordinary diving and snorkeling sights, Namale Resort and Spa hosts only 20 couples at a time, with over 125 staff to serve them. No wonder some of the world's most influential executives and celebrities have found their bliss at Namale, including actors **Russell Crowe, Edward Norton, Anthony Hopkins, and Meg Ryan;** entrepreneur **Jeff Bezos;** producer **Quincy Jones;** fashion icon **Donna Karan;** and NBA coach **Pat Riley**—just to name a few. The resort's world-class staff is committed to providing guests with an authentic Fijian vacation experience. Namale is where every request is met, every want is anticipated, and every expectation is exceeded. For more information, guests

can call USA (1-800-727-3454), international (1-858-381-5177), or visit
online at www.namalefiji.com.

ROBBINS-MADANES:
CENTER FOR STRATEGIC INTERVENTION

Anthony Robbins and Cloé Madanes joined forces to train therapists and
professional coaches in the most effective and integrated tools for creating personal, family, and organizational breakthroughs. Together they have
trained more than 15,000 therapists and coaches worldwide. Therapists are
trained in the exact methodology of Tony Robbins intervention strategies
and are tested for effectiveness over the course of one year—or, for more
advanced mentoring, three years. The center's mission is to find solutions to
interpersonal conflicts, to prevent violence, and to contribute to the creation
of a more cohesive and civil community. A strategic interventionist navigates
a variety of scenarios ranging from individual problems to those of the family, the peer group, the organization, and the larger social system.

www.robbinsmadanes.com

FORTUNE PRACTICE MANAGEMENT

Fortune Management is the nation's leading practice management company. Combining the expertise of Tony Robbins with the business expertise of Fortune Management, clients learn how to enhance their practice's
brand, increase referral-based business, increase patient volume and reten-
tion, and stay ahead of the competition. Fortune provides an unparalleled

combination of coaching, consulting, and training through customized seminars, personal coaching, and support systems designed to enrich the professional, personal, and financial lives of health care practitioners. Our mission is to provide professional health care teams with management expertise, resources, and solutions that will significantly improve their practice.

www.fortunemgmt.com

UNLIMITED TOMORROW

Unlimited Tomorrow, a technology and innovation company founded by Easton LaChappelle, produces products that enable humans to do the impossible. The company currently focuses on constructing affordable, lightweight, low-profile "exo-suits" and "exoskeletons" (robotic suit arms and legs). These suits will make it possible for paralyzed individuals to walk again. At age 14, founder Easton LaChappelle made his first robotic hand built from Legos, fishing wire, and electrical tubing. With his gradual improvement, the hand turned into an arm, and then advanced to a 3-D-printed invention operated by the mind. After an encounter at a science fair with a seven-year-old girl whose prosthetic arm cost $80,000 (and would need to be replaced when she outgrew it), LaChappelle was inspired to turn his prototype into a practical and affordable device. Not only were his designs amazingly effective, but also they have reduced the cost to less than $1,000. President Barack Obama invited LaChappelle to the White House and shook hands with one of his arms. He has traveled the world spreading the message of the unlimited tomorrow we all have available to us, including a TED Talk. Easton has even worked at NASA on the Robonaut project, developing a new telerobotic interface.

www.unlimitedtomorrow.com

BUSINESS AND FINANCIAL ELEVATION COMPANIES

CLOUDCOACHING INTERNATIONAL

CloudCoaching International is a dynamic, award-winning behavioral integration service. We utilize the cloud to drive maximum targeted-sales increases with sustainable growth for enterprise-level organizations. By combining the most effective CRM tools with optimized sales and sales management processes, we insure rapid and sustainable sales performance improvement. In 2013 CloudCoaching International was the winner of *Elearning!* magazine's "Best of Elearning! Award for Sales Training." **We have served more than 50% of Fortune 500 companies and have over three decades of proven experience.**

www.CloudCoachingInternational.com

ADVISORS EXCEL

At Advisors Excel, launched in 2005, our mission is to add unending value to the top independent financial advisors we serve across all 50 states. With a focus on retirement income planning, ARC has partnered with Advisors Excel to build and promote additional products and services that will help create a guaranteed lifetime income plan for the millions of Americans who have uncertainty regarding their retirement income future. Today Advisors Excel has grown to become the nation's largest annuity wholesaler.

www.AdvisorsExcel.com

LIFETIME INCOME

Lifetime Income, an additional joint venture with Advisors Excel, is a trusted source for helping individuals create and access a personalized guaranteed lifetime income plan. By using the power of guaranteed income annuities—and new forms of longevity insurance—the online system will help individuals formulate a "personal pension" plan that best fits their goals and source the highest income payouts available. Lifetime Income has a network of over 500 retirement income specialists across all 50 states.

www.LifetimeIncome.com

AMERICA'S BEST 401K

America's Best 401k (AB 401k) is a revolutionary company that is disrupting the status quo of high-cost 401(k) plans that plague the vast majority of American businesses, their employees, and their respective families. **America's Best 401k combines exceptional value, high-touch service, ultra-low-cost investment options** (index funds), and a straightforward and transparent fee structure. We also provide employer fiduciary protection, all of which are strategically combined to create an unparalleled and cost-efficient solution.

www.americasbest401k.com

MYPOWERCFO

For more than three decades, Tony Robbins has helped business owners maximize growth and save costs. Recently ARC partnered with some of the most reputable global accounting firms to provide virtual CFO services for a fraction of the full-time equivalent cost. MyPowerCFO was created to help companies maximize profitability, expose cash "leaks," and reveal inefficiencies in order to take the immediate steps to rectify their challenges (along with the assistance of a professional). MyPowerCFO offers a free tax-efficiency analysis for companies in the United States, United Kingdom, and Australia.

www.MyPowerCFO.com

MyPowerCFO Partners Include

MARCUM LLP

Established in 1951, Marcum LLP is one of the largest independent public accounting and advisory services firms in the United States. Ranked 15th nationally, Marcum LLP has partnered with Tony Robbins to offer the resources of 1,300 professionals, including over 160 partners in 23 offices throughout the United States, Grand Cayman, and China. Headquartered in New York City, the firm's presence runs deep, with full-service offices located strategically in major business markets.

www.MarcumLLP.com

HW FISHER & COMPANY

HW Fisher & Company, Tony Robbins's UK partner, is a commercially astute London-based organization with a personal, partner-led service aimed at entrepreneurial small and medium enterprises (SMEs), large corporates, and high-net-worth individuals. Founded in 1933, the practice is composed of 29 partners and approximately 260 staff, supplying a range of services spanning audit, corporate taxation, private client services, VAT, business recovery, and forensic accounting.

www.hwfisher.co.uk

HALL CHADWICK

Hall Chadwick is Tony Robbins's Australian partner and the fifth largest accounting group in Australia, servicing clients in every major capital city. Since 1886, Hall Chadwick has provided leading-edge solutions, and has an enviable reputation for its customer service. Hall Chadwick is also a member of the AGN International accounting group, an association of independent accounting firms from around the world. The AGN network has an international presence represented by more than 500 offices in more than 83 countries, with a total of more than 9,500 partners and staff worldwide.

www.hallchadwick.com.au

A NOTE ON SOURCES

Since this book expanded to more than 600 pages, in order to be efficient on additional space, we put the bibliography online. To access it simply go to tonyrobbins.com/masterthegame.

INDEX

PERMISSIONS

ABOUT THE AUTHOR

TONY ROBBINS is a bestselling author, entrepreneur, and philanthropist. For more than 37 years, millions of people have enjoyed the warmth, humor, and the transformational power of Mr. Robbins's business and personal development events. He is the nation's #1 life and business strategist. He's called upon to consult and coach with some of the world's finest athletes, entertainers, Fortune 500 CEOs, and even presidents of nations.

Robbins is a founder of or partner in more than a dozen companies in industries as diverse as a 5-star Fijian island resort to custom 3D-printed prosthetic limbs. Through the Anthony Robbins Foundation and his matching funds, Tony feeds 4 million people per year in 56 countries. He has also initiated programs in more than 1,500 schools, 700 prisons, and 50,000 service organizations and shelters. He lives in Palm Beach, Florida.